The Science of Perception and Memory

THE SCIENCE OF PERCEPTION AND MEMORY

A Pragmatic Guide for the Justice System

Daniel Reisberg

OXFORD
UNIVERSITY PRESS

UNIVERSITY PRESS

Oxford University Press is a department of the University of
Oxford. It furthers the University's objective of excellence in research,
scholarship, and education by publishing worldwide.

Oxford   New York
Auckland   Cape Town   Dar es Salaam   Hong Kong   Karachi
Kuala Lumpur   Madrid   Melbourne   Mexico City   Nairobi
New Delhi   Shanghai   Taipei   Toronto

With offices in
Argentina   Austria   Brazil   Chile   Czech Republic   France   Greece
Guatemala   Hungary   Italy   Japan   Poland   Portugal   Singapore
South Korea   Switzerland   Thailand   Turkey   Ukraine   Vietnam

Oxford is a registered trademark of Oxford University Press
in the UK and certain other countries.

Published in the United States of America by
Oxford University Press
198 Madison Avenue, New York, NY 10016

Library of Congress Cataloging-in-Publication Data
Reisberg, Daniel.
The science of perception and memory : a pragmatic guide for the justice system / Daniel Reisberg.
pages cm
Includes bibliographical references and index.
ISBN 978-0-19-982696-4 (hardback)
1. Memory.   2. Perception.   3. Cognitive psychology.   I. Title.
BF371.R374 2015
153.1'2024364—dc23
2014012603

9 8 7 6 5 4 3 2
Printed in the United States of America
on acid-free paper

For Friderike, who intelligently, insightfully, lovingly,
Improves everything that I do

CONTENTS

PREFACE

A robbery victim tries to remember who was present at the crime scene. A witness to a mugging stood 30 yards from the attack and later identifies the perpetrator from a lineup. A teenager approaches a school counselor reporting sex abuse that happened years earlier. A medical patient recalls the doctor saying that the pain in her side wasn't worrisome and, now that the tumor is much larger, she's suing. An investigation of insider trading hinges on someone's recall of exactly what was said at a business meeting.

In these and countless other examples, our ability to perceive and remember is crucial for the justice system—whether our focus is on criminal cases or civil, or, for that matter, administrative or family law. The problem, though, is that the evidence provided by perception and memory is fallible. Even under conditions we might call "optimal," our eyes can deceive us and our memories are sometimes incomplete— or (worse) mistaken. And, obviously, the justice system is often confronted with less-than-optimal conditions—people who had only a brief view of an event or a view with poor lighting; victims who are reporting precise details of conversations that took place long ago. How should we think about these points? How often do our eyes or memories deceive us? Is there some way to avoid these errors by gathering our memory-based evidence in just the right way? And, if we can't control the evidence gathering, can we at least specify the circumstances in which perceptual or memory errors are more likely and when less? Then, once the evidence is in hand, is there some means of evaluating a person's recollection to decide whether his or her report is accurate or not?

The questions in play here have been discussed within the legal community for years. Comments about memory or perceptual errors are commonplace in court rulings and law school curricula. But where can we find answers to these questions? It turns out that perception and memory are central concerns for research psychologists—scientists who investigate the functioning of the mind. I am one of these researchers, and, as a group, we're rather different from what most people think of as "psychologists." We have laboratories, not clinics; we are trained in statistics, not modes of therapy; our expertise is in research design, not clinical diagnosis. We do experiments, collect data, and draw conclusions in a fashion tightly controlled by the standards and practices of the scientific community. And, in many studies, the research has been carefully tuned to provide information directly useful for the justice system.

Results from these studies are slowly percolating into the legal world, and research psychologists are already advising the courts, consulting with attorneys, and training investigators. In many states, interview procedures with children have been designed in ways explicitly guided by what we know about children's memories and how children respond to various forms of questioning. In some jurisdictions, police use the so-called cognitive interview when questioning witnesses—an interview procedure based on what we know about adult memory. In still other cases, the courts rely on psychological research in assessing the reliability of an identification; more and more states are relying on this research in constructing their ID procedures.

We need to acknowledge, though, that the enthusiasm for this information flow hasn't been universal. Some people in the justice system argue that the scientific data aren't reliable or that the data are just not relevant to the issues at play in the courtroom. Other people are convinced there's an inherent bias in the research—and so (they claim) the science might be useful to a criminal defender but to no one else. Still others believe the science contributes little beyond common sense. Indeed, not so many years ago, I sat in a courtroom, listening as the attorneys debated the admissibility of my testimony. After hearing their arguments, the judge ruled: "I've been evaluating eyewitness evidence for my whole career without Dr. Reisberg's help, and I see no reason why I need him now." And, with those words pronounced, I was dismissed.

In this book, I'll explain why these concerns are all misguided. But I'll also do more than that: I want to lay out, in accessible form, what it is we know so that this information is readily available to judges, attorneys, investigators, and anyone else associated with the justice system. The topics I'll be discussing (and the data underlying my claims) are already covered in various publications, but often these publications are written by people without scientific training. As a result, the presentation is sometimes less authoritative, and perhaps even less accurate, than it needs to be, and, in any case, does a poor job of conveying the "scientific muscle" that sustains the authors' claims. In other cases, by contrast, the relevant information is conveyed in volumes written by the researchers themselves. These texts are excellent and certainly authoritative. But they're often dense in ways that make them difficult for nonspecialists to understand. My aim in this book, therefore, is to forge a middle path: I'll try to convey this material in a way that is sophisticated, current, and fully grounded in the best available science, but also in a way that makes the material accessible and, above all, useful.

The book has a modular structure, with each chapter tackling a well-defined topic. Each chapter is then divided into blocks, with entry tags providing information about what the block seeks to accomplish—what issue it seeks to address. My hope is that some diligent readers will read through the presentation in sequence. I have tried to set up the book, though, so that readers pressed for time, seeking help with a specific issue, can use the modular structure to find just the bits they want, treating the book as a succession of targeted handbook entries. In all cases, though, I hope the book's structure allows swift and efficient access to the information the reader needs.

In Chapter 1, Foundational Issues, I discuss the scientific roots of the work described in the book. As I've noted, claims about perception and memory come from the field of research psychology and also from neuroscience and cognitive science, and so we need to ask: What are these fields? Are their results solidly enough established and an accurate-enough reflection of real-world complexities so that they can be taken seriously by law enforcement or admitted into court?

The next two chapters provide foundation of a different sort by laying out, in general terms, what we know about perception (Chapter 2) and memory (Chapter 3), with a focus on how these crucial human capacities operate in settings of interest to the justice system. Chapters 4 and 5 then tackle a specific type of perception and memory: the perception and recognition of faces. Chapter 4 is concerned with a broad set of questions about face memory, providing the basis, in Chapter 5, for examining what we know about the identification procedures that are used (or that might be used) in criminal cases.

Chapter 6 then turns to a different type of memory and considers how well people remember voices and conversations they have heard. Memory for voices is, of course, relevant to a different ("earwitness") type of identification. Memory for conversations brings us to questions relevant to both civil litigations ("When did you hear the stock was going to be issued?") and criminal cases (for example, cases alleging conspiracy or cases trying to discern someone's intent). In this chapter, I also consider how well investigators remember their own wording when they questioned a witness—and thus whether we can count on their reports of whether they put ideas into someone's mind or led the witness.

In Chapter 7, I turn to the topic of lies. I discuss the distinction between lies and false memories and consider the factors that are relevant to deciding whether an individual is telling one or experiencing the other. The chapter also discusses the detection of lies, both by interviewers and through technical means like polygraphy or functional magnetic resonance imaging (fMRI). How accurately can we distinguish honest individuals from deceivers or true statements from lies?

Chapter 8 tackles reports of a different type: potentially false reports of one's own actions—and thus false confessions. What leads someone to make a false confession? How often do false confessions emerge? Is there a way to distinguish a false confession from an accurate one?

In Chapter 9, I change perspective. The book so far has covered perceptual and memory errors pertinent to witnesses, victims, and investigators. But there is another regard in which perception and memory matter for the legal system: jurors' memory. After all, jurors often need to recall complex arguments, evidence, or instructions, and there's typically a delay between when jurors first gain this information (perhaps an idea posed during voir dire or evidence presented early in a trial) and when they use this information in deliberation. Moreover, jurors often need to remember the source from which they gained the information: Was a specific point, raised in deliberation, actually covered in evidence? Or was the point promised during opening statements but never delivered during trial? Or perhaps was the point part of the pretrial publicity that should not be considered during deliberation at all? I'll consider the evidence pertinent to all of these issues—including the evidence that bears on whether some of the proposed aids for jurors (such as note-taking) actually have an effect.

Finally, Chapters 10 and 11 turn to children's memories. The logic here parallels that in Chapters 4 and 5, with the first chapter in each pair providing crucial background, and the latter chapter in the pair turning specifically to questions about investigative procedures. In these two final chapters, we are seeking to ask whether (or, more sensibly, when) we can count on a child's report for a crime the child has witnessed (or, worse, a crime for which the child has been the victim). My focus in this section is on how children remember and report on abuse. I consider both the memories themselves and also so-called symptom evidence (i.e., psychological patterns that might result from the abuse and which therefore might be used as evidence for the abuse). I also discuss recovered memories—memories of abuse that seem to emerge only after a delay of many years.

Before diving into all of this material, though, I want to head off a common misunderstanding: I've spoken with judges, attorneys, and police officers about these issues, and many of them are concerned that all this research tends to challenge witnesses' perception and recall. They fear, therefore, that attention to this research will encourage skepticism about witness evidence and therefore undermine law enforcement and prosecution efforts.

I argue throughout the book, though, that this concern is without basis. To be sure, there are cases in which one factor or another signals a risk of perceptual or memory error, and, in those cases, we do need to be cautious—and perhaps even skeptical—in interpreting a witness's report. In other cases, though, we might look for factors that might have pulled a witness off track and find none; in such cases, the science might be used to bolster the witness's credibility. This point rests on the fact that human perception is generally accurate (and, in fact, rather precise). Likewise, human memory is, in general, relatively complete, long-lasting, and correct. Of course, errors do arise, but the errors are the exception, not the rule, and so we usually can count on witness evidence. Moreover, the errors in perception or memory do not occur randomly; instead, known factors encourage the errors, and so, by examining a specific case, we can often determine whether errors are likely in that setting or not. Thus, part of my motivation in writing this book is to highlight the reliability of witness evidence—so that police and the courts can step away from baseless challenges to a witness's report and can, when the circumstances are right, put more weight on witness reports.

Perhaps more importantly, it's my hope that we can use the catalog of possible problems in witness evidence as a basis for improving witness evidence. Many scientists have been pursuing this effort in the collection of ID evidence—using what we know about face memory in order to obtain better identifications. A similar effort has played a central role in cases involving children: By specifying what can go wrong in child interviewing, we can assemble a list of "do's" and "don'ts" for the professionals who conduct these interviews. In this fashion, the science has already produced better procedures—codified in clear professional guidelines—that help investigators to collect evidence from children that's stronger, clearer, and less vulnerable to challenge.

On these grounds, the science I'll be describing in this book should be useful to everyone in the justice system. Sometimes the science will undermine a witness's evidence. Sometimes the science will bolster the evidence. Best of all, often the science can help us to collect better evidence. But, with all of these possibilities in view, I think it's a mistake to argue that the science favors "one side" or the other.

Of course, I understand that our courts operate on an adversarial system, and so I fear some readers will be skeptical about the optimistic views I've just expressed. Even so, it's my hope that everyone in the justice system wants to maximize the quality of the information being considered and to seek ways of distinguishing good information from bad. The science can help us move toward these crucial goals, and this book is my small contribution to this endeavor.

ACKNOWLEDGMENTS

Many people helped me with this endeavor, and I'm grateful to them all. Don Read gave me the benefit of his enormous expertise in psychology; Alafair Burke provided important insights from her perspective as an attorney and former prosecutor. Alex Houston provided fabulous help in the effort of double-checking and documenting the research data throughout the book. And then, at OUP, Catharine Carlin was wonderfully encouraging in the early steps of this project, and Joan Bossert, Louis Gulino, and Ryan Cury have provided great support in the process since then.

I'm also profoundly grateful to the many police officers, attorneys, and judges I've worked with over the years. Many of them have read sections of the manuscript; some read all of it, and all have provided comments that substantially improved the book. More importantly, all of these individuals have collectively taught me an enormous amount about the justice system, and along the way helped me to see both the strengths and the limitations of my science. And, odd though it might be, I'm also indebted to the crime victims and the defendants whose cases I've worked on; they've taught me just how important it is to get these issues right.

I'm also grateful to Jacob (a lawyer-to-be) who, with loving intent, kept pushing me to write this book, because he understood how much I needed to write it. Solomon, in turn, never lets me forget what careful scientific analysis looks like, and that helps to keep me on track. And, of course, Friderike has read every page of this volume, and her challenges and critiques were always rooted in a mix of thoughtfulness that was deeply serious and support that was wonderfully loving.

And, finally, I write in loving memory of my father. My debt to both of my parents is immeasurable. Among many other gifts, they taught me to choose my battles, but also taught me that, when the issue really matters, you have to fight for what you believe in.

CHAPTER 1

Foundational Issues

Starting in Chapter 2, we'll tackle substantive issues about how perception and memory operate and how investigations might be structured to maximize the quality of witness evidence. In this chapter, though, we'll set the broad context. We'll discuss the scientific status of psychological research—and, with that, the admissibility of this research under a *Daubert* or *Frye* standard. We'll also consider one of the common, but misguided, objections to this science—namely, that the research simply confirms common sense.

A. IS THIS SCIENCE?
The Relation Between Clinical and Research Psychology

For many people, the word "psychology" conjures up images of a one-on-one conversation between a therapist, listening attentively, and a client (they're usually not called "patients") describing life's challenges—perhaps difficulties in the client's marriage, or concerns about depression, or problems in dealing with stress. This sort of image, however, is misleading in many ways and fails utterly to convey the other face of psychology—psychology as a research discipline.

The field of psychology is, in truth, better thought of as *two* fields, one that we can broadly call "clinical psychology" and one that we can broadly call "research psychology." There are, to be sure, psychologists who live in both of these worlds (and happily so, because the two domains can help each other in important ways and, arguably, *need* each other). For the most part, though, the clinicians and researchers are distinct groups, with different types of training, different skills, and different knowledge, and these groups provide very different types of information for the justice system.

Clinical psychologists are generally trained as health care professionals, with an emphasis, of course, on mental health. These psychologists are skilled in the diagnosis, treatment, and, in some cases, prevention of mental problems. They help people who suffer from depression or anxiety; they help people to overcome compulsions or even addictions. They help people cope with stress. They can provide individualized assessment, telling you what someone's intelligence level is, or whether the person suffers from schizophrenia, or whether the person is competent to stand trial, or perhaps eligible for an insanity defense. In important ways, the work these psychologists do resembles (or overlaps with) the work done by psychiatrists, social workers, and counselors (although each of these professions is different from the others in some ways, including the educational background that can lead to each).

Research psychologists, in contrast, are trained not in diagnosis or treatment, but in the standard methods of science. They have laboratories, not clinics. They usually work in an academic setting, not in a hospital or mental health facility. Unlike clinicians (who are often licensed by a state agency), researchers have no licenses because there is simply no such thing as an officially approved "research license." Instead, researchers establish their credibility through educational and academic credentials (usually a Ph.D. in a field that involves scientific training and a post at a reputable institution). Far more important, quality control in the world of research is carried out not by some governing agency but in the fashion that's standard in the scientific world: by means of peer review. (I'll say more about peer review later in the chapter).

Many people outside of the academic world don't realize that research psychology even exists—and hence the misleading image that launched this chapter. Part of the reason is numerical: Clinicians outnumber psychology researchers by a substantial margin. And part of the reason is functional: Ordinary citizens often interact with clinicians (as therapists, counselors, and so on) but may never encounter a researcher. It's important to emphasize, therefore, that research psychology is a long-standing and well-established enterprise. Research psychology has been part of the university curriculum for a century. The *Journal of Experimental Psychology* began publication in 1916; in that year, *Psychological Review* was already publishing its 23rd volume. In more recent years, research psychologists have won a half-dozen Nobel prizes and are well represented in the U.S. National Academy of Sciences, alongside biologists, chemists, and physicists.

Psychology researchers pursue a range of detailed questions about why exactly people see what they see, remember what they remember, think what they think, and feel what they feel. The research is often multidisciplinary: To understand vision, for example, one needs to understand some fundamental points about the physics of light and the biology of the eyeball and the brain. To understand thinking, we often need to draw on insights from logicians studying deduction or economists studying choice; we sometimes test our proposals by building computer models designed to simulate a process or by comparing our claims to events in the nervous system. Indeed, this merging of methodological perspectives is the source of the term *cognitive science*, a label given to the multidisciplinary effort of asking questions about the mind. The constituents of cognitive science include psychology, anthropology, philosophy, computer science, linguistics, and *neuroscience* (which is itself an amalgam of the many disciplines aimed at an understanding of the nervous system).

Within research psychology, which specialties are likely to be useful for the justice system? *Cognitive psychologists* study perception, attention, and memory, and therefore can provide the justice system with information about these topics (topics crucial, of course, for evaluating witness evidence). *Social psychologists* study how people perceive each other, think about each other, and are influenced by each other. They can therefore provide information about witness evidence (because, after all, witnesses are usually reporting on an encounter with another human being). *Developmental psychologists* are concerned with how people change and grow across the lifespan and so can provide important information about memory in children or in the elderly, and also information about some of the important complexities of communicating with young children.

Defining Science

Should research psychology be taken seriously as a scientific discipline? The answer lies, of course, in the definition of science. Specifically, any scientific endeavor starts by formulating *empirical claims*—claims about the factual world that, ultimately, could be shown to be true or false. Science then tests those claims in a rigorous manner, using established tools and procedures. Those tests must satisfy strong requirements at every stage: in the formulation of the testable claim itself; in the design of the test procedure; and in the collection, analysis, and interpretation of data. Then, once the interpretation is in place, the entire sequence must be subjected to the critical scrutiny of other scholars, checking for flaws of any sort. It is only when the interpretation has survived this scrutiny that it can be taken seriously. And, of course, if the pattern of the data conflicts with a claim, then the claim needs to be adjusted or set aside. It is not acceptable, in the scientific world, to assert an empirical claim as true if there are no data to support the claim, and it is surely not acceptable to continue asserting a claim if there are data that contradict the claim. (For more on psychology's status as a science, see Malpass, Ross, Meissner, & Marcon, 2009.)

The Importance of Replication

It is also important that, in science, very few claims rest on just a single finding. There are several reasons for this, but one key reason is that, with all of our safeguards (checks on the reliability and validity of our measures, appropriate sampling procedures, and so on), there is always a chance that a result may emerge just as a fluke. (For more on what a "fluke" might be in this setting, see the later section on "Known or Potential Error Rate.") Science needs to guard against this possibility, and one way it does so is via *replication*—repeating an experiment (perhaps with an identical procedure, perhaps with some variation) in a new setting with a new experimenter and a new group of participants. If the result emerges again, this strengthens the claim that the earlier finding wasn't a fluke and also indicates that the result is robust enough to show up despite changes in the exact circumstances.

All of these requirements apply to any science, and they certainly apply to the study of psychology. Of course, the courts have developed their own criteria for evaluating the admissibility of scientific evidence or scientific testimony, and I will turn to those criteria in a moment. But, by any conventional definition, the inquiries conducted in psychology laboratories satisfy the requirements of "science," and, on that basis, the claims offered by psychologists, coming out of their research, deserve the same status as those offered by biology, chemistry, or any other scientific enterprise.

B. IS THE SCIENCE APPLICABLE TO "REAL-WORLD" CASES?

There is, however, an important concern attached to the courts' use of psychological research. To explain this point, let's start with a problem that scientists themselves need to address. Imagine that a psychologist wanted to learn which witnesses are more likely to have accurate memories and which are less so. As a first step toward answering this question, the psychologist might wonder, for example: Are women better at remembering events than men are? To find out, he recruits a dozen men and a dozen women, asks each to recount what he or she did the afternoon before, and then assesses these recollections for their level of detail.

This inquiry would, in fact, tell us little. As one problem, notice that this procedure provides no way of asking whether the recollections are accurate. Perhaps the women report more details, but get these details wrong. Or, as a different concern, notice that we may not have a "level playing field" here. Perhaps the women's lives actually contain more interesting, more distinctive events, and their lives are therefore easier to remember. If so, then their memories may be no better than men's, but they will nonetheless remember more because their lives are overall more memorable.

Let's emphasize, though, the role of the word "perhaps" in the previous paragraph. We said that *perhaps* the women are getting the details wrong and that *perhaps* their lives contain more interesting events. We certainly don't know that these suggestions are correct, and, indeed, we have no basis for suspecting that they're correct. But these suggestions *might be* correct, and that is enough to make the outcome of this (fictitious) experiment ambiguous. If we conducted the experiment, we would have no way to conclude anything with certainty. Or, to put the point broadly, if a result is ambiguous, it can sustain no conclusions: If there's more than one plausible way to think about the data, we don't know which way is correct, and so we can draw no claims from the data.

The logic behind these points is straightforward: Scientists would rather say nothing than say something wrong, and they would rather say nothing than say something that is unwarranted by the data. As a result, the operative rule is indeed: When there is ambiguity in the data, say nothing.

The Advantage of Controlled Settings

How do scientists—and psychologists in particular—address the concern just raised? In most cases, our path forward involves bringing the question into the laboratory: To continue with this (admittedly artificial) example, we could arrange for men and women both to witness the same event, perhaps a movie that we show them. We then let some predetermined amount of time go by before we question them about what they saw. And, because we showed them the movie, we know exactly what was in the movie, and so we can easily check the accuracy of their recall. Moreover, since our two groups saw the *same* movie, we now have a "clean comparison"—a comparison between men and women in which all other factors are held constant, thus isolating the factor (the gender difference) that we wanted to learn about.

The advantages of this approach (i.e., the benefits of scientific control) can be illustrated with numerous examples. As one case, Yuille and Cutshall (1986) interviewed witnesses to an actual crime and found that witnesses who experienced the most stress (by their own report) were also the witnesses most accurate in describing the event. This observation might imply that stress promotes memory, but there is an interpretive problem here: The witnesses who were most stressed by this crime were also the witnesses positioned closer to the crime (presumably this is why they felt the most stress), and therefore they actually had a better view than less-stressed witnesses. We need to ask, therefore, whether their better memory was a product of the stress or of their viewing opportunity. There is no way to determine this in the Yuille and Cutshall data, and that is the point here: In the laboratory, we can control circumstances and isolate the variable of interest (e.g., stress) with other factors held constant; studies outside of the laboratory, like the Yuille and Cutshall study, do not allow us this advantage. (And, by the way, data indicate that stress typically undermines memory rather than improving it; see Chapter 2.)

Addressing the Problem of Artificiality

The controls provided by the laboratory are valuable, but introduce their own problem. Returning to our example, if we know how men and women remember *in the laboratory,* does this tell us how they remember in other circumstances? (Perhaps women are more impressed by the laboratory setting and thus try harder in our tasks.) Likewise, if, in our study, we find a difference in how men and women remember the movies we show them, can we draw conclusions about how they remember other materials? (Perhaps men are less interested in cinema and so pay less attention to the film, in comparison to women.)

The point of all this should by now be obvious: Psychologists often move into controlled environments to gain scientific power, but, in doing so, they pay a price of artificiality. How can we address this concern? How can we make certain that lessons we draw from the research world are truly applicable to the "real world"?

The answer has several elements. First, we do what we can to minimize the artificiality in our studies—and so we take steps to narrow the gap between the circumstances in our experiments and the circumstances we ultimately want to understand. Moreover, we often do "hybrid" studies that are conducted in a controlled manner but carried out in a realistic (nonlaboratory) setting. Thus, studies of how stress affects memory are sometimes conducted in doctors' offices, probing the memories of patients undergoing actually stressful medical procedures. Likewise, studies of how inattention can influence perception (and therefore memory) sometimes probe how well or how poorly people remember objects in their day-to-day environment.

Second, we can use the methods of science to study the artificiality itself. As an example of this kind of testing, Haber and Haber (2001) wondered whether it matters that research participants in the laboratory know that they are in an experiment. Do they perhaps take the procedure less seriously because they know it is "only" an experiment? Or perhaps are they more attentive because they know their memories will be tested? Haber and Haber checked on these possibilities by means of a complex design that compared identification accuracy (choosing the perpetrator from a lineup) in two groups of studies: some in which people knew they were in a research experiment and some in which they did not know this. The data show no difference, suggesting that this (possible) worry is less pressing than it might initially seem.

Similarly, many studies have presented research participants with a video of a crime or a staged crime, with the participants merely bystanders to the event and not actually involved in the event. Does this contrast—bystanders versus victims—matter? If so, then this, too, would be a challenge to the realism of our studies and the value of our data. But, again, this is an issue that can be explored through research: Hosch and Cooper (1982; see also Hosch, Leippe, Marchioni, & Cooper, 1984, or, as a related study, see Ihlebaek, Løve, Eilertsen and Magnussen, 2003) compared several conditions: In one, participants were bystanders to an event; in another, the participants were fully involved in an event. As we will see in Chapter 6, this contrast does matter for some issues (thus, you are better able to remember a conversation if you were involved in the conversation rather than merely hearing it). However, the Hosch and Cooper data suggest that this concern can, in the case of eyewitness reports, be set aside.

Third, and perhaps most importantly, it is often possible to "cross-check" the data from controlled studies against data collected from real-world settings. Thus, for example, many laboratory studies show that people are less accurate when making *cross-race identifications* (a Caucasian recognizing an African American or vice versa) than when making *same-race identifications* (e.g., a Caucasian recognizing a Caucasian; see Chapter 4). Is this finding replicable in actual crime investigations? We can find out by (among other options) examining real police records and asking how often actual crime victims can identify their assailants in same-race crimes and how often in cross-race crimes. These field data are themselves open to more than one interpretation, but we can surely ask if the field data are as we'd expect them to be, based on the data from controlled studies. In fact, they generally are (e.g., Platz & Hosch, 1988), and it is this convergence between controlled studies and field studies that reassures us that our data are indeed providing a realistic portrait of how perception and memory function.

Likewise, we know that, in the laboratory, eyewitnesses often make errors, selecting from a simulated lineup someone who is not the person they saw in a simulated crime. Does this pattern reflect the reality of actual crimes? As we will see in Chapter 4, it does, and studies of actual police files suggest that real witnesses to real crimes choose someone innocent from a lineup at least 20% of the time.

This cross-checking needs to be done again and again, issue by issue, because some findings from the laboratory will turn out to be replicable in field settings whereas others will turn out not to be. Of course, for some findings, replicability is inevitable. (For example, the structure of the eyeball will be the same in the laboratory or outside of it, and so data patterns caused by this structure will inevitably hold up in the field data, just as they appear in the lab.) Far more commonly, though, we need to probe the replicability, treating any concerns about artificiality in the same way we would treat any empirical issue: as a matter to be investigated through appropriate study, using the standard methods of science.

C. IS PSYCHOLOGICAL SCIENCE ADMISSIBLE UNDER THE *DAUBERT* STANDARD?

One of the ways psychological science can be used by the justice system is via courtroom testimony delivered by a suitably chosen expert. Presumably, the expert can, in many circumstances, provide a framework that will inform the finders of fact as they seek to interpret the evidence. But this raises a question: Is this sort of testimony reliable and helpful? Or, more bluntly, is it admissible?

In U.S. federal court, the standard for admissibility is laid out in the so-called *Daubert* trilogy, a succession of three U.S. Supreme Court cases: *Daubert v. Merrell Dow Pharmaceuticals; General Electric Co. v. Joiner;* and *Kumho Tire Co. v. Carmichael.* Many states have adopted their own versions of the *Daubert* rulings; a few states have retained the older *Frye* standard (see the later section on "General Acceptance" and also Section D, targeted on the *Frye* standard).

The *Daubert* ruling has also influenced Canadian courts. The admissibility of experts in Canada is broadly governed by the standards laid out in *R. v. Mohan*, a ruling that emphasized that expert testimony must be relevant to the case and also necessary in assisting the trier of fact. Like the *Daubert* ruling in the United States, *Mohan* puts the trial judge in the position of "gatekeeper," deciding if the science is admissible or not. And, just as in the United States, Canadian courts are clear that the expert evidence should be excluded if its probative value is outweighed by its likely prejudicial impact. Some years after *Mohan*, though, the Canadian Supreme Court clarified these rules in *R. v. J. (J. L.)*. Here, the Court ruled that *novel* science could be admissible, and it endorsed criteria echoing those in the U.S. *Daubert* ruling (but also noted that *Daubert* is rooted in the U.S. rules of evidence, which differ somewhat from those in place in Canada).

What is the *Daubert* standard? The court ruling emphasizes a number of criteria that define the scientific method and which make scientific knowledge "reliable." (Note, though, that the Supreme Court made it clear that these criteria are nonexclusive [and so other criteria may be considered] and nondispositive [and thus do not, on their own, settle the question].) The specific criteria listed in the *Daubert* ruling are (1) falsifiability, (2) peer review, (3) known or potential error rate, (4) existence of standards and controls, and (5) general acceptance. Subsequent rulings (and some state rulings) add a further important criterion: (6) sufficient facts or data.

Falsifiability?

The scientific community and the courts agree that scientific claims must be testable, and, for the past half-century, scientists have usually understood "testable" to mean "falsifiable." In other words, scientists are generally skeptical about the idea that a claim can be *verified*—that is, proven true. There are several reasons for this position, including the idea that the facts will always fit with a *vague* theory (because a vague theory can accommodate any fact pattern). If, therefore, we were to count a theory as "proven" when the theory fits with many facts, then we would routinely gather "proof" for vague theories—and that's an unacceptable prospect for science. (Think about how easily we could prove claims like, "Sometime soon, something interesting will happen," or "either tomorrow will be fun for you, or it won't." For theories like these, proof is cheaply acquired and of no value whatsoever.)

To avoid this prospect, scientists insist that their theories be specific enough so that it is clear which facts would fit with the theory and which facts would not. That latter clause rules out vague theories and also theories that build in too much flexibility (so that they have an escape clause no matter how the data turn out). And, of course, that clause also means that the theory is falsifiable: That is, there are facts that might emerge that would be incompatible with the theory and that would force us to abandon the theory.

To put this point slightly differently, a theory is testable only if it makes "risky predictions"—predictions that might turn out not to be true (e.g., Popper, 1963). If a theory has made these predictions and has *not* been falsified, this bolsters our confidence that the theory is correct. At that point, we would say that the theory is "confirmed." A theory that makes "risk-free predictions," in contrast, is going to fit with the facts no matter what those facts are, and hence the idea of "confirmation" loses its meaning.

These principles are certainly respected by psychology research. Our experiments do involve risky predictions. Our professional journals insist that claims be falsifiable. Indeed, the undergraduate curriculum in psychology often highlights examples of theories that are not falsifiable (Sigmund Freud's theorizing is a favorite example) and showcases for students the reasons why this status is unacceptable for a scientific claim. In these ways, falsifiability is woven into the fabric of our field—and so psychology satisfies this criterion.

Subjected to Peer Review and Publication?

Scientists use the term *research literature* to refer to scholarly articles published on a particular topic—usually articles appearing in specialized professional journals. Scientists take a result seriously only if it appears in this literature, and the reason is straightforward: Papers are published in the literature only when they have survived a rigorous evaluation process.

To understand this process, consider what happens when a researcher hopes to get a paper published. The researcher sends the manuscript to the editor of one of the field's journals. The editor, in turn, sends the manuscript to carefully selected reviewers—usually experts on the topic covered in the paper. In most cases, the manuscript is stripped of identifying information (the name of the authors, the authors' institution) before it is sent to the reviewers, to avoid bias. (And, I should mention, this latter step seems to be successful: For the vast majority of the papers I've been asked to review, I have no idea who the paper's authors are.)

The reviewers read the paper and provide a written report for the editor—evaluating the paper's strengths and weaknesses and cataloguing any concerns, whether large or small. Based on these evaluations, the editor reaches a decision about the paper's fate: accepted, rejected, accepted pending revisions, rejected with suggestions for improvements, and so on.

In this process, the reviewers are understood to be the manuscript authors' "peers" and hence the name *peer review*. The notion of "peers" reflects the idea that all scientists have equal status in this process (and so a paper will not be published merely because the author is famous or based at a prestigious institution). The reviewers are also the authors' peers in another sense: The reviewers understand the paper's methods and analysis, just as the author does; they understand the theoretical framework, just as the author does. Hence, there is no risk that the reviewers will simply defer to the author's superior knowledge. Instead, the reviewers will provide expert-level, well-informed evaluation—just what we want.

The peer-review process is arguably the only path forward for science: Who else, besides a researcher's peers, has the training and expertise with which to evaluate a perhaps technical, perhaps sophisticated paper? And, with this process, journals are quite selective; most scientific journals reject the majority of submitted manuscripts. (Rejection rates of more than 70% or even 80% are common at the field's top journals.) It seems reasonable, therefore, that the "consumers" of research (other investigators, for example) take a paper seriously when it has (and *only* when it has) survived this gauntlet.

Of course, sometimes good papers get rejected; lower quality papers sometimes sneak through. However, if a weak paper does end up in print, readers of the journal are likely to respond in some way—writing rejoinders or seeking to publish their own studies in rebuttal to the original paper. Here, the field is relying on a broader form of peer review (with the journal's readers now serving as the peers) and, for this purpose, the passage of time is important. Scientific debates can take years to unfold, and this slow pace creates an opportunity for rebuttal to an already-published paper, if appropriate, and allows other researchers a chance to publish their own work, perhaps challenging the initial finding. Indeed, we mentioned earlier that it is rare for researchers to draw a claim from a single study; it is likewise rare that researchers draw strong conclusions from a single paper. Instead, the passage of time will lead to an accumulation of papers on a topic, all of which have been through the peer-review process. If there is a consistent pattern across all of these papers, and if the claims have survived all the challenges, then, finally, the claims are accepted as firmly established.

Does the field of research psychology rely on this process? The answer is a clear "yes." Does the field, as a result, rely on a succession of specialized and sophisticated journals? The answer is again a clear "yes," and a listing of the journals can be found on the websites of the American Psychological Association, the Association for Psychological Science, and the Psychonomic Society (and others). Thus, on these criteria as well, research psychology passes the *Daubert*-defined test.

Known or Potential Error Rate?
Defining "Error Rate" in Terms of Probabilities

The *Daubert* ruling (and the various state rulings derived from it) asks whether a method has a "known or potential error rate." This notion is easily understood when evaluating a specific procedure or a specific measure: What is the error rate associated with, say, the polygraph as a lie detection device? We can, with appropriate studies, determine what percentage of the people telling lies are correctly identified as such via a polygraph examination and what percentage of truth-tellers are falsely accused. We can then use these percentages as our estimates of the *error rate* for this procedure. (We return to this example, and the assessment of the polygraphy, in Chapter 7.)

The idea of "error rate" is less transparent, though, when evaluating a broad claim resting on many different experiments. Consider, for example, a scenario in which an expert testifies that an eyewitness's *degree of certainty* provides little information about whether the eyewitness's recall is correct or not. (We'll return to this claim in Chapters 3 and 5.) In other words, the expert testifies that research has shown only a weak correspondence between someone's confidence in a memory and the accuracy of that memory. What is the error rate associated with this claim?

The answer to this question is somewhat complicated and we'll walk through the details in the next two subsections. For readers who don't want the details, however, here is a brief summary of the argument: Researchers want to avoid making claims that are not justified by evidence. (As we said earlier, scientists generally prefer to say nothing rather than say something wrong.) This sentiment leads researchers to ask, for any observed pattern in their data, "Could the pattern be a mere fluke? The product of some sort of lucky accident?" Statistical procedures allow researchers to ask these questions in a precise fashion and, in particular, allow them to calculate the probability of the results indeed being a mere fluke.

From this base, we do know the "rate of error" associated with each of our claims. More precisely, we know the probability that a claim is not warranted by the data. And, perhaps more importantly, researchers draw conclusions from the data only if this probability is very low—less than one-in-twenty when considering a single experimental result, and much, much lower when considering a fabric of results drawn from multiple experiments.

Type 1 and Type 2 Error

There are two types of errors one can make in research: concluding from the data that a hypothesis is correct when in reality it is not, and concluding from the data that the hypothesis is wrong when in truth it is correct. In most cases, researchers try to be as cautious as they can and so they generally regard the former error (technically called a *type 1 error* or, in more common terms, a false alarm) as more troubling than the latter (a *type 2 error* or false negative, or—less formally—a "miss"). Again: Scientists would rather say nothing than say something wrong. Hence, it's better to overreject claims than to overaccept; that way, you are unlikely to say something that is wrong. As a result, many statistical procedures are designed explicitly to avoid type 1 errors—the false alarms.

Therefore, when a judge in a *Daubert* hearing asks about the error rate associated with a research claim, the answer can be framed in terms of the field's statistical methods. Specifically, we can provide the judge with information about the risk of a type 1 error—the risk that the expert is offering a claim not justified by the evidence. But how is the risk calculated, and how great is the risk?

In most cases, statistical procedures begin with the *null hypothesis*—that is, the hypothesis that, in reality, there is no systematic difference between the conditions or groups being compared. The statistics are then designed to ask: If the null hypothesis were true, then how likely is it that the study would have produced the pattern of results actually observed? Or, to put this differently, the null hypothesis is essentially a claim that any differences that are observed must be the result of chance fluctuation in the data. Framed in this way, the statistics are asking: What is the probability of getting the results observed in a study purely by chance? What is the probability that the results are just a fluke?

A simple example may be useful here: Imagine that you are tossing a coin and have just observed that the last eight tosses have all been "heads." You wonder: Could the coin somehow be biased? The null hypothesis here would be that the coin is *not* biased, so that any departures from a 50–50 distribution of "heads" and "tails" is just a matter of random chance. In this case, some simple calculation would tell you that, if the null hypothesis is correct here, the probability of observing your result (eight heads in a row) is roughly 0.4%. In other words, if you did this "experiment" 1,000 times with a fair coin, you might get this result, just by chance, in 4 of those 1,000 tries. Hence, this result *could* happen by chance, but it is the sort of observation that would happen only rarely by chance. You are therefore likely to conclude, since you got this result on your very first try, that the succession of eight "heads" is probably not the result of mere chance, and thus you would conclude that your coin is indeed biased.

The logic is the same when scientists evaluate their data. Statistical procedures are used to calculate the exact probability of getting the observed results just by chance, just by a lucky accident. This probability is described as a "p-value," and a p-value must be calculated for every comparison a researcher wishes to make. (Thus, a single experiment will often require many p-values if the researcher wishes first to compare *this* aspect of the data and then *that* aspect, and so on.) If the p-value is high (i.e., a high probability), then there is a substantial likelihood that the data might be the product of mere chance—and, if so, we draw no conclusions from the data. Conversely, if the p-value is low, then it's quite unlikely that the results came about by chance, and so the risk of a false claim—a type 1 error— is correspondingly low.

How are p-values calculated? The mathematical details aren't necessary here, but, in general, three considerations are in play in these calculations. First, how large a difference is there between the conditions (or groups) being compared? (This difference is referred to as the "effect size," and, all things equal, larger effect sizes are less likely to come about by chance and so yield smaller p-values; we'll have more to say about the term "effect size" in a later section.) Second, how consistent are the data? (All things equal, data patterns that are more consistent—less variable—are less likely to come about by chance and so, again, yield smaller p-values.) Third, how many observations did the researcher make? How many points of data are there? (All things equal, data patterns based on more observations are less likely to come about by chance, and so, once again, yield smaller p-values.) Let's note, though, that these three considerations can be traded against each other. (If the effect size is large and the variability is small, you need fewer observations. If the variability is large, you either need a larger effect size or more observations. And so on.) But, in any case, it is a straightforward matter, for a given comparison, to calculate the relevant p-values and thus to determine the danger that the result might be a matter of sheer chance. We take the result seriously only when that probability—the level of danger—is very, very low.

So What is the Error Rate?

Scientists want the risk of a type 1 error to be low—but how low is "low enough" to justify drawing conclusions? By convention, when evaluating a single study, researchers employ the criterion that we alluded to earlier, a criterion defined as "p <.05." In other words, researchers will draw conclusions from an observed difference only if the probability of obtaining this result just by chance is less than 5%. Or, turning this around, researchers will draw conclusions only if the odds are 19-to-1 that mere chance wouldn't produce the result.

This 5% rule is, however, merely the cut-off for acceptability, and many results in the literature have much lower p-values associated with them. (Thus, the research literature often contains results that are reliable at a level of $p < .01$ or $p < .001$, and thus results for which the risk of a type 1 error is 1.0% or even 0.1%, respectively.) In addition, we need to be clear that the $p < .05$ rule describes how researchers think about single, isolated results—the product of just one comparison, in one study. This is crucial because, as we've said, scientists are rarely guided by a single result. Instead, scientific claims rest on broad patterns of interlocking results, with different studies replicating an original finding, evaluating concerns about that finding, or testing claims about the mechanism that led to the finding, and so on. As the fabric of evidence grows, the likelihood of the results being a matter of chance necessarily gets lower and lower. On this basis, the actual risk of error for a research claim is much lower than 5%. (We will return to this point when we turn to the statistical procedure known as meta-analysis.)

Where does all of this leave us with regard to the *Daubert* standard? The rate of error for a scientific claim can be construed as the likelihood that the claim might not be justified by the research evidence. In other words, the Court's request for a rate of error can be addressed with the researchers' calculation of the probability of a type 1 error. This error rate is known because it is the result of precise calculations. And the error rate is guaranteed to be low because results will be taken seriously by the scientific community only when the results "pass" this statistical test.

Existence of Standards

Training in Research Methods

Another criterion named in the *Daubert* ruling is the existence of standard research methods, and this criterion is easily met by research psychology. The methods of the field are routinely covered as part of the educational curriculum—both at the undergraduate level and in graduate training. Indeed, this training usually begins with the very first "Intro" course; most textbooks for this course include a chapter on research design and statistics. In Ph.D. programs, courses in methodology are nearly universal.

Measuring Mental Attributes

In most studies, psychologists use measurements that are straightforward and objective. For example, if we are studying the relation between identification accuracy and a witness's degree of certainty, we can assess identification accuracy by simply noting whether the witness chose the suspect from the lineup or did not; we assess degree of certainty by asking the witness to provide us with a number—perhaps a percentage, with 0% indicating a guess and 100% indicating total confidence.

In some cases, though, research demands the construction of novel measures. For example, we will see in Chapter 8 that the risk of false confession is elevated if a suspect happens to have a lower-than-average level of *intelligence* or a higher-than-average level of the personality trait of *compliance*. Of course, research on these points is possible only if we have a means of assessing someone's level of intelligence or compliance, and, in addition, we obviously need some basis for claiming that these assessments are trustworthy.

Psychologists have well-defined procedures for developing and evaluating a measurement scale (whether we are considering a scale that assesses some mental *capacity,* like intelligence, or one that assesses a *trait,* like compliance). We also have clear standards that these scales must meet before they are used in research. Among other points, a measurement scale must be *reliable*—that is, consistent in what it measures. In some cases, the focus is on consistency *within* the measuring tool (are *these* questions really measuring the same capacity as *those* questions?); in other cases, the focus is on consistency *across time* (if I test you today, will I reach the same conclusion as I did based on last week's test?). Perhaps more importantly, a measurement scale must also be shown to be *valid*—that is, measuring what it purports to measure. The test's reliability and validity are central aspects of the test's *psychometric properties,* and these properties must be assessed and documented before any measurement scale can be used.

Enforcing the Standards

We've now said that psychology—like any science—has clear standards for how research should be conducted, but how are those standards enforced? Part of the answer is already in view: via the journals' peer-review process. Reviewers are certainly alert to possible problems in a study's design or statistical analysis, and papers will not make it into print if problems are detected.

However, we should acknowledge that, in a small number of cases, unscrupulous researchers have fabricated data, and so bogus (but seemingly sensible) papers have made it into the journals. In other cases, researchers have become mercenaries, and so will (among other options) testify in court in a fashion that serves a defendant or a plaintiff but that deliberately misrepresents the scientific evidence.

When the research community detects these cases, we deal harshly with them. If a professional journal learns that a paper is based on some sort of false reporting, the paper is removed from the body of scientific evidence: The paper is officially retracted, and subsequent researchers will not rely on that now-retracted paper as a source of evidence. In addition, a variety of sanctions are likely so that the researcher is, in effect, cut off from the field. Thus, if a researcher is found to be dishonest, that researcher will no longer receive funding from granting agencies, will no longer be asked to serve as a reviewer for the journals, will no longer be invited to contribute chapters to edited volumes, will no longer be invited as a speaker, and more. In many cases, the researcher's home institution will conduct its own investigation and offer some form of censure, including the option of dismissal from the institution. Overall, the research community puts a high value on its own credibility and the credibility of its results and reacts strongly to anyone who puts that credibility in danger.

General Acceptance?

In federal court, the *Daubert* criteria replaced the older *Frye* standard, but, even so, the *Daubert* ruling incorporates the notion that was central for *Frye*—the idea that "general acceptance" of a scientific claim is an indicator of reliability. This notion is discussed in full in Section D, but, overall, there is no question that the methods and procedures of research psychology are generally accepted, and, as already discussed, are enshrined in the curriculum and peer-review process. But what about individual results or individual claims? For these, general acceptance cannot be taken for granted and has to be determined on a case-by-case basis. As it turns out, there are straightforward means through which we can assess the degree of acceptance, within the scientific community, for this or that claim, and we will consider these means in a moment.

Sufficient Evidence?

Scientific claims must rest on good methods *and* good evidence drawn from those claims. After all, no matter how careful one's procedures, a claim cannot be taken seriously if the evidence for it is thin. But this point—like the issue of general acceptance (see Section D)—must be evaluated on a case-by-case basis. Overall, though, let's note that there is an enormous amount of research relevant to the topics covered in this book. For example, Cutler and Penrod (1995, p. 68) estimated some years ago that eyewitness psychology had been the subject of more than 2,000 research publications; the number has obviously grown since then. There are similarly large quantities of research on children's memories, the detection of lies, and so on.

In addition, the studies discussed in this book, focused on questions of immediate interest to the justice system, are rooted in a far broader context, one created by many other studies that collectively provide the methodological and substantive foundation for the data described here. Some of these other studies are focused on basic operating principles of perception and memory (and research on these broad topics has been ongoing in hundreds of laboratories for well over a century). Other studies examine the functioning of the nervous system and how the nervous system supports perception and memory. Still other studies probe the statistical and methodological assumptions that underlie our research. Studies of eyewitness memory must be consistent with the evidence provided by all of this research, and if (say) a claim about eyewitness memory conflicted with claims about memory in other domains, this would be a puzzle demanding immediate attention. More strongly, the fabric of evidence in all of these arenas provides a large, mutually supportive set of scientific facts, and it is this full set of facts that makes us confident the science is working properly.

D. IS THE SCIENCE ADMISSIBLE UNDER A *FRYE* STANDARD?
General Acceptance of Method

The notion of "general acceptance" is one of several *Daubert* criteria, but was, of course, central for the older *Frye* criteria still employed by many states (including California, Florida, New York, and Washington). As discussed in Section C, the notion of general acceptance is straightforward if we are asking whether research psychology's *methods* are generally accepted. To be sure, there are occasional debates about methodology—for example, whenever a new method is introduced. And, even for established methods, there are occasional challenges; indeed, any vital science encourages these challenges as a way of always remaining open to criticism and always open to improvement in its methodological claims. But, as discussed earlier, the central methods of psychological research are widely accepted, invariably covered in the curriculum, documented in textbooks at various levels, and so on.

General Acceptance of Empirical Findings

What about psychology's *findings*, or its *empirical claims*? Are these generally accepted? Many psychologists view this as an issue to be settled through research. In other words, we can, in effect, measure general acceptance. Specifically, we can poll the investigators who have expertise on a particular topic or (more broadly) poll investigators who are familiar with the relevant data and in these ways find out what proportion of these investigators agree with a particular proposition and how many of them regard the proposition as well established.

This sort of survey data has been collected for some research topics, including research on the polygraph (Iacano & Lykken, 1997) and also research on eyewitness testimony (e.g., Benton, Ross, Bradshaw, Thomas, & Bradshaw, 2005; Kassin, Ellsworth, & Smith, 1989; Kassin, Tubb, Hosch, & Memon, 2001). These surveys tell us, not surprisingly, that investigators regard some points as well-established (and so there is general acceptance of these points) and regard other points as uncertain and in need of further study. Hence, general acceptance has to be considered on a point-by-point basis.

Let's be careful, though, not to overinterpret these surveys-of-experts. As one concern, these surveys provide a snapshot of a particular historical moment and so reflect researchers' beliefs at the time the survey was conducted. We need to be alert, therefore, to the possibility that subsequent data may strengthen a claim that the researchers regarded as not-yet-established or perhaps undermine a claim that the researchers thought was secure.

In addition, these surveys (like any research study) can be scrutinized—and sometimes criticized—by other researchers and, of course, by attorneys as well. Did the survey include the proper selection of experts? Was there perhaps some bias in how the experts were chosen? Were the questions phrased appropriately? Questions like these can be and sometimes have been raised in challenge to these "general acceptance" surveys. (For an example of these challenges, see Bailey & Mecklenburg, 2009.)

It is therefore prudent to check the surveys against other forms of evidence. As one option, we can assess general acceptance by counting up papers in the literature: How many support a proposition? How many—through argument or data—challenge the proposition? In addition, psychologists have issued a number of white papers on topics relevant to the justice system. In any field, a *white paper* is intended as an authoritative report, usually commissioned by some well-established organization, designed to summarize evidence and educate readers about a particular topic. In psychology, white papers have been commissioned by a number of our professional organizations. For example, the American Psychology-Law Society (AP-LS) assembled a blue-ribbon panel of experts in 1998 to summarize, in a wide ranging and authoritative way, the state of the art on eyewitness identifications (Wells et al., 1998); the AP-LS commissioned another white paper, in 2010, to summarize the available research on police-induced (false) confessions (Kassin et al., 2010b).

As yet another indication of "general acceptance," the Association for Psychological Science (APS) publishes a journal entitled *Psychological Science in the Public Interest*. The APS describes this journal as publishing reviews that are "written by blue ribbon teams of specialists representing a range of viewpoints, and are intended to assess the current state-of-the-science." (This quotation appears alongside the masthead in each issue of the journal.) Articles in this journal have covered the research on lie detection (Vrij, Granhag, & Porter, 2010), eyewitness evidence (Wells, Memon, & Penrod, 2006), adolescent decision making (Reyna & Farley, 2006), and the psychology of confessions (Kassin & Gudjonsson, 2004). These reviews are both a valuable source of information for anyone in the justice system and also provide a prima facie basis for claiming that these results are broadly enough accepted to have appeared in these authoritative reviews.

Finally, various professional organizations, including the American Psychological Association and the American Psychiatric Association, have filed amicus briefs that are directly relevant to issues described in this text. These briefs are available online, indexed by issue,[1] and thus provide a valuable resource for litigators. Of course, these briefs advocate for the organizations' own position, but, even so, they are subjected to a rigorous review process relying on the broad expertise of the organizations' membership and are carefully documented. Thus, the existence of these briefs provides yet another indication of the general acceptance of the relevant findings.

---

1. For example, see http://www.apa.org/about/offices/ogc/amicus/index-issues.aspx

E. DOES THE RESEARCH GO BEYOND COMMON SENSE?

The *Daubert* ruling requires more than scientific reliability; the ruling also makes clear that scientific testimony can be admitted at trial only if the testimony will "assist the trier of fact to understand or determine a fact in issue." There are several ways to unpack this requirement, but one element is straightforward: The testimony won't "assist the trier of fact" if the testimony simply reiterates what the trier of fact knows already.

Likewise, Canada's ruling in *R. v. Mohan* emphasizes that expert testimony will be admissible only if the testimony is "necessary" in assisting the trier of fact. Of course, the testimony will not be at all necessary if it simply reaffirms propositions the trier of fact already understands and accepts. So here, too, we need to ask: Does psychology research provide information that goes beyond common sense?

We all have a lifetime's experience in perceiving, and this experience makes it plain that our perception generally serves us well—and so we manage to catch the softball that's tossed to us or steer our car through traffic without suffering some vehicular catastrophe. But, in addition, we all know that our perception sometimes fools us—and so we know what it's like to see a friend down the block but then discover, when we approach, that the person is someone else altogether.

Likewise, a lifetime of experience has told each of us that our memories are usually accurate—and so we find our car just where we remember parking it, and we have no trouble remembering where we spent our last birthday or the plot of our favorite movie. But we also know that our memory sometimes lets us down: Sometimes, we try to recall a name, or a fact, and we "draw a blank." And, occasionally, our memories are just mistaken: You vividly recall mailing the letter but find the envelope still in your pocket. You recall the dinner party one way, but your spouse recalls it very differently; one of you, it would seem, must have it wrong.

On these grounds, no one needs research to establish both the broad accuracy of perception and memory and the risk of error. If these were the points offered by expert testimony, then the testimony surely would be unnecessary, covering points already within the ken of the ordinary juror. Indeed, one prosecutor in Oregon commented, "I have never called a witness as an expert on memory myself; there are 12 of them sitting in the jury box. Someone testifying that 'memory can be false' seems to be akin to saying that most people have noses on their faces" (Robben, 2012).

Let's be clear, however, that no expert would testify simply to make the point that "memory can be false." That is indeed a matter of common sense. On many other issues, though, common-sense ideas about perception and memory turn out to be *mistaken*—markedly overstating some truths and understating others and, in many cases, offering claims that have no basis in fact whatsoever. The blunt reality, therefore, is that research can offer claims that are a substantial improvement on common sense.

Examples illustrating these points are easy to find. For example, jurors surely know that memory errors occur and may also understand that these errors can sometimes be "planted" through suggestive questioning. (A question like, "You did see the gun, didn't you?" may lead someone later to recall a gun, even if there was none.) However, jurors almost certainly underestimate the risk of this sort of memory contamination. Indeed, in one study, college students were surveyed about their perceptions of various risks (Wilson & Brekke, 1994). These students were largely unconcerned about the risk of someone biasing their memory with leading questions. According to the survey results, they regarded this risk as roughly equivalent to the risk of someday being kidnapped by space aliens. As it turns out, though, the students' assessment was mistaken: Studies make it plain that just a word or two of leading can produce memory errors in roughly a third of the people questioned (see Chapter 4). Surely, the danger of extraterrestrial abductions is much lower than this.

As a different example, many people have the view that significant emotional events are somehow "burned" into the brain and hence never forgotten. Thus people announce with conviction that "I'll never forget the events of 9/11" or " . . . the day I got married" or " . . . what he looked like when he pulled the trigger." There is a kernel of truth in these claims because these significant, emotional, distinctive events do tend to be well-remembered. But, here, too, common sense is in tension with the facts. As we will discuss in Chapter 3, it is easy to document large-scale errors in these singular, significant memories. The accuracy of these memories, in other words, is far from guaranteed, and the "burned into my brain" notion is therefore just wrong.

In fact, this point can be made more broadly—leading us to another contrast between common sense and scientific evidence. People routinely offer descriptions of their own memories: "I'll never forget how she . . ." or "I remember it as though it's yesterday . . ." or, more bluntly, "I'm certain that what happened was . . ." In other words, people offer assessments of their *degree of certainty* or their *confidence* that a particular memory is correct, and they plainly regard these assessments as useful: They are more likely to voice or take action on memories recalled with certainty compared to memories that they're less sure about. Likewise, several studies indicate that jurors are more likely to believe a witness who is confident in his or her recall compared to a witness who hedges or expresses doubts (see Chapter 9). Indeed, judges themselves often highlight the witness's confidence as an indicator of the witness's memory accuracy. For example, in one prominent ruling (*Neil v. Biggers*, 1972), the U.S. Supreme Court explicitly noted that "the factors to be considered in evaluating the likelihood of misidentification include . . . the level of certainty demonstrated by the witness at the confrontation."

But here, too, common sense pulls us off track. We'll review the relevant data in Chapter 3, but for now we note simply that, in many circumstances, there's little correspondence between witnesses' degree of memory certainty and their memory accuracy. Thus, if we follow the dictates of common sense and put more faith in memories expressed with confidence, we will routinely choose to disregard accurate memories and routinely put our trust in misleading information.

Surveys Documenting Common Sense

These broad points—about the limitations of common sense—can be confirmed more formally. In many studies, researchers have surveyed individuals in the jury pool to find out what they believe about perception and memory. Other surveys have targeted other groups, and so we have information available to us about "common-sense beliefs" among police officers, attorneys, and trial judges—with a specific focus on what these individuals know about eyewitness memory, the impact of leading questions, factors making false confessions more likely, and more. In all of these cases, we can then compare these common-sense beliefs to the results of careful scientific research, and thus we can find out in a direct fashion whether the science is (or is not) within the ken of the nonscientists.

It cannot be surprising that the views of all these groups are aligned with the science on some points (e.g., Desmarais & Read, 2011). After all, ordinary experience surely teaches us *something* about how our eyes and ears work and how often our memories are correct. Moreover, the research community and the mass media do what they can to publicize the results of scientific studies, and so nonresearchers are certain to learn more as time goes by. (As one paper put it, any "evaluation of lay knowledge has a limited shelf life"; Desmarais & Read, 2011, p. 208.) But it is also true that jurors, police officers, and professionals in the justice system have numerous beliefs about memory that are patently inconsistent with what we know to be true, based on careful science. In short, then, the claim that psychological research reiterates common sense is an empirical (i.e., testable) claim, and, on a range of topics, this claim is demonstrably false.

We have already mentioned some examples—the common-sense underestimation of the risk of false memory or the common-sense overreliance on degree of certainty as an index of memory accuracy. Here is a different sort of example: Many people seem to believe that the eye can sensibly be compared to a camera and memory to a video recorder. As we will see in Chapters 2 and 3, these comparisons are misleading in crucial ways and lead to a number of errors concerning the accuracy of memory and the ways in which we might evaluate or elicit memories. Misleading or not, though, these comparisons are often endorsed. In one survey of 1,300 potential jurors in Washington, D.C., 48% thought that memories were indeed like video recordings (Schmechel, O'Toole, Easterly, & Loftus, 2006). Similarly, Simons and Chabris (2011) surveyed almost 2,000 individuals and found that 63% believed that memory works like a video recorder. Their survey also indicated that 55% of the respondents believed memory could be enhanced through hypnosis (not true); 48% believed that memory is permanent (again: not true). (Also see Wise, Safer, & Maro, 2011; for some possible complications about surveys like these, however, see Alonzo & Lane, 2009.)

What about other topics? In a 1992 survey, potential jurors were asked whether they agreed with a series of 21 claims about eyewitness reliability; the participants offered claims out of step with the available science for 15 of the 21 topics (Kassin & Barndollar, 1992). Likewise, Benton et al. (2006) surveyed 111 jurors in Tennessee and found gaps between juror knowledge and the science on many issues. Fewer than half of the jurors, for example, had views in line with the science with regard to the importance of pre-lineup instructions, the poor relationship between someone's degree of certainty and the likelihood of memory accuracy, or the often-documented difference between "same-race" and "cross-race" identifications. In fact, jurors disagreed with the experts on 87% of the issues examined in this study. (For other surveys revealing common-sense beliefs about witness memory, see Deffenbacher & Loftus, 1982; Noon & Hollin, 1987; Seltzer, Venuti, & Lopes, 1990; Schmechel et al. 2006.)

Likewise, a survey by Henkel et al. (2008) asked what ordinary citizens believe about confessions and false confessions. In the survey, many citizens (correctly) acknowledged that false confessions can and do arise, but then endorsed a number of false claims about *when* and *how* false confessions emerge. And it's not just ordinary citizens who have these beliefs: As part of the interrogation process, many police officers rely on the so-called Behavioral Analysis Interview (BAI) for detecting lies (see Chapter 8). Many of the central ideas that underlie the BAI are fully in tune with common-sense notions about how people telling lies are likely to behave (e.g., Masip, Herrero, Garrido, & Barba, 2011), but, unfortunately, these notions are out of step with the facts—a finding that reflects poorly both on common sense and on the BAI itself.

The Bias Built into Common Sense

Jurors' beliefs are not just out of step with the science; more strongly, common-sense beliefs reveal a consistent *bias*. Overall, jurors tend to overbelieve eyewitnesses and to overrely on confession evidence. In one study, for example, researchers presented a sample of registered voters with crime scenarios, each of which was based on a previously conducted empirical study; the study participants were asked to estimate the likelihood of a correct identification by the eyewitnesses in each of these scenarios (Brigham & Bothwell, 1983). Overall, 84% of the respondents overestimated the accuracy rates. Moreover, the amount of overestimation was substantial; in one of the scenarios, for example, only 12% of the eyewitnesses had made a correct identification; the voters, in contrast, given the particulars of the scenario, estimated that 71% of the IDs would be correct.

Related data come from studies in which research participants are presented with a case and asked for a "verdict." In one study, participants were provided only circumstantial evidence in a case summary; 49% of the participants voted to convict. When a single, vague eyewitness account was added to the evidence, the conviction rate jumped to 68% (Sigler & Couch, 2002).

More positively, though, jurors do shift their views once they have received new information. Thus, in one study, mock jurors who had heard expert testimony spent considerably more time discussing eyewitness identifications during jury deliberations (Hosch, Beck, & McIntyre, 1980). In a different study, exposure to expert testimony resulted in increased juror attention to identification conditions and also to better post-trial knowledge of the factors influencing identification accuracy (Cutler, Penrod, & Dexter, 1989; for more on this broad topic, see Hosch, Jolly, Schmersal, & Smith, 2009; Leippe & Eisenstadt, 2009; Leo & Liu, 2009; Read & Desmarais, 2009; Schmechel et al., 2006).

The Limited Value of Anecdotal Evidence

Many factors contribute to this contrast between common sense and scientific evidence, but part of the explanation lies in the fact that common sense is often informed by *anecdotal evidence*. This term refers to evidence that is informally collected, stored only in memory, and conveyed (as an "anecdote") only in broad form.

With just one observer and no documentation, there is obviously room to question whether an anecdotal report is true at all. If we get past that issue, we still need to ask why a particular anecdote is recalled and reported. An obvious possibility here is that the anecdote is recalled because it "stands out" in memory—presumably because the remembered episode is somehow distinctive. But, if so, then we probably should not draw general conclusions from what is apparently an unusual case.

Anecdotal evidence often takes the form of a "man who" story: "What do you mean that cigarette smoking causes cancer? I know a man who smoked 8 packs a day and lived to 103." "What do you mean that suggestive questioning can mislead a witness? I recall a witness who was asked countless leading questions, but wouldn't budge in her story." Or, as a variant: "What do you mean that pretrial publicity prejudices a jury? I remember a case in which there was voluminous inflammatory publicity, but the jury still acquitted the guy." Reports in this form are common but suffer from obvious problems (they may or may not be accurately recalled; they rest on single cases that may or may not be representative, etc.). Hence, these reports cannot be persuasive.

F. THE POWER OF META-ANALYSIS

How can we avoid the perils associated with anecdotal evidence? More broadly, how can we make sure that scientific claims are an improvement on common sense? Part of the answer, as we've already seen, lies in systematic data collection, objective recording of the data, and conclusions that reflect *all* of the data (and not just a few notable cases). But part of the answer, in addition, lies in collecting a *lot* of evidence—to make sure a pattern is reliable, to make sure the data pattern emerges in diverse settings.

Once we've accumulated lots of data, though, how exactly do we combine the results to examine the overall picture? For many years, this combination was achieved through a *literature review*—a qualitative cataloguing of the available evidence, typically published in one of the professional journals that specializes in publishing review articles. However, in recent years, psychologists have shifted to *quantitative* reviews, relying on a method known as *meta-analysis*—literally, an analysis of other analyses.

A meta-analysis begins by defining its *inclusion criteria*—clearly stated, carefully justified rules for determining which studies will be included in the analysis. Once the inclusion criteria are laid out, all studies that meet these requirements must be included. In this way, meta-analysis rules out any sort of "cherry picking" in which one might favor results consistent with one's beliefs and disregard contrary findings.

With the data set now defined, meta-analysis involves a precisely defined statistical procedure for pooling all of the results, and this compilation of studies leads to one of the many strengths of meta-analysis: A typical experiment in psychology might involve 100 participants; meta-analyses, in contrast, routinely include findings from thousands of participants and therefore diminish any concern about small or idiosyncratic samples. Meta-analyses also pool findings from diverse procedures (provided that the procedures satisfy the inclusion criteria) and thus allow us to ask whether a result holds up across this diversity. If it does, we have learned something important: The result is not dependent on any specific details in a particular procedure because the result emerges reliably even when we change the details.

We need to offer a caution, however, with regard to how one reads a meta-analysis. Let's start with the fact that different studies in psychology often use different measures: One study might rate performance on a 1–5 scale, another might use a binary right-or-wrong scale, another might assess performance in terms of percentages. To combine these studies, as a meta-analysis does, the various results must all be converted to a common metric. This quantitative lingua franca takes the form of a generic measure called "effect size." Thus, an effect size is computed for each of the studies within a meta-analysis, and then the meta-analysis averages these various effect sizes together. (We first met the term "effect size" in our earlier discussion of error rates.)

Meta-analytic data are therefore often summarized in terms of effect sizes. But, of course, this measure (by design) is an abstraction, and so, to help readers digest meta-analytic results, effect sizes are often "back-translated" into more familiar, qualitiative terms and so are described as "small," "medium," or "large." This back-translation is done systematically; for example, meta-analyses often calculate a statistic known as a Cohen's *d,* and there are specific cut-offs, using this statistic, for calling an effect size small, medium, or large.

Let's be clear, however, that the cut-offs for these descriptive labels are merely conventions and so there is a danger of overinterpreting these labels—especially since, in the justice system, an effect labeled "small" by the statisticians might be deeply consequential for a particular defendant or a particular litigation. For example, one meta-analysis asked whether jurors' verdicts were influenced by exposure to potentially prejudicial pretrial publicity (Steblay, Besirevic, Fulero, & Jiminnez-Lrente, 1999). The data did show a reliable effect, but (by the standards of meta-analysis) the effect was deemed "small" (although appreciably larger in some settings than in others). Does this mean the courts can ignore the effect? In response, let's bear in mind that the "small" label is an arbitrary statistical one and certainly not assessed in terms of, say, pragmatic criteria tied to real-world impact.

Moreover, one might argue that, in the ideal, there would be *no impact* of pretrial publicity on a verdict because the jurors should be influenced only by the evidence heard in the courtroom. On this basis, a reliable (but "small") effect seems to reflect a violation of a defendant's due process rights. We will not attempt to resolve this point here, but we certainly do want to emphasize the need for caution in interpreting the (again, arbitrary) descriptors often associated with meta-analytic results.

Moderator Variables

A meta-analysis provides an overall summary of the data, deliberately cutting across all sorts of procedural variations. But meta-analysis can also examine these variations in order to ask, in essence, when an effect is stronger and when it is weaker. For example, different studies of pretrial publicity effects have focused on different types of crimes (homicide vs. sexual assault vs. drug crimes); meta-analysis allows us to ask whether type of crime is a *moderator variable*—a factor that can make the publicity's effect weaker or stronger. (And, in fact, type of crime is a moderator of the publicity effect; for more on pretrial publicity, see Chapter 9.)

Moderator variables in meta-analysis can also serve another function: They contribute to the quality control needed in all research. For example, one might be concerned that studies of pretrial publicity have often relied on university students for their research participants, and these students might not be typical of the citizens in the broader jury panel. To check on this possible problem, one can treat type-of-participant as a moderator variable in a meta-analysis of the publicity effects. As it turns out, the data indicate that this is an important moderator—and the effect of pretrial publicity is *stronger* in studies that have drawn their participants from the community's venire, rather than a university; hence, studies of university students may understate the effects of this publicity (Steblay, Besirevic, Fulero & Jiminez-Lorente, 1999).

Similarly, meta-analyses typically seek as large a data set as possible—and often this includes studies that are not yet published. Thus, a researcher setting out to do a meta-analysis will communicate with researchers working on or near the target problem, and will collect unpublished findings from them. This step obviously gives us a broader pool of data, but is also risky, given the fact that the publication process is designed to weed out flawed studies (see the earlier discussion of peer review). To address this concern, meta-analyses usually treat publication status (published in a peer-reviewed journal vs. not) as a moderator variable. If this variable has no impact on the data, that is reassuring; if it does moderate the data pattern, further scrutiny is required.

Fail-Safe Numbers

Clearly, meta-analyses provide many benefits: Because of their explicitly defined inclusion criteria, we can count on these analyses to be comprehensive summaries of the available data. Because they summarize data from diverse procedures, meta-analyses can tell us whether a result is robust despite variations in method, research group, or stimulus type. Analyses of moderator variables allow us to fine-tune our claims by specifying when an effect will be stronger and when weaker. Moderator variables also allow us to address methodological concerns, telling us (for example) whether an effect holds up as we move into more realistic settings.

Meta-analyses also provide another advantage: Scientific research is an ongoing enterprise, and new data continue to come in; new discoveries arise that can confirm (or sometimes challenge) current claims. Scientists regard these points as strengths of our method, providing evidence of scientists' open-minded insistence on placing data above doctrine—and so scientists are always willing to be shown wrong if new data point that way. In the eyes of many people, though, these attributes of science are worrisome: Why should they listen to the scientists if, perhaps, the claims confidently offered by science today will simply be reversed in a few years? Why listen to the scientists' input if science is such an unfinished business? In fact, this issue was raised by the U.S. Supreme Court in its *Daubert* ruling, which noted: "Scientific conclusions are subject to perpetual revision. Law on the other hand, must resolve disputes finally and quickly." What the courts need, therefore, is evidence (the Court continued) "designed not for the exhaustive search for cosmic understanding but for the particularized resolution of legal disputes."

Psychologists find it gratifying to learn that (according to the Supreme Court) we may be searching for "cosmic understanding," but, even so, the ruling raises the question: How can we bridge the gap between these two traditions, satisfying both the requirements of the science and the needs of the justice system? Part of the answer looks to the past; part looks to the future. Looking to the past, we can ask, for any particular claim: How long has the claim been available to the scientific community and thus open to scrutiny? How often have results central to the claim been replicated? Questions like these provide a means of asking whether a result has fared well in the test-of-time. If it has, scientists are likely to count the claim as solid and ready for "export" and use.

But we can also look to the future, and this is a point for which meta-analysis is again helpful: The mathematics of meta-analysis allow researchers to calculate what is called a *fail-safe number*. This is literally a calculation of how many new studies we would need, all coming in with data different from what we have so far, in order to un-do, or cancel out, the pattern to date. If the fail-safe number is low, then it is easy to imagine that we might in fact suffer a reversal of our claims with just a few additional studies. If the fail-safe number is high, we can be confident that the risk of reversal is correspondingly low. In this way, we can use the meta-analysis calculations to provide a quantitative response to the worry about whether today's scientific claims will still be around in the days or decades to come.

G. BUT EACH OF US IS DIFFERENT FROM EVERYONE ELSE

There is one last substantive issue to tackle in laying out the foundations for psychology's use in the justice system, and the issue begins with an important observation: When researchers advise the justice system, they are unlikely to have interviewed or evaluated any of the participants in the immediate dispute. (This point provides another contrast between researchers and clinical psychologists—who may well have done an "assessment" of one or more of the litigants.) Indeed, in cross-examination, I am often asked if I have interviewed the victim, or even met the victim? Have I interviewed the witnesses or the defendant? When the answer is "no" to these questions, the issue arises: How, then, can I offer testimony about the perception or memory of these individuals?

This point takes its apparent force from the obvious fact that each of us is, of course, unique in some way. One might argue, therefore, that the application of research to a specific legal matter is really a form of crude stereotyping—as if we were assuming that all children were alike (so that we could make blithe claims about "children in general") or that all robbery victims were the same (allowing sweeping generalizations about all of them).

What is the Response to this Concern?

It's surely true that individuals differ in many ways, but it is also true that, in many aspects, we are all alike. In some regards, these points of resemblance are inevitable, inasmuch as we all have the same human biology (and thus your brain has the same structures as mine; your neurons communicate with the same neurotransmitters as mine; and so on), making it certain that there will be important points of resemblance, from one person to the next, in the functioning of perception and memory.

In other regards, this issue of resemblance is—again—a point to be settled by research. Careful, appropriately designed studies can tell us which properties of memory are shared from one person to the next, and which properties are not. Indeed, the statistics in use for research examine just this point, asking whether a data pattern is consistent across the various individuals included in the study. (And, of course, other precautions are in place to ensure that these individuals are representative of the broader population.) Needless to say, any testimony from psychological science will then showcase these shared principles, and will stay away from claims that might not be applicable to people in general (and hence will stay from claims that might not be applicable to the individuals involved in the instant case).

Our Claims Are Probabilistic

At the same time, let's not overstate these points about resemblance because—of course—people are different from each other, and not everyone shows the patterns documented in psychology research. These patterns are consistent, but that does not mean universal. Thus, to return to an earlier example, the data tell us that people have more difficulty making cross-race identifications, but this does not mean that every person shows this effect, and it certainly does not mean that every cross-race ID is mistaken. Put differently, psychological claims will almost always be probabilistic—that is, couched in terms of probabilities or perhaps in terms of risks. The risk of error is greater with a cross-race ID than a same-race ID, the probability of an accurate memory is greater if someone is asked open-ended questions rather than close-ended, and so on.

In essence, then, psychology research offers the justice system a type of "risk analysis." Take, for example, a case involving an eyewitness identification. A researcher might point to factors in the case that have been shown to promote memory accuracy and also to factors that have been shown to undermine accuracy. Then, in light of those factors, the researcher could help the finder of fact understand whether the risk of error for this particular witness was high or low.

Let's emphasize that, in this setting, the researcher would be advising the court about *risk*, not about *error*. The reason, simply, is that the witness's identification might be correct even if factors on the scene indicate a high risk of error. Conversely, the witness might be incorrect even if factors indicate a low risk. (After all, not every cigarette smoker develops emphysema; being at "high risk for disease" is different from having the disease. Likewise, some nonsmokers do develop this disease; being at "low risk" is no guarantee of health.) In this fashion, the probabilities we can derive from research will help the finder of fact in evaluating the risk of error—but then it is of course up to the finder of fact, not the researchers, to decide whether an error occurred in the instant case or not.

Why Research Will *Not* Comment on a Witness's Veracity

The points just covered also help with another issue. Let's begin with the fact that jurists of all sorts are clear that it is improper for one witness to comment on the veracity of another witness; doing so would invade the province of the trier of fact. On this basis, one might be concerned about the propriety—or, for that matter, the admissibility—of a researcher's commentary on a witness's perception or memory; this does sound dangerously close to the forbidden comments on another's veracity.

This concern, however, is misplaced, and the previous section explains why. Indeed, the issue here is one for which the strictures of the law and the nature of science are perfectly aligned: A research psychologist's testimony will not and cannot offer information about a specific witness or a particular victim. Instead, the testimony would (as already discussed) simply identify the risks involved in that case: the risk of a perceptual or memory error or perhaps the risk that someone innocent, exposed to certain pressures, will produce a false confession. It would then be up to the court to decide how the risk was (or was not) realized in that specific case.

The Contrast Between Research Psychology and the Forensic Sciences

These last few paragraphs also highlight the differences between research psychology and the so-called forensic sciences—finger print analysis, forensic chemistry, and so on. These other endeavors, unlike research psychology, seek to offer claims about the particular case being litigated—and so (for example) the fingerprints from the actual crime scene are sent off to a crime lab where a forensic expert will determine whether the prints match the defendant's or match other prints in some database.

Or perhaps a forensic chemist analyzes the contents of a pill bottle to determine whether the bottle contains poison.

This sort of forensic testing has been prominent in the public's view (in part because of popular TV shows) but has also been the subject of severe criticism (e.g., Fisher, 2008; Harris, 2012; Kassin, Dror, & Kukucka, 2013; National Research Council, 2009; Simon, 2012). Critics have voiced concerns about the accuracy and objectivity of some of the testing done in these crime labs. People have also raised questions about the scientific foundation for some of this work—and whether some of the forensic sciences are sciences at all.

My concern here, however, is not with these challenges to forensic science. Instead, I simply want to highlight how different this sort of endeavor is from the research described in this book. As should be clear by now, the input from research psychology is not providing an evaluation of the specific facts or the specific individuals involved in a case. Instead, psychological science will (as discussed) simply provide the framework that finders of fact can then use in evaluating the case evidence. As a consequence, we're again led to a familiar bottom line: Psychological research will not provide a comment on the veracity of any particular witness or victim.

H. IS THIS SCIENCE BIASED TOWARD THE DEFENSE?

I have now dealt with most of the issues involved in the foundation for psychology's contribution to the justice system. But there is one more issue that should be addressed.

One of the challenges sometimes offered to research psychology is an accusation of bias. After all, to the degree that we highlight perceptual or memory errors, we seem to be engaged in an effort toward undermining witness evidence, and, in most litigation, it's the plaintiff who brings the evidence. On that basis, one might think that the research is likely to challenge the plaintiff's or the prosecution's case and thus tilt the argument toward a "not guilty" verdict.

There are, however, several responses to this suggestion, any of which (I believe) would be persuasive. Let's start with the premise that what the science contributes is simply a catalog of risk factors that can promote witness errors. This premise is mistaken. Instead, the science tells us, first, that perception and memory are accurate more often than not, and so any blanket effort toward challenging witness evidence is unmistakably misguided. In addition, the results of research can be understood either as offering a catalog of risk factors or as offering exactly the opposite—a listing of the factors that indicate memory or perceptual accuracy. Thus, a longer delay before recalling a conversation can be counted as a risk factor for memory accuracy; a shorter delay is one of the indicia of reliability. An exposure to a face in poor lighting suggests a risk of mistaken ID; a better lit exposure suggests the opposite. And so on. In this fashion, the available science should be useful to both sides in any litigation, with the prospect that both sides can better assess the strengths and the weaknesses of their witness evidence and thus gain a more realistic understanding of the case.

In addition, perhaps the better use of psychological science is not in the courtroom at all. Instead, the preferred use, for many aspects of the science, may be as a guide for training investigators, including law enforcement. After all, surely it is better to collect high-quality evidence from the outset rather than quarrel in a courtroom about whether the evidence is reliable or not, whether it deserves much weight or little. Better quality evidence can speed the exoneration of the actually innocent and can also facilitate the prosecution of those who have committed crimes.

This last point—about better quality evidence—gains force when we realize that many errors in the justice system are, in fact, "double errors." A mistaken identification or a false confession, for example, will potentially send someone innocent to jail *and* will allow the actual perpetrator to go free (and perhaps commit other crimes). There can be no question, then, that all of us—defenders, plaintiffs, and society more broadly—are well served by getting the best evidence we possibly can, and scientific research can surely help us in that endeavor.

CHAPTER 2

Perception

What Can a Witness See?

Many people compare the eye to a camera and memory to a video recorder. After all, both the eye and the camera have a lens, an adjustable opening for controlling the entry of light, and a light-sensitive surface that detects and records the input. Both memory and a video recorder take "input," provide storage for some period of time, and then allow some sort of "playback."

These comparisons, however, are misleading on many levels and can lead to a variety of errors in the justice system. As an initial example, consider a strategy sometimes used in cross-examination in an effort toward impeaching an eyewitness: The attorney asks the witness question after question about an event and soon discovers that the witness recalls some facts but not others. Thus, for example, the witness might remember the perpetrator's words but not his clothing, or he might recall the clothing but be mistaken about where various people in the scene were standing. Later, during closing, the attorney asks the jury: "How can we trust this witness's recall? With so many gaps in the witness's recollection, it's clear that the witness was not paying attention. We therefore cannot rely on what the witness says."

Notice, though, that this argument assumes the camera + video recorder view. After all, when a camera is on and operating, it takes in whatever is in front of the lens. A camera that "missed" some point that was directly in the line of sight would, therefore, be a strange camera indeed. Likewise, if memory were like a video recorder, then we should worry if the playback has gaps or errors. If your actual video recorder or DVD player skipped every other second or was missing half the image, that would be a serious malfunction.

But this logic does not apply to perception or memory. Instead, both of these capacities are inherently selective. People perceive only part of what is in their view and then recall only part of what they perceived. Therefore, if a witness cannot recall some aspects of a crime, this merely tells us that the witness wasn't paying attention to everything in the scene. And given what we know about the limits of attention, a witness *can't* pay attention to everything. Thus, it is simply inevitable that a witness's memory will be incomplete, and it is an error to use that incompleteness as a basis for distrusting the witness.

If the camera + video recorder idea is mistaken, what is the correct view of perception and memory? In this chapter and the next, we tackle this broad topic. Our main focus in this chapter is on perception; we'll tackle issues of memory in Chapter 3. As we'll see, though, these two broad topics are interwoven in important ways; nonetheless, we'll separate them to the extent possible.

A. SELECTIVE, CONSTRUCTIVE, INTEGRATIVE

There is a broad range of scientific research, conducted over the past century or so, examining perception and memory function. Much of that research is not focused on issues central to the justice system, but the simple fact is that the eyeballs people use to witness a crime are the same eyeballs they use in other settings; the neural tissue that helps someone remember a bank robber's voice is also used for other aspects of memory. For these reasons, much of what we know about perception and memory is unmistakably relevant to the issues at play in this book.

Psychologists distinguish different types or aspects of perception, but, across all of these distinctions, we can identify certain traits that characterize all of our intellectual commerce with the world. First, our perception of the world is *selective*. As we will see, we routinely fail to perceive objects—even large, prominent objects—directly in front of our eyes. This is not because we are careless or inattentive; instead, the selectivity is inevitable given the basic workings of the visual system. Likewise, our recollection of the past is, under the best of circumstances, also selective, and we routinely fail to remember many aspects of our experience, including aspects that we might ordinarily deem "highly memorable."

Second, perception and memory are both *constructive*: We supplement what we perceive and what we remember by drawing on our broader fabric of knowledge—in essence, "filling in the gaps" with inferences based on other things we know or expect. This construction is not capricious; instead, it is guided by straightforward principles and these principles allow the construction to be *accurate* more often than not: Our inferences about bits-not-seen or bits-not-remembered are usually correct. Even so, we do make mistakes. Moreover, we typically have no way of separating the bits we actually perceive from the bits we've (unconsciously) filled in with inference, and so, if mistakes occur, they are generally undetectable. Likewise, we usually have no basis for separating the bits we actually remember from the bits we've (unconsciously) reconstructed after the fact, and so, again, we have enormous difficulty in spotting our own inferences and hence our own mistakes.

Third, it's important that our memories are not filled with separate "files," each representing a single episode in our past. Instead, the many bits of information in memory are woven together, and this is generally helpful for us: The weaving together provides us with a coherent fabric of knowledge rather than a huge catalog of isolated factoids. But we pay a price for this cohesiveness because the weaving together creates a risk that we will lose track of which bit of information we gained from which source, and we may end up confused about what we saw in *this* episode and what we saw in *that* episode. In this fashion, memory is *integrative*; that is, it compiles distinct episodes into a unified package, and, again, this is both helpful (because it helps us to link related bits of information) and harmful (because it risks confusion about source).

B. PERCEPTION IS SELECTIVE

Occasionally, psychological experiments gain enormous notoriety, and one prominent example is the "invisible gorilla" experiment (or, actually, *experiments,* because there are several). In one version of this experiment, participants watched a computer screen that showed a team of players in white shirts passing a ball back and forth; the participants had to signal each time the ball changed hands. Interwoven with these players and visible on the same screen was another team wearing black shirts, also passing a ball back and forth; participants were instructed to ignore these players.

Participants easily did this task, but were so intent on the white team that they didn't notice when another player wearing a gorilla costume walked through the middle of the game, pausing briefly to thump his chest before exiting (Neisser & Becklen, 1975; Simons & Chabris, 1999; also Mack & Rock, 1998).

This effect emerges even if participants are "on guard," trying not to be fooled. In my classroom, for example, I show students the "gorilla video," and, of course, most of them don't see the ape. Then I point out the gorilla, and students are chagrined to have missed it—and, crucially, they're motivated not to be fooled again. Moments later, I show them a different video, also containing an unheralded gorilla. This time, forewarned, students do detect the ape but now fail to notice other prominent aspects of the scene (such as the fact that one of the players simply leaves the game and walks off-screen midway through the video or the fact that the curtain forming the entire backdrop for the video inexplicably changes from one color to another).

This perceptual selectivity is easily demonstrated when viewers are looking at a video on a computer or projection screen. Remarkably, though, the same failure-to-perceive can be documented with "live" events that the viewer is actually participating in. In one study, an investigator (let's call him "Leon") approached pedestrians on a college campus and asked for directions to a certain building. During the conversation, two men carrying a door approached and deliberately walked between Leon and his conversational partner. As a result, Leon was briefly hidden (by the door) from the other person's view, and, in that moment, Leon traded places with one of the men carrying the door. A second later, therefore, Leon was able to walk away, unseen (i.e., still hidden by the door), while the new fellow (who had been carrying the door) stayed behind and continued the conversation.

Roughly half of the people tested failed to notice this switch. They continued the conversation as though nothing had happened—despite the fact that Leon and his replacement were wearing different clothes, had easily distinguishable voices, and so on. When asked directly whether anything odd had happened in this event, those (many) participants who had not noticed the switch commented only that it was rude that the guys carrying the door had walked right through their conversation (Chabris & Simons, 2010; Simons & Ambinder, 2005).

A related observation draws on an often-discussed topic: the distracting power of cell phone conversations. A number of studies have shown that drivers on the phone (whether a hand-held or hands-free model) are less likely to notice large landmarks along their path, more likely to miss their exit, slower to notice other cars' change in position, and so on (Strayer, Drew, & Crouch, 2006; Strayer & Johnston, 2001). But it's not just drivers who show this pattern: In one study, researchers observed pedestrians walking across a public square. If the pedestrian was walking with a friend (and so engaged in a "live" conversation), there was a 71% chance the pedestrian would notice the unicycling clown, just off the pedestrian's path. For pedestrians engaged in a cell phone conversation, only 25% detected the clown (Hyman, Boss, Wise, McKenzie, & Caggiano, 2010).

Before pressing on, we should mention two side points. First, why is it that a "live" conversation with a friend has a different impact from a phone conversation? Part of the answer lies in the fact that the friend can also see the clown (or, in a car, can also see the exit or the upcoming construction) and can draw your attention to these things. In addition, if your path or the circumstances become complicated, your conversational partner can see this—either by looking out of the car's window or by observing your tension and focus. In these settings, your friend will helpfully slow down his or her side of the conversation, and this adjustment diminishes the potential for distraction (e.g., Drews, Pasupathi, & Strayer, 2008).

Second, we should mention that some of the procedures described here (e.g., the gorilla passing through the basketball game or the exchange behind the door) are captured in video clips available online. The clips are quite persuasive and so (if admitted) worth showing to a jury. To find the clips, search the Internet for "change blindness" or "invisible gorilla."

Chabris and Simons (2010) call attention to some of the real-world implications of these findings. For example, they discuss reports of traffic accidents in which a driver says, "I never saw the bicyclist. He came out of nowhere. But then—suddenly—there he was, right in front of me." Or, as a more mundane case, you go to the refrigerator to find the mayonnaise (or the ketchup or the juice) and fail to find it, even though it is directly in front of you.

In these cases, we lament the neglectful driver, and your inability to find the mayonnaise may cause you to worry that you're losing your mind as well as your condiments. The response to all this, though, is to realize that these cases of failing-to-see are entirely normal. Perception is inherently selective, and, just as important, perception requires more than "merely" having a stimulus in front of your eyes. Perception requires some work.

The Anatomy of the Eyeball

Why is perception selective? The first step toward an answer lies in the anatomy of the eye. Light enters the eye, is focused by the cornea and lens, and forms an image on the back surface of the eyeball: a surface called the *retina*. The retina contains cells called *photoreceptors*—cells that are sensitive to light—and there are two types of photoreceptors. The *rods* respond even to low levels of light but are poor at discerning detail. Rods are also insensitive to differences in hue and so cannot distinguish red from blue from green. (Rod vision does allow you to distinguish a red traffic light from a green one, but that is because these lights differ in *brightness* as well as in hue.) The other type of photoreceptors, the *cones,* require more light to operate at all but are color sensitive and quite sensitive to detail.

Rods and cones are not distributed uniformly across the retina. Instead, cones are concentrated in the center of the retina, in an area called the *fovea.* When you "point your eyes" at a target, therefore, what you are doing is positioning your eyes so that the target's image falls on the cone-rich fovea; this allows you to see the details of the target. If you want to pick up detailed information from some other aspect of the visual world, you need to move your eyes so that some new target falls on the fovea.

Let's now add a flurry of further points. The fovea itself is relatively small. As a rough approximation, hold your fist out at arm's length, with your thumb pointed upwards (the classic "all's well" gesture). Point your eyes at your thumbnail. In this position, the image of the thumbnail virtually fills your fovea—making it plain how restricted a portion of visual space falls into this region. (Some authors playfully describe this simple comparison as providing a "rule of thumb" for describing the fovea's size.)

Second, we've already indicated that your ability to see detail (technically called *visual acuity*) is much better for objects in foveal view (and hence: falling on a region rich in cones) than it is for objects at the periphery of your vision (and so falling on a region filled primarily with rods). Let's emphasize, though, that acuity isn't just weak at the very edges of your visual world. Instead, acuity drops off rapidly as we move away from the fovea. There are various ways to measure this drop, but, as a crude description, let's give a score of 100% to your ability to see detail right in front of your eyes; this is your acuity at its best. For an object that is, say, 10 degrees off your line of sight, your acuity score drops to about 30% of this optimum. For an object 20 degrees off your line of sight, the score drops to about 15% of this optimum. These are not small differences, and thus the fall-off in acuity, away from the fovea, is dramatic.

Third, humans are only able to move their eyes four or five times per second. More frequent eye movements are just not possible. In addition, our eye movements rarely provide us with a thorough, wide-ranging inspection of the visual scene. Instead, we point our eyes again and again at the relatively few targets within the scene that are of special interest to us. (We say more about this pattern later in the chapter.) The end result is that we never point our eyes at all at the majority of positions within the scene.

Let's now put these pieces together. The visual input we receive is surprisingly limited—four or five thumbnail-sized views each second, with the same views often repeated from one second to the next, and with little detail (and no information about hue) available for positions *away from* these small views.

How do these facts matter for the justice system? In one study, researchers showed viewers a video reenactment of an armed robbery and literally tracked where viewers were pointing their eyes while observing this event (Loftus, Loftus, & Messo, 1987). The data showed a strong tendency for the viewers to point their eyes at the robber's gun—with the consequence that the viewers simply could not discern details elsewhere in the scene, including details of what the robber's face looked like. (We have more to say about this pattern later, in a section entitled Weapon Focus.)

The Role of Attention

The anatomy of the eyeball, however, is only one source of perceptual selectivity. Another crucial limit derives from how people pay attention, with the relevant evidence coming from many sources. In some experiments, researchers "overload" their participants by giving them complex tasks or multiple simultaneous tasks and then ask what the participants can perceive in this setting. In these circumstances, participants' ability to notice things in the world is often dramatically compromised. (This is, for example, what is going on in the various cell-phone experiments.) In other studies, participants are misled about the upcoming stimuli, so that they "prime" themselves for one input but receive a different one. In this setting, perception is slowed and may fail altogether. In still other studies, participants do not expect an input to arrive and so have no reason to pay attention. Here, too, perception is undermined, with a huge majority of people failing to perceive clearly "visible" targets directly in their line of view (Mack & Rock, 1998; for a broad review of these issues, see Reisberg, 2013a).

C. THE "GRAND ILLUSION OF PERCEPTION"

There are thus many ways to document the selectivity of perception, with the evidence often drawing on demonstrations of how much we fail to see in the world before our eyes. Crucially, though, people often seem not to notice this selectivity. In various experiments, participants are surprised (and perhaps embarrassed) when we point out, within the visual input, large objects that they had overlooked or when we show them how easily we can swap out an object within the scene, replacing it with something altogether different, without their noticing the exchange (Simons & Rensink, 2005). In other words, people seem to experience what some writers call the "grand illusion of perception"—a strong subjective sense that their perception of the world is complete and uniformly detailed, even though it is plainly not.

In the same vein, people are often surprised to learn how little detail they are able to discern just a few degrees away from the current focus of vision and likewise are surprised to learn that perception of hue in the visual periphery is dependent on a mix of inference and memory—and not on the visual input per se. Apparently, then, people have the impression that they *can* see detail and color out at the edges of their vision—even though they demonstrably cannot.

For all of these reasons, one might fear that people will often be overconfident in their own powers of observation and overready to blame others who fail to see some seemingly prominent input. This fear is well-founded. In one study, researchers described to people (but did not show to them) some of the displays we have already mentioned—the gorilla walking through the middle of the basketball game or Leon "escaping" from a conversation by trading places with the fellow who had been carrying the door. The people in the study were asked directly: Do you think you would miss these events, if you were in the actual study?

In one version of this study, 83% of the participants predicted they would detect the events described to them; in the actual experiment, by contrast, only 11% of the participants had noticed the change (Levin, Momen, Drivdahl, & Simons, 2000). Plainly, people believe their perception is more complete, more encompassing than it actually is.

D. PERCEPTION IS CONSTRUCTIVE

Thanks to the selectivity of perception, we perceive *less* than one might expect, given the stimulus information available to us. But there is also a regard in which we perceive *more* than one might expect because our perceptual apparatus often supplements the input with inferences and interpretations.

This *constructive* side of perception is easy to document. As one example, consider the two "tables" shown in Figure 2.1. Of course, these are drawings of tables—two-dimensional representations drawn on a flat page. However, odds are good that you automatically and uncontrollably perceive these drawings as if they were three-dimensional shapes—two tables viewed from slightly different vantage points. Moreover, this interpretation of the drawing is not something that you "add" to your perception as some sort of postscript or codicil. Instead, this interpretation is part of, and woven into, your perception and thus ends up shaping the perception itself—in this case, producing a compelling illusion.

What is the illusion here? In the drawing, each "tabletop" appears as a parallelogram, but which parallelogram is longer—the one that depicts the tabletop on the left or the one on the right? Which parallelogram is narrower? In fact, the two parallelograms are exactly the same shape and size. (If you were to cut out the parallelogram on the left, rotate it and slide it over, it would coincide perfectly with the parallelogram on the right. You can, if you wish, persuade yourself on this point, without defacing the book, by laying a thin sheet of paper on top of this page and tracing the outline of the left table's top. Then slide the tracing to the right, rotate it, and overlay it on the right table's top.)

In this illusion (and in countless others as well), you are a victim of your own interpretive process. Your visual system interprets the drawings as though they were three-dimensional and then "adjusts" the perception of the drawing according to this

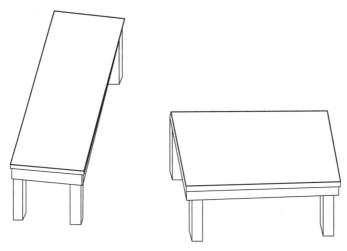

Figure 2.1:
The role for interpretation in perception. Simple illusions make the point that our perception of the world routinely supplements the input with inferences and interpretations. And, because we're interpreting, it's possible for us to misinterpret. Here, the tabletop on the left seems longer and narrower than the one on the right. However, the two parallelograms are exactly the same shape and size.

(mistaken) assessment of depth. It is thus your own adjustment, as you view the drawing, that creates the illusion.

Of course, we've illustrated this point with a simple drawing, but, as we'll see later in the chapter, related effects of interpretation (and misinterpretation) can be demonstrated with more complex inputs and in settings outside of a psychologist's laboratory.

E. SPECIAL CIRCUMSTANCES

Our perception of the world is, of course, generally accurate. This point is evident, for example, in the simple fact that we are able to move around in the physical world, guided by vision, without a series of calamitous collisions. This success in perceiving, however, does not change the fact that, in many circumstances, the selectivity of perception will lead us to miss conspicuous (and potentially important) inputs. Likewise, there is no question that the constructive nature of perception leaves us vulnerable to misinterpretation and illusion.

What lessons should the justice system draw from this overall assessment? The answer—not surprisingly—depends on the circumstances. The risk of perceptual error is low (although not zero) in the leisurely, well-lit, nondistracting, often-predictable settings in which we conduct most of our daily lives. But the risk is markedly higher in other settings. Let's look at some of the relevant parameters.

Darkness

Many criminal activities take place outdoors at night—and hence in relative darkness. Some crimes take place indoors but in limited lighting. How do these factors matter? The answer starts with common sense: namely, that it's difficult to see things in the dark. If there were any dispute about this point, witnesses in one study viewed someone at the end of twilight, and were later essentially random in their subsequent identifications of this person (Yarmey, 1986; also see Loftus, 1985; Wagenaar & Van der Schreir, 1996).

The available evidence, however, allows us to be more specific on this issue. First, let's emphasize that illuminations can vary continuously over an enormous range—from circumstances that might be described as "pitch black" to circumstances that are brightly lit and with many options in between. Let's also emphasize that what matters for perception reaches beyond the physical measurement of the light—a measurement that might be done with a photographer's light meter. The reason is that our eyes vary in their sensitivity to light, and so we need to evaluate the illumination levels "through the eyes" of the witness.

When you move from a lit room into the darkness, your eyes adjust, a process called *dark adaptation*. The speed of adaptation is uneven: The early adaptation is very rapid (less than a second), thanks to the swift adjustment of the pupil in the eye (allowing more light to enter the eyeball). A second aspect of adaptation takes nine or ten minutes as the cones on the retina adjust to the lower light levels. A third aspect takes roughly 30 minutes as the rods adjust. (The rods adjust more slowly because, with their high level of light sensitivity, they will have been "overstimulated" by the strong illumination in the room you exited, before you came into the dark, and so they need more time to "recover.")

These time estimates, though, must be understood as crude approximations because the speed of this process depends on other factors, including how brightly illuminated the initial scene was (in essence, how much light was the eye exposed to before the adaptation began), the age of the witness (dark adaptation is slower in older witnesses), and other factors as well. (Certain drugs, for example, influence dark adaptation, in part because they influence pupil diameter.)

For these reasons, if a particular case involves action at low-light levels, investigators are well advised to explore the issues just raised (the light levels the witness just exited, the age of the witness, and possible drug use). No matter how these details play out, however, bear in mind that, in low-light levels, perceivers must rely on rods (and this is called *scotopic vision*) and not cones (*photopic vision*). This fact is the consequence of a point noted earlier: rods are (for reasons of anatomy and biochemistry) able to function at low light levels; cones require a higher level of illumination. Why is this distinction—between scotopic and photopic vision—important? Recall that the rods are insensitive to differences in hue and much less sensitive than cones to details in the visual scene. As a result, if a scene is dimly lit, then witnesses' ability to perceive detail or hues will be deeply compromised. If these visual attributes matter for a case, then facts about vision can be crucial for investigators seeking to understand the case.

Let's also mention in passing that, in the ideal, the light levels would be observed and recorded by the police officers first arriving on the scene (i.e., by the officers arriving soon after the crime). These observations need not be technical; it is helpful, for example, just to know whether a police officer can easily read a street sign at a distance of 10 feet, or can easily see the colors of someone's clothing. It is likewise helpful to know which lights in a room were turned on, whether curtains were open or closed, or exactly where the crime scene was relative to the nearest streetlight. Unfortunately, facts like these are often not recorded, and so the attorneys need at some later point to infer the light levels. This is worrisome: Sky conditions may be different on the night the attorneys make their observations than they were on the night of the crime, light bulbs that were shining on the crime may not be shining later, and so on. This point should be flagged, then, as a straightforward way that, with better report writing, police officers can improve the quality of evidence in many crime investigations.

The "Rule of 15"

For many purposes, the qualitative comments in the previous section will suffice. In some settings, though, investigators may need a *quantitative* treatment of lighting issues. For this purpose, Wagenaar and Van der Schrier (1996; De Jong, Wagenaar, Wolters, & Verstijnen, 2005) have proposed a guideline that they refer to as the "rule of 15."

Wagenaar and Van der Schrier examined face recognition under circumstances that were certainly favorable for perception: Participants in the study were calm, focused, and tested after a very short delay. From this base, the researchers asked: What other factors were needed for these observers to reach an "acceptable" level of accuracy? Wagenaar and Van der Schrier proposed that an error rate greater than 10% would be unacceptable for most investigations, and so they evaluated their data by asking under what circumstances would accuracy be at least 90%.

The answer to this question is the "rule of 15": Identification accuracy will reach the desirable level of accuracy, these researchers argue, if the illumination level is at least 15 lux *and* the viewing distance is no more than 15 meters. (We say more about viewing distance in a moment.) The term *lux* refers to a measurement of how much light is illuminating a surface, and, to translate this measure into more familiar terms, Wagenaar and Van der Schreir note that a dimly illuminated interior space is generally lit at 30 lux, whereas urban areas with bright street lights are illuminated at only 10 lux. Therefore, a view of someone directly under the street light might (barely) allow this ("acceptable") level of accuracy, but a view of someone not directly under the street light would entail an "unacceptable" risk of error.

Of course, the claims here rest on a specific definition of "unacceptable risk," and one might challenge this definition (cf. Horry et al., 2014). Likewise, one might argue that actual witnesses (excited, distracted, and tested at a delay) will perform less well than these test subjects and so might need more illumination and closer viewing distances. With these cautions noted, however, the Wagenaar and Van der Schreir "rule" does provide an often-quoted guideline in thinking about crime scene illumination.

In thinking about a scene's illumination, it's not enough just to ask how much light there was. It is also important to consider the source, and therefore the direction, of the lighting. For example, if a crime takes place outdoors at night, the crime scene may be illuminated by just a few lights directly overhead. These lights may create enough illumination, but in some cases will also cast strong shadows, and this can change perception in a variety of ways.

What is the concern here? The answer begins with the (obvious) point that strong shadows will leave some aspects of the scene in (semi)darkness, even if the rest of the scene is well lit. Investigators need to be alert to this issue when making claims about what witnesses could or could not see.

In addition, perceivers actually *use* shadow information as a cue in judging depth. (This truth is well-known to generations of summer camp counselors who make their faces look strange and frightening while telling a campfire ghost story simply by lighting their faces from below with a flashlight.) The power of this depth-from-shading cue is evident, for example, in Figure 2.2A. Most people perceive this pattern as depicting six "bulges," roughly in an eyes-nose-and-mouth configuration, against a backdrop of multiple "dimples." Figure 2.2B, in contrast, shows the same figure now turned upside-down. This inversion obviously reverses the pattern of shading, and this reversal is enough to turn bulges into dimples and vice versa.

Note, though, that the visual system's use of shadow information rests on certain (implicit) assumptions about how concave or convex surfaces are ordinarily lit. When those assumptions are mistaken (as they can be in settings with artificial light), our perception can be pulled off track. As a result, strong shadows can distort many facial features—the salience of cheek bones, the depth of wrinkles, the prominence of eyebrows, and more—potentially undermining the likelihood of an accurate identification later on. (For further exploration of how changes in illumination from one view to the next can "drastically undermine recognition performance," see Liu, Chen, Han, & Shan, 2013.)

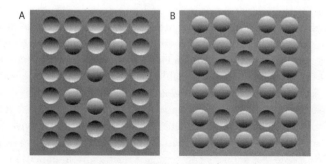

Figure 2.2:
The perception of depth is influenced by shadows. The panel on the left is generally perceived as containing six "bulges," roughly in an eyes-nose-mouth configuration. The panel on the right shows the exact same figure, but now turned upside down. The inversion reverses the pattern of shading and turns the bulges into dimples.

Eyeglasses

I am almost embarrassed to mention a further factor: whether the witness wears prescription lenses (in the form of eyeglasses or contact lenses) and whether the witness had these lenses in place at the time of the crime. Nonetheless, I do mention this factor for two reasons: First, it obviously matters (what witnesses can see is surely shaped by whether they're wearing their glasses or not). Second, this factor is often overlooked. I have consulted in many cases in which investigators sought to determine, months after a crime, whether crucial witnesses were wearing their glasses or not. My hope, of course, is that by mentioning these points I will encourage police officers in their reports (and investigators in their thinking) not to overlook this concern.

Distance

Common sense tells us that it is easier to see things close up than it is to see things far away. Research allows us, however, to go well beyond common sense and to specify how far might be too far.

Some of the best work on this point has been done with faces, and we earlier mentioned the so-called "rule of 15." The idea of this "rule" is that the ability to recognize faces is acceptably accurate only if the face was viewed from a distance no greater than 15 meters (roughly 50 feet; De Jong et al., 2005; Wagenaar & Van der Shreier, 1996; but also see Horry et al., 2014; Lindsay, Semmler, Weber, Brewer, & Lindsay, 2008).

We can, however, be more precise here. Accuracy for facial identification gradually improves as the viewing distance drops from 20 meters or so down to 12 meters (about 40 feet). At smaller distances (from 12 meters down to 7; roughly 20 feet), the benefits of closer viewing are detectable but slight. Then, once someone is within 7 meters of the target, there is virtually no advantage from even closer viewing (Horry et al., 2014; Wagenaar & van der Schreir, 1996).

What about distances greater than 15 meters? One study examined what we can think of as a "best-case scenario" (Loftus & Harley, 2005): Participants in this procedure were trying to recognize highly familiar faces, such as those of celebrities, and were cued in advance whose face they might see. (Roughly, the procedure is one in which research participants are told: "In the next block of trials, you will be seeing faces drawn from the following list of 16 celebrities . . .") Prior to the test trials, participants were also shown photos of these celebrities to remind them of the celebrities' appearance. In addition, the participants were all calm and focused on their task; the illumination was fine, and the air was clear.

In this procedure, participants recognized 80% of the celebrities (and, in some conditions, more) at a viewing distance of approximately 30 feet (roughly: 10 meters; so, performance here was actually somewhat worse than we would expect from the "rule of 15"). At greater distances, recognition accuracy fell off, and (for example) at a distance of 64 feet (about 20 meters), the error rate was greater than 40%. By 128 feet (about 40 meters), performance was quite poor—with more than 80% of the identifications now mistaken.

Here is a different way to think about these data: Within 34 feet (10 meters), accuracy was decent—at least 75% (although, again, slightly worse than we might expect, given the "rule of 15"). Beyond a distance of 75 feet (25 meters), recognition accuracy was generally below 25%. Thus, between the closer viewing distance (10 meters) and the farther (25 meters), the test subjects' performance fell from being correct three-times-in-four to being wrong three-times-in-four.

Let's emphasize again, though, that these are "best-case" estimates. After all, in most crimes, witnesses are not trying to recognize highly familiar celebrity faces. Instead, they are likely to get only a brief view of an unfamiliar face, perhaps at low lighting; they then try to identify that same face only at a delay, when they are shown a police lineup. Performance in these settings is likely to be appreciably worse than that observed in the study just described. In addition, in some cases, atmospheric conditions need to be taken into account. (Mist, for example, or dust in the air, will degrade a witness's ability to see clearly at a distance.) Therefore, some downward adjustment of the numbers offered here will often be necessary.

Finally, in describing their study, Loftus and Harley (2005) also offer an important note of caution: They describe a criminal trial that hinged on an identification at a distance of roughly 450 feet. After the verdict was in, some of the jurors "confirmed that they did their own experiment in broad daylight during a break. They had one or more jurors pace off a given distance and then they all stood and decided if they could recognize them" (p. 64). Of course, this "experiment" was problematic at many levels: Jurors are instructed not to do their own "research," but to rely only on information admitted into evidence. Moreover, even if the experiment were permissible, its results were surely misleading: The crime took place in the evening, and hence light levels were probably low. The jurors, in contrast, did their experiment with good illumination. The crime was fast-paced and involved four assailants in complex actions. The jurors' experiment was slow-paced and involved people standing still while they were being viewed.

Most important, the witness to the crime was trying, at this distance, to perceive and perhaps memorize never-seen-before faces for a subsequent ID. The jurors, on the other hand, were viewing a face they knew well (one of the other jurors) and asking each other some version of, "You can still see it's Fred, can't you?" These are massively different situations, and performance is certain to be vastly better in the latter task than in the former. (Indeed, there is a broad pattern of evidence telling us that it is easier to confirm an already identified face than it is to perceive and identify a new face; see Chapter 4.) Despite all of these points, notice that jurors thought this was a reasonable experiment to conduct.

Viewing Angle

In some cases, witnesses view a scene not just from an awkward distance, but also from an awkward viewing angle. For example, I have testified in armed-robbery cases in which the perpetrators forced their victims to lie down on the floor. The victims' only view of the perpetrators' faces, therefore, was from floor level, trying to look up at a sharp angle, out of the corners of their eyes.

Sometimes it's not the *witness* who has an unusual viewing angle; it is instead a *video camera*. Many crime scenes are covered by video surveillance, but often the camera for the surveillance is placed in some high position (so that it has an unobstructed view of a wide area). As a result, the camera tells us what the perpetrator looks like *if viewed from ceiling height,* and investigators (or jurors) then need to decide if this is what a suspect (or defendant) might look like if viewed from that same height.

Humans are certainly capable of a process termed "imaged rotation," in which they imagine a form rotated into a new angle and then make judgments about what the form would look like from this new angle (e.g., Cooper & Shepard, 1973; Reisberg, 2013a, 2013b). However, these judgments are sometimes slow, often need practice, and are especially difficult with complex, unfamiliar objects (such as a face). On this basis, I would urge caution whenever someone has seen a face from one (perhaps extreme) angle and is now trying to recognize the person from a rather different angle. (For more on the difficulties of "translating" one viewing angle of a face into another, see Jenkins, White, Montfort, & Burton, 2011.)

In some circumstances, however, we can sidestep the difficulties just described. Specifically, I have, in a variety of cases, urged investigators or attorneys simply *to stand on a chair* or to climb a step-ladder and then take a photo of their suspect (or client) from this vantage point. This photo will then provide a direct comparison with the image (of the actual perpetrator) recorded by a high-positioned video camera. This photograph would likely be inadmissible at trial, but can provide attorneys and investigators a means of comparing different views of a face with no concerns about the difficulties of imaged rotation.

Event Duration

The duration of an event is also important, and, again, some of the best science on this point concerns the perception (and subsequent identification) of faces. Specifically, research shows a clear relationship between the amount of time that a witness has to observe someone and the likelihood of an accurate identification later on.

It cannot be surprising that brief views lead to less accurate identification (Bornstein, Deffenbacher, Penrod, & McGorty, 2012; Horry et al., 2014; Memon, Hope, & Bull, 2003; Shapiro & Penrod, 1986; Tredoux, Meissner, Malpass, & Zimmerman, 2004). However, the precise relationship between viewing time and identification accuracy depends on other factors (e.g., lighting, attention, the amount of time that passes between the initial view and the subsequent identification procedure). Overall, though, the effect of duration is quite substantial. As an illustration, some studies document high levels of accuracy (90% or so) if people have as long as 45 seconds to view a face, but accuracy falls off dramatically (roughly 30% correct IDs and hence 70% errors) if the exposure duration is cut to 10–12 seconds (Memon et al., 2003; for more on this point, see Chapter 4).

Event Complexity

In the earlier discussion of viewing distance, I described a jury "experiment" in which jurors observed a calm episode (with other jurors standing at a prescribed distance) and drew conclusions from this "experiment" about an excited and complicated episode (four assailants attacking several individuals, one of whom was killed). Does this difference in complexity matter?

Two broad considerations are relevant here. First, we have already mentioned the importance of attention in supporting perception (and, arguably, in making perception possible at all). With a complex event, your attention will be taxed because there is, to put it bluntly, a lot to "take in"—different actions and different players. As one result, the accuracy of identifications goes down if the witnessed event was complex (e.g., Clifford & Hollin, 1981).

Second, overloading someone's attention can produce a specific type of error called a *conjunction error*. This term refers to a situation in which someone correctly perceives the features or elements of a scene but is confused about how these elements were "assembled." The classic version of this error is demonstrated in lab studies that might show, say, a red T and a blue Q. If the perceiver's attention is taxed, however, the person might (correctly) report seeing something red and something blue and might also report the T and the Q. However, the person might (with confidence) report having clearly seen a blue T and a red Q (Prinzmetal, Presti, & Posner, 1986).

Do similar errors happen with more complex stimuli? In one study, participants viewed several faces and ended up misremembering which face wore which expression (Neel, Becker, Neuberg, & Kenrick, 2012). Moreover, this perceptual error was not random; instead, the mistakes were (as we might expect) guided by other beliefs and, in this case, by gender stereotypes. Thus, if they lost track of which face had been displaying anger, the participants were more likely to make the mistake of perceiving the male face as angry rather the female face. As the authors put it, men "grab anger" from neighboring faces. In contrast, though, women's faces tended to "grab" expressions of happiness from neighboring faces.

These conjunction errors have important implications for the legal system. Imagine a crime involving several assailants. In such cases, the courts might need to determine which of the assailants were the "watchers" and which were the "punchers" or, perhaps, need to determine which of the assailants wielded the knife. With a complex event—especially a fast-paced complex event—there is room for error about these crucial points.

Attention

We have already argued that perceiving depends on attention, and thus people can fail to perceive a stimulus if they are not suitably primed and attentive. Let's pause to elaborate this theme in several ways.

What does it mean for a witness to be "attentive?" As a start, we might ask: Was the witness daydreaming, sleepy, or drugged? Or was the witness highly alert? If the witness was not (in this broad fashion) attentive, this would undermine the witness's ability to focus on *anything,* with important implications for what the witness will later remember.

But we also need to ask a more fine-grained question: What was the witness paying attention *to?* Even if the witness was fully alert and highly vigilant, perception of the world is (as we've said) selective, and so knowing that a witness detected (or failed to detect) one aspect of a scene or perceived (or misperceived) one detail tells us little about what else the witness perceived.

How can we find out what exactly a witness was focused on? We turn later to an approach that seems *not* to be fruitful: simply asking the witness, after the fact, what he or she was paying attention to. But, if we set that option aside, what can we do instead? In truth, there is no simple answer.

Research tells us that certain visual inputs do tend to catch someone's attention, but the key word here is "tend," and there are few guarantees on this topic. Even so, brightly lit stimuli and moving stimuli do tend to catch people's attention. Faces tend to catch people's attention, all other things equal. But, more powerfully, what someone pays attention to is heavily influenced by the interests and curiosity of the viewer. A classic demonstration of this point comes from a study by Yarbus (1967). He showed his participants the image shown at the top-left in Figure 2.3. The other panels in the figure show the pattern of eye movements of the viewer when given various instructions—to judge the ages of the people shown in the picture, to estimate from the picture how long the visitor had been away, and so on.

As a further complication, even if we know what *objects* in a scene someone was focusing on, we still need to ask what *aspects* or dimensions of those objects the person was paying attention to. To see how this matters, consider an informal demonstration: Find someone who is wearing a wristwatch and ask them what time it is. Then immediately ask them to look at the ceiling, and, in this new position, ask them *to describe their own watch.* Are all 12 numbers shown on the watch's face? Or just numbers at the compass points? Are the numbers in italic? Are there serifs on the numerals? Most men will be unable to answer these questions, even though they looked at their watch just a moment ago, when you inquired about the time. In that glance at the watch, they were paying attention to the time itself and not the watch's appearance—and so failed to perceive what they did not attend. (This demonstration works less well with women, who, because of the patterns built into our culture, may enjoy the watch as an item of jewelry as much as a timepiece and so may pay closer attention to the watch's exact appearance.)

The point, then, is that it is not enough to know that someone "was alert and attentive"; we also need to know what the person was attentive *to.* Likewise, it is not enough to know the nature of the visual scene in front of a viewer because how viewers point their eyes, within that scene, depends on the viewers' priorities. Moreover, even if we do know exactly where the person was pointing his or her eyes, we still need information about the person's goals because attention to one aspect of an

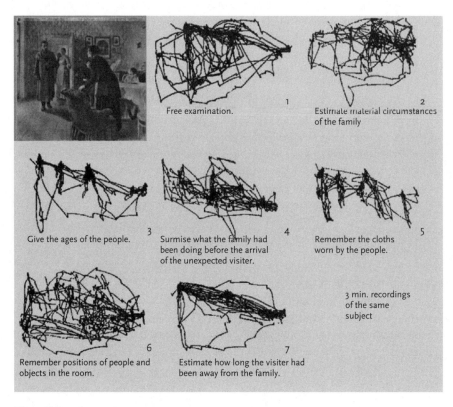

Figure 2.3:
Eye movements depend on goals. Panel 1 shows the path of a viewer's eye movements when simply allowed to view the picture on the top left for three minutes. Panel 2 shows the path of a viewer's eye movements when asked to estimate the wealth level of the family in the picture. Panel 3 shows the eye movements when a viewer was asked to estimate the ages of the people in the picture. (From Yarbus, A. F. (1967) *Eye Movements and Vision*, New York, Plenum Press. Fig. 109, pg. 174, Ch. 7: Eye movement records for one subject while viewing the painting "An Unexpected Visitor." With kind permission from Springer Science and Business Media.) Permission granted by Springer via Rightslink.

object (e.g., the time shown on the watch) can allow utter neglect of (and ignorance about) other aspects of the object.

We should also mention that most of our examples here involve attention to *visual* stimuli. Similar points can be documented, though, for *auditory* stimuli: In this domain as well, people routinely fail to notice what they did not attend. In this domain as well, attention to one aspect of a stimulus (e.g., attention to the *gist* of a conversation) often entails neglect of other aspects (e.g., the exact wording of sentences or the qualities of the voice itself; for more on these points, see Chapter 6.)

Weapon Focus

As we have seen, attention matters enormously for perception, but it is often difficult to know what it was within a scene that someone paid attention to. Nonetheless, in some cases, we can make some strong inferences about what a person was focused on and thus strong inferences about what the person is likely to remember.

Sometimes, inferences about someone's focus are supported by particular details of the case. I participated in one trial in which a male witness described in detail the hairstyle of another male who had been at the crime scene. Attorneys were skeptical of this description until they learned that the witness worked part-time as a hair stylist, cared deeply about styles, and tended always to notice other people's styles. In a different trial, a robbery victim identified the perpetrator as part of the police investigation. She also told the police that she noticed the perpetrator the moment he entered her shop because she was struck by how much he resembled one of her cousins. This certainly sounds like a witness who had reason to notice and pay attention to a face, and this point bolstered her identification.

In other cases, the situation itself provides indications of what a witness paid attention to. Imagine a robbery of a retail store: The robber comes in, voices a threat, and hands a sack to the clerk who fills the sack from the cash drawer; the robber then leaves. This sequence is likely to take less than a minute, and this brief duration limits the witness's opportunity to view and pay attention to the robber. (For more on limited duration views, see earlier discussion.) In addition, the clerk must spend some moments looking down at the cash drawer to guide his hands as he reaches toward the money and moves it into the sack; moments spent this way are, of course, moments *not* spent looking at the robber. If, in addition, the clerk casts his or her eyes around the store (perhaps seeking help, perhaps looking for a second robber) then these steps, too, take some time. In this fashion, we can plausibly reconstruct how the clerk paid attention to the various elements within the scene and thus (among other points) what the clerk's opportunity was to view (and memorize) the robber's appearance.

One aspect of this reconstruction, however, is complicated. A number of investigators have highlighted the role of so-called *weapon focus*. This term refers to a tendency for witnesses or victims to focus attention on a knife or gun, if one is in view, with the consequence that they pay less attention to other aspects of the scene. In other words, the witnesses may develop what is commonly called "tunnel vision" and, on this logic, will offer descriptions of the crime that are less complete compared to witnesses to (or victims of) crimes without weapons. (For similar claims about "tunnel vision," see the discussion in the section on the effects of drugs and alcohol and also the section on the effects of emotional arousal.)

There is an obvious common-sense basis to the weapon-focus idea. After all, what could possibly be more interesting, and more urgent, for witnesses than to know where the weapon was, whether the weapon was pointed at them, whether the perpetrator's finger was on the trigger, and so on? But, in addition to this common-sense logic, numerous studies have confirmed the existence of weapon focus. Some of these studies have involved the presentation of crime videos that either did or did not include a weapon, with the studies then probing research participants' memories for the crime. Other studies have involved staged events; still others have used real-life episodes—asking, for example, whether children lock their attention on to the doctor's hypodermic needle when about to receive an injection. These studies have reliably shown a weapon-focus effect. The effect is detectable in memory data (with participants exposed to a weapon routinely having better memory for that weapon compared to a control object and *worse* memory for all else in the scene compared to participants not exposed to a weapon). The effect is also detectable in participants' eye movements (with more time spent looking at the weapon; Loftus, Loftus, & Messo, 1987; Stanny & Johnson, 2000). And the effect is large: In one study, memory accuracy for a "perpetrator" was 33% if the perpetrator was carrying a weapon (in this study, a potentially threatening hypodermic syringe), compared to 64% accuracy if the perpetrator was carrying a nonthreatening object (in this study, a pen; Maass & Köhnken, 1989). On all these grounds, it's not surprising that the weapon-focus effect also emerges when we pool the data from many studies via a meta-analysis (Steblay, 1992).

Other studies suggest that you actually don't need a weapon to produce the weapon-focus pattern. Imagine, for example, that you enter a bank and notice that one of the other customers is carrying a live ferret. Here, too, it seems plausible that this unexpected, interesting input will serve as an "attention magnet" (a term coined by Laney, Heuer, & Reisberg, 2003), with the result that you'll focus your attention on the ferret, notice many details of the ferret's appearance, but fail to notice other aspects of the scene. (For demonstrations of a weapon-focus pattern without a weapon, see Pickel, 1998; also Erickson, Lampinen, & Leding, 2014.)

There is, however, a complication here, drawing on evidence from actual police cases. Several studies have examined reports of real crimes that *did* involve a weapon and reports that *did not*. In light of the weapon-focus pattern, we would expect witness identifications to be more common and more accurate in crimes without weapons (i.e., crimes that lacked the "attention magnet" that a weapon supposedly creates). The data, however, have been mixed. Tollestrup, Turtle, and Yuille (1994) found a weapon-focus effect in some measures (e.g., how often witnesses selected, in an identification procedure, the police suspect) but not in other measures (e.g., the accuracy of witness estimates of the perpetrator's age, height, or weight). Other studies show no effect of a weapon's presence on any measures (Behrman & Davey, 2001; Cooper, Kennedy, Hervé, & Yuille, 2002; Valentine, Pickering, & Darling, 2003).

What should we make of this pattern—with an apparent conflict between the research data (which reliably show a weapon-focus effect) and the studies of actual police cases (which often do not show this effect)? The answer is not clear (although, for some suggestions, see Pickel, 1998; 2006), but one possibility hinges on event duration: Perhaps people initially focus on the weapon, but, if the event lasts long enough, they take the opportunity to explore the scene more broadly (see, for example, Steblay, 1992, p. 421; also Wells, Memon, & Penrod, 2006). This suggestion draws strength from a recent meta-analysis that suggests, first, that a weapon focus effect *can* be observed in nonlaboratory ("real-world") environments, and, second, that the effect is significantly reduced if the target event is longer in duration (Fawcett, Russell, Peace, & Christie, 2013).

In light of this mixed pattern, though, I would urge practitioners *not* to assume a weapon-focus effect in crimes involving weapons (or other unusual objects). To be sure, sometimes the witnesses themselves tell you about weapon focus. Sometimes they say things like, "I couldn't take my eyes off the gun," or "All I could think about was that gun." Sometimes they provide impressively detailed descriptions of the gun. In such cases, it does seem that a weapon-focus effect is on the scene, and this should invite concern about how accurately the witness perceived, or will remember, other aspects of the event. Beyond these cases, though, the status of weapon focus is—in my view—still uncertain.

The Interplay Between Perception and Memory

This chapter is about perception, not memory (we'll turn directly to a discussion of memory in Chapter 3 and beyond). There are, however, many points of contact between these two broad topics, so we can't separate them altogether. In one direction, let us flag three influences: First, you cannot remember what you did not perceive in the first place, and so, if perception is selective, then it's inevitable that memory will be as well. After all, you can't get water from an empty bottle, and you can't read information off a blank page. In the same way, you can't recall information that was never put into memory in the first place.

Second, if perception is constructive, then these effects, too, will be carried into memory: Your memory provides a record of what you perceived, and, if your perception was shaped by prior knowledge and inference, then it is this knowledge-and-inference-based perception that is stored in memory. Hence, what you will recall will necessarily echo these earlier effects.

Third, memory distortions (and memory errors of various sorts) are more common for events that were not perceived clearly from the start. One reason for this pattern is that memory distortions often arise from an effort toward filling in gaps in what you can recall, and gaps are more likely for events that were not fully and accurately perceived. Another reason is that you often receive further information about an event after experiencing the event itself. (That further information might come from media coverage, from co-witnesses, or from suggestive questioning by an investigator.) In ways we will discuss in later chapters, you will be more strongly influenced by these outside influences if you lack a strong "anchor"—that is, if you lack a strong recollection, on your own, for what actually occurred. And, of course, you'll lack this anchor if you only had a dim or partial perception of the original event. Thus, problems in perception during an event leave you more vulnerable to memory contamination afterward.

Memory for Viewing Opportunity

But there is also a different type of contact between memory and perception because we often count on memory to find out what someone perceived. We ask witnesses, for example, to tell us (perhaps months after a crime) how good the lighting was at the crime scene, how close they were standing to the people they are describing, for how many seconds the robber's face was in view, or exactly what they were paying attention to within the scene.

In fact, this reliance on witness memory for viewing opportunity is woven into several crucial court rulings. For example, the evaluation of eyewitness identifications is governed, in U.S. federal courts (and in many state courts as well) by principles laid out in the 1972 *Neil v. Biggers* ruling and the 1977 *Manson v. Braithwaite* ruling. Both of these rulings (correctly) note the importance of the witness's opportunity to view the perpetrator (an opportunity depending on factors such as distance, duration, and lighting) and also the witness's degree of attentiveness to the perpetrator. The problem, however, is that, in most cases, we have no objective, reliable means of documenting these important factors, with the result that courts routinely rely on witness memory for these points.

We are therefore led to ask: How accurate are people in recalling these points? How well can people remember their own viewing opportunity? A series of studies is illuminating here, and we will have reason to revisit these studies in Chapter 3 (when we discuss the confidence someone places in his or her own memory) and in Chapter 5 (when we discuss identification procedures). For now, though, here is the basic paradigm: Witnesses are exposed to a crime (in some studies, the crime is shown in a video that the research participants watch; in other studies, the participants were actual witnesses to a real crime). Some time later, the witnesses are shown a photo lineup and asked if they can identify the perpetrator. Then, half the participants are given some feedback, along the lines of, "Good; you picked our suspect" or even something more general, such as "You've been a good witness." The other half of the participants, however, are given no feedback at all. (In some studies, a third group is given *negative* feedback: "The guy you picked actually wasn't our suspect.") All participants are then asked further questions, including a question about how certain they are in their identification and also questions about the *basis* for their identification—that is, how good a view they got. (For some exemplars of this paradigm, see Garrioch & Brimacombe, 2001; Luus & Wells, 1991.)

The brief words of feedback given to some participants have a powerful effect. Participants who receive confirming feedback indicate much higher levels of confidence in their identification—presumably because the feedback allows them to set aside any doubts they had about the ID and perhaps even to forget that they had harbored these doubts. More important for present purposes, the feedback also causes an odd sort of memory distortion: Participants who received confirming feedback now seem to recall that the lighting at the crime scene was pretty good, that they were standing close to the perpetrator, that they were paying full attention to the perpetrator's face, and so on. Figure 2.4 depicts the data from one study in which some participants got positive feedback, confirming their selection from the lineup, and others got negative feedback, indicating that they'd chosen someone who wasn't the suspect. The figure summarizes the percentage of the participants in each group who gave the highest possible ratings in response to the researchers' questions (responses of 6 or 7 on a 7-point scale). Thus, these are, in essence, participants who indicated that they could not possibly have been more certain, that their view could not have been better, and so on (Wells & Bradfield, 1998).

In the figure, there are obviously large differences between the two groups (again, with one group receiving positive feedback and one group receiving negative

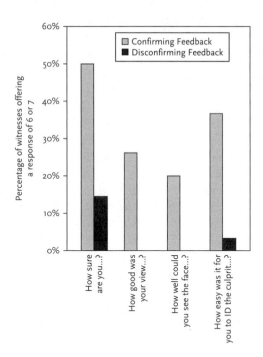

Figure 2.4:
The impact of feedback. A few words of encouragement have a powerful effect on a witness's recollection. Here, some of the witnesses were given confirming feedback, indicating that their selection from a lineup was in fact the police suspect; other witnesses were given disconfirming feedback. In both groups, the figure shows the percentage of these witnesses who gave the highest possible ratings in response to the researchers' questions (e.g., said they were as certain as they possibly could be; said that their view couldn't have been better, and so on).

feedback). Let's be clear, though, that these difference must be understood as reflecting *errors*. The reason, of course, is that all participants in this study saw the same crime. If memory for viewing opportunity were accurate, we would get the same report about viewing opportunity from the two groups. But, plainly, we get different reports, forcing the conclusion that the feedback has distorted participants' memory.

These effects are understandable, though, given what we know about memory: Like perception, memory, we've said, is constructive. (More precisely, we should say that memory is "reconstructive.") For both of these cognitive achievements, people rely on a "mix" of the information actually available to them (provided by the eyes or through recall) and other things they believe—using the latter to supplement, interpret, and sometimes to *shape* the former. (We have more to say about these points in Chapter 3.) Hence, if you now have reason to believe (thanks to an experimenter's feedback) that you made a correct identification, it's reasonable for you to infer that you must have gotten a good view after all. Thus, you reconstruct that the lighting, duration, and so on, must have been favorable. The trick, though, is that this inference is seamlessly woven into your "recall," and so you report a mistaken *memory*, not an inference.

Memory for Event Duration and Viewing Distance

The studies just described involve some sort of feedback (such as a police officer confirming an ID choice or someone telling a witness that the same selection was made by a different witness). Importantly, though, memory for viewing opportunity can be poor even without this feedback. In one study, witnesses viewed a simulated bank robbery that lasted 30 seconds. Later, the witnesses estimated that the event lasted (on average) 147 seconds, and so the witnesses were off by more than 400%. Moreover, this effect was remarkably consistent, and all but two of the witnesses overestimated the event duration (Loftus, Schooler, Boone, & Kline, 1987; also see Peterson & Wright, 2002; Pigott, Brigham, & Bothwell, 1990; Shiffman & Bobko, 1975; Yarmey, 2000; but for a demonstration that some people are systematically better at estimating duration than others, see Attard & Bindemann, 2013). Importantly for many legal cases, people are especially poor at estimating durations if they were *stressed* at the time of the event; stress can lead to even greater overestimates of duration (Sarason & Stroops, 1978).

People are likewise poor in estimating and then remembering distances: In one study (Lindsay et al., 2008), participants tended to underestimate distance (and so reported being closer than they actually were) for distances smaller than 100 feet or so; the error then *reversed* (and so participants offered *over*estimates) when the actual distance was greater than 100 feet. In many circumstances, participants misjudged distance by as much as a third. When asked to use *ranges* to describe their distance estimates ("I was at least __ feet away, but no more than __ feet away"), the actual distance was outside of the reported range in more than half the cases.

The key, then, is that we simply cannot rely on memory for viewing opportunity. Put differently, we need to guard against the peculiar error of trying to evaluate one aspect of memory (for example, an ID of the perpetrator) by means of another aspect of memory (what the witness recalls about his or her opportunity to view). Instead, we need other means of evaluating these crucial determinants of perceptual accuracy—distance, duration, lighting, and so on. We certainly need to distinguish between *documented* viewing opportunity and *remembered* viewing opportunity. The former is a deeply important consideration in evaluating witness evidence; the latter, unfortunately, is often misleading. (These points have many implications, including the deep questions they raise about the logic built into some court rulings—such as *Manson v. Braithwaite*; we return to this issue in Chapter 5.)

Perceiving: The Effects of Expectations

In evaluating perception, we also need to consider factors "inside the viewer"— including the knowledge and expectations that the viewer brings to a situation. The reason is rooted in a point we have already made: Our perception and our memory are constructive in important ways—adding elements that we believe are likely to be in place, even if we did not experience them directly, and adding interpretations for patterns that on their own might be ambiguous. Psychologists refer to these steps as "top-down" processes—processes that draw on knowledge and expectations to supplement (or guide the interpretation of) information picked up directly from the world. (Sometimes the term "knowledge-driven" is used in place of "top-down," and the information pick-up itself is usually said to involve "bottom-up" or "data-driven" processes.)

Earlier, we considered some top-down effects with simple line drawings, and we saw that the perceiver often ends up "seeing" more than is actually in the stimulus. But do similar effects emerge when we consider the complex stimuli someone encounters in the world? Brewer and Treyens (1981) invited their research participants to wait briefly in an academic office, prior to an experiment's start. Moments later, just after leaving the office, these participants were quizzed about the office's contents. As it turns out, the office had been carefully set up so that the bookshelves were full of various objects—but contained no books. Nonetheless, even though the participants had been sitting in the office just a minute ago, and even though there had been nothing to distract the participants while in the office, roughly one-third of them "recalled" having seen bookshelves full of books.

One might quibble about whether this is a perceptual error or a memory error (since there was a minute or so of delay between being in the office and the "recall" of the office contents). In either case, though, the data are clear in showing that a substantial number of participants reported that they had indeed seen books, apparently influenced by their expectations for what an academic office is likely to contain. This study therefore provides a testimonial both to how little people pick up from their environment, if not specifically paying attention to the target (and so the participants didn't note the bookless shelves), and how easily witnesses' reports can be shaped by their broader knowledge and expectations.

Here is a more troubling case: In several studies, research participants have played a "video game" in which human figures suddenly pop into view on the computer screen. The participant's task is to press a button if the figure is holding a weapon but to do nothing if the figure is holding some benign object (e.g., a soda can or a pack of cigarettes). The data show that participants are quicker in pressing the button if the figure holding the weapon is an African American than if he was a white. Likewise, participants are more likely to produce a "false alarm" (mistakenly pushing the button) if the figure holding a neutral object is an African American (for discussion, see Correll, Park, Judd, & Wittenbrink, 2002; Correll et al., 2007).

Close analysis of these data suggests that this effect depends on participants' "response criterion"—that is, on how much perceptual evidence participants require before deciding that, yes, they were seeing a weapon (and so should press the response button). When the figure on the computer screen was a black, participants' response criterion was lower—and so the participants were more easily persuaded that the figure did have a weapon.

How might this pattern emerge in "real-life" cases? The studies just described were in fact designed to explore a tragic case in New York City in which four white police officers shot and killed an unarmed African man. The police officers were searching a Bronx neighborhood for a rape suspect when they spotted Amadou Diallo—a man born in Liberia who happened to match the description of the suspect. The officers identified themselves as policemen and Diallo reached into his pocket, apparently intending to withdraw his wallet. Believing that he was reaching for a gun, the police opened fire, and 19 of their shots hit and killed Diallo. As it turns out, Diallo was not reaching for a gun—because he had no gun. Plainly, then, the officers had concluded there was a weapon on the basis of too little evidence.

The Effects of Injuries

This is a book rooted in psychology, not biology or medicine. Nonetheless, there are some topics for which biomedical considerations must enter our discussion because, on some points, we cannot describe perceptual or memory functioning without the relevant biology. Consider, for example, the fact that witnesses or victims to crimes are sometimes injured in some way; how does this affect their ability to perceive and then to report what they perceived? Likewise, these injured parties are often medicated in some way; how does this influence their reports?

Any damage to the body—for example, the blood loss caused by a wound—causes widespread problems, disrupting the function of the musculature, the digestive tract, respiration, and more. But the effects of biomedical harm are especially visible in the organ that places the heaviest demands on the body's oxygen and energy supplies: the brain. In fact, the human brain weighs only 3 pounds, more or less, and so for most people comprises only 2% of their biological tissue. Even so, the brain is a biologically expensive organ to maintain and consumes up to 20% of the oxygen used by the body (Raichle, 2001). The brain is also especially sensitive to toxins (and, in fact, receives "purer," "cleaner" blood than the rest of the body, thanks to a special filtration system called the blood–brain barrier). It is no wonder, then, that medical problems almost anywhere in the body can cause disruption of brain function.

What happens, therefore, if someone has been knifed or shot and loses a lot of blood? The medical profession uses the term *hypovolemic shock* to refer to a state resulting from a severe decrease in blood volume. A range of problems can cause this form of shock, but the list of mechanisms surely includes blood loss through wounds, vomiting, or some drugs. Hypovolemic shock is commonly subdivided into four stages, and the third and fourth stages are the ones of special interest in the present context: One of the identifying marks for Stage 3 is, in fact, an alteration in mental status (including confusion and anxiety); Stage 4, in turn, is often marked by loss of consciousness (Kelley, 2005).

It is not surprising that hypovolemic shock can disrupt perception and memory for events unfolding while the person is in shock. But hypovolemic shock can also have a retroactive effect because this shock can disrupt *memory consolidation* (Dudai, 2004). This is the biological process that moves newly acquired memories out of "temporary" storage and into a more enduring form. The process is largely automatic and thus requires no "mental work." In fact, consolidation proceeds perfectly well even if the person is asleep. (Indeed, some researchers suggest that sleep can *promote* the consolidation process; e.g., Buzsáki, 1998.)

What consolidation does require, however, is that the person remains reasonably healthy so that there will be no disruption to the biological steps needed to turn new and fragile memories into longer lasting ones. In addition, consolidation requires *time* because consolidation is a surprisingly slow process, unfolding in the hours after the target event. Until those hours have passed (i.e., until the memory is consolidated), the memory is fragile and easily knocked out of existence by various forms of physical duress.

On this basis, a wound (and the resulting blood loss) can interrupt the consolidation of a memory acquired hours earlier. As a result, the person establishes no memory for the earlier episodes and will certainly be unable to recall the earlier episodes. Let's be clear, though, that there is no firm rule here about memory loss, and the likelihood of memory loss depends on many factors (including the extent of the blood loss, how abrupt the blood loss was, how rapidly the person received medical treatment, how much time had elapsed between the to-be-remembered event and the onset of the blood loss, and more). Nonetheless, investigators should not be surprised if shock is accompanied by a loss of memory for events in the hours prior to the onset of the shock.

A similar form of memory loss—technically called *retrograde amnesia*—can be observed in circumstances not involving blood loss or shock. Blows to the head can disrupt memory consolidation. Extreme sleep deprivation or extraordinary levels of stress can have the same effect. Thus, it is not surprising if a victim of a horrific automobile accident finds himself unable to recall the accident or the hours leading up to the accident. Similarly, consider a soldier who manages to function well in the heat of battle but returns to camp at the end of the day, physically and emotionally exhausted, desperately short on sleep, having just undergone many hours of stress. In this case, it is entirely plausible that the soldier will wake up the next morning with no memory of the previous day's events—a case of battlefield amnesia caused by the biological duress that undermined memory consolidation (cf. McNally, 2003).

But what if, in any of these circumstances, the person *does* offer a report—perhaps a vivid, detailed report, delivered with certainty—about the moments leading up to a wound or the moments leading up to the car crash? One possibility that must be considered is that this person somehow escaped the retrograde effects of the wound or the car crash. As we indicated earlier, memory loss *can* be produced by these circumstances, but, even in extreme cases, an accurate, relatively complete memory is possible. (For related points, see Chapter 3's discussion of so-called *critical-incident amnesia*.)

Another possibility that must be considered, though, is that this "memory" is no memory at all but instead an after-the-fact reconstruction, describing how the person *believes* the event unfolded. (For more on this sort of reconstruction, see Chapter 3.) Plainly, therefore, someone's memory-based report must, in this setting, be interpreted with caution.

The Effects of Drugs and Alcohol

Witness reports can also be disrupted by another type of biological influence—the effect of drugs and alcohol (see, for a broad review, Soraci et al., 2007). Many prescribed drugs can cause some degree of amnesia, and some of these drugs are routinely given in hospital emergency rooms or as precursors to medical procedures.

The list of relevant drugs here is long (and continuously changing) but includes sedatives, antianxiety medications (e.g., drugs in the benzodiazepine family), and some analgesics. In a case involving hospitalization, therefore, investigators are well advised to check with medical experts to learn whether the constellation of drugs used may interfere with perception or memory.

In addition, many recreational drugs also have amnestic effects. These drugs include the benzodiazepine family just mentioned and also marijuana, which can disrupt both the formation of new memories and the recall of older memories (Pope, Gruber, Hudson, Huestis & Yurgelun-Todd, 2001). Disruptions of perception and memory are also associated with alcohol consumption. For example, in one study, participants who had witnessed an event were asked to identify the perpetrator using a "show-up" procedure. (See Chapter 5 for more on show-ups.) For participants with low levels of blood alcohol (BAC values under .04), a large majority (78%) correctly said that the suspect they were viewing was not the perpetrator. For participants with higher BAC levels, performance was markedly worse, and now roughly half of the participants (52%) mistakenly identified the suspect as being the perpetrator (Dysart, Lindsay, MacDonald, & Wicke, 2002).

In addition, alcohol is often alleged to shape how the now-drunken person pays attention, and some researchers argue that alcohol can produce its own version of "tunnel vision," often referred to as "alcohol myopia" (cf. Soraci et al., 2007). The idea here is that a drunken person takes in only a fraction of the information that would be noticed by someone sober. However, this "narrowing" is not inevitable: In one study, researchers approached people who were drinking in bars, measured their blood alcohol level, and showed them a crime video. A few days later, the researchers tested memory in these "crime witnesses." The results showed a clear effect of drinking, with moderately and highly intoxicated individuals recalling up to 33% fewer details than people who were not drunk (Oorsouw & Merckelbach, 2012). But, contrary to the idea of alcohol myopia, there was no selective impairment of peripheral details. Hence, the status of the myopia pattern remains uncertain (also see Compo et al., 2012; Harvey, Kneller, & Campbell, 2013).

Before pressing on, though, let's pause for a methodological point. The study just cited is realistic in the sense that participants were recruited in a real-life setting in which they were drinking as they ordinarily might. However, the study provides a clear example of the limits associated with "field studies." The concern here is that the more-intoxicated individuals may have differed from the sober individuals in some fashion *other than* the alcohol itself. (Perhaps the more-intoxicated individuals were drinking heavily because they were in the midst of a stressful period in their lives; if so, it might be the stress, rather than the alcohol, that is guiding their memory.) Hence, the study is suggestive but needs to be interpreted with caution.

Let's also note that the effects of drugs and alcohol must be considered together. The reason is straightforward: The effects of the various drugs we've been discussing are synergistic, such that alcohol (for example) amplifies the memory effect of many drugs and vice versa (White, 2003). Hence, the total impairment is generally greater than the "sum of its parts."

One further point is tied to popular lore about alcohol: Many people endorse the notion (celebrated, for example, in Charlie Chaplin's classic film *City Lights*) that events experienced while drunk will be forgotten later, after the person has sobered up, but then *remembered again* the next time the person is intoxicated. This pattern might seem plausible in light of evidence for well-documented *context reinstatement effects*—i.e., the greater likelihood of remembering if, at the time of recall, one is back in the same context and has the same perspective that one was in at the time of experiencing an event. (We discuss these effects in Chapter 3.) However, despite this plausibility, the evidence for this pattern with alcohol is at best uneven (see Weissenborn & Duka, 2000).

Alcoholic Blackouts

Alcohol can also, in some circumstances, produce *blackouts*. These blackouts are generally associated with blood alcohol levels of .15% or higher, but there is debate about this issue, and so we cannot point to a firm cut-off for the level of intoxication needed for a blackout. Some authors suggest that a level of .25–.30% is needed (Julien & DiCecco, 2010), but one study suggested that blackouts are possible with blood alcohol levels as low as .06% (Wetherill & Fromme, 2011; also see Ryback, 1970). A crucial complication for any of these estimates, though, is that we also need to consider the drinking *rate,* with alcoholic blackouts more common if the person became abruptly intoxicated, as opposed to someone who gradually built up a high level of alcohol in the bloodstream. Thus, blackouts are more likely if someone gulped his drinks, drank on an empty stomach, or was drinking hard liquor rather than beer (e.g., Perry et al., 2006; White, 2003; White, Singer, Kraus, & Swartzweider, 2004).

There is also some suggestion that people with a history of blackouts may suffer a new blackout with a relatively low BAC. Likewise, some studies indicate that genetic factors may play a role in this domain, with some individuals especially vulnerable to blackouts because of their innate constitution (Hartzler & Fromme, 2003; Nelson et al., 2004; Wetherill & Fromme, 2011; White, 2003).

Even with these complexities, someone's blood alcohol level surely plays a role in precipitating a blackout, but what if we don't have a blood alcohol measurement for a particular person? (For example, police rarely get a blood alcohol measurement for *crime witnesses,* although the measurement, if available, would often be of enormous value—cf. Evans, Compo & Russano, 2009.) We can at least approximate this measurement by relying on a count of drinks consumed. To be sure, this translation is crude because someone's blood alcohol level also depends on the person's body weight, level of body fat, and other factors, and we have also emphasized the role of *drinking rate*, which matters both for blood alcohol level and for the overall risk of a blackout. Even so, blackouts are likely if someone has had (roughly) seven or eight "drink equivalents," with these equivalents sometimes defined as 1 ounce of 80 proof liquor *or* 4 ounces of wine *or* 12 ounces of beer. Then, for each hour *after* drinking, we can, as a rough rule of thumb, subtract one "drink equivalent." As a related yardstick, some people rely on a "Widmark calculation," which suggests that

BAC falls roughly .015% for each hour that passes after consuming alcohol (Posey & Mozayani, 2007).

How common are alcohol-induced blackouts? In a survey of 772 undergraduates, 40% reported a blackout in the previous year (White, Jamieson-Drake, & Swartzwelder, 2002; also see Knight, Palacios, & Shannon, 1999). Many of the people in this survey also reported that, while drunk, they had engaged in a range of activities they could not remember later—activities that included vandalism, unprotected sex, driving, and spending money (also see Goodwin, 1995).

These last observations draw our attention to an important aspect of blackouts and intoxication overall. In some cases, alcohol consumption can cause someone to "pass out"—that is, to lose consciousness—and this is consistent with the notion, held for many years, that alcohol diminishes activity level throughout the central nervous system. It has become clear, however, that alcohol's effects on the nervous system are more selective: diminishing activity in some areas far more than others. This is why it is possible for someone who is heavily intoxicated to remain conscious, talk, drive, and engage in other complex activities—while also losing the capacity to establish new memories (Goodwin, 1995; Lee, Roh, & Kim, 2009). Therefore, there is a clear separation between "blacking out" and "passing out," with the former far more common.

As a related point, it is important to distinguish *en bloc* and *fragmentary* blackouts. En bloc blackouts are more extreme and involve a complete loss of any recollection of the period of extreme intoxication. Fragmentary blackouts, in contrast, are much more common and involve memory loss for specific events within the period of drunkenness (e.g., Goodwin, Crane, & Guze, 1969; Hartzler & Fromme, 2003; Jennison & Johnson, 1994; White et al., 2004). Often, fragmentary blackouts go unnoticed, and so, later, the person may not realize that elements are "missing" from the memory record. However, cues and probes can draw the person's attention to the gaps in his or her recollection.

There is also some suggestion that reminders can help the person to recall the "forgotten" bits (e.g., Goodwin, Cranke, & Guze, 1969b). However, this point is difficult to interpret because, in some cases, this "recall" may involve some sort of after-the-fact inference or reconstruction. ("I guess I must have driven the car because how else did I get here?")

Fragmentary blackouts can also sometimes be *retroactive*. In other words, imagine someone who is sober during an episode but then engages in a bout of binge drinking. Studies document that the initial episode might, in this case, not be recalled "even though there was no alcohol on board at the time" (Lee et al., 2009, p. 278). Similarly, Goodwin et al. (1970) observed memory impairments that began early in an episode of drinking, when blood alcohol levels were still low (but rising).

What produces these retroactive effects? The answer likely involves a process discussed earlier: memory consolidation. In other words, high levels of blood alcohol may be a further factor disrupting consolidation and thus can prevent the formation of enduring memories for events that may have occurred early in (or even well before) the current round of drinking.

Perhaps most importantly, we should emphasize that there is generally no pattern to the gaps in a fragmentary blackout: It is not the case, for example, that exceptional events are recalled but mundane events are forgotten (or vice versa). It is likewise not the case that emotional events or more consequential events are more likely to be recalled. Instead, the pattern of memory loss in a fragmentary blackout is—as far as we can tell—essentially random.

The Effects of Emotional Arousal

A crime victim or witness is likely to be emotionally aroused—feeling angry, or afraid, or sad about a state of helplessness. The victim or witness is also likely to feel some amount of stress—a state that typically involves the combination of feeling threatened and also powerless to remove the threat. How do these factors shape perception and memory?

Emotion has multiple effects on perception and on memory. Some of these effects are best understood in terms of psychological mechanisms. (For example, emotion can change the meaning of an event and thus can shift what the person deems worth paying attention to.) Other effects are best understood biologically. (Among other points, emotion involves a shift in body chemistry that influences the consolidation process; see Cahill & McGaugh, 1995; Hamann, 2001.) But, whatever the mechanism, we can still ask: How are emotional events remembered?

Common sense suggests that emotion improves memory—and most people think back to singular, highly emotional events in their lives and offer comments like, "I'll never forget that day . . ." or "I remember it as though it were yesterday . . ." We'll have more to say about this sort of recollection in Chapter 3, when we discuss what are called "flashbulb memories." For now, though, let's note only that common sense does contain an element of truth here, and there are surely circumstances in which emotional arousal does improve memory. There are other circumstances, though, in which the emotion seems to produce its own version of "tunnel vision," a pattern sometimes referred to as "memory narrowing." In this pattern, emotion seems to improve memory for the "central" aspects of an episode but undermines memory for other aspects. (See, e.g., Reisberg & Hertel, 2004; for related discussion, see the earlier section on weapon focus.)

In addition, the *strength* of the emotion must be considered. Moderate levels of emotion do seem to help memory (either for the entire episode or just for the episode's center). Much stronger emotion, however, may have the opposite effect—undermining memory. The reason is likely to be stress, on the idea that situations that trigger very strong emotion are also likely to be highly stressful. Thus, a witness might feel the emotion of anger, but also feel helpless and endangered, and the latter reactions (and the biological changes that go with them) work against attention and memory.

In light of this mixed pattern, we should avoid sweeping claims that apply to all sorts of memory for all sorts of emotional events. (For examples of more finely tuned proposals, see Laney et al., 2003; or Levine & Pizarro, 2004.) Even so, emotional events are, overall, better remembered compared to less arousing events. But note that this claim is rendered in relative terms. Emotional memories (like all memories) do fade as time goes by, and substantial memory errors are possible in emotional recall, just as they are in the recall of more mundane episodes. (Again, we return to this point in Chapter 3.)

The Effects of Stress

We have already alluded to a related point—the impact of stress—and the evidence on this point is clear. Stress interferes with perception and memory. This is evident in research looking at the biological impact of stress (e.g., Kim, Song, & Kosten, 2006). It is also evident if we consider studies designed to assess stress in what one research team called "witness circumstances." In a 2004 meta-analysis, investigators reported that, across a range of studies, stress reduced correct identification rates from 59% (observed in low-stress circumstances) to 39% (Deffenbacher, Bornstein, Penrod, & McCorty, 2004).

Another often-cited study confirms this result: The study involved soldiers in the U.S. military who were undergoing survival training. As part of the training, the soldiers went through a highly realistic simulation of a prisoner-of-war interrogation; some soldiers were exposed to a higher stress interrogation (including a threat of physical violence) and others to a lower stress procedure. One day later, the soldiers were asked to identify their interrogators from a lineup. In this study, 60% of the soldiers in the low-stress condition were able to identify their interrogators; only 30% in the high-stress group were able to do so. A troubling 38% of the soldiers who had undergone a low-stress investigation made a *false* identification (selecting someone who was, in fact, not the interrogator), but the false identification jumped to 56% for those who had undergone a high-stress interrogation (Morgan et al., 2004).

Other lines of evidence confirm this pattern: In one study, researchers questioned people who had just visited an especially frightening "haunted house" (the *London Dungeon*) in a British amusement park. Participants were asked how anxious they'd been while in the haunted house and were also asked if they could identify a specific person they had seen inside the haunted house. Those who reported low anxiety were successful in identifying this person 75% of the time; those who reported higher anxiety identified the target only 18% of the time (Valentine & Mesout, 2008). In yet another study, 212 adults who had received inoculations were asked to identify the nurse who had administered the injection; the researchers assessed the degree of stress by measuring how much each patient's pulse rate increased during the injection. Identification accuracy was worst for the patients whose pulse rates had increased the most (Peters, 1988).

Yet another study examined police officers, probing their memory for events experienced as part of their training (Hope, Lewinski, Dixon, Blocksidge, & Gabbert, 2012). They, too, show the effects of stress—with increased stress associated with poorer recall of the target event and more errors in identifying the people involved in the event. (For still more evidence showing stress effects in children, see Rush, Quas, & Yim, 2011.)

F. OVERVIEW

We have covered a wide range of topics in this chapter, starting with the perception of simple line drawings and moving to the perception of more complex events. Our main focus was on perception, but we have strayed into the obviously related topic of memory, and, at several junctures, into the more specialized topic of face memory. (We have much more to say about memory and faces in Chapters 3, 4, and 5.) And, in several passages, we have noted that it is difficult to know whether limitations in witnesses' (or research participants') reports are best understood as limitations in what they *saw* or in what they *recall*—again showcasing the interplay between perception and memory.

Overall, though, the key messages of this chapter are easy to describe: There is no question that our perception of the world is typically accurate and typically objective. But there is also no question that our perception is *selective* and *constructive*—we perceive only part of the information that is optically available to our eyes or acoustically available to our ears, and then we interpret the inputs we do receive and often supplement those inputs based on knowledge and expectations.

Hence, we cannot take the accuracy of perception for granted, but, conversely, this cannot lead us to a wholesale skepticism of perception. Instead, we can be specific about some of the circumstances in which perceptual errors are more common, and, in that fashion, we can often provide a "risk assessment" for a given case. This assessment will surely not tell us whether a given witness is correct or is incorrect. The assessment should, however, help the finder of fact to determine the level of danger that an error has occurred, which should, in turn, help the finder of fact to decide how much weight to give a witness's report.

CHAPTER 3

Memory

General Considerations

A. SELECTIVE, CONSTRUCTIVE, INTEGRATIVE

We noted in Chapter 2 that the human eye is sometimes compared to a camera, and human memory is sometimes compared to a video recorder. As we've discussed, though, these comparisons are misleading. Your perception of the world is selective and constructive in ways that a camera is not, and these traits are inevitably carried over into memory. Thus, if you failed to perceive some event, then the relevant information was never recorded into memory and cannot be recalled later. Likewise, if perception is constructive, then your memory will be, too. Your memory provides a record of what you perceived, and thus what you recall will reflect the interpretation and assumptions woven into your perception.

But, in addition, memory is shaped by a further influence because memory is also *integrative*. The idea here is that our memories for various episodes are not stored in separate "files," each kept apart from all the others. Instead, all of our memories are heavily interconnected, with each containing many links to other memories. As we will see, these links are helpful for us (and, arguably, they are necessary), but the benefits come at a price. The connections create a risk that memories will "bleed" into each other, so that, for example, a witness might remember seeing a red truck near the crime scene when, in truth, the witness merely heard about the red truck from another witness. Likewise, connections between a specific memory and other, more generic knowledge can allow the other knowledge to intrude into our recollection. Thus, a witness might remember the robber threatening violence merely because threats are part of the witness's cognitive "schema" for how robberies typically unfold. In this case, schematic knowledge has intruded into recall of a particular episode.

In this chapter, we'll explore these points, providing an intellectual foundation that we will rely on in subsequent chapters. Along the way, we'll consider the gaps in memory (i.e., aspects of an episode that someone later on fails to remember) and also the prospect of memory errors (cases in which the episode as remembered is different from the episode as it actually unfolded). We'll also examine some of the steps we might take to detect memory errors. (For a fuller summary of memory function, see Reisberg, 2013a; for a sophisticated application of these fundamentals to forensic cases, see Davis & Loftus, 2007.)

B. MEMORY AS A "NETWORK"

Many theorists describe memory as a huge network of interconnected nodes. Thus, imagine that you are witness to a collision between two cars. Your memory for this event will end up connected to your recollections of other episodes—perhaps your recollection of other events you've observed at that location, or your recollection of conversations you later had about the crash, or even your recollection of car crashes you've seen in the movies. Your memory for the collision will also end up linked to ideas that were merely part of your understanding of the episode or somehow triggered by the episode.

The Benefits of Connections

These connections, linking one memory to many others, help you in crucial ways. As one benefit, the connections are essential for memory retrieval. Imagine, for example, that you're trying to recall what happened immediately after the collision. You'll start by activating nodes in memory that represent some aspect of the episode—perhaps your memory of the fear you felt when you heard the brakes squealing. Activation can then flow outward from that specific memory to the nodes representing other, related memories, and then can flow from these to still other memories. Eventually, the activation can flow into nodes representing the information you seek, concerned with (let's say) the fist fight between the two drivers. In this fashion, connections among memories serve as "retrieval paths," guiding your search through memory.

Links among memories also help in another way: Think about all the times in your life when you have been with a particular friend. These episodes are related to each other in an obvious way, and so they are likely to become interconnected in your memory. This may cause difficulties if you want to remember, let's say, whether you had a particular conversation in this episode or that one. For many purposes, though, you *want* the memories to merge into each other because this will allow you to join information gained in one setting with information gained in other settings. Thus, as the memories blur together, what you'll hold in memory will be a united package that contains all of your knowledge about your friend. In this fashion, the weaving together of separate episodes actually provides a mechanism through which you acquire general knowledge, integrating bits that you picked up in multiple, distinct experiences.

Memory Schemata

So far, we've been considering connections among specific memories: Your memory of a conversation with your friend on Tuesday is linked to your memory of a conversation with him on Saturday. Your memory of what you saw on the day of the car crash is connected to your memory of what you heard on the news about the crash. Just as important, though, are connections to your *memory schemata*.

Let's start with the fact that you enter most settings in your life with a considerable amount of background knowledge—about the situation and the players in it. Thus, imagine that you walk into a bank. This setting is familiar to you, and you know a lot about what's likely to happen here. You'll probably step to a desk and do some quick paperwork (perhaps filling out a deposit slip). You'll then wait in line for a moment, then approach a teller, exchange a few friendly words, go through the steps of your transaction, and then leave. Your knowledge of all these steps is often referred to with the Greek word *schema* (plural: *schemata*). Schemata summarize the broad pattern of what's normal in a situation. Thus, your bank schema tells you that the bank is likely to have chairs in it, but no piano; your dentist's office schema tells you there are likely to be magazines in the waiting room, and so on.

When you're in the bank, or the dentist's office, or wherever, you rely on your schema to help you understand what's happening. In the bank, for example, you're not surprised if you see quantities of cash being handed back and forth. You are not alarmed if you see an armed guard, and you're not puzzled if the guard asks you to take off your sunglasses. Your schema tells you that these are normal elements in a bank visit, and you instantly understand how they fit into the broader framework.

Schemata also help when the time comes to recall how an event unfolded. This is because there are often gaps in your recollection—either because there were things you didn't notice in the first place or because you have gradually forgotten some aspect of an experience. In either case, you can rely on your schemata to fill the gaps. Thus, in thinking back to your bank visit, you might not remember waiting in line. Nonetheless, you can be reasonably sure you did wait, in a standing position (and not sitting), several feet back from the counter. On this basis, you're likely to include the wait in your "recall" of the bank trip, even if you have no specific memory for it. In this way, you'll (unwittingly) supplement what you actually remember with a plausible reconstruction based on your schematic knowledge. And, in most cases, this after-the-fact reconstruction will be correct because schemata do, after all, describe what happens most of the time.

C. EVIDENCE FOR THE "NETWORK"

We've now described some of the benefits that derive from memory connections: The connections serve as retrieval paths and thus allow you to locate information in memory. The connections link related episodes and so help you to integrate information gained in one setting with information gained in other settings. The connections also tie specific experiences to your generic knowledge—your schemata—in a way that promotes understanding during an event and aids (and can supplement) recall later on.

As we've suggested, though, there's a price to be paid for these gains. The links between *this* episode in memory and *that* episode gradually knit the two episodes together. As a result, you can lose track of the "boundary" between the episodes, and, more precisely, you can easily lose track of which bits of information were contained within which event. Thus, you become vulnerable to so-called *intrusion errors,* in which a bit of information encountered in one context "intrudes" into another context.

In the same fashion, as your memory for an episode becomes more and more interwoven with other thoughts you've had about the episode, it can become difficult to keep track of which elements are linked to the episode because they were, in truth, part of the episode itself and which are linked merely because they were associated with the episode in your thoughts. This, too, can produce intrusion errors—so that elements that were part of your thinking get misremembered as being actually part of the original experience.

The broad idea, then, is that memory connections both help and hurt recollection, and this suggestion is easy to confirm. Classic studies demonstrated this point with simple stories (e.g., Owens, Bower, & Black, 1979), and similar effects can be demonstrated with stimuli as straightforward as word lists, even if research participants are explicitly warned about the types of errors that can occur and strongly encouraged to avoid these errors (Gallo, Roberts, & Seamon, 1997; McDermott & Roediger, 1998).

Here's an example: In one study, half of the participants read the following passage (Owens et al., 1979):

Nancy arrived at the cocktail party. She looked around the room to see who was there. She went to talk with her professor. She felt she had to talk to him but was a little nervous about just what to say. A group of people started to play charades. Nancy went over and had some refreshments. The hors d'oeuvres were good but she wasn't interested in talking to the rest of the people at the party. After a while she decided she'd had enough and left the party.

The remaining participants read the same passage, but with a prologue that set the stage:

Nancy woke up feeling sick again and she wondered if she really were pregnant. How would she tell the professor she had been seeing? And the money was another problem.

All participants were then given a recall test in which they were asked to remember this story as exactly as they could. What should we expect here? The prologue made the story easier to understand—that is, it made it easier for the participants to see how the story's elements were linked to each other. These linkages, in turn, could serve as retrieval paths—and so should support recall. On this basis, we would expect better recall from the participants who saw the prologue, and that is indeed the result—participants who saw the prologue recalled 50% more of the story's actual content.

At the same time, the story's prologue is also likely to encourage certain inferences—for example, that the professor had gotten Nancy pregnant. This proposition is not part of the story but is certainly implied by the prologue, and thus it will likely be part of the participants' understanding of the story. If it's this understanding that guides recall, then the prologue will also hurt memory accuracy—by encouraging intrusion errors. This is indeed the actual result, and participants who had seen the prologue made four times as many intrusion errors as did participants who had not seen the prologue.

Schema-Based Errors

A different line of evidence concerns the types of errors we would expect if perception and memory are guided by schemata. Bear in mind here that your schemata tell you, in essence, what's typical or ordinary in a given situation—what sorts of things you'll generally encounter in a bank or what types of furniture you'll usually find in a motel room. As a result, any reliance on (or intrusions from) schematic knowledge will reflect this knowledge about what's typical and thus will make the world seem more "normal" than it really is and will make the past seem more "regular" than it actually was.

Here's an example: In 1992, an El Al cargo plane lost power in two of its engines just after taking off from Amsterdam's Schiphol Airport. The pilot attempted to return the plane to the airport but couldn't make it; a few minutes later, the plane crashed into an 11-story apartment building. The building collapsed and burst into flames; 43 people were killed, including the plane's entire crew.

Ten months later, researchers questioned 193 Dutch people about the crash, asking them in particular, "Did you see the television film of the moment the plane hit the apartment building?" More than half of the participants (107 of them) reported seeing the film, even though there was no such film. No camera had recorded the crash; no film (or any reenactment) was shown on television (Crombag, Wagenaar, & van Koppen, 1996; for similar data, with people remembering a nonexistent film of the car crash that killed Princess Diana and Dodi Fayed, see Ost, Vrij, Costall, & Bull, 2002; also Jelicic et al., 2006; but also see Smeets, Telgen, Ost, Jelicic, & Merckelback, 2009).

In a follow-up study, the investigators surveyed another 93 people about the plane crash. These people were also asked whether they'd seen the nonexistent TV film, and then they were asked detailed questions about exactly what they had seen in the film: Was the plane burning when it crashed, or did it catch fire a moment later? In the film, did you see the plane come down vertically, or did it hit the building while still moving horizontally at a considerable speed?

Two-thirds of these participants "remembered" seeing the film, and most of them confidently provided details about what they had seen. When asked about the plane's speed, for example, only 23% prudently said that they couldn't recall this point. The others gave various responses, presumably based on their "memory" of the film.

This is not a case of one or two people making a mistake; most of the people questioned seemed to have a detailed memory of the nonexistent film. In addition, let's emphasize that this plane crash was an emotional and much-discussed event for these participants; the researchers were not asking them to recall a minor occurrence.

What's going on here? The Dutch participants' memories distorted reality by making the past seem more regular, more typical, than it really was. After all, the Dutch survey respondents probably hear about most major news events via a television broadcast, and these broadcasts typically include vivid video footage. Thus, the past-as-remembered seems here to have been assimilated into the pattern of the ordinary. The event as it unfolded was unusual, but the event as remembered is typical of its kind—just as we would expect if understanding and remembering were guided by our knowledge of the way things generally unfold.

In Chapter 2, we argued that perception is constructive, and we proposed that this pattern is inevitably carried over into memory. The experiment just described, however, suggests a different regard in which memory is constructive—or more properly *reconstructive*: In "recalling" the plane crash, the participants were likely engaged in an (unconscious, uncontrollable) effort toward reconstructing what "must have been." Thus, guided by their current beliefs and broader knowledge, they created an account of what (they believed) happened in the previous episode, although they were likely convinced they were simply recalling the episode and not reconstructing it. (For another example of this sort of after-the-fact reconstruction, see Chapter 2's discussion of memory for viewing opportunity.)

D. FALSE MEMORIES

We've so far given a handful of examples of memory errors. But how common are these errors? In what settings do the errors occur, and what sorts of errors occur? Let's look at the details.

Leading Questions

Most people readily agree that witness responses can be shaped by leading questions. But how heavy-handed do leading questions need to be in order to have an effect? Does subtle leading also have an impact? And how long-lasting is the effect of a leading question? Can the effect be undone later on, by returning to neutral, nonleading questions?

In an early study, Loftus and Palmer (1974) showed participants a series of projected slides depicting an automobile collision. Some time later, half the participants were asked, "How fast were the cars going when they hit each other?" Others were asked, "How fast were the cars going when they smashed into each other?" The difference here ("hit" vs. "smashed") is slight but did have an effect. Participants in the "hit" group estimated the speed to have been 34 miles per hour; participants in the "smashed" group estimated 41 miles per hour—roughly 20% higher.

What is critical, though, is what comes next: One week later, the participants were asked in a neutral way whether they had seen any broken glass in the slides. Participants who had been asked the "hit" question tended to remember (correctly) that no glass was visible; participants who had been asked the "smashed" question, though, often recalled the broken shards of glass, apparently misled by the leading question they had been asked earlier.

It seems, then, that leading questions can be rather subtle—with just a single word having a large impact. In fact, this point is easy to illustrate, and (for example) people are more likely to remember seeing a weapon if asked, "Did you see the gun?" rather than "Did you see a gun?" In addition, leading questions can have far-reaching effects: In the study just described, the error about the broken glass emerged after several days' delay and in response to neutral, careful questions. It would seem, then, that once the damage to memory is done, it remains.

What caused this memory error? When the research participants were asked about broken glass, they actually had two events in memory to draw on—their memory of the original video, in which they saw the car crash, and their memory of being asked about the cars' speed. These two events are obviously related and surely linked to each other in memory. This creates a danger of the two memory records bleeding into one another—so that elements in one record ("smashed," and, with this word, thoughts about a more violent encounter) are (mis)remembered as being involved in the other record. It's this dynamic, made possible by the memory connections, that leads to the memory error.

As a quick aside, we should note that there are several ways that this dynamic can unfold (Wright & Loftus, 2008). Perhaps you recall both the original version of the event (the one you actually saw) and the version suggested by the question, and lose track of which is which. Perhaps you didn't notice initially what was on the ground (and so didn't register whether there was broken glass or not), and so you simply accept the suggestion in the subsequent memory. Or perhaps you have two memories (from the original event, and from the questioning), and your recollection blends these together. Researchers have taken various steps to tease apart these possibilities, but, for the justice system, these options all lead to the same place—with different events interacting in memory, potentially creating memory errors.

The Breadth of Settings that Cause the "Misinformation Effect"

In the study just described, the question asked of participants implied (via the word choice of "hit" vs. "smashed") how they ought to think about the target event. In other studies, participants have been asked questions that contain actual misinformation about an event—and so the resulting memory errors are often referred to as the "misinformation effect." For example, participants might be asked, "How fast was the car going when it raced by the barn?" when, in truth, no barn was in view. In other studies, participants have been exposed to descriptions of the target event that allegedly were written by other witnesses. They might be told, for example, "Here's how someone else recalled the crime; does this match what you recall?" Of course, the "other witness" descriptions contain some misinformation, allowing us to ask if our participants "pick up" these false leads (e.g., Paterson & Kemp, 2006; also Edelson, Sharot, Dolan, & Dudai, 2011). In still other cases, participants view a film and then discuss the film with other participants who (they think) have seen the same film, but who have actually seen a somewhat different film. In this setting, each participant can unwittingly provide misinformation for the other (e.g., Hope, Ost, Gabbert, Healey, & Lenton, 2008; Loftus & Greene, 1980; Zajac & Henderson, 2009).

In other cases, participants generate the misinformation for themselves. For example, participants can be asked, "In the video, was the man bleeding from his knee or from his elbow after the fall?" Even though it was clear in the video that the man wasn't bleeding at all, participants are forced to choose one of these options (e.g., Ackil & Zaragoza, 2011; Chrobak & Zaragoza, 2008; Zaragoza, Payment, Ackil, Drivdahl, & Beck, 2001), and so it is their own response that introduces misinformation into their thoughts.

These procedures differ from each other in obvious ways, but they are all variations on the same theme. In each case, the participant experiences an event and is then exposed to a misleading suggestion about how the event unfolded. Then, some time is allowed to pass. At the end of this interval, the participant's memory is tested. And in each of these variations, the outcome is the same: A substantial number of participants—as many as one-third of the participants in some studies—end up incorporating the false suggestion into their memory of the original event.

Let us be clear, then, about three points: First, there is no indication that participants in these studies are being deceptive in any way; instead, they are reporting the past as they recall it—but their recall has been shaped by the misinformation. Researchers use the term "false memory" to describe these sincere, honest memory errors. (We return to the distinction between false memories and lies in a later section and again in Chapter 7.) Second, there is no "proper procedure" or "best procedure" for producing a false memory. Instead, a wide variety of sequences will have this impact, provided that the sequence includes an event, some misinformation about the event, and the passage of a bit of time. Thus, we can use subtle procedures (carefully worded questions) to plant false information in someone's memory, or we can use a more blatant procedure (demanding that the person make up the bogus facts). We can use printed stories as our to-be-remembered materials, movies, or live events. In all cases, it is remarkably easy to alter someone's memory, with the result that the past as the person remembers it differs from the past as it really was. (For more on research in this domain, see Chan, Thomas, & Bulevich, 2009; Frenda, Nichols, & Loftus, 2011; Laney, 2013; Oeberst & Blank, 2012; Seamon, Philbin, & Harrison, 2006; Sharman & Powell, 2012.)

Third, the fact pattern just described (including the point that these are memory errors and not deceptions in any sense, and also the wide variety of procedures that produce these effects) is just what we would expect in light of the network-based theory we have described. Related events are linked to each other in memory. Questions and conversations about an event will be linked in memory to the record of the original event. These links are—we again emphasize—helpful for many purposes but also create a risk of error.

We have used the term "misinformation effect" to describe this error, but it is also useful to apply a broader label: These errors are examples of *source confusion* because, in each case, the person is correct in recalling that a particular bit of information was somehow part of his or her past but then is confused about the source of the information—and so recalls it as part of the original event when, in fact, the information came into the person's experience via some other route.

Misinformation from Imagination

In the studies described so far, the memory errors are "externally induced." The experimenter asks a leading question, supplies some misinformation, or demands that the witness concoct an answer to a nonsensical question. However, there is nothing in the logic we are developing that depends on these points, and so similar errors should be observed even without these outside influences.

In some studies, researchers have examined how people remember their own dreams (e.g., Johnson, Kahan, & Raye, 1984) and documented instances in which an event appeared in a dream but is then recalled as actually occurring. This sort of confusion arises often in children, and many parents have had to comfort a child who wakes up terrified about the monsters in the room; parents deal with this situation by lovingly murmuring, "it was only a dream." But similar confusion can be documented in adults (Kemp & Burt, 2006; Kemp, Burt, & Sheen, 2003). This confusion is relatively rare, perhaps because dreams are often quite bizarre and so can be dismissed as "not real" on that basis alone. Nonetheless, this confusion is possible, and it provides further indication of the diversity of pathways that can lead to memory error.

Possible Limits on the "Misinformation Effect"

What sorts of memory errors can be produced via the misinformation effect or via source confusion more broadly? The answer, in brief, is: all sorts. We have mentioned that researchers have led participants to remember broken glass when really there was none and to remember barns when there were no buildings at all in view. Similar procedures have altered how people are remembered—so that with just a few "suggestions" from the experimenter, witnesses remember clean-shaven men as bearded, young people as old, and fat people as thin (e.g., Christiaansen, Sweeney, & Ochalek, 1983; Frenda et al., 2011). Indeed, when later asked to identify a suspect (e.g., from a police lineup), witnesses will often select someone whose appearance includes a detail supplied to the witness only through misinformation (e.g., Loftus & Greene, 1980).

How far down this road can we travel? Can we plant memories for entire events that never happened at all? In one study, college students were told that the investigators were trying to learn how different people remember the same experience. The students were then given a list of events that they were told had been reported by their parents; the students were asked to recall these events as well as they could, so that the investigators could compare their recall with their parents' (Hyman, Husband, & Billings, 1995).

Some of the events on the list had, in fact, been reported by the participants' parents. Other events were bogus—made up by the experimenters. One of the bogus events was an overnight hospitalization for a high fever; in a different experiment, the bogus event was attending a wedding reception, with the student described as having accidentally spilled a bowlful of punch onto the bride's parents.

The college students were easily able to remember the genuine events (i.e., the events actually reported by their parents). In an initial interview, more than 80% of these events were recalled, but none of the students recalled the bogus events. However, repeated attempts at recall changed this pattern, and, by a third interview, 25% of the participants were able to remember the embarrassment of spilling the punch, and many were able to supply the details of this (entirely fictitious) episode. Other studies have yielded similar results, with participants led to recall details of particular birthday parties that, in truth, they never had (Hyman et al., 1995) or an incident of being lost in a shopping mall even though this event never took place, or a fictitious event in which they were the victim of a vicious animal attack (Loftus, 2003; 2004; also see Chrobak & Zaragoza, 2008; Geraerts et al., 2009; Laney, Morris, Bernstein, Wakefield, & Loftus, 2008; and many more).

Other researchers have taken a further step and have provided participants with "evidence" in support of the bogus memory. In one procedure, researchers obtained a childhood snapshot of the participant, and, with a few clicks of a computer mouse, created a fictitious picture showing the child and his or her parent in the wicker basket underneath a hot-air balloon. With this prompt, many participants were led to a detailed recollection of the hot-air balloon ride—even though it never occurred (Wade, Garry, Read, & Lindsay, 2002). Another study used an unaltered photo, showing the participants' second-grade class. This was apparently enough to persuade participants that the experimenters really did have information about the participants' childhood. Thus, when the experimenters "reminded" the participants of an episode of their childhood misbehavior, the participants took this reminder seriously. The result: 65.2% of the participants seemed to remember the target episode, even though it had never happened (Lindsay, Hagen, Read, Wade, & Garry, 2004; although also see Garry & Wade, 2005).

Notice that these studies have involved adult participants. What about children reporting on crimes they have witnessed or crimes of which they have been the victims? We say much more about children's memories in Chapters 10 and 11, but, for now, let's note only that false memories can also be documented in children, and, in fact, evidence suggests that children (especially preschool-aged children) are in most procedures more vulnerable than adults to this sort of memory "planting."

What, then, are the limits of false memory? It seems clear that our memories can sometimes be mistaken on small details (was there broken glass in view?), but our memories can also fool us in larger ways: We can remember entire events that never took place. We can remember emotional episodes (like being lost in a shopping mall) that never happened. We can remember our own transgressions (spilling the punch bowl, misbehaving in the second grade), even when they never occurred.

Factors Moderating the Misinformation Effect

Not surprisingly, some circumstances make false memories more likely; other circumstances make these errors less likely. Attention to these circumstances, therefore, can be enormously useful for the justice system, allowing us to decide, for a given case, whether the risk of false memory is especially high, especially low, or somewhere in between.

Memory errors are certainly more likely for distant events than for recent events (we return to this notion in a later section). Smaller errors (e.g., misremembering just one aspect of an actual event) are more likely than larger errors (e.g., remembering an entire episode that never took place at all). Similarly, errors are more likely for peripheral aspects of an event than for central (and probably closely attended) aspects. However, all of these factors interact—and, as time goes by, larger and larger errors can occur, even for points at the center of the event.

False memories are also more likely if the person hears the misinformation from a trusted source or from multiple sources. Better still, false memories are more easily planted if the person doesn't just hear about the false event but, instead, is urged to imagine how the suggested event unfolded—an effect referred to with the ironic term *imagination inflation*. In one study, participants were given a list of possible childhood events (going to the emergency room late at night, winning a stuffed animal at a carnival game, getting in trouble for calling 9-1-1). Participants were asked to "picture each event as clearly and completely" as they could, and this simple exercise was enough to increase participants' confidence that the event had really occurred (Garry, Manning, Loftus, & Sherman, 1996; also Mazzoni & Memon, 2003; Sharman & Barnier, 2008).

In addition, false memories are more common if the misleading suggestion is bolstered in some fashion. For example, if someone has previously given you accurate information, this person has established his credibility, increasing his impact if he now gives you false information (e.g., Zhu, Chen, Loftus, Lin, & Dong, 2010). We saw a related result in the earlier section, in studies involving actual or doctored photographs. This sort of "evidence" clearly promotes false recollection.

Two other factors are also important, one regarding the basic plausibility of the event, the other involving the degree to which the person who holds a false memory is hurt by the memory. These factors are the focus of the next two sections.

The Effect of Plausibility

Imagine that someone asks you a series of leading questions about your meeting with Julius Caesar. Or imagine that someone offers you misinformation suggesting you were wounded in a skirmish on Mars. Surely, you would easily and accurately reject these suggestions because common sense tells you these events could not have happened.

In the same vein, we noted earlier that false memories suggested by dreams are rare because the suggested events can often be ruled out as impossible. No matter how vivid your dreams of flying without mechanical aids over the nearby mountain, you will be confident that this aerial adventure never took place.

The idea, then, is that false memories can arise only if you believe the suggested event is possible. Indeed, we might consider a stronger claim: false memories can arise only if the suggested event seems possible and plausible. If correct, these limits could be crucial for the justice system because, in some cases, witnesses or victims do report outrageous events—events at the edge of what most people would count as plausible. Perhaps, then, these are events for which we can set aside concerns about false memory.

There is, in fact, evidence consistent with these ideas. In one study, researchers tried to plant in Jewish participants a memory for the episode in which the participants had taken first communion. The researchers also tried to plant in Catholic participants a memory of a ritual Jewish dinner—complete with Shabbat candles, a loaf of challah, and other aspects of this event that takes place every Friday in many Jewish households. The results were straightforward: Only 10% of the Catholics and none of the Jews fell for the suggestion (Pezdek, Finger, & Hodge, 1997). Apparently, it is more difficult to plant implausible memories.

Other evidence, however, makes it clear that judgments of plausibility are—at best—a thin shield against memory error. As one consideration, we know that many people have vivid memories for events that most of us consider highly implausible—for example, memories for being abducted by space aliens (Clancy, 2005; Mack, 1994). Or, as a different case, some people claim they recall events that occurred when they were just one day old (Spanos, Burgess, Burgess, Samuels, & Blois, 1999); some people claim they recall events that occurred decades prior to their birth. Thus, the plausibility of an event is very much "in the eye of the beholder," and so we should hesitate in proclaiming an event implausible and hence not the sort of thing that could be planted through outside suggestion. (For another illustration of this point, see Pezdek & Blandón-Gitlin, 2011; Rubin & Berntsen, 2009.)

Even for a single individual, views about plausibility can be quite malleable, and often a bit of argument can persuade someone that a particular account, initially doubted, is in fact entirely reasonable. Thus, even if judgments of implausibility do protect someone from false suggestion, this protection can sometimes be overcome (e.g., Mazzoni, Loftus, & Kirsch, 2001).

As a related point, even if you start out firmly convinced that an event did not happen, this belief does not shelter you from a subsequent "memory" for the event. We alluded to one relevant study earlier: In this procedure, participants were given suggestions about a previous episode—and the participants responded in ways that indicated plainly that they knew the suggestions were false. Nonetheless, a few weeks later, the participants confidently "recalled" episodes that, just a few weeks earlier, they (correctly) insisted had never happened (Chroback & Zaragoza, 2008). Thus, "once believed to be false" (or even "once known to be false") is no protection against "eventually believed." (For more on these issues, see Hyman, 2000; Pezdek & Blandón-Gitlin, 2011; Pezdek, Blandón-Gitlin, & Gabbay, 2006; Scoboria, Mazzoni, Kirsch, & Jimenez, 2006; Sharman & Scoboria, 2011; Thomas & Loftus, 2002.)

Even with all these complications, it remains true that (all other things equal) it is easier to establish a plausible memory than an implausible one. For purposes of the justice system, therefore, it is important to ascertain (to the degree possible) whether the person recalling a memory started out believing the event to be unlikely. Assessment of this point can often provide information about the risk of error.

The Role for Motivation

When people lie, they typically have some motivation to lie—perhaps motivation to gain something, or to avoid harm, or to protect someone else, or even motivation to hurt someone else. When someone has a false memory, in contrast, motivation plays less of a role. A false memory is, we've said, a type of confusion and can occur even when there is no motivation that would favor the confusion. Thus, the absence of some gain from a memory cannot be used as a basis for rebutting a suggestion that a memory is false.

Nonetheless, motivation can play a role in fostering false memories. We have already alluded to one aspect of this role: Sometimes a person is motivated to lie, and the lie can then "evolve" into a false memory. But, in addition, motivation can also contribute to false memories through another mechanism. The key here is that false memories are more likely if the person actively engages an idea, perhaps returning to the suggestion again and again in his or her thoughts, perhaps trying to imagine how the event might have unfolded. These mental steps are, of course, more likely if the suggested memory is somehow attractive (or perhaps just *intriguing*) to the person, and so, via this path, motivation can facilitate the creation of a false memory.

In many cases, though, the motivation to adopt (or, at least, to consider) a suggested memory may be complex. Consider, for example, an adult who now recalls some awful childhood event. If the remembered event was painful or shameful, one might think the person gains nothing from this memory; instead, it hurts the person to hold these memories. Nonetheless, there may be what clinical psychologists call "secondary gain" that derives from the memory. Perhaps the person gets long hoped for attention and respect. Perhaps the person is excused from various responsibilities. Perhaps the person at last gains the powerful feeling reflected in statements like, "Finally, my life makes sense, and I see why all these bad things happened to me," or "At last, I realize that the bad things in my life were not my fault." Thus, anyone evaluating the memory and seeking to decide if the memory is accurate or not should weigh these possibilities.

E. EFFORTS TOWARD DETECTING MEMORY ERRORS

Let's pause to put things in perspective. The suggestion coming from research is not, and cannot be, that our memories are generally unreliable. There is surely no reason to be skeptical about every witness's recall or every victim's. Indeed, our memories are accurate far more often than not.

Moreover, memory errors do not happen randomly, and this point provides a huge benefit for investigators. Relying on what we know about the causes of memory error, an investigator can examine a case and assess the *risk* of error. Was the witness questioned in a neutral fashion, or, better still, was the witness report spontaneous (i.e., with no questioning)? If so, then concerns about leading questions can be set aside. Was the witness exposed to other sources of information about the target event—from other witnesses or the media? If so, these are possible sources of memory contamination, and they increase the risk of error. Did the witness regard the target event as plausible? Did the witness gain anything from the recollection? These factors, too, can guide the evaluation of risk for a particular memory.

One might hope, in addition, that we can gain some leverage by examining the memory itself or by examining the person as he or she relates the memory. The science relative to these points, however, is for many people surprising.

Degree of Certainty

People sometimes announce that they're confident in their recall ("I distinctly remember her yellow jacket; I'm sure of it"), and sometimes they say the opposite ("Gee, I think she was wearing yellow, but I'm not certain"). Sometimes, these assessments are even more extreme, and people occasionally say things like, "I'll never forget that day; it's burned into my brain, and I can recall it as though it were yesterday." And at the "least certain" end of the range, people sometimes preface their recall with qualifiers like, "If I had to guess, I'd say that . . ."

People take these assessments quite seriously. They are more willing to take action based on confident memories than hesitant ones, and they are guided by similar sentiments when they listen to others. In the courtroom, juries place more weight on a witness's evidence if the witness expresses confidence during the testimony; juries are often skeptical about testimony that is hesitant or hedged (Brigham & Wolfskiel, 1983; Cutler, Penrod, & Dexter, 1990; Loftus, 1979; Wells, Lindsay, & Ferguson, 1979; see also Chapter 9).

In fact, this notion of trusting confident recall is explicitly included in some courtroom procedures. Judges often instruct juries to put more faith in confident witnesses, less faith in hesitant ones. Likewise, consider how courts proceed if a defendant challenges an identification procedure. If the judge decides that the procedure was indeed suggestive, then the judge must seek other information to determine if the ID is still reliable. Court rulings propose various factors as relevant to this determination, but the witness's "level of certainty" is prominent, on the idea that higher levels of certainty indicate a more trustworthy identification. (We return to this procedure for evaluating IDs in Chapter 5.)

This is an issue, however, on which common sense, juries, and the courts are all mistaken. Many studies have systematically compared people's confidence when they are reporting a correct memory with their confidence when they are reporting a false memory, and the pattern of evidence is clear: In many settings, there's little relationship between memory confidence and memory accuracy. Any attempt to categorize memories as correct or incorrect based on someone's confidence, therefore, will be riddled with errors. (For some of the evidence, see Busey, Tunnicliff, Loftus, & Loftus, 2000; Roediger & McDermott, 1995; Shaw, McClure, & Dykstra, 2007; Sporer, Penrod, Read, & Cutler, 1995; Wells, Olson, & Charman, 2002.)

Quantifying the Relation Between Certainty and Accuracy

What is the evidence on these points, and, with that, what exactly is the relationship between certainty and accuracy? The answer to this is complicated because the link between certainty and accuracy depends on the circumstances. It will be helpful, though, to look at some "best-case" estimates—and thus the most generous reading of what we can learn from someone's degree of certainty.

One way to assess certainty involves a "between-subjects" comparison. Technically, this means that the data involve measurements from different people; so, imagine that 100 individuals each have an opportunity to observe the target event. We can then ask each individual to describe the event (and so their recollections will, in crude terms, either be right or wrong), and we can ask each person how certain he or she is in this recall.

This sort of comparison allows us to ask: Are the more confident witnesses also the witnesses who are more accurate? Or, more generally, as the confidence level increases, does the probability of a correct memory also increase? The answer to this question is typically provided by a *confidence-accuracy correlation*, a statistical measure of the relationship between these two variables.

In the best of settings, this correlation takes a value of roughly +.40 (e.g., Sporer et al., 1995) and is often lower (e.g., Brewer, Keast, & Rishword, 2002). What should we make of this? Wells, Olson, and Charman (2002; also Smalarz & Wells, 2013) offer a careful analysis. They note that if (for example) the overall accuracy rate among all participants is 50%, then a +.40 correlation translates into 70% of the high-confidence witnesses being correct and only 30% of the low-confidence witnesses being right. This is not a trivial difference—and hence there is information in the confidence assessments. But this information is surely of limited value because, in these estimates, highly confident recall is mistaken almost a third of the time.

In addition, let's emphasize that these are best-case estimates. Correlations lower than +.40 have routinely been reported in the research literature, and we will have more to say about this point in a moment. (Also see Sporer et al., 1995, for further discussion of factors that will sometimes lead to a lower correlation between accuracy and confidence.) Moreover, the estimates in the previous paragraph assume an overall accuracy rate of 50%. Rates departing from 50% will erode what we can learn from the level of certainty.

Here is a different way to approach the issue, one that yields what is called a *calibration curve* for confidence. Skipping the details, we can create a calibration curve by showing a single witness, let's say, 100 faces, and then, later on, testing this witness with 200 faces—100 of which are repeated from the earlier set and 100 of which are novel. For each of the test faces, we ask two questions: "Is this one of the faces you saw earlier?" and "How certain are you for this face?"

From these data, we can group together all of the faces for which the person was 100% sure and ask: For how many of these was the person's response correct? Likewise, we can group together all of the faces for which the person was 90% sure and ask: For how many of these was the response correct? And so on for other levels of confidence.

If a person's confidence was perfectly "calibrated" to accuracy, then we might expect people to be 100% accurate when they say they are 100% certain; 90% accurate when they say they are 90% certain, and so on. And, encouragingly, calibration curves obtained with this procedure are far from random: When someone says, for example, that she is 60% sure, she is more likely to be correct than if she had said 50%. More broadly, as the expressed level of certainty goes up, the likely accuracy (in this procedure) goes up. Perhaps more importantly, though, these curves reliably show an overconfidence pattern: People who say they are 90% certain tend to be accurate less than 90% of the time. People who say they are 80% certain tend to be accurate less than 80% of the time. Once again, therefore, we find reason to be cautious about someone's assertion of his or her own certainty. (For more on this issue, see Wells, Memon, & Penrod, 2006; for some of the factors influencing confidence calibration, see Brewer & Wells, 2005; Palmer, Brewer, Weber, & Nagesh, 2013; Read, Vokey, & Hammersley, 1990.)

Why Is Certainty a Poor Gauge?

How could this be? How could people be so often mistaken in evaluating their own memories—so that, for example, they tell us they're certain about their recall, but their recall is flatly wrong? For that matter, how could it be that a witness has an exquisitely detailed, fully accurate recollection of an event, but timidly expresses great doubt about the memory? In tackling this issue, it is useful to ask where confidence estimates come from. How does each of us assess the "quality" or "strength" of our own memories?

If asked how confident you are in one of your memories, you will likely be influenced by a mix of considerations. Some of the considerations are tied to the memory itself. (Is the memory rich with sensory detail—what things looked and sounded like? Does the memory seem complete?) Other considerations are tied to the experience of remembering: Did the memory come to mind easily and quickly? And still other considerations are external to the memory: Do you have other reasons to doubt your own recall? Your swift (and largely unconscious) answers to all these questions will determine whether you feel certain in the memory's accuracy, feel like you're merely guessing, or something in between.

The considerations just listed are all sensible, and this is why your degree of certainty is far from random. One problem, though, is that we sometimes ask people to assess their memories in the absence of these indicators. For example, sometimes police investigators ask a witness: "How confident are you that you'll recognize the culprit if you see him again?" In that case, the person has not yet had an opportunity to try making an identification and so has no way to tell how easy the identification process will be. Perhaps it is unsurprising, therefore, that—lacking this important cue—confidence forecasts made before an ID procedure are poor indicators of accuracy in the subsequent identification (e.g., Cutler & Penrod, 1989).

In addition (and perhaps more troubling), these various indicators, used by all of us in assessing our own memories, can be shaped by factors that have no impact on memory accuracy. When these other factors are on the scene, therefore, your confidence will change—sometimes upward, sometimes downward—with no change in the accuracy level. These shifts will therefore erode the correspondence between degree of confidence and accuracy—and can, in some circumstances, obliterate the correspondence.

As a concrete example, think about what happens when someone is asked about an event again and again—so that the person gains practice, in essence, in recalling the event. The person is likely to offer (roughly) the same report each time, and, with no change in the memory's content, there's certainly no change in the memory's accuracy. However, with practice, the retrieval itself will become easier and more fluent. The practice may also allow the person to "flesh out" the memory, perhaps relying on some amount of reconstruction to add a detail here, a bit of background there. These small changes—an increased sense of fluency in reporting the memory and an increased number of details—will generally elevate the person's confidence (and, in fact, evidence suggests that people do become more confident in their recollection when they tell and re-tell and re-tell what happened; Granhag, Strömwall, & Allwood, 2000; Odinot, Wolters, & Lavender, 2009; Shaw, 1996; Shaw et al., 2007). In short, then, repeated testimony creates a scenario in which there is an increase in confidence with no corresponding change in accuracy—and so a scenario in which we gradually weaken any connection between confidence and accuracy.

Similarly, imagine two police lineups. In one, the suspect's picture is surrounded by five fillers, each of whom looks quite similar to the suspect. In the other lineup, the same suspect's picture is surrounded by five fillers whose faces are markedly different from the suspect's. A witness will likely have an easier time making a choice from the second lineup because the first lineup demands careful scrutiny among close options. If the witness now relies on this sense of easiness or difficulty in judging confidence, then the witness will be more confident with the second (more diverse) lineup—and, in fact, this pattern can be documented: Using less-plausible fillers in a lineup does inflate witness confidence (e.g., Charman, Wells, & Joy, 2011). This pattern is not a result of the witness having a clearer, stronger memory; instead, confidence is inflated here simply because the investigation is artificially and externally making the witness's selection easier.

Here is another way the value of memory confidence can be eroded: Imagine what happens if we subtly persuade witnesses, after they have drawn some information from memory, to set aside any doubts they might have about this information. In Chapter 2, for example, we mentioned studies in which participants witnessed a crime and then, later, were asked if they could identify the culprit from a group of pictures. Some of the participants were then given feedback ("Good, you identified the suspect"); others were not. This feedback could not possibly influence the accuracy of the identification because the feedback arrived only after the identification was done. But the feedback did influence confidence, and witnesses who had received the feedback expressed a much higher level of confidence in their choice than did witnesses who received no feedback (Douglass, Brewer, & Semmler, 2010; Douglass, Neuschatz, Imrich, & Wilkinson, 2010; Steblay, Wells, & Douglas, 2014; also Semmler & Brewer, 2006; Wells, Olson, & Charman, 2002; 2003; for similar data with children as eyewitnesses, see Hafstad, Memon, & Logie, 2004; for the inverse effect, in which *negative* feedback decreases confidence levels, see Charman & Wells, 2012).

This effect emerges even if witnesses receive feedback from someone who is not an authoritative figure—for example, a co-witness (e.g., Goodwin, Kukucka, & Hawks, 2013; Skagerberg, 2007). Related effects can be observed if the feedback and the confidence assessment are delayed by 48 hours (Wells et al., 2003) or if the feedback is relatively diffuse—and so, in one study, witness confidence was elevated merely by hearing the test administrator say, "Thank you, you have been a really great witness" (Dysart, Lawson, & Rainey, 2012). The effects are long-lasting (Neuschatz et al., 2005) and are evident even in witnesses who affirm that they were unaffected by the feedback they received (Smalarz & Wells, 2013; Wells & Bradfield, 1998). In all cases, with confidence inflated but accuracy unchanged, any linkage between confidence and accuracy is undermined. (For other factors contributing to the disconnection between accuracy and confidence, see Heathcote, Freeman, Etherington, Tonkin, & Bora, 2009; Lampinen, Meier, Arnal, & Leding, 2005; Sampaio & Brewer, 2009; Sharman, Manning, & Garry, 2005; Shaw et al. 2007; Wells et al., 2006.)

Do these shifts in confidence level happen in real police cases—that is, outside of the laboratory? Wright and Skagerberg (2007) studied real witnesses to real crimes and found that, even in this consequential setting, feedback elevated witness certainty and thus undermined the information value of witness certainty. But, in addition, Garrett (2008) explored this issue in the context of the DNA exoneration cases—cases in which someone had been wrongfully convicted but then exonerated through DNA evidence. (We'll say more about the DNA exonerations in Chapter 4.) Garrett reports that almost all of the witnesses in these cases were quite certain in their courtroom identifications—identifications that, thanks to the DNA evidence, we now know were mistaken. However, Garrett goes on to note that, according to police records, these same witnesses had "earlier not been certain at all" (pp. 63–64). Clearly, confidence levels can shift, and, specifically, can shift in ways that lead the courts to accept, and to be persuaded by, weak evidence.

Finally, before moving off this topic, we should reiterate that witnesses are neither random nor foolish when they assess their degree of certainty in a memory. Of course, you are certain that you know your own name, and you're also certain that you do not know George Washington's grandmother's name, and your level of certainty is well-placed in both cases. (Washington's grandmothers were, of course, named Mildred and Mary.) Nonetheless, many circumstances can drive a substantial wedge between certainty and accuracy,.and it is entirely plausible that these circumstances (including repetition or feedback of various sorts) will arise in a forensic case. As a result, we are left in a setting in which degree of certainty is at best a poor index of memory error.

Level of Detail

A different criterion used for evaluating memory is the level of detail in the memory—on the idea that false memories (or lies) are likely to contain little detail. One might suppose, therefore, that if the recollection is detailed, it is unlikely to be a false memory and thus likely to be accurate.

There is a kernel of truth here, based on the idea that false memories, when initially created, do tend to be sparse—perhaps just a broad sense that an event happened, with little elaboration. As the event gets reported and re-reported, however, details get added. (For a study of this growth in a false report in children's recollection, see Ceci, Crotteau-Huffman, Smith & Loftus, 1994; for a view of this process in adults' memory, see, e.g., Hyman et al., 1995.) Thus, with a bit of time (and some repetitions), a false report can become fully elaborate and detailed, undercutting the usefulness of level of detail as a means of detecting memory error.

As a different approach, some researchers have examined the types of details included in memories known to be true and memories known to be false, asking whether this sort of analysis might allow us to assess veracity. Some of these comparisons have been guided by a theoretical framework known as *reality monitoring* (Johnson & Raye, 1981). This term refers to the process through which we all try to decide which of our thoughts (and which of our memories) correspond to actual events and which are passing fantasies, chance associations, or even recall of dreams. Other comparisons have been done under the rubric of *criterion-based content analysis* (CBCA). This analysis (done by a carefully trained evaluator) scores a memory on various measures, allowing a comparison between true memories and false ones (Vrij, 2005; Vrij & Mann, 2006).

We will have more to say about these quantitative assessments in Chapter 7, when we consider options for telling truths from deliberate lies. For now, though, we will simply say that this sort of analysis is promising but seems to be of limited pragmatic value. Specifically, if we examine a large number of true memories and a large number of false memories, we find that the two groups do differ on average. However, the data show enormous overlap between the scores for true memories and scores for false memories, with the result that a particular score (say, from a CBCA analysis) is rarely diagnostic of truth or falsity.

Consistency

Often, attorneys seek to impeach a witness's report by highlighting inconsistencies in the report—contradictions within a single report (e.g., a single interview with the police) or changes between what is said in one conversation and then what is said in a subsequent conversation (including testimony in the courtroom).

Unfortunately, this strategy fits poorly with the available science. It is certainly true that if a witness once reports that a car was white and later reports that it was blue, at least one of these reports must be false. If a witness reports that the intruder did have a knife and also says he did not have a knife, then only one of these claims can be correct. The more ambitious question, though, is whether we can use inconsistencies in some aspects of a witness's recall as a means of evaluating other aspects: If a witness contradicts himself once or twice, does that mean we can not trust the witness in general?

We alluded to this issue in Chapter 2 (in our discussion of the selectivity of perception), but what are the data? One study asked participants to recall an event twice, and the study took various steps to encourage a shift in the participants' perspectives at the time of the second recall, essentially inviting inconsistencies (Gilbert & Fisher, 2006). This allowed the researchers to scrutinize the ways in which a witness might change his or her story—facts the witnesses recalled on the first effort at remembering but left out in their second effort; facts not remembered initially but then included in the second report; and facts remembered one way in the first recall but then remembered differently on the second try. The researchers also calculated overall accuracy scores for the participants in order to ask what the relationship might be between overall accuracy and the various types of inconsistency.

In this study, "additions" and "subtractions" in recall were quite common, but—crucially—not correlated with overall accuracy. Said differently, the witness's shifting on how (or whether) one point was described provided no information about whether that witness would be accurate in reporting other points. Thus, this common strategy for impeaching testimony seems misguided, and, for our purposes, apparently we cannot use consistency of recall as a gauge of memory accuracy.

F. A REPRISE OF THE VIDEO RECORDER VIEW

Researchers have invested considerable energy in seeking means of distinguishing accurate memories from false ones. In some cases, the research is guided by theory (e.g., claims about reality monitoring); in other cases, the research is guided by the common-sense criteria (e.g., claims about a witness's degree of certainty). Researchers have considered the content of these memories, the subjective "feel" of these memories (Marche, Brainerd, & Reyna, 2010), and also the biological underpinnings of these memories (e.g., Schacter & Loftus, 2013). In all cases, though, the outcome is the same: There are, so far, no reliable indicators that will let us decide whether a memory is accurate or not, leaving us no trustworthy basis for assessing a particular memory-based report. (For more on these issue, see the upcoming section on "Should Emotionality Bolster Credibility?")

Where does this leave us? As we've indicated, the answer is surely not to become skeptical about all memories. We have said repeatedly that our memories serve us well most of the time. Our memories are correct more often than they're wrong. Nonetheless, some skepticism about memory is needed because, as we have also noted again and again, memory errors can occur and can be large and consequential.

In addition, notice that the patterns we have described provide further argument against the "video recorder" view of memory. We argued earlier that the input to memory involves processes that are selective and constructive in ways that the input to a recorder is not. We can now add that the storage in memory is far more dynamic than that in a video recorder: If you record your favorite television show or take a video of a child's birthday, the information stored on a disk or computer drive stays there unchanged—and so the playback, sometime later, will be a faithful echo of the information acquired at the outset. If there is any alteration at all, it is likely to be a gradual erosion of the recording, as time goes by. However, that is not the way memory works. Instead, newly arriving information is added to and integrated with information in storage, providing updates and elaborations. This is reflected, for example, in the misinformation effect, with new information altering how you recall the past.

One can argue that, in this regard, your memory is appreciably better than a video recorder, with your memory updating older, partial information and replacing it with new and more elaborate information. In obvious ways, this will leave you with a more sophisticated, richer understanding of your world, drawing on the full range of your experiences, no matter when that information arrived. At the same time, the problems this creates for the justice system should by now be obvious.

But the differences between memory and video recorder don't stop there because memory also differs from an electronic recorder in its playback. Consider, for example, the role of schema-based reconstruction, in which someone uses inference, based on general knowledge, to fill in gaps in their recollection. This step is more sophisticated, more active, than a recorder's (mostly passive) playback, and (on the positive side) allows the person to supplement his or her recall with other information, filling in gaps in what he or she actually does recall. But here, too, a process that usually serves us well creates a risk of error and creates a danger that "recall" is supplemented by inferences rooted in information that arrived long after the target event. Again, the concerns for the justice system are obvious.

G. REASONS FOR FORGETTING

Our emphasis so far in this chapter has been on memory errors—cases in which a witness sincerely (and perhaps confidently) says things about a past event that are just wrong (i.e., different from what actually occurred). But there is another way our memories can let us down—namely, forgetting.

Let's start, though, by setting aside a prominent example of "forgetting" that turns out not to be forgetting at all. Imagine meeting someone at a party, being told his name, and moments later realizing that you don't have a clue what his name is—even though you just heard it. This common experience is not the result of ultra-rapid forgetting. Instead, the experience stems from a failure in acquisition. You were exposed to the name but barely paid attention to it and, as a result, never learned it in the first place.

What about "real" cases of forgetting—cases in which you once knew the information (and so plainly had learned it), but no longer do? For these cases, one of the best predictors of forgetting (not surprisingly) is the passage of time. Psychologists use the term *retention interval* to refer to the amount of time that elapses between the initial learning and the subsequent retrieval; as this interval grows, you're likely to forget more and more of the earlier event (cf. Read & Connolly, 2007).

This pattern actually involves three distinct mechanisms: One mechanism is *decay*. Just as wind and rain gradually erode mountains, various biological processes gradually erode memory connections, and so, purely as a function of passing time, memories fade and can eventually disappear. A second mechanism is dubbed *interference* and grows out of the fact that new learning can interfere with older learning. Via this mechanism, the passage of time is correlated with forgetting but does not cause forgetting directly. Instead, the passage of time creates the opportunity for new learning, and it is the new learning that disrupts the older memories.

A third contributor is *retrieval failure*. After all, the ability to locate information in storage is far from guaranteed, and (in ways we will explore) retrieval is more likely if your perspective at the time of retrieval matches that in place at the time of learning. If we now assume that your perspective is likely to change as time goes by, we can make a prediction about forgetting: The greater the retention interval, the greater the likelihood that your perspective has changed and therefore the greater the likelihood of retrieval failure.

All three of these mechanisms—decay, interference, and retrieval failure—contribute to forgetting. These various mechanisms lead to different consequences, though, for how rapidly forgetting unfolds and also for the prospects of "undoing" forgetting.

H. THE SPEED OF FORGETTING

More than a century ago, Ebbinghaus (1885/1913) showed that the speed of forgetting is uneven, and modern work has confirmed Ebbinghaus's claim again and again. Forgetting is rapid at first, and so much of the information loss occurs soon after the target event. Thus, even a short delay in an investigation can have a large impact on memory (e.g., Deffenbacher, Bornstein, McGorty, & Penrod, 2008; Shapiro & Penrod, 1986). But then the pace of forgetting slows down, and so there is less forgetting in the second hour after an event than there was in the first, less forgetting in the third day after the event than there was in the second.

Nonetheless, forgetting continues, and so more and more information is lost as time goes by.

There is, however, considerable variation within this overall pattern. Thus, there will always be more forgetting in the first hour than in the second, but there will be variation in *just how much forgetting* we'll see in that first hour (and so on). Among other considerations, forgetting is slower for materials that were well-learned at the start. Forgetting also tends to be slower for emotional materials, a point we return to in a moment.

Another factor is also crucial: Forgetting can be dramatically slowed if someone occasionally "revisits" a memory. As an example, one heroic researcher kept careful notes on the events that filled each of her days, sort of like keeping a detailed diary (Linton, 1975; 1978; 1982; 1986). After certain intervals, she would select an event from the diary and test her own memory for what had transpired; this recollection could then be checked against the written record. The data showed impressive memory accuracy for these mundane events—more than 65% remembered after three years. But, in addition, the researcher sometimes retested her memory for a given event. In this way, we can ask about the effect of the revisit because, after all, the experience of testing memory constitutes a reencounter with the original episode. (Thus, the first test provides a revisit that may benefit the second test.) This process of retesting had an enormous impact: For those events previously tested, forgetting after three years was cut in half, from more than 30% with no revisit down to 16% with one revisit.

Related data have been obtained in academic settings: Students obviously have to take exams, and each exam forces them to "revisit" the course materials. These revisits, we've just suggested, should slow forgetting, and, on this basis, exams can help students hang on to the material they've learned. Several studies have confirmed this optimistic suggestion—that is, have shown that the step of taking a college exam can promote long-term retention (e.g., Carpenter, Pashler, & Cepeda, 2009; Halamish & Bjork, 2011; Karpicke, 2012; Karpicke & Blunt, 2011; Karpicke & Roediger, 2010; McDaniel, Roediger, & McDermott, 2007; Pashler, Rohrer, Cepeda, & Carpenter, 2007).

Of course, let's also flag a danger here: Each revisit to a memory creates an opportunity for the person to weave new information (new insights, new perspectives, or information gathered from other sources) into the original memory. As a result, a revisit to a memory can have two effects—making it less likely that the event will be forgotten but more likely that the recall may be compromised by intrusions from other knowledge.

I. TECHNIQUES FOR UNDOING FORGETTING

We have just considered the prospect of slowing down forgetting by means of occasional revisits to a memory. But what if the forgetting has already occurred? Are there ways to "undo" forgetting? Here, we can quickly catalog what doesn't work and what does.

For years, many law enforcement agencies relied on forensic hypnosis, based on the idea that a hypnotized person could mentally "return" to an earlier event and remember virtually everything about the event, including aspects the person didn't even notice (much less think about) at the time. Similar claims have been made about certain drugs—sodium amytal, for example—with the idea that these, too, can help people remember things they otherwise never could.

Many studies have examined these claims, and the evidence is clear: Neither of these techniques improves memory. Hypnotized participants often do give detailed reports of the target event, but this isn't because they remember more; instead, they're just willing to say more in order to comply with the hypnotist's instructions. As a result, their "memories" are a mix of recollection, guesses, and inferences—and, of course, the hypnotized individual cannot tell you which of these are which (Lynn, Neuschatz, Fite, & Rhue, 2001; Mazzoni & Lynn, 2007; Spiegel, 1995). Likewise, the drugs sometimes given to improve memory work largely as sedatives, putting an individual in a less guarded, less cautious state of mind. This state allows people to report more about the past—not because they remember more, but simply because in this relaxed condition they're willing to say more.

There is, however, a procedure that does diminish forgetting—although through much more mundane mechanisms. Bear in mind that at least some forgetting can be understood as retrieval failure: The information you seek is in your memory, but you are for the moment unable to locate this information. In this setting, we can often help you by providing "retrieval cues" that might guide your search through your own memory.

This "guidance" will not restore memories that have been lost to interference or decay, and it will certainly not unearth memories for information that was never learned in the first place. It is also crucial that this guidance, when offered to a witness, not suggest to the person what might have happened (because, in that case, we have left the domain of retrieval support and entered the domain of the misinformation effect). But, to the extent that the person has lost information through retrieval failure, and to the extent that we can guide the person in a neutral fashion, we should be able to improve memory—and the evidence confirms this expectation.

Some of the evidence comes from studies of the so-called *cognitive interview*, a technique explicitly designed to aid law enforcement with the goal of maximizing the quality and accuracy of information obtained from witnesses (Fisher & Schreiber, 2007). This interview involves multiple elements, one of which is "context reinstatement," a procedure for recreating the psychological state the person was in during the remembered event. The interview also is designed to provide a diverse set of retrieval cues, on the idea that the more cues provided, the greater the chance of finding a successful cue. Studies—both in the laboratory and the field—confirm that this procedure is effective, moving us forward both theoretically (by confirming the role of retrieval failure within forgetting) and pragmatically (by improving the information available to law enforcement). (For some of the evidence that this interview does indeed work, both in crime simulations and in actual police investigations, see Bembibre & Higueras, 2012; Colomb, Ginet, Wright, Demarchi, & Sadler,

2013; Memon & Higham, 1999; Memon, Meissner, & Fraser, 2010; for evidence of the effectiveness of this interview with children, see Verkampt & Ginet, 2010.)

J. THE ROLE OF EMOTION

Common sense tells us that forgetting does not occur at all for some special events, and so people say things like, "That afternoon is burned into my brain," or "I'll never forget the day in which . . ." or "You know—some things you just never forget." This notion has been in circulation for many years: More than a century ago, William James, a founding figure in research psychology, wrote: "An impression may be so exciting emotionally as almost to leave a scar upon the cerebral tissues" (James, 1890, p. 670).

There is an element of truth in these sentiments, and, as we have mentioned, emotion does slow the process for forgetting (cf. Reisberg & Heuer, 2004.) However, both James and common sense overstate the facts because memories for emotional events (like all memories) do eventually fade. Hand in hand with this, we can certainly document errors—and sometimes large errors—in how emotional events are remembered.

Flashbulb Memories

We have already considered examples relevant to this point (e.g., the Dutch participants who, in remembering a highly emotional plane crash, recalled seeing a film that actually did not exist). Similarly, Morgan et al. (2013) were able to document memory errors produced by postevent misinformation in soldiers' recall of a highly emotional, highly stressful training episode. Still other evidence comes from the study of so-called *flashbulb memories*. These are memories of extraordinary clarity, typically for highly emotional events, retained despite the passage of many years (Brown & Kulik, 1977). Many Americans, for example, have flashbulb memories for the moment in 2001 when they first heard about the attack on the World Trade Center. They report that they remember the event "as though it were yesterday," and they can recall details of where they were at the time, what they were doing, and whom they were with. Many people say that they can recall the clothing worn by people around them, the exact words uttered, and the like. (Other public events that have produced this sort of memory include the 1986 explosion of the space shuttle Challenger, Princess Diana's death in 1997, and the news of Michael Jackson's death in 2009.)

Remarkably, though, these memories sometimes contain substantial errors. For example, Hirst et al. (2009) interviewed more than 3,000 people soon after the September 11 attack on the World Trade Center, asking them questions designed to probe the usual content of flashbulb memories: How had they first heard about the attack? Who brought them the news? What they were doing at the time? These individuals were then re-interviewed a year later, and more than a third of the participants (37%) provided a substantially different account in this follow-up. Even so, the participants were strongly confident in their recollection (rating their degree of certainty, on a 1–5 scale, at an average of 4.41). The picture was the same for participants interviewed three years after the attack, with 43% of these participants offering different accounts than they had initially, but with an average confidence level of 4.25.

Other studies have yielded similar data (e.g., Neisser & Harsch, 1992; Talarico & Rubin, 2003; 2007; Wagenaar & Groeneweg, 1990). Indeed, across studies, what seems remarkable about flashbulb memories is neither their accuracy nor their "stability" from one telling to the next. Instead, what is remarkable about flashbulbs is simply the level of certainty with which these events are recalled.

Other data, however, seem to tell a different story, and some flashbulb memories do seem marvelously accurate. The key message, then, is not that flashbulbs are likely to be mistaken. Instead, the key here is that we cannot take the accuracy of these memories for granted—despite someone's protestations that they are 100% certain about the memory—because the accuracy of these memories is, like the accuracy of any memory, uneven. The "burned into the brain" proposal is mistaken.

Should Emotionality Bolster Credibility?

Earlier in the chapter, we discussed ways in which we might try to decide whether a particular memory was accurate or not, but, as we saw, research on this issue is discouraging. False memories are recalled with just as much certainty as true memories; there is no reliable difference in the level of detail or the degree of consistency from one telling to the next. These points are, of course, echoed in our current discussion: From the point of view of the person who has a flashbulb memory, there's no detectable difference between an accurate flashbulb and an inaccurate one: Either will be recalled with great detail; either will be recalled with enormous confidence. In either case, the memory can be intensely emotional.

Let's pause, though, to elaborate on this issue. Plainly, emotionality, whether associated with the original event or experienced during the recollection, is no guarantee of memory accuracy. Nonetheless, is there some link between emotion and accuracy, so that we can use degree of emotionality as an index of veracity? The idea here is that people might feel more emotional in recalling a real event than they would in recalling a fiction; if so, intense emotion during recollection might be an indicator of memory accuracy.

This suggestion is plausible but mistaken. In one study, researchers measured heart rate, skin conductance, and muscle tension in individuals who were recalling an episode in which they had been abducted by space aliens (McNally et al., 2004). Most people would count this as a false memory, and yet the memory was associated with a psychophysiological response essentially identical to the response triggered (in other individuals) by memories known to be true (e.g., the response observed when soldiers recalled an episode of combat). Data like these make it clear that emotionality, during recall, is a poor index of veracity.

Sometimes, though, attorneys approach this issue from a different perspective and use the emotionality of the alleged event to bolster the credibility of someone's recollection of the event. To make this concrete, imagine that 6-year-old Amy has reported that she was abused by her Uncle Jeff, and she describes how frightened she was during the abuse. Jeff, however, steadfastly denies the allegation. Imagine further that there is no incriminating evidence beyond Amy's report, and so Jeff's trial (and possible conviction) rests largely on whether the jury believes Amy or not.

What should we make of this? In cases with this profile, I have heard prosecutors argue this way: Amy, by her own report, was emotional during the crime, and this emotionality cannot be surprising given the events Amy is describing. Moreover, we know from many studies that emotional events tend to be more fully remembered in comparison to neutral events. Therefore, the prosecutor concludes, this is a case in which memory is likely to be accurate, and so we should trust Amy's recollection.

This argument, however, is flawed. It is true that emotional events tend to be well remembered (e.g., Buchanan & Adolphs, 2004; Reisberg & Heuer, 2004). If, therefore, Amy really was abused, then odds are good that she would remember the abuse for a long, long time. The problem, though, is that we do not know for sure if Amy was abused; that point is precisely what would be at issue in Jeff's trial.

To make certain this point is clear, let's cast this issue in terms of Figure 3.1. As we have seen, research confirms the effect implied by the arrow on the left: emotion (all things equal) does promote memory. This effect is why one can legitimately argue that "If an actual emotional event occurred, then we will likely observe detailed recollection of the event." But this framing of things obviously starts with the *emotional event* and looks *forward* in time to the recall. The situation in a trial, though, is the opposite: Here, the witness is recalling the event, and we are trying to look *backward* in time, trying to learn about the event that allegedly gave rise to this memory. In this situation, we also need to consider the arrow on the right side of Figure 3.1 because research tells us that external forces can create false memories of emotional events, including a false memory of being frightened during the

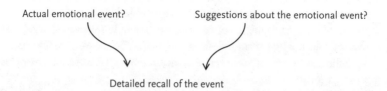

Figure 3.1:
The ambiguity of detailed reports. Advocates sometimes argue this way: "The events alleged by this victim surely would have been emotional. Emotional events are well remembered. Therefore, we can trust the victim's memory." This argument is flawed. It is true that emotional events are generally well-remembered (depicted here as the arrow on the left). But emotional recollection can also come from other sources—including leading questions or other forms of suggestion (arrow on the right). Therefore, a complainant's report of an emotional event cannot, by itself, tell us that the event occurred.

supposed event. Thus, it is okay to argue "If emotional event, then memory;" the research amply confirms this claim. But it is not legitimate to reverse the assertion and claim "If memory, then emotional event." Or, to put this one more way, an assertion like "the event would have been emotional and memorable *if the allegations are true*" can not imply that "the allegations are true." This is a simple point of logic, but the logic is sometimes muddied in the courtroom.

Emotionality and "Tunnel Vision"

Let's also add that, even when emotional memories are accurate, they are likely to be incomplete. We alluded to this point in Chapter 2, when we noted that emotion can cause a species of "tunnel vision." In other words, emotion seems, in many circumstances, to narrow someone's attention, so that the person is more alert to "central" aspects of the event but less sensitive to (and less likely to remember) more "peripheral" aspects (Berntsen, 2002; Reisberg & Heuer, 2004). There are multiple reasons for this, including brain mechanisms through which emotion seizes attention and disrupts the processes through which the person might otherwise seek to control his or her attention voluntarily (Phelps, 2012; as a common-sense example, consider drivers who are moving past a traffic accident and seem unable to prevent themselves from slowing down to "rubber-neck," gawking at the cars or people involved in the accident).

There is room for debate about how exactly the central and peripheral aspects of the event should be defined (Burke, Heuer, & Reisberg, 1992; Levine & Pizarro, 2004; Phelps, 2012), and this certainly limits the usefulness of these notions for the justice system. Nonetheless, the main point is clear: Just as we cannot count on the correctness of emotional memories, we cannot count on their completeness. We can often detect gaps in emotional memories, and we can often detect errors (perhaps encouraged by the gaps) in an otherwise correct emotional memory.

"After-the-Fact" Emotion

Before leaving the topic of emotion, we need to add a final layer to this discussion: Sometimes, an event takes on emotional significance only in retrospect. A witness stood in line behind another customer, waiting for service at the bank. The other customer steps up to the teller, transacts his business, and then leaves—and only then does the witness learn he was a bank robber. Or a parent becomes suspicious that her daughter has been abused and so thinks back over the last months and realizes the significance of an odd comment the child made some time back or the importance of the peculiar way the child acted when last visiting Uncle Joe.

Let's bear in mind that, in these scenarios, the witness and the parent were not emotional about, and put no special emphasis on, the target events when these events were unfolding. As a result, there is no reason to believe these events were carefully attended to or richly encoded into memory. Later on, the person realizes the importance of the events, and this realization is likely to spur extra effort at recalling the events. We therefore have a combination of not much information recorded into memory at the outset and substantial effort at recall. This is a setting, in other words, in which the witness is trying hard to offer a recollection without much to draw on—and hence a situation likely to rely heavily on after-the-fact reconstruction. More bluntly, this is a situation in which the risk of memory errors is high. Even more bluntly, this is an aspect of emotion—again, arising only after the to-be-remembered event—that can work against memory accuracy, even though other aspects of emotion are likely to promote accuracy.

K. TRAUMATIC EVENTS

We have said a great deal about the memory effects of moderate—and perhaps even strong—emotion. We need to carry the discussion one step further, though, and ask how traumatic events are remembered. If someone has witnessed a homicide, can we count on the accuracy of his or her testimony in trial? If someone suffers through the horrors of a rape, can we count on this person's recollection of the horrific event?

Remembering Trauma

Evidence suggests, in fact, that most traumatic events are well remembered for many years; indeed, victims of some atrocities seem plagued by a cruel enhancement of memory, leaving them with extra-vivid and long-lived recollections of the terrible event (e.g., Alexander et al., 2005; Goodman et al., 2003; Peace & Porter, 2004; Porter & Peace, 2007; Thomsen & Berntsen, 2009). In fact, people who have experienced trauma sometimes complain about having "too much" memory and wish they remembered less.

This enhanced memory is best understood in terms of a mechanism we met in Chapter 2: memory consolidation. This process is promoted by the conditions that accompany bodily arousal, including the extreme arousal typically present in a traumatic event (Buchanan & Adolphs, 2004; Hamann, 2001). But this does not mean that traumatic events are always well remembered. There are, in fact, cases in which people who have suffered through extreme events have no recall of their experience (e.g., Arrigo & Pezdek, 1997). In addition, we can sometimes document substantial errors in someone's recall of a traumatic event (Paz-Alonso & Goodman, 2008). We need to ask, therefore, why some traumatic events—in contrast to the broader pattern—are *not* well remembered.

In some cases, the forgetting of a traumatic event can be understood simply in terms of the person's age. Specifically, people have difficulty recalling events (traumatic or otherwise) from the first years of life (see Chapter 10), and so a failure to recall early trauma may just be part of this broader pattern. In other cases, traumatic events are accompanied by sleep deprivation, head injuries, or substance abuse, each of which can disrupt memory, making it unsurprising that these traumas aren't recalled (McNally, 2003). In still other cases, the extreme stress associated with the event can disrupt the consolidation processes and so no memory is ever established (Hasselmo, 1999; Joëls, Fernandez, & Roozendaal, 2011; McGaugh, 2000; Payne, Nadel, Britton, & Jacobs, 2004; for more on stress effects, see Chapter 2).

However, the possibilities just catalogued need to be understood as the exceptions and not the typical pattern. The available evidence suggests that traumatic events are recalled—and, as we have mentioned, often recalled more vividly than the person would wish. (For evidence of memory errors, however, in the recall of highly stressful events, see Morgan et al., 2013.)

Critical-Incident Amnesia

There has been some discussion in the law enforcement community about a pattern called *critical-incident amnesia* (e.g., Grossman & Siddle, 2004; Rivard, Dietz, Martell, & Widawski, 2002; also see Hulse & Memon, 2006). This term rarely appears in the research literature, but is endorsed by a number of police officers and attorneys. The idea here is that, if you are involved in a fast-paced and stressful incident, you may not be able to remember the incident immediately afterward. You need a day or two to calm down and gather your thoughts, and only then will you be able to recall what happened.

Claims about critical-incident amnesia arise, for example, in cases that hinge on how police officers remember violent incidents they have been involved in. For example, when there is an officer-involved shooting, the officer is sometimes uncertain at first what happened. After a day or so, however, the officer can provide a narrative describing the target event.

Similar patterns are sometimes alleged for crime victims. I consulted in one case in which the victim of an assault told police, right after the crime, that he could not describe his assailants. He reported that "they came out of nowhere . . . It was too dark . . . They blind-sided me . . ." A few days later, though, the victim was able to describe the event in more detail—recounting the conversation he had with his assailants before they hit him and offering some words describing the assailants. In this case, the prosecution argued that we should trust the latter report because the former merely reflected critical-incident amnesia.

However, we need to be cautious here and the evaluation of these apparently-recovered memories is far from certain. It is certainly true that high stress can interfere with perception and memory, and so some degree of amnesia, after a stressful event, will often be observed. It is also undeniable that a highly-stressed individual may have difficulty in providing a coherent report about an event, and so this individual might well provide a fuller, more detailed account after calming down a bit. But it is also true that a day or two's delay creates a danger that the person will be exposed to other influences that can shape the memory. The delay can also allow someone to engage in the sort of after-the-fact reconstruction that we have discussed in other contexts. In the latter case, the apparent "recovery" of the memory once the person has calmed down is no recovery at all.

This concern about reconstruction is shared by law-enforcement professionals writing about critical incident amnesia. In the words of two often-cited authors, "Within 72 hours, the final and most complete form of memory will occur, but it will be at least partially 'reconstructed' (and therefore somewhat 'contaminated') after the inevitable process of integrating available information from all other sources (media)" (Grossman & Siddle, 2001, pg. 1).

The key, then, is that a delay in report may improve memory (because the now-calmed witness is a better reporter) and also may compromise memory (because of the influence of reconstruction and the risk of contamination from outside sources). It is far from clear how these forces should be weighed against each other, and in light of this ambiguity—and in light of the scarcity of evidence on this topic—care is needed in interpreting claims about this form of apparent memory recovery.

Repression

Memory recovery also plays a central role within one last topic—and it is a topic that is highly controversial. Many clinical psychologists and a smaller number of research psychologists are convinced that people can defend themselves from painful memories by somehow pushing those memories out of view—a deliberate process of self-protection that serves to "bury" or "hide" these memories so that they cease to cause pain. Older texts refer to a process of memory *repression*, a notion that arises largely from the writings of Sigmund Freud. More recent texts refer to a process of *dissociation*—roughly, the idea that people can protect themselves by taking steps that create a sense of "psychological distance" between them and the painful recollection. (For modern—and somewhat specialized—versions of these claims, see Freyd, 1996; 1998; Terr, 1991; 1994.)

Practicing clinical psychologists are broadly receptive to these claims. In one study, clinicians were asked about memories that had been "repressed" and then "recovered." The clinicians said that they found memories like these to be quite credible, and a clear majority of the clinicians indicated that, in their view, such memories were "mostly" accurate or perhaps even always accurate (Magnussen & Melinder, 2012; also Patihis, Ho, Tingen, Lilienfeld, & Loftus, 2013).

Jurors seem to have similar views. In one survey, 73% of the jurors polled in 2006 thought that it was possible to repress and later recover a traumatic memory from childhood. Two-thirds of the jurors were skeptical about the claim (commonly offered by memory researchers) that recovered memories are often false or distorted (Benton, Ross, Bradshaw, Thomas, & Bradshaw, 2006).

Many researchers, however, have expressed deep skepticism about repression or dissociation claims (for overviews of the debate, see Piper, Lellevik, & Krizer, 2008; Patihis, Ho, Tingen, Lilienfeld, & Loftus, 2014; Smith & Gleaves, 2007). Several lines of evidence support this skepticism, including the straightforward fact that painful and even traumatic events tend (as we have mentioned) to be better remembered compared to neutral events, not less well remembered—the opposite of what one would expect if self-protective mechanisms were on the scene.

Of course, sometimes events are so painful, so frightening, that they produce a level of stress that disrupts memory. In this case, the events will not be remembered, but this is not an issue of repression. Instead, the level of stress creates a situation in which no memory is ever established, and so there is no prospect of "recovering" the memory later.

The Debate About Repression

The debate about repression (and dissociation) is ongoing, and so anyone in the justice system is well-advised to be cautious about claims made in this arena. However, a handful of research studies are routinely showcased as favoring the repression idea, and so anyone pursuing these issues needs to understand these studies.

One often-mentioned study here is by Corwin and Olafson (1997). They describe a case in which a young woman had (they claimed) repressed and later recovered a memory of abuse. However, some years later, researchers, using public records and a succession of interviews, were able to gather further information that was not included in Corwin and Olafson's original report, information showing that the memory in question was almost certainly false. As a result, the Corwin and Olafson study cannot be cited as offering documentation of repression. The study is at best controversial (and so should be excluded in any court insisting on "general acceptance" for scientific evidence) and is, according to many commentators, flawed in fatal ways (see, e.g., Geis & Loftus, 2009; Loftus & Guyer, 2002a; 2002b; Tavris, 2008).

Another study routinely mentioned in support of repression is described in a pair of publications by Williams (1994; 1995). In this study, 129 subjects were interviewed almost 20 years after their earlier reports of having been abused as children. An impressive number of these participants seemed to have forgotten about the abuse and then later recovered the memories (as should be possible if the memory was repressed, but still present, in the participants' minds).

However, the Williams study is in several ways problematic. As one concern, some of the women in this study were just 10 months old at the time of the alleged abuse. This is an age at which the normal development of memory virtually guarantees a pattern of "infantile amnesia" in which no episodes, traumatic or otherwise, are recalled. On this basis, there is no surprise when Williams reports (as she did in the first paper in this pair) that there is no memory of the trauma, and there is a deep puzzle when Williams reports (as she did in the second paper in the pair) that a "memory" has been recovered. (A substantial quantity of evidence—discussed in Chapter 10—makes it clear that autobiographical memories are not established at this young age, and, if no memory was established, then there is no memory to be "recovered" later.) These points demand that we regard the "recovery" with skepticism.

More troubling, Williams's main evidence that memories were "lost" and then "recovered" comes from a question asked of her study participants, "Was there ever a time when you did not remember that this had happened to you?" A key issue here is whether we can rely on someone's ability to answer this question accurately, and, in truth, there is powerful reason not to rely on this. We know, for example, that people routinely make mistakes about when they did or did not know something, did or did not remember something. In some settings, we can document a "I knew it all along" bias, in which people claim to have known things during time intervals in which they did not know the relevant information. In other settings, we can document the opposite bias (playfully called the "I forgot it all along" bias), in which people claim not to have known things during time intervals in which they demonstrably did know the relevant information (Schooler, 1999; also see Roese & Vohs, 2012). On this basis, Williams's main line of evidence—"I had forgotten about this"—involves a form of data in which we can have little confidence.

For these and other reasons, the Williams studies—like the Corwin and Olafson paper—do not justify claims about repression. (For other worries about the Williams data, see Laney & Loftus, 2005; Loftus, Garry, & Feldman, 1994; Loftus & Ketcham, 1996; Piper et al., 2008.) These points are then joined by the fact that—as we mentioned—painful and also shameful events—are typically well remembered and not "repressed" at all (see Chapter 10). Researchers therefore seem justified in their skepticism about the repression notion.

We might add, however, that even if the evidence for repression is problematic, we lack a compelling reason to assert that the repression-and-recovery pattern never occurs. (Indeed, it is generally difficult in science to show that something never occurs.) A more cautious conclusion, then, is that this pattern is possible but perhaps rare and certainly not well-documented. Thus, any claims about "recovered memories" should be viewed with caution but cannot be dismissed out of hand. (I might mention that, on this point, I am more cautious than some of my colleagues, and one can find stronger denials of the repression idea; e.g., Loftus & Ketcham, 1996.)

Continuous Versus Discontinuous Memories

How, then, should we proceed if—for example—a 25-year-old, after years of silence, reports on an event that occurred in her childhood? Many clinical psychologists would count this as evidence for the recovery of a repressed memory, but there are several more plausible possibilities to consider here. Perhaps the adult has always remembered the horrible event but has kept silent for years out of fear or shame, and only now has she found the courage to speak out. Or perhaps the adult has always recalled the event but is coming forward now because he or she has discovered that the alleged abuser has access to some other child, and so the complaining witness is bringing forward the accusations to protect this other child. In still other cases, accusers indicate that they had long believed that a disclosure would be met with inaction at best and skepticism at worst, and this led them to silence. They are coming forward now, though, because they are convinced that at last they will be believed. Or—as one more option—perhaps the person had always remembered the acts but did not realize they were acts that should be reported and possibly prosecuted. ("He always hugged me, and it was only years later that I realized he shouldn't have been putting his hands down there.")

From a memory perspective, there is little to be said about any of these shifts from silence to disclosure. In cases involving long-delayed reports, therefore, a researcher would want to ask: Can we find out if the memory is "continuous" (always known to the accuser but not reported) or "discontinuous"? If the former, there is no need to worry about the dynamic of memories lost-then-found. We would, however, still need to be alert to the fact that these cases typically involve someone remembering an event from the distant past, and so (here as always) we need to scrutinize the memory with care. In such cases, the passage of time has likely created an opportunity for the person to encounter other ideas, other information, about the now-remembered events, and these points demand concern about possible memory contamination and possible memory error. Thus, we still need to be alert to the possibility that these long-delayed reports may in some cases be entirely false—troubling and consequential instances of false memory.

Retrieval Failure Versus Repression

What if there is reason to believe that the memory was "discontinuous"—so that the memory had been unavailable and unknown for some period of time? Here, we need to consider whether the memory might have dropped from view simply because of the pattern of retrieval failure that we have already discussed. This is, as we said earlier, a pattern in which you lose track of a memory simply because you are unable to locate the memory within the vast warehouse of your stored recollections. However, if a suitable reminder comes into view, you will recall the event.

In some ways, the pattern of retrieval failure resembles the sequence of repression and recovery. In both cases, a memory is lost from view for a period of time but then returns to view. There are, however, crucial differences between these two mechanisms—one rooted in the ordinary function of memory and one rooted in a proposal about self-defense. These differences turn out to be enormously useful for the justice system because we can often use the characteristics of retrieval failure as a means of evaluating a memory in a particular case.

There's no debate about the reality of retrieval failure. This form of "temporary forgetting" can and often does occur, but—crucially—this type of "forgetting" is eliminated if a suitable retrieval cue is provided. This point allows us to distinguish retrieval failure from repression, and, pragmatically, an account in terms of retrieval failure becomes much more plausible if (a) seemingly potent retrieval cues were absent during the period of not-remembering, accounting for the failure to recall the target memory, but (b) seemingly potent retrieval cues have now arrived, accounting for the reappearance of the memory.

Notice, then, that the circumstances just described can make a discontinuous memory more credible. If these circumstances are in place, then the pattern of a memory lost-then-recovered would fit with well-established and uncontroversial principles of memory functioning. Thus, imagine someone who is abused by a family friend who lives briefly in the child's home when the child is, say, four years old. The child then moves to another part of the country and so sees neither the home nor the friend for many years and is instead immersed in a new physical and social environment. Under these circumstances, the abuse may well fall out of the child's thinking because the obvious reminders (sight of the house, sight of the abuser) are not available. Thoughts of the abuse are likely to arise, though, if the victim returns to the original home or sees the abuser after many years. The presentation of these retrieval cues will, in most cases, swiftly bring the long-lost memory to mind.

But what if circumstances like these are not in place? As an alternative scenario, imagine someone who has allegedly suffered abuse but claims to have had no memory of the abuse for many years despite being repeatedly exposed to cues associated with the abuse. Let's say, for example, that the person often sees the (alleged) abuser, is regularly in the physical setting in which the abuse supposedly took place, and is involved in some number of conversations about abuse and abuse-related topics. But then, one day, the abuse does come to mind, even though we can discern no new and especially powerful retrieval cue. In this scenario, the memory failed to surface even though it probably should have (because decent retrieval cues were available), and then did surface even though it should not have (because no new and more effective cue was presented). In this example, the "memory" does not function as a memory typically would, thus inviting the suggestion that it is not a bona fide memory at all.

Evaluating Apparently Recovered Memories

How, therefore, should an investigator proceed in cases that seem to involve a recovered memory? For reasons just discussed, the investigator should try to determine if the memory was continuous or discontinuous and, if the latter, what sorts of retrieval cues have been available during the time in which the memory was absent and what retrieval cues were in place when the memory reappeared.

It is also useful to know how exactly the memories emerged. Was it in response to some suggestion or questioning (perhaps from a parent or a friend)? Did the memories emerge (as some recovered memories do) in therapy? Some therapists are convinced that a client's troubles are likely the result of long-forgotten abuse, and, if so, the therapist may seek confirmation of this notion during the therapy sessions. Even if therapists scrupulously avoid leading questions, bias might still lead them to shape their clients' memory in other ways: by giving signs of interest or concern if the clients hit on the "right" line of exploration, by spending more time on topics related to the alleged memories, and so forth. In these ways, the climate within a therapeutic session could guide the client toward finding exactly the "memories" the therapist expects to find. (Indeed, for evidence suggesting that memories recovered in therapy may be especially prone to error, see Geraerts, Schooler, Merckelbach, Jelicic, Haner, & Amabadar, 2007.)

In addition, we can ask whether the recovered memories have the traits normally observed in genuine, accurate memories. For example, was the event traumatic? If so, it is peculiar that the memory was ever lost (through retrieval failure or any other mechanism) because traumatic events, we've said repeatedly, tend to be well remembered. Was there a repeated series of events, occurring over many months? If so, then this, too, would make it peculiar if the memory was lost for a time because repeated events tend to be better remembered (although often the repeated events blur together, so that one loses track of which event was which). In these ways, we can ask roughly whether the "loss" of the memory makes sense in light of what we know about how memory functions in general. (For further discussion of recovered memories, see, among others, Geraerts et al., 2007; 2009; Ghetti et al., 2006; Giesbrecht, Lynn, Lilienfield, & Merckelbach, 2008; Kihlstrom & Schacter, 2000; Loftus & Guyer, 2002a, 2002b; Read, 1999.)

L. SOME FINAL THOUGHTS

Where, then, does all of this leave us? Perception does not operate like a video camera; memory does not operate like a video recorder. Perception and memory are, we have argued, more active, more dynamic than these electronic devices and are, in particular, selective, constructive, and integrative in ways that the devices are not. These points are, we have repeatedly said, positive features of these human processes and provide each of us with a better-informed, more sophisticated, more current understanding of the world around us. We gain these benefits, though, at a price—a sometimes diminished recollection of the objective details of our experience.

Over and over, though, we have warned against a cynical conclusion from all of this because the fact remains that our perception and memory are accurate more often than not. Indeed, it is hard to imagine that evolution would have tolerated a creature whose beliefs and memories were routinely out of step with reality. And, consistent with this optimistic note, researchers have offered a number of estimates of the overall accuracy level of memory for forensically relevant information (see, e.g., an estimate from Simon, 2012, based on a broad swath of data—including Christianson & Hübinette, 1993; Köhnken, Milne, Memon, & Bull, 1999; Woolnough & MacLeod, 2001; Yuille & Cutshall, 1986; Yuille, Davies, Gibling, Marxsen, & Porter, 1994.)

These overall assessments, however, are of limited use. Instead, we need (and can provide) a more finely tuned estimate of memory accuracy by considering the details of a particular event and a particular witness. It is precisely that consideration that we have aimed at in this chapter and throughout this book.

CHAPTER 4

Witness Evidence

The Steps Leading to an Identification

We turn now to a type of memory that surely deserves its own treatment—the memory a witness or victim might have for the visual appearance of a criminal and, with that, the procedures for obtaining an accurate eyewitness identification. In this chapter, we examine the steps leading up to an identification—including factors that influence how well the face is "encoded" into memory. Then, in Chapter 5, we'll turn to the crucial next step: the procedure through which police seek to obtain identification evidence.

A. FACES ARE SPECIAL

There are many reasons why identifications based on facial appearance deserve special coverage in a book like this. These identifications are, of course, a potent form of evidence and among the most influential factors in determining a jury's verdict. But, in addition, the scientific evidence demands that we separate our discussion of *face memory* from the broader discussion of memory in general. The reason, in brief, is that the processes through which we perceive and remember faces are different from the processes used for the recognition of other objects (including, for example, the recognition of voices or weapons or vehicles). And, as we'll see, the specialized nature of face recognition has numerous implications for the justice system.

Evidence that Faces Are Special

Damage almost anywhere in the brain can lead to substantial and often tragic disruption of someone's life. For example, some forms of brain damage produce a pattern known as *agnosia*—an inability to recognize familiar inputs. Agnosia is typically limited to one sensory modality or another, and so someone with visual agnosia might fail to recognize a spoon or a rose that is out in plain view, but be able to instantly identify the spoon if allowed to explore it with touch or identify the rose from its scent.

In some cases, agnosia is even more specialized, and people who suffer from *prosopagnosia* lose their ability to recognize faces even though their other visual abilities are intact. This pattern seems to imply a neural structure involved almost exclusively in the recognition and discrimination of faces, and, of course, it's this structure that's damaged in people suffering from prosopagnosia (Behrmann & Avidan, 2005; Burton, Young, Bruce, Johnston, & Ellis, 1991; Damasio, Tranel, & Damasio, 1990; De Renzi, Faglioni, Grossi, & Nichelli, 1991).

Related evidence comes from studies of people who have intact brains. Neuroimaging techniques (such as positron emission tomography [PET] or functional magnetic resonance imaging [fMRI] scans) allow us to examine activity patterns in a person's brain when he or she is looking at faces and compare these to the patterns of activity when the person is examining some other target. These studies indicate that face recognition selectively activates a brain site often called the *fusiform face area* (FFA), again indicating specialized neural tissue devoted largely to face recognition.

Finally (and perhaps most importantly for the courts), face recognition also *functions* differently from other forms of recognition and seems to be governed by its own principles. We will have more to say about this point as we proceed, but, for now, here is a single example: There is debate about whether (or the degree to which) recognition of houses, teacups, or automobiles is "viewpoint-dependent"—that is, more accurate and more efficient from some angles of view than from others. There is no debate about this point, however, for faces: People are much worse at recognizing inverted (or sideways) faces than they are at recognizing other inverted (or sideways) stimuli, and so plainly face recognition is dependent on "proper" orientation in ways in which other stimuli are not (e.g., Diamond & Carey, 1986; Thompson, 1980; Yin, 1969; for a different view of these data, though, see Rakover, 2013).

There is, we note, some debate about how exactly we should read all these data. Some researchers argue that face recognition really is *sui generis* and that the FFA is appropriately named—and thus it really is the fusiform *face* area, specialized for the perception of faces. Other researchers offer a slightly different claim: Instead of distinguishing "face perception" from other forms of perception, they distinguish "expert-level discrimination of individuals" from other forms of perception. According to this view, face perception is an instance of this expert-level discrimination, but there are other types of perception that also fall into this specialized category. (For example, think about expert bird watchers who have developed remarkable skill in distinguishing types of warblers or judges at dog shows who have developed exquisite skill in telling individual dogs apart. According to this alternative view, these people, too, rely on the FFA for their perceptual expertise.)

This disagreement—although important—may be inconsequential for the courts. On either of these accounts, the processes used for, the brain centers involved in, and the level of skill evident in face recognition are all plainly different from those involved in most other forms of perception. We can debate whether faces are the *only* type of visual input that is special, but the research community agrees: Faces are special.

"Holistic" Perception

But what is it that makes face recognition distinctive? Evidence suggests that we recognize most objects by starting with a catalog of the object's parts. "Four right angles? Must be a square. Long legs, long neck, and spots? Must be a giraffe." Face recognition, in contrast, seems not to depend on an inventory of a face's parts; instead, this recognition depends on "holistic perception." In other words, the recognition depends on complex relationships created by the face's overall configuration—the spacing of the eyes relative to the length of the nose, the height of the forehead relative to the width of the face, and so forth.

Of course, a face's features still matter in this holistic process. The key, however, is that the features can't be considered one by one, apart from the context of the face. Instead, the features matter by virtue of the relationships and configurations they create. It's these relationships, and not the features on their own, that guide face recognition (cf. Rhodes, 2013).

We will have reason to circle back to holistic perception and what it implies several times in this chapter. For now, though, as an example of the evidence favoring this notion, consider the so-called *composite effect*. In an early demonstration of this effect, Young et al. (1987) combined the top half of one (highly familiar) face with the bottom-half of another, and participants were asked to identify just the top half. This task was very difficult if the two halves were properly aligned. In this setting, participants seemed unable to focus only on the top half; instead, they inevitably viewed the top of the face as part of the whole and so were misled by the (unfamiliar) relationships created by this composite and could not attend only to the (familiar) features in the face's top half. The task was much easier, though, if the halves were misaligned (e.g., if the bottom half of the face was slid even slightly to the right, breaking the continuity of the face outline, the nose, and so on). In this setting, the stimulus itself broke up the configuration, making it possible to view the top half on its own. (Also see Gauthier & Bukach, 2007; McKone & Robbins, 2007; for related results, see Amishav & Kimchi, 2010.)

B. HOW ACCURATE IS FACIAL RECOGNITION?

Across the evolutionary history of our species, it has surely been crucial that humans be able to distinguish friend from foe, clan-mate from stranger. Indeed, this simple point surely played a role in guiding our evolution such that we ended up with neural circuits (e.g., those in the FFA) specialized for just this sort of perception, just this sort of recognition.

On this basis, we might expect that facial recognition would be quite accurate—relying on specialized neural machinery and very well practiced. To assess this claim, though, we need to make a crucial distinction: one between *recognition* and *identification* (cf. Bruce, Burton, & Hancock, 2007).

Recognition Versus Identification

If you are witness to a crime, you are probably observing a perpetrator who previously was a stranger to you; you are seeing that person for the first time at the scene of the crime. Then, a while later, based on that, perhaps brief, exposure, you might try to *identify* that person from a mug book or perhaps a police lineup. In contrast, imagine that you have seen Allen around the neighborhood many times and easily recognize him whenever you see him. Now imagine that you are standing outside of a club when Allen approaches, threatens you, and steals your wallet. Again, sometime later, you are looking at a mug book or lineup, and you make a selection—but now you are looking to *recognize* Allen in the pictures.

The difference at stake here is not a qualitative difference; instead, it is a matter of degree: At one extreme, you may never have seen the perpetrator before. Or perhaps you saw the perpetrator once before, briefly, and only in passing. Or perhaps you have seen the perpetrator three times before and had a conversation with him. Or (now moving to the other extreme) perhaps you have seen the perpetrator dozens of times and often interacted with him at length. Plainly, there is a wide range of options here.

Let's ignore the fine-grained distinctions for now and focus just on the extremes—and so let's focus on the difference between, say, a witness's encounter with a previously unknown person and a comparable encounter with someone who the witness knows well from other occasions. A witness in the latter situation will have a vastly easier time spotting the perpetrator in a lineup, compared to a witness trying to identify an unfamiliar, just-once-viewed stranger (e.g., Reder et al., 2013). Recognition of a familiar face is also less vulnerable to guiding and outside influence than identification of a previously unknown face.

This contrast should not be surprising. After all, with an unfamiliar face, you must, during a brief encounter, memorize the face; researchers would say that you need to *encode* the face into your memory. But when Allen (say), already familiar to you, approached to steal your wallet, you did not have to create a memory representation of his face; you already had one. All you needed to do was link the current event to that trace in memory—an appreciably easier process than creating a face trace in the first place.

But just how easy is it to recognize an already familiar face—that is, to recognize a previous acquaintance who now comes into your view? Common sense suggests an answer: Think about the enormous number of friends, family members, work acquaintances, celebrities, or politicians whom you recognize the moment you see them (in person, in photos, or on a screen). This informal observation suggests that recognition of familiar faces is indeed easy and accurate.

Research confirms this point and tells us that recognition of familiar faces remains accurate even if it has been years since you last encountered the face. In one study (Bahrick, Bahrick, & Wittlinger, 1975), researchers tracked down the graduates of a particular high school—people who had graduated in the previous year, and the year before, and the year before that, and, ultimately, people who had graduated 50 years earlier. All of these alumni were shown photographs from their own year's high school yearbook. For each photo, they were given a group of names and had to choose the name of the person shown in the picture. The data for this task show impressive accuracy and remarkably little forgetting as the years went by: Performance was approximately 90% correct for participants tested just 3 months after graduation, roughly the same after 7 years, and the same after 14 years. In some versions of the test, performance was still excellent after 34 years.

In another version of this task, participants were shown faces from their graduation year's yearbook and had to come up with the names on their own. Here, too, performance was impressive. Participants who had graduated 25 years earlier (and who, therefore, had not seen these faces for a quarter-century) were still able to name half of the faces shown to them.

The facts are different, though, for the identification of unfamiliar faces. In this situation, as we've said, you only have one typically brief, often stress-filled chance to observe (and memorize) the person's face. You cannot link that memory to other information about the individual (e.g., the person's name or memories of other events in which you've seen this person) because you have no such information. We've said that this type of memorization is more difficult, but just how difficult is it?

The DNA Exonerations

There are now more than 300 cases in the United States in which someone has been convicted, served a lengthy period in jail, but was eventually proved innocent thanks to DNA analysis that was not available at the time of the trial. These cases have been scrutinized by legal scholars, journalists, and scientists, and all parties agree: Mistaken identifications account for roughly three-quarters of these wrongful convictions. Said differently, bad IDs account for more of these cases than all other causes combined. These witness errors include cases in which witnesses testified that they were absolutely certain they were correct in their identifications; there are also cases in which the identifications had been made by law enforcement professionals; there also cases in which there were multiple identifications of the defendant. In all cases, though, we know that these identifications were mistaken because the DNA evidence tells us the defendant was innocent. (For a similar pattern drawn from a much larger set of exonerations, readers may want to examine the National Registry of Exonerations, described online at www.law.umich.edu/special/exoneration/Pages/about.aspx.)

Plainly, therefore, eyewitness errors occur in real life cases and seem to be a serious problem for the justice system. Many authors have provided authoritative, scholarly overviews of these cases (see, e.g., Connors, Lundregan, Miller, & McEwen, 1996;

Garrett, 2008; Gross, Jacoby, Matheson, Montgomery, & Patil, 2005), but, for readers who want a closer, "more human" view of DNA exoneration, Jennifer Thompson-Cannino and Ronald Cotton have co-authored a truly remarkable volume (Thompson-Cannino, Cotton, & Torneo, 2009). Jennifer Thompson was a crime victim who identified the wrong man as her rapist, sending this innocent man to jail for 10 years. Ronald Cotton is now her friend, but he is also the man she falsely accused in 1984.

There is, however, room for debate about these exoneration cases. To anticipate, we will argue that eyewitness errors are, in fact, quite common, and so concern about the DNA exonerations has not misled us and has pointed us toward the correct conclusion: Identification evidence is more fragile, more often mistaken, than many people believe, and indeed the exoneration cases may understate the problem (e.g., Wells, Greathouse, & Smalarz, 2012). Ironically, though, the DNA exonerations themselves may not be the best way to support this conclusion.

What is the nature of the debate here? As one consideration, any wrongful conviction is tragic, but perhaps we should compare the number of DNA exonerations to the vast number of convictions overall in the United States, over the same time span. The point is, of course, that the exonerations represent only a minute fraction of this much larger set, and, on that basis, one might celebrate the fact that mistaken IDs have been documented in such a small proportion of all convictions. (For discussion, see Simon, 2012, pp. 4–5.) Indeed, in support of this view, one might consider the numbers suggested by the New Jersey Supreme Court in its often-cited ruling in *State v. Henderson*. The Court reached beyond the DNA exonerations and ended up with an estimate that "approximately 7,500 of every 1.5 million annual convictions for serious offenses" can be traced to misidentifications. This is simultaneously an alarmingly high number of errors, but it is also a small proportion (0.5%), perhaps inviting the upbeat conclusion that 99.5% of the identifications are likely to be secure.

Second, the exoneration cases derive from a limited range of crimes (mostly sexual offenses, which leave DNA evidence behind), and these may not be representative of all crimes (Smith & Cutler, 2013). In addition, the exonerations have each derived from a sustained effort toward postconviction relief, and gaining this relief is an expensive, lengthy process. As a result, agencies (such as the Innocence Project) choose with care which cases to pursue. Hence, the convictions selected for DNA scrutiny are likely to be just those cases that seem worrisome on other grounds. Extrapolating from the exonerations, therefore, to make claims about convictions in general may not be warranted. (For other concerns about the exoneration cases, see Flowe, Finklea, & Ebbesen, 2009; Smith & Cutler, 2013.)

Evidence from Case Studies

However, there is no reason to get drawn into a debate about the DNA exonerations. The reason is that other evidence makes it clear that the exonerations are, in truth, pointing us toward the right conclusion—namely, that identification evidence is, in fact, surprisingly error-prone.

We can, for example, gain further information from a small number of highly realistic case studies. In one study, a young man entered a bank and attempted to cash a money order. The amount on the money order, however, had obviously been altered (from $10 to $110), and this triggered the bank teller's suspicions, leading to an irate exchange with the man, who then left the bank. A few hours later, investigators came to the bank and asked the teller if she could identify the suspect from a photomontage.

As it turns out, this event had been staged, allowing researchers to determine how accurate IDs would be in this scenario. The data are striking: If the young man's picture was not in the photomontage, 37% of the tellers tested still made a choice—that is, chose someone entirely innocent (Pigott, Brigham, & Bothwell, 1990).

Other studies have collected similar data (e.g., Brigham, Maas, Snyder, & Spaulding, 1982; Krafka & Penrod, 1985; Platz & Hosch, 1988). These studies collectively involve hundreds of ID attempts, and, across these studies, more than a third of the participants chose a foil from a target-absent array.

How Good Could We Be?

Another line of research takes a different approach: The exact appearance of a face can vary depending on the person's emotional expression, the camera angle, the lighting, the person's fatigue state, and so on. Thus, how someone looks in one photograph may be rather different from how that same person looks in another photograph, or in a video, or if viewed "live." Evidence suggests these differences do matter and can significantly impair recognition (Jenkins, White, Van Montfort, & Burton, 2011; Megreya, Sandford, & Burton, 2013). Indeed, authors of one recent paper commented that a change in illumination from one image of a face to another image of the same face can "drastically" undermine recognition performance (Liu, Chen, Han, & Shan, 2013).

Davis and Loftus (2012) use these ideas as a basis for asking how good identification can possibly be, even in near-ideal circumstances. They describe studies in which participants were allowed to make side-by-side comparisons of live actors and a photograph, and asked (essentially) "Does *this* photo show *that* person?" Here, there is no issue of "information loss" caused by a delay, because the photograph and target person were in view simultaneously. Even so, studies with this set up yield error rates between 15% and 33%, perhaps suggesting a "ceiling" on the accuracy of photographic identifications with previously unknown faces. (For evidence that people can improve their performance in this task, though, if provided practice and feedback, see White, Kemp, Jenkins, & Burton, 2014.)

An older study makes the same point: Kemp, Towell, and Pike (1997) studied supermarket cashiers who were performing their normal (and well-practiced) routine in which they had to decide whether the photo shown on a shopper's credit card matched the shopper's face. The cashiers knew they were being tested and had to complete a response sheet after each transaction indicating their confidence in their assessment of the credit card. To encourage accuracy, the cashiers were told they could earn a cash prize if their performance was at a high level. Even with these (presumably helpful) factors in place, performance was quite poor, and only 67% of the cashiers' decisions were correct. (Bear in mind that, since the credit card photo either did or did not match the shopper's face, *random* decisions would still be correct 50% of the time; hence, the cashiers' performance was only slightly better than chance.)

Evidence from Archival Studies

Another line of evidence focuses on mistaken convictions documented through means other than DNA exoneration. These cases, spanning the past century, lead to a familiar conclusion: Eyewitness errors are a prominent source of these mistakes. (For a broad review, see Malpass, Ross, Meissner, & Marcon, 2009; also Radelet, Bedau, & Putnam, 1992, for a review focused specifically on capital cases.)

Other researchers have gained access to police records in order to ask how well real witnesses have done in identifying real suspects. In these studies, we can ask how often witnesses choose the police suspect from the lineup, but let's be clear that this response is ambiguous: We have no iron-clad way of telling whether the suspect in each case was the actual perpetrator. Hence, we cannot equate "suspect-choices" with "correct choices." We can, however, be sure about one type of error—cases in which a witness selects a "known innocent" from the lineup—that is, selects a filler known not to be involved in the crime and included in the witness's options simply to make sure the lineup had the right number of people in it.

In a study by Slater (1994), based on reports from 843 witnesses who collectively had viewed a total of 302 lineups, 36% chose the police suspect, but 22% chose an innocent foil as the perpetrator. Wright and McDaid (1996) surveyed more than 1,500 identification attempts in actual cases based on more than 600 lineups; in their data, 39% of the witnesses selected the suspect; 20% chose one of the foils. (Notice, then, that 41% made no identification, and so, of the identifications offered, more than a third were filler selections.) Wright and Skagerberg (2007) documented a 21% rate of filler choices. Behrman and Davey (2001) examined almost 300 police cases in Sacramento, California, and reported that 24% of the identifications in live lineups were selections of fillers; in another study, Behrman and Richards (2005) reported a 15% rate of choosing fillers. Valentine, Pickering, and Darling (2003) analyzed 640 identification attempts in London, England; in their data, 22% of the eyewitnesses chose fillers. (Again, this means that, of the identifications offered, 38% were incorrect.) Horry, Memon, Wright, and Milne (2012) examined identification decisions (from video lineups) from 1,039 attempts in England; the filler identification rate was 26%. (Also see Horry, Halford, Brewer, Milne & Bull, 2014, for a study of 709 witnesses who, overall, made 18% filler selections.) Or, in yet another study, Wells, Steblay, and Dysart (2012) drew their data from a field study comparing simultaneous and sequential lineups (more on this comparison in Chapter 5); if we focus on just their simultaneous lineups (i.e., the conventional procedure), they report an 18% rate of filler choices.

The consistency of these numbers is striking, with various studies all yielding values of roughly 20% filler choices. Let's emphasize, though, that this is the percentage of *all witnesses,* including those who made no choice at all. In most prosecutions, there would be no role for these "unable-to-choose" witnesses, and so plausibly we should focus just on those witnesses who made *some selection.* We have already indicated that, if we do focus in this fashion, the data indicate that at least one-third of all witness choices are mistakes.

Moreover, in these analyses, we are only considering one type of error—selections of a known innocent. The total error rate will also include cases in which the witness selected the suspect, but the suspect is not the perpetrator. Thus, the numbers just mentioned likely *under*state the actual error rate in identifications.

We should mention, though, that a few studies do paint a different picture. For example, Mecklenburg, Bailey, and Larson (2008) report a much lower rate of filler selections (9.2%) in their data, and they cite a New York City study with an even lower rate of filler selections. However, there has been considerable debate over whether the Mecklenburg study was properly conducted, and so it is not clear what to make of these numbers (cf. Schacter et al., 2008; Steblay, 2011).

A different caveat about these data is more substantial: One of the strengths of these archival studies lies in the fact that there is no "cherry-picking" of the data. Instead, these studies include all the identifications attempted during the test period. This raises a question, however, of whether we are being misled by some number of identifications attempted by peripheral witnesses or witnesses questioned only weeks after the crime. On that basis, one might hope that at least some of these errors would be "filtered out" in subsequent steps (in the investigation or in trial; for a different broad concern about these data, see Horry et al., 2014).

Nonetheless, the broad pattern of the evidence is clear, and we are getting a consistent message from these archival studies *and* the case studies *and* the DNA exonerations *and* the "best-case" estimates (think about the supermarket cashiers). Overall, there really can be no question that witnesses make bad picks from lineups with surprising (and alarming) frequency.

Target-Present Versus Target-Absent

In the prior few sections, we have mentioned several percentages of error in witness identifications. One of the recurrent themes in this book, however, is that we should be wary of overall assessments of perception or memory. There are circumstances in which these processes serve us well and provide us with complete and accurate information; there are also circumstances in which these processes go astray. In place of overall assessments, therefore, we need to examine the data at a finer grain.

This point is well exemplified by the distinction between *target-present* (TP) and *target-absent* (TA) lineups. Target-present lineups are those that include the actual perpetrator. Here, a correct response would be selecting the perpetrator; an error would either be picking the wrong person or making no choice at all. Target-absent lineups are those in which the actual perpetrator is not included in the lineup. Here, the correct response would be refusing to make a choice; an error would be making any selection at all.

One glimpse of how this distinction matters comes from a meta-analysis comparing lineups with showups (Steblay, Dysart, Fulero, & Lindsay, 2003; we will return to this analysis in Chapter 5). This study pooled data from eight published papers and so reflects the results from more than 3,000 participants. This analysis indicates that, with target-*present* lineups, participants chose someone innocent (one of the fillers) 24% of the time. With a target-*absent* lineups, participants chose someone innocent almost twice as often—43% of the time.

The point here is also illustrated by a commonly cited study by Gary Wells (Wells, 1993). Participants in this study viewed a crime, and then half were shown a six-person target-present lineup. More than half (54%) chose the culprit; 35% chose one of the fillers. For the remaining participants, the actual culprit was simply removed from the lineup, and so they were shown a five-person target-absent lineup. Denied the option of choosing the actual culprit, these participants simply shifted their selection to the next most likely candidate, and so 68% of the participants selected one of the five fillers.

These findings have an immediate implication: To the extent possible, investigators should try to ensure that they are using target-present lineups because errors are less common here than in target-absent lineups. As a result, it is probably unwise to engage in a practice employed by some investigators: using lineups early in an investigation as a way of "clearing the brush"—that is, excluding otherwise plausible suspects. Likewise, police officers should probably avoid a "fishing expedition" in which they construct lineups with little evidence merely in the hope of stumbling across the perpetrator's identity.

How important are these considerations? Wilford and Wells (2013, p. 29) frame this issue in terms of the "base rate" of using target-absent lineups (i.e., what proportion of all lineups are target-absent). They argue that this base rate "drives mistaken identification and accurate identification rates more than perhaps any other variable."

System Variables, Estimator Variables

Many other variables also play a role in governing identification accuracy, and, as a way of bringing order to this catalog, some years back Gary Wells (a deeply influential researcher in this arena) suggested that we can divide these factors into two broad categories (Wells, 1978; also Fulero, 2009; for a more recent discussion, see Wilford & Wells, 2013): *Estimator variables* are factors that we have no control over, but which we can use as a basis for evaluating a particular identification. These variables include how well lit the crime scene was, how much time went by between the crime and the identification, and so on. By tracking these variables, we can offer law enforcement and the courts an assessment of the risk of identification error in that specific case.

In contrast, *system variables* are variables that influence performance but that we do have control over. We can use system variables to evaluate an ID (e.g., Were proper instructions given? Were the faces used in a photo lineup sensibly selected?). More importantly, we can use system variables in a proactive fashion: We can, in other words, *adjust* the system variables to maximize the likelihood the witnesses will identify perpetrators and minimize the likelihood that witnesses will mistakenly identify someone else or will "miss" the perpetrator in the lineup.

For policy makers (or anyone writing guidelines for the justice system), the distinction between estimator and system variables is crucial because, to put the matter simply, system variables provide us with opportunities for improving identification procedures; estimator variables do not (but are valuable for other purposes). If we want to work toward better procedures, therefore, system variables must be our focus.

General Impairment Versus Suspect Bias

The distinction between system and estimator variables is often mentioned in the research literature and has made its way into some judicial rulings. In many settings, however, I believe a different contrast is more useful—the one separating *general-impairment factors* and *suspect-bias factors* (Wilford & Wells, 2013).

General-impairment factors are those that will make it more difficult for the witness to make any identification at all—for example, dim lighting at a crime scene or a distracting environment when the identification is attempted. (Note, by the way, that the first of these is an estimator variable and the second is a system variable.) Suspect-bias factors, on the other hand, are those that might guide the witness toward selecting the suspect from a lineup (e.g., prior familiarity with the suspect [estimator] or a poorly constructed photospread [system]).

General-impairment and suspect-bias factors interact with each other—and so a biased photospread will have more impact if the witness got a poor view in the first place. Even so, advocates are well-advised to keep these categories separate. To see why, consider a case in which a witness only viewed the perpetrator from, say, 50 yards away and with poor lighting, but who then later selects the suspect from a lineup. In this setting, the distance and lighting (general-impairment variables) provide no explanation for why the witness chose the suspect and not someone else; hence, a defense presentation showcasing just the distance and lighting would necessarily be incomplete.

C. WHAT DID THE WITNESS SEE?

In Chapter 2's discussion of perception, we considered many factors that can influence perceptual accuracy, and these factors obviously matter for the special case we are now considering—seeing (and later being able to identify) someone's face. It will be helpful, therefore, to review several of these factors here.

Lighting

It is obviously more difficult to see things in the dark than it is in the light. We can, however, add some important refinements to this claim: First, we noted in Chapter 2 that low light levels make it especially difficult to perceive *details* or *hues*. Both of these aspects of perception depend on cone vision, and cones operate poorly at low light levels. Second, when we discuss light levels, we often learn less than we need from "objective" measures such as those provided by a light meter or recorded via a camera. There are several reasons for this, including the fact that a camera's overall light sensitivity and its sensitivity to different wavelengths is different from the sensitivity of the human eye. The human eye, in addition, *varies* in its sensitivity, influenced by such factors as time-in-the-dark (governing the process of dark adaptation), the light levels the person had been exposed to prior to the crime (again relevant to dark adaptation), the person's age, the person's drug history, and more.

Even with these complications, though, light levels are surely relevant and need to be considered (albeit on a case-by-case basis). The angle of illumination is also important. During the day, light reaches the face from many sources (the sun, of course, but also from the many other surfaces that reflect ambient light toward the face). This pattern of illumination from several directions tends to diminish shadows. At night, though, with light coming from just one or two sources, there will often be strong shadows, and (as discussed in Chapter 2) this can distort perception overall and the perception of depth in particular.

Viewing Distance, Viewing Quality

Just as important is viewing *distance* and also the quality of a witness's vision (e.g., whether the person is near- or far-sighted), and these points need to be considered both at the crime scene (how far away was the witness from the crime?) and at the time of the identification. In a field showup (defined in Chapter 5), for example, the witness sometimes views the suspect only from a distance. Even with a photo identification, however, we cannot take the quality of the witness's vision for granted: I testified in one trial in which the witness reported that she'd barely been able to see the photomontage through her tear-filled eyes. In another trial, the witness, during his testimony, needed to take out his glasses to view the montage the attorney was handing him; the witness had not, however, been wearing his glasses when the police had initially shown him the montage.

Some agencies address this issue in a sensible and direct fashion: The San Francisco Police Department, for example, asks in their ID forms whether the person making the ID wears glasses or contact lenses. If the answer is "yes," the form requires the investigating officer to indicate whether the person making the ID was wearing these corrective lenses at the time of the original incident and at the time of the ID itself. Unfortunately, other agencies do not take this simple precaution, and so this is a point to keep track of in evaluating an ID.

Duration

We all understand that it will be difficult to identify a face that was viewed only briefly. However, people seem to be surprised by just how important the viewing duration is and by how little information is gained from viewing a face for only a few seconds.

Shapiro and Penrod (1986), based on a meta-analysis of identification studies, report a linear trend linking exposure time and identification accuracy: As exposure went down, accuracy proportionally went down as well. More concretely, though, consider a study by Memon, Hope, and Bull (2003). They showed witnesses a realistic videotape of a crime. Tested 45 minutes later, 90% of the participants who had seen the perpetrator for 45 seconds were able to identify him (although 41% of the participants shown a target-absent lineup picked someone innocent). In contrast, only 32% of the participants who had seen the perpetrator for 12 seconds were able to identify him, and a remarkable 85% of the participants in the 12-second condition, when shown a target-absent lineup, picked someone innocent. Thus, with a 12-second view and a target-absent line-up, mistaken identifications outnumbered correct responses by almost six-to-one.

Attention

Chapter 2 also emphasized the role of attention in governing perception, but how do we find out what a person was paying attention to during a crime? Sometimes, the case facts provide important clues. For example, Chapter 2 mentioned a case in which a witness commented on someone's hairstyle, and it turned out that the witness was a hair stylist and so cared deeply about (and tended to notice) such things. I also consulted on a case in which a witness made no mention of tattoos on the perpetrator but was insistent the perpetrator was wearing a short-sleeved shirt. As it turns out, the defendant had enormously prominent tattoos on his face, neck, and arms. These tattoos surely would have drawn the perceiver's attention *if* they were on the scene, and so the absence of the tattoos in the witness description was quite informative.

In addition, we noted in Chapter 2 that we need to know more than just what *object* someone is paying attention to. People usually have options for what they will focus on *within* the object, and the choice of options can have important implications for memory. In the earlier chapter, we gave an example of looking at a wristwatch: Someone who looks at the watch to find out what time it is may pay little attention to the font of the numerals and so may end up with no memory for the font. But how does this apply to faces?

Recall our earlier discussion of the "holistic" nature of face perception and thus the notion that we generally recognize faces by means of their overall configuration: how tall the face is relative to its width, the height of the nose relative to the eye spacing, and so on. Against this backdrop, consider studies in which researchers have urged participants to focus on features, urging them to pay attention to the exact shape of the nose, for example, or the precise thickness of the lips, or curve of the jaw. These instructions actually impair identification accuracy (Tanaka & Farah, 1993), presumably because these instructions draw viewers' attention away from the complex set of relationships often needed for face recognition. In other words, the instructions urge viewers to focus on the parts, rather than the (more informative) whole.

To be sure, sometimes a person does have an especially distinctive feature (remarkably thin lips, unusually bushy eyebrows, or a salient scar on the cheek). In such cases, noticing the feature will be helpful. (I consulted in one case in which the witness reported that his assailant had several large numbers tattooed on his forehead. A suspect was detained, minutes later, a short distance from the crime scene and indeed had the described tattoo. Identification in this case was not difficult.) But, in the more common cases, a feature orientation actually seems to be counterproductive.

For all these reasons, investigators should do all they can to learn (or, at least, reconstruct) what a witness paid attention to during the target event. Does the witness's report indicate that he or she paid attention to the face? Was the witness's attention perhaps drawn to aspects of the scene other than the face? And, importantly, if the witness was focused on the face, can we gain any information about how he or she was thinking about the face? In Chapter 2, I mentioned a shopkeeper who commented to the police that she had noticed the perpetrator because he resembled her cousin; this seems to be a witness who was in fact thinking about overall appearance and so a witness who should provide a strong ID. In contrast, imagine someone who says: "I really wanted to nail the guy, and so, during the robbery, I did everything I could to memorize his face. I tried to focus first on his eyes, then on his nose, then his chin . . ." This person has good intentions but a bad strategy and may be a less reliable witness.

Weapon Focus

We should also reprise another issue that came up in Chapter 2, concerned with so-called *weapon focus*. The idea here, again, is that if a weapon is on the scene, witnesses are likely to focus their attention on it. With this focus, the witness will end up paying less attention to other aspects of the scene—including the perpetrator's appearance. The result, of course, would be that identifications are less reliable in crimes involving a weapon (including perhaps, an implied weapon—such as a hand suspiciously held in a coat pocket), in comparison to crimes with no weapon.

This pattern—greater attention to the weapon, less attention to the face, and hence less accurate identifications—has been confirmed many times in the laboratory, and the size of the effect is impressive. In one study, the presence of a gun within a (videotaped) event cut the rate of correct identifications in half—from 35% correct identifications in the no-weapon condition to 15% in the weapon condition (Loftus, Loftus, & Messo, 1987).

However, we mentioned in the earlier chapter that several studies have scrutinized the records of actual police investigations, sorting these into a set of crimes in which a weapon was brandished and a set in which no weapon was in play. In these studies, in contrast to the lab data, good IDs are not less likely in "weapon crimes" than "non-weapon crimes," and, indeed, this is one of the few (and therefore notable) cases in which the simulation studies do not line up with the data from the field.

Even with this contrast in view, most researchers remain confident that the weapon-focus pattern is real and have offered various conjectures about why the pattern is not evident in police files. One plausible notion focuses on the duration of crimes, on the idea that actual witnesses do focus on the weapon initially, just like participants in the simulation studies. If the crime continues, though, witnesses eventually have an opportunity to shift their attention to the perpetrator's face, an opportunity not afforded by the briefer events typically studied in the simulations.

For now, the state of the art is unsettled. In some cases, the police reports make it clear that the witness was focused on the weapon. (And so the witness might say, "All I could see was that gun pointing at me . . .") In many other cases, however, caution suggests that we remain neutral about the importance of this factor—counting it neither as favoring nor undercutting the likelihood of a good identification.

Emotion

Another issue discussed in earlier chapters is also relevant here because a considerable quantity of evidence indicates that emotional arousal tends to improve memory, especially for aspects of an event that we would consider "central." However, it is not the case that "more emotion" uniformly points toward "better memory" and hence "better identifications." The reason is that, at some point, a witness can become so emotional that the emotionality disrupts the person's ability to focus, perceive, and eventually to remember (e.g., Deffenbacher, Bornstein, Penrod, & McGorty, 2004; Morgan et al., 2004; for more on stress, see Chapters 2 and 3).

Alcohol

It cannot be surprising that drunkenness undermines someone's ability to focus his or her eyes and attention and hence can undermine memory. But how exactly does alcohol influence face memory?

Drunkenness during an event can obviously compromise memory encoding. At high enough levels, drunkenness can produce blackouts—and hence no memory for an event (see Chapter 2). But, to understand alcohol's effects on facial recognition, we need a more precise analysis because the impact of inebriation depends on the circumstances. For example, when participants in one study were shown a target-present showup (so that they could detect and respond to the familiarity of the person shown), alcohol consumption had little or no effect on correct identification rates (Dysart, Lindsay, MacDonald, & Wicke, 2002). The data were different, though, if participants were shown a target-absent showup: The false identification rate in this condition was markedly higher (52%) for participants with a high blood alcohol level, compared to 22% for those with a lower blood alcohol level.

Disguise

Often, perpetrators try to make their faces difficult to identify via disguises of one sort or another. But how effective are disguises? The answer—inevitably—is variable because much depends on the face, and much depends on the disguise. Overall, though, disguises can have a powerful effect, especially if they hide an otherwise distinctive feature (e.g., Mansour et al., 2012; also see Davies, Shepherd, & Ellis, 1979).

Disguises can be effective, however, even if they obscure none of the face's features. The key here is that a disguise can alter the configuration of the face and, as we have discussed, it is generally the configuration that makes a face identifiable. To see how this works, consider the impact of a pullover cap, worn low. The cap will alter the vertical extent of the face and thus can change a dimension that provides a reference frame for evaluating other aspects of the face's appearance.

In one study, for example, a perpetrator wore a pullover cap in one condition but not in the other. Witnesses then saw the perpetrator with no hat in the line-up. Witnesses who had seen the perpetrator with no a hat during the crime (and thus undisguised) were accurate 45% of the time in their identifications; witnesses who had seen him wearing a hat (and so disguised) were accurate only 27% of the time (Cutler, Penrod, & Martens, 1987; also see Cutler, 2006; Hockley, Hemsworth, & Consoli, 1999; Mansour et al., 2012; MacLin & Malpass, 2003; Patterson & Baddeley, 1977).

Figure 4.1 provides a comical demonstration of how effective 'disguises' can be, even if the disguise hides none of the face's features. The figure depicts the so-called Clinton-Gore illusion (Sinha & Poggio, 1996). This term refers to a widely circulated photo showing former Vice-President Gore standing behind former President Clinton. The trick, of course, is that the two faces shown in the picture are identical. What distinguishes the two men is their position relative to the microphone and their hair, and these two points are sufficient to fool many people into missing the fact that the two faces are the same.

Finally, we should mention that some changes in appearance, functioning as "disguises," are not deliberate. Imagine, for example, an undisguised perpetrator who decides to grow his hair longer or to shave his beard. Or imagine a perpetrator who is in the midst of a drug-use episode during a crime but is then drug-free when photographed for a lineup. Drug use often changes the state of various muscles in the face (relaxing some, tensing others), thus changing overall appearance. These changes, too, can compromise witness accuracy.

Figure 4.1:
The "Clinton-Gore illusion." The two faces shown here are identical. What distinguishes the two men in the picture is their position and their hair, and these facts are enough to create the illusion that the picture shows former Vice-President Gore standing behind former President Clinton. Permission granted by Pawan Sinha and Tomaso Poggio, MIT.
web.mit.edu/bcs/sinha/papers/clinton_gore_nature.gif

Cross-Race Identification

We have alluded to another crucial factor guiding identification accuracy: race. The key is neither the witness's race on its own, nor the perpetrator's. Instead, the key is the relation between the witness's and perpetrator's race because people are appreciably better at recognizing individuals from their own race than they are in recognizing individuals from other races. A summary of the relevant evidence can be found in Meissner and Brigham's (2001) meta-analysis, pooling data from 5,000 research participants and 39 different studies. Overall, their analysis shows that the rate of correct identifications was 40% higher when participant and target were of the same race, compared to the situation when they were of different races. Conversely, the rate of false identifications (choosing someone innocent) was 56% higher when the participant and the target were of different races, compared to same-race identification attempts. This is, in other words, a powerful effect.

The question often arises of whether this effect is somehow tied to a witness's degree of prejudice or the witness's attitudes toward people of other races. Likewise, is the effect diminished if someone lives in an environment that is racially heterogeneous? The answer to the first question is "no"; there is no clear evidence of a link between racial attitudes and the cross-race effect. The answer to the second question is mixed. There is some suggestion that considerable contact with individuals of other races can diminish the cross-race effect, but the evidence is uneven, so that we simply need to be cautious about this point (Meissner & Brigham, 2001; for an intriguing discussion of the origins of the cross-race effect in *infants,* see Anzures et al., 2013).

Researchers are beginning to explore the boundaries of the cross-race (or, more ambitiously, "cross-group") phenomenon. Specifically, most of the evidence regarding this effect comes from white and African-American research participants trying to identify either white or African-American faces. A smaller quantity of data shows similar effects for whites and Asians seeking to identify each other. But, more broadly, similar patterns may emerge with many other groups (Brigham, Bennett, Meissner, & Mitchell, 2007). For example, there may be a cross-*age* effect similar to the cross-race effect, with people somewhat better at identifying individuals of their own age (Havard, Memon, Laybourn, & Cunningham, 2012; Rhodes & Anastasi, 2012; Wright & Stroud, 2002). How far this pattern extends, however (Whites identifying Native Americans? Native Americans identifying Latinos?) simply remains to be seen.

Finally, we note that the magnitude of the cross-race effect depends on circumstances, and so this effect will be more important for some investigations than for others. For example, cross-race identification seems to be especially impaired if the target faces were viewed in a group rather than individually (Pezdek, O'Brien, & Wasson, 2012). Conversely, one study suggests that intoxication impairs same-race identification more than cross-race identification, and so the size of the cross-race effect may be *diminished* if witnesses are intoxicated (Hilliar, Kemp, & Denson, 2010). And—crucially—there is obviously a diversity of faces within any racial group, and the size of the cross-race effect is shaped by the specifics of the face being viewed. Thus, viewers are more likely to associate a face with criminality if the face is "stereotypically African" (i.e., with some combination of darker skin, wider nose, and fuller lips; see, e.g., Blair, Judd, Sadler, & Jenkins, 2002; Eberhardt, Goff, Purdie, & Davies, 2004; Kleider, Cavrak, & Knuycky, 2012), and a "more African" face may also produce a larger cross-race effect in identification.

D. WHAT HAPPENS AFTER THE CRIME?

In the previous several sections, our focus has been on the circumstances of a crime: What was the lighting or the viewing distance? What was the witness paying attention to? But we also need to consider factors subsequent to the crime itself, prior to the identification attempt.

The Passage of Time

The amount of time that passes between an incident and an identification is (as noted in Chapter 3) called the "retention interval" and has a powerful impact on eyewitness identifications. (For some of the evidence, see, e.g., the meta-analysis reported by Deffenbacher et al., 2008; also see Dysart & Lindsay, 2007*b*.) More specifically, though, how rapidly do people forget a once-viewed face? The answer depends on the various factors already described in this chapter, on the idea that a lengthy, calm, and attentive view will lead to a stronger memory that will fade more gradually. But, as an illustration of the data pattern, consider a study included in the Deffenbacher meta-analysis: Pigott et al. (1990) tested memory in 47 bank tellers who had, for roughly two minutes, interacted with a stranger attempting to cash a forged money order. (The tellers were not aware at the time that the event was staged.) In a lineup conducted right after the incident, identification accuracy was quite good. Accuracy dropped by roughly 20%, though, if the identification procedure was delayed by just four hours. Tellers tested after a week had only a 50% chance of making an accurate ID. Notice, then, that (as we described in Chapter 3) the loss of memory is not uniform. Instead, the greatest loss happens soon after an event; forgetting then continues at a slower rate as time goes by. (For other studies comparing identification rates soon after a crime to those after a delay, see Behrman & Davey, 2001; Valentine et al., 2003.)

Is the Forgetting of Faces Irreversible?

Is there some way to "undo" the forgetting of a face? Overall, the answer seems to be no. Consider, for example, the "cognitive interview." This procedure, discussed in Chapter 3, is the best-documented technique for helping people recover apparently lost memories. Evidence suggests, however, that this procedure does nothing to help people "unforget" faces they have seen (Finger & Pezdek, 1999).

One study, however, points toward a more encouraging conclusion: The study employed a variant on the cognitive interview, guided by the fact that face recognition is (as we have discussed) "holistic." The so-called *holistic cognitive interview*, therefore, tries to encourage memory by drawing the witness's attention to the overall configuration of the face. In essence, the procedure invites the individual to think globally about the person being recalled: Did he or she seem friendly? Smart? Aggressive? Early results suggest that this approach may help bring the image of the person's face back to mind (e.g., Frowd, Bruce, Smith, & Hancock, 2008), holding open the prospect that, with this specialized interview, people can be led to fuller, more accurate recall of a face. The data on this point, however, are so far thin, and this is plainly an issue on which more research is needed.

Verbal Descriptions

Once the police have a suspect, they can present the suspect (or the suspect's picture) to the witness and ask if the witness recognizes the suspect. But what information can a witness provide before there is a suspect—information that might lead the police to the suspect? The answer, typically, is that investigators ask the witness to describe the face. That description can then be used by police as they narrow their search for the guilty party. In many cases, the description is also used later, at trial, to bolster an ID. And, in some cases, if there are inconsistencies between the description and a subsequent ID, defenders can use these as a basis for challenging the ID.

However, all of these uses of verbal description may be ill-advised. Several studies have examined the quality of these verbal descriptions, and, in truth, the quality is low. Often, the descriptions are relatively sparse: The witness might mention the perpetrator's gender and race and might say a bit about what the perpetrator was wearing—but these descriptors, even in combination, generally do little to narrow the field of possible suspects. (And, of course, clothing can be changed and so is of little value for the longer term.) Often, witnesses report their estimates of the perpetrator's height, weight, and age, but these estimates are commonly mistaken, sometimes by a wide margin. When pressed for more specific points (presence or absence of facial hair, for example), witnesses often indicate that they cannot recall these points.

Let's also be clear that witness descriptions are not just vague; they are often *wrong*. This latter claim is rooted both in laboratory studies and in scrutiny of actual court cases. Often, witnesses are mistaken about hair color, facial hair, skin tone, and more. (For a glimpse of the evidence, see, among others, Clark & Tunnicliff, 2001; Darling, Valentine, & Memon, 2008; Fahsing, Ask, & Granhag, 2004; Meissner, Sporer, & Schooler, 2007; van Koppen & Lochun, 1997; Wells, 1993.)

As a separate consideration, can we use a witness's verbal description as a basis for evaluating the witness's subsequent ID? If a witness has given a particularly full description, should we then put more faith in the ID? If the witness's verbal description contains errors, should we put *less* faith in the ID? The answer is "no" for both questions, because it turns out that there is little correspondence between the accuracy or completeness of a description, on the one side, and the likelihood of a correct identification, on the other. With this, there is no reason to challenge an ID simply because it is out of step with an earlier description provided by that witness (e.g., Pigott & Brigham, 1985; Meissner et al., 2007; Wells, 1985).

These points, for many people, seem contrary to common sense: A witness who offers a complete, detailed description would seem to be an attentive witness, perhaps a witness with a particularly good memory, and perhaps even a witness with a good memory *for faces*. It would seem sensible, then, that this is a witness who is more likely to make an accurate (and trustworthy) ID. Common sense, however, misleads us here, and part of the reason rests on something we have mentioned several times—the holistic nature of face recognition. We recognize faces on the basis of the entire configuration, and the relationships that define this configuration are often difficult to name or describe. (I cannot recall ever seeing a witness description along the lines of "the perpetrator's eyes were widely spaced relative to the vertical extent of his face," or "the thinness of the lips seemed out of proportion to the width of the nose.") By default, then, descriptions of faces tend to focus on the more readily verbalized individual features ("sharp chin, big nose, high cheek bones," and so on). As a result, this is a setting in which we can distinguish two types of information: the holistic information relevant to the recognition itself and the (less accurate, less discriminating) feature information relevant to the verbal description. In light of this contrast, it becomes less surprising that the quality of someone's description is separate from the likelihood of an accurate identification.

We can push this point one step further: If, in viewing a face, instructions explicitly encourage witnesses to focus on features, this will *help* the witnesses to give a better description but will undermine their ability to identify the face in a lineup. Conversely, instructions that encourage global judgments when the face is in view undermine the person's ability to describe the face but lead to better IDs (Meissner et al., 2007; Wells & Hryciw, 1984).

Indeed, think about what happens if we simply ask witnesses, shortly after a crime, to describe the perpetrator's face. This request may draw the witnesses' attention to the face's individual features (since it is these, and not the configuration, that can be described verbally), and this shift in focus can lead the witnesses to emphasize features in their subsequent thinking about the face. This sequence of events can produce an effect dubbed *verbal overshadowing,* in which the step of describing the face (a step that promotes a "feature focus" and draws attention away from the face's configuration) can actually undermine identification accuracy in a subsequent ID procedure.

The verbal overshadowing pattern has been documented in several studies (Meissner et al., 2007; Wells, Rydell, & Seelau, 1993). However, a number of studies have not shown this effect, and there are some suggestions that appropriate instructions can reverse this focus on features (e.g., LaPaglia & Chan, 2012). Therefore, the research certainly does not imply that police should cease asking for descriptions on the fear that the descriptions might undermine witness accuracy. But investigators should be alert to the fact that a verbal description can, in some settings, interact with what witnesses pay attention to in a face and how they remember the face.

Composite Drawing

There is one more way in which investigators can learn from a witness what the perpetrator looked like: Sometimes, witnesses help police to create a composite drawing of the perpetrator. In some jurisdictions, these composites are created by selecting features from a database of various noses, various eye shapes, and so on. In other jurisdictions, computer systems are used to generate the drawing; in still other cases, the composites are created through a complex (and nonstandardized) conversation between the witness and a police artist.

In light of this variability in procedure, it is difficult to make broad claims about the quality of these composites (Davies & Valentine, 2007; Kovera, Penrod, Pappas, & Thill, 1997). Some of the composites are surely of high quality (closely resembling the perpetrator), and many are not. However, three general points can be made. First, in many circumstances, the creation of the composite depends on the witness's ability to recall (and often to describe) the face (e.g., to describe the person to the police artist). Therefore, the low quality of these descriptions often constrains how good the composite drawing can be.

Second (and related), in many procedures, the creation of a composite depends on a feature-by-feature analysis of a face. This will be true, for example, if the procedure requires the witness to select proper eyes, a proper nose, and so on. Ironically, then, a witness who focused on someone's features during the crime may be better positioned to create a composite, but—with this focus on features rather than the overall configuration—less able to make an accurate identification. (For discussion, see Carlson, Gronlund, Weatherford, & Carlson, 2012; Wells & Hryciw, 1984.)

Third, even in the best of settings, there will be some degree of inaccuracy in the composite drawing, and, of course, the witness will have seen the composite. Indeed, the witness will (inevitably) have seen the composite more recently than the original face and may also have had a chance to scrutinize the composite for a longer time period than he or she had to see the perpetrator. As a result, the face-as-drawn will now be well established in the witness's memory and will be well-linked to the witness's memory of the original crime.

This set of circumstances makes it likely that witnesses will suffer some degree of "memory interference" from the composite drawing, with any inaccuracy in the drawing serving to dilute and distort the witnesses' original memory. On this basis, the rate of identification error may be higher for witnesses who have helped to construct a composite drawing, compared to witnesses who have not helped to create (or viewed) a composite. Several studies confirm these points (e.g., Jenkins & Davies, 1985; Mauldin & Laughery, 1981; Wells, Charman, & Olson, 2005; Wells & Hasel, 2007). Hence, composites will surely continue to be a necessary tool for law enforcement, but they should be used sparingly, given both the concern about their quality and concern about the prospect of the composite undermining witness memory.

CHAPTER 5

Identification Procedures

The risk of error in an identification is shaped by all of the factors reviewed in Chapter 4. But there are still more factors to consider: the various aspects of the identification procedure itself and also steps that can occur immediately after the identification. Let's emphasize that these are factors typically under the control of law enforcement (and so they are *system* variables, not *estimator* variables). As a result, these factors create an opportunity for improving the identification process, allowing us to move toward procedures that will increase identification accuracy—thus aiding the prosecution of the actually guilty and helping to protect the innocent.

A. THE FORMAT OF THE IDENTIFICATION PROCEDURE
Lineups Versus Showups

In many crimes, witnesses are shown a single photograph or a single individual and asked—roughly—"Is this the guy?" This procedure is usually called a *showup* and is contrasted with a *lineup*, in which the suspect is shown along with some number of other options (termed "fillers" or "distractors").

How common are showups? The answer varies from jurisdiction to jurisdiction and even from investigator to investigator within a jurisdiction, and so it is not surprising that estimates of frequency vary broadly (roughly: from 30% to 77%; Goodsell, Wetmore, Neuschatz, & Gronlund, 2013). Overall, though, it appears that roughly half of the identification procedures run by the police may be showups (e.g., Behrman & Davey, 2001; Flowe, Mehta, & Ebbesen, 2011; Gonzalez, Ellseworth, & Pembroke, 1993).

In some cases, the showup is conducted shortly after the crime: Police officers search the vicinity for plausible suspects; if they find one, they often do not have probable cause for an arrest or even any reason to transport this suspect. Indeed, at this stage, the suspect is often detained merely because he or she is in the neighborhood of the crime and resembles (perhaps only roughly) a witness description. However, these considerations provide a basis for detaining the suspect briefly, transporting the witness or victim to that location, and allowing the witness or victim to view and perhaps identify the suspect.

Most authorities agree, however, that this procedure is inherently suggestive. As one illustration, a "model policy" published in 2010 by the International Association of Chiefs of Police (IACP) states "The use of showups should be avoided whenever possible in preference for the use of a photo array or a lineup." This policy goes on to indicate specific boundaries on when showups should be used: "Use showups only when the suspect is detained within a reasonably short time frame following the offense," and "Do not use single suspect showups if probable cause to arrest the suspect has already been established."

Other guidelines echo these sentiments. For example, the California Commission on the Fair Administration of Justice issued its "Final Report" in 2008. The report says that "A single subject showup should not be used if there is probable cause to arrest the suspect" (p. 11). The Report goes on to urge that "lineups or photo spreads should be used for remaining witnesses after an identification [from a showup] is obtained from one witness."

Is the concern about showups justified? Data overall suggest that showups conducted in an optimal fashion, in optimal circumstances, may not be problematic. However, note the cautions built into the previous sentence, and showups are in truth fragile procedures—procedures in which things can easily go wrong.

Here is a glimpse of data reflecting what is arguably the best-case scenario: A 2003 meta-analysis compiled results from studies that, on aggregate, involved more than 3,000 research participants (Steblay, Dysart, Fulero, & Lindsay, 2003; also Dysart & Lindsay, 2007a). Summing across studies, overall accuracy rates were *higher* for showups than for lineups (69% vs. 51%), but, to a large extent, this was because participants were more likely to make a selection (and hence less likely to make no choice) for lineups. To see how this plays out, let's focus on target-present procedures (these are procedures that include the actual culprit in a showup or lineup). Across the many studies included in this meta-analysis, 46% of the participants looking at a showup said (roughly) "that's him," and, of course, with a target-present showup, 100% of these responses were correct. In contrast, with lineups, a much larger percentage of the participants—71%—made a selection, but, of these, only 64% chose the suspect. (The remainder chose one of the fillers.) Combining these numbers, the overall accuracy rates for target-present procedures are virtually tied: For showups, 46% of the selections made were correct (this number is 100% of the 46% of the witnesses who made a choice); for lineups, 45% of the selections made were correct (this number is 64% correct for the 71% of the witnesses who made a choice).

What about target-absent procedures (procedures in which the culprit is not one of the choices available to the witness)? In this setting, participants were still more likely to make a selection with lineups (43% make a selection) than with showups (15% make a selection). But note that with a target-absent procedure—lineup or showup—any choice is necessarily an error (because the correct response is "none of these"). Hence, the error rate is appreciably higher with lineups than with show-ups—by roughly 3 to 1.

These data might seem to encourage the use of showups (with equivalent accuracy rates with target-present lineups and many fewer errors with showups if the presentation is target-absent). Indeed, the authors of the meta-analysis conclude that "overall, the results present surprising commonality in outcome between presentation formats and—specific to target-absent displays—an apparent contradiction of the ambient knowledge that showups are more dangerous for innocent suspects than are lineups" (p. 535; for more recent data documenting similar ID rates with showups and live lineups, see Valentine, Davis, Memon, & Roberts, 2012; for some concerns, however, about how exactly we should assess the overall accuracy of show-ups, see Goodsell et al., 2013).

The Case Against Showups

Other considerations, though, add some complications to our assessment of show-ups, and argue in favor of the strong words of caution offered by (among others) the IACP. Let's start with the fact that there is another (and arguably more sensible) way to consider the data from the meta-analysis: With a target-absent lineup, as we have said, 43% of the research participants shown a lineup make a choice (and because the target is not included in the lineup in this condition, all of these choices are errors). With a target-absent showup, only 15% of the participants make a choice. The overall error rate, therefore, is plainly lower with showups than with lineups. But should our concern be with the "overall" error rate? With a lineup, we might expect these incorrect choices to be distributed among the various lineup members. Hence, if 43% of the participants make a (mistaken) choice and there are six faces shown in the lineup, then each face might be chosen only 7.2% of the time (43% divided by 6). Thus, an innocent suspect included in a six-person lineup is twice as likely to be chosen with a showup (15%) as with a lineup (7.2%).

Second, the data show that error rates for showups increase markedly if an innocent suspect happens to bear some resemblance to the suspect. In other words, showups on their own may not be problematic, but showups that offer the witness a plausible choice can be highly problematic. Indeed, the meta-analysis indicates that, if we focus on studies in which an innocent suspect does resemble the culprit, the error rate for showups is 50% higher than it is for lineups (Steblay et al., 2003).

Third, the accuracy rate with showups depends on how promptly after the crime the showup is conducted. Thus the IACP model policy mentioned earlier is justified when it urges that showups be used only if the suspect is detained "within a reasonably short time frame following the offense." But what is "a 'reasonably short time frame"? One study examined 500 identifications in actual police cases. When the showups were performed within minutes of a crime, they were just as accurate as lineups. If the showups were delayed, however, by just two hours, more than half the witnesses mistakenly "identified" someone in a showup, compared to a rate of only 14% false identification with (target-absent) photo lineups (Yarmey, Yarmey, & Yarmey, 1996; see also Dysart & Lindsay, 2007*b*).

Research studies also make it clear that showups are heavily influenced by what is called "clothing bias," in which witnesses are likely to select someone innocent in a showup if the suspect happens to be wearing clothing similar to that worn by the perpetrator. This bias can be demonstrated (although in a weakened form) even if the clothing is not especially distinctive (Dysart, Lindsay, & Dupuis, 2006; Gonzalez et al. 1993; Yarmey & Yarmey, 1997). Indeed, witnesses often confirm the presence of clothing bias in the comments they make about their own showup IDs. In cases I have reviewed, for example, it is common for witnesses to acknowledge that "I knew it was him because that's his coat," or "the first thing I noticed was the sweatshirt," and so on.

Finally, showups lack an important safeguard that is built into any lineup procedure. Imagine a witness who does not remember the perpetrator's face but is determined nonetheless to make an identification. (Perhaps the witness is angry and distressed that the investigation might be stalled if there is no identification. Or perhaps the person just wants to show that he or she has a good memory.) How will this play out? With a lineup, this casual, careless witness has an 83% chance (5 out of 6) of selecting one of the "fillers," someone known to be innocent. The officer will then immediately know that the witness has made a bad pick and will discount the identification. In a showup, in contrast, this careless witness will say "yes" to the only option in view, and the officer has no way to tell if this is a genuine identification or just a selection for the sake of making a selection. As a result, the error will not be discounted, and thus a bad pick in a showup can be misleading and deeply consequential.

Live Lineups Versus Photos

Movies and television routinely depict a scene in which a crime witness stands behind a one-way mirror and watches as six suspects shuffle in, each holding a number. One by one, the suspects step forward, perhaps say a few words, perhaps turn left or right, and then step back. This scene is a poor reflection of how identifications are usually conducted. In the United States, it is far more common that an ID is collected via photographs: Wogalter, Malpass, and McQuiston (2004), for example, surveyed police and reported that photo lineups are roughly three times more common than live lineups. Thus, the witness might see a page with two rows of photos and three photos in each row. The witness then makes a judgment from this *photomontage* (or "photo lineup," "photospread," or, less formally, a "six-pack"). The photos might be booking photos, driver's license photos, or photos taken from some other source.

In the United Kingdom, in contrast, identifications are routinely conducted in specialized facilities known as "identification suites." For many years, witnesses were shown a live lineup (an "identity parade") in these suites; now, in many jurisdictions across the UK, witnesses are instead shown a succession of *videos*, produced by the Video Identification Parade Electronic Recording (VIPER) system. Each suspect is in view for approximately 15 seconds, looking initially into the camera, then slowly turning left and right to provide a profile view.

How do photo lineups compare to video lineups or live lineups? Several studies have asked this question, and the results are mixed, but with some indication that dynamic images (whether live or on video) lead to better identifications than do static images (photographs) and that video lineups may be less prone to bias than static lineups (e.g., Valentine & Heaton, 1999). There is also some suggestion that, in actual police investigations, electronically presented identifications lead to better identifications compared to live lineups—but these benefits may reflect the lineup composition and not the medium per se (Valentine & Heaton, 1999; Valentine et al., 2003; for an examination of formats when children are witnesses, see Havard, Memon, Clifford, & Gabbert, 2010; for examination of rates of *identification error* when children are witnesses, see Pozzulo, 2006). Specifically, in constructing a live lineup, police typically use as fillers people who happen to be around at the time of the lineup, and these people may not be well-matched to the suspect. (For more on "matching," see the section on Choosing the Fillers.) In constructing a photo or video lineup, in contrast, police often draw on large prerecorded databases (i.e., collections of other photos or other videos). As a result, live lineups often contain lower quality fillers, a factor that can undermine accuracy.

But why are the data "mixed" in comparisons between photo lineups and video (or live) lineups? The reason, in brief, is that video and live lineups do provide more information to the witness, but the value of this information is low, and this "extra" information is often ignored by witnesses.

This assessment is rooted in several facts. First, some suspects are distinctive in their posture, body shape, or movement, and this point will sometimes produce an advantage with video or live lineups (which can, of course, provide this broader information; cf. Cutler & Penrod, 1988). However, most people are rather ordinary in these regards—and so they have a body shape close to the average—with the result that this advantage of video or live lineups is likely to be small and inconsistent.

In addition, even when there is information in someone's posture or body shape, witnesses are likely to ignore this information. During the crime itself, witnesses are more likely to focus on the perpetrator's face, and, indeed, studies of eye movements confirm that, in most events, viewers spend a lot of the event duration pointing their eyes at the faces in the scene (see Chapter 2). Then, during the identification, evidence suggests that, if the suspect's face is visible and at least somewhat distinctive (relative to the other faces in the lineup), witnesses tend to ignore bodily appearance (Rice, Phillips, Natu, An, & O'Toole, 2013)—and so, in essence, they focus on the lineup options "from the neck up."

Third, live lineups and (in some versions) video lineups can provide audio information—specifically, a sample of the suspects' speech. But here, too, we lose little by omitting this information: Overall, voice recognition is less accurate than face recognition, and so "voice-less" identifications are giving up a cue of uncertain quality. In addition, when both visual and auditory information are available, witnesses seem to suffer some sort of distraction or interference and do less well in identifying either (McAllister, Dale, Bregman, McCabe, & Crotton, 1993; Yarmey, 1986; for more on voice identification, see Chapter 6).

For these reasons, it is not surprising that the advantages of video or live lineups are small and inconsistent. Moreover, let's note that these points also have implications for in-court identifications. These identifications are sometimes lauded because (among other points) they allow a full-body view and allow the witness to hear the suspect's voice. As noted, though, these points of praise for in-court IDs are not well-grounded in fact. (We will return to the topic of in-court identifications later in the chapter.)

Sequential Versus Simultaneous Lineups

There has been considerable debate in recent years about another way that lineups can vary: In a *simultaneous* lineup, all of the faces (typically, six) are in view at the same time. In a *sequential* lineup, the faces are brought into view one by one and the witness must make a yes-or-no decision for each before seeing the next.

The theory behind the sequential lineup is straightforward: With a simultaneous lineup, witnesses may adopt what is called a "relative-judgment strategy." The idea is that the witnesses ask themselves, "Of these faces, which one looks most like my memory of the criminal?" This strategy is unproblematic if the perpetrator is in fact included in the lineup because presumably the perpetrator will look more like the face in the witness's memory than anyone else will. (After all, the memory is a memory for the perpetrator.) But consider what happens if the police have targeted the wrong individual (and so the lineup is target-absent). In this case, it is a matter of simple logic that, no matter who is in the lineup, someone will look "more like" the perpetrator than the others do, and so, if this is the basis for selection, the witness will go ahead and select this (innocent) person's picture.

The situation is different, though, with sequential lineups. (And here we'll start with a "pure" version of the sequential lineup, in which witnesses are allowed only one pass through the pictures; we'll return in a moment to a situation in which witnesses are allowed a second or third "lap" through the lineup.) In this setting, with pictures in view only one at a time, direct, side-by-side "comparison shopping" is not possible. And, with other pictures still to be viewed, the only comparison a witness could make is "best of the ones I've seen so far," and this is a weak basis on which to make a choice. As a result, the sequential lineup should encourage an "absolute-judgment strategy," in which witnesses ask themselves, for each picture, "Is this face close enough to my memory to justify a selection?"

The idea, then, is that the shift from simultaneous to sequential lineups will have little impact with target-present lineups (because, in that case, the relative-judgment strategy is unproblematic). The sequential lineup should be preferable, though, with target-absent lineups (because here the sequential lineups will discourage the bad picks invited by the relative-judgment strategy). These predictions turn out to be largely correct, with a number of laboratory studies indicating little difference between simultaneous and sequential procedures with target-present lineups but with sequential lineups producing a considerable benefit (and, specifically, fewer "bad picks") if the suspect is not present in the lineup (Steblay, Dysart, Fulero, & Lindsay, 2001; Steblay, Dysart, & Wells, 2011).

As we have emphasized many times, however, it is important to confirm laboratory findings with field data, and, in fact, the sequential lineup has been several times tested with actual police investigations. One widely publicized test seemed to contradict the laboratory data and suggested that simultaneous lineups were preferable (Mecklenburg, Bailey, & Larson, 2008). However, several authors have argued that this study was seriously flawed. Some of the problems were conceptual, based on how this field study was designed (Schacter et al., 2008). But, in addition, there were flaws in how the study was implemented, because the set of crimes investigated via simultaneous lineups was different from the start from the set of crimes investigated via sequential lineups (Steblay, 2011). As a result of this contrast, there is no way to interpret the study's outcome because the comparison, to use the common phrase, was not conducted on a "level playing field."

A more compelling study was subsequently conducted under the supervision of the American Judicature Society. (A full report, released in 2011, is available through the AJS web page, at www.ajs.org/wc/ewid/ewid_report.asp). This study evaluated roughly 500 identifications that had been conducted in actual police cases in four jurisdictions nationwide. In these data, sequential and simultaneous lineups produced virtually identical rates of "correct picks" (i.e., selecting the suspect)—27% sequential versus 26% simultaneous. (Statistical analyses indicate this difference is small enough that it is plausibly a matter of measurement error and not a genuine difference.) The lineup procedures differed markedly, however, in their rates of "bad picks," with simultaneous lineups producing 50% more of these (18% vs. 12%).

These results seem to provide strong support for the sequential procedure. Even so, debate about the sequential lineup continues, with part of the debate focused on the theory behind the sequential lineup. We have already discussed the idea that this new format encourages absolute judgments rather than relative judgments. A different possibility is that the sequential lineup simply encourages witnesses to be more cautious in their selections. (Technically, the idea is that sequential lineups encourage a more conservative "response criterion.") As a result, the sequential lineup decreases both the number of incorrect choices *and* the number of correct choices.

This challenge to the sequential lineup does have some basis in fact—because studies typically do show a decrease in accurate picks with this procedure alongside the decrease in bad picks. Even so, most researchers believe there are powerful reasons to prefer the sequential lineup over the more traditional simultaneous lineup. Among other considerations, studies continue to show that the benefits of the sequential lineup (the decrease in mistaken selections) are statistically much larger than the costs (the decrease in correct selections). In addition, some large-scale studies (including the American Judicature Society study just described) have failed to document this supposed cost of the sequential lineup. (For glimpses of this sometimes heated debate, however, see Clark, 2012; Clark, Moreland, & Gronlund, 2014; Dobolyi & Dodson, 2013; Gronlund, Anderen, & Perry, 2013; Gronlund, Carlson, Dailey, & Goodsell, 2009; Gronlund, Goodsell, & Amderson, 2012;

Gronlund, Wixted, & Mickes, 2014; Malpass, Tredoux, & McQuiston-Surrett, 2009; McQuiston-Surrett, Malpass, & Tredoux, 2006; Mickes, Flow, & Wixted, 2012; Wells, 2014; Wells, Steblay, & Dysart, 2012; Wixted, Gronlund, & Mickes, 2014.)

There has also been continuing discussion about the exact procedure that should be used with sequential lineups. For example, there is a broad concern that, with a sequential lineup, witnesses will become nervous as they progress through the lineup, with their reasoning something like this: "I'm almost at the end of the series, and I haven't made a choice yet. I guess I need to pick someone soon, before I'm completely through my options." On this basis, witnesses might become overeager to make a selection later in the series, and correspondingly careless. We can solve this problem, though, by not telling the witness how many faces there are in the series and perhaps encouraging the witness to believe that the series of faces may be quite long. On this basis, the witness will feel no pressure to make a choice ("before it's too late") when looking at the fourth, fifth, and sixth faces, and so will not become careless when looking at these faces (Horry, Palmer, & Brewer, 2012).

Likewise, we mentioned earlier that, in the "pure" version of the sequential lineup, witnesses are allowed to examine the photos just once—with no provision for a second or third "lap" through the pictures. The concern, of course, is that these subsequent laps might allow precisely the sort of comparisons, from one face to another, that this lineup procedure is trying to prevent. A study by Steblay et al. (2011) indicates that this concern is well-founded: Witnesses do make more selections from the lineup if they are allowed a second lap through the pictures, but these additional selections tend to include more errors than correct identifications; as a result, the overall accuracy of the lineup (measured, as one option, as the ratio between accurate picks and inaccurate ones) is better with just one lap through the pictures (also see Horry et al., 2012). It remains to be seen, however, whether law enforcement will adopt the strict procedure (with no laps allowed) that these findings suggest is best; if not, then we may lose some of the hoped-for benefits of the sequential lineup.

How should we put all these points together? Overall, the data do favor the sequential lineup over the more traditional (simultaneous) format. However, policy makers considering a shift in procedure should be alert to the studies suggesting that this shift may not be cost-free and that the benefits of the sequential procedure may depend on the details of how these lineups are implemented. Even so, most researchers would recommend a change to the sequential lineup, pointing to the research findings (from both lab and field) indicating that this change can powerfully increase the overall accuracy of witness identifications.

B. WHO'S IN THE LINEUP?
Choosing the Fillers

In the late 1990s, the U.S. Department of Justice issued a set of guidelines for collecting eyewitness evidence; the guidelines are available on several sites online.

Among other suggestions, the guidelines direct law enforcement (p. 29) to "include only one suspect in each identification procedure" and to "select fillers who generally fit the witness' description of the perpetrator." Above all, the guidelines note that "The investigator shall compose the lineup in such a manner that the suspect does not unduly stand out."

But what does it mean for the suspect to "stand out"? We can distinguish two ways in which this requirement might not be met—and thus two ways in which a lineup might be biased. First, in some lineups, the suspect stands out on visual grounds—his picture is bigger, or darker, or on a distinctively colored background, making it immediately different from the other pictures. In some cases, the suspect's picture looks angrier than the others, or more frightened, or more like a "stereo-typical criminal" (Flowe & Humphries, 2011). This sort of bias, inherent in the visual images themselves, is sometimes called "oddball bias."

Second, in some lineups, the suspect does not stand out visually but is the only suspect who is a plausible choice in light of other information known to the witness. For example, imagine a lineup in which the photos show men ranging in hair length and also varying in their skin tone. In this scenario, it might be difficult to argue that there is an oddball bias because the pictures are diverse enough so that no single picture stands out on its own. But now imagine that the witness insisted to the police that the perpetrator was a pale-skinned guy with very short hair. The witness is likely to remember these words and so is likely to exclude from consideration the four or five photos incompatible with this description. As a result, only one or two of the photos shown is plausible, and so there is a problem of "plausibility bias." The photo lineup nominally has six photos in it, but the witness will only take one or two of these photos seriously as options. The *nominal size* of the lineup might be six, but the *functional size* is much smaller, and hence the lineup is biased, drawing attention to the suspect's face.

Before pressing on, we should note that a lineup can be biased *away* from the suspect as well as toward him. Concretely, I have observed lineups in which one of the fillers stands out (either through oddball bias or by virtue of being an especially good match to the witness description). In this case, a pick of the suspect is all the more impressive. But, in such a case, a witness not choosing the suspect has provided an ambiguous response: Perhaps the witness has only a poor memory of the crime, or perhaps the witness's memory is fine, but the witness was drawn off track by the biased lineup. (In this sort of case, then, the defense might argue that the witness's failure to pick the suspect is exculpating, but this argument would actually be unpersuasive: The failure to make a pick might reflect a biased lineup rather than an innocent defendant.) These observations make it clear that bias in either direction, toward or away from the suspect, can be problematic.

Avoiding oddball bias is straightforward: If the photos are uniform, with every picture the same size, on the same background, and so on, oddball bias is not a concern. But this bias can be avoided even with a nonuniform set of photos: If three of the photos are large and three are small, then the witness will likely realize that variations in size are irrelevant to the procedure; if each photo shows someone in a different color shirt, then this attribute won't draw attention to the suspect. The key is that the photos should either be uniform *or* should vary a lot; in either case, worry about oddball bias can be set aside.

What about plausibility bias? Here, the investigator has a choice: He or she can choose fillers who visually resemble the perpetrator or can choose fillers who fit the witness's initial description of the perpetrator (i.e., the description typically collected early in the investigation, soon after the crime). Most research indicates that the latter strategy is preferable, and identification accuracy tends to be higher when the fillers are matched to the witness's description rather than to the suspect's appearance.

Let's acknowledge, though, that there is ongoing debate about the relative advantages of matching to description as opposed to matching to suspect. (See, among others, Clark & Tunnicliff, 2001; Clark, Rush, & Moreland, 2013; Darling, Valentine, & Memon, 2008; Fitzgerald, Price, Oriet, & Charma, 2013; Gronlund et al., 2012; Tunnicliff & Clark, 2000; Wells, Rydell, & Seelau, 1993.) Even so, evidence does suggest that, in most circumstances, match to description is preferred.

But if, in fact, match to description is preferable, why should this be? One plausible answer begins with a point already mentioned: If a witness has offered a description to the police, then he or she is likely to carry some version of that description in memory at the time of the lineup. As a result, the witness is likely to use that description as a guide in making a selection. Thus, if the witness described the perpetrator as having (say) long hair and a narrow face, then the witness will scrutinize the lineup for faces having these traits. (This is, of course, the concern we alluded to in defining plausibility bias.) From the investigators' perspective, though, we want the witness to look at all of the faces in the lineup and to make a selection based not on a match to a verbal description, but on a match to some sort of visual memory. This goal is achieved if multiple (and perhaps all of the) faces in the lineup match this description.

At risk of redundancy, here is a different way to make this point. There is no value for law enforcement if the witness's pick from the lineup simply echoes information already available. Imagine a witness who has already told the police the perpetrator was skinny, had big eyes, a large mustache, and thin lips, and now selects from the lineup the only option who has all of these traits. In this scenario, the witness is merely reaffirming a description already given. Indeed, even if the witness had no memory other than this description (i.e., no visual sense of the perpetrator's face), he or she might still make this same pick. In fact, imagine that the witness had told these descriptions to someone else who was not a witness to the crime. That person would presumably make the same pick from the lineup, guided by these descriptors, thus making it plain that, in this scenario, the lineup choice provides no information beyond a repetition of assertions already in the police reports.

The Mock-Witness Paradigm

We have just discussed what police might do (and arguably should do) to minimize bias in a lineup. But how can we decide if they have succeeded in this effort? How can we decide if a lineup is biased or not? Traditionally, the courts have relied on a subjective assessment—and specifically have relied on whether the montage appears biased to the judge, the attorneys, and the jury. The scientific community has argued, however, that an objective measure of bias is far preferable—and, in particular, a measure of bias that is quantifiable, not influenced by any individual viewer's (potentially idiosyncratic) assessment, and immune to the prejudice that any person attached to the case might have. Moreover, let's emphasize that whether a lineup is biased is to some extent "in the eyes of the beholder." Thus, what we need to ask is whether the lineup was biased *in the witness's view*, because this is the bias, if present, that would have guided the witness's choice. So how can we find out if a lineup was biased for a particular witness?

Let's start with the fact that the witness's perspective may be different from that of the judge's or attorneys'. These professionals, after all, have likely seen many photo lineups during their careers, and so they have a sense of how lineups vary in their lighting, in the face's position within each picture, and so on. In contrast, the actual witness may never have seen a photo lineup before, and it is plausible that the montage may look differently if viewed through "naïve eyes."

Note also that the actual witness presumably came to the montage with no prior information about the suspect and so, in this regard, may have a perspective different from that of the attorneys or, for that matter, the jurors. (By the time the jurors see a photo lineup entered as evidence in a trial, they have heard other elements of the trial and seen the defendant sitting in the courtroom; these are obviously experiences that the actual witness did not have prior to seeing the montage.) Hence, if we want to know how the photo lineup looked through the witness's eyes, we need to deal with these concerns as well.

Finally—and most importantly—someone who looks "attractive" or "mean" or "crazed" in one person's eyes may not have these traits in another person's view. Someone who strikes one viewer as "light-skinned" may appear different to a viewer with a different comparison base. Someone who looks "Asian" to one viewer may appear to be Korean and not of some other Asian ethnicity to a more discriminating perceiver. Thus, on these grounds, too, we want to find out how the lineup appears to people with a perspective similar to the witness's.

For all of these reasons, researchers are skeptical about a reliance on judges', attorneys', or jurors' perceptions in judging a lineup. There is simply no reason to believe that the lineup will look the same through these person's eyes as it did through the witness's. Instead, researchers recommend a procedure called the *mock-witness paradigm* as a measure of lineup fairness (Malpass et al., 2007; McQuiston & Malpass, 2002; Wells & Bradfield, 1999). This paradigm is widely used, standardized in its procedure, and broadly accepted in the scientific community. Numerous studies have evaluated this procedure and confirmed that it does accurately detect bias that might be present in a specific photo lineup.

For this procedure, an investigator recruits "mock witnesses"—people who will, in effect, serve as simulators for the witness. These are people who did not see the crime and so have no memory of the crime to draw on. When we ask them, therefore, to make a selection from the montage, they cannot possibly be guided by a memory of the crime. Instead, their selection can only be guided by any bias that might be inherent in the montage, and that is, of course, what the paradigm is intended to measure.

Following the logic already in view, we want mock witnesses who have a background as similar as possible to that of the actual witness. They should be of the same race and gender as the actual witness and of roughly the same age. They should have the same degree of experience with viewing montages as the witness. (In most cases, this means no experience at all.) If possible, mock witnesses should be recruited from groups who live in neighborhoods with the same ethnic mix as the actual witness's neighborhood. In all of these regards, we're guided by our goal of asking how the montage looked through the actual witness's eyes, and it's this goal that demands recruitment of mock witnesses likely to have a similar perspective.

The mock-witness procedure is then run with a clearly defined script (a script that can then be made available for scrutiny to any interested party). The person using this script (i.e., the person administering the procedure) should not know which photo in the montage is the police suspect. In this way, this administrator is "blind" to any outcome that might be desired by the parties in the case and so cannot possibly influence the results toward or away from that desired outcome. (In running this procedure, I sometimes recruit a student assistant, making certain that the student will follow the script, but also making certain that the assistant does not know who the suspect is. I have sometimes worked with attorneys who hire an investigator to run this procedure using the same requirements.)

In this procedure, mock witnesses are generally told that the procedure is assessing a lineup used in an actual police case; this point should encourage the mock witnesses to take their (somewhat peculiar) task seriously. In addition, we have already noted that actual witnesses are likely to recall the description of the perpetrator that they gave to the police and will be guided by that description in their inspection of the lineup. Therefore, as part of the overall effort toward matching the mock witnesses' perspective to that of the actual witness, the mock witnesses are given this description. Thus, they are told that, soon after the crime, a witness described the perpetrator as tall and thin (or short and pale, or whatever the words were, relying on the exact words contained in the police reports).

If the photomontage in a case is fair, then the photo of the suspect will not stand out in any way, either visually (through oddball bias) or via a match with the description (i.e., plausibility bias). In this case, the mock witnesses will, in truth, have no systematic basis for making their selections. Therefore, they will be forced to choose at random, and so their choices should spread out evenly across the six photos—with each photo receiving its "fair share": one-sixth of the choices (roughly 17%). If, in contrast, the defendant's photo is distinctive or especially plausible as a choice, then this photo will stand out even to these viewers who (again) have no knowledge of the crime. On this basis, the photo will receive more than its one-sixth share, and hence we can use the size of the share as an objective indication of bias.

To make this concrete, an attorney brought me one case in which a witness had described the perpetrator as having a "thin" face. The police developed a suspect and placed his face into a photomontage. In my perception, the suspect's picture stood out in the montage because his face did look (by my standards) rather thin, and none of the other pictures looked thin to me at all. However, this evaluation could not be taken seriously—what if my standards for "thinness" were different from the witness's? And, worse, I looked at the montage already knowing who the suspect was, and it is plausible that this biased my assessment.

This is a scenario in which a mock-witness procedure can be useful, and, in fact, we ran the procedure: We recruited several dozen individuals of the same age, gender, and ethnicity as the witness, and (skipping some details) we told them: "A crime witness described the perpetrator of the crime as 'thin.' On this basis, which of these photos do you think is most likely to be the perpetrator?" Roughly two-thirds of these mock witnesses chose the suspect's picture—making it clear that the picture did stand out and that, from the witness's point of view, the photomontage did draw attention to the suspect.

This sort of test has (in my work and much more broadly) been used with many photospreads, and, in my own experience, I can say that most spreads survive this test. In other words, with most photospreads, the mock witnesses do choose in an essentially random fashion, indicating no bias. This is an important point because it provides assurance that this procedure is not setting an unrealistically high standard.

But is bias measured in this fashion actually detecting what we want it to measure? Let's say that we evaluate a particular photospread with the mock-witness procedure and find that it is biased. In other words, a large proportion of the mock witnesses—people who have, by definition, not seen the crime—choose the suspect's picture. Does this mean that witnesses who *have* seen the crime will be less accurate if their memories are probed with this photospread? The answer is yes, and studies indicate that lineups that are biased (according to this measure) do indeed undermine witness accuracy (e.g., Malpass, Tredoux, & McQuiston-Surrett, 2007). On this basis, this does seem a reasonable measure to use in any case in which lineup bias is suspected as a problem.

Altering the Pictures

One last point about photospreads can be dealt with quickly: Sometimes a witness describes the perpetrator as having a prominent tattoo, scar, or some other obvious identifying mark. In some cases, these marks are themselves enough to allow an identification, but, in other cases, there is still a need for a lineup: Was it *this* man with a scar who attacked you? Or perhaps *this* man with his scar?

These cases create a challenge for investigators: How can they find pictures to fill out the lineup—pictures that match these (arguably unusual, perhaps unique) descriptors? The answer is contained in the Department of Justice guidelines, mentioned earlier. Those guidelines explicitly invite investigators to *alter the photographs* used in a photo lineup. Specifically, the guidelines urge investigators to "create a consistent appearance between the suspect and fillers with respect to any unique or unusual feature (e.g., scars, tattoos) used to describe the perpetrator by artificially adding or concealing that feature" (pp. 29–30). Of course, these changes must be guided by the overarching principle (already quoted) that the "investigator shall compose the lineup in such a manner that the suspect does not unduly stand out," but, with this proviso, there is no obstacle (from the perspective of law enforcement or the perspective of research) to altering the pictures. Therefore, if the perpetrator had a knit cap on during the crime, it seems plausible that the investigator might add a knit cap to all of the pictures in the lineup. If the perpetrator had a moustache at the time of the crime or was wearing sunglasses, these features, too, can be added to the pictures. With the obligation that they not draw attention to the suspect, these changes can, in some cases, increase the likelihood of an accurate identification. (For more on this point, see Badham, Wade, Watts, Woods, & Maylor, 2012.)

C. INSTRUCTIONS
"May or May Not Be Present"

Witnesses often seem hesitant to reject a lineup—that is, they prefer not to say "I'm sorry, but I don't recognize any of these guys." In some cases, this preference may derive from the witness's trust in the police and, with that, the belief that the police would launch an ID attempt only when they have a strong suspect. On this basis, many citizens will assume that the perpetrator's face is included in the lineup, and so they will be hesitant to reject the lineup.

In other cases, the witness might think that rejecting the lineup would reveal that he or she had been inattentive during the crime or has a bad memory—again, suggestions that many witnesses would prefer to avoid. In addition, it seems inevitable that witnesses to (or victims of) a crime will be eager to see the investigation and prosecution move forward; they certainly don't want to do anything that might obstruct the investigation. This, too, can shape how they approach the lineup because witnesses might fear that rejecting the lineup will slow police progress in solving the crime.

For all these reasons, there is a concern that witnesses, not wishing to reject the lineup, will go ahead and make a selection even if they are not certain. Their specific selection, in this setting, will likely be guided by the relative-judgment strategy already described: They will select the individual in the lineup who (relative to the other options) most resembles their memory of the perpetrator.

These various suggestions all lead to the prediction that we can improve identification accuracy by providing instructions, just before an identification attempt, that offset the attitudes just described. And, in fact, this prediction turns out to be correct. Different jurisdictions each have their own version of the preidentification instructions, but the key element is to let the witness know that the perpetrator may or may not be in the lineup and that saying "I recognize no one" is a legitimate response. Some jurisdictions add the point that it is just as important to clear innocent persons from suspicion as it is to identify guilty parties. Some jurisdictions also note that the investigation will continue even if the witness is unable to make a response.

We'll refer to this family of instructions as the MOMN instruction (our own abbreviation for "*may or may not be there*"). Studies indicate that this instruction does have a large impact. In one meta-analysis, the data indicated little effect of the MOMN instruction if the perpetrator was actually included in the lineup (although, for debate on this claim of "no cost," see Clark, 2005; 2012; Clark et al., 2014; Steblay, 2013; Wells, Memon, & Penrod, 2006). However, the instruction markedly decreased false identifications with target-absent lineups (Steblay, 1997; 2013; Wells, Steblay, & Dysart, 2012).

Most researchers strongly recommend, therefore, that the MOMN instruction be given and argue that if this instruction is not given, then the risk of a false identification is sharply increased. Note also that this instruction is appropriate for all identification procedures, and it is therefore worrisome that some jurisdictions require a MOMN instruction for lineups but have no such required instruction for showups.

Note in addition that simply providing the MOMN instruction may not be enough especially because, in some jurisdictions, the phrasing of this instruction seems (to my eye) rather clumsy, so that understanding is not guaranteed. (For example, in some jurisdictions, witnesses are told that "the fact that the photographs are shown to you should not influence your judgment." I've never been sure what this sentence is trying to convey.) This therefore provides an obvious point in which police procedures could be improved—by, at the least, asking witnesses if they have understood the instruction and, better, seeking some means of confirming this understanding.

In addition, in some investigations, the police provide the MOMN instruction but then undercut the instruction in some way. Occasionally, an officer might convey, via tone of voice perhaps, that the instruction is just a required ritual and not to be taken seriously. Or perhaps an officer might inadvertently "leak" information (verbally or non-verbally) that suggests to the witness that, despite the MOMN instruction, the perpetrator *is* present in the lineup.

How serious are these concerns? In one study, participants were given appropriate instructions (including the MOMN instruction) before viewing a target-absent lineup (Quinlivan et al., 2012). In this setting, a number of participants (39%) still made a selection from the lineup (and, of course, with a target-absent lineup, any selection is by definition an error). Another group of participants was run through the same procedure (including the MOMN instruction) but were led to believe that they would be able to pick out the "right person" in the lineup. In other words, they were led to an expectation that could undermine the MOMN sentiment. The effect of this expectation was powerful—doubling (to 83%) the number of lineup selections (again, all of which were necessarily incorrect with a target-absent lineup).

Proper instructions can also be undermined if witnesses know how other witnesses have responded to the same lineup; here, too, expectations about the lineup seem to trump instructions. In one study, some participants were told that a co-witness had selected photo number 2 from the lineup. In this setting, 15% of the participants decided to make the same selection—even though, in a control condition (in which participants heard no information about a co-witness), zero participants chose photo number 2 (Hasel, 2012; for related data, see Levett, 2013).

As one more illustration, Pezdek (2009, p. 36) envisions a case in which, after a crime, an eyewitness has no contact with the police for several months "and then suddenly the stolen property is returned and she is asked to attend a lineup." In this setting, the witness seems quite likely to assume the lineup does contain the suspect, no matter what words of instruction are offered. Hence, in this and other such cases, it is worth asking, when evaluating an identification, both whether the proper instructions were given and whether the instructions were understood and believed.

Finally, as an important complication, let's note that we often don't know what instructions were given to a witness or whether subsequent communication (or the circumstances) somehow undercut the instructions. The reason, in brief, is that identification procedures are often documented poorly (if at all). In one national survey, 33% of police investigators indicated that they keep no written report on their identification procedures (Wogalter, Malpass, & McQuiston, 2004). This pattern provides one of several reasons why we should applaud the advice given by the many groups that "live lineup procedures and photo displays should be preserved on video tape, or audio tape when video is not practicable" (from the Final Report of the California Commission on the Fair Administration of Justice, although similar sentiments can be found in many other best-practice guidelines).

The Appearance-Change Instruction

In some jurisdictions, instructions given to a witness also include another element—a reminder that people's appearances can change from one circumstance to another. Sometimes, the instructions go a step further and mention specific features that can change (hair style or length, or the presence of facial hair). Sometimes, the instructions go even further and urge witnesses to focus on features that cannot change (like shape of the nose or size of the eyes). We refer to this family of *appearance-change instructions* with the abbreviation ACI.

There is an obvious common-sense appeal to the ACI. After all, appearances do change: In some cases, the perpetrator might have worn a disguise during the crime. In other cases, the perpetrator's face may have changed in an unplanned way. (Perhaps the perpetrator chose, for reasons of aesthetics, to shave his head.) Sometimes, the booking picture (or driver's license photo) shown to the witness is from years ago. For these and other reasons, it seems sensible to remind witnesses about changes and to encourage them to look past these various changes.

In addition, police officers report that witnesses often ask questions or express misgivings during an ID procedure: "I think number 2 looks like him, but I remember him as being thinner." Or, "I think number 3 looks right, except for the moustache." Sometimes, the witnesses request guidance in these circumstances—should they make a pick despite these differences? By including the ACI, the police officer can deal with these comments before they arise and in this way minimize the conversation that takes place during the ID effort and thus diminish the risk of the conversation somehow biasing the witness.

Despite these common-sense arguments, it turns out that there is little evidence to support use of the ACI, and at least some evidence suggesting that the ACI may be a bad practice. At the time of this writing, there are only a few published papers examining the impact of the ACI (Charman & Wells, 2007; Molinaro, Arndorfer, & Charman, 2013; Porter, Moss, & Reisberg, 2013), and these papers indicate no benefit at all from including the instruction, even if the culprit's appearance *had* changed between the crime and the ID (i.e., even in the circumstance in which the ACI is most likely to help). What the ACI seems to accomplish instead is an increase in a witness's willingness to make a selection at all, including both good selections (i.e., picking the culprit) and bad.

What is going on here? One possibility is that the ACI provides witnesses with an easy way to "explain away" a mismatch between their recollection of the perpetrator and the photos in front of them. Thus, the ACI might encourage witnesses to say to themselves something like, "This photo doesn't look quite right, but perhaps that's not because it's the wrong guy. Perhaps it's the right guy but his appearance has changed, just as the detective told me it might." In this fashion, the ACI might encourage witnesses to make a selection despite differences between their memory and the face now in view, potentially producing a greater number of false identifications.

We should be clear that these suggestions about the relevant mental processes are speculative. Nonetheless, the point remains that there is essentially no evidence supporting use of the ACI and at least some evidence suggesting that this instruction does more harm than good.

D. DOUBLE-BLIND

One last step is concerned with how investigators should run an identification—a suggestion that the identification should be "double-blind." This term derives from scientific testing (including medical testing) in which neither the test administrator nor the test subjects knows what condition of the study the testee is in. Thus, in a medical setting, neither the administrator nor test subject knows whether the pills being given are the new medicine actually being evaluated or a placebo given to some participants merely to provide a basis for comparison.

In the context of forensic identifications, the term "double-blind" refers to a situation in which the person interacting with the witness (the person who hands the witness the photomontage, for example, and likewise the person who records the witness's response) does not know who, within the lineup, the suspect is. The notion here is that, with this set-up, there is no way for the administrator to guide or influence the witness, thus guaranteeing that the witness's choice is determined only by the witness him- or herself.

Let's emphasize that the notion of double-blind testing does not rest on some implied accusation of the police (cf. Austin, Zimmerman, Rhead, & Kovera, 2013). Instead, the idea here is that even the most careful, cautious investigator in the world might still "leak" cues to the witness—leaning forward slightly when the witness focuses attention on the suspect's picture, holding his breath momentarily, or smiling briefly. These cues might be entirely inadvertent, unwitting, and perhaps even uncontrollable—but there is a danger nonetheless that the witness will detect and be influenced by these cues.

Double-blind testing also guards against another concern: In principle, an identification procedure ends when a witness has made a selection or perhaps has announced that he or she cannot choose. In reality, though, an investigator has considerable control over when the procedure "ends" (see Wells & Quinlivan, 2009). To see how this might play out, imagine two witnesses: The first looks at the montage and selects the police suspect; the second looks at the montage and selects one of the fillers. A police officer might well end the identification session after the first witness's pick, but wait patiently after the second witness's selection, in the hope that the latter witness might reconsider this choice. Or, as an alternative, imagine that a witness has equivocated: "I can't tell; I'm torn between choosing 2 and 3." If neither of these photos shows the suspect, a police officer might end the session and write in the police report "The witness could not make a selection." But if one of these photos shows the suspect, the officer might choose to wait a moment, or even utter some words of encouragement, in hopes that the witness might select the "proper" photo.

Does this sort of cueing really matter? In one study, the lineup administrator remained silent while the participants in one condition viewed the lineup (Clark, Marshall, & Rosenthal, 2009). In another condition, if the participant had not made a selection after 12 seconds, the administrator made a comment along the lines of "take your time," or "there's no rush." In a third condition, if there was no selection after 12 seconds, the administrator asked whether any lineup member resembled the perpetrator more than any other. These various manipulations had little impact with target-present lineups, but, with target-absent lineups, both of the latter conditions increased choosing rates (and, again, with target-absent lineups, an increase in choosing is necessarily an increase in errors).

Other studies add to the concerns here. For example, data show that witnesses are more likely to choose someone from a lineup if the lineup administrator believes that person to be the target even when the administrator provides no overt expression of that belief (Greathouse & Kovera, 2009; Phillips, McAuliff, Kovera, & Cutler, 1999; Russano, Dickinson, Greathouse, & Kovera, 2006). Witnesses also express more confidence in their choices if they have selected someone the lineup administrator believes to be the target—again, in the absence of any overt signals about this belief (Garrioch & Brimacombe, 2001).

In all of these cases, the lineup administrators were presumably doing their best not to convey signals to the witness and were probably convinced they had succeeded in this effort. Just as importantly, the witnesses also believed they were uncued by the administrator: In some studies, witnesses have been asked directly whether they had received any signals or guidance in making their choices. The data show that witnesses can be influenced even when they deny any awareness of cues given by the person administering the lineup (Clark et al., 2009; also see Haw & Fisher, 2004).

Finally, some law enforcement professionals object that double-blind testing might be cumbersome, requiring pairs of detectives to work together so that (roughly) Officer X will administer the lineups for Officer Y's cases, and vice versa. The logistics of this arrangement might be complex—but are unnecessary because double-blind testing can be implemented in other, simpler ways. For example, some authors recommend the "envelope method," in which each of the photos for the photospread is placed in a separate, unmarked envelope, and the investigator then shuffles the envelopes before handing them to the witness. The investigator then steps back, so that he or she cannot see the photos as the witness removes each from the envelope. In this setting, the investigator has no way to tell which photo a witness is considering at each moment, thus diminishing the risk of the investigator guiding the witness's choice.

As a related suggestion, we note that, in some jurisdictions, lineups are presented on laptop computers, and presentation on computerized tablets or smart phones is also an option. (The small screen of a smart phone might demand a sequential lineup, which might on its own be an advantage.) If the relevant device is in the hands of the witness, then, again, the officer could step back and not have a view of the lineup, in this way providing (the equivalent of) double-blind administration. All of these options seem desirable and feasible.

E. THE WITNESS'S RESPONSE

We already surveyed (in Chapter 4) what happens at the crime scene and then, afterward, in the time interval leading up to the identification. In this chapter, we've discussed what happens in the identification procedure itself. However, we still need to consider what happens next—when the witness makes (and, often, offers a justification for) a choice.

The Witness's Exact Words

In some jurisdictions, witnesses record their responses to a lineup by means of a form, along the lines of:

"I recognize ___ #1 ___ #2 ___ #3 ___ #4 ___ #5 ___ #6
Or: ___ I did not recognize any of the pictures."

Such forms do provide objectivity and consistency, but are also problematic because we can often learn a lot from the specific words witnesses use in responding to a lineup. In some cases, witnesses say words like, "Well, of these, #4 is the closest." That phrasing seems to indicate the relative-judgment strategy described earlier in the chapter and, as discussed there, that strategy is worrisome. In other cases, witnesses hedge their identifications, "Number 5 looks like him," or "If I had to choose, I'd say Number 3." The justice system should be alert to the fact that neither of these is a clear identification and should certainly be alert to the contrast if later on the witness offers a stronger phrasing ("I'm sure it's him").

After all, we noted in Chapter 4 that face memory is unlikely to improve with time, and so we need to ask what might have caused the change from an initial tentative selection to an ultimate firm and confident choice. (We'll return to this issue in a few pages.)

In addition, notice that the explicit response choices described here blur together two options: A witness who is certain the perpetrator is *not* in the lineup would select "I did not recognize any of the pictures." A witness who simply cannot judge one way or another would also select the same response. Hence, this menu of responses provides no way to distinguish these two witnesses. Does this matter? To be sure, neither of these sentiments ("I'm sure it's none of these" vs. "I don't know") would count as an identification, and so, in most cases, neither would contribute to a prosecution. But law enforcement does have reason to care about this distinction because the "none of these" response (but not the "I don't know" response) might convince police that their suspect is innocent.

These points invite a question: Can *witnesses* distinguish between these two options? Weber and Perfect (2012) report a procedure in which witnesses were given response options that explicitly distinguished between "It's none of these" and "I don't know." With this distinction in place, there was virtually no impact on the number of correct choices but a substantial decrease in the number of mistaken "He's not there" responses. Hence, the inclusion of this overt response choice seems an easy, inexpensive way to clarify what the witness is telling the police.

Why Did You Choose Number 4?

Sometimes witnesses offer explanations of their choices: "I know it's him because of those eyes." Or "I'll never forget that mouth." Sometimes, police officers request these explanations: "What is it about number 5 that made you pick him?" And at least some attorneys believe that an identification deserves more weight if it can be explained in this fashion—if, for example, the witness says, "I recognized the nose." (I have, for example, been confronted with exactly this point in cross-examination, when an attorney was looking to shore up an identification.)

It is not clear, however, what to make of these explanations. Without question, some people do have distinctive features, and so we should take a witness seriously when he asks, "How could I not remember that eagle tattoo?" or " . . . that jagged scar?" But such cases are rare, and, as we noted in Chapter 4, most face recognition is based on relationships within the face, rather than individual features. Moreover, there is no reason to think people are aware of the specific relationships that guide their identification (for confirmation of this point, see Rice et al., 2013). Even if they are aware of these relationships, they may have difficulty in describing them. As a result, it will often be the case, first, that people do not know why they chose a face, and, second, that the "explanations" people offer may be misleading. In other words, the assertions offered by the witness may not be explanations at all but instead may be the witness's best after-the-fact estimate of why the face appeared familiar. (See, for example, Wilford & Wells, 2010; also Wells, Memon, & Penrod, 2006.)

Match to Description

Similar remarks apply to another way that investigators seek to evaluate an identification: If a witness had earlier offered a description of the perpetrator (e.g., to police detectives, right after the crime), investigators sometimes compare that description to the eventual identification. If there is a significant mismatch (the witness described the perpetrator as bald but has now chosen someone red-headed), this point is used to discredit the identification. If there is a close match, this point is used to bolster the identification.

This use of descriptions for evaluating an identification is by no means limited to police investigators. Trial judges also use descriptions for this purpose, a procedure that is enshrined in several court rulings, including the often-cited federal ruling in *Manson v. Brathwaite*. This U.S. Supreme Court ruling lays out several criteria for deciding when an identification is admissible even if suggestive procedures were used in obtaining the ID. Specifically, the ruling lists several "factors to be weighed against the corrupting effect of the suggestive procedure in assessing reliability," and one of the factors is the accuracy of the witness's prior description of the criminal.

We'll have more to say about the *Manson* ruling later in the chapter. For now, though, let's focus on this use of the witness's description as a means of evaluating (and perhaps bolstering) an ID. As Wells and Quinlivan (2009) point out, there are several problems here. One is that the courts sometimes deem a description to be "accurate" because it matches the appearance of the defendant. This notion, however, seems to assume that the defendant is, in fact, the culprit—exactly the point at issue in the trial. (What if the description happens to be massively *in*accurate in describing the perpetrator but matches the defendant perfectly? If we rely on match-to-defendant as our means of assessing the description, we would be misled in this scenario; for other concerns see Meissner, Sporer, & Susa, 2008.)

In addition, imagine two witnesses. One has provided no description of the culprit. The other has told the police that the culprit was light-skinned, thin, and bald, and she now selects someone from the lineup who has just these traits. How should we interpret this pattern? Should we put more faith in the second witness? Bear in mind here that, as we have already noted, witnesses are likely to remember at least the gist of their own descriptions and are likely to be guided by this knowledge in making a selection from the lineup (cf. Lindsay & Wells, 1980; Wells, 1984; Wells et al., 1993). Hence, we cannot rely on the description as corroborating the lineup selection because the influence of the description on the pick *virtually guarantees* a correspondence between these two. Returning to our pair of witnesses, then, if we put more faith in the second witness, we are giving the witness (undeserved) "credit" for a correspondence that was close to inevitable.

Confidence

Often, witnesses will directly express their degree of certainty in an ID selection. Sometimes, the witness will use some qualitative expression: "I'm sure," "I know it's him," "I'd guarantee that's him." And sometimes the witness will use some quantitative expression: "100% certain," "9 out of 10."

We argued in Chapter 3, however, that courts should give less weight to these certainty estimates than they do. In optimal circumstances, there is a (weak) relationship between degree of certainty and likelihood of a correct answer, and, on this basis, a witness's degree of certainty can provide some information and should be noted. But the key here is the phrase "optimal circumstances" because it is easy to find settings in which the relationship between certainty and accuracy is zero.

In Chapter 3, we discussed some of the factors that govern a witness's expression of certainty and also some of the circumstances that can alter the degree of certainty. In fact, the ease with which certainty can be changed has led to a substantial body of research exploring *confidence malleability*—the potential for shifts in someone's degree of certainty thanks to a variety of external factors (for a review of research on this topic, see Bradfield Douglass, & Pavletic, 2012; Leippe & Eisenstadt, 2007; Steblay, Wells, & Douglass, 2014; for a survey of factors that contribute to confidence malleability, see Chapter 3).

How should these points guide law enforcement? We have noted that, in optimal circumstances, there is a connection between confidence and accuracy, and so a witness's degree of confidence can provide information and thus should be recorded. To maximize the quality of this information, though, investigators should do all they can to ensure (or at least approach) "optimal circumstances." The witnesses' degree of confidence should therefore be collected immediately after the identification, with no cues (verbal or nonverbal) provided between the selection and the confidence statement. (This is another regard in which double-blind administrations provide a powerful safeguard.) Then, as the investigation continues, it should be this initial statement of certainty that is used in evaluating the ID. If the witness subsequently changes his or her statement of confidence, this late-arriving report should be viewed with skepticism and perhaps discounted altogether as likely the result of confidence malleability.

Speed of Choice

One last aspect of the witness's response has perhaps received less notice than it should—the *speed* with which the witness makes a selection. In some trials, attorneys point to the witness's lengthy inspection of the lineup, perhaps an inspection taking five minutes or more, and argue from this that the witness was careful, systematic, and hence more likely to be correct. Unfortunately, though, this argument has things backward. Recognition memory tends to be relatively fast. Slower identifications may therefore reveal the presence of a relative-judgment or the presence of a witness who initially had doubts and was somehow talked out of those doubts.

In fact, several studies document a consistent relationship between speed of response and likelihood of an accurate response. Dunning and Peretta (2002), for example, report that witnesses who need less than 10–12 seconds to make an identification tend to be quite accurate (almost 90% accurate IDs); witnesses who take more than 12 seconds are appreciably less accurate (50%; also see Ross, Benton, McDonnell, Metzger, & Silver, 2007; Smith, Lindsay, & Pryke, 2000).

Researchers would, however, warn against adopting some sort of "cut-off" in deciding which identifications to trust. One reason is that the "time boundary" separating accurate IDs from inaccurate ones varies from one circumstance to another (e.g., Weber, Brewer, Wells, Semmler, & Keast, 2004). Nonetheless, the fact remains that faster identifications do tend to be more accurate than slower ones.

F. MISPLACED FAMILIARITY

We have now finished our "chronological sweep" through the events associated with an identification, starting in Chapter 4 with the crime itself and the interval afterward; then moving in this chapter to the lineup presentation and the witness response. However, we still need to deal with three further issues, starting, first, with the possibility that a culprit might look familiar to a witness for some benign (noncriminal) reason. Second, we need to step away from issues of a criminal investigation and turn to issues of trial, asking specifically about the science relevant to a pretrial decision about an identification's admissibility. Finally, we turn to the drama of an in-court identification.

Familiarity Versus Recollection

In Chapter 4, we argued that the recognition of a familiar face ("Oh look, there's George Clooney") is very different from the sort of identification relevant to most criminal cases. Forensic identifications are typically based on a single, brief view of a face that had never been seen before, in contrast to the multiple, lengthy, contextualized views you have had of Clooney (or any other face that is familiar to you).

We argued in the previous chapter that familiarity with a face promotes memory accuracy. Specifically, we argued that *recognition* (of a familiar face) is generally more accurate and less susceptible to outside influence than is *identification* (of an unfamiliar, once-viewed face). However, it turns out that there are also settings in which familiarity can have the opposite effect and can actually undermine memory accuracy.

What produces this seeming paradox? The brain system that supports your sense of familiarity is separate from the brain system that supports what is called *recollection*. The former system tells you *that* a face (or a song or a place) is familiar; the latter system does the "bookkeeping" and tells you *why* the face (or song or place) is familiar. The latter system, in other words, tells you where and when you encountered the face and so specifies the source of the familiarity.

The separateness of these two systems is evident in a common experience: You pass someone on the street, or perhaps you see a face in a movie (or on television), and you immediately know that the face is familiar. But, with deep frustration, you cannot recall *why* the face is familiar and so over and over you ask yourself, "Where do I know that guy from?" In this setting, the familiarity system has functioned properly and has told you that the face is familiar. But the recollection system has let you down, leaving you clueless about why the face is familiar.

A variation on this circumstance is, unfortunately, more insidious: Sometimes you (correctly) realize that a face is familiar, and you believe you know why the face is familiar—but you are wrong about the latter point. As a result, you have actually experienced someone in one setting, but, in your memory, you've mistakenly "transferred" him into another setting, and this is why this error is sometimes referred to as "unconscious transference"—the brain's version of a computer's cut-and-paste operation.

This type of confusion is easy to document. In one study, witnesses viewed a video showing three women in a supermarket; one of the women in the film was shown stealing some items. Later, the witnesses were shown a lineup and asked if they could identify the thief. As it turns out, the lineup did not contain the actual thief but did show another woman from the video, and more than half the witnesses (falsely) identified her as the culprit. Apparently, the witnesses (correctly) realized that this woman's face was familiar, but they lost track of why it was familiar, leading to their identification error (Davis, Loftus, Vanous, & Cucciare, 2008; see also Ross, Ceci, Dunning, & Toglia, 1994).

In another study, participants received a massage and also spoke with a researcher. When tested a month later, almost half the participants were confused about which face belonged to the masseuse and which to the researcher (Mueller-Johnson & Ceci, 2004). Thus, at a one-month delay, the participants correctly registered both of these faces as familiar but had lost track of which face was which.

Many studies have documented these errors, and so there is no question that these errors often occur. A few studies, though, have not documented these errors (cf. Read, Tollestrup, Hammersley, McFadzen, & Christensen, 1990), reminding us that unconscious transference is not inevitable. Let's acknowledge, therefore, that (of course) sometimes people *do* realize why a particular face is familiar to them. Moreover, although the existence of these errors is clear, there is room for debate about how we should *label* these errors. The term "unconscious transference" is used in many contexts (including some court rulings) but may be misleading. Indeed, in some cases, these errors may result from an entirely *conscious inference*: "Gee, that guy looks familiar, and the police are showing me faces of people who, they believe, may have been at the crime scene, and so I suppose that he looks familiar because . . ." Hence, we may be better served by a shift in terminology—referring to these errors as cases of "misplaced familiarity" or "source confusion" (on the idea that you are mistaken about the source of the familiarity).

The Impact of Benign Contact

Misplaced familiarity can be created in many ways, including benign contact that has nothing to do with the matter being investigated. For example, Simon (2012, p. 77) notes a case in which a man was misidentified as the perpetrator in an assault. The error was likely the result of the fact that the innocent man was indeed familiar to the victim because, three days before the assault, "he came to the victim's house to see a motorcycle that the victim's son was selling." Simons describes another case in which a man who worked in a hospital was misidentified by a victim who happened to be a nursing student at that hospital. Simons also notes cases in which witnesses have "erroneously identified people who lived down the street from them, worked for the same company, resided in the same apartment complex, or previously visited the victim's apartment or building." In still other cases, the mistaken identification has been triggered by the witness first seeing someone's face in the media and then later seeing the same face in a lineup or in the courtroom. Across all of these cases, the pattern is the same: At the time of the identification, the witness correctly registers the face as familiar but makes a consequential error in assessing *why* the face is familiar.

As yet another example, I testified in a trial in which a woman had been a victim of a robbery and easily picked the defendant out of a photo lineup as the robber. As it turns out, though, the defendant had a persuasive alibi and could not possibly have been the robber. How did the error arise? The defendant was a devoted jogger, running several miles each week, and one of his preferred jogging routes took him right by the victim's house. The odds are good, therefore, that the victim had seen him in passing but had no reason to take special notice of the man jogging by. This is a clear example of a circumstance that will produce familiarity without much recollection, and this is why, when the woman saw the defendant's picture in the lineup, she correctly noticed he was familiar but made a mistake about why.

Of course, the woman's error in this case was not foolish or capricious. After all, consider the circumstances: She was looking at a lineup shown to her by the police. She likely assumed that one of the men in the lineup was the robber. One face seemed familiar, and she had no recollection that would have provided an alternative (and correct) explanation for this familiarity. In this setting, it was an entirely reasonable inference—albeit mistaken—that the defendant was familiar because he was the robber.

In light of this broad possibility, investigators are well-advised to ask whether a face picked from a lineup might be familiar to the witness for some benign reason. Do they live in the same neighborhood? Ride the same bus? Shop in the same stores? If so, investigators need to consider the possibility that the ID may be the result of misplaced familiarity.

Of course, there is a problem in all of this: We have said that familiarity *promotes* memory accuracy (that was our George Clooney example and is a point considered at length in Chapter 4) and also that familiarity can *undermine* accuracy (via misplaced familiarity). How can we separate these two effects? As a rough rule of thumb, one can ask: When you see Devon, do you know his name (even if, at that moment, you can't think of the name)? If you do not know his name, do you know *why* he is familiar (e.g., because you've seen him around the neighborhood, know he's a friend of Jeff's, or whatever)? Do you recall the last time you saw him? If any of these questions—essentially "contextualizing" the familiarity—get a "yes" answer, then Devon is likely to be familiar enough to promote memory accuracy when you see him. If, in contrast, seeing Devon leaves you only with a vague sense of familiarity, a feeling that you cannot contextualize, then we are in the range in which familiarity can have the opposite effect, undercutting identification accuracy.

Mug-Shot Bias

The previous section concerned settings in which benign contact can produce misplaced familiarity. A similar pattern can arise through exposure to a face during the course of a police investigation. In one study, for example, participants initially witnessed a staged crime. Two or three days later, they were shown "mug shots" of individuals who supposedly had been the "criminals" in the initial event, but, it turns out, the mug shots showed entirely different people, people who had not been part of the crime at all. Finally, after four or five more days, participants were shown a lineup and asked to select the individuals seen in the very first step—the simulated crime. The data showed a large effect of source confusion, with fully 29% of the witnesses "accusing" individuals they had only seen in the mug shots. Apparently, the witnesses correctly noted that these individuals seemed familiar but then made an error about why the faces were familiar (Brown, Deffenbacher, & Sturgill, 1977; this study was actually modeled after a case evaluated by the U.S. Supreme Court in *Simmons* et al. *v. United States*, 1968).

Here is a variation on the same theme: Steblay, Tix, and Benson (2013) showed eyewitnesses two lineups, separated by a two-week interval, with an innocent "suspect's" picture shown in both of the lineups. Witnesses who mistakenly picked the (actually innocent) suspect in the first lineup carried the error forward to the second lineup and thus repeated their error. What's more important for present purposes, though, is that many witnesses who correctly did not pick the (innocent) suspect in the first lineup reversed this decision and picked him from the second lineup, apparently guided by a sense of familiarity with this twice-viewed photo.

How large are these effects? The Brown et al. study just cited reported a 29% error rate. A more recent survey of the evidence (via meta-analysis) found that 37% of the research participants tested chose an actually innocent person from a lineup if they had earlier seen that person's mug shot; in contrast, the choosing rate for this innocent person was just 15% for participants who had not been shown the mug shot. Apparently, the impact of the mug shot is considerable (Deffenbacher, Bornstein, & Penrod, 2006; for other mechanisms also contributing to mug-shot bias, see Godfrey & Clark, 2010; Valentine et al., 2012).

G. PRETRIAL ASSESSMENTS OF ADMISSIBILITY

Courts have long acknowledged that eyewitness identifications are sometimes mistaken and have also acknowledged that some of these mistakes may be the result of investigative error—with the state somehow suggesting to the witness who he or she was "supposed to" select from a lineup (or showup). The courts have consistently held, however, that there is no reason to exclude from a trial all instances of suggestive identifications. Instead, the courts generally rely on a two-step decision process, laid out in federal court in two Supreme Court rulings: *Neil v. Biggers* (1972) and *Manson v. Brathwaite* (1977). In this process, a judge must first ascertain whether the ID procedure was, in fact, suggestive in some way. If not, there is no admissibility issue to be discussed. If the procedure was suggestive, then, as the second step, the judge must decide whether the suggestive procedure actually did some harm. In other words, in light of the totality of the circumstances, does it seem likely that the witness choice would have been the same even with a neutral, nonsuggestive procedure? If so, then the suggestiveness is not a problem, and the identification is allowed into trial. If not—if the identification choice was likely shaped by the suggestive procedure—then the judge may rule the identification to be inadmissible.

There is surely a common-sense appeal to this two-step sequence, one based on the idea that a suggestive procedure will do no harm if someone has a strong enough, clear enough memory. Imagine, for example, that you are shown a lineup and asked to pick out your mother's picture. Let's say that your mother is shown in Position 4, but the lineup is strongly suggestive, guiding you toward the face in Position 3. Perhaps the investigator even asks, "It's number 3, isn't it?" Despite these pressures, you'll recognize Mom.

Nonetheless, scholars have raised deep questions about the adequacy of the *Biggers* or *Manson* procedures, and some states have been reviewing their version of these procedures. In 2011, New Jersey significantly revised its ID procedure in *State v. Henderson.* In 2012, Oregon went further and, in *State v. Lawson,* soundly rejected this two-step evaluation. Other states are considering their own revisions; for example, as of this writing, Massachusetts is still reflecting on the report submitted by the Supreme Judicial Court Study Group on Eyewitness Evidence; the report contains specific recommendations that may lead to substantial reforms. Agencies outside of the judiciary are also weighing in on these issues: The IACP issued a report in November 2013 that offers numerous recommendations about how identifications should be conducted, and, at the time of this publication, a report from the U.S. National Academy of Sciences (specifically, from the Committee on Scientific Approaches to Understanding and Maximizing the Validity and Reliability of Eyewitness Identification in Law Enforcement and the Courts) is expected soon. (For a broad review of the science relevant to the *Manson* criteria and thus to all of these rulings, see Wells & Quinlivin, 2009.)

What exactly is the concern here? Let's start with the first step in *Manson's* two-step evaluation. In 2012, the U.S. Supreme Court asserted (in *Perry v. New Hampshire*) that this step should be guided by due-process concerns. A pretrial evaluation of an ID is therefore launched, the majority concluded, only if the suggestiveness of the procedure is the result of circumstances "arranged by law enforcement officers." If "no improper law enforcement activity" is involved in the case, then the ID can still be challenged, but only through other means (cross examination, jury instructions, and so on). In her dissent, though, Justice Sotomayor argues that eyewitness evidence "derived from suggestive circumstances . . . is uniquely resistant to the ordinary tests of the adversary process." Moreover, she argues that concerns about due process should lead to a broader demand: namely, that evidence be presented at trial only if the evidence is demonstrably *reliable,* and unreliability, she notes, can be produced either by state action (as the majority ruling asserts) or through other influences.

Justice Sotomayor's claims are well-supported by the available research, and the data tell us, for example, that jurors do find eyewitness identifications to be compelling, even with cross-examination or cautionary instructions (see Chapter 9). Likewise, the scientific evidence suggests little systematic difference between "police-arranged" and other forms of influence on a witness. Both types of influence (police-arranged and not) can bias memory, can produce ID errors, can inflate witness confidence, and so on. Nonetheless, the 8-to-1 ruling in *Perry* does limit the pretrial evaluation of identifications and likely allows the jury to hear about many unreliable identifications.

State rulings, however, need not follow this standard. Oregon's *Lawson* ruling (for example) does emphasize the need for reliability in identification evidence. As a result, the *Lawson* ruling sets aside the distinction, crucial for *Perry,* between police-arranged and other forms of influence. Indeed, in discussing reliability and with an explicit reference to *Perry,* the Oregon ruling rejects the "purposeless distinctions between suggestiveness and other sources of unreliability."

What about the second step in *Manson*? As already noted, this ruling lists various factors that might suggest an identification is acceptable even with a suggestive procedure. Specifically, the ruling highlights five criteria: (1) the witness's ability to view the person later identified, (2) the degree to which the witness was paying attention to the person, (3) the quality of the description the witness offered police soon after the crime, (4) the amount of time that passed between the crime and the identification, and (5) the degree of certainty the witness expressed in the identification.

Some of the concerns about this list should be obviously immediately. In Chapter 3 and in this chapter, we have discussed the fact that degree of certainty is, in the best of circumstances, a weak indicator of memory accuracy. Hence, the unalloyed inclusion of this factor is arguably a mistake.

Likewise, we have discussed the fact that the quality of someone's verbal description is also a poor indicator of memory accuracy (e.g., Meissner et al., 2007). Worse, we mentioned earlier that whenever witnesses make a choice from a lineup, their choice is guided by their recollection of how they described the suspect early on. Thus *all picks* (accurate or not) tend to be consistent with the description (whether the description is accurate or not). It makes little sense, therefore, to use "consistency with the description" as an indicator of veracity.

The *Manson* Factors Are Incomplete

Just as important are the omissions from the *Manson* criteria. In Chapter 4, we noted that cross-race identifications are less accurate, and so a suggestive procedure is more likely to produce an error if a case hinges on a cross-race ID. Yet this factor is absent from the *Manson* list. The same words can be said for extreme stress or the presence of a bleeding wound. These factors, too, erode memory, and hence would increase the harm from a suggestive procedure, but they are not included in the *Manson* criteria.

In addition, the *Manson* ruling enumerates criteria that we might use in evaluating an identification but omits a further (and crucial) point: The factors that influence an identification *interact with each other*. Thus, the passage of time (one of the criteria) will have a larger effect on memory if the memory was not well established in the first place (perhaps because of a poor viewing opportunity—one of the other criteria). Thus, a poor view will, in essence, amplify the impact of passing time. Likewise, if a view was brief, it becomes all the more important that the witness use that opportunity well. Hence, attention becomes more important if the viewing opportunity was limited—again, one factor amplifying another. (For discussion of this sort of interaction among influences, see Malpass, Ross, Meissner, & Marcon, 2009; also see Pezdek, 2009, especially p. 36; Pezdek, 2012, pp. 119–120; Wells, Memon, & Penrod, 2006, especially p. 51.)

The *Manson* Factors Are Vague

It is also notable how little guidance the *Manson* factors provide for a trial judge (or, for that matter, for the appellate courts). The *Manson* criteria do mention the witness's opportunity to view the criminal—a truly important factor—but leave it up to a judge to decide how this opportunity might be evaluated. As described in Chapter 4, we know a lot about these points. (Research can, for example, help the court to decide how far away is too far, or how exactly low light levels can shape vision.) However, the *Manson* ruling provides no instructions (or reminders, or incentives) that would link a judge's assessment of "opportunity to view" to the science relevant to these issues.

The concern is similar for the factor of "attention." This, too, is a crucial consideration, but, once again, the *Manson* ruling provides minimal guidance for how this factor might be assessed. Consider, for example (as Wells & Quinlivin [2009] suggest) a witness who was determined to remember her assailant's appearance and so paid rapt attention to the shape of the assailant's nose and the shape of his eyes. This witness was clearly paying attention but was attending to features, not the face's overall configuration, and the relevant research says this focus might impair subsequent identification, not help it. With examples like this one in view, it seems clear that merely asking "was the witness paying close attention?" is insufficient for the court's needs.

Documented Versus Remembered Factors

A further problem concerns how the courts learn about such crucial factors as a witness's opportunity to view the criminal or the witness's degree and focus of attention. In many cases, the courts travel the obvious path and simply ask the witness about these points, often at a pretrial hearing, often many months after the crime: "How far away were you standing? Was there anything obstructing your line of view? How clearly could you see his face?" In this way, courts rely on the witness's recollection of these points, and that is a problem.

As we mentioned in Chapter 2, memory for "view" and "attention" is often inaccurate. To name just one example, one limit on a witness's opportunity to view a crime is duration, and yet Chapter 2 discussed research showing that people are quite poor at retrospectively assessing duration. That earlier chapter also argued that people are quite poor in estimating or remembering distance.

Likewise, Chapter 2 also discussed the myriad effects of postidentification feedback. This feedback produces an inflation in witness confidence and also a distortion in witness memory for the viewing circumstances. When, for example, a witness hears, "Good, you selected our suspect," the witness seems to think something along the lines of "I got the right guy, so I guess I got a good view after all." This unconscious, unwitting, and uncontrollable line of thought leads witnesses to recall the duration of their view as being longer than it was, to recall the lighting as being better than it was, to recall themselves standing closer to the target than they actually were, and so on.

In light of these facts, we surely want to distinguish between a witness's *documented* opportunity to view and a witness's *remembered* opportunity to view and, likewise, the witness's *documented* focus of attention and the witness's *remembered* focus. In each pair, the former point ("documented" opportunity or attention) is crucial: You cannot remember a face if you had no opportunity to see the face in the first place, and you will not remember a face if you paid no attention to it. But the latter point in each pair ("remembered" opportunity or attention) will, in many cases, carry no information. As we mentioned in Chapter 2 and reiterate here, our ability to remember these points is poor overall. Worse, our memory can be compromised (and distorted) by various influences (including feedback), thus making a poor memory even worse.

The Circularity in the *Manson* Logic

The points just raised actually reveal a deep problem in the two-step logic described in the *Manson* ruling (after Wells & Quinlivan, 2009). Recall that, according to this ruling (and others, in both federal and state courts), a trial judge must first decide if an ID procedure was unduly suggestive. If the procedure was suggestive, this triggers a second step in which the judge now must decide if the ID is nonetheless admissible. In other words, in this second step, the judge determines whether the suggestive procedure did any harm.

To see the problem here, consider a concrete case. Imagine that a crime victim reports that the robber had an especially big nose. Some time later, the police show this victim a photomontage containing one photo that shows a big nose and five small-nosed fillers. When the victim chooses the only plausible photo, the police applaud and say, "That's our suspect."

This procedure—with a biased lineup and postidentification feedback—is surely suggestive and presumably would trigger the second step of the *Manson* review. But here let's bear in mind that the biased lineup and the feedback have multiple effects. These factors will, we have said, produce an inflated sense of certainty in the witness and will also trigger a bias in how the witness remembers her viewing opportunity and her degree of attention. But, of course, these are some of the indicators that the *Manson* ruling relies on in evaluating the identification. Thus, the *Manson* ruling has us check on suggestiveness by using indicators that are themselves shaped by—and, indeed, compromised by—the suggestiveness. Hence, there is circularity here because we are trying to detect a problem (an ID biased by a bad procedure), but we are relying on evidence that is systematically undermined by the very same bad procedure. Or, to put the point bluntly, we are allowing the suggestive procedure to manufacture its own bona fides—a circumstance that is circular and self-defeating for the justice system.

Once more, though, we note that state courts have the option of departing from (and improving on) this federal standard, and here, too, the Oregon *Lawson* ruling provides an instructive example. (For purposes of full disclosure, I should mention that I testified as the defense expert in the trial that eventually led to this ruling by Oregon's Supreme Court.) We have already mentioned that this ruling sets aside the distinction between state-produced suggestiveness and other forms of influence; this ruling also puts the burden on the party bringing the ID forward—usually the state—to show that the ID is reliable. But, in addition, the ruling offers a lengthy catalog of the (many) factors that can influence an identification and also takes judicial notice of the studies documenting confidence malleability. The ruling also notes the potential circularity built into the *Manson* logic. Specifically, the ruling acknowledges that witness reports of the *Manson* factors (or, in Oregon's version, the *Classen* factors) "can be inflated by the suggestive procedure itself. That fact creates in turn a sort of feedback loop in which self-reports of reliability, which can be exaggerated by suggestiveness, are then used to prove that suggestiveness did not adversely affect the reliability of an identification. That result is contrary to the scientific research establishing that suggestiveness *adversely* affects reliability."

It remains to be seen whether other states will follow Oregon's lead here or how exactly this ruling will shape trial decisions in Oregon. In the meantime, there is no question that some states (and not just Oregon) are taking notice of, and changing procedures in light of, the science relevant to the *Manson* ruling and identifications in general.

H. IN-COURT IDENTIFICATIONS

We turn, finally, to one more way in which identifications emerge in the legal system: At a key moment during a trial, an attorney asks a witness: "Do you see, in this room, the person who robbed you?" (or ". . . raped you," or ". . . fired the gun," or whatever). The witness says yes; the attorney asks, "Can you indicate that person?" The witness indicates the defendant, and the attorney intones, "Let the record show that the witness has indicated the defendant."

In-court identifications are high drama and will likely be part of the courtroom sequence forever. It should be clear from the discussion so far, however, that in-court identifications have little probative value. As one concern, in-court identifications are inevitably suggestive: In the courtroom, it is obvious from the seating arrangement who the defendant is. The witness also knows that the police and prosecution believe the defendant is guilty. The witness is also likely to be aware of other evidence that (according to the prosecution) points toward the defendant's guilt. In most cases, the witness knows that he or she has already made an identification of this individual and may be ashamed to reverse this assertion.

All of these facts put some pressure on the witness to make an identification of the defendant. To be sure, there are occasions in which a witness, in court, is unwilling to make an identification. But, even so, the circumstances of an in-court identification are exactly the opposite of those we seek for a fair pretrial identification (e.g., with nothing drawing attention to the suspect, with an admonition clearly reminding the witness that the perpetrator may or may not be present among the faces shown, and so on).

We have also seen that people are often better at realizing *that* a face is familiar than they are in recalling *why* the face is familiar. Thus, in court, the witness might (correctly) realize that the defendant's face is familiar and sensibly conclude that she has seen his face before. But then the witness might make an error about where she had seen the defendant before, perhaps mistakenly concluding that he looks familiar because she saw him during the crime, when, in actuality, he looks familiar because she saw him in the courthouse corridor, at an arraignment, or in a newspaper account of the crime. In other words, this is a setting ripe for the error we earlier called misplaced familiarity.

Furthermore, the speed of the justice system is less than anyone would wish, and trials often take place months (or years) after a crime. Therefore, there has been ample opportunity for the witness's memory of the crime to fade. As a result, the witness does not have much of an "internal anchor" (i.e., a good and clear memory) to guide the identification, thus making the witness all the more vulnerable to the concerns already listed.

Finally, we have also discussed some of the putative benefits of an in-court identification: The witness can see the full body, the pattern of movement, and the posture of the defendant. Perhaps the witness can hear the defendant's voice. As we noted earlier, though, research suggests that these "extra" sources of information are of little value and may actually undermine the witness's use of the most important information— the face itself. So, here, too, in-court identifications fall short of their promise.

For all of these reasons—the impact of a suggestive identification procedure, the risk of misplaced familiarity, the effect of passing time—we should be skeptical of in-court identifications. These IDs are dramatic and often persuasive, but they are— because of the concerns enumerated—of little value as evidence.

CHAPTER 6

Memory for Voices and Conversations

Someone who has witnessed an event—including a crime—has potentially gained a lot of information. The person knows what happened and can describe the sequence of actions to investigators. The person has seen the other people present in the event and will perhaps be able to identify these people later. But, in addition, the witness has heard what transpired during the event, and this can give rise to two types of memory: First, the witness may remember the *voices* of the various speakers, and this memory provides a possible basis for a subsequent identification. In other words, police may provide the earwitness with a "voice lineup" in hopes of getting an (auditory) identification. Second, the witness may remember *what was said*—the content of the conversation and perhaps the phrasing. This information, too, can often be crucial for investigators.

In this chapter, we tackle these two types of memory—memory for voices and for conversation. How accurate is this memory? In what ways might this sort of memory be different from the types of memory we have already considered? And what is the best way to gather this sort of memory—that is, to find out what someone heard?

A. MEMORY FOR VOICES

There are many circumstances in which criminals might be best identified via their voices. Imagine a crime that takes place in the dark, for example, or one in which the criminal stands behind the victim. Imagine a crime in which the criminal is wearing a disguise—including, perhaps, a full mask. Or imagine a crime that does not involve face-to-face contact—e.g., a bomb threat or some form of harassment heard over the telephone. In any of these scenarios, an identification via voice might be central for an investigation and eventually a prosecution.

Recognition Versus Identification

How accurate is voice identification? What factors can make this identification more accurate, or less? Before tackling these questions, we need to reiterate a distinction introduced in Chapter 4 in discussing faces: On the one side, it is relatively easy to recognize an already familiar voice, one that you have encountered in many circumstances ("I immediately knew that was Sam's voice; I've known him for years"). On the other side, the challenge that confronts a typical earwitness is much more difficult: The earwitness is likely hearing the target voice for the first time during the crime itself, and he or she somehow needs to memorize the sound of the voice during this (perhaps brief) episode, then recall that voice later on. These tasks—recognizing a familiar voice and identifying a stranger's voice heard just once before—are plainly distinct, and we must not confuse them. (We'll focus here on the *functional* distinction between recognition and identification; for discussion of the *neural* distinction between these two cases, see Van Lancker, Cummings, Kreiman, & Dobkin, 1988.)

Let's start with the recognition of a familiar voice, a task that is easy, generally accurate, relatively fast, and that can survive a fair amount of acoustic distortion. These points are evident in the simple fact that most of us know immediately who we're talking to when a friend begins a phone conversation with the three syllables of, "Hi, it's me." (This recognition proceeds even though the tiny speaker within a phone cannot produce high-fidelity sound.) Likewise, most of us immediately recognize the voices of various celebrities and world leaders when we hear them in a movie or on TV (e.g., Abberton & Fourcin, 1978; Hollien, Bennett, & Gelfer, 1983), and it is true that mothers can distinguish their own infant's cry from the cries of other infants (e.g., Formby, 1967). (For some complications, though, involving the recognition of familiar voices, see Yarmey, 2001; 2007.)

Even a small degree of familiarity is helpful: Yarmey (2001) showed that people are more likely to recognize even a casually familiar voice than they are to recognize a voice they have heard only on a single occasion. As familiarity increases, though, recognition accuracy improves.

How Accurate Is Voice Identification?

In many crimes, the earwitness has had no prior experience with the critical voice and heard the voice only once, during the crime. In this setting, there is no possibility of recognizing the speaker ("Ah—it's Dan!") and then remembering the person's name. Instead, the earwitness must somehow remember the voice itself and then try to "match" this memory to a voice in a lineup. How accurate are these identifications?

Evidence suggests overall that voice identification is, in fact, quite difficult, and performance levels tend to be low. As a benchmark, one study indicated that the likelihood of a correct identification for a voice heard once and for a relatively brief amount of time is about 30% (Yarmey, 2007). We can also ask how often people, in trying to identify a voice, falsely select a different voice (i.e., choose a voice that had not been heard before); in one study, 36% of the witnesses made this error (Yarmey, 2001).

We can also ask how well earwitnesses do with target-absent voice lineups, for which the correct response is "none of these." In one study, only 28% of the participants gave this correct response; in another study, only 16% correctly rejected the lineup; in the third study, only 2% correctly rejected the lineup. (Yarmey [2007] offers a review of these and related studies.)

As a different gauge of accuracy, we can compare face and voice identifications. In one study, memory was tested via a showup procedure (i.e., with participants offered just one option, as they would be with a law enforcement field showup). The proportion of correct responses was twice as high for faces as for voices (57% vs. 28%). When memory was tested with lineups (six faces to choose from or six voices), the margin was even greater—46% correct for faces; 9% for voices (Yarmey, 2007).

A different contrast between faces and voices involves the capacity of each to trigger other memories. When we see someone, does this encourage recall of a previous event in which we encountered that person? How about when we hear the person's voice; does this encourage recall of the prior event? Evidence suggests that faces are appreciably more powerful than voices as memory triggers—whether the face and voice belong to a celebrity, someone who is familiar to us, or someone we have encountered only once (Brédart & Barsics, 2012).

The Cues Used for Voice Identification

What cues or attributes do people rely on in identifying voices? The answer varies because voice perception is in some ways opportunistic, with the features used for identifying a voice varying from one voice to the next. Thus, some voices can be identified by focusing on their timbre; others are identified by focusing on their pace and rhythm; still others are identified by focusing on the idiosyncratic pronunciation of particular speech sounds. (Here, we should note that voice identification via an analysis of sound spectrograms tends to rely on timbre and is not all that accurate; see Hammersley & Read, 1996; National Research Council [1979].)

Evidence for these various claims comes from studies that ask participants to identify altered voices. For voices recognized by their pitch or timbre, recognition accuracy is still good even if the voice is played backward (a manipulation that does not change pitch or timbre), although this alteration does undermine recognition for voices recognized by their pace or timing. In contrast, recognition of voices recognized by their pace or rhythm is disrupted if these timing cues are (electronically) altered (Van Lancker, Kreiman, & Emmorey, 1985; Van Lancker, Kreiman, & Wickens, 1985).

In addition, many voices are distinctive in some fashion (especially high-pitched, for example, or especially nasal), whereas other voices are (acoustically and subjectively) more "ordinary." Not surprisingly, this distinctiveness matters: In one study, a group of participants rated a succession of voices for how "typical" each seemed. Then, a second group of participants heard these voices and later tried to identify them. The data showed that voices identified as "typical" by the first group of participants were harder to identify by the second group—and often confused with other typical voices (Mullennix et al., 2011).

Just how important are these differences from one voice to the next? In one study, participants heard roughly 45 seconds of speech, then tried to identify the voice 30 minutes later (Philippon, Cherryman, Bull, & Vrij, 2007). For one of the target voices, 20% of the ID attempts were correct; for another, 60% were correct—plainly, the individual voice does matter. Another study indicated that the nature of memory errors also varied from one voice to the next: Listeners tended to recall low-pitched voices as being even lower than they actually were and remembered high-pitched voices as being even higher than they were (Mullennix, Stern, Grounds, Kalas, Flaherty, Kowalok, May, & Tesmer, 2010).

In addition to these variations from one voice to the next, there are variations even for a single voice, and these also matter for identification accuracy. For example, sometimes an individual speaks slowly; sometimes the same person speaks rapidly. Individual speakers also change the pitch and loudness of their voice, influenced by how excited they are, whether they are moving around (and so perhaps breathing more heavily), whether they are in a noisy environment, and so on. Likewise, if someone is under stress, this changes many aspects of the voice, including pitch, pace, and timbre (Hollien, 1990; Jessen, 1997).

Moreover, people often try to disguise their voices. Thus, people deliberately change the pitch or pace of their speech, and some use a disguise that effectively eliminates cues about the voice's timbre: they whisper (Künzel, 2000; Yarmey, 2001; 2007). All of these factors contribute to the difficulty of recognizing voices. (We'll have more to say about disguises and other voice changes later—see "The effect of voice changes.")

Face-Voice Interactions

What happens when witnesses both see and hear someone at the time of the crime? Does this combination—obviously providing more information—improve identifications? We alluded to this point in Chapter 5, in discussing live lineups, and, disappointingly, the answer seems to be "no." Evidence suggests that these two sources of information don't supplement each other. Instead, they seem to compete for the witness's attention, so that any attention focused on one of these modalities requires that less attention be focused on the other modality.

This interference, however, is asymmetrical: Facial recognition is slightly less accurate if the witness has both seen and heard the target. In other words, the presence of the auditory information has only a small effect on the accuracy of subsequent visual identifications. The effect is larger, though, in the opposite direction, and, when witnesses can hear and see a perpetrator, the presence of this visual information can seriously compromise the witness's ability to identify the voice later (e.g., McAllister, Dale, Bregman, McCabe, & Cotton, 1993; Stevenage, Howland, & Tippelt, 2011).

Describing Voices

In many investigations, investigators ask witnesses for a verbal description of a voice. In some cases, the descriptors involve categories, and so an earwitness might indicate the speaker's gender or ethnicity, perhaps whether the speaker sounded "educated" or not, and so on. In other cases, the descriptors specify traits of the voice itself (accented or not, high-pitched or low-, rapid or slow, "gravelly" or "raspy" or "breathless"). How accurate are these descriptions?

People do reasonably well in identifying the gender and ethnicity of a speaker, although performance is far from perfect (Yarmey, 2007). Listeners can often tell, for example, whether the speaker is Caucasian, African American, or Chicano (Purnell, Idsardi, & Baugh, 1999). Somewhat surprisingly, many listeners can make reasonable estimates of the speaker's age, height, and weight, especially if the speaker is male (e.g., Krauss, Freyberg, & Morsella, 2002). There has been debate, though, about the limits on this information about age, and one research group recommends that earwitnesses only provide generic age information ("young adult" vs. "older adult") rather than numerical estimates (Cerrato, Falcone, & Paoloni, 2000).

Listeners can also provide other information: They'll often report, for example, whether the voice was distinctive in some way (with a lisp, or an especially nasal voice, and so on). In many cases, the listeners will have some sense of the speaker's emotional state (excited or calm, happy or sad). But it's also common for listeners to draw unwarranted conclusions about a voice—making inferences, based on a brief speech sample, about the speakers' personality, visual attractiveness, and profession. There is little reason to believe these latter perceptions are accurate, inviting caution in how we use this information.

Let's also note that a listener's description of a voice is vulnerable to other influences and so, in this regard, is just like any other form of memory. Imagine, for example, that a witness hears a voice and then subsequently learns that the speaker lived in an area with a strong regional dialect, or subsequently learns that the speaker tended to speak quickly. These after-the-fact bits of information can easily alter what the witness recalls hearing.

As an example of this pattern, participants in one study received training on the speech cues that they were told could signal either honesty or deception in the speaker (Boydell, Barone, & Read, 2013). The participants then listened to a speaker's account of a crime and had to judge whether this person was lying or being truthful. Participants then received feedback that either confirmed or disconfirmed their assessment of the suspect. Finally, participants were asked to rate how often, in the suspect's speech, they had heard the various cues they had been instructed to detect. The results showed a clear effect of the feedback, with participants shifting their memory for what they heard based on the feedback they subsequently received.

The Effect of Timing

Voice identification is compromised if the initial exposure to the voice was brief; as a rough rule of thumb, the listener needs at least 30 seconds to encode a voice into memory (Yarmey, 2007). Let's be clear, though, that this is only a crude estimate, and we have already noted that some voices are more easily identified than others and therefore some voices will be recognized with shorter exposures.

Obviously, then, investigators want to know the duration of a witness's exposure to the target voice, but here we encounter a familiar problem: As we have seen, people are generally poor at estimating and recalling durations, and they tend to overestimate durations. These points have been documented in many settings, including exposure durations for voices (Yarmey, 2007). Thus, investigators are well advised to seek other means of determining the duration of exposure—including, of course, steps of reconstructing, based on other information, what the duration was likely to have been.

In addition, several factors can offset the effect of a brief exposure, and, in some conditions, voices can be properly identified even if the initial exposure was merely two seconds (Bricker & Pruzansky, 1966). As one consideration, identification is improved if the witness has heard a variety of speech sounds (as opposed to hearing someone say the same phrase over and over). Accuracy is also improved if the witness actually converses with the target person as opposed to simply hearing the target's voice (Yarmey, 2007).

Hearing a voice on separate occasions seems also to improve memory (e.g., Solan & Tiersma, 2003). In one study, all participants heard 60 seconds of the target voice and were later asked to identify the voice. One group heard the voice in an uninterrupted exposure; two weeks later, only 29% of the participants were able to identify the voice. A different group heard the same 60 seconds of voice, but divided into smaller segments and heard over three consecutive days. All of these participants were able to identify the voice later on (Deffenbacher et al., 1989). However, this effect may interact with overall duration, and this benefit was not obtained if the entire exposure to the voice was merely 30 seconds long. In that case, it did not matter whether participants heard the voice in one uninterrupted segment or in several segments; in both conditions, recognition performance was poor.

Finally, what about the other aspect of timing—the passage of time between hearing the voice and the subsequent identification attempt? (This time period, we noted earlier, is referred to as the retention interval.) Memory for voices shows a standard "forgetting curve" (see Chapter 3), but the exact form of the curve depends on various parameters—including how long the initial exposure was, how distinctive the voice was, and so on. As a result, sweeping claims about the forgetting rate are difficult to justify. One study showed a 50% accuracy rate for voice IDs after one week, 43% after two weeks, and only 9% after three weeks (Yarmey, 2007; but also see Kerstholt, Jansen, Amelsvoorty, & Broeders, 2006). Other studies, in contrast, have shown virtually no difference between a one- and two-week delay (Bull & Clifford, 1984).

Do the Exact Words Matter?

When witnesses hear a speaker, they hear him or her saying certain words, uttering certain phrases. One might expect, therefore, that identification will be enhanced if, in a voice lineup, the target and fillers utter the same words—that is, utter words spoken during the commission of the crime. Evidence suggests, however, that this return to the words used during the crime provides little advantage: Identification is just as good if, during the voice lineup, the speakers talk about some altogether different topic (e.g., Hammersley & Read, 1985; Yarmey, 2007).

Many people find this result to be surprising, but the explanation is straightforward: Even if suspects utter the same words they used during the crime, they are likely, during the lineup, to say them with a different intonation, at a different pitch and speed. These differences defeat the sort of "template matching" we might have hoped for by using just the "right" words.

Efforts Toward Distinguishing Good and Bad Voice IDs

It is plain that errors do occur in voice identification. Can we find a means of filtering out these mistaken identifications? More broadly, can we find a way to assess voice identifications, with the obvious goal of deciding which IDs are at high risk of error and which are at lower risk?

We have already discussed some of the relevant considerations: What was the duration of exposure? How long was the retention interval? Is the target voice distinctive? But, in addition and as with other forms of memory, common sense suggests that we might put more trust in an identification made with certainty ("I'm sure that's the voice I heard that night") than in one offered with doubts and qualifications ("I suppose that, if I had to guess, I'd pick No. 4"). As with face identifications, however, confidence turns out to be a poor index of voice identification accuracy: The correlation between confidence and accuracy for voice identification is close to zero, in large part because people tend to be far too confident in these judgments and consistently underestimate their risk of error. One author summarized the data by noting that potential jurors are "highly unrealistic in their commonsense predictions of the accuracy of speaker identifications" and that people "vastly overestimate the accuracy of identifications" (Yarmey, 2007, p. 117).

Perhaps, then, we should seek other means of assessing voice identification. As one option, perhaps we should put more trust in voice IDs by witnesses who have demonstrated their memory prowess in other ways. Imagine, for example, a witness who is able to give a rich and detailed description of the voice prior to the ID procedure. This sounds like a witness who did a good job of encoding the voice into memory—and therefore a witness more likely to provide an accurate identification. Similar claims might apply to a witness who seems able to provide a lengthy, apparently verbatim report of what the speaker said. Again, we might expect an accurate ID from this attentive, retentive witness. Unfortunately, though, neither of these suggestions is correct—and data show no advantage in the accuracy of identifications for witnesses who gave a detailed description of a voice or for witnesses who seem able to recall exactly what the speaker had said (Yarmey, 2001).

Identifier's Characteristics

A different route for assessing identifications focuses on the traits of the witness. For example, people with musical talent or training do seem to have some advantage in perceiving and remembering voices (Köster et al., 1998). Likewise, and perhaps unsurprisingly, expert phoneticians seem more accurate in recognizing voices than are people without this expertise (Hollien, 1990; Hollien & Schwartz, 2000). In contrast, there is no evidence for a difference between men and women in their ability to remember voices nor any evidence for an advantage in this regard for law-enforcement professionals.

Witnesses seem to be more successful in recognizing a voice that spoke words in the witness's own language (e.g., Köster & Schiller, 1997; Thompson, 1987). Several factors likely contribute to this effect. In their own language, witnesses can "segment" the speech stream into its constituent words, allowing them to judge the pronunciation of these words and assess the pace of the speech. In an unknown language, segmentation is difficult (and perhaps impossible), denying witnesses access to these cues. Moreover, witnesses hearing their own language may detect unusual stress patterns or idiosyncratic pronunciations—again, cues unavailable to someone without some proficiency in that language.

Even if the speaker is using the witness's own language, the witness will have greater difficulty in a subsequent identification if the speaker has a strong foreign accent. Again, various factors contribute, including the fact that, in this setting, the listener must spend considerable effort to understand the speech. Mental effort spent in this way is effort not spent on thinking about or encoding into memory the sound of the voice itself, leading to poorer memory for the voice later on (Pickel & Staller, 2012).

The Effect of Voice Changes

We earlier mentioned another complication for voice recognition: the occasion-to-occasion changes that can take place for a single voice. Some of these changes involve deliberate efforts at disguise, but many do not. For example, a perpetrator might be excited or angry during the crime, and these emotions can alter the pitch and pace of the perpetrator's voice. Intoxication can also change the pattern of someone's speech (including the timing of the speech and the pitch; Hollien & Martin, 1996). In addition, a perpetrator might yell or whisper during a crime, and these shifts alter many of the acoustic properties of the voice.

Whispering is, in fact, commonly used as a means of disguise, and so are deliberate changes in pitch (often, trying to speak with a lowered pitch). These disguises can be effective (Hollien, Majewski, & Doherty, 1982), and whispering is especially so (Procter & Yarmey, 2003). In one study, the recognition rate was 89% for familiar voices, but only 77% for whispered familiar voices (Yarmey, 2001). The impact of whispering was even larger for unfamiliar voices, decreasing identification rates from 66% to 22%.

We note in passing that the study just cited also included a separate group asked simply to forecast how accurate voice recognition would be in the various conditions. In keeping with other results, these forecasts were impressively optimistic—with estimates that participants would recognize 91% of the familiar whispers (14% higher than the actual result) and would recognize 74% of the unfamiliar whispers (and so 52% too high).

Proper ID Procedures

As with any form of evidence, earwitness identifications need to be collected properly. This point seems obvious, but bear in mind that voice identifications are relatively rare and so many law enforcement professionals have no experience in designing and implementing a voice identification lineup. The resulting improvisation can often invite error.

As one example, I participated in a case that involved a telephone bomb threat. Based on other evidence, the police developed a suspect and arrested him. The media announced the arrest, and so the earwitness knew that someone named "Josh" was in jail awaiting trial.

For the identification procedure, the police used a recording of a phone call that Josh made from jail to a friend. The phone call began (as most jail calls do) with a prerecorded message, advising the friend that the call was from a jail inmate and that the call was being recorded. Then, during the call, the friend called Josh by name, and the tone of the conversation made it clear that Josh was sometimes badly behaved.

This conversation was then played for the earwitness—including the message indicating that the call was from an inmate, the use of Josh's name, and the comments about Josh's behavior. No other conversation was played (i.e., the procedure was a voice showup, not a lineup), and the earwitness was asked to make an identification 18 months after her initial exposure to the voice, when she heard the bomb threat. (It should be no surprise that the judge ruled the ID inadmissible.)

What should a proper procedure include? Witnesses should be given an admonition ("the actual perpetrator's voice may or may not be included . . ."), just as they are with photo lineups. A lineup (with five fillers) is preferable to a showup. In the lineup, the suspect's voice should not stand out for any reason (including oddball bias or plausibility bias, as discussed in Chapter 5). If the suspect's voice is recorded over the telephone, then several voices in the lineup should be as well. (For more on identification of voices heard over the telephone, see Yarmey [1991].) If the suspect is speaking spontaneously (i.e., not from a script), then the same should be true for other (and perhaps all of the) voices in the lineup. It does not matter if all the voices are speaking the same words, nor does it matter if their words are matched to those spoken at the crime.

The witness's response should be recorded verbatim, and the witness's certainty collected immediately, before any further information is provided to the witness. If possible, the lineup should be conducted in a blind manner (i.e., conducted by someone who does not know which voice is the suspect's). The investigator should also seek to ascertain whether the witness might be familiar with the voice for some benign reason. Finally, the investigator should be very cautious in trusting the witness's recollection of the duration of hearing the voice because, as we have noted, this sort of memory is fragile (just as it is with faces), often inaccurate, and certainly open to outside influence.

B. MEMORY FOR CONVERSATIONS

So far in this chapter, our emphasis has been on an earwitness's ability to describe or identify the voice of a specific speaker. Often, though, the justice system turns to earwitnesses for another reason: to hear their recollection of what was said during a key event. This sort of memory is relevant to civil litigation ("When did you hear the stock was going to be issued?" "What was said at the business meeting?"). Memory for spoken messages is also relevant to many criminal cases. In some cases, the issue of prior intent is central (imagine a witness testifying that she heard the defendant say "Let's go kill him"). In other cases, there are allegations of conspiracy (and so a witness might recall conversations planning the crime). In still other cases, the crime itself is verbal (think about allegations of harassment, or abuse, or threat), and words once spoken can provide key information about these points. And, as one more example, criminal investigations are often shaped by "hearsay confessions"—including cases in which a jailhouse snitch reports another inmate boasting about a crime (cf. Neuschatz, Lawson, Swanner, Meissner, & Neuschatz, 2008; Swanner & Beike, 2010).

In some cases, earwitnesses provide information about whether a conversation happened at all. ("Did the doctor warn you about a procedure's side effects?"). Sometimes, the exact words are crucial. ("Did he say 'I did it' or 'we did it'?") In other cases, what matters is the sequence ("Did she mention the gun before you did, or only after?"). In still other cases, what matters is who the conversation participants were. ("Was George there when you said that to Marie?"). Plainly, memory for conversation is multidimensional.

Memory for conversation is also crucial for another purpose: We know that witness memory can be shaped by how the witness was questioned, and so, for example, juries might (and perhaps should) give more weight to witness utterances that were spontaneous and less weight to utterances suggested by the interviewer. For this reason, we want to know how a conversation with the witness unfolded: What questions were asked? How were they phrased? Were some questions repeated? Was feedback provided? In many investigations, our only evidence for these points comes from memory—and, specifically, an investigator's memory of how he or she questioned a witness, or perhaps a parent's memory of how he or she questioned a child. Can we count on these memories?

Conversation: Some Initial Observations

Memory for conversations is powerfully shaped by two intertwined themes. We'll begin with a broad overview of these themes, and then slow down to expand these points and examine the evidence relevant to each.

First, in most conversations, what people care about is not the exact sequence of words. Instead, what they care about—and so pay attention to and think about—is the "propositional content" of the conversation—the underlying gist. Said differently, listeners are generally trying to discern the message a speaker is conveying and often have little interest in how exactly the message was conveyed.

Note the immediate implication of this point: If people are focused on the gist, then they are likely to remember the gist and not the wording. Hence, we should expect from the outset that people will have difficulty in recalling how utterances were phrased or how exactly a conversation unfolded.

Second, in virtually all conversations, a huge amount of information goes unsaid, but the conversational participants effortlessly make inferences to fill in the bits not overtly expressed. This filling-in is made possible by the fact that participants in a conversation draw on their "common ground"—beliefs shared by the individuals in that conversation. When there is no common ground, the risk of misunderstanding is obviously increased.

Again, note the implication: We've just said that the gist of a conversation depends on inferences and assumptions. We've also said that people tend to remember the gist of a conversation and not the actual words spoken. Putting these pieces together, we're led to the expectation that people will often blur together in their recall propositions that were actually expressed and those that were merely implied. Said differently, people will often recall fragments of conversation that were not spoken at all.

The Priority of Gist

Right now, you, the reader, are looking at this page. Odds are good, though, that you have been paying little attention to the type font of these words or the exact structure of the sentences. Instead, you've likely been paying attention to the intended meaning of the passage and perhaps the implications of this gist for your work.

In Chapters 2 and 3, we discussed the linkage between attention and memory. Almost 20 years ago, Daniel Goleman offered a pithy summary of this linkage: "Memory," he wrote, "is attention in the past tense" (Goleman, 1996, p. 95). Perhaps Goleman thought this phrasing *too* pithy, though, because he immediately expanded this profound idea, noting that "what you remember now is what you noticed before."

In light of these points, what will you remember about this passage if quizzed, say, a day from now—or even 10 minutes from now? The prediction has to be that you will not remember the font or the phrasing because these did not catch your attention. (Or, rather, they wouldn't ordinarily have caught your attention. Your attention may now have shifted to these points, however, because of the content of this passage.) What you will likely remember is the gist of the passage, or, more precisely, your understanding of the gist, because that is what you were focusing on.

By the same logic, though, sometimes you will remember the exact wording. For example, you may have paused to contemplate (and enjoy) Goleman's pithy phrase.

The exact wording, then, was at that moment the focus of your attention—making it more likely that you will remember that wording. In the same vein, if this passage contained a superb alliteration or an especially eloquent turn of phrase, these points, too, might catch your view and thus stick with you. For that matter, if the phrasing suddenly became rude or included some obscure vocabulary, that too would attract attention and likely be remembered.

Memory for Wording

There is a wealth of evidence confirming the predictions just made—whether we are probing memory for a printed passage, a spoken narrative, or, returning to the focus of this chapter, a conversation. (For some of the classic data, see Bartlett [1932] and Bransford [1979]. For an excellent overview of memory for conversation, see Davis and Friedman [2007]. For the broader fabric of research describing the importance of attention and understanding in shaping what people remember, see Reisberg [2013a].)

As an illustration of the data pattern, consider an early study by Sachs (1967). Participants in the study heard a 24-sentence verbal passage. At various points, the passage was interrupted, and participants were presented with a test sentence. Their task was to decide whether this test sentence was identical to one of the sentences they had just encountered in the passage.

Sometimes, the test sentence arrived immediately after the target sentence was presented, so that the retention interval was effectively zero. In this condition, performance was excellent, and study participants easily detected any changes in the target sentence. The outcome was different, though, if just 80 syllables of new material intervened between the target and test—a delay of approximately 27 seconds. In this situation, participants were still accurate (roughly 80% correct) in detecting changes that altered the target sentence's meaning. However, with even this brief delay, participants were clueless in detecting changes in a sentence's form, with an accuracy level of 50%. (Let's emphasize that this level reflects essentially random responding. After all, with just two response options—"identical" versus "changed"—participants could reach this level of success if they based their responses on a coin toss rather than on a memory.)

Similar results have been obtained with participants hearing isolated sentences rather than connected discourse and with participants reading sentences rather than hearing them. Performance remains poor even if participants are explicitly warned about the nature of the upcoming memory test. In study after study, with just a few seconds delay, people generally have immense difficulty in recalling exact wording.

Memory for (Understood) Gist

On the positive side, though, people are rather good at recalling the gist of verbal inputs they have encountered—or, more precisely, the gist as they understood it.

Some of the evidence comes from studies that manipulate understanding (through the provision of hints or cues); the results show that steps that improve understanding routinely lead to better memory. Other evidence comes from studies that assess understanding, with the data routinely showing that deeper levels of understanding, assessed just after an encounter with verbal material, are predictive of better memory for that material days (or even years) later. (For some of the relevant evidence, see Bransford, 1979; Bransford & Johnson, 1972; Conway, Cohen, & Stanhope, 1992.)

Conversely, if someone *mis*understands a verbal input (including a conversation), or if the input is out of step with the person's broader understanding of the world, these factors can lead to a distortion in memory—one that brings the memory into alignment with the person's beliefs, at the cost of memory accuracy (e.g., Davis & Friedman, 2007). As a related point, if the person understands some aspects of the material but not others, results consistently show that memory will be more accurate for the elements that are understood, compared to those elements that were (for that person) unfamiliar, unclear, or opaque (for classic data, see Bartlett, 1932).

Linked to all of these points, memory for verbal material—and for conversations in particular—is improved if the person is somehow involved with the material—and so (in the case of a conversation) is one of the participants, not just a passive listener (e.g., Hammersley & Read, 1985). Presumably, this is because involvement demands that the person focus on, keep track of, and to some extent anticipate the conversation—considerations that will promote attention and understanding, and hence memory.

When Do People Remember the Verbatim Wording?

We have already indicated, though, that there will be systematic exceptions to the claims just made. Specifically, people should remember verbatim content (and not just gist) if the specific wording caught their attention—if, for example, the wording made the statement noticeably rude or particularly eloquent.

Several studies confirm these claims (e.g., Keenan, MacWhinney, & Mayhew, 1977; Kintsch & Bates, 1977; Murphy & Shapiro, 1994). In one study, for example, the researchers audio-recorded an academic seminar (Keenan et al., 1977). Later, the participants in that seminar were tested to see how well they remembered the sentences actually uttered. For most of the sentences, the data showed the by-now familiar pattern: The participants rejected test sentences (deeming them unfamiliar) if the test sentences were at odds with the gist of the discussion in the seminar. However, the participants seemed to have no memory of how exactly this gist was "packaged" and therefore could not distinguish between test sentences identical to those uttered in the seminar, and test sentences that were plausible paraphrases of those uttered.

The pattern was different, though, for sentences that the researchers categorized as having "high interactional content." These were sentences that managed, in their specific phrasing, to convey details of the speaker's intentions or beliefs, or extra information about the speaker's attitude toward the listener. For these sentences, memory for gist was still quite good, but so also was memory for phrasing.

Beyond the Information Given

We earlier mentioned that a great deal of information goes unsaid in a conversation and that conversational participants draw on their "common ground" to fill in these unspoken bits. This filling-in actually goes on at many levels—including a constructive process that changes not just someone's understanding of the conversation, but also their perception of the speech sounds themselves. Thus, in one early study, researchers recorded a number of naturally occurring conversations and, from these recordings, spliced out individual words. These words were then presented, now in isolation, to research participants. With no context to guide them, the participants were able to identify only half of the words. If restored to their original context, however, so that participants could use the context to supplement what they were hearing, word identification was nearly perfect (Pollack & Pickett, 1964).

In other cases, listeners' (or readers') filling-in provides the narrative "glue" that holds a conversation or a narrative together. As a simple illustration, consider this brief story (adapted from Charniak, 1972):

Betsy wanted to bring Jacob a present. She shook her piggy bank. It made no sound. She went to look for her mother.

This four-sentence tale is easy to understand but only because you provide important bits of background. For example, you weren't at all puzzled about why Betsy was interested in her piggy bank, and so you easily understood why the story's first sentence led naturally to the second. This is because you knew that things one gives as presents are often things bought for the occasion, that this purchase requires money, and that money is kept in piggy banks. Without these facts, you would likely have been bewildered about why a desire to give a gift would lead someone to her piggy bank. (Surely, you did not think Betsy intended to give the piggy bank itself as a present.) Likewise, why did Betsy shake her bank (as opposed to just looking at it)? What did she learn from the bank's silence? Why did she next go her mother? You can easily answer these questions, and your answers reflect the background knowledge that you used to fill in the "gaps" in the story.

In the Betsy and Jacob example, your contribution involves low-level common-sense knowledge. But now consider this example (after Pinker, 1994, pp. 146–147):

Woman to man: I'm leaving you.
Man in response: Who is he?!

Here, you make sense of the exchange by drawing on your knowledge about the vicissitudes of romance, allowing you easily to fill in the relevant soap-opera script.

Examples like these make it easy to see how often listeners (and readers) provide background information, allowing them to hear more in a verbal input (i.e., to identify the words), to make sense of the input (as in the Betsy and Jacob story), and to support further inferences from the input (as in the "I'm leaving you" sequence). These points are crucial when we ask how and how well people understand verbal inputs. The same points are crucial when we ask how people remember verbal inputs.

The Risk of Mishearing

Most conversations go smoothly forward, with the participants easily able to understand each other. Sometimes, though, things go awry, and people do find themselves at cross-purposes with their conversational partner ("Oh—I thought you were talking about *his* clothes, and not . . ."). Happily, these occasions seem to be rare, but can we specify when this sort of misunderstanding is more likely and when less?

The risk of misunderstanding will obviously go up if the actual stimulus information—the acoustic signal reaching your ears—is impoverished or distorted. This setting would be one in which you are forced to rely heavily on interpretation, with a corresponding risk of misinterpretation.

In some cases, a poor-quality acoustic signal is the result of background noise masking the speech. Or, imagine someone screaming as loudly as they can. In that setting, the loudness of the sound (and probably the emotion that triggered the screaming) can strain the musculature that produces speech, compromising the speech signal. In still other cases, details of the physical environment can disrupt the production, transmission, or detection of speech sounds. For example, I testified in a case in which a young girl had reported being touched inappropriately by a neighbor. The first report of this offense was overheard by the girl's mother when the alleged victim told her sister about the touching one night at bath time. The two sisters were in the tub; the mother was supervising the bath, but busy with her own activities (and looking away from the tub) while the children were bathing.

Notice, first, that the mother was not a participant in the girls' conversation but was merely a witness to the conversation. As we mentioned earlier, this point on its own creates a risk of misunderstanding. Second, the mother was paying attention to her own concerns and only casually listening to the girl's conversation. This factor—the mother only giving the conversation part of her attention—enhances the risk of misperception (Davis & Friedman, 2007). Third, consider the fact that this was *bath time*: Water was flowing into the tub, and the children were moving the bath water around. These are important sources of noise, masking the speech signal itself and forcing any listener to rely less on this acoustic input and more on inference. (Researchers would refer to the noise in this setting as "white noise," a term indicating that the noise contains a mix of different frequencies; white noise is particularly effective in masking other noises in the environment.) Fourth, consider the acoustic properties of an ordinary bathroom: The room is filled with large, flat, glossy surfaces—tiles, mirrors, bare floors, and walls. These surfaces do a fine job of reflecting sound waves. These reflections can make someone's voice sound richer and fuller (this point is part of why each of us sounds glorious when we are singing in the shower), but also undermines the clarity of the acoustic signal, again demanding more inference (to fill in what wasn't heard) and thus increasing the risk of mishearing.

Finally, note that the mother was not looking toward the children when she (reportedly) heard the initial disclosure. One might think this is irrelevant, inasmuch as "hearing" is an activity that depends on the ears, not on the eyes. However, this common-sense notion is misleading because ordinary speech perception is heavily influenced by visual cues: People routinely supplement what they hear with information gleaned from the sight of the speaker's face; this visual input is especially important if the speech is difficult to hear (as it likely was in this bathroom scenario). The visual input also becomes more important if the speech is difficult to *understand*, as it would be if the speech contains utterances that are puzzling or simply unexpected (Reisberg, McLean, & Goldstein, 1987).

Of course, in the case we are considering, the mother immediately started questioning her daughter to learn more, and we will return to this type of questioning later in the chapter and (from a different perspective) in Chapter 10. The key point, however, is that this is a circumstance ripe for mishearing, and it illustrates why a consideration of the circumstances is often essential.

The Importance of Common Ground

The previous section focused on the physical setting in which a conversation takes place. Just as important, though, is the *psychological* setting and—perhaps unsurprisingly—misunderstandings are more likely if the speaker and listener bring different assumptions and background to the conversation—that is, if they do not share common ground (Clark, 1996; Holtgraves, 2002).

Questions about common ground—and, specifically, whether common ground is shared in a particular conversation—need to be addressed on a case-by-case basis. Even so, a pair of illustrations may be helpful.

Misunderstanding in a conversation—and consequently errors in memory—is especially likely if the conversational participants differ in their social and educational background and in their professional roles. I consulted in one case, for example, in which a medical doctor insisted that he had told a patient to check back with him if a certain symptom persisted. The patient insisted that the conversation had never taken place, and, of course, the symptom had grown worse, leading to accusations and litigation.

In this situation, there are obvious concerns about common ground (Davis & Friedman, 2007; DiMatteo, 1985; Schneider, 1998). As an initial point, the pragmatic demands of medical practice often encourage physicians to be brief with their patients, leading to conversation that may be elliptical and thus in need of supplement (i.e., inferences drawn from a *hoped-for* common ground). In addition, doctors and patients may use different terms for symptoms and also different terms in describing subjective qualities (e.g., what does "moderately painful" mean?). Points that may be obvious to a doctor may not be obvious to the patient and vice versa. For all of these reasons, the risk of misunderstanding in these conversations is substantial, and the risk of memory error by either the doctor or the patient will be high. (For evidence bearing on these various points, see Davis & Friedman, 2007.)

Concerns about common ground are also prominent if the conversational participants have different views about the nature of their conversation. Consider, for example, the "conversation" that takes place between a police investigator and a suspect in an interrogation room. The courts are clear, of course, that a suspect's statement will be inadmissible if the investigator makes explicit promises or threats during the interrogation. Investigators are careful, therefore, not to make any promises or threats. However, investigators can (and often do) *imply* promises or threats. For example, I have reviewed many interrogations in which police officers make statements along the lines of these (the quote is fictitious, but closely modeled after actual transcripts):

> You know, I have to write a report after we're done talking, then it's up to the D.A. to decide what happens next. What do you think the D.A. will do if the report says you refused to cooperate and lied to us? And what do you think will happen if the report says you cooperated and manned up to what you did, and said you were sorry?

This is a setting in which the investigator and suspect are likely to have different understandings of the conversation—they are, in effect, "playing by different rules." The investigator's perspective emphasizes the specific words actually spoken (words that do not contain an explicit promise or threat). The suspect, on the other hand, is likely to adopt a perspective that is sensible in most settings—one that (as we have seen) focuses on the gist of the exchange, with minimal attention to how that gist is expressed. The suspect, in other words, "hears" the (suggested) promise and threat, even though the investigator uttered neither.

Can we document this misunderstanding? In one study, Kassin and McNall (1991) had participants read transcripts of criminal interrogations. Later, the participants were asked to forecast the jail sentence the suspect would receive if she confessed to the crime and the sentence if she continued to deny the charges. The results indicated that an interrogator's "maximizing" (a technique of emphasizing the strength of the evidence and the seriousness of the crime) did indeed convey the message that punishment would be harsh and, in fact, conveyed essentially the same message as an explicit threat of punishment. Conversely, "minimizing" (a technique of mentioning mitigating factors) conveyed the message that punishment would be lenient and had the same impact as an overt promise of leniency. (For more on interrogations and confessions, see Chapter 8.)

Other Roles for Knowledge

Common ground is not the only way in which knowledge shapes your understanding and memory of a conversation. Imagine, for example, that you talked with Ann last month about her divorce. Two days later, Fran had told you what *she'd* learned from Ann about the divorce. In this setting, there is a substantial risk that you'll end up "remembering" your conversation with Ann in a fashion that incorporates Fran's insights (Davis et al., 2005).

Likewise, imagine that you've talked with Ed on several occasions about his business plans. Later, you will surely have difficulties recalling which comments were made in which conversations. Remarkable evidence on this point comes from a detailed case study of (White House Counsel) John Dean's memory, when Dean tried to recall his Oval Office conversations with President Nixon (Neisser, 1981). Dean was questioned closely about these conversations (e.g., during the investigation of the Watergate Scandal that ended the Nixon presidency), and it later came to light that Nixon had secretly tape-recorded the conversations. Thus, we can now compare Dean's recall with what was actually said in the Oval Office, and his recall shows a consistent pattern: Dean was reasonably accurate in recalling the gist of the conversations, but made error after error in recalling which elements belonged in which conversation. In essence, these repeated episodes had blurred into each other, leaving Dean unable to distinguish the various conversations in his recall.

Who Said What?

The errors just discussed are both examples of *source confusion*—a notion we first introduced in Chapter 3. Source confusion can also take another form in memory for conversation: confusion about *who said what*.

Errors in this category are easily demonstrated (Davis & Friedman, 2007), and the errors are often guided by social categories. Thus, a remark made by one of the women in the room will be misattributed to some other woman; a comment made by one authority will be misremembered as coming from another authority. These errors are also guided by prior knowledge: If you know that Matt often complains, then you are likely to (mis)remember Al's complaint as having been voiced by Matt.

Errors about source can even include people remembering that *they* introduced an idea into the conversation when, in reality, the idea was first offered by someone else. This latter pattern is sometimes dubbed "unconscious plagiarism" and has been demonstrated in many settings. The error is more likely, however, at a longer delay and if the person now misremembering did alter or elaborate the idea in some fashion (e.g., Brown & Murphy, 1989; Defeldre, 2005; Stark & Perfect, 2006).

Remembering How You Questioned a Witness

We still need to address one more somewhat specialized topic: How well do people remember interviews or interrogations that were conducted as part of an investigation?

We saw in Chapter 3 that it is relatively easy to guide a witness—by asking suggestive questions, by highlighting certain topics, by providing positive feedback for some answers but not others. In assessing witness evidence, therefore, we need to know how the witness was questioned—and perhaps give less weight to the witness's report if the witness was led in some way.

Or, as a different example, consider an interrogation that eventually elicits a confession from the suspect. Here, we need to know whether the suspect's statement was coerced or not. And if the statement includes details about the crime, did the suspect come up with this information or was it suggested by the interviewers? In the former case, this guilty knowledge provides corroboration for the confession; in the latter case, it would not.

In some cases, we have a recording of the interview or the interrogation, and the recording can, of course, tell us whether the witness was led or the suspect coerced. Often, though, the recording covers only part of the crucial conversation. Often, there is no recording at all. As a result, our information about these conversations generally comes from the investigators' memories: when they describe (in a police report perhaps, or on the witness stand) who said what and in what sequence, what words were used, what comments were offered; and so on.

In light of our discussion so far, the concern about these memories should be obvious: It is likely that investigators will recall the gist of these conversations—or, more properly, the gist as they understood it. It is unlikely that they will recall the details of how the conversation unfolded: how questions were phrased; whether it was the investigator or the witness (or suspect) who first mentioned a point; whether questions were asked once or repeated; and so on. Unfortunately, though, these are exactly the points we would need to evaluate the interview and thus to determine the evidentiary value of the interview.

The importance of these issues is especially clear when the interview subject is a child. We know that children are highly vulnerable to suggestive questioning—and can, by improper questioning, sometimes be intimidated into silence and sometimes guided to unwarranted reports (see Chapters 10 and 11). Hence, it is urgent to know exactly how (and how often) the child has been questioned. Moreover, let's note that many investigations involving children are triggered by a conversation between a mother and her child—a conversation in which the child makes some important and often highly troubling disclosure. Can we count on mothers to recall the content of these crucial conversations?

One often-cited study focused on mothers' recall of a conversation with their four-year-old children. The study began with a brief session in which the researchers met with each child and engaged in some fun activities (with the mother absent). Then, immediately afterward, each mother was invited to question her child to find out what had happened during this play session. The key part of the study, however, took place three days later, when the mothers were questioned about how exactly their conversations with their children had unfolded (Bruck, Ceci, & Francoeur, 1999).

The mothers were quite accurate (88%) in recalling the gist of their conversations with their children, but they had great difficulty in recalling details of the conversation. For example, mothers were correct only 18% of the time in recalling whether a remark from the child had been spontaneous or prompted by a question. Mothers also underestimated their own role in shaping the conversation (and so, for example, recalled only 16% of the questions they had asked).

In this study, the mothers were also shown transcriptions of sentences they might have uttered in the conversations with their child, and they were asked whether the transcriptions were correct. Here, too, performance was poor, and mothers routinely accepted inaccurate transcriptions—including ones for which the researchers had omitted crucial elements. In some cases, the transcription left out the mother's explicit suggestion to her child or the mother's encouragement on a particular point; even with these omissions, the mothers still judged the transcriptions to be correct. In other cases, the transcription attributed to the child a comment that had actually been uttered by the mother; these transcriptions, too, were often judged correct. And, remarkably, the overall pattern of these data was essentially the same for a group of mothers who were alerted at the very start of the experiment that their memories would later be tested; this extra step (and the extra care it presumably elicited in the mothers) did virtually nothing to improve memory accuracy.

Similar results have been obtained with professional interviewers; they, too, tend to under-remember their own role in shaping the conversation. In one study, more than 80% of the interviewers' questions were not reflected at all in the interviewers' subsequent recollection of an interview (Warren & Woodall, 1999). Another study focused on actual forensic interviews conducted by trained investigators (with, on average, 12 years of experience in conducting these interviews). The researchers compared audio recordings of these interviews to the investigators' notes, taken contemporaneously (and, presumably, verbatim) during the interviews themselves (Lamb, Orbach, Sternberg, Hershkowitz, & Horowitz, 2000; see also Gregory, Schreiber-Compo, Vertefuille, & Zambrusky, 2011; Solan & Tiersma, 2003). One might think these data provide the "best-case scenario"—trained interviewers, important interviews, contemporaneous notes (and so no loss of information because of days of forgetting). Nonetheless, the data echo the pattern already described: The notes dramatically understated the interviewers' role in the conversation, and so, for example, made many of the children's remarks seem spontaneous when the remarks had instead been elicited by an explicit prompt. Indeed, there was no mention in the notes of almost two-thirds of the investigators' substantive remarks and, worse, no mention of 53% of the interviewer utterances that the researchers counted as suggestive.

C. MEMORY FOR CONVERSATIONS AND FOR VOICES: OVERVIEW

There are obvious commonalities between the material in this chapter and the material in earlier chapters. In this chapter, for example, we have had occasion to revisit the role of attention in guiding memory. Moreover, we have again seen that what matters for memory is not just "attention overall," but something more specific. Thus, someone might be paying full attention to a conversation—but that generally means attention to the ideas being expressed, and this focus entails less attention to (and so worse memory for) other aspects of the conversation, such as the voice qualities of the speaker or the actual words used.

Another recurrent theme involves the role of someone's broad knowledge in shaping what they perceive and what they remember. Thus, in Chapter 2, we discussed the role of "top-down" processes—mental steps that draw on assumptions and inferences to fill gaps in your perception and to guide interpretation of what you perceive. In the same fashion, we've emphasized in this chapter that, in listening to a conversation, people routinely draw on assumptions and inferences to fill in bits that are poorly heard or entirely unspoken.

In some ways, therefore, the discussion in this chapter parallels the content of earlier chapters. This point is itself important, inasmuch as the claims offered here can be seen as confirming a much broader pattern of evidence tied to how memory functions in many different domains.

CHAPTER 7

Lies

In our discussion so far, we have assumed a cooperative witness, ready to share information with law enforcement and attorneys. The witness may not remember all the information we need and may make mistakes in recalling the past. But at least the witness is trying to share what he knows.

Obviously, though, the justice system often encounters a different situation—one in which a witness is not cooperative and tries to deceive investigators. Anyone assessing witness evidence therefore needs to consider this other scenario: namely, *witnesses who lie.*

In this chapter, we start by examining strategies that have long been in place for lie detection—strategies that focus on the emotional state of the person who's lying. The idea here is that this person is likely to be anxious or tense while telling the lie, and so we can detect lies by detecting these states. This idea is at the center of many interviewers' attempts at lie detection; it is also central for lie detection via the polygraph. As we will see, though, there's little evidence to support these notions, and we should probably be seeking other approaches to lie detection.

A. HOW ACCURATELY DO PEOPLE DETECT LIES?

Police investigators, parole officers, and other professionals do their best to decide if someone is lying to them. Many nonprofessionals—including jurors—often need to make the same determination. We might ask at the start, therefore, how accurate these determinations are, and the answer is disappointing. The blunt reality is that most people do a poor job in lie detection, with accuracy rates not much better than one might achieve by blind guessing. Let's look at the data.

Lies Versus False Memories

We need to start with one preliminary, and it involves a point that has been in view in other chapters: It is easy to imagine that an investigator's (or juror's) challenge in evaluating a witness is to decide if the witness is lying or being truthful. This framing of the issue, however, is misleading. As one rather obvious point, a witness might be honest in some statements but not in others, and so a more fine-grained assessment is needed. But, even for a single statement, an investigator needs to bear in mind that there are three options to consider, not just two: (1) A witness might be telling a lie. (2) Or the witness might be accurately reporting what happened. (3) Or the witness may be honestly, sincerely reporting the past (so that the witness is not lying) but may be mistaken (and so the witness is not offering the truth).

The key here, of course, is that false memories (honest but mistaken reports on the past) are distinct from lies, and the detection of false memories is an entirely different matter from the detection of lies. For lies, one might seek indications of insincerity, but a false memory is sincere. For lies, one might focus on someone's motivation, on the straightforward idea that people lie in order to gain something or to avoid some undesired outcome. As discussed in Chapter 3, in contrast, motivation can be relevant to a false memory but often is not, and this provides another regard in which false memories are distinct from lies.

In addition, there are often "hybrids" that weave together truths, lies, and false memories. As one example, a lie can build on a true account but deliberately omit or alter some crucial element. As a less obvious case, someone can start out lying but, after telling the lie a few times, can be drawn in by the deception and end up believing it. In this case, the lie has evolved into a false memory.

These (and other) complications can cloud assessments of witness evidence. However, these complexities do not alter the fundamental fact that witnesses sometimes do tell straightforward lies. Sometimes they insist that they do not know the answer to a question when, in fact, they do. Sometimes they offer denials for statements they know to be true. Sometimes they offer an account that they know is at odds with the facts. Cases like these will be our focus in this chapter.

Measuring Lie-Detection Accuracy

Researchers use a variety of techniques to measure the accuracy of lie detection. Overall, though, this measurement requires two elements. First, we need "stimulus materials"—recordings (or live performances) of known lies and known truths. Second, we then present these materials to our test subjects and ask them to tell us: Are they seeing (or hearing) a truth? Or are they seeing (or hearing) a lie?

In some studies, the "stimulus materials" are in the form of videotapes showing some individuals telling the truth and some not; test subjects view these tapes in order to evaluate them. In other studies, the materials are audiotapes of people telling the truth or telling a lie; the test subjects have to make their judgments based only on this auditory information. In still other studies, we supply our test subjects with transcripts of someone telling the truth or someone lying. And, finally, in other studies, our test subjects interact with a live performer who is either telling the truth or lying, and, again, the test subjects must decide on the veracity (or the mendacity) of this performer.

Studies also differ in who the speakers are. In some studies, the speakers are actual criminals, explicitly asked to tell lies as part of the research project. In other studies, the speakers are criminals who are lying for their own reasons, separate from the research project. (Researchers can draw this sort of recording from videotapes of police interrogations or from reports in the media.) In still other studies, university students or even professional actors have been asked to lie about their opinions or previous events. Finally, in still other studies, the stimulus materials involve people who have first been instructed to engage in a (pretend) crime and then to lie about it (e.g., Ekman, O'Sullivan, & Frank, 1999; Kassin & Fong, 1999; Leach et al., 2009; Vrij et al., 2008).

There are, to be sure, concerns about some of these studies: University students may be less-practiced in lying than full-time criminals. People lying about low-stakes matters (e.g., what they saw in a nature video) may be less motivated to deceive compared to people lying about a consequential crime, and one might think that the less-motivated lies will be easier to detect (cf. DePaulo, Lanier, & Davis, 1983; Mann, Vrij, & Bull, 2004). Alternatively, people explicitly invited to lie by an experimenter may be calmer than people who are on their own choosing to lie, and this may make their lies harder to spot (e.g., Leach et al., 2009). Even so, there is an impressive level of consistency in the data, despite the diversity of procedures and participant pools, and it is this consistency that suggests our portrait of lie detection is reasonably accurate.

In this research, note that the research participants have two response options: The statement they are hearing is either a truth or a lie. If the participants therefore chose their response by *tossing a coin* they would get the right answer 50% of the time. It is daunting, therefore, that, in most procedures, the observed level of accuracy is in the vicinity of 55–60%—somewhat better than coin tossing, but not by much. One recent meta-analysis, for example, found an average accuracy rate among untrained participants of 54% (Bond & DePaulo, 2006). Another study found an accuracy rate of 55% among police officers and secret service agents (Vrij, Granhag & Porter, 2010). One study of prison inmates found somewhat better performance, with the inmates achieving 65% accuracy in distinguishing (videotaped) lies from true statements (Hartwig, Granhag, Strömwall, & Andersson, 2004). A different study found that government agents were 63% accurate in identifying true and false statements about theft and only 43% accurate (worse than tossing a coin) in distinguishing true from fabricated emotions (Bond, 2008; Mann et al., 2004).

Alongside of these averages, though, we should note that studies indicate considerable variability from one perceiver to the next. For example, Leach et al. (2009) reported chance levels of lie-detection accuracy overall (i.e., no better than a coin toss) but also found a wide range of performance levels. Their worst participants were only 29% accurate (and so were wrong more often than right and would have done better by guessing randomly). However, their best participants were 75% accurate—far from perfect, but appreciably better than chance. And a tiny number of people are said to be "lie-detection wizards"—reportedly able to detect lies with 90% accuracy or better. These individuals are extremely rare (only a few dozen have been identified, in a process that has screened more than 10,000 individuals), and it is not at all clear how they achieve their accuracy. We should also mention, though, that there is debate about the status (and perhaps even the existence) of these lie-detection "wizards" (e.g., Bond, 2008; 2012; O'Sullivan & Ekman, 2004; Vrij & Granhag, 2012). Even with this debate acknowledged, the key point remains: Lie-detection accuracy is immensely variable but, overall, rather poor.

The picture is different, though, if we ask people to assess their own levels of lie-detection performance, because people reliably overestimate their own success. For example, one study surveyed 600 police officers across the United States (Kassin et al., 2007). These officers understood that their lie-detection performance was far from perfect, but their self-assessment was nonetheless quite generous: Reflecting on their own experience, they claimed that they could spot lies (averaging across officers) 77% of the time—a level of accuracy notably higher than objective measurements have revealed.

Moreover, even though law enforcement professionals are generally no more accurate in their lie detection than ordinary citizens (cf. Vrij, Granhag, & Porter, 2010), the professionals tend to be more confident in their ability to detect lies (e.g., Leach, Talwar, Lee, Bala, & Lindsay, 2004). Other data, however, make it clear that there is little to no relationship between someone's confidence in his or her lie-detection judgments and the accuracy of those judgments (DePaulo, Charlton, Cooper, Lindsay, & Muhlenbruck, 1997).

What is going on here? Why is lie-detection performance generally so poor, and what is the source of this (apparently) misplaced confidence? The answers will emerge across this chapter, but in a nutshell the key is this: Many people have strong ideas about what the "tells" are that reveal a lie, and they are confident in their lie-detection ability because they know they are using these presumably helpful cues. As it turns out, though, these widely shared ideas are wrong, and the cues people usually rely on are not helpful. Thus, by relying on these cues, people do poorly in lie detection, and their confidence is unwarranted.

Detecting Children's Lies

Before we press on, is performance any better with children's lies? Can these be detected? Once again, the data are discouraging. Let's start, though, with the simple fact that children do tell lies (Vrij, 2002). Even preschool children are capable of deception, although their lies are often just one word, such as saying "yes" when the answer is "no." Preschool children are also capable of deceiving by withholding information, especially if coached or encouraged to do so. And, of course, as children grow, their ability to lie improves. Thus, school-aged children are able to tell more elaborate and fully plausible lies, and, again, coaching matters, so that their lies become more sophisticated if someone has instructed them in some way.

Let's also bear in mind that although young children (e.g., preschoolers) are often inept in lying, they are also inept in reporting actual events, and this makes it more difficult to spot the lies. In addition, young children are often confused about the distinction between reality and fantasy (we return to this point in Chapter 10), and so fantastical elements are sometimes included both in a child's lies and in the child's sincere reports. This complexity, too, can undermine adults' ability to spot deception in children. Moreover, with a little practice in telling a lie, children become much more skilled (e.g., Saykaly, Talwar, Lindsay, Bala, & Lee, 2013), and this adds to the difficulty of detecting their lies.

In light of all these points, it is unsurprising that adults are relatively unskilled in detecting children's deceit. As an example of the relevant research, one study focused on children's lies of omission, that is, the deliberate withholding of information. Adults detected these lies with accuracy levels greater than chance—but, even so, performance levels were poor (Nysse-Carris, Bottoms, & Salermo, 2011). With three- and four-year-olds, adults detected these lies only 62% of the time (bearing in mind that the adults could achieve 50% accuracy by basing their response on a coin toss rather than on their assessment of the child). With five- and six-year-olds, performance was in the same ballpark, with 65% of the lies detected.

Evidence suggests that parents are better at detecting children's lies than non-parents, and lie detection is better if one focuses on the child's narrative rather than the child's nonverbal behavior (Vrij, 2002). However, these points do not change the main message that performance levels here are generally low.

Does Training Improve Lie Detection?

It seems, then, that study after study reveals poor performance when people try to discern whether someone is telling them the truth or not. This pattern has been documented when research participants are trying to evaluate adults who are telling lies and when they evaluate children who are telling lies. The data are similar if we examine the performance of university students in detecting lies or if we instead test police investigators and government agents.

Remarkably, performance levels are not much better if we test people who have been explicitly trained in lie detection. One large-scale meta-analysis found that explicit training had a substantial impact on interviewers' "response criterion" but not on their actual sensitivity to lies (Meissner & Kassin, 2002). In other words, the training did not improve interviewers' actual ability to tell lies from truths. However, the training did lead interviewers to a more lax criterion—and so, trained interviewers needed less information and less certainty before proclaiming someone a liar compared to untrained interviewers. As a result, the trained interviewers were less likely to "miss" detecting a lie, but they were also more likely to produce a "false alarm" response—declaring a truth-teller to be a liar.

Studies also suggest that, after training, interviewers tend to be more confident in their ability to detect lies even though the training has, in fact, produced little improvement in their ability (Akehurst, Bull, Vrij, & Köhnken, 2004; Kassin & Fong, 1999). And, worse, at least some forms of training seem to undermine lie-detection performance, so that trained interviewers end up less accurate than untrained ones (Kassin & Fong, 1999).

What about a different form of training—the on-the-job training that investigators derive from years of experience as a police detective or parole officer, interviewing suspect after suspect? Here, the data are mixed. On the positive side, lie-detection skill is better among some professional groups (e.g., agents of the U.S. Secret Service; Ekman & O'Sullivan, 1991), and this advantage may to some extent be attributable to training and experience. On the negative side, though, we have already mentioned that poor lie-detection performance can be documented even among police officers, and so on-the-job experience is no guarantee of lie-detection skill.

Why doesn't experience help police officers to become better lie detectors? Part of the problem lies in the fact that police often enter a conversation with a suspect with strong ideas about whether the subject is being truthful. (If, for example, police already have evidence suggesting a suspect's guilt, they are likely to presume that the suspect will lie during their interview.) These preconceptions can potentially blind the interviewer to cues that might, in actuality, have improved lie detection; more broadly, these preconceptions can render the work experience much less useful in fostering lie-detection skills.

B. DETECTING LIES VIA SIGNS OF EMOTION

Thus, even with training, even with years of experience, most people are rather poor at detecting lies—with performance levels barely better than random guessing. Why is this? Why is lie detection so hard?

We have already suggested an answer to these questions, an answer that starts with the fact that most people have strong intuitions about how liars look or behave. Many people believe, for example, that liars will not look you in the eye and that they often have shifty eyes, moving their gaze abruptly from point to point. Likewise, many of us believe that liars tend to fidget, shaking their foot perhaps, or jiggling a leg. Other people are convinced that a specific shift in gaze direction is a signal for deception—a liar, they believe, is likely to gaze off to the left while lying.

Beliefs like these can be documented in a variety of ways—including surveys of ordinary citizens or surveys of police officers. These ideas are even woven into popular fiction. In his New York Times Bestseller, *The Fifth Witness*, Michael Connelly included a passage in which the narrator wanted "to pick up all body movements as I tried to read him. He was already displaying some of the classic tells of a dissembler—avoidance of eye contact, inappropriate smiling, constant hand movement" (p. 132). In *No Mark Upon Her*, Deborah Crombie writes "He watched Atterton's face for the tick that would betray foreknowledge, for the quick involuntary shift of the eyes that signaled deceit" (p. 208). William Heffernan, in *The Dead Detective*, writes

"There was a slight movement of his eyes to the left when he answered, which Harry picked up on. It was a classic tell. It didn't mean the young minister was lying, but it did indicate that he was not answering the question in a completely truthful manner" (p. 138). And so on.

These various ideas seem to rest on the notion that lies will be emotionally arousing in one fashion or another. Perhaps the person telling the lie is anxious, troubled by the prospect of being caught in the lie. Perhaps he is tense, because he knows he is engaged in a blameworthy act. Perhaps he is excited or feeling some sense of antagonism toward the questioner. In any of these cases, the proposal would be that we can detect the lie by detecting signs of these emotions. But with this common-sense logic now spelled out, what is the relevant science?

The History and Logic of the Polygraph

The idea that someone telling a lie will be anxious or agitated has a long history, and, across the centuries, has been used as a means of detecting lies. It is said, for example, that the ancient Chinese would have a suspect chew a few grains of rice and then spit them out. The idea here is that a dishonest suspect would be anxious, and the anxiety would lead to a dry mouth. Therefore, if the rice was dry when spit out, this was an indication of deception.

The logic is similar for a more modern means of detecting lies: the polygraph. To be precise, the term "polygraph" merely refers to the measurement device used in the lie-detection procedure—a device that keeps track of the subject's blood pressure, pulse, breathing pattern, and perspiration rate. These measurements can, however, be interpreted in conjunction with a specific questioning protocol—usually some version of the Control Question Test (CQT)—and this is the basis for the lie-detector test (e.g., Meijer & Verschuere, 2010).

Many individuals played key roles in the development of modern polygraphy. A medical student named John August Larson (1892–1965) is often credited as the inventor of the polygraph, in 1921. Also important was the systolic blood pressure test proposed by William Marston (1893–1947). Marston was an especially interesting character because, in addition to his work as a psychologist and inventor, he was also the creator of the comic book character Wonder Woman. (Note, by the way, that one of Wonder Woman's important weapons was her "Lasso of Truth." When someone was caught by this golden lasso, they were unable to lie—and so Wonder Woman, like her creator, took seriously the task of lie detection.)

Use of the polygraph was controversial from the start, and the admissibility of polygraph evidence was at the center of a U.S. Supreme Court ruling in 1923, in *Frye v. United States*. In this case, the trial court had ruled that polygraph evidence should not be admitted, and the ruling was upheld on appeal. Of course, this ruling is familiar to most legal scholars because the resulting "*Frye* rule" (i.e., the notion that a scientific claim must be "generally accepted" before it can be admitted) prevailed in U.S. courts for many years and is still the standard used by many state courts.

In any case, several inventors improved on Larson's and Marston's devices, and one noteworthy improvement was suggested in 1945 by John E. Reid—familiar to many readers because of his association with the "Reid technique," perhaps the most commonly used interrogation technique in the United States. (For more on this technique, see Chapter 8.) Thus, with links to comic books, a crucial (and still consequential) court ruling, and John Reid, polygraphy has had a noteworthy evolution.

Stepping away from history, though, how does the CQT proceed, and how successful is it? Generally, the test relies on three types of questions (Griesel & Yuille, 2007): *Irrelevant* questions are designed to provide a reading of the subject's reactions when answering a benign, trivial question. ("Are the walls in this room blue?"). Probable-lie ("*control*") questions are questions most people will lie about; these are intended to provide a reading of the subject's reactions when telling a lie. ("Have you ever lied?" "Have you ever broken the speed limit?") *Relevant* questions, finally, are the questions of main interest: "Did you rob the bank?" or "Did you touch her skin?"

The subject's physiological responses are measured for each type of question and then compared across questions. The idea here (roughly put) is that, if the response to the relevant questions is weaker than that to the probable-lie questions, then the subject has passed the test and will be scored as not-deceptive. If the converse is true (greater response to the relevant question), the subject will be scored as deceptive. (And, of course, often the test yields an intermediate outcome and is deemed "inconclusive.")

Note, though, that the responses being measured (heart rate and so on) are not in any direct way indicators of veracity. Instead, they are indicators of bodily arousal, excitement, or stress. (More precisely, these measures are indications of arousal in the *sympathetic branch* of the *autonomic nervous system*—a part of our biology that among other functions helps us to respond to threat.) In other words, the polygraph is, in its basic logic, resting on the idea that we can use degree of excitement (or, perhaps, degree of tension, agitation, or anxiety) as an indicator of deception because people telling a lie are, presumably, excited, tense, or anxious about their lies. But are they?

Assessments of the Polygraph

Advocates of polygraphy (including businesses with a commercial interest in the procedure) claim accuracy rates of 90–95% (or higher). The community of researchers, however, has been skeptical about these claims and has published data indicating much lower accuracy rates. Most studies concede that the polygraph is correct more often than not, and so the instrument does give us some information (e.g., Ben-Shakhar & Elaad, 2003; Fiedler, Schmid, & Stahl, 2002; Griesel & Yuille, 2007; Iacono & Lykken, 1997; Kircher, Horowitz, & Raskin, 1988). However, the error rate is substantial in many studies, and the "90% accurate" claim is certainly overgenerous

In fact, the sources of this error rate are easy to see. Some people do not become excited when telling their lies and so will pass the CQT. Some truth-tellers are highly anxious about the matter being investigated, and this anxiety will in some cases be registered by the CQT as deception. For these reasons, it is inevitable that the CQT is far from infallible.

In addition, there are several countermeasures designed to undermine the CQT (e.g., Honts & Kircher, 1994). One broad measure is for the subject to engage in relaxation exercises before and during the test, so that anxiety and arousal are low in response to all of the CQT questions. A different strategy is to engage in some activity (e.g., mental arithmetic) during the probable-lie (control) questions to increase the bodily response to these questions and to seek to relax during the relevant questions (to decrease the response). These strategies will alter the contrast between these two categories of question, making it more likely that the exam will show the subject to be truthful.

In light of these various concerns, it is perhaps unsurprising that, in 2003, the U.S. National Academy of Sciences expressed great reservations about the CQT, conceding that the test "may have some utility" but concluding overall (p. 212) that there is "little basis for the expectation that a polygraph test could have extremely high accuracy."

Before leaving this section, though, I should mention that there is considerable complexity attached to any claims about the overall accuracy of the polygraph, and, in truth, realistic claims about "overall accuracy" may not be possible. (The problem, in brief, is that the accuracy rate varies considerably, depending on a statistic called the "base rate.") Thus, if you have a case for which polygraphy plays a central role, you should dig into the details. Those details, however, are not essential for purposes of this book.

The Common-Sense Indicators of Deception

Stepping away from these complexities, though, let's return to our main agenda: How (and how well) can we detect lies? We have been focusing on the polygraph, but what about interviewers trying to detect lies? What cues do they focus on? What cues should they focus on?

We mentioned earlier that people have strong intuitions about how people look when they're telling lies and how they behave. Here's one more illustration of these intuitions: I once evaluated a case in which a police report contained the following details: "I was watching [X]'s reactions and body language to Detective [Y]'s questions. I made the following observations. 0135 HRS—Detective [Y] asked [X] where he was on the [dates]. [X]'s right foot began tapping. It had not tapped until that point in our interview and it only tapped for about 5 seconds. 0238 HRS—Detective [Y] was talking about [X] about his work history around the time of the crime. [X] was saying he worked for a mechanic. . . . I saw [X]'s right foot began tapping slightly again for about 5 seconds."

Cases like this one make it clear that investigators often have well-defined views about cues that signal deception. But are these views correct? Many researchers have explored this issue, and the data are clear: Cues like shifty eyes or fidgeting are actually of little value. One study, for example, showed that the accuracy of deception detection was *lower* among interviewers who consistently rely on these common-sense cues (Mann, Vrij, & Bull, 2004). Another study showed that training programs that emphasize these cues seem to undermine lie detection, although this training does increase participants' confidence in their judgments (Kassin & Fong, 1999).

Other studies have asked research participants to decide if a statement was a lie or not and have varied the medium of presentation—video versus audio versus transcript. One might expect that performance would be best when the participants can see the potential liars on video, but the result is otherwise: Performance is better when participants read a transcript or (in some studies) hear the audio, rather than viewing a videotape of the speaker. Why is this? With a transcript or audio, participants do not have the option of watching for shifty eyes or fidgeting. Therefore, these presentations do not allow participants to rely on these low-value cues; instead, the participants have to rely on the content of the lie—a point that leads to better lie detection (Bond & DePaulo, 2006; Bradford, Goodman-Delahunty, & Brooks, 2013; Davis, Markus, & Walters, 2006; Mann, Vrij, Fisher, & Robinson, 2008).

Observation and Measurement of Liars

Further evidence on this issue comes from studies that directly scrutinize the people telling lies, comparing them to truth-tellers. The research strategy here is to collect videotapes (or audiotapes or transcripts) of people telling known lies and known truths and then to ask directly how the two groups differ.

The available data are summarized in an often-cited meta-analysis by DePaulo, Lindsay, Malone, Muhlenbruck, Charlton, and Cooper (2003). They pooled data from more than a hundred studies, each of which had compared the actual behaviors of liars and truth-tellers. This rich dataset allowed DePaulo et al. to evaluate 158 possible cues that might be used to distinguish lies from truths, and their data do reveal differences between liars and truth-tellers, but the differences are small and emerge only when we consider the average scores of many liars in comparison to the averages for many truth-tellers. Put differently, the differences, although detectable in the statistics, are of negligible value in evaluating individual cases. Thus, liars and truth-tellers do not reliably differ in the classic "tells" of shifty eyes or fidgeting. In fact, they do not differ markedly on any dimension. There is no actual analog to Pinocchio's nose.

There is, however, a more positive way to think about the DePaulo et al. data. These data tell us that liars and truth-tellers do, as we have acknowledged, differ in various ways (albeit with considerable overlap between the groups). This point leaves open the possibility that we might somehow aggregate the various indicators—each of which is weak on its own—and in that fashion try to distinguish the two groups.

What cues might contribute to this aggregate? In the DePaulo et al. data, liars do provide (on average) slightly fewer details. They tend (on average) to be somewhat reticent and thus let the interviewers take up more of the conversation. They also (on average) take various steps to create some distance between themselves and their report and between themselves and the interviewer. Thus, they tend (on average) to use passive voice more often in comparison to truth-tellers; they are more likely to phrase things negatively (reporting on what didn't happen or what wasn't present); they also create a physical distance by, on average, leaning back a little. They also tend to be a bit more tense, although the tension is not revealed by any single cue (such as fidgeting); instead, they just broadly *seem* tense, and this state is again detectable only through an aggregation of several different cues. One noteworthy aspect of this tension, though, is in the muscles used to produce speech, with the result that, on average, people telling lies speak at a slightly higher pitch than truth-tellers.

It remains to be seen whether some means of lie detection might be created that somehow pools these various indicators. (It seems possible that the lie-detection wizards mentioned earlier may be relying on this sort of aggregate cue; the same may be true for professional gamblers, who claim they can tell when their opponents are bluffing. However, these suggestions are largely unexplored.) In the meantime, the fact remains that each of these cues is weak, and—again—there is enormous overlap between liars and truth-tellers in all of these dimensions. Perhaps, therefore, we should seek some other approach, one that does not rest on these common-sense cues or tells. This possibility has been prominent in recent research.

C. MICROEXPRESSIONS

People routinely display their emotions in a facial expression—smiling when happy, frowning when angry, and so on. Some of the facial indicators of emotion are, however, quite subtle—involving relatively small movements and lasting only a fraction of a second. These so-called *microexpressions* seem largely involuntary—which means that they will occur even when people are doing all they can to conceal their feelings (e.g., Freitas-Magahlaes, 2012). Some authors have suggested, therefore, that close scrutiny of these microexpressions can be used to detect deceit. Other authors, however, suggest that microexpressions cannot reveal a lie, but do reveal otherwise-hidden emotions —including emotions that are out of step with what a person claims to remember or claims that he or she is feeling (Matsumoto & Hwang, 2011a; 2011b; Porter & ten Brinke, 2008).

No matter how they are employed, though, the detection of microexpressions usually requires explicit training—for example, training in the use of the so-called Facial Action Coding System (Ekman, 2009; Ekman & Friesen, 2003). Various law enforcement agencies (including the Federal Bureau of Investigation and the Transportation Safety Administration) are exploring this training, and, more broadly, the use of microexpressions, and these fleeting, subtle cues may play a large role in lie detection in years to come. For now, though, we flag this avenue of research as promising but not yet established and, in any case, centered on a cue often unavailable for untrained individuals—including, of course, most law enforcement professionals, attorneys, or jurors.

D. KNOWING TOO MUCH; KNOWING TOO LITTLE

Our discussion in this chapter so far has focused largely on the person telling a lie, asking how he or she behaves, or sounds, or talks. Can we make more headway if we instead focus on the lies themselves? What information is offered? Is too much information provided, or perhaps too little?

What "Should" Someone Remember?

I participated in a case some years ago in which a young girl reported that she had been the victim of a night-time assault years earlier. She was able to provide exquisite detail about the event—including how many times she had blinked to convince herself she was truly awake and exactly the words spoken. Yet she was clueless about large-scale matters, such as bodily positions during the assault.

How should we think about this report? Other evidence tells us that emotional events are generally well remembered, but eventually do fade from memory (see Chapter 3). We also know that, within an emotional memory, central materials are more likely to be recalled while inconsequential details may never be encoded into memory. On these grounds, I was skeptical about the young girl's report. She knew too much about some points (the number of blinks) and too little about other points (the assault itself). Apparently, the jury agreed, and the defendant was acquitted.

Notice, then, that we can sometimes evaluate a witness's or victim's report by asking, in a broad, qualitative way, "What *should* be remembered?" in a case like the one being considered. Of course, we need to be careful here because people differ in what they remember, and—crucially—in how (and how much) they choose to report about prior events. Likewise, we know that people remember best what they attended most closely, but people also vary, from one person to the next and from one occasion to the next, in what catches their attention. For all these reasons, the "what should be remembered?" perspective must be applied with caution.

Statement Analysis

Perhaps we can do better, though, with a more formal, more systematic assessment of a witness's, victim's, or suspect's report. One procedure that has been explored is called Criteria-Based Content Analysis (CBCA). This procedure (which we first met in Chapter 3) was developed more than 50 years ago, with an initial focus on the evaluation of children's statements in cases involving allegations of child abuse. In more recent years, the CBCA has been used with adults as well and for a broad range of events.

In using the CBCA, trained judges evaluate someone's statements with regard to a list of specific criteria; these include logical structure, quantity of detail, descriptions of interactions, reproduction of conversation, accounts of subjective mental states, admitting lack of memory, and more. The evaluator decides, for each criterion, whether the report does or does not have the relevant attribute. The final score is then simply a count of how many of these criteria are present, with higher scores indicating a greater likelihood of veracity.

The CBCA has some validity, and people telling the truth do, in general, gain higher scores than people telling lies (Akehurtst, Manton, & Quandte, 2011; Griesel & Yuille, 2007; Vrij, 2005; for related data, indicating measures that might distinguish true and false trauma narratives, see Peace & Porter, 2011). On this basis, it is sensible that results from the CBCA are admissible in many jurisdictions (including Germany, where the CBCA is widely used, and several other northern European countries). There are, however, concerns about the CBCA: First, the analysis is done with written statements and so is possible only if there is an accurate record of the target material. Second, successful use of these criteria requires well-trained evaluators (Hauch et al., 2010) and, in at least some cases, these evaluators seem to rely on a mix of the CBCA scores and their own intuitions (cf. Akehurtst et al., 2011), and it is unclear how much of their decision making is carried by the intuitions. Third, statements need to be of adequate length for the CBCA to be applied, and so the procedure is of little value either for brief statements or for the analysis of single statements within a larger narrative (Raskin & Esplin, 1991). Fourth, CBCA scores can be influenced by factors independent of veracity: Thus, scores tend to be higher if the statements being evaluated involve familiar events rather than unfamiliar ones (Pezdek et al., 2004); the scores also tend to be higher with older children in comparison to younger ones (Vrij, 2005); scores may also be influenced by someone's motivation to lie, whether the lie has been coached in some fashion, and whether the person offering the "memory" is lying or instead offering a sincere but false memory (Ruby & Brigham, 1997). CBCA scores may also depend on the specific event being recalled, and—if the report is a lie—on whether the story has been made up from scratch, or instead borrows elements from an actual (truthful) memory (Sporer, 2014). Interpretation of CBCA scores is also complicated by an ongoing disagreement about how exactly the test is scored (Sporer, 2014)—with some authors preferring a 0 or 1 assessment for each of the criteria, and others preferring other schemes (e.g., a 0, 1 or 2 score for each criterion). Overall, then, the CBCA is a promising and often useful tool, but it is of limited value in many circumstances; indeed, one reviewer argued that its results "are not accurate enough to be admitted as expert scientific evidence in criminal courts but might be useful in police investigations" (Vrij, 2005, p. 3).

Similar remarks apply to another type of statement-validity assessment: one based in a reality-monitoring framework. The notion here is that each of us experiences thoughts from many difference sources: Some of our thoughts are rooted in specific memories, others are based on inferences, others are fantasies. Researchers have therefore asked: In day to day life, how does each of us sort through this variety, so that (one hopes) we trust the memories but are (usually) not fooled by the fantasies? From this base, can we develop an assessment that might allow us to evaluate someone else's memory—and, in particular, might allow us to distinguish true reports from false ones?

Like the CBCA, the reality-monitoring (RM) approach evaluates written statements—and so requires an accurate transcript of adequate length. Also like the CBCA, the RM assessment is done by raters with extensive training. Unlike the CBCA, however, the RM is explicitly rooted in theory—specifically, in a set of theoretical claims about how memories, inferences, and fantasies differ—and also claims about the cues we all spontaneously use (with varying degrees of success) to tell these categories of thought apart (Johnson & Raye, 1981). Thus, in this type of analysis, memories are evaluated for their inclusion of perceptual information (visual details, sounds, smells, and so on), context information (when and where did the event take place), memory for feelings (e.g., how did the person react), and more.

The RM approach is again promising and may in some circumstances distinguish true reports from false ones (e.g., Memon, Fraser, Colwell, Odinot, & Mastroberardino, 2010). However, the approach is far from infallible. For example, in one study, the scores distinguished true memories from false ones in only two of the three samples studied and only for younger children (under eight years old; Roberts & Lamb, 2010). In addition, evidence suggests that reality-monitoring scores are influenced by factors other than deception (including the character of the actual event, motivation to deceive, and questioning style), further eroding the value of this approach for forensic purposes. Overall, one thorough review described the full pattern of evidence as "mixed" and suggested that the differences between truthful and deceptive accounts were "quite small" when assessed through the lens of reality monitoring (Sporer, 2004, p. 90).

Guilty Knowledge

Yet another path toward lie detection focuses more specifically on the content of the (possible) lie and focuses in particular on what someone does or does not know about a target event. As we will see, though, this path brings us back to lie detection by "machine" rather than by an interviewer.

Imagine that a robbery victim was wearing a bright red shirt. This trivial detail would probably not make it into the news reports and so would not be widely known. However, the robber himself would likely have noticed the bright hue. Hence, if our suspect does know the shirt color, this seems incriminating: The suspect has "guilty knowledge"—knowledge that would likely be known by the perpetrator but not by someone innocent.

Needless to say, a suspect is likely to deny any knowledge about the crime—including the shirt color in our example. Investigators have various options, however, for going beyond a suspect's overt responses, and one of these options is at the heart of a procedure initially called the Guilty Knowledge Test but more recently dubbed the Concealed Information Test (CIT; Rosenfeld, Ben-Shakhar, & Ganis, 2012).

The term *orienting response (OR)* refers to an automatic response that humans (and many other organisms) make whenever an interesting or informative stimulus appears in the environment. In some settings and in some organisms, the OR is evident in an eye movement: You direct your gaze toward the new input. In other settings and in other organisms, the OR can be detected when the organism literally "perks up its ears," thus maximizing sensitivity to an auditory input.

The OR is also detectable in subtler ways—including signs that can be picked up by a polygraph. As we noted earlier, the polygraph itself (the measuring instrument) is simply a means of recording various indices of bodily arousal (breathing rate, blood pressure, pulse rate, perspiration, etc.). We can use the polygraph for lie detection, therefore, only by taking an additional step, and, traditionally, that step (as we described earlier) involves the CQT—comparing the test subject's state in response to relevant, irrelevant, and control questions. It is possible, however, to use these measurements of bodily activity in an entirely different way—including the momentary burst of arousal that is associated with the OR.

A more sophisticated means of detecting the OR involves brain wave measurement via an electroencephalogram. Specifically, if someone hears or sees a mostly monotonous succession of stimuli, and there is some sort of "oddball" within this series, the oddball reliably triggers a brain wave pattern known as the P300—a shift toward a more positive voltage (hence the "P") occurring roughly 300 milliseconds after the oddball arrives. Many types of oddball will trigger the P300, including the presentation of a high-pitched tone within a series of low-pitched sounds, the presentation of a tool amid a series of fruit names ("apple, banana, pear, cherry, pliers . . ."), and more. Importantly, though, the P300 is also triggered by the presentation of a familiar item within a series of unfamiliar items or the presentation of a meaningful item within a series of meaningless ones.

How can we turn these ideas into a lie-detection procedure? Imagine that we monitor someone's moment-by-moment bodily state while showing the person, on a computer screen, a question like: "Was the victim's shirt blue? . . . yellow? . . . red? . . . white?" The notion here is that the suspect will likely insist that he does not know the answer and may (in some procedures) even be instructed to sit silently while reading the question (and the various options). Nonetheless, one of the proffered options will be familiar and meaningful for the guilty party; that option would not be in any way distinctive for someone other than the guilty party. We can therefore ask: Does this "oddball" within the options trigger an OR, detectable through polygraphy or as a P300? In this fashion, no matter what knowledge the suspect denies having, we can detect the distinctive response to the guilty knowledge—and in that way detect the knowledge.

Several variants on the CIT have been proposed—some offered by researchers and some by commercial ventures. For example, one firm, under the label of "Brain Fingerprinting," uses brain waves as a means of detecting guilty knowledge; another firm, with the label, "No Lie MRI," uses neuroimaging scans (and functional magnetic resonance imaging [fMRI] scans in particular) in roughly the same way.

Do these procedures deliver what they promise? The evidence is mixed on the fMRI-based procedures (whether used for the detection of guilty knowledge or used for some other form of lie detection), and fMRI lie detection has several times been deemed inadmissible in court (e.g., Moriarty, 2008; also Langleben & Campbell, 2013; Pardo & Patterson, 2013; Rosenfeld, et al., 2012; Satel & Lilienfeld, 2013; Schacter, Chamberlain, Gaesser, & Gerlach, 2012; Schacter & Loftus, 2013). One summary, a few years back, simply stated that "the published literature reveals no data that provides unambiguous evidence regarding the sensitivity and specificity of fMRI-based neuroscience methods in the detection of lies at the individual-subject or the individual-event levels" (Wagner, 2010, p. 22).

But, setting the fMRI debate aside, other studies with other measures confirm the value of the CIT. And, in some ways, this value is almost guaranteed: There is no question that the orienting response exists and can be triggered by the presentation of a familiar stimulus within a series of unfamiliar options. There is likewise no debate about the fact that the OR can be detected through various changes in bodily state, even without an overt verbal response. These points provide a firm grounding for the CIT and make it nearly inevitable that the test will succeed.

Even so, there are important limitations on the CIT: This procedure is accurate in distinguishing liars from truth-tellers only if the procedure includes an adequate number of test items—that is, multiple facts that only the guilty party would know. One meta-analysis suggests five or more as a reasonable cut-off here (Ben-Shakhar & Elaad, 2003). To see why, and returning to our example, perhaps the test subject is innocent and shows a strong response to "red" as the shirt color only because he's rather fond of his own red shirt. That response, in our test, would be indistinguishable from a response actually indicating guilty knowledge about the victim's shirt. To avoid this sort of ambiguity, we need numerous test items—a situation in which it is unlikely that, just by coincidence, each of the "guilty" items is meaningful for the test subject for some benign reason.

The problem, of course, is that the availability of test items depends on the case facts: A test item is suitable for the CIT only if the investigators can be confident that the perpetrator would know the relevant information and that someone innocent would not know (and could not infer) this information. Finding facts in this category can be difficult and often requires that the initial investigation of the case be conducted with the CIT in mind so that suitable information can be collected from the start. This point obviously sets boundaries on the usefulness of this procedure. (For other concerns about whether the CIT, well-tested in the laboratory, will survive the translation into actual crime investigations, see Satel & Lilienfeld, 2013.)

E. ROUTES TO IMPROVING DECEPTION DETECTION

Where are we so far? Various traits and behaviors are, we've said, statistically associated with deception (DePaulo et al., 2003), but the statistical linkage is weak. The analysis of microexpressions seems promising, but, at best, its use requires extensive training. Statement analyses like the CBCA and RM do reasonably well in detecting some lies but can be pulled off track by various factors, and in any case require trained raters and a statement of adequate length. The CIT seems promising but is only possible if the case facts permit it.

With these points in view, it seems natural to ask what other paths might be open to us. Is there some better way for investigators to detect lies?

Interview Style

There are many ways to approach an interview with a suspect (or witness), and, from the perspective of lie detection, some approaches are better than others. For example, some interviewers use a more "accusatory" style that begins with an explicit assertion by the interviewer of the suspect's wrong-doing and continues from there with an aggressive tone. Other interviewers use a more neutral "information-gathering" style, relying heavily on open-ended questions and letting the interview be guided by answers to these questions. Evidence suggests that information-gathering interviews are in several ways superior—producing more information overall and also eliciting more cues (verbal or nonverbal) that might help the interviewer detect deceit (Vrij, Mann, & Fisher, 2006; for more on this contrast in interview styles, see Chapter 8's discussion of the difference between the United States and British styles of interrogating suspects). An information-gathering tone also increases the "load" on the interviewee, a point that will become important in a moment.

In addition, an investigator often enters an interview already knowing some relevant information. In this setting, one option is to put the information into view right at the start. This step offers a powerful message to the interviewee—namely, that the investigator is knowledgeable and has other sources of information with which to check the interviewee's claims. Plausibly, this message will persuade the interviewee that deceptive answers will likely be detected, and this may deter the interviewee from lying.

An entirely different option is to keep the information hidden, only mentioning it late in the interview (if at all). This strategy creates the possibility of detecting lies if the interviewee, not seeing the danger, makes some assertion that the investigator knows to be false. Likewise, this strategy creates the possibility that the interviewee will commit to a particular assertion that (unknown to the interviewee) is contradicted by the interviewer's advance knowledge. The interviewer can then confront the interviewee with the contradiction, perhaps leading to a reversal in the interviewee's story and perhaps leading to new disclosures.

Evidence suggests that the latter strategy—with the interviewer (at least initially) hiding what he or she knows—leads to better interviews and better lie detection (Hartwig, Granhag, Strömwall, & Kronvist, 2006). Indeed, one study compared interviewers who had been trained in the "strategic use of evidence" with those who had not and showed considerable improvement in lie detection (Hartwig et al., 2006).

Cognitive Load

Telling lies typically involves some work: You have to invent a story, trying to make sure it is plausible and either in line with the available facts or not checkable through the facts. You have to decide how closely the lie should resemble the truth. (The closer they are, the easier it will be to create the lie. But the closer they are, the greater the risk that the lie may reveal more than you intend.) You also need to draw on your intuitions about what a memory "ought to" include. (If you experience an event, how many of the details will you remember after a week? After a month? If you're creating a lie, you want to simulate this level.)

From this base, a number of researchers (especially Vrij and colleagues—e.g., Vrij & Granhag, 2012) have proposed that we can detect lies by detecting the observable consequences of all this mental work. They also propose steps to increase the effort needed to lie (in the scientific jargon, increase the "cognitive load"), thereby making it more difficult to lie and more difficult to lie well.

Detecting Effort

An emphasis on the role of mental effort in lying leads to numerous suggestions about how we might improve lie detection (Vrij, 2004; also Vrij & Granhag, 2012; Vrij et al., 2008; although, for some concerns about this perspective, see Buckley, 2012; Frank & Svetieva, 2012). As an initial step, the interviewer certainly wants to be alert to various signs of mental effort, and there are, in fact, many signs to watch for. For example, the cognitive burden of constructing a deception often forces someone telling a lie to keep their story relatively simple, and so we can sometimes detect the effort by tracking an account's overall complexity. Thus, concretely, liars often use fewer first-person pronouns and fewer "exclusive" words (such as *except*, or *but*, or *without*); these patterns are indications of diminished linguistic and narrative complexity (Newman, Pennebaker, Berry, & Richards, 2003). The effort needed to create the lie may also leave the liar less flexible in how the (fictitious) narrative is reported, and so someone telling a lie will have more difficulty if asked, say, first to report on an event verbally and then to draw a picture and narrate the event based on his or her own drawing (Leins, Fisher, & Vrij, 2012).

As a related point, Vrij, Edward, and Bull (2001) report that interviewers are more accurate in detecting lies if the interviewers are literally asked, "how hard is the person thinking?" rather than being asked "is the person lying?" This shift in the question may have two benefits. First, the "how hard" question draws the interviewer's attention to attributes (in the speaker's account and behavior) that may reveal the mental effort and thus the lie. Second, by *not* asking the "is she lying" question, we make it less likely that the interviewer will focus on the cues that (according to common sense) are indicative of lies (like fidgeting or shifty eyes). Because, as we have seen, these cues are actually not indicative of deception, we can improve lie detection by drawing attention away from them.

Maximizing the Effort Needed to Lie

Interviewers can also take steps to increase the liar's mental workload and thereby make the liar's efforts easier to detect. Among other options, the interviewer can ask detailed follow-up questions, requiring suspects to elaborate on what they have said. These elaborations force the suspect to go beyond the story that he or she has already prepared—demanding new constructions on the spot. (Again, these points will be relevant to the

British style of interrogating suspects, discussed in Chapter 8.) It can also be helpful to ask the suspect to describe the incident in reverse sequence. (What happened last? What happened before this?; Vrij et al., 2008) This sequence will be unprepared and unrehearsed, potentially creating a cognitive "overload" that causes the liar to falter.

In addition, the interviewer is well-advised to ask unexpected questions (e.g., Lancaster, Vrij, Hope, & Waller, 2013; Shaw et al., 2013). The idea here is that people planning to lie often prepare their lies in advance (i.e., before the interview begins). Because of this preparation, the work needed to construct the lie will already have happened before the interviewer arrives on the scene, and, of course, this will make it more difficult to detect the work (and hence the lie). To defeat this strategy, the interviewer wants to ask unanticipated questions, questions for which the person has likely done no preparation.

What sorts of unanticipated questions are best? Among other options, the interviewer can capitalize on the fact that many aspects of an event are likely to be memorable but regarded as not worth reporting; these aspects are likely not to be included in the prepared story. Vrij offers the example of reporting on a vacation; the travelers are likely to remember, but not bore their audience with, details of how exactly they purchased their tickets or which suitcases they took. Hence, someone preparing a lie about a vacation might not think to include these details and might be caught off guard if asked about these points.

Acknowledging Our Limits

One last point is also worth mentioning: In several ways, the justice system would be well served simply by acknowledging how difficult lie detection is. As we have seen, overall accuracy rates are quite low, and many investigators seem overconfident in their ability to detect lies. Against this backdrop, perhaps it would be a step forward to correct this overconfidence and help investigators gain a more realistic sense of their lie-detection abilities. Plausibly, this would allow investigators a more accurate evaluation of their evidence and thus improve their investigations. The same would be true for attorneys and triers of fact: They, too, might be well-served by a more accurate appraisal of their own lie-detection skill.

Beyond this point, though, let's be clear that the final word on lie detection is surely not yet written. In the last few pages, we have mentioned a number of new approaches to lie detection, including the CIT and interview procedures designed to maximize cognitive load and then to detect this load. Ongoing research is exploring these possibilities and will likely lead us to new and better procedures, and, overall, to various means of improving lie detection accuracy. Or, as a different path forward, we may able to fine tune some of our current claims, so that, for example, we will eventually be able to define circumstances in which we *can* count on interviewers' ability to detect lies. (For a possible lead on this point, with people seeking to detect high-stakes, highly emotional lies, see ten Brinke & Porter, 2012). On these grounds, this chapter has summarized the state of the art, but there is reason to hope that performance levels in lie detection will improve in years to come.

CHAPTER 8

Confessions

There may be no stronger form of evidence than a confession from a suspect. Indeed, in *Bruton v. United States,* the Supreme Court noted that a confession is "probably the most probative and damaging evidence that can be admitted." Eighteen years later, in its 1986 ruling in *Colorado v. Connelly,* the Court noted that "the introduction of a confession makes the other aspects of trial superfluous and the real trial, for all practical purposes, occurs when the confession is obtained." (For more on the power of confessions, see Appleby, Hasel, & Kassin, 2013.)

We're well served, therefore, when people guilty of crimes confess what they have done. Their confessions provide evidence that helps us achieve justice and promote public safety. But, of course, there's another side to this story because we know that sometimes innocent people confess—taking responsibility for crimes actually committed by others or taking responsibility for crimes that never occurred at all. In such cases, the power of confession evidence makes it likely that the innocent party will end up in jail. And, tragically, in many cases a false confession produces a "double error"—putting someone innocent in prison and simultaneously allowing the actual perpetrator to escape prosecution.

We therefore need to ask: How often do false confessions occur? Why do some people falsely confess? What evidence should we examine in trying to decide whether a particular confession might be false? We tackle all these issues in this chapter.

A. HOW COMMON ARE FALSE CONFESSIONS?

Common sense tells us that people prefer not being punished rather than being punished. Most rational people would, of course, prefer to be free rather than in prison; few people would volunteer to pay a financial penalty when they have the option of avoiding the penalty. On these grounds, one might think that false confessions would be rare and would emerge only in conditions of considerable coercion— because, after all, a false confession leaves someone vulnerable to punishment for whatever transgression he or she has now confessed to. Evidence suggests, though, that false confessions are not all that rare and emerge even in the absence of what most people think of as coercion. Let's look at the data.

Estimates of False-Confession Frequency

No one really knows how often false confessions occur. We can, however, provide some ballpark estimates—but with cautions attached to each estimate. In 2007, Kassin, Leo, Meissner, Richman, Colwell, Leach, and La Fon surveyed 631 police officers, examining the officers' beliefs and practices on many points. Among other questions, the police were asked to estimate how many of the confessions they'd seen were actually false. The average estimate was 4.8%.

How should we interpret this number? It seems plausible that police would prefer not to undermine their own evidence—evidence that, in many cases, they have developed through their own efforts (e.g., through an interrogation that they conducted). On this basis, it seems likely that police would tend toward understatement in answering Kassin et al.'s question, and so we might suspect that their responses (again, averaging to 4.8%) may well be an underestimate. Let's tentatively say, therefore, that the actual number of false confessions is some number greater than 4.8%.

A different number comes from the DNA exonerations that we have already discussed. As described in Chapter 4, there are reasons to be cautious about the exoneration data; nonetheless, these data do give us a window into the judicial process, and it is striking that, among the more than 300 cases documented so far, roughly one-quarter have included some sort of confession or self-incriminating statement.

Related data come from a broader survey of exoneration cases (including many not rooted in DNA evidence) reported by Gross, Jacoby, Matheson, Montgomery, and Patil (2005). In their data, 13% of the adult cases involved confessions (and because these were exoneration cases, these are obviously false confessions). Troublingly, 44% of the cases involving juveniles also included confessions (we have more to say about juveniles in a few pages).

A different sort of data come from surveys of specific populations, asking them directly whether they had ever offered a false confession in response to an interrogation. In these cases, one might worry about the honesty or accuracy of this self-disclosure, but the data are worth looking at even so: In one survey of prison inmates, for example, 12% claimed to have included a false confession in their own evidence (Gudjonsson, 2003; also see Kassin & Gudjonsson, 2004). In another, extremely ambitious study, researchers surveyed 23,000 juveniles in seven countries. Roughly 11% of these indicated that they had been interrogated by the police at some point, and, within this group, 14% reported having made some sort of false confession (Gudjonsson, Sigurdsson, & Sigfusdottir, 2009). In yet another study (Malloy, Shulman & Cauffman, 2014), researchers interviewed 193 teenage males incarcerated for serious crimes; 35% of the sample claimed to have made a false statement to authorities (either a false confession or a false guilty plea).

Again, let's note that any of these numbers should be interpreted with caution—especially when we realize that the categories of "correct" and "false confession" are less clear-cut than one might think. Often, suspects offer a genuine, truthful confession, but police investigators press them for more—and so the suspects elaborate on their misdeeds or falsely admit to further violations. These "hybrid" cases are important on their own, and the courts, in evaluating a confession, need to be alert to the often-overlooked possibility that *part* of the confession is true and part is not. For present purposes, though, these cases make it more difficult to specify how common false confessions are.

Even with this complication, the available data do provide a ballpark expectation for what the actual rate of false confession might be. The police estimate of 4.8% is likely too low; the 25% rate from the DNA exonerations (and, again, an even higher rate for juveniles) may not be representative of the broader set of criminal investigations; hence this estimate may be too high. (For more on this range of estimates, see Drizin & Leo, 2004.) Within this range, however, two points seem undeniable: First, and reassuringly, the vast majority of confessions are likely to be accurate. But, second, false confessions occur often enough to be deeply troubling, especially when we acknowledge the power of confession evidence in the courtroom.

B. WHY DO PEOPLE CONFESS?

Why do people confess—either to crimes they did commit or to crimes for which they are innocent? The answer has several parts because different people confess for different reasons. Some people confess because they long for notoriety. Some people confess because mental illness has led them to lose track of what is real and what is not. Some people confess as a deliberate effort toward confounding and misleading law enforcement. But what about ordinary people, in ordinary circumstances? Here, too, multiple mechanisms are in play, but three broad forces are worth emphasizing and help us understand the specific factors that can make a confession more likely.

Confessions as a Choice

In most interrogations, it is clear what the investigators want to hear. Indeed, often the investigators model the story, offering fairly explicit suggestions about how the alleged events might have unfolded. The suspect is therefore faced with a simple choice: "Should I assent to this account the investigators are laying out for me, and say 'yes, I did it,' or not?"

In this setting, the suspect will likely ask him- or herself: "What will happen if I give in and confess, and what will happen if I refuse to confess?" A confession will, of course, be more likely if the suspect decides the former consequences are preferable to the latter—that is, if the suspect decides there are better reasons to confess than not to. In essence, then, the suspect is doing a cost-benefit analysis—weighing the perceived costs of confessing against the perceived benefits and making a decision based on these considerations.

In some cases, this cost-benefit comparison is done consciously and deliberately, as a suspect mulls over his or her options. In other cases, this weighing of factors is done outside of awareness, and so we can regard the cost-benefit analysis not as a thoughtful exercise in decision making, but as an unconscious combination of pushes and pulls, with some notions pushing the suspect toward a confession and others pulling in the other direction. The result then depends on which forces prevail.

As we see later in this chapter, a lot of evidence confirms this view of confessions. Speaking broadly, though, the evidence falls into four interrelated categories: First, many studies tell us that a confession is more likely if the suspect is, for one reason or another, inept in his or her decision making. Thus, confessions are more likely if suspects are not thinking very clearly (e.g., because of depression or fatigue), are impulsive in their decision making, or simply do not understand the stakes in a police investigation.

Second, we also review evidence that confessions are more likely if someone overestimates the benefits of confessing. Thus, for example, confessions are more likely if the interrogation is especially aversive—because this point increases the perceived benefit for the suspect of bringing this obnoxious experience to a close. Likewise, a wealth of evidence tells us that juveniles and adolescents are often more alert to the short-term effects of their actions than they are to the longer term consequences. In an interrogation room, therefore, they are more sensitive to the immediate gain of exiting the interrogation compared to the longer term consequences they may suffer after offering a confession.

Third, we also consider evidence that confessions are more likely if someone underestimates the cost of confessing. In many cases, for example, innocent suspects are persuaded that the investigators will eventually confirm their innocence and let them go. On that basis, the suspect might believe there is no cost attached to a confession because the confession will ultimately be dismissed as bogus. Hence, the only consideration is the gain from confessing—namely, the escape from an aversive interrogation.

Fourth, suspects are sometimes persuaded in an interrogation that they will be convicted no matter what they say. This circumstance reframes the decision as a choice between "be convicted with a confession" or "be convicted without a confession." This is again a setting in which suspects might believe there is no cost to confessing (because they will be convicted either way) but a hoped-for benefit: some degree of leniency. It is not surprising, therefore, that this reframing of the decision has a powerful effect on suspects' decision making.

Let's emphasize once more that the claim here is not that suspects are consciously tallying the pluses and minuses of confessions, calculating the utility of their various options. To be sure, some suspects do go through this deliberate process, but most do not. Even so, we will soon see many pieces of evidence that fit well with the logic just described, and in this way the evidence confirms that the notion of "confession as choice" provides a powerful way to think about when confessions happen and why.

Social Pressure

Confessions are also evoked by another mechanism often working in concert with the choice process just described. That other mechanism, though, is best understood in social, not cognitive, terms.

Most of us have a set of well-practiced, virtually automatic responses that we make in social situations. If someone gives us a gift or shows us a kindness, we have an inclination to reciprocate. If someone makes an assertion, it is easier to accede than to disagree. If someone frames an issue in a certain way, we often accept that framing rather than insisting on our own perspective. In these and many other regards, our tendency is to "get along" and to act in a way that sustains a social interaction rather than disrupts it.

These social tendencies can be documented in a wide range of situations and certainly come into play whenever someone is interacting with a bully. Most individuals are hesitant to take the confrontational or even aggressive stance that might allow them to stand up to the bully. For most of us, it is far easier to give in to the bully, at least temporarily—with the hope of escaping from the bully's pressure and presence and thus ending the encounter.

How powerful are these social tendencies? One answer comes from a classic series of studies that involved relatively mild social pressure. In these studies, participants were shown cards with various lines on them and had to make a judgment about the lines' length. The key, though, is that participants were in groups when they made these judgments, and the other members of the group were (without the actual participant knowing it) working with the experimenter. In the first few trials, these other people would offer correct responses, putting the actual research participant at ease. On a subsequent trial, though, these other people would announce an incorrect response before the actual participant could voice his or her decision; the question was whether the participant would give in to this group pressure (Asch, 1956).

The judgments in this experiment were actually quite easy, and, in the absence of any group pressure, virtually every participant gave accurate responses. When the group pressure was present, however, roughly a third of the participants' answers were wrong, and, across the experiment, three-quarters of the participants gave in to the group pressure in at least one trial.

How do these ideas apply to an interrogation? The police are exerting social pressure. Often, they are kind to the suspect, inviting reciprocation. Often, the police frame the issue in a particular way ("Are you some sort of depraved villain, or are you just a guy who made a single mistake?"), luring the suspect into accepting their (often biased) presentation of the options. The police will also make strong assertions ("You know, a witness saw you at the scene"), and the pattern of ordinary conversation will lead the suspect to accept this statement at face value. All of these points, of course, allow the police to control the conversation and to navigate the suspect toward a confession.

More strongly, police do sometimes engage in behavior that one might categorize as "bullying." They aggressively tell the suspect, "No one is going to believe you." They might express impatience and perhaps even yell at the suspect, "How long are you going to keep us here?" They position themselves so that they are uncomfortably close to the suspect, so that the suspect feels physically hemmed in and "invaded." They arrange for multiple interviewers, so that the suspect feels (and is) "outnumbered." In these ways, the interrogation may indeed involve some version of bullying, and, for most people, it is easier to give in to bullies than resist them.

Internalized False Confession

In many cases, suspects offer a confession to the police but then emerge from the interrogation insisting (to friends, family members, or their attorney) that they are not guilty and that their confession was false. The mechanisms we have just considered—framed in terms of choice and social pressure—obviously apply to such cases. In other cases, though, suspects offer a false confession but then end up (mistakenly) believing their own confession. Researchers refer to this pattern as an *internalized false confession*—one in which an innocent person genuinely believes he or she is guilty.

This pattern seems bizarre to many people and gives rise to questions about whether the suspect might be mentally ill and delusional. However, the explanation for this pattern is more mundane. In earlier chapters, we discussed various cases in which someone honestly (and perhaps vividly) recalls a past event even though the event never happened at all. Most examples of these false memories involve events for which the person was a victim or a witness, but false memories can also occur for your own actions—and thus provide the basis for an internalized false confession.

In Chapter 3, we discussed factors that can encourage a false memory, and several of these factors are relevant to police interrogations. Often police insist, over and over, that the suspect did commit the criminal offense. Often, the police assert that they have other evidence (physical evidence or information from witnesses) confirming the suspect's guilt. Perhaps the police lay out, in some detail, the narrative of how they believe the criminal event occurred. Steps like these can powerfully encourage the creation of false memories (see Chapter 3)—so that the suspect comes to believe in his or her guilt and ends up "remembering" the guilty actions, even if the suspect is factually innocent.

This perspective suggests that internalized false confessions will be more likely in suspects who happen to be highly suggestible—and, as we will see, evidence confirms this point. In addition, let's note that false memories are more easily created in people who do not have a clear recollection of what actually occurred. (Thus, for example, if you vividly remember your dinner at home last night, I will have a difficult time creating in you the false memory that you actually ate the meal in a restaurant.) This point explains why false memories are more easily created for events in the distant past compared to more recent occurrences. But, in this context, let's note that many criminal suspects were inebriated in the hours surrounding a crime and so simply cannot recall what actually occurred. Let's also note that some suspects experience enormous stress associated with the criminal event, and this point, too, can impair memory. As a result, suspects often lack the recall that might help them resist outside suggestion, allowing police to move the suspects through a sequence we can roughly describe as "I guess that might have happened," leading to "I guess that did happen," leading to "Yes, I did pull the trigger."

Internalized false confessions surely arise in actual police investigations. The clearest demonstrations of this pattern, however, come from the laboratory, and here we need to acknowledge some important ethical issues: For purposes of science, do we want to expose our research participants to the stress of a false accusation? Do we want to risk the possibility that we will persuade our innocent participants that they have done something bad, should feel shame, and should present themselves for punishment? Mindful of these issues, no sane researcher would endanger participants by launching a false accusation of, say, an assault or an armed robbery, no matter how important the scientific hypotheses at stake. Researchers have therefore turned to accusations of (and potentially confessions of) much milder "crimes," in the hope that—even with these lighter transgressions—we can gain insight into the dynamics of interrogation and confession.

One important line of research, for example, uses a paradigm developed by Saul Kassin (e.g., Kassin & Kiechel, 1996; we should also acknowledge that Kassin—an enormously influential researcher in this domain—is the source of many of the ideas throughout this chapter): In this paradigm, participants are invited into the laboratory for a procedure that ostensibly involves fast typing. They are warned, however, that the software running the study has a weak spot: The software will freeze, they are told, and the study will be ruined if the participant happens to hit the "ALT" key on the keyboard. Participants are explicitly warned, therefore, not to hit this key. As the procedure progresses, however, the software is (unbeknownst to the participants) preprogrammed to freeze at a certain point, allowing the researcher to accuse the participants of having hit the forbidden key and, in some conditions, to provide evidence (e.g., an eyewitness) that the participants did indeed hit the key. The question, then, is whether participants will confess to this error and perhaps even come to believe that they committed this (non-existent) "crime."

Obviously, the transgression in play here (pressing a forbidden key and causing the researcher's computer to freeze) is trivial in comparison to the real-world crimes for which the police seek actual confessions. In Kassin's studies, no one is accusing the research participants of murder, child abuse, or rape; the participants know that their alleged misdeed will not lead to years in prison. (Indeed, Joseph Buckley, president of John E. Reid and Associates, the nation's leading trainer of police interrogators, has dismissed these experiments as "ridiculous"; Starr, 2013.) Even so, we can still draw insights from this research regarding the sorts of factors that encourage or discourage a false confession, insights that, of course, we can then confirm (or perhaps disconfirm) with subsequent and more realistic studies.

So, what happens in the Kassin studies? A stunning number of participants confess to the fictitious crime (e.g., Kassin & Kiechel, 1996): If the procedure had been reasonably fast-paced (making it plausible that the participant might have slipped and hit the ALT key), 65% of the participants confess. If, in addition, a "witness" says essentially: "I saw you hit the key," then all of the participants confess. Crucially for present purposes, though, many participants end up believing that they did indeed hit the ALT key. Thus, after leaving the study, 65% of the participants in the fast-paced + witness condition continue admitting their guilt to another person who is, they believe, not in any way connected to the research. In addition, more than a third of the participants are able to supply details about their misdeed, describing exactly how and when they hit the ALT key, even though they never did.

Thus, we need to bear in mind that a confession is, in many circumstances, a report on what the person remembers—with the suspect apparently recalling his or her transgressions. As such, confessions are vulnerable to all of the influences that guide other types of memory—including the prospect for substantial memory errors leading, in some cases, to a person falsely confessing *and* falsely remembering his or her own misdeeds.

C. WHAT SORTS OF PEOPLE ARE AT RISK FOR FALSE CONFESSION?

As we will see, many factors play a role in encouraging a confession, and let's note at the outset that these factors can encourage both true and false confessions. We therefore need to be alert to the fact that an outright condemnation of these factors is unwise. After all, surely we do want actually guilty suspects to be prosecuted efficiently, and that aim is promoted if actually guilty suspects confess. Even so, evidence suggests that at least some of these factors have a disproportionate effect on the innocent and therefore do more to encourage false confessions than genuine ones. As a result, these factors can lift the percentage of confessions that are false, and this is troublesome—and a point we return to later.

Overall, though, it will be helpful to divide the relevant factors into three broad categories. One category refers to the type of person the suspect is; that is, the capacities, traits, and (in some circumstances) mental illness that, in general, characterize the suspect. These are characteristics that the suspect had long before any police contact. A second category refers to the suspect's status right at the start of a police interview and thus to any duress the person may be under during the interview. Thus, independent of what the suspect is like overall, what was the suspect like on that day? Fatigued? Hungry? In need of drugs, medication, or even nicotine? Was the suspect drunk or hungover? These factors, too, need to be considered. Then the third category (unsurprisingly) concerns the interrogation itself: how, in what circumstances, and at what length the interrogation is conducted.

Adolescents and the Mentally Impaired

We have several times referred to the DNA exonerations, and, as we have discussed, the exonerations offer us a window through which we can try to assess what goes on in actual police cases. With that context, it is important that, of the DNA exoneration cases involving some sort of confession evidence, roughly 35% involved suspects who were juveniles, had some form of mental impairment, or both.

This pattern is then echoed by other studies: Drizin and Leo (2004), for example, describe a database of 125 proven false confessions; 33% of these involve juveniles. Gross et al. (2005) have also examined cases of wrongful convictions. As we mentioned earlier, their data indicate that, among adults, the false confession rate was 13%; the percentage jumps to more than 40% among exonerated juveniles, and to 75% among the youngest juveniles in their data set (12- to 15-year-olds). (Also see Goldstein, Condie, Kalbeitzer, Osman, & Geier, 2003; Grisso et al., 2003; Kassin et al. 2010b; Norris & Redlich, 2012; for a court ruling echoing these concerns about young people in the justice system, see *J. D. B. v. North Carolina*, 131 S.Ct. 2394 (2011).)

The data are likewise troubling if we focus on the mentally impaired. For example, Drizin and Leo found that 22% of the exonerees in their database were intellectually disabled according to standard intelligence test scores. (For an examination of the concerns when the suspect is both a juvenile and suffering from mental illness, see Redlich, 2007.)

Multiple mechanisms underlie these data patterns (cf. Norris & Redlich, 2012). To name just a few of these: Juveniles and the mentally impaired may be unable to understand their rights and may, without comprehension, waive these rights. Thus, they are denied this important safeguard (e.g., Fulero & Everington, 1995; 2004; Goldstein et al., 2003; Grisso, 1998; Oberlander & Goldstein, 2001; O'Connell, Garmoe, & Goldstein, 2005). Second, adolescents and the mentally impaired also tend to be more suggestible than adults (Gudjonsson, 2003; Kassin & Gudjonsson, 2004; Kassin et al., 2010b) and often show a pattern of "going along" with outside pressures, a pattern sometimes called *acquiescence bias* (Finlay & Lyons, 2002; Shaw & Budd, 1982). Third, members of these groups are often impulsive in their decision making and inclined to discount risk. These points may be linked to the slow development of the brain's prefrontal cortex, a structure that plays a crucial role in decision making and in the inhibition of inappropriate behaviors, and, it turns out, a structure that is not fully mature until someone is roughly 25 years old (e.g., Casey, Jones, & Hare, 2008). This slow brain development may in turn provide the explanation for another important point: namely, that adolescents tend to be keenly sensitive to immediate gratification and broadly insensitive to the long-term repercussions of their acts (Owen-Kostelnik, Repucci, & Meyer, 2006).

For all of these reasons, adolescents and the mentally impaired will often discount the likely consequences if they do confess, underestimate the probability of receiving those consequences, and will be powerfully motivated to seize the immediate benefit of escaping the interrogation pressure in any way they can find. In addition, individuals in these groups may not understand what is at stake in the interrogation itself and may not appreciate the seriousness of their situation (e.g., Clare & Gudjonsson, 1995). Indeed, many attorneys describe defendants who have offered comments like, "I thought I could go home if I just said yes to their questions," or "I was sure they'd figure out I wasn't guilty, so it didn't matter what I said to them."

In addition, individuals with mental disabilities can have difficulty communicating, thus clouding their comprehension of questions asked during interrogation and making their responses difficult to interpret. With this, individuals with disabilities often develop a pattern of relying on authority figures for information and guidance, and, of course, this makes them especially vulnerable to suggestion within an interrogation. These individuals may also have difficulty remembering their experiences, leaving them more open to an investigator's suggestion of what happened and also leaving them less able to provide exculpating evidence (including memories that may lead to an alibi).

Mental Illness

Various forms of mental illness are also associated with an increased likelihood of confession and, with that, an increased risk of false confession. Redlich (2007), for example, found that 22% of prison inmates who suffered from mental illness self-reported a false confession compared to reports of false confession from only 12% of inmates without mental illness (Sigurdsson & Gudjonsson, 1996; also Redlich, Kulish, & Steadman, 2011).

In fact, there are several reasons why mental illness is associated with confession (Kassin et al., 2010b). Some forms of mental illness (e.g., schizophrenia) are accompanied by delusions, so that a person being interrogated might lose track of which actions he has committed and which he has merely imagined. Other forms of mental illness (e.g., major depression) involve a strong sense of hopelessness, encouraging a suspect to believe he or she will be convicted no matter what else happens, and so he or she might as well confess in hopes of leniency or at least in hopes of ending the interrogation. A sense of hopelessness or anxiety can also make the police interrogation seem especially aversive, increasing the suspect's inclination to do anything possible—including confessing—to exit the interrogation room. Likewise, research suggests that the various symptoms associated with attention deficit/hyperactivity disorder (e.g., inattention, impulsivity) may also elevate the risk of false confession, plausibly because the symptoms of this disorder increase the danger that the suspect will not be able to focus on and think clearly about the risks in play in an interrogation.

In some cases, mental illness (and various forms of personality disorders) can lead someone to be less assertive and so more easily swayed by the police or to be rash and impulsive and so less likely to think about the longer term consequences of confessing. In still other cases, mental illness and various personality disorders are simply associated with poor decision making, and, again, this can undercut someone's ability to choose between confessing and not confessing.

Compliance and Suggestibility

Often, defense attorneys retain a clinical psychologist to do an evaluation of their client. When this happens, the factors we have been considering (intelligence, mental illness) are routinely assessed. But, in addition, there are two specialized measures that are relevant to confessions but often not part of the "standard" test battery.

Gudjonsson (2003) explicitly designed the Gudjonsson Compliance Scale (GCS) and Gudjonsson Suggestibility Scale (GSS) to evaluate a pair of factors directly relevant to events in the interrogation room: Roughly put, the GCS asks, "Do you do what I tell you to do?" More precisely, this scale is designed to measure how vulnerable someone is to outside pressures, including the social pressures exerted by police interrogators. People with high scores on this scale tend to be conflict-avoidant, acquiescent, and eager to please others.

The GSS, on the other hand, asks (again, putting it roughly), "Do you do believe what I tell you to believe?" This scale is designed to measure how readily someone will pick up suggestions from others and turn them into new beliefs. High scores here indicate that someone tends to accept and repeat back assertions he or she has heard, tends to have a poor memory overall, and is likely to be less assertive than most other people.

Both of these factors, compliance and suggestibility, are statistically linked to confession rates and thus important to consider in evaluating confession evidence. (We should also note that the GSS is designed to measure how suggestible in general someone is. However, suggestibility can also be increased by specific circumstances, including sleep deprivation and alcohol withdrawal [see Blagrove, 1996; Kassin & Gudjonsson, 2004]. Hence suggestibility is important on its own and can become even more so in some circumstances.)

Impulsivity and Substance Use

The broad trait of impulsivity also increases the likelihood of a confession: Someone who is impulsive is likely to give in to the pressures of the moment (including police pressure to admit to a crime) with little concern about longer term consequences. But impulsivity, in turn, is itself associated with other relevant traits and behaviors. We have already mentioned that adolescents are often impulsive, and this is one of the reasons for the increased likelihood of confession among adolescents. Likewise, research suggests that impulsivity is more of a concern among cigarette smokers, alcoholics, and other substance users (Baker, Johnson, & Bickel, 2003; Bickel & Marsch, 2001; Bickel, Odum, & Madden, 1999; Kollins, 2003; Reynolds, Richards, Horn, & Karraker, 2004). The exact nature of the linkage here is uncertain: Perhaps people who are impulsive to begin with may be more likely to seek out and use these various substances. Or, perhaps, the use of these substances can encourage someone to enjoy, and give in to, the pleasures of immediate gratification. One way or the other, evidence does suggest an association between substance use and impulsivity and thus between substance use and increased likelihood of confession.

Innocence

Some years back, Saul Kassin (e.g., Kassin, 2005; Kassin et al., 2010b) noted another—ironic and arguably tragic—factor that can put someone at increased risk for a confession, and specifically for a false confession. That factor is *factual innocence of the crime.* Kassin notes several lines of evidence suggesting that people who are innocent are more likely to waive their Miranda rights and more likely to cooperate fully with the police. In essence, these people seem to proceed on the idea that "I did nothing wrong; I have nothing to hide; I want to help the police." Moreover, Kassin suggests, these people seem to believe that their innocence is obvious to others (even though it is not), and so they are influenced by an "illusion of transparency."

With these attitudes in place, innocent suspects will often accept police suggestions at face value and will be largely unguarded in their responses during a police interview. In many cases, they will be convinced that their innocence will eventually be proven through further investigation. As a result, they perceive the "cost" of confessing to be low ("I'll confess now, but I'm sure we'll get it straightened out soon") and certainly low in relationship to the gain of ending a perhaps frightening, perhaps exhausting police interview. With this comparison of costs and benefits in place, the risk of a false confession is, of course, elevated.

D. DURESS

I testified in one trial in which the suspect had a history of suicidal depression, a lifelong pattern of acquiescing to others' needs or demands, a mental age of 14 or 15 (although she was chronologically 24 when interviewed by the police), and a GCS score of 20 (the highest possible score on this test). All of these points left this woman especially vulnerable to police pressure. If she was guilty of the crime, the police would have had a relatively easy time eliciting a confession. If she was actually innocent, the risk of a false confession was high.

It also turns out, though, that this woman came to the police station in a state of duress, and we need to consider this fact as well. Specifically, the woman came to the police station after a night in which she had gotten no sleep. She had not eaten anything for many hours. She had also smoked some marijuana the night before. For all these reasons, a polygrapher decided that her test results were uninterpretable and recorded this sentiment in the police report on the polygraph.

Police questioning of this woman began immediately after the (uninterpretable) polygraph, and that leads us to ask what the impact would be of the woman's status at that point: no sleep, no food, recent drug use, and now the stress and fatigue produced by just having undergone a polygraph examination. In truth, this cluster of factors is likely to have produced multiple problems: First, these various forms of duress (and/or altered state) can disrupt someone's cognition and make it more difficult for a suspect to recall prior events that might provide exculpating evidence. Second, poor memory can also render someone less certain about what did happen at the time of a crime and hence more open to police suggestion about what might have happened. Third, the same factors can undermine someone's decision making and thus make the person more inclined to prefer confessing and its immediate rewards over not confessing. These factors might also disrupt someone's ability to think through what will happen if they do confess or if they do not.

Fourth, these same factors can help to make the police questioning more aversive. ("I'm tired. I'm hungry. I'm desperate to get out of here.") This state would increase the person's motivation to escape the situation (and hence lead to an exaggerated sense of what is gained through confessing).

The case just described may be the extreme, simply because of the accumulation of factors, but similar logic applies to many other cases. Imagine a suspect who is a habitual cigarette smoker but has no opportunity for a nicotine break during police questioning. Or imagine someone who is distraught over some recent event. (A ferocious quarrel? Having witnessed a horrific accident?) These points, too, can disrupt someone's cognition and make the police questioning more troubling—increasing the likelihood of bad memory, bad decision making, poor critical thinking, and a strong wish to escape the situation by any means possible.

Duration

All of these points about the suspect's status, both immediately before and then during an interrogation, interact with another obvious concern: the length of the interrogation itself. If someone is hungry, weary, or nicotine-starved at the start of an interview, he will grow more so as the interview wears on. If other priorities make someone impatient to leave the police station, this feeling, too, will likely grow as the interview progresses. In addition, a lengthy interrogation can interrupt the suspect's eating or sleep schedules, and these points add to the duress experienced by the suspect. Indeed, lack of sleep is especially important here, inasmuch as sleep deprivation can itself lead to poor decision making, increased despair and suggestibility, and certainly to an enhanced desire simply to escape the stressful circumstances (cf. Harrison & Horne, 2000). And, if the person is a substance user, a lengthy interrogation is likely to produce a withdrawal state, amplifying all of the concerns already listed (for discussion of the effect of alcohol withdrawal on suggestibility and compliance, see Gudjonsson et al., 2004).

On these grounds, we might expect that longer police interviews will be more successful in eliciting confessions (both genuine and false), and evidence confirms this expectation. In Drizin and Leo's (2004) survey of actual police interrogations, the durations tend to be between 30 minutes and 2 hours. But, in their scrutiny of confessions subsequently proven to be false, the average duration was 16.3 hours. Roughly a third lasted between 6 and 12 hours; another third lasted 12–24 hours. (For more on interview duration, and specifically on how a longer interview encourages people to focus on the immediate gain of escaping repetitive questioning, see Madon, Yang, Smalarz, Guyll, & Scherr, 2013.)

E. THE NATURE OF THE INTERROGATION

So far, we have considered who the suspect is over the long term (and so the suspect's intelligence level, history of mental illness, and personality) and also what the suspect's state is at the start of and during the interrogation (is the suspect tired? hungry? hungover? in need of nicotine or some other substance?). It cannot be surprising, though, that the nature of the interrogation itself is also crucial: What is the content of the interrogation? What is its tone? What promises or threats are implied?

Much of the research on these issues has focused on the technique pioneered by John Reid. Many law enforcement professionals learn this interrogation style through training at the firm of John E. Reid and Associates; indeed, this firm trains more interrogators than any other company in the world. The Reid technique is also described in several books, including Inbau, Reid, Buckley, and Jayne's *Criminal Interrogation and Confessions* (2001; for a historical perspective on this technique, including an account of a false confession elicited by John Reid himself, see Starr, 2013). Many U.S. law enforcement professionals have been trained in this technique, and many others have learned aspects of this technique second- (or third-) hand through colleagues. Still others have received Reid training, but then improvise from this base according to their own judgment and the particulars of a specific interview. (On these grounds, perhaps we should not talk about "Reid interviews," but "Reid-influenced interviews.") For all of these reasons, the strategies included within the Reid technique are evident in interrogation room after interrogation room, and this leads to a number of questions: What are these techniques? Are they effective in eliciting confessions? How much do these techniques risk false confessions?

The Behavior Analysis Interview

Practitioners of the Reid technique agree that their procedure is confrontational, manipulative, and, in various ways, coercive. Are these aspects of the procedure a problem? Kassin and Gudjonsson (2004, p. 36) provide one answer: They describe an episode in which John Buckley, president of John E. Reid and Associates, was asked whether the Reid procedure lures innocent people into false confessions; his response was, "No, because we don't interrogate innocent people."

How do Reid-style interviewers arrange for this protection? Their procedure relies on an important safeguard—namely, that questioning should begin with a nonaccusatory Behavior Analysis Interview (BAI) explicitly designed to ascertain whether the suspect is being deceptive or not, withholding information or not. Based on the BAI, the interviewer decides whether to move on to the more coercive procedure, taking this step (one hopes) only for deceptive and presumed guilty interview subjects.

In the BAI, the interviewer asks questions designed to make the suspect anxious and to elicit behaviors allegedly diagnostic of deception. Often, the interviewer will ask, "What do you think should happen to someone who does this sort of crime?" Sometimes the interviewer will "bait" the suspect by suggesting that the interviewer has (or will soon have) evidence of the suspect's guilt. Throughout, the interviewer is instructed to be on the lookout for signals of anxiety and therefore deception—including long pauses before responding, gaze aversion, frozen posture, and more (Inbau et al., 2011). The Reid Institute seems convinced this is an effective procedure, and their website asserts that, according to their own research, interviewers trained in this procedure can correctly identify truthfulness 85% of the time (see www.reid.com/services/r_behavior.html).

Unfortunately, the Institute has not made its research public, and the evidence that is public points toward a very different conclusion: namely, that these behaviors are not diagnostic of deception and that the BAI therefore fails in its goal. Indeed, in one study (Vrij, Mann, & Fisher, 2006), 40 participants were interviewed using the BAI, and the data were coded according to the guidelines recommended by Inbau et al. (2011). On point after point, the results from the study were the opposite of those predicted by the BAI instructions, with deceptive participants showing fewer of the BAI signs than the truthful participants.

Other results confirm this pattern: One study tested law enforcement professionals to ascertain how successful each was at detecting deception. These professionals were then asked what cues they pay attention to in this task. Those who reported paying attention to the cues specifically highlighted by the BAI were systematically worse in detecting deception compared to others who did not report using these cues (Mann, Vrij, & Bull, 2004; also Vrij, Granhag, & Porter, 2010). Likewise, in a study we mentioned briefly in Chapter 7, Kassin and Fong (1999) used the Reid training protocols to instruct research participants in how to conduct the BAI. Compared to control participants who did not receive this training, those using the BAI were less accurate in detecting deception.

Overall, then, the safeguard supposedly provided by the BAI seems at best ineffectual and perhaps makes lie detection even less effective. The result, therefore, is that some number of guilty individuals will appear honest in the BAI and so will not be subjected to a procedure designed to gather incriminating evidence—a point that will undermine investigations and prosecution. Likewise, some number of innocent suspects will be judged dishonest in the BAI, and so they will be subjected to the manipulative, often deceptive practices of a Reid-style interview.

Reid Interrogations Are "Guilt Presumptive"

In the Reid protocol, interviewers are encouraged to step into a full interrogation only if they are convinced the suspect was deceptive in the initial BAI procedure. Indeed, this protocol makes a clear distinction between "interviews" and "interrogations." An interview should involve open-ended questions, is exploratory (not accusatory) in tone, and broadly involves the investigator listening more than talking. In an interrogation, the tone is accusatory, questions are likely to be leading, and, although investigators will tell suspects they want to hear their "side of the story," the investigators will do a lot (and perhaps most) of the talking as they control and guide the conversation in ways set out by the Reid procedure.

The key, then, is that investigators begin an interrogation already believing (correctly or not) that the suspect is likely to be guilty of the crimes being investigated, and, in this fashion, Reid-style interrogations are "guilt presumptive" (Kassin & Gudjonsson, 2004; Kassin et al., 2010a, b). To see how this matters, let's first set some context, using an illustration suggested by Simon (2012). Imagine that you are talking with someone and believe that person to be an extrovert. You probably wouldn't ask, "Have you ever tried to be just a little bit outgoing?" (although that might be a reasonable question to ask an introvert). Instead, you might offer a question that builds on your own assumption, perhaps asking: "What would you do if you wanted to liven things up at a party?" Let's also imagine, though, that you are mistaken, and you're actually conversing with someone who is introverted. Your question about livening up a party might encourage this person to focus on the (rare) occasions in which he has done something that was boldly outgoing, and so you may make the person sound extroverted (by focusing on these atypical cases), even if he is not.

Some terminology may be helpful here. Your behavior in this setting illustrates a pattern broadly known as *confirmation bias*. This term refers to a wide range of behaviors, all of which have the effect of protecting (and often strengthening) the beliefs someone already has—and so confirming those beliefs (see Reisberg, 2013a; for more on the role of confirmation bias in forensic science, see Kassin, Dror, & Kukucka, 2013). In the example just sketched, your question about the party seeks confirmation and elaboration of something you already believe and, in fact, is likely to elicit that confirmation.

But we can also focus more broadly—not just on your question, but also on how the other person responds. From this perspective, this hypothetical conversation illustrates a *self-fulfilling prophesy*. Your question encouraged a response that fit with your initial belief and confirmed your expectations. Thus, your question didn't just seek confirmation; instead, it structured the conversation in a fashion that made confirmation quite likely.

The broad idea, then, is that your expectations often shape how you act and also shape how others respond to you. But, beyond these informal descriptions, what's the evidence? In one study, pairs of people interacted via a voice-only link and so could not see each other (Snyder, Tanke, & Berscheid, 1977; also Snyder & Swann, 1978). One person in the pair (let's say "Jack") was told at the outset that the other person (let's say "Jill") was visually quite attractive, and this expectation led Jack to ask questions that allowed Jill to showcase her positive traits and talk about events in which she was attractive to others. As a result, people like Jill, assumed to be attractive by their conversational partners, actually ended up "sounding" more attractive. This point was confirmed when, later, recordings of these conversations were played for an altogether different person—let's call him "Jesse." Crucially, Jesse had no prior knowledge of Jack or Jill, had never seen either, and certainly did not know that Jack came into the conversation with certain beliefs. Jesse's only information, in other words, came from the audio recording of Jack and Jill's conversation. But, if Jesse heard a conversation in which Jack had presumed Jill to be attractive, Jesse concluded that Jill did indeed sound like an attractive individual. Alternatively, if Jesse heard a conversation in which some other Jack presumed some other Jill not to be attractive, then Jesse concluded Jill didn't sound attractive at all. Thus, Jack's expectations succeeded in changing Jill's self-presentation, which in turn had an impact on an entirely independent judge.

The relevance of all this to the interrogation room should be obvious. Imagine that police believe their suspect is guilty and therefore expect her to be tense and evasive. From this base, there is a substantial risk that police questioning will *cause* the suspect to have the anticipated qualities. In this way, the police expectations become self-fulfilling, confirming law enforcement's initial beliefs.

In fact, one study examined directly how this dynamic can play out in forensic interviews: Kassin, Goldstein, and Savitsky (2003) arranged for some of their research participants to steal $100 (as a "mock theft"); other participants were innocent of the crime. A separate group of participants then served as interviewers of these "suspects." Half of these interviewers were told prior to the interview that the suspects were likely to be innocent; half were told the suspects were likely to be guilty. (Thus, there are four combinations here, with the suspect actually "guilty" or not, and the interviewer believing in the suspect's "guilt" or not.) Then, finally, audiotapes of these interviews were played for yet another group of participants who rated their impressions of both the "suspects" and the "investigators."

In this study, investigators who believed the suspect to be guilty exerted more pressure on the suspect for a confession. They also made the suspects sound more anxious. "Condition blind observers who later listened to the tapes also perceived suspects in the guilty-expectations condition as more likely to have committed the mock crime. The presumption of guilt . . . thus set into motion a process of behavioral confirmation, shaping the interrogator's behavior, the suspect's behavior, and ultimately the judgments of neutral observers" (Kassin & Gudjonsson, 2004, p. 42).

Ironically, this data pattern was strongest when a guilt-assuming investigator was paired with an actually innocent suspect. "Apparently, interrogators who expected that their suspect was likely guilty did not reevaluate this belief even when paired with innocent people who issued plausible denials. Instead, they saw the denials as proof of a guilty person's resistance—and redoubled their efforts to elicit a confession" (p. 42).

Finally, before moving on, we should note that, when asked, most police officers will indicate that their goal in an interrogation is to learn the truth and not necessarily to gain a confession from the suspect. We should emphasize, then, that the notion of guilt-presumptive interviews is not intended as a challenge to this sentiment, nor is the notion of guilt-presumptive interviews intended as an accusation of police misconduct. In their interviews (or, more properly, their interrogations), police *are* seeking the truth—but if they enter the interrogation already convinced that the suspect is guilty, then the interview will still be guilt-presumptive. In other cases, though, police enter the interrogation uncertain about the suspect's guilt, but they conduct a guilt-presumptive interview anyhow, presumably on the assumption that this strategy will yield good evidence. The key here, though, is that this assumption will generally be wrong—with serious consequences for the quality of the evidence and of the investigation overall.

Reid-Style Interrogations

We still need to ask, however, what interrogations actually involve. Just how manipulative are they (or aren't they)? Are there some aspects of the interrogation that are more diagnostic (i.e., effective in producing true confessions but not false ones) and other aspects that are less diagnostic?

The full Reid procedure lays out the interrogation sequence in great detail—with step-by-step instructions and even a detailed description of what the interrogation room should look like. As we have mentioned, though, many investigators learn the Reid procedure only second- or third-hand, and many improvise on their own from the basic Reid outline. Rather than describe the full procedure, therefore, it will be more useful to rely on a "distilled" description (cf. Hasel & Kassin, 2009).

Overall, the Reid-derived or Reid-related procedure involves three main elements: *isolation, confrontation,* and *minimization.* The three elements are woven together into a complex sequence, but it will be helpful to describe them separately.

Isolation

If the path toward confession involves decision making, the police want to define the set of available choices in a way that favors law enforcement. Thus, for example, they may want to focus the suspect's attention on just two options—confessing to a one-time lapse, or admitting to being a committed criminal capable of (and perhaps guilty of) many transgressions. (They might therefore pose the question, "Are you just a guy who made a one-time mistake, or are you some kind of predator?") For this purpose, having the suspect isolated is of considerable value, allowing the police total control over the flow of information and the framing of the issues. Thus, the suspect should have no contact with other individuals—and so the suspect should have no allies in the room, or even a window to look out of, perhaps to seek allies; the suspect should not have access to a cell phone; and so on.

Likewise, if the path toward confession involves social pressure, isolation is again important. Once isolated, the suspect is cut off from other resources, including friends or sources of support, and so the only "social connection" available is via the police themselves. This makes the connection to the police all the more important and maximizes the effectiveness of social influence originating with the police.

Isolation also makes the interrogation more unpleasant. The suspect is denied usual comforts (including breaks when the person wants them or the momentary distraction and relief that might be provided by a window to look out of). The isolation also leaves the suspect in the dark about how the investigation is unfolding or what is happening with friends, and these points can increase the suspect's sense of uncertainty and anxiety and thus increase the incentive to escape this obnoxious setting. This anxiety can also undermine a suspect's thoughtfulness (including the capacity to make a reasoned assessment of the arguments for or against confessing).

For all of these reasons, it cannot be surprising that police questioning is typically done in a windowless, undecorated, clock-less, bare room. The suspect usually sits in an unpadded, armless metal chair. Cell phone use is forbidden, and often the suspect's cell phone is taken away. In many cases, the suspect is also led to feel powerless in a variety of ways—and so the timing of breaks is entirely up to the police, and "breaks" may actually take the form of the police leaving the room, with the suspect left sitting alone, unsupported, and undistracted, for many minutes. Little (or no) information is given about outside events, when the questioning will stop, and so on. All of these points make a confession more likely—and, if the suspect is factually innocent, make a false confession more likely.

Confrontation and Refusal of Denials

Often, police questioning begins with some conversation to establish rapport (increasing the effect of social influence by the police) but soon moves to confrontation. The confrontation is sometimes done gently (see the section on minimization) but is always firm: The police make it clear that they are utterly convinced the person is guilty. If the suspect offers denials, these are dismissed, interrupted, or ignored. With unwavering confidence, the police may assert that the suspect's denials are illogical or perhaps just implausible. The police may counter the denials by offering specific accounts of how they believe the criminal action took place. (This last is valuable for several reasons, including the fact that the suspect needs to do little beyond assenting in order to confess.)

Why is police rejection (or ignoring) of denials important? In this setting, the suspect can easily draw the conclusion that denials will always be rejected, so that renewed denials will simply lead to a continuation of the interview. It would not be absurd, therefore, for a suspect to conclude that the only way to end the questioning is by giving the police what they apparently want—acquiescence rather than denials and hence a confession. Thus, the prospect of interminable questioning can itself provide an incentive for the suspect to confess.

In addition, the continued rejections are likely to be aversive for the interview suspect. It is uncomfortable for most of us not to be believed, not to be trusted. It is tiresome for all of us to go over the same points in a conversation again and again. In these ways, the continued rejections make the conversation more obnoxious, more wearying—points that increase the motivation to end the conversation (by confessing) and also erode the thoughtfulness that might lead someone not to confess.

Confrontation via "Evidence"

Investigators will often introduce evidence into an interrogation in order to convince the suspect that they know he or she is guilty and that the court will surely reach the same conclusion. Thus, investigators might mention that some other witness saw the suspect at the crime scene, or they might mention physical evidence that confirms the suspect's guilt. United States law also permits police officers to confront a suspect with entirely fictitious evidence—claiming they have a witness, fingerprint, or confession from a co-conspirator even when they have no such thing.

Here is an example of this technique: I reviewed one case in which a detective was trying to elicit acknowledgment from a suspect that he was indeed present at a fist fight. "[The suspect] became more nervous and asked to leave. I told him he could and as he walked out of the interview room, I showed him a photo lineup that I had made with [his picture included]. On this photo lineup I had [the suspect's] photo circled and a fake signature signed at the bottom. When I showed [the suspect] this photo lineup, I told him that I knew he was at the fight on [date]. I again asked [him] if he was involved in the fight and he said to me you already know I was."

In some cases, suspects are told that they failed a polygraph (whether they did or not). More gently, police ask questions like, "What would you say if I told you you'd failed the polygraph?" Indeed, a reliance on (sometimes fictitious) polygraph evidence during the "post-polygraph interview" is common enough—and effective enough—in eliciting false confessions that the National Research Council has explicitly warned against this use of the polygraph, noting that this use can easily encourage false confessions (National Research Council, 2003).

The presentation of evidence (genuine or not) is often successful in eliciting confessions, and, the stronger the evidence is perceived by the suspect to be, the greater the likelihood of a confession (Deslauriers-Varin, Lussier, & St-Yves, 2011; also see Kassin & Kiechel, 1996; Kassin et al., 2010b). Why is this form of confrontation so powerful? First, the evidence presented during questioning will often contribute to the suspect's feeling of being trapped—and hence will increase the suspect's sense of powerlessness and isolation. Second, the evidence also shapes the suspect's understanding of his or her options: If evidence points toward guilt, then (as we have mentioned) the suspect may well perceive his options as "be convicted *with* a confession" or "be convicted *without* a confession." If those are indeed the only possibilities, a suspect might rationally choose a confession—even a false confession—in hopes of leniency.

Moreover, the presentation of fictitious evidence can literally alter a suspect's reality. We know that evidence from others can change how someone perceives the world; that was evident in the Asch studies of line-length perception, mentioned earlier. We also know that external evidence can alter someone's memory (see Chapter 3). In these ways, the presentation of evidence might do more than just persuade the suspect to confess; more powerfully, the presentation of evidence might actually persuade an innocent suspect that he or she is guilty.

Finally, in addition to presenting evidence, police will sometimes persuade a suspect that they will soon have incriminating evidence: "We're waiting for the lab to tell us that your DNA was at the scene," or "The hospital will let us talk to her in the morning; we already know she's going to say you were the driver." These promises of evidence-to-come are also powerful in eliciting confessions (Perillo & Kassin, 2011), but here we need to distinguish two cases: If the suspect is guilty, these bluffs can encourage a confession for the reasons already sketched: "I'm going to be found guilty with or without the confession, so I might as well confess so that I'll appear cooperative." What if the suspect is actually not guilty? Here, the bluffs invite a different line of thought: "The new evidence, when it arrives, will exonerate me, and so the police will get it right in the end. Therefore, I might as well confess now to end this horrible interview, knowing that the new evidence will protect me from any consequences of the [false] confession." But, of course, if the promise of evidence-to-come is a bluff, then this "rescue" from the false confession will never arrive. The dark consequences of that point should be obvious.

Before moving on, we should note that the presentation of fictitious evidence is acceptable to the justice system—but only up to a certain point. When the interrogators' lies become "patently coercive," the resulting confesson may be ruled inadmissible. This point was central, for example, in a 2014 ruling in New York state, in the case of *People v. Adrian P. Thomas*. The court ruled that "not all deception of a suspect is coercive, but in extreme forms it may be." Subsequent rulings, however, will be needed to clarify the definition of "extreme forms" of deception.

Minimization

It is extremely common for interrogators to develop "themes" within an interrogation that can provide a face-saving way for the suspect to admit wrong-doing. The themes can provide some sort of moral excuse or justification for the crime or can make the crime seem more "normal"—the sort of thing almost anyone might do. (One volume, published by the Reid firm, lists thousands of these themes; Senese, 2005). Among other options, these themes might suggest the crime was "spontaneous, accidental, provoked, pressured by peers, drug induced, hormone induced, or otherwise justified by circumstances" (Hasel & Kassin, 2009, p. 65). In cases involving violence, the police may suggest that the suspect's actions can be understood as self-defense. In cases involving sexual crimes, it is common for police to slide into crude stereotypes, with comments such as: "After all, the way she was dressed, how could you resist?" or even "She's certainly an attractive girl, and I'd be tempted, too."

In other cases, the theme might concede that the crime was bad but contrast it with something worse. For example, we mentioned earlier the two alternatives often offered by the police: They tell the suspect that they have seen two types of criminals—"a guy who made a one-time mistake" and "a genuine pervert who does this sort of thing over and over." The police might then ask the suspect which he is and even express the hope: "I believe—and I hope I'm right—that you're just one of the guys who made a mistake."

Again, minimization has multiple effects. At the least, this strategy can change how suspects perceive their options. Specifically, confessing may not seem so awful a step if you're confessing to something that is understandable or excusable. In addition, minimization can also imply to the suspect that a confession will be met with leniency because the suspect is confessing to something not so bad, not entirely blameworthy. Of course, police are not allowed to offer any sort of deals during an interrogation, and they are certainly not allowed to offer promises in return for this or that concession from the suspect. Nonetheless, the minimization will often be understood by the suspect as virtually a promise of leniency.

Indeed, police sometimes take steps to encourage this understanding. They sometimes, for example, describe other cases they have worked on in which some other suspect committed a similar offense, confessed, and then experienced a good outcome. They might say that this other suspect got "credit for stepping up." They might even say that the prosecutor reduced the charges against that suspect or that the suspect was acquitted. Of course, the police are not promising a similar outcome for the current suspect's case, but the implication is nonetheless clear.

Similarly, in some cases, police will say words along the lines of, "Look, I've got to write a report on all of this, and then I give my report to the D.A. Do you want me to write a report that says you're a guy who made a mistake, or a report that says you're a hardened criminal?" (We first met this example in Chapter 6.) Or perhaps the police say, "Which is better, a report that says you were cooperative, or a report that says you stone-walled?" These formulations certainly do not promise leniency but do remind the suspect that there will be a permanent record of the confession and that record will be carried forward to other steps in the justice system. It seems plausible that the suspect might draw from these points the idea that the now-minimized crime will be punished less harshly.

In fact, we have some evidence that suspects do make this inference. Specifically, Kassin and McNall (1991) had their participants read a transcript of an interrogation that elicited a confession, and the participants were asked what they thought the likely sentence would be if the suspect, having confessed, was convicted. Participants who read a transcript that offered minimization predicted a shorter sentence—exactly as did other participants who read a transcript that contained an *explicit promise* of leniency.

We alluded to the Kassin and McNall study in Chapter 6, in our discussion of common ground. There, we noted that the police and the suspect have different perspectives on the "conversation" taking place in an interrogation room. The police in this setting often rely on the premise that the exact words spoken are crucial, and so there is no problem if they offer broad hints about a possible promise or threat. The suspect, in contrast, relies on a perspective that is more common in conversations: As we noted in the earlier chapter, it is normal for a great deal to go unsaid in a conversation; indeed, there is often little difference, in determining how people understand a conversation, between ideas literally expressed and those merely implied. Likewise, there is often little difference in how a conversation is remembered between ideas expressed and ideas implied. But, of course, an interrogation is not an "ordinary conversation," and, in an interrogation, a hint of a promise is not (in the court's eyes) a promise. Hence, this is a situation in which a misunderstanding is likely *and* likely to be consequential.

This implied promise of leniency takes on special importance if the police have already convinced the suspect that he is likely to be convicted with or without a confession. (And, again, this belief in the suspect is encouraged both by the refusal of the suspect's denials and by the police presentation of other evidence—even if bogus evidence—"proving" the suspect's guilt.) In that setting, the suspect may give less thought to *whether* he'll be convicted and focus instead on what will happen *after conviction*. As a result, a path that might lead to leniency will seem especially attractive. In essence, the suspect is already convinced he's going to fall and is now trying to arrange for a soft landing.

Finally, we should mention that minimization (and its implied promise of leniency) may be especially powerful for suspects who are, in truth, not guilty. Russano, Meissner, Narchet, and Kassin (2005) used a laboratory paradigm in which participants were explicitly required to work individually on a project, neither helping nor being helped by other people in the room. Later, participants were accused of violating this rule and (specifically) accused of "cheating" by giving help to others. Many participants confessed to this violation, and this confession was more likely if minimization was used in the questioning of the participant. Crucially, though, minimization had more of an effect on innocent suspects, actually tripling the frequency of false confessions in this group.

Leverage via Other People

In some interrogations, police also seek another form of leverage—by encouraging the suspect to protect other people. I have, for example, seen interrogations in which the police say words along these lines: "If it wasn't you who pulled the trigger, it was your husband; he was the only other person there." Here, the suspect may wish to protect a spouse (or, in other settings, a fellow gang member or some other person), providing a different form of pressure that can lead to a confession.

It is also common for police to use the victim's status as a form of leverage. In cases involving child sexual abuse, police will ask, "You know that she still loves you, right? Do you realize how she's going to feel when she hears you're calling her a liar? And do you want other people to think she's a liar? Is that fair to her?" Or, as a more extreme variant, the police will tell the suspect that a confession is needed in order to save the victim's life. For example, in cases involving physical abuse of a child, the child often needs medical care, and it is common for police to tell the suspect that the doctors will not know what treatment is appropriate until they know exactly what happened. This assertion by the police is a lie and in most cases makes no sense medically, but it places powerful pressure on the suspect to confess in order to save the child.

Sometimes, police also rely on a different aspect of the social world—how the suspect will be perceived by others. For example, the police might describe a pair of crimes—one in which the perpetrator confessed ("stepped up," "manned up," "was honest about it," and so on) and one in which the perpetrator denied wrong-doing. The police then invite a social judgment: "Which of these guys would you admire more?," using this point to emphasize the apparent benefits of confessing.

The Reid Technique Overall

It should by now be clear why the Reid technique is so powerful. In the interrogation room, the suspect is isolated and without resources. The suspect has few choices—and the choice of not confessing is, in effect, ruled out. The police take steps (via minimization) so that the suspect seems to be confessing to something not so bad. They imply leniency. They use other people as leverage. And the police can persist in these efforts with no time limit. The interrogation can go on for hours, and this duration has several effects. The suspect will grow tired and so less thoughtful about the options. The process will grow more aversive, so that the suspect's eagerness to escape the situation will grow. The extended conversation will likely make it plain to the suspect that a thousand more denials of the crime will still have no effect. And the length of the interview provides the police with ample opportunity to try new perspectives, new forms of pressure, that might lead the suspect to provide the confession at last.

Police officers can also apply another type of pressure: They may tell the suspect that the interview (more accurately, the interrogation) is the suspect's "only chance" to offer his "side of the story." They may announce that, once this interview is over, they will hand the case over to someone else (probably a prosecutor). As a result, suspects are convinced that they do not have the luxury of carefully mulling over their options, consulting with a friend, or reflecting on what the police officers have said. Thus, suspects are pressed into making a decision while still in the interrogation room—and hence while under the stress and duress of the interrogation itself.

Given this accumulation of many factors, it should be no surprise that the Reid procedure is indeed effective, drawing on powerful psychological processes. The technique leaves many suspects believing that their only meaningful option is to surrender to police insistence that they're guilty and to comply with the police instruction that they should confess. In this fashion, the Reid technique achieves what it sets out to achieve, eliciting confessions in (by some estimates) more than half of the people interrogated. There is, however, a real danger that at least some (and perhaps many) of these confessions are false.

F. THE PEACE MODEL

We have been focusing on Reid-style interrogations because, as we noted earlier, this procedure is by far the most common style of interviewing in the United States. We should pause, though, to acknowledge that other models are available for how law enforcement should interview suspects, including the "PEACE" model.

The PEACE approach to interviewing grows out of the 1984 Police and Criminal Evidence Act in Britain, and, in the past dozen years, it has been used throughout England and Wales. PEACE style interviews are designed to be nonaccusatory and information gathering, in contrast to the confrontational approach used in the Reid technique. The goal of a PEACE interview is not to obtain a confession but is instead to gather as much information as possible so that the police (and, eventually, a jury) can make a fact-based determination of the suspect's involvement in the crime.

The term "PEACE" refers to the five parts of this interviewing strategy: *Preparation and Planning, Engage and Explain, Account, Closure,* and *Evaluate.* In the *Preparation and Planning* stage, interviewers plan the upcoming interview in detail and are encouraged to have intimate knowledge of the case file before starting the interview. In the

Engage and Explain step, interviewers establish rapport with the suspect and engage the person in conversation. Then, in the *Account* step, police rely on open-ended questions to elicit as full an account of the key events as they can. Then, in *Closure,* the officer summarizes the information and provides the suspect an opportunity to correct or add information. Then, in *Evaluate,* the information now gathered can be assessed within the broader context of the investigation.

Within these steps, the emphasis is plainly on information gathering, with a focus on the content of what the suspect is saying and not on the suspect's nonverbal behavior. Investigators are instructed not to pay attention to anxiety as a cue to lying, and they are not allowed to offer bluffs (or outright lies) to the suspect about other evidence that they supposedly might have. Above all, investigators try to maximize the information they gain from the suspect—circling back to elements already described in order to gain more detail. Investigators stay alert for inconsistencies in the suspect's account and for factual points that can be confirmed or challenged through other evidence.

Does this procedure work? Does it elicit information useful for—indeed, needed by—the criminal justice system? The evidence is encouraging. Let's start with the fact that the PEACE procedure is rooted in the same principles as the cognitive interview, described in Chapter 3, and we already know that the cognitive interview is effective in eliciting fuller recall from witnesses—and presumably from suspects as well. In addition, we saw in Chapter 7 that lie detection seems better when interviews emphasize content and cognitive load rather than seeking signs of anxiety, and this point, too, seems to favor the PEACE procedure. Finally, this procedure is also guided by the principles built into the interview protocols recommended for children (Chapter 11), with an emphasis on invitational and open-ended questions. These principles are drawn directly from research and so provide another line of support for the PEACE approach.

More directly, though, there is no indication in the historical record that prosecutions became more difficult when investigators in Britain shifted to the PEACE strategy. Moreover, a recent meta-analysis compared information-gathering interviews like PEACE with accusatory interviews (like those rooted in the Reid technique). The authors concluded that "When directly contrasted with one another, information-gathering methods of interrogation prove more diagnostic—they elicit a greater proportion of true confessions, while significantly reducing the likelihood of false confession" (Meissner, Redlich, Bhatt, & Brandon, 2012; p. 31; also see Kassin, Appleby, & Torkildson Perillo, 2010a). Thus, the PEACE procedure does seem a viable alternative to the confrontational approach widely used in the United States, and American law enforcement would be well advised to examine this British model.

G. POTENTIAL CORROBORATION FOR A CONFESSION

We said earlier and here reiterate: The vast majority of confessions (whether from Reid-style or PEACE interviews) are likely to be accurate and true, but, even so, there is no doubt that false confessions do occur, and this point is obviously visible to law enforcement. (We have mentioned the Kassin et al. [2007] survey, documenting this point.) Let's therefore set aside the naïve idea that police investigators will accept every confession they obtain or learn about. Instead, the police will, in many cases, be alert to the possibility that a confession might be false and seek further evidence to check on this possibility. (Indeed, in some jurisdictions, statutes require this further step and demand some form of corroboration for a suspect's admissions.)

Confession Contamination

What further evidence can corroborate or perhaps undermine a confession? In many cases, the suspect provides details about the crime—about the words said, the layout of the crime scene, and more. Often there is no way to check on this information, but, even so, these details can make the confession more persuasive, either for investigators or for a jury (Appleby, Hasel, & Kasin, 2013). In other cases, the suspect provides information that can be confirmed ("You'll find the gun if you look in the basement"), and this "guilty knowledge" can be quite incriminating. (For more on guilty knowledge, see Chapter 7.)

However, let's flag the need for caution in interpreting this "extra" information provided by the suspect. In many cases, this information is endorsed by the suspect but was introduced into the interrogation by the police. The police might, for example, have suggested to the suspect how the crime unfolded or how they believe it unfolded. Those suggestions might then be echoed by the suspect—and perhaps even believed by the suspect (see Chapter 3)—but, again, in this scenario, the information provided by these details was put into the conversation by the police. Hence, the suspect's endorsement of this information has little evidentiary value.

The concern at issue here is sometimes dubbed "confession contamination"— information deriving from the interrogators but then included in the suspect's confession. Sometimes this contamination is evident in a recording of the interrogation, but often it comes from earlier, unrecorded conversations. In the latter case, we might hope for guidance from the interrogators' memories ("Who mentioned the body's location first? Was it you or was it the suspect?") but, as we discussed in Chapter 6, we cannot put much faith in this type of memory. Memory for conversations is often inaccurate, and people often recall utterances as arising spontaneously when, in fact, the utterances were explicitly cued by a question or prior statement.

Investigators are explicitly warned that they should avoid this sort of contamination (e.g., Buckley, 2006). Even so, there is no doubt that the contamination occurs. For example, Garrett (2010) scrutinized 38 cases in which DNA evidence had shown that the suspects' confessions were false. In 36 of these cases, court records indicated that the defendant had detailed "guilty knowledge," and this knowledge had encouraged law enforcement to accept the confessions as accurate. But, of course, because this study was focused on exoneration cases, we know that the defendants were innocent and so had not gained their insider's knowledge through participation in the crime. Instead, in these 36 of 38 cases, the confessions had apparently been contaminated by law enforcement (also see Garrett, 2012; Leo, Neufeld, Drizin, & Taslitz, 2013; Nirider, Tepfer, & Drizen, 2012).

Checking the Confession Against Other Evidence

Sometimes, a police investigation yields independent evidence that seems to corroborate a confession. Imagine, for example, that a suspect has confessed to a homicide but said nothing about the weapon. Let's now imagine that the gun used in the crime is found under the suspect's bed or that the suspect's DNA is found at the crime scene. These points certainly seem incriminating and powerfully suggest that the confession is true.

Even here, though, there is a complication: Often the other evidence in an investigation is to some extent ambiguous. Fingerprints were found at the crime scene but they are smudged, and so some judgment is required in deciding whether they match the suspect's prints or not. An eyewitness is reasonably sure she saw the suspect fleeing the scene of the robbery but has doubts about the identification. In cases such as these, there is a danger that investigators' knowledge about the confession can corrupt these other forms of evidence.

How does this corruption emerge? Imagine a well-trained fingerprint analyst contemplating an ambiguous match between the suspect's prints and latent prints found at a crime scene. If the analyst knows that the suspect has confessed, this knowledge can encourage the analyst to "perceive" a match, even if the quality of the fingerprint evidence is, at best, uncertain. (The notion in play here is plainly linked to our earlier discussion of *confirmation bias*.) Dror and Charlton (2006) document exactly this pattern: In their study, actual fingerprint analysts shifted their views about fingerprint evidence (from "ambiguous" to "match") once the analysts heard about a confession. Clearly, the concern here must be taken seriously.

A similar pattern has been observed with eyewitness identifications: Hasel and Kassin (2009; also Hasel, 2012) had their participants view a theft, and then participants tried to make a selection from a lineup. A few days later, the participants were told that another suspect—not the person they'd selected from the lineup—had confessed. Having heard this new information, many witnesses seemed to gain "new memories" for the perpetrator's appearance. Indeed, almost two-thirds of the witnesses who had initially made a selection from the lineup now changed their minds about their decision and offered a new response that brought their ID into alignment with the confession.

Does this pattern emerge in actual criminal investigations? Kassin, Bogart, and Kerner (2012) explored this issue by scrutinizing the records from DNA exoneration cases. As a first step, they sorted these cases into those that did contain a confession (roughly 25% of the cases) and those that did not. (And, again, since these are exoneration cases, we know that these confessions are false.) The analysis next asked: What other evidence was there in the case that had favored the wrongful conviction? It turns out that the confession cases included more "incriminating evidence," in addition to the confession, than the nonconfession cases did. (And, once more, "incriminating" is in quotations here because we know these defendants to be innocent.)

What happened in these cases? One possible account is that, once the (false) confession was in view, investigators sought—and *found*—other evidence that would corroborate the confession. But, of course, since the confession was later learned to be false, the other evidence "confirming" the suspects' guilt would also have been misleading. Or, to put this more bluntly, the concern is that the presence of the false confession somehow corrupted subsequent steps of the investigation, leading the investigators to find other evidence that we now know to be bad evidence.

Of course, this account assumes a temporal sequence: If the bad evidence was available before the confession was obtained, then the confession could not possibly be the source of or have led to the discovery of the bad evidence. But this concern is easily set aside: Kassin et al.'s (2012) scrutiny of these exoneration cases suggests that the confessions were obtained before the other "corroborating" evidence was collected. This bolsters the troubling suggestion that the confession did play a causal role in guiding the interpretation of this other evidence—evidence we now know to be bogus. (For a discussion of the dynamics that can promote these errors, see Simon [2012], especially chapter 2; for a similar account describing the potential for bias in prosecutors, see Burke [2010]; for more on the role that confirmation bias can play when investigators check on a confession, see Kassin et al., [2013].)

H. VIDEO RECORDS OF INTERROGATIONS

The material in this chapter is highly worrisome. We want the police to collect high-quality evidence, and the collection of confessions is, of course, an especially valuable and powerful tool. At the same time, we have seen that false confessions do occur, and we now see that these confessions, once in place, can compromise the subsequent investigation, so that a bad confession encourages the collection of more bad evidence.

There is, however, a safeguard that has been recommended by many researchers and policy makers: a requirement for a video recording of an interrogation, from the very start to the very end, so that the interrogation can be evaluated later. In many cases, this evaluation will provide compelling assurance that the interrogation was conducted in an entirely appropriate manner; thus, the video record will serve to corroborate the confession and shut down challenges. In other cases, the video record will make it completely clear how and with what details the suspect confessed, again strengthening the confession. And, of course, in some cases, the video record will allow us to find potential problems in the interrogation, so that we can later make a sensible judgment about how much weight to give the confession.

There are, however, two concerns here. One concern is not surprising: Often a suspect is questioned for some time before the video recorder is started, and this common practice substantially undermines the value of the video record. A second concern, however, is less obvious—and involves the *camera angle* from which an interview is recorded.

Researchers have known for years that many aspects of a social interaction are open to interpretation. Consider an ordinary conversation: Was it Alec who guided the selection of topics, or did Jody and Matt play an equal role in shaping what was discussed? Was it Jody who set the tone, or someone else? Answers to questions like these can, in many settings, color our overall understanding of the conversation and can likewise influence the conclusions we draw from the conversation.

Moreover, the answers to these questions can be guided by factors influencing the *perceptual salience* of one conversation member or another. In one early study (Storms, 1973), half of the observers viewed a video recording of a conversation between two people—let's call them A and B—but with the video showing the view over Person A's shoulder and thus showcasing Person B. The other half of the observers were shown a video record taken from the opposite perspective (i.e., from behind Person B), and thus showcasing Person A. When later questioned about the conversation, observers in both groups had a biased perception, in both cases emphasizing the importance of the person who had been on screen. That person, perceptually salient for these observers, was regarded as playing a larger role in shaping the conversational direction, setting the agenda, influencing the tone, and so on.

How do these points apply to confessions? One might think that, in video recording an interrogation, the focus should be on the suspect. In that way, the video will allow viewers to see as much as possible about the suspect's posture and facial expressions; the video will keep the viewers' attention on what the suspect says or agrees to. The research just cited, however, suggests that this suspect-focus (perhaps a focus that does not show the interviewer on screen at all) will bias observers' interpretation, leading the observers to understate the interviewer's role in guiding the conversation. As a result, this camera angle might make observers less alert to the ways in which the interviewer encouraged the confession, making the confession seem "more voluntary" than it actually was.

Does this effect really happen? In a series of studies, Lassiter and his colleagues have shown that it does (e.g., Lassiter, Geers, Handley, Weiland, & Munhall, 2002; Lassiter & Geers, 2004). In these studies, some of the research participants view a video recording of an interrogation but with the video showing just the suspect; other participants see a video showing the suspect and the interrogator. In some procedures, still other participants see no video recording at all but merely hear the interrogation. In this research, Lassiter and colleagues have varied the crime being investigated (e.g., rape vs. drug trafficking vs. burglary) and also how much other information the participants had about the alleged crime (and so, in some studies, participants viewed a several-hour video depicting the trial). The data come from studies of university students, studies of nonstudents drawn from the jury pool, and also studies of judges (recruited at a judicial conference at the University of Illinois College of Law). Across all of these (and other) variations, the data show that observers regard a confession as more "voluntary" if the video shows only the suspect. Perhaps more troubling, observers who see a suspect-focused video are less able to distinguish true confessions from false ones in comparison to observers who see a video showing both the suspect and the interrogator (Lassiter & Geers, 2004).

In light of these results, it seems clear that a proper video record of an interrogation should cover the entire time period in which a suspect is being questioned *and* should show the viewer the interviewer as well as the suspect. Videos that do not fulfill these requirements fail to provide the safeguard we need (Kassin, Drizin, Grisso, Gudjonsson, Leo, & Redlich, 2010b.)

I. HOW CAN ALL OF THIS MATERIAL BE USED?

Throughout this book, the goal has been to provide useful material, and so it seems appropriate to end this chapter by highlighting how the science reviewed in this chapter points the way to improvements in extant practices. (For more on these points, see Kassin et al., 2010b.)

Let's acknowledge once again that we want actually guilty perpetrators to confess. Accurate, truthful confessions promote public safety, preserve resources in the justice system, and serve the aims of justice. But, in addition, we all want to avoid (or, at least, be able to detect) false confessions. In this way, we protect the innocent and again promote public safety because, by not distracting investigators with bad confessions, we help investigators to locate and collect evidence about the actual perpetrators.

With this context, it's gratifying how many policy suggestions flow from research in this domain. To name just a few: Researchers—and the lessons learned from Great Britain—would encourage American investigators to explore, and perhaps adopt, the PEACE method. Researchers would also propose videotaping all questioning of suspects, with a camera position that shows both the suspect and the interviewer. The data also suggest that the presentation of fictitious evidence and the use of "promises" of evidence to come are especially powerful in promoting false confessions, and these practices should be limited or perhaps eliminated. The data are also clear that certain populations (adolescents, individuals who are mentally disabled, people with mental illness) are especially vulnerable to police pressure and should not be questioned with procedures resembling the Reid technique. And, when using the Reid (or Reid-derived) technique, interviewers need to re-evaluate their reliance on the BAI—a procedure that fails to deliver on its promise and encourages guilt-presumptive interviews.

In addition, the science also provides a basis for evaluating interrogations through a consideration of the suspect's traits, his or her state, and the interrogation itself in order to ask whether indicators of "false-confession risk" are in place or not. This evaluation, in turn, can then help decision makers (a police officer choosing how to pursue a case, a prosecutor deciding whether to indict, a juror evaluating the evidence) to give a suspect's admissions the appropriate weight. Let's be clear, though, that the role of the science here is to *evaluate* the confession and not solely to *challenge* these statements. Indeed, when defense attorneys bring me confessions to evaluate, I routinely tell them, based on my assessment of the case and guided by the available science, that I see no grounds for challenging the confession, and they should probably be looking for a good plea deal. In other cases, though, scrutiny will lead us to a sense of caution for a particular confession and an enhanced scrutiny of other case facts.

In these and other ways, therefore, research on confessions can help us to improve the procedure through which confessions (or admissions of any sort) are collected and to improve the assessment and weighting of these statements. In this fashion, there is no question that the science can help us to make better use of this crucial form of evidence.

CHAPTER 9

Jurors' Cognition

So far, this volume has been concerned with the perceptions and memories of people directly involved in a litigation: witnesses, victims, and suspects. But there are related issues to examine with regard to another constituency: *jurors*.

In this chapter, we focus on three broad questions: First, we'll consider the influence of pretrial publicity (PTP; in the media, on the Internet, or even in community gossip). Are jurors influenced by this publicity? What remedies—if any—can undo the effects of this publicity? Second, we will turn to the information jurors *should* be influenced by—information presented during trial. How well do jurors remember what they have heard in testimony? Are there steps we can take to help jurors remember? Finally, separate from questions of memory are questions of perception, and we will explore some of the factors that govern how jurors perceive evidence: What sorts of witnesses do jurors tend to trust? What cues do jurors rely on in deciding whether to trust a witness?

As we will see, these various issues will lead us to a number of concerns about jurors' performance—limitations in their memories, errors in their judgment. Let's therefore note right at the start that we'll close the chapter with a rather positive assessment of jury decision making, and we will highlight some of the evidence that jurors seem to make the correct decisions far more often than not.

Before leaping in, though, we should note that this chapter leaves aside research on several important topics. For example, there is research on how well jurors understand and are influenced by judicial instructions. There is also research on how jury deliberation proceeds (and thus how a jury foreperson is chosen, what the process of polling entails, and so on; e.g., Levet, Denielsen, Kovera, & Cutler, 2005). We omit these points, not because the research is uninteresting (far from it), but because discussion would take us far from our main agenda—that is, from our focus on issues of perception and memory. (For a glimpse of research on jury instructions, though, see Cruse & Browne, 1986; Devine, 2012; Lieberman, 2009; Mitchell, Haw, Pfeifer, & Meissner, 2005; Ogloff & Rose, 2005; Steblay et al., 2006.)

A. THE EFFECTS OF PRETRIAL PUBLICITY

Many judicial matters receive little public notice; the only people who hear about the case are those directly involved (victims, witnesses, family members, friends, and so on). Sometimes, though, investigations or trials do attract attention—perhaps because the crime itself is notable or because prominent people are involved. In these cases, there may be news reports about the case; there may be discussions in social media or in blogs. Information may spread through flyers posted in the community or gatherings in support of (or in memory of) a victim. For some cases, members of the public have access to online information (e.g., websites listing registered sex offenders or sites listing recent arrests), and they may share this information with friends and neighbors.

Often, PTP covers only the basic facts: "The grocery store was robbed. Robbie Robber has been arrested. The trial will be next month." Sometimes, though, the information is prejudicial in one way or another, and so, for example, Imrich, Mullin, and Linz (1995) found that 27% of the newspaper reports they scrutinized described the suspect in a negative fashion. In contrast, just 5% of the reports explored the possibility that the defendant might be innocent. (See Dixon & Linz, 2002, for more evidence confirming this pattern.) In addition, news of a crime often emerges during the initial investigation, and, at this early stage, virtually all information comes from the police and thus is shaped by the police perspective. Then, both at early and later stages, evidence that might be inadmissible at trial can leak into public view (despite the American Bar Association's [2000] clear position on the types of information lawyers should *not* disseminate). Moreover, the media often convey information likely to be emotionally inflammatory—interviews with victims, horrific photographs, reports that highlight the tragedy of the case, and more.

We should also mention that these concerns enlarge when we consider PTP conveyed online by blogs or comments on newspaper websites. These outlets are often unconstrained by an editor's judgment or a website's policies. Publicity of this form is often authored by people with strong views (and strong emotions) about the crime being discussed. And, indeed, anyone who has surveyed these outlets realizes that the comments are sometimes ill-informed and occasionally vicious.

Unmistakably, then, PTP can be prejudicial, and, as we will see, research confirms that jurors are indeed influenced by PTP. In addition, research also informs us about the mechanisms leading to this influence, and, troublingly, an understanding of these mechanisms leads to the conclusion that the common judicial remedies for PTP are virtually guaranteed to fail.

Documenting PTP

If an attorney or judge is concerned about PTP effects, the first step must be to document the PTP itself. In many cases, this simply involves a "cataloguing" of what has been reported in the news media, including print and broadcast media, and also information sources on the Internet. As we discuss later, PTP can include both factual elements (e.g., a news report describing exactly how a crime unfolded) and emotional elements (e.g., billboards reminding people of the victim's tragic fate or candlelight vigils to express community concern about the crime). These two types of publicity often overlap (a news report can be both informative and emotionally upsetting), but the key is that both types matter, and both must be catalogued in any effort toward documenting PTP. (For more on the emotional effects of PTP, see Ruva, Guenther, & Yarbrough, 2011.)

Documenting the PTP, however, is not enough. We also need to ask whether potential jury members have noticed this information and been influenced by it. Thus, it is common for attorneys to hire a consultant (essentially a pollster) who can conduct a community survey, asking how deeply the PTP has "penetrated" into the community and assessing the degree to which the PTP has led people to pretrial views about what the verdict should be (cf. Vidmar, 2002; Vidmar & Judson, 1981).

Research Methods for the Study of PTP

In various courtrooms, I have heard attorneys (or judges) draw conclusions about PTP by reflecting on specific cases in which they had been involved. For example, they might point to a particular trial that had been preceded by inflammatory pro-prosecution publicity but that had resulted in an acquittal. ("Don't you remember *State v. Jones*? There was an avalanche of publicity, and he still was acquitted. Obviously, then, juries can set the publicity aside.")

Taken at face value, anecdotes of this sort might imply that PTP has no effect and can be ignored. But, of course, no one believes PTP guarantees a particular verdict, and obviously evidence in a trial can sometimes overcome PTP effects. Thus, there will inevitably be cases in which the PTP points in one direction, but the verdict goes in the other direction. For this reason, we learn little from consideration of individual cases. (For more on the limitations of "anecdotal evidence," see Chapter 1.) Instead, what we need to ask is whether PTP *generally* has (or doesn't have) an effect; that's the question that will allow us to evaluate concerns about PTP for a particular upcoming trial. And we can't decide this point about PTP's overall effects by looking at an anecdote or two; instead, we need a broader pattern of evidence.

The situation is no better if claims about PTP rest on a formal study or two ("Smith et al. published a paper in 2003 showing that . . ."). The reason, in brief, is that some studies do show an effect of PTP, and some do not. Thus, if you "cherry pick" through the evidence, you can support either the conclusion that PTP is likely to matter for an upcoming trial or that it is not. Any reasonable assessment, therefore, must be based on all of the research evidence, rather than individual studies.

Even when we turn to broader sets of evidence, though, there's still a complication to be considered: Attorneys sometimes offer a comparison between a set of cases with PTP and a set without publicity, and offer an argument such as: "The conviction rate seems similar in the two groups of cases. Therefore, the publicity has no effect, and so we have no reason to worry about pretrial publicity." The problem here is that trials with PTP often involve more inflammatory crimes and (often) more experienced counsel compared to trials without PTP. If, therefore, we do find a differ-ence between "PTP cases" and "no-PTP cases," this difference might be attributable to the PTP *or* to the difference in crimes *or* to the difference in attorneys. As such, the cause of the difference is uncertain, and no conclusions can be drawn. Likewise, if we find no difference among these groups, the concern remains: Perhaps the PTP did have an effect, but this effect was masked by other variables. In either case, the "evidence" here is without force.

How, therefore, should we study PTP effects? We obviously need a set of studies broad enough to support general claims. We also want studies that provide a "level playing field," so that we have a fair comparison between cases with PTP and those without. And, as in other domains, we're well served by a diversity of studies to ensure that we're not misled by some flaw inherent in a single style of data collection.

What methods contribute to this diversity? In some studies, we can compare, for a single trial, community members who have seen a lot of the publicity and commu-nity members who have not and ask whether the former group is more likely to have prejudged the case. In other studies, we can (again, for a single trial) compare two groups of community members: those in a city in which the case has received much publicity and those in a nearby city in which there has been less PTP.

In still other cases, researchers create simulated trials with "mock jurors"—peo-ple who are trying to judge the case as actual jurors would. In some of these stud-ies, the participants read transcripts of a trial; other more realistic studies have participants view a lengthy video of a trial. Other studies, more realistic still, have participants view a "live" performance of the trial. In all of these cases, some of the participants are exposed beforehand to PTP; other ("control") participants are exposed to neutral material.

These studies with mock jurors allow researchers to create exactly the compari-sons they need, so that they can test specific hypotheses about PTP effects. As we discussed in other chapters, though, the scientific power of these studies is pur-chased at a price: The studies are in several ways artificial, and it is plausible that par-ticipants in an academic study will behave differently than jurors in an actual trial. As always, therefore, researchers take care to "cross-check" the simulations against real cases, so that we end up with the best of both worlds: The simulations provide sci-entific muscle, and the "cross-check" provides assurance that our data really capture the real-world phenomena that we want to understand. (For examples of some of the real-world studies, see the studies catalogued in Fulero, 2002; Devine, Buddenbaum, Houp, Studebaker, & Stolle, 2009; Studebaker et al., 2002; Studebaker & Penrod, 1997; 2005.)

Does PTP Have an Effect?

With these methodological points in view, what are the data? As we have mentioned, some studies show little influence of PTP, but many studies show a powerful effect (e.g., Dexter, Cutler, & Moran, 1992; Greene & Wade, 1988; Hoiberg & Stires, 1973; Hvistendahl, 1979; Kerr, Kramer, Carroll, & Alfini, 1991; Kramer, Kerr, & Carroll,

1990; Moran & Cutler, 1991; Ogloff & Vidmar, 1994; Otto, Penrod, & Dexter, 1994; Padawer-Singer & Barton, 1977; Rollings & Blascovich, 1977; Simon & Eimerman, 1971; Studebaker, Robbenolt, Penrod, Pathak-Sharma, Groscup & Devenport, 2002; Sue, Smith, & Pedroza, 1975).

To assess this broad pattern, a meta-analysis by Steblay et al. (1999) combined the data from 44 studies, with the aggregate results drawn from a diversity of methods and almost 6,000 research participants. The meta-analysis confirmed what many have long suspected: PTP does have an impact. Specifically, the meta-analysis found that jurors exposed to PTP were appreciably more likely to endorse a guilty verdict compared to jurors not exposed to PTP.

In addition, in Chapter 1, we noted that meta-analyses routinely provide a "fail safe" number: a count of how many new studies would be needed, all with findings contrary to the current pattern, to "cancel out" the current pattern. This number allows us to assess the risk that the currently documented pattern might be reversed as new studies come in, if those studies turn out to contradict the data so far. If the fail-safe number is high, then a reversal of the pattern seems unlikely, and, in the Steblay et al. meta-analysis, the researchers report that "the fail-safe N for this group of studies is 2,755, indicating that this large number of non-supportive studies would be necessary to change the conclusions" (p. 223). In short, there is little to worry about on this issue.

We should mention, though, that, by the standards of meta-analysis, the overall effect in the Steblay et al. study would be counted as statistically "small to moderate," and, in some ways, the modest size of the effect cannot be surprising: Jurors take their responsibility seriously, understand that PTP is not evidence, and presumably do their best to ignore the PTP in choosing a verdict. Nonetheless, the PTP does have an effect, working through mechanisms we will describe in a moment.

In addition, in interpreting this description of PTP's impact, recall a point we made in Chapter 1: The descriptive levels used for meta-analysis ("small," "medium," "large") are simply mathematical conventions, offered by statisticians as a step toward "back-translating" the technical results of a meta-analysis into more familiar language. (Thus, for example, an effect size is deemed "small" if a statistical measure called Cohen's d has a value of .2 or smaller.) Let's be clear, though, that an effect called "small" by this standard may still be deeply consequential. As an illustration of this point, consider an early study of the effects of a daily aspirin on someone's likelihood of having a heart attack (Rosnow & Rosenthal, 2003). According to statistical standards, the effect was deemed "trivial" in size—but, pragmatically, the effect was large enough so that the researchers decided it was unethical to continue the study; instead, they contacted all of the research participants who'd been taking a placebo and urged them to start taking a daily aspirin.

In addition, the PTP meta-analysis makes it clear that any overall assessment of effect size must be regarded with caution in this domain. The reason is that, in some settings and with some factors in place, the effect of PTP is rather large; in other settings, it is smaller. Therefore, this is territory in which we learn little by focusing on the "average" effect; the meta-analysis itself tells us that we need to zoom in for a closer view of targeted subsets of the research evidence.

When is the PTP effect larger? The meta-analysis tells us that PTP effects are especially strong in studies that draw their participants from an actual venire, asking about the impact of real PTP on an actual trial. In contrast, the effects are weaker in "simulation" studies done on university campuses and relying on students as the research participants. Ironically, therefore, the simulation studies alluded to earlier may understate the size of PTP effects.

The data also show that PTP effects are stronger if participants are exposed to multiple points of information within the PTP, rather than just one or two. Furthermore, studies that present participants with real PTP (drawn from the media, as opposed to PTP created by the researchers) also show stronger effects. The analysis also indicates that PTP effects are stronger for some crimes than for others (for example, greater for drug cases and for cases involving murder or sexual abuse). Pretrial publicity effects are also greater if a longer period of time had elapsed between exposure to the PTP and the research participants' judgment; we return to this point later.

Source Confusion

In light of the results summarized so far, most researchers regard PTP's effects as well-established (for an overview of more recent data, see Devine, 2012). Researchers have therefore moved on to what is sometimes referred to as the "second wave" of research—an examination of the causes of PTP effects.

One important cause involves a mechanism we have encountered in other chapters; namely, "source confusion." As we have discussed, the idea here is that our memories have evolved, in essence, to integrate information from many sources so that we end up with a coherent pattern of knowledge and not a set of unassembled "factoids." The benefits of this integration, however, come at a cost—and, specifically, research suggests that we often lose track of which bits of information we got from which source. Thus, we are often correct in remembering that we did at some point encounter a certain idea, but we make an error in recalling the source of that idea (i.e., where we got the information from).

Source confusion can be documented in a wide range of circumstances, making it, in most researchers' view, inevitable that this confusion can occur in the courtroom. After all, our brains don't contain one set of memory circuits used for trial-related material and a different set of circuits for other types of material. Instead, the same type of memory is used for both, essentially guaranteeing that jurors—like people in any other setting—will be vulnerable to source confusion, including confusion about what information they gained during the trial and what information they gained in other settings.

If, however, there were any question about these points, studies have asked specifically if source confusion can be observed in the courtroom (e.g., Ruva, McEvoy, & Bryant, 2007). The procedure here is straightforward: Jurors are exposed to PTP, then to a trial, and then questioned about which pieces of information came from which source. In these studies, source confusion has been observed in individuals' recollection of real trials in which they have served as jurors and also observed in research participants' recollection of simulated trials. In the data, source confusion is evident even when the information in the PTP was inaccurate (as sometimes it is) or if the information would have been inadmissible if it had been presented in trial.

This research also shows (unsurprisingly) that source confusion is more likely if the trial is long or complex. Source confusion is also increased if the PTP was encountered some time back; apparently, the passage of time makes it more difficult for people to do the "bookkeeping" of recalling where they got their information. This point is obviously relevant to an observation already mentioned—that PTP effects grow stronger if there is a delay between the presentation of the PTP and the trial.

It is also important that source confusion seems, in research studies, not to be eliminated by jury deliberation. Jurors do correct each other during deliberation; however, the jurors who do the "correcting" are not always the jurors with the most accurate memories, and hence, the "correcting" can sometimes exacerbate source confusion (cf. Pritchard & Keenan, 2002).

As an illustration of these various points, consider a study by Ruva, McEvoy, and Bryant (2007). They had mock jurors read news articles containing PTP that was biased against the defendant; the "jurors" later viewed a videotaped murder trial, then deliberated and finally offered a verdict. The participants were also specifically admonished not to use any information they had obtained before the trial itself. Nonetheless, the data showed a clear effect of the publicity, with the PTP influencing perception of the defendant's credibility, the verdict, and participants' preferred length for the sentence. Most important for present purposes, an explicit check on the research participants' memory revealed many source confusion errors, even after deliberation. For point after point, the participants (correctly) remembered that they had read about certain facts in the PTP, but they also (falsely) recalled that this information was reiterated in the trial itself.

Source Confusion and the PTP Remedies

To the extent that PTP has its effect via source confusion, what does this imply for the potential remedies for PTP? One common remedy is a continuance, but let's be clear that the delay caused by a continuance does not "erase" the PTP information from jurors' minds. Instead, the delay will merely drop the information into what is called *marginal status*: After the continuance, the jurors cannot easily recall the PTP's content, but the information still resides in their memories and will likely be brought back into view by a suitable reminder—for example, the start of the trial or the onset of new publicity when the trial begins after the continuance.

Worse, the continuance also has another effect on memory: As we have said, the delay inherent in a continuance can make source confusion more likely. (Thus, concretely, a juror might forget the specific experience of hearing a bit of information in a news broadcast; all that remains in the juror's memory is the gist of the information, with the juror now unable to recall where the information came from.) Hence, a continuance will sometimes make PTP effects worse, not better (cf. Ruva & McEvoy, 2008).

Let's also emphasize that source confusion is indeed *confusion,* with jurors genuinely uncertain about how they obtained their information. In light of this confusion, there is no way that a juror could follow a judge's explicit instruction to ignore the PTP. (Ignoring pretrial information is possible only if you know which information came from pretrial sources.) By the same logic, this confusion renders irrelevant a juror's solemn promise, during voir dire, to set aside the PTP information. (Again, you can set aside this information only if you recognize this information when you encounter it, and this is precisely what you cannot do if suffering from source confusion.)

Confirmation Bias

A second mechanism is also pertinent to PTP effects; namely, confirmation bias. This term (which we met in earlier chapters) refers to a family of well-documented effects all involving the tendency to interpret information through the "lens" of our current beliefs. Thus, we are more likely to notice evidence consistent with our views; we also tend to take information at face value if it is consistent with our current beliefs but challenge evidence not consistent with our views; we tend to interpret ambiguous evidence in a way that favors our views; we are likely to give greater weight to evidence consistent with our views; and so on. Plainly, then, multiple mechanisms contribute to the confirmation bias pattern. (For discussion of confirmation bias, see Reisberg, 2013a.)

Pretrial publicity can contribute to confirmation bias in several ways. In the extreme, PTP can persuade jurors that the defendant truly is guilty. More modestly, PTP can make the defendant's guilt seem plausible to the jurors, so that they'll need little additional evidence to become convinced that he is indeed guilty. Alternatively, the PTP can simply lead jurors to a negative view of the defendant's character. (On this last point, we note that, in most circumstances, courts forbid testimony about a defendant's prior bad acts. Part of the logic here is that such testimony might lead the jury to believe the defendant is a bad person and on that basis alone likely to be guilty of the charges now at issue. Note, however, that PTP can have roughly the same impact on the jury; for evidence on this point, see Ruva et al., 2011.)

Can we demonstrate these effects directly? In one study, some participants were presented with PTP, and others were not. All participants were then presented with testimony from a succession of witnesses and asked, after each witness, their impression of the witness's evidence. Specifically, the participants were asked to rate the witness's evidence on a scale ranging from "strongly favors the defendant's case" to "strongly favors the prosecution's case" (Hope, Memon, & McGeorge, 2004). The results showed (among other points) that participants who had been exposed to PTP found prosecution witnesses more compelling and perceived the incriminating evidence to be more powerful compared to jurors not exposed to PTP. It would seem, then, that jurors' views of the evidence were shaped by the framework they brought to the trial from the very start—a framework created by PTP.

Notice, in addition, the potential here for a cyclic effect: In this study, PTP encouraged an initial pro-prosecution leaning. This leaning colored how the jurors interpreted the evidence and, specifically, made incriminating evidence seem more powerful. This perception of the evidence, in turn, strengthened the pro-prosecution leaning, creating a stronger bias in how the jurors would interpret the next bit of evidence. Around and around we go, with the jurors' bias coloring how they read the evidence, which strengthened the bias, which further colored how they read the subsequent evidence.

And, again, jury deliberation does not eliminate this pattern. Ruva and LeVasseur (2012) scrutinized the deliberation by 30 "mock juries." The data showed once more that PTP powerfully influenced the jury verdict, and, despite a judge's admonishment not to use the PTP, jurors who mentioned the PTP during deliberation were rarely corrected by their fellow jurors. Most important for present purposes, jurors who had been exposed to PTP tended, in deliberation, to discuss ambiguous trial facts in a fashion that supported the prosecution's case. Thus, in addition to whatever direct effects the PTP might have had on the verdict, the PTP also colored jurors' interpretation of the evidence actually presented in trial.

Confirmation Bias and the PTP Remedies

We noted early on that PTP can take two different forms: "Factual PTP" concerns information the juror might have encountered prior to the trial, including information about the crime or the defendant. "Emotional PTP" concerns factors that provide no information but that set an emotional tone for the trial. As we've said, these two categories overlap (and so a news broadcast might include factual and emotional elements), but the distinction is important for several reasons, including the fact that the passage of time seems to have little effect on emotional PTP. In other words, people generally remember their affective response to the crime (a response of horror, anger, or sadness) even when they have forgotten most of the relevant information. As a result, emotional PTP can trigger confirmation bias at a long delay—even with a continuance.

In addition, we have already noted that a continuance does not erase factual PTP from jurors' memories. Thus, after the continuance, reminders can bring this form of PTP back into the jurors' minds, again triggering confirmation bias. For multiple reasons, then, a continuance will have little impact on this form of jury bias.

Moreover, let's be clear that confirmation bias is generally an automatic, unconscious process, built into the ways in which people gather and use information from the world around them. Confirmation bias, therefore, is not the result of jurors being careless, lazy, or irresponsible, and neither is it the result of jurors misunderstanding their task. For all of these reasons, confirmation bias will remain in place even with the best of juror intentions—including intentions formed in response to a judicial instruction or intentions formed as a result of a pledge during voir dire to ignore the PTP. Hence, these remedies, too, are generally ineffectual.

Pretrial Publicity Remedies Overall

As we said earlier, jurors understand that PTP is not evidence and that they should render a verdict based only on trial evidence. Presumably, then, they do all they can to set the PTP aside. Nonetheless, PTP does have an effect and can create bias—and sometimes powerful bias—during a trial. And, as should be plain by now, the available research encourages skepticism about the often-employed remedies for PTP (cf. Studebaker & Penrod, 1997). To reiterate: A continuance has little effect on emotional PTP, and factual PTP, even if "forgotten," will be refreshed in jurors' memories by the start of the trial itself (cf. Kramer, Kerr, & Carroll, 1990). In addition, a continuance can encourage source confusion and so can actually increase the impact of PTP.

Second, deliberation seems not to offset PTP effects. This was evident in the 1999 meta-analysis (Steblay et al., 1999), which observed reliable PTP effects even after jury deliberation. Other, more recent studies (cited in the previous pages) have confirmed this point.

Third, judicial instructions to ignore PTP seem, in various studies, to have little effect, and the discussion so far explains why: A juror faithfully following the instructions would still be vulnerable to source confusion and so might be sincerely convinced he or she was relying on trial evidence and not on information picked up from PTP, even though the information did indeed come from the PTP. Likewise, a juror might, in compliance with a judge's instruction, be careful to rely only on trial evidence but not realize that his or her view of this evidence had been colored by the PTP.

Worse, studies indicate that judicial instructions can sometimes have a "boomerang" effect and make jurors more likely to rely on PTP (or other forms of inadmissible evidence; see, for example, Sue, Smith, & Gilbert, 1974; or, more broadly, Lieberman & Arndt, 2000). There are several reasons for this pattern, including the fact that the instructions highlight the inadmissible information, making it more salient for jurors and thus increasing its impact on the verdict.

Fourth, what about voir dire? Often, jurors are asked to pledge, during voir dire, only to consider information admitted in trial. However, for reasons we have already described, this pledge has little effect. Thus, PTP effects can easily be detected even among jurors who have promised to lay aside any pretrial information they have encountered. (Fulero [2002] offers a catalog of relevant studies.)

In addition, during voir dire, jurors are often asked to forecast how they will make their judgments. They are, for example, sometimes asked questions along the lines of "Will you be able to set aside what you have heard about this case?" or "Will you remain open-minded and follow instructions?" There are obviously concerns here about jurors' candor in answering these questions, questions tantamount to asking jurors whether they will be good citizens and reasonable or bad citizens and unreasonable. But, beyond this point, there is no reason to think that jurors can answer these questions accurately. A wealth of research makes it clear that our thoughts, values, and behaviors are often shaped by unnoticed "priming" from stimuli we have encountered and also by implicit (again, unnoticed) associations that exist in our memories. The consequence of this is that we often do not know why we acted as we did or why we reached this or that conclusion. Thus, in the case of jury decision making, jurors often will not know during deliberation to what extent they are being influenced by PTP. On this basis, it is pointless to ask jurors, in voir dire, whether they will be influenced by PTP. The simple reality is that jurors—no matter how careful, thoughtful, and responsible they are—cannot know the answer to this question, and we learn little by asking them the question (cf. Rose & Diamond, 2008; Studebaker & Penrod, 2005).

These points are well-rooted in a wide swath of scientific studies. But, more directly, a few studies have asked directly whether jurors can assess their ability to resist PTP effects. For example, Butler (2007) compared death-qualified jurors to those who were not death-qualified. She found, first, that death-qualified jurors (using the criteria in Florida's 12th Judicial Circuit) were more likely to believe, based on the PTP, that the defendant was guilty. But, second, she also found that death-qualified jurors were more likely to assert that the PTP would have minimal impact on the defendant's right to due process. Notice, then, the gap between *being sensitive to PTP*, and *acknowledging the influence of PTP*: Death-qualified jurors are higher than average on the first, but lower than average on the second.

Likewise, Moran and Cutler (1991) found that community members who (pretrial) knew more about a case were more likely to believe (pretrial) that the defendant was culpable. (This point simply echoes the often-documented effect of PTP.) But, in addition, Moran and Cutler found no correlation between pretrial knowledge and a community member's willingness to admit partiality. Apparently, the PTP had biased these potential jurors, but left the jurors either unable or unwilling to detect their own bias.

Finally, there is a danger that voir dire may enhance PTP effects rather than eliminate them. We mentioned earlier that judicial instructions sometimes highlight the PTP, making this inadmissible information more salient in jurors' thoughts; questions to jurors during voir dire can have the same effect. And, of course, if the passage of time has allowed the PTP to fade from jurors' memories, then the questions will themselves be a powerful reminder, calling the contents of the PTP back to mind.

Where, then, does this leave us? In truth, many researchers suggest that a change of venue may be the only remedy for PTP likely to succeed. Obviously, though, there are other concerns about a change of venue, and, pragmatically, judges hesitate to grant a motion for this change. Even so, the evidence on PTP effects is clear, and the implications for remedies other than a venue change are discouraging.

B. JURORS' MEMORIES FOR TRIAL EVIDENCE

So far in this chapter, we have asked whether jurors are influenced by information they should in truth ignore or forget; namely, information acquired outside of the courtroom. But what about information inside the trial?

Trials vary enormously in their length and complexity, and so the memory burden on jurors is sometimes relatively light and sometimes enormous. Even in a simple trial, however, various factors may work against accurate memory for the trial evidence. Consider, for example, the fact that people are better able to remember a conversation if they were participants in the conversation rather than passive witnesses to the conversation. Obviously, jurors do not participate in the exchanges between an attorney and a witness, and so in that sense are passive witnesses to the exchanges—a point that works against memory.

In addition, in most trials, jurors receive crucial information about their task (in the form of the judge's instructions) only when testimony is complete (i.e., just before deliberations). As a consequence, while hearing the testimony, jurors may not know which pieces of information are crucial (and so worthy of special note, special attention) and which are not, and this too can work against memory. (For research on the benefits of "preinstruction"—instruction given to jurors at the very start of the trial—see Ogloff & Rose, 2005.)

For these and other reasons, jurors' accurate recollection of the trial information is by no means guaranteed. Beyond these general points, though, research indicates a number of factors that can make accurate memory more likely, or less.

The Impact of Stories

One often-cited account of jury decision making is the so-called *story model* (Pennington & Hastie, 1993; also Huntley & Costanzo, 2003). In this context, *story* refers to a narrative account formed in the jurors' minds that describes the sequence of events that led up to the jury trial (the offense, perhaps the circumstances that precipitated the offense, the investigation, and so on). Typically, multiple stories will be available (one offered by the plaintiff, one offered by the defense, and perhaps alternatives from other sources), and the proposal is that jurors settle on a verdict by deciding which story is best. Overall, the preferred story will likely be the one that seems most complete, most coherent, and most in tune both with the facts and with other beliefs the jurors hold about how human affairs unfold.

The story model is typically mentioned as an explanation of jury decisions, but the model also has implications for juror memory. The central idea here is linked to comments we offered in Chapter 3 regarding "schema effects." As we saw in that earlier setting, our memories are often organized in terms of a "schema" or "script" that summarizes a certain type of situation. (The term "schema" is usually applied to types of settings; the term "script" to types of events.) Thus, we might have a "kitchen schema" that tells us the room is certain to contain a stove and probably a refrigerator as well; the kitchen schema also tells us that a television might be present, but a sofa will surely not be. Likewise, we might have a "restaurant script" that tells us the plausible sequence when one dines out: entering the restaurant, being seated and given menus, ordering, eating, paying, and leaving.

In Chapter 3, we discussed some of the ways that people rely on this generic knowledge to organize (and supplement) their memories of a specific kitchen, a specific restaurant meal, and so on. We also noted that the framework provided by a script or schema helps people to remember aspects of their experience that fit easily into this framework. Unfortunately, though, elements that do not fit with the framework are often forgotten or perhaps remembered in a distorted form so that the recollection, now with its altered content, does fit with the framework.

This pattern has been documented in many settings (for a broad review, see Reisberg, 2013a), and so it cannot be surprising that the pattern can also be demonstrated in jurors. To see how this plays out, bear in mind that attorneys often use their opening statement to present a story—a narrative describing the plaintiff's or defense's account of the relevant events—and this use of opening statement is well-advised. Among other effects, jurors are more likely to remember trial evidence if they have one of these stories in mind from the trial's start. Not surprisingly, this benefit is more visible if the testimony then presents the trial evidence in "story sequence"—first the earliest events in the story, then later events, and so on (Kerstholt & Jackson, 1998).

There is, however, a downside to these points: Once jurors have adopted a story about the trial, evidence consistent with the story is more likely to be remembered; evidence inconsistent with the story may be forgotten. In addition, jurors can sometimes "remember" evidence that was not presented during the trial at all—but which is consistent with the story.

The Effect of Deliberation

A verdict obviously depends on the jury, not on individual jurors. That is, jurors must work together, as a group, to deliberate about the trial and eventually choose their verdict. One might hope, therefore, that jurors will engage in a collaborative effort toward remembering, so that, for example, a juror who has forgotten (or misremembers) some bit of evidence will be reminded (or corrected) by other jurors. In this way, the jurors' shared memory after deliberation might be more complete and more accurate than the individual jurors' memories before deliberation.

Studies suggest that this beneficial effect does occur—but, in truth, the improvement in memory after deliberation is quite small, and, in at least some cases, deliberation may actually undermine jurors' memory for the evidence (Hirst, Coman, & Stone, 2012). We saw our first indication of this point earlier in the chapter, in our discussion of PTP, but obviously the issue arises again when considering jurors' memory for trial evidence.

Why does deliberation produce only a small benefit? In the jury room, the people most likely to speak up about the evidence are generally the jurors who are most confident that they recall the trial well. As we have repeatedly seen, however, confidence in one's memory is not always an indication that the memory is accurate. Therefore, the people who speak up may be asserting incorrect information, and, if they impose their recollection on others, they can actually undermine others' memories (Cuc, Ozuru, Manier, & Hirst, 2006). In addition, at least some studies suggest that people tend to believe the first person who speaks up in recalling an event (or in recalling some piece of evidence); this tendency, too, can undermine the benefit of deliberation for the simple reason that the most accurate recall may not belong to the first speaker (Wright & Carlucci, 2011).

Note-Taking and Juror Questions

In some jurisdictions (and, more narrowly, in some judges' courtrooms), jurors are allowed to take notes during the trial, and one might think that this step would help jurors to recall the testimony they have heard. Does it?

Before turning to the evidence, we should acknowledge that some scholars have expressed reservations about the note-taking practice. As one concern, jurors might take a lot of notes early in the trial but then grow tired of this practice. If they later rely on their notes, this pattern might lend disproportionate weight to early testimony (well recorded in the notes) compared to later testimony. As a different concern, jurors may differ in their inclination to take notes. If, in deliberation, the jury puts their trust in the notes, this could give disproportionate weight to those jurors who wrote down a great deal relative to those who did not. Then, as yet another concern, many students realize that, if they get swept up in taking complete notes, they may end up spending less time and effort listening to the presentation they are trying to record—and so note-taking ends up "competing with" listening and paying attention.

Researchers have sought evidence to address these concerns and also to evaluate the overall effect of juror note-taking. Encouragingly, studies suggest that note-taking does not create the various problems just listed: The note-taking seems not to favor just one portion of the trial, seems not to be distracting, and does seem to be reasonably accurate. Moreover, jurors generally like the option of note-taking, and so having this option may foster a more positive attitude in jurors, which may in turn lead to better juror performance. But, in the end, does note-taking improve juror memory? The available evidence suggests that it does, but the effect is small (Devine, 2012; Ogloff & Rose, 2005). Hence, we should welcome this remedy, but not put too much weight on it (Heuer & Penrod, 1994).

What about another innovation allowed in some courtrooms—a provision for jurors themselves to ask questions of witnesses? These questions are typically submitted in writing to the judge, at the end of the witness's testimony. The judge screens the questions (to make certain they are appropriate) and reads the admissible ones to the witness. There is little scientific evidence that would allow an evaluation of this procedure, but it does seem plausible that this procedure will be worthwhile. Among other gains, this step would likely encourage jurors to be more engaged, more "active listeners" as they hear trial testimony—a point that could aid both comprehension and memory.

C. JURORS' PERCEPTION OF WITNESSES

Questions about jurors' memory are of obvious importance for the justice system. But just as important are questions about jurors' *perception*—including their perception of witnesses as they try to decide how much weight to give each bit of testimony.

What Makes a Witness's Recall Persuasive?

A number of studies have presented research participants with (simulated) trial evidence—via a transcript, video, or, in some cases, a live performance. These studies vary certain aspects of the witness presentation in order to ask: What aspects of the testimony make a witness more persuasive, more credible, and what aspects do the reverse?

Jurors tend overall to believe eyewitnesses, and they put considerable faith in witness narratives and eyewitness identifications (Boyce, Beaudry, & Lindsay, 2007; Yarmey, 2007); as we discussed in Chapter 6, they also tend to believe earwitnesses. Jurors are especially likely to believe witnesses who express certainty in their recollection and tend to distrust those who admit a lack of confidence in their own recall (e.g., Brigham & Bothwell, 1983; Cutler, Penrod, & Dexter, 1990; Lindsay, Wells, & Rumpell, 1981; Luus & Wells, 1994; Smalarz & Wells, 2013; Wells, 1984; Wells, Lindsay, & Ferguson, 1979; Wells, Memon, & Penrod, 2006). Jurors also put more trust in a witness who provides more detail rather than less. Finally, jurors also use a witness's consistency as an indicator of reliability, on the notion that a consistent witness is a trustworthy witness (e.g., Berman & Cutler, 1996; Berman, Narby, & Cutler, 1995; Devenport, Kimbrough, & Cutler, 2009; for a review of all these issues, see Devine, 2012; Semmler, Brewer, & Bradford Douglas, 2012.)

These considerations (confidence, detail, and consistency) seem to trump other assessments, with the result that jurors are often unimpressed by other relevant factors—including the presence and possible influence of a disguise, the passage of time between a crime and the subsequent identification, and missteps in the identification procedure itself (e.g., poor instructions). These latter factors, which we know to be relevant to witness accuracy, have only a small impact on jurors' perception and are easily eclipsed by a witness's expression of certainty (e.g., Cutler et al., 1990; also Wells, Greathouse, & Smalarz, 2012; although for some indications that confidence doesn't completely eclipse other concerns, see Bradfield & Wells, 2000; Tenney, MacCoun, Spellman, & Hastie, 2007).

Before pressing on, though, let's emphasize that, in all of these cases, jurors seem to be relying on cues of questionable value. In Chapters 3 and 5, we considered the relationship between memory accuracy, on the one side, and either confidence or detail, on the other. There we saw that these indices are (at best) only weakly associated with memory accuracy. What about consistency? In some cases, the inconsistencies involve flat contradictions—if, for example, a witness tells investigators both that an event happened indoors and that it happened outdoors. Here, common sense says that one of these contradictory assertions must be wrong, and so inconsistency does signal that there is some sort of error here.

In other cases, though, the inconsistencies are of a different sort. It is common, for example, for a witness to recall some points in one interview but different points in a subsequent interview. (Hence, some bits of information "fall out" of the narrative as we move from one interview to the next, and other information may appear for the first time only in a later interview.) Inconsistencies like these are sometimes used to impeach a witness, with the changes in memory interpreted as an indication that the recall overall cannot be trusted.

However, we argued in Chapter 3 that this impeachment is unwarranted. As one concern, it is certainly possible for a witness to forget the event as times goes by, and this immediately explains why information might be present in early reports but not in later ones. What about shifts in the opposite direction? Bear in mind here that getting information out of memory—the step called "memory retrieval"—is not effortless and can sometimes fail. As a result, there are circumstances in which an initial effort at retrieval provides only a subset of the information in storage and in which a subsequent effort provides a different subset. In some cases, the person will be aware of these changes. (Think of the near-caricature image of someone slapping his palm onto his forehead as he proclaims with relief, "Oh, *now* I remember . . .") In other cases, though, the person may not realize he has provided different (and new) information in the most recent effort at recall.

In Chapter 3, we mentioned a study that examined these shifts in recall. Gilbert and Fisher (2006) had research participants view a simulated crime, and then had the participants recall the crime twice—once after a few minutes and then again two days later. Moreover, the study included various steps designed to encourage a shift in the participants' perspective at the time of the second recall. The researchers' hope here was that this shift would lead participants to approach their own memories with a new set of retrieval cues and thus encourage recall of information that might have been overlooked in the first retrieval effort.

In this study, changes in what participants recalled were quite common, and especially so for participants who had, through instructions, shifted perspective between their retrieval efforts. Most important, though, the researchers asked whether these shifts in memory—that is, inconsistencies in the witnesses' report—were indicators that the witness was unreliable. Specifically, the researchers were able to ask, for each of their study participants, how many changes there were between the participant's first and second recall and also how accurate that participant's memory was overall. The data showed no correspondence between these measures—and so no indication that an inconsistent witness is likely to be an unreliable witness. Hence, there is no justification for discrediting a given witness's report simply because new details enter the witness's account in subsequent recall efforts or because early details drop out of the report. (For more on jurors' skepticism about witnesses sometimes remembering more as time goes by, see Oeberst, 2012.)

Finally, let's also note the impact of "feedback" effects. We have described the base result in other chapters; in a typical experiment, an eyewitness is asked to make an identification from a lineup and then told "Good, you selected our suspect." These five words of feedback reliably lead witnesses to greater certainty in their ID, and also lead to various forms of memory distortion—and so, after receiving the feedback, witnesses recall their viewing opportunity as being appreciably better than it really was.

Studies suggest that feedback effects don't just affect witnesses; they also affect jurors. Specifically, feedback to a witness (during the investigation) makes the witness's testimony (at trial) more compelling, and makes it more difficult for jurors to tell apart accurate and inaccurate IDs. This effect remains even if the witness is subjected to cross examination: In one study, witnesses were asked, during cross, whether they had received feedback after making an ID, and whether they had been influenced in any way by that feedback. Even with these issues in view, feedback (given long before the trial, during the investigation itself) leads to more compelling testimony that in turn erodes jurors' ability to evaluate the identification (e.g., Smalarz & Wells, 2014).

Detecting Lies

Triers of fact sometimes hear witnesses who, despite the penalties for perjury, have powerful reasons to lie while on the stand—and so they hear testimony from defendants who wish to deny their crimes or from friends and family of the accused trying to help the person. How do jurors (or, for that matter, judges) deal with this challenge?

Evidence central for this issue is summarized in Chapter 7. There, our primary focus was on investigators' ability to detect lies from suspects, but the research data apply to judges and jurors as well and are easily summarized: First, people are generally inept in detecting deception—and so they are often unable to decide which witnesses are lying and which are truthful. Second (and related), people tend to rely on a small number of "common-sense signals" for spotting lies—signals that include gaze direction, fidgeting, and other signs of nervousness. As it turns out, none of these signals is reliably associated with deception, making it unsurprising that deception detection is poor. Third, it is common in the courtroom for attorneys to exhort jurors to pay close attention to witness demeanor to spot the lies—likely underscoring the cues that jurors were paying attention to on their own. This exhortation is likely to be counterproductive in light of the data suggesting that the best cues to deception are often "story cues"—the exact content of the witness's account—and not the visual cues contained within demeanor. In this regard, the instruction often given to jurors may make their ability to spot lies worse, not better. (And, again, for evidence supporting these various claims, see Chapter 7.)

We should also mention one other issue that is largely untouched by scientific research: Courtrooms are a solemn place, with a well-defined set of procedures and a number of prominent rituals—including the oath that each witness must swear before giving testimony. Witnesses know that their testimony is being scrutinized by many individuals and probably know that the penalties for perjury can be severe. It seems plausible that witnesses might be less likely to lie in these circumstances, thus making questions about lie-detection accuracy less urgent. But it also seems plausible that lie detection might suffer in this setting because the finders of fact might assume that the setting makes lying less likely, so that they are less alert to the possibility that a particular witness might be lying. These are intriguing possibilities, but the claims here are untested, and so this point rests as a possible focus for future research.

Assessing Confessions

Finally, research has examined another aspect of juror perception—namely, jurors' understanding of confession evidence—and the data are straightforward: Jurors are powerfully influenced by confessions. In one study, participants read about several trials, each hinging on a different type of evidence (a confession, an eyewitness to the crime, or character evidence; Kassin & Neumann, 1997). The participants found the confession evidence to be far more incriminating than the other evidence types.

What happens if the trial evidence suggests the confession may have been the result of coercion? Kasin and Sukel (1997) presented their participants with a summary of a murder trial. In one version, the participants learned that the suspect was in pain during the interrogation and had been questioned aggressively by a detective waving his gun around. When asked directly, these research participants judged this confession to be coerced and asserted that it did not influence their assessment of the trial. However, the participants' proposed verdicts made it clear that they *were* influenced by this confession—and so they were much more likely to choose a guilty verdict, in comparison to participants who did not hear about the confession at all. This effect remained in place even in a condition in which the research participants were strongly admonished by the judge to discount the confession if they thought it was coerced. (For more data showing the noneffect of judicial instructions on this point, see Kassin & Wrightsman, 1981.)

In another study, participants learned that a confession had been given in response to an overt promise of leniency. The participants understood this confession to be involuntary but were persuaded by it anyhow and judged the suspect to be guilty (Kassin & Wrightsman, 1980; 1981).

Why Do People Tend to Overbelieve Even Coerced Confessions?

Can we explain why participants fail to discount confessions that, by their own assessment, are coerced? Several factors contribute. As one consideration, many jurors believe that even a coerced confession is likely to be accurate, and moreover may have the view that pressuring a suspect toward a confession is simply good police work. (Indeed, it is plausible that many coerced confessions—like most confessions overall—*are* accurate.) Hand in hand with this, jurors underestimate how often false confessions occur and believe that false confessions are likely only if the defendant suffers from some form of mental illness (although see Costanzo, Shaked-Schroer, & Vinson, 2010). The result is that jurors routinely discount the possibility of a false confession if they believe the defendant to be sane (Chojnacki, Cicchini, & White, 2008; Henkel, Coffman, & Dailey, 2008).

Yet another factor is the tendency for confessions—even false ones—to contain "signs of veracity" (Garrett, 2010; Kassin, 2012; Kassin, Meissner, & Norwick, 2005; Leo et al., 2013; Wallace & Kassin, 2012). For example, confessions sometimes include references by the suspect to his or her own thoughts, feelings, and motives during the (supposed) commission of the crime. These references can turn a bare-bones confession ("Yes, I did it") into one that is vivid, compelling, and "rings true."

Further "corroboration" for a confession can come from mention, within the confession, of various crime facts, facts that make the confession more concrete and detailed and hence more believable. These facts may include details supposedly known only to the perpetrator and hence provide evidence of "guilty knowledge." (For more on this point, see Chapters 7 and 8.)

Of course, the problem here is that all of these bits of information—the references to thoughts and feelings, the mention of various crime facts—may have been supplied to the suspect by the interrogators, sometimes through leading questions, sometimes through photos of the crime scene, sometimes through actual visits to the crime scene. As a result of this "confession contamination," these various signs of veracity are often less useful than jurors suppose. (For more on confession contamination, see Chapter 8.)

Indeed, some researchers suggest that police interrogators often engage in a process of *shaping* a confession. Specifically, interrogators sometimes suggest to the suspect "how and why the crime occurred, providing possible motives and plausible explanations; correcting, suggesting and filling in missing crime-relevant information . . . As a result, contaminated/formatted false confessions contain not only non-public crime facts, but a coherent and compelling story-line, motives and explanations, detailed and vivid crime knowledge, displays of emotion (including crying), description of the confessor's thoughts and feelings (both before and after supposedly committing the crime), displays of catharsis and remorse, requests for forgiveness and even expressions of voluntariness" (Leo et al., 2013).

Finally, one more factor encourages jurors to believe confessions; this factor involves a pattern so strong and so widespread that researchers refer to it as the "fundamental attribution error" (Blandon-Gitlin, Sperry, & Leo, 2011; Kassin & Gudjonsson, 2004; Kassin, Drizin, Grisso, Gudjonsson, Leo, & Redlich, 2010; see also Ross, 1977). This term refers to the strong tendency for people to underestimate (and perhaps neglect altogether) the powerful role of the situation in shaping someone's behavior and a corresponding tendency for people to assume that a person's behavior is the result of the person's beliefs and personality. Thus, in evaluating a confession, jurors are likely to discount the role of situational pressures (the circumstances of the interrogation, the social influences, the suggestive questioning) and also to discount the individual's state coming into the interrogation (e.g., the level of hunger or exhaustion, or the need for some habitually used drug). As a result, jurors are likely to discount factors that we know are crucial in eliciting a false confession.

The Importance of Camera Angle

We should also reprise a further point mentioned in Chapter 8—an aspect of confession evidence that encourages jurors to make the fundamental attribution error. In many jurisdictions, the interrogation leading to a confession is videotaped, but often there is no recording of the sometimes lengthy interview that led to the confession. Hence, a suspect might be questioned by the police for hours with no recorder running. It is only at the end of this sequence, when the suspect is finally ready to admit guilt, that the recorder is at last turned on. As a result, the evidence provided to the jury (i.e., the video itself) showcases the suspect's admission, but provides no record of the situation that led to the admission. This configuration obviously focuses the jurors' attention on the confession and not the situation—a pattern that makes the fundamental attribution error even more likely.

Moreover, most jurisdictions record suspects' confessions with the camera zoomed in to show just the suspect; often the interrogators themselves are entirely off-camera (and hence audible but not visible). This format seems sensible, on the common-sense idea that we especially want to view the demeanor and body language of the suspect; these cues, we might think, will be particularly helpful in evaluating the suspect's behavior (including the confession).

There are, however, two problems here. First, as we saw in Chapter 7 and have reiterated here, demeanor and body language are not all that useful in evaluating a suspect's narrative. At best, therefore, this video format is showcasing cues of questionable worth. At worst, the format actually encourages viewers to focus on these low-value cues.

Second, Chapter 8 mentioned a series of studies by Lassiter (e.g., Lassiter & Geers, 2004) that make it clear that this video format encourages the fundamental attribution error. These data tell us that by focusing the camera on the suspect, we encourage viewers to think about the suspect as shaping (and indeed causing) the sequence of events in the interrogation room, and likewise we draw their attention away from any consideration of the unseen influences, including the interrogator's utterances and nonverbal behavior. As a result, research participants (and, in some of Lassiter's studies, actual jurors, attorneys, and judges) end up less alert to suggestive questioning or coercion and less able to discriminate true confessions from false ones.

D. JURY PERFORMANCE: OVERALL

Once again, the material in this chapter is worrisome. In evaluating witness testimony, jurors often rely on indicators (confidence, detail, consistency) that are of little value, and they routinely neglect factors (described in Chapters 3, 4, and 5) that are plainly important. Jurors' ability to recall trial evidence when they move into deliberation is uneven, and we cannot rely on the deliberation itself to correct memory errors or fill memory lapses. Jurors, like all the rest of us, seem inept in detecting lies and assess witness veracity by relying on indices that are, in truth, not informative.

Jurors rely on confession evidence in forming their verdicts even when it is plain that the confession was involuntary. Then, on top of these concerns, we have alluded to the further fact that jury comprehension of judicial instructions seems, in many settings, to be variable at best and often weak.

A cynical conclusion from all of this might be that we should abandon all hope of good jury decision making—especially when we realize that the cases reaching juries are the more difficult cases being litigated. (After all, if a case is straightforward, with evidence clearly favoring one decision or another, then the litigants are likely to resolve the case before trial. Cases that reach trial, therefore, are typically those with a less obvious, less predictable outcome—putting an even heavier load on the jury.)

Despite these concerns, evidence powerfully suggests that juries typically reach the "right answer"—if we count as correct the verdict a judge would have given if there were no jury. Many studies over the years have confirmed this convergence between juries' verdicts and judges'. To be sure, there has been debate over many of these studies, but the overall pattern of the evidence remains (e.g., Bornstein, 2006; Diamond & Rose, 2005). In addition, a number of studies have made it clear that the single most important determinant of jury verdicts is the strength of evidence in the trial—just as it should be. (For an overview of the research on this point, see Devine, 2012.) Apparently, then, juries somehow rise above the problems we have described in this chapter. Our conclusion probably should not, therefore, be a lamentation about the poor quality of jury perception and memory. Instead, our focus should be on the factors that can sometimes undermine jury performance and sometimes nurture it, with the prospect of using this focus to work toward better performance overall.

CHAPTER 10

Children's Memories

Sadly, children sometimes get swept up in the justice system. Sometimes they are witnesses to crimes and, with alarming frequency, are victims of crimes. What do we know about their ability to report some horror they have witnessed or experienced?

In many crimes involving children, there is physical evidence, but, to interpret that evidence, we often need to rely on a child's memories. (How did the child get bruised? Was it perhaps an accident? Who caused the bruises—a parent or someone else?) In other cases, crimes involving children leave no physical evidence. This is certainly true for many forms of sexual abuse—including groping, oral contact, or exposure. When investigating these crimes, the child's report is sometimes our only source of information. We therefore have powerful reasons to ask how fully we can rely on children's testimony and also on whether there are preferred procedures for obtaining that testimony. Those points are the central concerns of this chapter and the next.

Discussion throughout this book rests on a broad base of scientific evidence, but this point deserves special emphasis with regard to children. There is a huge research enterprise that has examined (and continues to examine) children's cognitive and social development, their language skills, their memory capacities, and more. Thus, in addition to the sources mentioned in these chapters, readers are well advised to consult other resources, including Bartlett & Memon, 2006; Lamb, Orbach, Warren, Esplin, & Herkkowitz, 2007; Lamb et al., 2011b; Melnyk, Crossman, & Scullin, 2007; Pipe, Lamb, Orbach, & Cederborg, 2007; Pozzulo, 2006, or, for that matter, a text-book on child development.

A. CHILDREN'S MEMORIES: SOME INITIAL DISTINCTIONS

Attorneys sometimes ask me for an overall assessment of children's memories, hoping that I can tell them that children's memories can or cannot be trusted. A moment's reflection, however, makes it clear that sweeping pronouncements on this point are unwise, thanks to the considerable variability in this domain—including variability linked to how we define memory accuracy, variability linked (unsurprisingly) to the child's age, and also variability (even for age-matched peers) from one child to the next. Let's examine these variations, starting with how we might define "memory accuracy."

Gist Versus Source Memory

As they grow, children have an enormous amount to learn. They need to learn about practical matters and social matters. They need to gain a broad set of everyday skills, ranging from the skill of dressing oneself to the skill of mastering and using language. They need to learn the names of friends and teachers and family members, that stealing is wrong, that vases break if you drop them, and that your parents will be pleased if you finish your spinach. The list obviously goes on and on.

Moreover, if the child is to end up with *usable* knowledge, all of this information must be cross-referenced and integrated, so that the facts gathered *here* are linked to facts gathered *there*, and information acquired in one setting is interwoven with information encountered in other settings.

Children are marvelously successful in this endeavor, but they pay a price for their remarkable learning capacity, because the process of integration and cross-referencing creates a danger—namely, that the child will lose track of where each piece of information came from. "Was this something that I saw for myself? Or merely heard about? Is this something I heard last week from my mom? Or an idea I came up with on my own?"

The issue here is one we have met in other settings throughout this book, because adults face roughly the same challenge: Adults, too, need to integrate and cross-reference the bits of knowledge they acquire; this integration makes our knowledge much more useful. But, as we have discussed, this integration creates a danger of "source confusion" and thus errors in recalling where each bit of knowledge came from.

Concerns about source confusion are greater for children, however, for multiple reasons. Among other considerations, children lack skill in the judgment process that researchers call "source monitoring." Hence, they are overall less accurate than adults in recalling the source of their knowledge. What underlies this lack of skill? The answer has several parts, but one part is straightforwardly biological: The brain tissues that support memory are still developing during the years of childhood, and so children literally have immature memories (e.g., Gogtay et al., 2006).

The key point, then, is that children are remarkably skilled in acquiring knowledge, but less good at keeping track of and remembering where they got their knowledge (cf. Lindsay, 2002). Thus they make mistakes about whether they saw something for themselves or heard about it from a friend, and mistakes about whether they experienced an event or learned about the event through some adult's questioning.

Researchers sometimes describe these points by noting that children are skilled in deriving the *gist* of their experiences (e.g., Reyna, Mills, Estrada, & Brainerd, 2007), but we need to be clear that gist is "in the eye of the beholder." In other words, the gist of an event (or message or conversation) consists of those elements the person understands to be central, and, of course, people differ in their understanding. Children do their best to understand the world around them, but they do so with limited tools: They have to rely on the (often limited) knowledge they have gained so far as a base for understanding new experiences and new information. As a result, children can sometimes add gist information to their knowledge base that is inaccurate, reflecting their immature misunderstanding of things they see or things they experience.

In light of all of these points, how should we describe children's memories? Children have a remarkable learning capacity, and this capacity serves them well in the sorts of learning they need day to day. They do misunderstand (and so misremember) some events, but, even so, one has to be impressed by how well children remember the gist of their experiences. The sort of remembering needed for the justice system, however, is often different because the justice system needs more than gist and can be misled by a child's misunderstanding of an event or a conversation. And, of course, the justice system can also be misled—sometimes in deeply consequential ways—by information for which the child has made a source error. These broad points arise again and again in this chapter.

The Importance of Language Acquisition

Not surprisingly, the child's age is also a key variable in determining the likelihood of gaining complete, accurate information from the child; age is also important for determining how easily the child can be pulled off track by outside influences (including inappropriate questioning). Let's start with some rough rules of thumb and then add some complexities.

The justice system depends on a specialized type of remembering: information provided through a verbal report and (in most cases) open to cross-examination. Obviously, then, we can obtain this type of memory only from children who have mastered language, and so the justice system is unlikely to receive evidence from children younger than three years or so.

What about a child who, at age three or four, is able to talk and seems to be reporting on events that took place a year (or more) earlier, before the child was able to talk? Should we trust these descriptions of events that unfolded when the (now verbal) child was still in a preverbal state? The naïve answer to these questions might run this way: Perhaps a preverbal child is able to "record" events into memory but is not yet able to report on the events. Once the child gains language skill, however, there is a means of sharing the memory, and so the event can now be reported.

This account might seem plausible but is wrong. As one concern, there is reason to question whether key brain areas in a toddler (areas in and around the hippocampus) are developed enough to support "autobiographical remembering." In addition (and certainly related), preverbal children lack some of the mental resources needed to "record" events into memory. Specifically, encoding an event into memory depends on the person's ability to understand the event, because this understanding allows the person to link elements within the event to each other and also to other aspects of knowledge. In addition, what gets recorded from an event depends on what the person pays attention to, and what the person pays attention to, in turn, again depends on understanding—so that someone who comprehends the basic structure of an event is likely to focus on elements that we all would consider central, whereas someone with no understanding might well focus on trivial minutiae.

These points about understanding and attention are important for many reasons, but, for present purposes, note that these points set limits on how well a very young child can establish memories: The young child will have only a limited understanding of an event and so will not be able to see the connections that support (and, on some accounts, are necessary for) memory. Moreover, a young child will have only primitive ideas of what to pay attention to within the event, and this, too, will constrain memory.

In addition, a preverbal child has not yet received what we can think of as "instruction in how to remember." This point rests on the idea that the acquisition of language skills allows a child to participate in conversations, and conversations, in turn, provide an enormous amount of information to the child about *what* and *how* to remember. Of course, when the child is very young, the conversations tend to be one-sided, with the adult doing most of the work of describing the remembered episode. ("Remember when we went to see Grandma, and she gave you a teddy bear?") As the child develops, the adult gradually retreats to a narrower role, asking specific questions to guide the child's report ("Did you see any elephants at the zoo?") and then, at a later age, asking only broader questions ("What happened in school today?"). Eventually, the child's narrative skill develops to a point at which the adult can just listen as the child reports on an earlier episode. Over this entire evolution, though, the questions asked, the sequence of questions, and the level of detail requested provide crucial guides for the child as he or she figures out what is worth reporting in an event, what the order of report should be, and, just as important, what is worth paying attention to while the event is unfolding (Fivush, 1998; 2002; Fivush, Haden, & Reese, 2006; Fivush & Nelson, 2004; Nelson & Fivush, 2000; Peterson & McCabe, 1994; Pipe, Thierry, & Lamb, 2007).

These points have many implications, but, for now, let's draw a narrow conclusion: A preverbal child has not yet engaged in the conversations that will eventually teach the child how to pay attention to, think about, and report on events. The preverbal child has also not yet gained the knowledge that will eventually flow in through conversations—knowledge that, when it arrives, will provide a vastly richer set of schemata for the child, guiding the child's attention, promoting understanding, and offering a broad set of potential connections in memory.

For all of these reasons, researchers would urge considerable caution in any case involving a child's verbal description of an event that took place in the child's preverbal years. If we do find this sort of early memory, investigators should consider the possibility that the memory is "second-hand"—with the child reporting on what he or she learned from others about the target event (Fivush, 2002).

Preschool-Aged Children

It is rare to find verifiable, first-hand, verbally expressed memory for events a child experienced before the age of 20–24 months (cf. Terr, 1988). Even for children who have reached this age, verifiable memories are generally observed only for children who are relatively advanced in their verbal prowess (Fivush, 2002).

The situation changes considerably though, when we consider children just a few months older, and autobiographical recall is easily documented with preschool-aged children—that is, children between, roughly, age 2½–3, at the lower end, and 5 or so, at the upper end. These children can provide reasonably complete, accurate, and detailed reports of their experience—but with a couple of important limitations. First, children of this age still have considerable difficulty with source monitoring and so are easily pulled off track in remembering the past if they are exposed to outside sources of information that might contaminate their recall. (We'll say much more on this point later.) Second, and related, children of this age are still "novices" at reporting the past and often need a lot of encouragement and support in constructing their memory-based narratives. In other words, children at this early age need a lot of adult guidance in describing their experiences, and this creates a danger of *mis*guidance; that is, a danger that the children's reports may be shaped and perhaps even distorted by the way they are questioned (e.g., Baker-Ward & Ornstein, 2002). This makes it crucial that children be questioned properly from the start. (Again, more on this point later.)

In addition, children of this age are in important ways still "novices" in language use. As a result, their vocabulary is often limited, and so they may not understand questions that are put to them and may not use words in the same way that an adult does (cf. Lamb et al., 2007; Saywitz, 2002). For example (here focusing on an issue of crucial importance for the justice system), children of this age often have odd notions of what "sex" is, and so, for example, may say "we had sex" merely to convey some form of snuggling. Similarly, children of this age are often unskilled in using the words and related concepts needed to convey dates and quantities, and so interviewers need to be cautious when the child says (for example) "we did it eight times," or "it was last month."

Children of this age also routinely find themselves in conversations in which they do not understand what is said to them—perhaps because an adult has used an unfamiliar word or a complex sentence construction. In these settings, preschool-aged children often give no signs of their confusion (i.e., do not request clarification; Saywitz, 2002; Saywitz, Snyder, & Nathanson, 1999). Instead, they make their best guess about what the adult intended, and so, rather than signaling their uncertainty, they respond as if they did understand. (Indeed, in one study, researchers documented 900 cases in which five- to seven-year-old children were asked confusing and complex questions; the researchers noted only nine instances in which the children indicated noncomprehension; Carter, Bottoms, & Levine, 1996.) This is, of course, another way for miscommunication to arise—with the children responding to a question as they understood it, but with a contrast between the child's understanding and what the adult intended.

In fact, this last point is easily documented—with preschoolers and even with older children. In one study, children aged five to eight were asked questions that were deliberately nonsensical. They might be asked, for example, "What do bricks eat?" or "Is a jumper angrier than a tree?" (This study was conducted in Britain; children there understand "jumper" to mean the clothing item Americans call a sweater.) For open-ended questions (like the one about bricks), children sensibly indicated they did not know the answer, or they indicated confusion. For close-ended questions, though (like the "jumper" question), many of the children did their best to respond, with roughly 80% of the children offering "answers" that (presumably) they regarded as plausible responses to a puzzling adult query (Waterman, Blades, & Spencer, 2002; 2004; see Chapter 11 for more on the contrast between "open-ended" and "close-ended" questions). Plainly, therefore, one has to be alert to this sort of miscommunication with children, and one cannot rely on children to signal when they have misunderstood. (For more on the effects of a child's emerging language skills, see Peterson & Warren, 2009.)

School-Aged Children

Not surprisingly, the concerns just expressed diminish as children get older: Older children are better at reporting on events and less vulnerable to source confusion. Let's emphasize, though, that the concerns diminish, but do not disappear, as the child matures. (Indeed, in Chapter 3, we discussed research with adults in which false memories were created through outside suggestion. There is no question, then, that vulnerability to source confusion does not vanish as one ages.) Older children are also better able to understand an interviewer's questions and to communicate their own intended meanings, and so miscommunication is less likely with older children. Indeed, by the time children have reached age eight or nine, many aspects of their memory and communicative competence approach those of an adult.

However, these points cannot be summarized simply by asserting, "The older the child, the greater the likelihood of an accurate memory report." This bald statement is roughly true but needs several qualifications. First, some studies do not show the expected age trend (Lamb et al., 2007). The explanation for this mixed pattern lies in the fact that younger children are more susceptible to outside suggestion, but older children are open to other problems. Older children are, for example, better able to supplement their recall with knowledge-based inference. In many cases, these inferences will be accurate—but sometimes they may not be, and, if so, an (unwitting) inference can lead to an error in describing an earlier event. (For demonstrations of this pattern, see Baker-Ward, Ornstein, & Starnes, 2009; Brainerd, 2013; Brainerd, Reyna, & Zember, 2011.)

Second, children of age 9, 10, or 11 are moving toward puberty and often become confused or embarrassed about issues linked to sexuality. As a result, children of this age may end up providing less clear, less complete reports on events pertaining to sexual touching, with confusion or embarrassment impeding their communication.

Moreover, children in the early stages of puberty will, in many cases, talk with peers more and more about sexual matters and may seek out information about sexual activities. For these reasons, children at this age may be exposed to a range of influences potentially shaping their memories of their own experiences. Bragging may also play a role—if, for example, a child boasts to peers about some sex-related experience, and this boast is overheard and taken seriously by, say, a mandatory reporter. (A mandatory reporter is an individual who, usually by virtue of his or her employment, has regular contact with vulnerable individuals and who is required by law to report suspicions of abuse to law enforcement.)

Overall, then, it is true that memory accuracy tends to be greater in older children than in younger children. However, we must not overstate this claim. Even older children (and adults) make memory errors, and some studies show little relationship between age and memory accuracy. More powerfully, in some circumstances, older children are *more* likely to omit information from their reports (e.g., because of embarrassment) and also more likely to make some types of memory errors (especially errors deriving from the child's inferences about the event). Hence, there is surely a linkage between memory accuracy and age, but with some complexity attached to this broad notion.

Differences Among Children

There is one more complication that we should mention, although there is less to say here than one would wish: Children differ from each other. Even at a single age, some children are better at remembering (and reporting on) the past than their peers. Likewise, in laboratory studies, many children make memory errors when asked about previous episodes, but many do not. Plainly, then, it would be useful if we could clarify which children are more likely to provide trustworthy evidence and which less so.

This issue has been scrutinized by researchers, but the state of the art is not overwhelming (see Dickinson, Poole, & Laimon, 2005). As we have discussed, the age of the child is a good (but imperfect) indicator of the likelihood of an accurate report. In addition, the verbal maturity of the child is a reasonable indicator (e.g., Bruck & Melnyk, 2004, although also see Lamb, Malloy, & La Rooy, 2011; Pipe et al., 2007a). This linkage to verbal maturity probably derives from points already discussed: More-verbal children have engaged in a greater number and greater range of conversations about the past and so have had more "training" in reporting on their life events. In addition, more-verbal children will obviously be better in communicating what they recall, thus decreasing the danger of miscommunication. Finally, more-verbal children will require less guidance and fewer prompts during an investigation, decreasing the risk of leading the child.

How can we measure the verbal maturity of a particular child? The most straightforward procedure is to check on the child's vocabulary—does the child know the meaning of *this* word? The meaning of *that* word? (Researchers refer to this point as the child's *receptive vocabulary*—the ability to understand words the child hears.) This sort of vocabulary test turns out, however, to be a poor predictor of memory. What matters instead is the child's expressive skill—the ability to offer a cohesive and well-structured narrative describing previous events (e.g., Peterson & Warren, 2009).

Stepping away from verbal skills, though, there is also some suggestion that *more intelligent* and *less creative* children may be less suggestible (e.g., Pipe et al., 2007b). A child's understanding of an event is also predictive of memory accuracy. Thus, for example, researchers have probed children's memories for a visit to a dentist's office or their memories for a medical procedure the child had undergone. Memory accuracy tends to be greater among children who had a greater understanding, in advance of these events, about what would happen to them (e.g., Baker-Ward et al., 2009).

Other evidence suggests that memory accuracy may be linked to the child's *attachment style*. This term refers to a theory-guided classification that describes how the child relates to others (typically, how the child relates to his or her primary caregiver) and how the child understands these relationships. (The child's understanding is often referred to as the child's "internal working model" of social relationships.) Children who are "securely" attached seem in some studies to have better memories and to be less suggestible (cf. Bruck & Melnyk, 2004; Chae, Ogle, & Goodman, 2009). However, we will not pursue this point here, mostly because information about a particular child's attachment style is rarely available to the justice system, making the link between attachment and memory less useful for forensic purposes.

Two other points, however, are worth mentioning: First, children also differ in how frequently they drift off into fantasy and in how often fantasy elements appear in their conversations. (We have more to say about the role of fantasy in a later section.) Children who are especially fantasy-prone may be more easily led by a questioner (and may, in fact, create their own fictions that they later come to accept as true accounts).

Second, children also differ in how often and how well they lie. Some children show a remarkable level of honesty and may even be aghast at the prospect of one person lying to another; other children lie routinely (sometimes to gain something, sometimes just for the pleasure of being deceptive). However, it is not clear how much weight investigators should place on this attribute, for several reasons. As we have already discussed, lies are different from false memories, and so, if a child is somehow mistaken about what happened in the past, then the child's report will be candid and sincere, and not a lie. In that sort of case, the child's proclivity toward lying is irrelevant. Moreover, an otherwise honest child can certainly be led to lie if suitably encouraged or sufficiently motivated. Hence, a history of honesty or dishonesty may be of little value in telling us whether the child is lying in a particular case. As a related point, the notion that a child has been honest in the past and hence can be trusted now assumes a level of consistency in the child's behavior. (Roughly, the assumption is: "Typically honest, therefore honest now," or perhaps the reverse: "Often dishonest, therefore lying now.") However, this assumption of consistency is not well founded. Indeed, one of the classic studies in psychology focused on just this issue: Hartshorne and May (1928) examined children's behavior in a variety of settings and documented that children who were dishonest in one setting (e.g., who cheated in a sports competition) might well be scrupulously honest in another setting (e.g., in the classroom). This study stirred up a long-lasting debate within psychology about the "cross-situational consistency" of behavior, but, more narrowly, it carries an important message for us here: Trying to assess a child's report based on the child's degree of honesty in other settings may be unwise.

Trial Competence

The previous section had a cautionary tone: We certainly want to assess the reliability of children who are offering pretrial evidence or testimony in court. We know that children differ from each other. But, overall, the available evidence does not allow strong claims about which children are more likely to be reliable informants and which are not.

There is, however, one regard in which trial courts are already making—and need to make—an evaluation of individual children, namely, in the assessment of a child's competence to testify. (For a broad discussion of children's trial competency, see Lyon, 2002; 2011.) Different jurisdictions have their own rules for assessing competence, but here we focus on two issues that cut across jurisdictions. First, if a child is once deemed incompetent to testify about a certain set of issues, can this decision be reversed when the child is older, so that the child is now allowed to testify on the same issues? Second, it is common for assessments of competence to rely heavily on whether a child can distinguish "telling the truth" from "telling a lie" and, related, can distinguish reality from fantasy. What do we know about children's grasp of these points?

I have consulted in several cases that included the follow sequence of events: A young child disclosed some victimization. The child was assessed by the court but deemed incompetent to testify. Some months went by—perhaps even a year or more—and the prosecution brought the case forward again based on the same evidence. Now the child was reassessed, deemed competent, and the case proceeded.

The sequence might make sense if, perhaps, we assume that the only limitation in the scenario just described lies in the "playback" process: On this view, a young child has not yet learned how to report on memories, but even so the memories are securely waiting "in storage." Eventually, though—perhaps with increasing maturity or perhaps through instruction—the child will learn how to report on these memories so that the case can go forward.

But this description of memory is just wrong. If, at an early age, the child's report blurs together reality and fantasy, truth and falsity, this is not just a problem in the child's *reporting* on episodes; it is likely to be a problem in the child's *understanding* of the episodes, and so the information residing in the child's memory may already be weaving together accurate and inaccurate information. The passage of time is not going to repair this concern; if anything, the passage of time will aggravate the problem, inasmuch as reality monitoring and source monitoring are less accurate for more distant events.

Moreover, we have already mentioned the link between language skill and memory. If, therefore, a child lacks communicative competence (and so is deemed incompetent for that reason), the child is likely to lack memory competence as well. As a result, what is "recorded" into the child's memory is, for this reason as well, likely to be a mix of accurate and inaccurate elements, and, again, there is no reason to believe that this confusion will dissipate as time goes by.

Finally, on top of these points, we need to bear in mind that memories fade as the retention interval grows longer (and so recollection at a delay is generally less accurate, less complete; see Chapter 3). The passage of time also creates an opportunity for new information to arrive—perhaps suggesting to the child what might have happened and what should be reported. Both of these points undermine the likelihood of an accurate report at a delay, adding to the concerns already described here.

Distinguishing Truth and Lies, Reality and Fantasy

The assessment of a child's competence to testify often hinges on whether the child understands the difference between truth and falsity and (related) the distinction between reality and fantasy. Research evidence, however, indicates some complexity for these determinations.

We will turn in Chapter 11 to the question of how proper forensic interviews with children should proceed. One element of proper interviewing is, however, directly relevant here: Often, a forensic interview begins with what is sometimes called "the truth/lie ceremony." The child might be asked, "Do you know the difference between telling a truth and telling a lie?" and, if the child says yes, the child is asked for a definition. Alternatively, the interviewer might point to an object in the room (e.g., the child's blue shirt) and ask, "If I said your shirt was yellow, would I be telling the truth or telling a lie?" Or, as another variant, the procedure sometimes relies on a procedure developed by Lyon and Saywitz (2000). As one step in this procedure, the child is shown a drawing of two girls looking at a pig. The interviewer points to one girl in the drawing and says, "*This* girl looks at the pig and says it's a pig." Then the interviewer points to the other child in the drawing and says, "*This* girl looks at the pig and says it's a fish. Which girl told the truth?"

In any of these variations, sometimes the truth/lies ceremony contains another element: The interviewer promises the child that he or she will tell the truth and requests a similar promise from the child. Then, at the end of the interview, the interviewer often returns to this topic, asking "Has everything you told me today been the truth?"

These steps resemble the steps taken in courtroom assessments of a child's competence, but do the steps achieve their goals? The answer is not clear, but one review of the research on this topic noted that "(a) there is little evidence that children who pass such questions report witnessed events more accurately than same-age peers who do not . . . (b) there is no evidence that providing simple instructions encourages children to filter out misinformation they have heard . . .; and (c) such questions only test children's understanding of lying, but they do not measure other cognitive milestones, such as memory-source monitoring, that might be related to testimony accuracy" (Poole & Lamb, 1998, p. 125, internal citations omitted, but see in particular Huffman, Warren, & Larson, 1999; Lyon, 2011; Pipe & Wilson, 1994; for some indications, though, that the truth ceremony can help, see Lyon, Malloy, Quas, & Talwar, 2008). In short, then, as part of a forensic interview, the truth/lie ceremony may provide little benefit. In the same fashion, questions about truth and lie may be less informative than one would wish as part of an assessment of trial competence.

What about the other arm of the assessment—the child's ability to distinguish reality and fantasy? Here, the complication lies in the fact that a child probed one way might seem fully able to distinguish these two categories, but the same child, probed in a different way, might be uncertain about this distinction. This contrast is (informally) reflected in the fact that many children continue to believe in the Tooth Fairy and Santa Claus even though, when questioned directly, they will (sensibly) tell an adult that dragons and Harry Potter are, of course, fantasy and not real. Likewise, most parents can recall a time when their son or daughter was watching a fantasy movie but cried out in genuine fear of the film villain—as though the make-believe villain posed an entirely real threat.

These observations suggest that the boundary between "real" and "not-real" is somewhat permeable for many children, and this point can be confirmed in research: In one study, three-year-olds were invited to imagine that a monster was inside of a box (Harris, 2000). The child was allowed to look in the box and could, of course, see that the box was empty, and so it's not surprising that the child confidently agreed with the interviewer that the monster was just make-believe. However, when the interviewer left the room briefly, the children often edged nervously away from the box—presumably motivated by the fear that sometimes pretend monsters can pose real danger.

In another study, three- and four-year-old children were quizzed about a number of figures: "Do you know who George Washington is? Is he real or pretend? Do you know who Snow White is? Is she real or pretend?" The same children were also asked questions in another format; they might be told, for example, about a girl who has a blanket that can make her invisible and asked: "Is she real or pretend?" Many children performed accurately on the first test (indicating that they did understand the difference between reality and fantasy) but performed poorly on the second test (implying the opposite conclusion; Corriveau, Kim, Schwalen, & Harris, 2009; for more on the interplay among fantasy, memory accuracy, and testimony, see Lamb, Malloy, & LaRooy, 2011a).

Overall, then, the scientific evidence may simply be in tension with the needs and goals of the justice system. To decide a particular case, a judge needs to make a binary decision: Should a child be allowed to testify or not? The need for this decision, though, sits alongside research indicating no bright-line separation here, no well-defined distinction between children who reliably understand the difference between reality and fantasy and those who do not. The resolution to this matter is not clear, especially given the blunt fact that the courts do need to make decisions about a child's trial competency. At the least, though, the available science urges caution about this determination. Perhaps more useful, if a child *is* deemed competent to testify, the issues raised here could surely be presented to a jury in hopes of aiding them as they wrestle with the challenge of assessing a child's testimony.

B. REMEMBERING SIGNIFICANT EVENTS

The previous sections have mentioned a number of concerns, including memory problems in preschoolers, the difficulty of assessing competence, and so on. But, against this backdrop, let's emphasize that memory reports from even young children can be accurate and complete provided that the children are questioned properly from the start. Children can (if properly questioned) show impressively detailed memory for day-to-day events and even better memory for distinctive, emotional events—presumably the sort of events that might be relevant to a criminal case.

Remembering Distinctive Events

Various studies have examined how children remember unusual or special events, events that stand apart from the mundane experiences of everyday life. For example, Fivush, Hudson, and Nelson (1984) interviewed 18 kindergartners after a class trip to a museum of archeology. The children's reports were impressively accurate even after a six-week delay. Fivush et al. also followed-up with these children a year later. Not surprisingly, they recalled less information at this delay, but what they did recall was still accurate.

What about events that are distinctive and *stressful*? Bahrick, Parker, Fivush, and Levitt (1998; Fivush & Sales, 2004) questioned three- and four-year-old children about an episode in which the children's houses had been threatened by a hurricane. For some of the children, the episode was highly stressful: Their houses had sustained substantial damage from the storm, including broken windows, partial collapse of portions of the house, and more. For comparison, data were also collected from a "low-stress" group, which included children whose families had prepared for the storm but whose houses had sustained little damage. In addition, a "moderate stress" group included children who had experienced damage to the perimeter of their home, but with the home itself left intact.

When questioned two to six months after the storm, children were able to recall both the gist of the event and many details, although the level of recall was lowest for the high-stress group, best for the moderate-stress group. The same children were re-interviewed six years later. Now there was no relationship between level of stress and overall amount of information recalled, but children in the high-stress group needed more prompts for their recall, suggesting perhaps that one of the long-term effects of the stress was a diminished willingness to come forward with much information. However, the children in the high-stress group could still recall a considerable amount of information when suitably prompted. (For more on how stress shapes children's memories, see Baker-Ward et al., 2009; Edelstein, Alexander, Saver, Schaaf, Quas, Lovas, & Goodman, 2004a; Fivush, 2002; Rush, Quas, & Yim, 2011.)

Remembering Medical Procedures

What about even more stressful events or events involving pain? Evidence on these points comes from studies of children who, for legitimate (and often essential) medical purposes, have been exposed to painful, frightening procedures, including injections, emergency room visits, and more. In many studies, researchers have managed to document what actually happened during these events; then, later, the researchers questioned the children to learn how the events were remembered.

For example, Burgwyn-Bailes, Baker-Ward, Gordon, and Ornstein (2001) probed memory for a hospital visit in which children had been treated for facial lacerations. Children between the ages of three and seven showed impressively complete and consistent recall of the event even after a year's delay. However, the delay did have an effect, and, for some of the questions put to the children, the frequency of wrong answers went from 12% in the initial round of questioning (soon after the event) to 22% in the one-year follow-up. Similarly, children in another study were questioned after a delay of five years about an injury that had required a hospital visit (Peterson, 2010). At this long delay, the children recalled appreciably less than they had in an earlier interview conducted soon after the hospital visit, but, even so, they still remembered many details about their injury (also see Peterson, 2012; Peterson & Warren, 2009).

The key message here, then, is that distinctive events seem to be well-remembered by children—even if these events involve some amount of pain. (We note, though, that this longevity in the children's memories may to some extent be encouraged by "reminder conversations" within the family in the months after the initial event.) Nonetheless, these memories do fade with the passage of time—and so, after a delay, children remember less and are more vulnerable to outside suggestion.

A different—but compelling—illustration of this pattern comes from studies of children who have undergone a voiding cystourethrogram (VCUG) procedure. This outpatient procedure involves an x-ray examination of the child's bladder. The child must first remove all of his or her clothing and put on a hospital gown. A doctor or nurse then cleans the child's genital areas and inserts a catheter through the urethra and into the bladder. Dye is then introduced into the bladder while a technician watches on a monitor. A parent may be in the room with the child, but will likely be wearing a lead apron (to protect from radiation exposure).

The procedure is described by physicians as "not painful," but one can imagine debate about this point, and, in any case, the procedure is surely embarrassing, frightening, and uncomfortable. How do these factors influence memory? Several research teams have examined memory for VCUG procedures, and the results are clear: Children as young as three years seem to remember these experiences reasonably well, even after a delay of several years. As one might expect, though, children who experience the VCUG procedure before age three are unable to demonstrate clear memory of the event (e.g., Baker-Ward et al., 2009; Edelstein et al., 2004a; Salmon, Price, & Pereira, 2002).

These data suggest that even traumatic events are likely to be well remembered by children. Indeed, one researcher noted that, like adults, children who have been traumatized often end up with more memory than they would wish, and "most children experiencing severe trauma report having difficulty not thinking about it, and often suffer from intrusive memories" (Fivush, 2002, p. 63).

Remembering Repeated Events

If a child witnesses a robbery or a shooting, this is likely to be a singular event in the life of the child. But if a child is the victim of abuse or neglect, then—tragically—the crime may have been ongoing for some time. As a result, the investigation may be asking the child to recall a cluster of repeated, similar events rather than a one-time occurrence. How does this influence memory?

Repetitions both help and hurt memory (Lamb et al., 2007; Lamb, Hershkowitz, Orbach, & Esplin, 2008; Pipe et al., 2007b; Powell & Thomson, 2002). The repetitions help to the extent that elements of the event are shared from one occurrence to the next. This sort of repetition makes it easier for the child to recall these multiply experienced elements. However, the repetition will pose a challenge for the child if he or she needs to recall elements that distinguish one event within the series from another. As one problem, the child is likely to lose track of which elements occurred in which episode. ("Did he give you the candy the *first* time or the *second* time?") The child may also develop a mental "script" for how these repeated events unfold and, with the passage of time, may rely more and more on this script in inferring what happened in a particular episode, rather than actually remembering that episode.

By similar logic, repetition interacts with the effect of suggestive questions. With repeated events, children will be more resistant to leading questions that concern "fixed" details—details that are consistently part of the repeated events. But, conversely, with repetitions, children are more vulnerable, and more likely to acquiesce, to leading questions about aspects that varied across the repetitions (Powell & Thomson, 2002).

C. THE CONCERN ABOUT SUGGESTIBILITY

Overall, then, the data are telling us that children can remember the past accurately, completely, and for a long time. Moreover, the types of events relevant to the justice system tend to be especially memorable for children because the events are distinctive, often stressful, and sometimes repeated.

We have, however, already signaled the other side of this story. We have mentioned that children can suffer from source confusion. We have mentioned that children are suggestible. We have emphasized the importance of proper questioning. But what are the specifics attached to these concerns?

The "Mr. Science" Experiment

Let's start with a description of a research study on children's suggestibility. This study is offered only as an illustration, because, of course, claims about children's memory (or any other topic) must be rooted in a much broader fabric of evidence. This study will, however, convey the pattern of the evidence and also highlight a number of crucial points.

Poole and Lindsay have conducted a number of "Mr. Science" studies (e.g., Poole & Lindsay, 1995; 2001; 2002; we first met this study in Chapter 3 but elaborate on it here). In one version of the study, a man (dubbed "Mr. Science") visited the children's school and met individually with each child. Mr. Science did a series of four "science demonstrations" with the child (e.g., using two funnels and a rubber tube to make a crude telephone). Then, three months later, the researchers mailed the children's parents a brief "story book," ostensibly describing Mr. Science's visit. The parents were encouraged to read this book with their child three times, much as they would read any story with the child. The book included descriptions of the actually experienced science demonstrations, but also some demonstrations that the child had not experienced. The book also described two events involving body touch that, in truth, had not occurred at all—an event in which Mr. Science put something "yucky" in the child's mouth and one in which Mr. Science touched the child's bare skin, pushing so hard on the child's tummy (to apply a reward sticker) that it hurt.

Importantly, the parents were explicitly warned that they should not accept as factual everything they read in the "story book." Specifically, they were told that not all children had experienced the same demonstrations, and that the story book therefore included some events that their own child had experienced and some that other children had experienced.

Shortly afterward, the children were interviewed by the researchers about the Mr. Science visit. The interview was conducted in a fashion carefully designed not to be leading or suggestive in any fashion. (In Chapter 11, we will have more to say about what this style of neutral interviewing must involve, and did involve, in the Mr. Science studies.)

This overall procedure yielded a rich and textured pattern of results. To highlight just a few points, many children absorbed into their memory the fictitious events described in the story book. As a result, many children offered false reports about the Mr. Science visit when questioned (again, in an entirely nonsuggestive, open-ended manner) at the end of the procedure. And, crucially, many of these false reports included suggested events that—if they had occurred—would have been unpleasant and therefore salient: In an early round of interviews at the study's close, roughly 30–40% of the children in each age group responded "yes" to questions about whether Mr. Science put something yucky in their mouths or hurt their tummies. In follow-up interviews, with slightly more careful questioning, these rates of false acquiescence *increased* for the three-year-olds (to 53%) and four-year-olds (to 58%), but decreased (to roughly 15%) for the seven- and eight-year-old children in the study.

There is much worth discussing in this data pattern, but a few points deserve special emphasis: First, no one tried deliberately to put ideas into these children's memories. Indeed, the parents were explicitly put on guard through an overt warning in the booklet that some of the elements contained within the booklet were not experienced by their child. Hence, false memories need not result from someone trying to "manipulate" a child. Second, the frequency of false memories is quite high here—with more than half of the children, on some measures, reporting events that never occurred. False memories are not rare. Third, there was no need for pressured or intense interviewing to produce these false memories; instead, the memories arose out of the simple experience of the child's reading through a story book with one of his or her parents just three times.

Fourth, the false memories were detected by the researchers in interviews at the end of the procedure that were neutral and objective; the false memories were often reported in response to open-ended questions. In fact, the actual script for the questioning ran this way: "Do you remember playing with Mr. Science? Good. I want you to tell me everything that happened when you were playing with Mr. Science. I wasn't in the room, so I don't know what happened" (Poole & Lindsay, 2001, p. 30). Thus, even though open-ended questions are vastly preferable in questioning a child, open-ended questions cannot on their own insulate the child from memory contamination.

Fifth, note that, for many children, these errors remained in place even when the memories were challenged. ("You know, there might have been some things in the story [that you read with your mom or dad] that you didn't really do, things that were only in the story"; Poole & Lindsay, 2001, p. 31). Apparently, once a false memory is established, the error cannot easily be reversed through careful questioning or challenge later on. Once the false memory is established, in other words, we cannot "unring the bell" or "unscramble the egg."

Sixth, let's emphasize that the false memories in this study were not limited to benign events; false memories regularly occurred for events that involved painful skin-to-skin contact (getting hurt when Mr. Science pushed on your tummy) or aversive to the child (something "yucky" in the mouth).

Factors Shaping Suggestibility

The Mr. Science studies are, of course, only a small part of a large research literature, and many other studies confirm that children can often be led to false reports. The Mr. Science studies provide a clear illustration, however, of the general pattern of this research: In study after study, children are exposed to some event, usually as part of their daily routine. The children are then exposed to some outside influence.

In some cases, this influence takes the form of a specific type of questioning (allowing us to ask, for example, whether children respond differently to "yes/no" questions than they do to other forms of questioning). In other cases, this influence takes the form of information imparted to the child by the experimenter or perhaps by others. Then, finally, there is some follow-up assessment of the child—but with this last step typically done in a neutral, nonleading way, in order to ask whether the effects of the earlier influence remain even if the child is now questioned in a non-suggestive fashion.

Studies employing this rough template have taught us a great deal about children's memories—including some important lessons about how often and how readily children's memories can be pulled off track. Crucially, though, these studies also allow us to catalog some of the factors that make suggestion easier in some circumstances than in others. This catalog is valuable for several reasons, among them the fact that it provides a basis for assessing the degree of risk for a false memory in an individual case. Specifically, we can scrutinize a given case in order to ask whether factors promoting suggestibility are present or absent. If many of these factors are present, concern about suggestibility and false memory has to increase; if few (or none) of the factors are in place, the concern is diminished. Let's be clear, though, that no single factor, no element within the catalog, is necessary, but each can contribute to the likelihood of a memory error, and so, the more of these factors that are in place, the greater the concern about false memory has to be.

Here, then, is a list of a dozen factors that one should keep track of when trying to discern whether a child may have been misled and thus whether the child's report might be an honest, candid instance of confusion, with the child "recalling" events that did not occur. This list is not exhaustive, and other researchers might structure the list somewhat differently. Nonetheless, I (and attorneys I have worked with) find this list useful as a way of guiding the examination of any particular case. (For evidence relevant to all of these points, see Bourg et al., 1999; Bull, 2010; Ceci, Crossman, Scullin, Gilstrap, & Huffman, 2002; Lamb et al., 2007; 2011b.)

1. *Directive questioning.* One powerful way to produce a false report is through leading or suggestive questions. Sometimes questions are overtly suggestive: "He touched you, didn't he?" Sometimes questions simply inject a previously unmentioned idea into a conversation (and so it's the adult and not the child who is the first to mention the removal of clothing or some such). Sometimes questions are phrased neutrally, but with a tone of voice that suggests the expected or desired answer. Children are alert to all of these cues and will often shift their answer to comply with the directive and to accept the suggestion. We also need to be clear here that what matters is not the intention of the questioner (e.g., whether the questioner means to lead the child or not). What matters instead is the perception of the child (i.e., whether the child perceives the presentation of the question, or the question itself, to imply that a particular answer is desired or expected).

2. *Feedback.* In many contexts, children receive feedback (from parents, teachers) that signals to them whether their behavior or utterances met with approval or did not. The feedback can take many forms—with the adults sometimes offering

an explicit verbal evaluation ("Yes, that's right," or "I'm not sure that's correct") and sometimes providing a nonverbal cue (a nod or a shake of the head). Sometimes the adults provide an elaboration of the child's utterance (thus implying an endorsement of the utterance) or their own version of events (implying a rejection). In still other cases, sometimes the adults express skepticism, perhaps outright ("Are you sure?") or by asking questions that highlight a concern about the child's account ("How could you see if it was so dark?"). Children are sensitive to all of this informational feedback and often shift their accounts in a fashion guided by this feedback. Of course, this sensitivity to feedback is usually helpful and is one of the reasons why children are so quick to learn new material. In the context of an investigation, however, this feedback can cement in place some responses and discourage others, powerfully shaping the child's report.

In addition to informational feedback, children are also sensitive to feedback of another sort. Imagine a child who mentions some event of victimization and immediately receives some form of emotional feedback—perhaps a flow of warm, loving support, or perhaps a greater amount of attention from some adult. Perhaps the feedback takes the form of a hug; perhaps the feedback is verbal ("You're very brave to be telling me this"). In all cases, the child has received a reward for offering the allegation, and this form of feedback will also have an effect of encouraging similar or expanded allegations. (See, e.g., Bruck, Ceci, Francoeur, & Barr, 1995; Lepore & Sesco, 1994; Saywitz, 1995.)

3. *Repeated questions.* Children are generally surrounded by adults who want to help them develop and learn. This help can take many forms, including a pattern of "forgiveness" if the child makes a mistake. The forgiveness can be overt ("That's not quite right; try again.") Or, in other settings, the adult can achieve the same goal by simply reasking the question—in essence pretending not to hear the child's initial response and generously offering the child another try.

Children understand this pattern, and thus understand that a repeated question is often an indication that their first answer was inadequate. Hence the repetition encourages a change in answer (e.g., Krähenbühl, Blades, & Eiser, 2009; Poole & White, 1991) and so provides yet another means through which adults can shape the child's report—accepting some answers (by not reasking the question) and refusing others (by repeating the question).

Repeated questions also have other effects. Questions that keep coming back to a certain topic provide information to the child about the conversation's "agenda." (In essence, the repeated questions lead the child to a conclusion along the lines of "I notice that we keep talking about Peter, and the swimming pool; that must be what this conversation is about.") In this fashion, the repetitions can highlight themes and thus signal to the child what he or she is "supposed to be" addressing in the conversation.

In addition, repeated questions can gradually make a topic more and more familiar, and this invites a problem we discussed in earlier chapters: As we have seen, people (both adults and children) are often better at saying *that* something is familiar than they are in recalling *why* something is familiar. This can lead to its own form of source confusion because the person can become confused about the source of the familiarity. More specifically, the error in play here is sometimes referred to as "misplaced familiarity" because, in this setting, the person has correctly noted that an idea is familiar but then makes an error in judging the cause of the familiarity.

Thus, when questioning a child, repeated questions—for example, questions about Peter and the swimming pool—will gradually make this conjunction of ideas more and more familiar. Eventually, this can trigger a source confusion error, with the child mistakenly believing that the conjunction is familiar because of some event involving Peter and the pool, when in fact the familiarity has come from a different source—being asked about Peter and the pool over and over.

4. *A trustworthy source.* From an early age, children are selective in who they trust most, and who they rely on, and this selectivity has important implications for an investigation. On the positive side, more-trusted adults are likely to gain better information from children—and so (for example) children will often be more honest, more open with their mothers than they will be with other adults (Goodman, Sharma, Thomas, & Considine, 1995). But, on the negative side, children are more accepting of information they receive from trusted sources. Thus, leading or suggestive questions, or information provided by tone of voice, can be more effective in shaping the child's report if these cues come from a trusted source. Of course, children can be misled by adults they have just met for the first time (and, in fact, this is the scenario in many research studies). Nonetheless, children are more easily led by someone they regard as an authority, or someone they have long trusted. (For discussion of how children's learning is guided by issues of trust, see Koenig & Sabbach, 2013; Liu, Vanderbilt, & Heyman, 2013.)

5. *"Your mother told me . . ."* When police question an adult suspect, they often confront the suspect with other evidence, including reports obtained from other witnesses. Thus, the police might say, "We heard from three people that you were in the bar that night," or "A neighbor saw you getting home late," or some such. Statements like these are a powerful means of influencing the suspect and are, for example, often used in eliciting a confession. (See Chapter 8.)

In roughly the same manner, children's reports can be shaped by reports of other "evidence." For example, interviewers might say something like, "Your mother told me you were upset about something," or "Your mother told me you said something about Sean. . . ." More strongly, an interviewer might say, "Your mother said you told her about Sean doing something bad . . ." These statements have a powerful impact on children, with the child often acquiescing to the suggestion whether the interviewer had heard anything from the mother or not.

6. *Information from peers.* We have been highlighting the role of authority figures and trusted adults in shaping a child's report; we also mentioned, though, that memories can be created through interactions with peers, and that point merits some expansion.

In one study, researchers arranged for a "magician" to visit a preschool and, during his performance he tried to pull a rabbit out of a hat—but failed; there was no rabbit. Immediately after the show, the children's teacher and an unfamiliar adult engaged in a scripted conversation in the children's presence, with the adult commenting that he "heard that the rabbit got loose in the school . . ." One week later, in response to open-ended questioning, almost a third of the children who overheard this conversation falsely reported having seen the fictitious rabbit.

Another group of children consisted of classmates of the children who had overheard this conversation. For this latter group, the only opportunity to learn about the alleged mishap with the rabbit was through conversation with their peers. Even so, in this group, 55% of the children reported, in response to open-ended questions, having seen the wayward bunny. Apparently, conversation among peers is enough, not only to influence a preschool child's beliefs, but also to shape what the child "remembers" about his or her own experience (Principe, Kanaya, Ceci, & Singh, 2006).

Notice that this case provides another example of source confusion: The reality is that children heard about an event (and so had only second-hand knowledge about the event), but many children ended up mistakenly believing they had seen the event (and so had first-hand knowledge). Thus, the children plainly ended up confused about (and wrong about) the source of their own knowledge.

7. *Plausibility.* We discuss in a later section the sorts of false memories that can, by one means or another, be planted in a child's recall. We should be clear, though, that some suggestions are more likely to succeed than others, and, in children as in adults, a suggestion will be more readily accepted if the suggestion seems plausible from the outset. (See Chapter 3 for more on the role of plausibility in creating false memories.)

In fact, plausibility matters for both the child and the adult who is questioning the child. To understand the influence on the adult, consider two scenarios: In the first, let's say that a child makes an ambiguous remark about being touched by Uncle Fred, and Mom has long suspected that Uncle Fred is a bad man who does bad things. It is easy to imagine that this mother might take her child's remark seriously and pursue it with vigor. Even if her child now insists that nothing has happened, the mother might still press her child, just to make certain. But now, in a second scenario, let's say that a child makes a similarly ambiguous remark about Uncle Joe, but Mom is convinced from the outset that this suggestion makes no sense; she firmly believes Joe could not have committed the suggested acts. In this case, the mother might not question her child at all or might question her only in a cursory manner, and she would likely accept the initial denial.

Likewise, let's say that Mom does have suspicions about Uncle Fred and preconceptions about what Fred may have done. In this setting, the mother is more likely to ask her child leading questions (in comparison to a mother who enters the conversation with no expectations) in order to ferret out information about Fred's misdeeds. A mother with preconceptions about what may have occurred is also more likely to ask yes/no questions in comparison to a mother without prior suspicions—and, in many cases, the yes/no questions will be phrased with "yes" as the expected answer (Bruck, Ceci, & Hembrooke, 1998; Quas et al., 2007; White, Leichtman, & Ceci, 1997).

On this logic, it is often helpful to know about the beliefs and expectations of the person who first questioned the child. Information about these points will, in many cases, allow us a plausible reconstruction of how that initial conversation unfolded. The reconstruction, in turn, can provide information about whether the questioning was suggestive or leading, or entirely neutral. We should pause to ask, though: Why a reconstruction? Why not simply ask the adult involved how the conversation unfolded? The answer lies in the likelihood that the adult will be unable to recall the relevant details of the conversation—a point we addressed in Chapter 6. Thus, the adult's memory seems to provide the most direct means of determining how a conversation unfolded, but, with the memory demonstrably unreliable, this is a circumstance in which we're well advised to rely instead on a thoughtful process of reasoning through how the conversation likely proceeded.

What about the other side of this point—the effect of plausibility on the child? Here, let's imagine that little Judy has, in various conversations, overheard adults in her family talking about sexual matters, including various forms of physical contact. Let's also imagine that Judy knows that cousin Sue was abused, and maybe she knows that Sue testified in her abuser's trial. As a result of these experiences, Judy will be familiar with the broad notion of sexual touching, and we earlier discussed the role of familiarity in creating false memories. In addition, Judy will now think it plausible that she might have experienced sexual touching (because, she has learned, this sort of touching does indeed happen). This perspective will make Judy less resistant to suggestions that she, too, has been abused, and hence more vulnerable to outside information suggesting that, yes, she has experienced some form of sexual contact.

8. *Stereotype induction*. A related factor is often dubbed "stereotype induction." Specifically, imagine a sequence in which you tell a child, "You know, Ron is really clumsy. Can you tell me what happened when Ron came to your class yesterday?" Or, equivalently, "I've heard that Sam is sometimes naughty. Do you know anything about Sam?" Sequences like this can lead children to report on Ron's clumsy acts or Sam's misbehavior even though nothing of the sort occurred (e.g., Ceci et al., 2002; Leichtman & Ceci, 1995).

Note that, in cases involving stereotype induction, children are "active partners" in the creation of the false memory. (We should mention, though, that this "activity" is evident in many other settings as well.) Thus, no one has to lay out for the child, "This is the narrative sequence I want you to endorse." Instead, the creation of a false memory often involves someone merely planting a "seed" ("Did grandpa touch you?"), and the seed can sometimes be rather diffuse ("Did grandpa do something bad to you?" or even "You know, grandpa sometimes does bad things."). From that base, the child can then develop a narrative about the (fictitious) event—perhaps on his or her own or perhaps via a "collaborative conversation" with an inquiring adult.

This pattern is certainly in place for stereotype induction but applies more broadly. Suggestions to children often do little more than "launch" the creation of a false memory. The details of the memory are, in many cases, supplied by the children themselves.

9. *A basis in truth*. When someone (adult or child) falls prey to a false memory, that person has in effect "moved" from an accurate and correct recall of what happened at an earlier point to an inaccurate, false recall of what happened. It

cannot be surprising that this "move" will happen more readily if there is only a short "distance" between the truth and the fiction, so that the past-as-recalled is in some ways similar to, or overlaps with, the past-as-it-actually-unfolded. For this reason, memory errors are more likely if the errors build on some element of truth, so that the past-as-recalled does not involve a wholesale fiction, but instead involves some elaboration (or distortion, or alteration) of an actual event. We shouldn't overstate this point because wholesale fictions can be created in someone's memory. Even so, a memory error is more likely if the error is, in essence, a small one.

Of course, even a small error can be deeply consequential. I testified in one case in which multiple witnesses confirmed that the children had been playing together in a swimming pool and engaging in the sort of rough-housing common in that setting. Older children had been picking up the younger children and tossing them into the air, letting the younger children then splash down into the pool. This tossing obviously required the older children to touch the younger children and to touch them in body areas that typically are not touched. All of this might be entirely innocent, but, in this case, one of the older boys was accused of sexually touching one of the younger children's genitals. We will never know if this truly was an error or not (although, in fact, the defendant was acquitted), but, if this report was an error, it was an error that was factually small but legally large.

10. *Delay*. The risk of false memories and the "size" of a false memory (i.e., how great the departure is from what actually happened) both grow with the passage of time. Several mechanisms contribute to these points. First, as times goes by, the memory for what actually happened in an earlier event will fade (see Chapter 3), leaving the person (child or adult) with less of an "anchor" that might help the person resist a tug toward a false memory. Second, the passage of time also creates more and more of an opportunity for outside influences to impinge on the child (more repetitions of questions, more stereotype induction, and so on). Hence, the risk of memory contamination goes up as time goes by.

Third, we also need to consider what happens if time goes by *after* a child has been exposed to some misleading or suggestive influence. Here, the key lies in the fact that the task of source monitoring (remembering where each bit of information came from) becomes more difficult as the days pass. As a result, a child might initially be aware that ideas about her step-dad's misdeeds only arose in a conversation with mom. With a delay, the child can lose track of this source of the ideas and come to believe that the misdeeds really took place.

Passing time also creates an opportunity for the child to tell and retell what has happened. These retellings will gradually make the narrative more familiar to the child (and so more persuasive *to the child*) and also more fluent (and so more persuasive *to an audience*). The retellings will also create an opportunity for feedback. This feedback can (in the child's perception) confirm the account, thus helping to secure the account in place. The feedback can also *improve* the account if, for example, adults somehow reveal their puzzlement when they hear an inconsistency or odd gap in the child's narrative. This feedback will often lead the child to alter the narrative in ways that will avoid this skeptical response.

All of these mechanisms, tied to the passage of time, can interact in a powerful way with points we discussed earlier. We have noted, for example, that it is easier to create a small error than it is to create a larger one. We can now extend this by saying: a larger memory error (e.g., one containing a lot of detail, multiple events, and many steps of narrative within each event) usually takes time to develop. In other words, false reports can appear rapidly (e.g., a false report on an event that happened just hours ago), *and* false reports can be remarkably elaborate. It is surprising, though, for a false report to have both of these traits—a fast appearance and a lot of detail. Elaborate false reports generally need time to grow.

11. *An initial lie.* In discussing stereotype induction, we noted that children are often "active partners" in creating a false memory, with someone else merely providing the seed of the alleged event and then the child elaborating on this seed. Children can also be active sources of false memories through another pathway—via their own lies.

In one study, children were shown a Disney movie, then asked a number of questions about what they had seen. Some of the questions were peculiar. The child might be asked, for example, whether a character was bleeding from his elbow or from his knee after a fall, when, in truth, it was plain in the movie that the character was not bleeding at all. The children were compelled to choose one of these options—and so, in essence, the children were required to say something that they knew was false. Days later, though, when the children were (neutrally, nonsuggestively) questioned about the video, many of the children were apparently drawn in by their own fabrication and now believed their own false statement (Ackil & Zarzoga, 1998).

The relevance of this study to criminal investigations should be clear: In some cases, one might fear that a child had lied to an adult (perhaps a parent, perhaps a police investigator) in response to the adult's overt pressure, to deflect blame for some transgression, or for some other reason. Then, weeks later, perhaps after repeating the lie several times, the child comes to believe his or her own lie. This shift—from a lie to a false memory—has numerous implications, including the fact that the child might now be quite persuasive to subsequent interviewers (or in testimony) because, in this scenario, the child is, in the end, offering a completely sincere, fully honest (albeit mistaken) report.

12. *Imagination, dreams.* The last entry in this catalog of considerations is related to the previous point. In some cases, a false memory can grow out of a child's imagination. For some children, the starting point is a dream, and, upon waking, the child might be confused about whether the dream was real or not. Indeed, as we mentioned in Chapter 3, many parents have had to comfort their frightened child who just awakened from a nightmare; the parents reassure the child, over and over, "It was only a dream. It was only a dream."

Sometimes parents are able to calm a child in this setting—but sometimes not. In addition, in some cases, the child might not think about or react to a dream on wakening but might instead remember the dream's content only after several weeks. In these (and related) scenarios, the risk of source confusion is plain—with a chance that the child might mistakenly accept the dream as a memory for an actual event.

Of course, one would still want to ask why a particular dream arose at all. To take a concrete example, if a child has not been exposed to pornography or other sources of sexual information, the child is unlikely to have dreams that depict vivid sexual episodes. Thus, in trying to argue that a memory grew out of a dream, an advocate should start by asking what may have triggered the dream in the first place.

Finally, false memories can also be "self-produced" in another way, linked to themes discussed in Chapter 3 (under the heading "The role for motivation"). Imagine an adolescent who has long been troubled in one way or another. Perhaps a young teen suffers from depression, has difficulty in forming relationships, or is concerned about his body shape. It is plausible that this adolescent will feel puzzled about where these problems came from; now, let's say that this individual happens to hear about another teen who developed similar difficulties after a history of abuse. Our adolescent might wonder, "Could that have happened to me?" To tackle this difficult and painful question, the child might try imagining various childhood scenarios, asking whether scenarios involving abuse feel "right" or "true" or "familiar." The difficulty, of course, is that the experience of imagining these events can itself create memories for the events. Indeed, one of the (many) ways to produce a false memory (e.g., in a research setting) is to instruct individuals to imagine this or that scenario; this procedure is powerful enough so that, as we noted in Chapter 3, researchers use the term "imagination inflation" to describe the ways in which imaging can foster false memories.

The Many Paths Toward Suggestion

We have now described many factors that can, in some circumstances, make a false memory more likely and, in other circumstances, less so. We reiterate: The list is not exhaustive, and no factor on the list is necessary. Nonetheless, the more of these factors that are on the scene, the greater the concern should be about a memory's veracity.

This list of factors also draws attention to another point, implicit in our discussion so far, that there is no "fixed procedure," no strictly defined "recipe," for producing a false memory. (Again, see Chapter 3 for related discussion, although there focusing on false memory in adults.) A false memory can be produced by deliberate leading, seeking to suggest a particular memory; a false memory can also be produced with no such intent. A false memory can be encouraged by conversations with an adult who has suspicions or fears about some previous event ("I think Grandpa Jo did something bad"), but it can also arise from interactions with adults who have no such suspicions. (Indeed, we saw in the Mr. Science study that adults can inadvertently produce a false memory even when they've been explicitly warned not to assume that certain events might have occurred.) A false memory can be created with leading questions, with neutral-but-repeated questions, or with neutral questions that happen to be preceded by some type of stereotype induction. Indeed, a false memory can be created with no direct questioning of the child at all—if, for example, the child merely overhears some relevant conversation, creates the relevant ideas as a lie, or draws the relevant ideas out of a dream.

Across all of this variety, though, note the consistent theme: False memories are created in children (just as they are in adults) when the child becomes confused about the source of his or her own ideas, the source of his or her own memories. That theme can be instantiated in dozens of ways, and that is part of the reason why false memories are so easily created and so often encountered. But it is this single theme that lies behind all of the cases we have considered.

What Can Be Suggested?

We still need one more strand in this overview of children's memories, and once again the issue here parallels one discussed in Chapter 3: Specifically, we have been discussing *how* children's memories can be pulled off track, but we also need to ask *how far* they can be pulled off track. What sorts of memory errors are possible?

The fast response here is that no one really knows the answer to this question, in part because there are powerful (and appropriate) ethical constraints on scientific research. Thus, no researcher would ever launch a project to ask questions like: Can you plant a memory in someone of being physically beaten? Can you plant a memory in someone of being raped, even if that person has never experienced this horrible crime? Such research would be repugnant to any scientific investigator, and, if that were not enough, this research would be forbidden by the institutional review boards (IRBs) that assess every research proposal to ensure ethical and legal acceptability.

Researchers have done what they can, however, to explore the limits of false memories while certainly honoring these ethical requirements. In the Mr. Science study, for example, we saw that researchers had no trouble creating a false memory of Mr. Science hurting the child's tummy or a false memory of Mr. Science putting something yucky in the child's mouth. Apparently, then, false memories can include "recall" of skin-to-skin contact and aversive events. In a different study, children were led to a false memory of an event in which they had gotten their finger caught in a mouse-trap (Ceci et al., 2002; Pezdek & Hinz, 2002), confirming that children can have false memories of painful events. In another paradigm (Quas et al., 1999), researchers questioned children about a stressful medical procedure that the children really had experienced but also asked suggestive questions about an entirely fictitious procedure (nose surgery). Almost half of the children (17 of 40) later reported that the nose surgery really had occurred (and so were describing a significant, emotional event), and 13 of these children (roughly a third of children tested) provided their own details about this (nonexistent) surgery. (For yet another example of children being led into false memories of a medical procedure, see Bruck et al., 1995.)

Let's pause, though, to acknowledge that there is some debate about these issues. Some writers have suggested that children are resistant to abuse-related suggestions; they conclude, therefore, that when reports of bodily touch arise in the justice system, these reports are unlikely to be the result of suggestion and hence unlikely to be false. However, I would urge skepticism about this broad claim because there is, in the end, no question about whether false reports of bodily touch can arise. They can. We have seen this point in various studies reviewed here; other studies echo this finding (cf. Melnyk et al., 2007).

What, therefore, is fueling this debate? In some studies, children have indeed resisted abuse-related suggestions and so do not develop false memories of being touched. However, this fact cannot be surprising, for reasons we have already discussed: As we have said, larger memory errors, involving more complex events or more consequential events, are more difficult to produce than smaller memory errors. For this reason, large-scale errors—including memories of being touched in some troubling way—will be observed only if the child is exposed to multiple influences or to relatively strong influences. Indeed, one review argued that, in the studies documenting resistance to suggestion, researchers had simply done too little to "plant" the suggestion—had not "repeated misleading questions over a short time period, exposed children to misleading stereotypes about target individuals, provided incentives to respond falsely, or included conditions that are often associated with recognition errors . . . All of these experimental conditions increase the susceptibility to suggestion" (Lamb et al., 2007, pp. 441–442).

In fact, we can easily show that various influences on a child have a cumulative effect, so that false memories are more frequent and can involve larger errors if multiple suggestive elements are in play. In one study, preschool children were exposed to repeated suggestions *and* instructions to imagine how the suggested events might have unfolded *and* selective reinforcement of responses that indicated acceptance of the suggestions. These steps continued across a series of interviews. In this set-up, a stunning 95% of the children assented to the false events (e.g., claiming they had witnessed a theft in their daycare center) by the third interview (Bruck, Hembrooke, & Ceci, 1997).

In another study, children were interviewed for less than five minutes about a stranger who had visited their daycare center (Garven, Wood, Malpass, & Shaw, 1998). Some of the children were interviewed in a fashion that included just one suggestive element. These children falsely accused the man of the suggested misbehavior only 17% of time. Other children, in contrast, were exposed to repeated suggestive questions and encouragement for making allegations about the man's misbehavior; these children, exposed to multiple influences, falsely accused the man almost 60% of the time.

We can reinforce these points, though, by drawing on evidence that comes, not from scientific research, but from the legal world itself: There are many reasons to study children's memory capacities, but part of the impetus comes from a handful of famous (or perhaps infamous) court cases in which children offered a succession of horrific and bizarre accusations leading to criminal trials of the people accused. In many of these instances, the children reported events that were almost certainly fictitious. For example, in the investigation of the McMartin Preschool case (in Manhattan Beach, California), children reported ritualistic sacrifice of babies (although no babies were missing), helicopter rides to the desert, and having spent time in a network of secret tunnels underneath the daycare center (Melnyk et al., 2007).

Similarly bizarre suggestions emerged in the investigation of the Wee Care Nursery School (in New Jersey) and the Little Rascals Day Care (in North Carolina). If (as seems sensible) we count these accusations as false, and if we assume (as seems plausible) that these accusations were sincerely offered by the children, we gain some insight into how far false memories can go. The conclusion seems to be that large-scale, consequential false memories can occur, and, addressing a point raised earlier, false memories for seemingly implausible events can also occur. In fact, one might conclude, based on these actual court cases, that if there is a limit on false memories, we have not found it yet.

Against this backdrop, though, let's reiterate a positive message: Across this chapter, we have mentioned the many paths that can lead to false memories in children and to the fact that, in some settings, false memories are quite common. We have now argued that false memories can be large in scale (think about those helicopter rides) and deeply consequential. None of this, however, should be taken as an argument for wholesale distrust of children's memories. Children's reports can be enormously accurate—especially if the children are questioned promptly and carefully. This point is crucial for us all because every one of us wants to support the prosecution of anyone who victimizes children. But what exactly does proper questioning of children involve? That question is our main concern in Chapter 11.

CHAPTER 11

Proper Investigations with Children

In Chapter 10, we emphasized that children can provide high quality-evidence—and, specifically, memory-based reports that are clear, complete, and accurate—provided that they are questioned properly from the start. And the simple reality is that we often need this evidence from children. After all, children sometimes do witness horrific events, and—tragically—they are far too often the victims of abuse. We therefore need children's testimony in order to prosecute wrong-doers. The inevitable question, then, is how should children be questioned to maximize the completeness and accuracy of their reports? We focus in this chapter on investigations in which the child was allegedly victimized: physically or sexually abused or in some fashion neglected. The points we cover, however, also apply to other cases of child evidence—for crimes they have witnessed, alibis they can confirm, and more.

A. THE INITIAL REPORT OF ABUSE

When a case alleges some sort of child victimization, the investigation will, in most jurisdictions, come under the control of an agency specifically prepared to deal with these crimes. Before the agency becomes involved, however, there is almost always an earlier step in which the child reported the alleged abuse to someone (a friend, parent, school counselor) who is typically untrained as an interviewer, unaware of the crucial importance of proper interviewing, and not prepared (or equipped) to document the initial round of complaints. Let's start with this earlier step.

The Importance of the First Interview

The early conversations with the child, in which an allegation first emerges, are crucial. If these early conversations shape the child's report or, worse, plant ideas in the child's memory, there may be no way to undo this memory contamination. As we noted in Chapter 10, the situation at issue here is one in which we cannot "unring the bell" or "unscramble the egg." Many studies make this point, including the Mr. Science study described in the previous chapter: In this study, the children's errors about the Mr. Science visit were created during conversations with their parents. However, the errors emerged (and were not eliminated) in a subsequent interview done carefully, neutrally, and relying heavily on open-ended, invitational ("Tell me what happened") questions.

Of course, in some cases, a child will have been exposed to outside influences, distorting the initial report, on occasions *prior to* the initial report. The child may have heard family discussion about some other abuse victim or some other abuser. The child may have had conversations with friends or family members about the now-accused suspect or perhaps broader conversations about sexual behaviors. In any of these cases, the conversation that takes place at the time of the child's first complaint is just one of the possible sources of contamination. But, even so, the conversation in which the allegations first emerge can be a powerful source of influence, and so we obviously want to know as much as we can about how this conversation unfolded. We want to know what was said to the child (what questions were asked; what feedback was provided); we also want to know exactly what the child said.

We should also be clear: There will be occasions in which information about these early conversations might be used to challenge a child's complaint—if, for example, leading questions were asked, or if the child's initial account is markedly different from a subsequent account. Surely, though, there will also be occasions in which information about these early conversations will bolster a child's complaint and therefore promote a prosecution. If, for example, there were no leading questions, or, better, no questions at all (because the child's complaint was entirely spontaneous), then concerns about leading can be set aside (although other possible concerns still need to be examined). Thus, information about the early conversations is neither "pro-defense" nor "pro-prosecution." Instead, this information can help us (as anyone would hope) to ascertain the facts of the matter.

The Need to Reconstruct the First Complaint

Few parents, grandparents, or neighbors routinely have a audio recorder running when talking with a child. The courts often rely, therefore, on adults' memories for the first conversation in which victimization was alleged. Thus, a grandparent might be asked, "What were you doing when the topic of touching came up?" or "What exactly did you ask your granddaughter?"

In Chapter 6, however, we argued that these memories are of questionable value. Several studies have examined how well parents recall their conversations with their children; other studies have examined the accuracy of notes taken by an adult, during or immediately after a conversation with a child. In both scenarios, the results are the same: Adults are quite good at recalling or recording in notes the gist of the conversation as they understood it. However, adults are poor at recalling or recording exactly how the conversation unfolded—including such details as how questions were framed (suggestively or neutrally), whether questions were repeated, whether it was the adult or the child who first introduced a topic into the conversation, and so on. And these are, of course, precisely the details we need if we are to assess the conversation as suggestive or not. In addition, adults' errors in misremembering these points tend to be systematic: Adults tend to underrepresent in their recall and notes their own role in the conversation and correspondingly tend to overrepresent the child's role. Thus, ideas are attributed to the child when it was the adult who first mentioned them, the child's utterances are described as spontaneous when they were in response to questions, and so on.

Notice, then, where all of this leads us: The early conversations about an allegation are immensely important, but we generally lack formal documentation of these conversations. It also seems that we cannot rely on adults' recall of the conversation, notes taken during the conversation, or journal entries recorded soon afterward. Putting these points together, it seems that we have no choice about how we must proceed: The courts obviously prefer (and should prefer) direct evidence about an event as opposed to plausible reconstructions about that event. Nonetheless, as we mentioned in Chapter 10, reconstruction will in many cases be our only option for judging how these early and crucial conversations unfolded.

How Do Adults Typically Talk to Children?

A number of researchers have scrutinized how adults ordinarily talk to children. In most cases, these studies involve straightforward recording of freely occurring conversations—as mothers try to find out what happened during their child's school day or what happened when the child visited the researcher's laboratory. (For glimpses of this work, see Fivush, Hazzard, McDermott, Sarfati, & Brown, 2003; Laible & Panfile, 2009; Mayall, 2008; Oppenheim & Koren-Karie, 2009.)

We alluded to some of this research in Chapter 10 when we discussed the role of early conversations in helping a child learn how to remember. In broad outline, though, this research tells us that adults often play an active role in shaping these conversations with children, especially when the children are young. Adults draw attention to obvious benchmarks within the episode that's being discussed ("What did you have for lunch?"). They provide a sequence for the narrative ("What happened right after lunch?"). They also supply elements of the report, especially if the child's report seems sparse ("Did you have sandwiches again?"). If the child is slow to respond, the adults often supply a possible answer ("Was it a cheese sandwich?"). In these and other ways, the adult plays a large part in shaping the content and sequence of the conversation.

In addition to conversational elements initiated by the adult, we also need to consider how adults respond to a child's utterances. If the child's statement seems odd, the parents may question it ("Are you sure?"). If the child's answer to a question is somehow puzzling, adults often repeat the question, a step that (as discussed in Chapter 10) can indicate to the child that the first answer was inadequate. If the child describes something embarrassing or frightful, the adult is likely to provide some supporting comment ("That must have been awful") or reassurance ("We'll make sure he never hurts you again").

All of these elements of feedback are, again, powerful means of shaping the conversation. But these points should not be understood as criticisms of adults' behavior (as if the adults were inept or manipulative in their conversations with children). Instead, these points are quite valuable because (as we have discussed) these various aspects of conversation help to teach the child how to report on events, how to conceptualize events, and what to pay attention to as an event is unfolding. Other elements of the conversation serve the emotional needs of the child (or, sometimes, of the adult) in important ways. Thus, there is nothing "wrong" with these conversations, even if, as we now see, these conversations are ill-suited for the needs of the justice system.

It is also important that the tone and content of an adult's conversation with a child will change if they are discussing a troubling or frightening event ("Where did that bruise come from?" "Did Uncle Joe touch you?" "Why was Mary in the bedroom with you?"). In these settings, a natural sense of urgency can make the adult impatient to learn what happened and especially eager to gather information about a specific set of possibilities: Did someone deliberately hurt the child? Was the child involved in some action that never should have happened at all? This urgency will likely shape the flow of questioning, and it also increases the risk that the adult might ask questions—perhaps suggestive questions—targeted on the concerning events. The atmosphere of these conversations also creates a danger that the adult may reveal—through tone of voice, gesture, or rhythm of speech—what the concern is, and this may itself be suggestive (signaling to the child what the suspicion is or who the suspect is).

The overall point, then, is that early conversations with a child are likely to contain many elements that a trained interviewer would scrupulously avoid—and thus there is a substantial risk that these early conversations can indeed shape the child's report. This risk grows if the adult entered the conversation with concerns or suspicions about the now-alleged actions, or if the adult came into the conversation already carrying some hostility toward the suspect in the case.

We also need to ask whether, after the initial disclosure, adults continue discussing the alleged actions with the child. I participated in one case in which a mother was convinced her child was not emotionally ready to discuss the alleged abuse with authorities. The mother therefore spent months "counseling" her own child, so that the child could eventually "use her words" in order to keep "that sick guy out of our lives." (The quoted words are from the mother's eventual conversations with police and testimony.) In cases like this, the fact of continuing conversation obviously amplifies the concern about an adult's shaping the child's report.

In some jurisdictions, law enforcement professionals take steps to address the possibility just mentioned. Specifically, once police or social workers learn of the initial complaint, they urge the adults close to the complaining child not to have further discussions about the concerning events. In essence, law enforcement tells the adults not to conduct their own investigation (or counseling), but instead to leave the case in the hands of properly trained professionals.

If this instruction is given and followed, this step provides a possible safeguard against further contamination of the child's memory. Thus, in investigating a case, it is useful to know if this instruction was given to the involved adults. It is likewise useful to determine (as best as one can) whether the adults were able or inclined to follow this admonition.

Finally, here's a somewhat different perspective on the nature and limitations of ordinary adult–child conversations. In the next section, we discuss interviews with children that are conducted by skilled, professional forensic interviewers. For now, though, let's focus just on the level of training these professionals receive, including formal training before they conduct their first interview and then careful supervision as part of a continuing education effort. This training ensures that these professionals will conduct interviews that are neutral, objective, and nonsuggestive.

Why is this extensive training needed? The obvious answer is that someone without this training is unlikely to conduct a neutral, nonsuggestive interview, and that is, of course, exactly the point we are seeking to establish in this section.

B. PROPER INTERVIEWING PROCEDURES WITH CHILDREN

Eventually (and one hopes, soon), cases that involve children are brought to the attention of the relevant authorities, and, from that point forward, the investigation is generally conducted by professionals, including a trained interviewer. We need to emphasize, though, that the quality of these interviews cannot be taken for granted. In the cases I have reviewed, the vast majority of the forensic interviews are well conducted; if there are concerns about the children's evidence in these cases, the concerns derive from events "upstream" from the formal interview. However, there are exceptions to this pattern. In some cases, forensic interviews begin well, but the interviewer seems to grow frustrated when the child is unable or unwilling to disclose the suspected events, and the interview lapses into poorer quality questioning. In other cases, the formal interview is conducted by someone who reportedly has been appropriately trained, but the quality of the questioning belies this report. Thus, in all cases, the forensic interview must be scrutinized with care; most are fine, but some are not.

What is the nature of these forensic interviews when they are well-conducted? The answer varies somewhat from jurisdiction to jurisdiction, but, overall, these interviews are designed with a close eye on various guidebooks, available online or in printed form, describing how cases involving child victims should be investigated. Some of these guides come from government agencies, some from the scientific community, and some from the interviewers themselves. The topics covered by the various guides include the training of interviewers, the documentation of the interview process, the planning of an interview, the building of rapport, the substantive questions to explore allegations, the use of props, the interpretation of the interview, adjustments in the interview for children with special needs, and more. And it is surely worth mentioning that these guidelines, offered by diverse agencies, overlap heavily; there is, in other words, a near-consensus on how these interviews should be conducted; this is not controversial territory. (For a sampling of these guidelines and some of the validation data for them, see American Professional Society on the Abuse of Children [APSAC], 2012; Anderson et al., 2010; Bourg et al., 1999; Brown et al., 2013; Lamb, Hershkowitz, Orbach, & Esplin, 2008; Lamb, La Rooy, Malloy, & Katz, 2011; Lamb, Orbach, Warren, Esplin, & Hershkowitz, 2007; The National Children's Advocacy Center, 2012; Orbach et al., 2000; Poole & Lamb, 1998; Saywitz & Camparo, 2014.)

Even with this (near) consensus, researchers and interviewers continue to seek ways to make these interviews even better. For example, there has been discussion of ways to improve the widely-used NICHHD protocol, and a number of investigators have pursued Saywitz's suggestion (e.g., Saywitz & Camparo, 2014) that certain types of focused questions can gain more information. Therefore the 'final word' in child interviewing is surely not yet written. Nonetheless, there are certainly well-established, well-documented, widely-accepted principles in view for how these interviews should proceed.

Once again, though, we should wave a caution flag: We have already said that most forensic interviews are done well, but some are not, and so all must be examined. In the same spirit, most of the established guidelines for forensic interviews are well-conceived and sensibly designed, but some are not, and so all must be examined. In other words, the quality and currency of the various guidelines—although generally excellent—cannot be taken for granted.

The Role of Science in Setting the Procedures

What is the basis for the procedures outlined in the guidebooks just mentioned? To some extent, the guides draw lessons from the experience of professional interviewers, experience that tells us which interview strategies have been effective in the past. More broadly, though, the various guidebooks are explicitly rooted in scientific research. The guides are clear that we need this research in order to know, going into an interview, what sorts of things we can count on children to remember and what sorts of things will children forget. Likewise, the guides are explicit that we need the research in order to know what sorts of questioning lead to accurate reports and what sorts of questions undermine children's recollection. Said differently, the perspective taken in these guidebooks resembles the perspective offered in the book you are now reading—namely, that careful and realistic scientific research provides crucial information for the justice system, information that can be used to design investigative procedures, and information that allows the courts to evaluate the evidence resulting from these procedures.

As an aside, I might mention that I have sometimes been challenged in the courtroom for presuming to comment on investigative interviews with children, inasmuch as I am not a trained interviewer, do not conduct interviews, and do not have a clinical practice in which I work with children. A powerful answer to this challenge, though, comes from the interview guidebooks we are discussing here. These guides—including those written by the forensic interviewers themselves—are clear about the need for a scientific foundation for best-practice interviewing. Thus, the evidence that I (or some other expert) would offer is precisely the evidence that the interviewers and government agencies, in the various guidebooks, are highlighting as essential for anyone seeking to understand the design and evaluation of proper interviewing.

The Interview's Start

Most guides for forensic interviewing suggest several initial steps of conversation, before the interviewer turns to the substantive concerns that triggered the investigation. In most jurisdictions, the interviewer must begin by orienting the child to the physical setting, and, if the interview is being recorded (as it should be), the interviewer should explain this to the child and get the child's consent for the recording.

Professional interviewers should also spend time, early in the interview, talking with the child about neutral topics. This early stage helps establish rapport between the interviewer and the child and may help an apprehensive child grow more comfortable in the interview setting. The early conversation can also provide important guidance for the interviewer, allowing the interviewer to gauge the child's level of comfort and level of verbal skill. (The latter point can then help the interviewer to frame utterances in a fashion fully accessible to the child.)

Often, this early stage of the interview involves an invitation to the child to describe some neutral event in detail: "Tell me everything about how you spent your day yesterday," or "Tell me everything about how you spent your birthday." This step provides further information about the child's verbal skill and also the child's skill as a reporter. The use of "invitational" open-ended questions in this phase of the interview also helps to establish expectations in the child regarding the type of discourse to follow (cf. Pipe, Lamb, Orbach, & Esplin, 2004), with the interviewer providing little direct guidance and with the information in the interview coming from the child, not the adult. Finally, this early step also creates an opportunity for gentle feedback as the interviewer seeks to convey—with regard to an utterly benign topic—what level of detail will be requested within the interview.

It is also common for an interview (especially with a younger child) to include early questions designed to check on the child's vocabulary. The child may be asked if a crayon is "under" or "over" a piece of paper or may be asked the color of a marker. The child may be asked to count to ten or asked which of two piles of markers has "more markers." Incorrect answers to these questions should be carefully noted and may indicate a level of verbal immaturity that demands caution in assessing the rest of the interview. Correct answers, however, are more difficult to interpret: A child who correctly labels "blue" and "red" may be inaccurate with other terms more central to the interview. Moreover, we mentioned in Chapter 10 that measures of a child's receptive vocabulary are poor indicators of the child's ability to remember events accurately or the child's level of suggestibility (e.g., Peterson & Warren, 2009). This point provides further reason to be cautious about this brief assessment of the child's vocabulary; a better sense of the child's language skills can come from the "narrative practice" described in the previous paragraph.

Finally, note also that this fast assessment of vocabulary may not detect a child's idiosyncratic use of other terms. (Imagine that Fred put his palm on his niece's buttocks. His niece, however, says that "Fred didn't touch me," but means only that he didn't touch her with his fingertips, because, for the niece, that's what "touch" means.) Hence, we must bear in mind that a child's doing well in this check on vocabulary is no guarantee of accurate communication.

The "Ground Rules"

The early part of a child forensic interview should also convey certain "ground rules" to the child for how the rest of the conversation will unfold. As we noted in Chapter 10, children sometimes hide their confusion about an adult's utterances and respond as best they can based on their (partial or mistaken) understanding of the adult. To avoid this problem, forensic interviewers should encourage children to speak up if they do not understand a question; the interviewer can promise to clarify the question if the child is uncertain what is being asked.

Similarly, interacting with a strange authority figure in this unfamiliar setting, children may have the idea that they are supposed to answer every question—and so they may try to answer questions even if they do not know the answer. Likewise, children may have the idea that they should not correct this authority figure (the interviewer) if the adult makes an error. For these reasons, it is important to advise the child that a response of "I don't know" is entirely acceptable and that the child should correct any error the interviewer makes.

Often, interviewers do more than admonish the child on these points. Often, the interview will offer an example: "What would you say if I asked you your gender?" (probing for an "I don't understand" response) or "What would you say if I asked you my cat's name?" (probing for an "I don't know" response). Sometimes, the interviewer will deliberately say something false (e.g., calling the child by the wrong name) to see if the child will correct the error. These steps are well-advised and provide reassurance that the child has indeed understood and will comply with these important instructions.

Children should also be advised that sometimes the interviewer will repeat questions but that this does not mean the child's initial answer was wrong or unacceptable. Instead, the child should be told that the interviewer may be confused or may have forgotten what the child said. Alternatively, the child can be told that the interviewer really cares deeply about the child's report, and so the interviewer might reask questions to make certain he or she understands what the child is saying.

How effective are these various ground rules? Obviously, the fact that the child corrects some of the interviewer's errors provides no guarantee that the child will consistently correct errors, and the fact that the child sometimes refuses to guess is no guarantee that there will be no guessing during the interview. Nonetheless, researchers have asked whether a clear statement of these ground rules makes an accurate report more likely. The data are mixed. Some studies show no effect; some do show a positive effect. One key factor, though, may be the child's age, on the simple notion that younger children often have difficulty following rules, even if they plainly understand the rules (for an overview, see Dickinson, Poole, & Laimon, 2005). Even so, the rules can surely head off at least some misunderstandings and so should be given.

Finally, forensic interviews typically involve some version of a "truth ceremony." In some jurisdictions, the interviewer asks the child if he or she knows what it means to tell the truth and elicits a promise that the child will only tell the truth during the interview. In other jurisdictions, the interview might test the child: "If I told you it was raining in here, would that be the truth or a lie?" In still other jurisdictions, interviewers use the Lyon and Saywitz protocol (2000). As we noted in Chapter 10, the benefits of this step are uncertain, but the truth ceremony has become a common feature in child forensic interviewing.

Proper Questions

Beyond these preliminaries, how does proper interviewing proceed? The answer has many elements; some of the relevant guidelines take hundreds of pages to address this issue. If the guidelines can be distilled down to one theme, though, it might be this: It is crucial that the flow of information in these interviews be from the child to the interviewer, and not the other way around. Hence, it is preferable to ask open-ended invitational questions ("Tell me what happened") rather than close-ended questions (i.e., questions that can be answered with a word or two). The interviewer should not signal what the topic is or who the person of interest might be. Instead, the interviewer should find a way to get the child to tell his or her story.

Often, this process begins with a series of open-ended prompts. For example, the interviewer might ask the child to list all the people in the child's household and, for each, might ask, "Tell me what you like" about that person and "what you don't like." Alternatively, the interviewer might ask the child if he or she knows the reason for the interview. (This approach can launch the conversation and can also sometimes reveal the degree to which prior conversations may have primed the child for the interview.)

With answers to these initial questions in view, the interviewer can request expansion, providing a framework but still posing open-ended invitations: "I wasn't there, and I really want to know what happened. Tell me everything you can about what happened." Or "Tell me how things began," and then "Tell me what happened after that." Then, later in the interview, once the basic outline of events has been provided by the child, the interviewer can circle back with more focused questions, to gain more detailed information. Even here, though, the interviewer should provide little in the way of guidance, by (for example) asking questions in "multiple-choice format": "Was it day time, night time, or something else?" "Was it inside, or outside, or something else?" (And here we note in passing that terms like "inside" and "outside" are sometime used in idiosyncratic ways by children and so may need follow-up questions for clarification.) Then, if the child presents new information in response to these close-ended questions, the interviewer can step back to open-ended inquiry: "Tell me more about that," or "Help me understand how that happened."

This broad strategy of not guiding the child pertains both to the sequence of questions (usually, open-ended first, then close-ended later) and also to the sequence of *topics*. Imagine a scenario in which, early on, the interviewer asks questions along the lines of "Do you know what good touch is and bad touch?," and then steps from there to "Tell me about Ted." In that setting, the child might well spot the fact that the interview is focused on a conjunction of topics—bad touching + Ted—perhaps leading the child to some misstatements about this conjunction. It would be preferable in this setting first to ask questions that might lead the child to name Ted (e.g., "Who else lives in your house?") and then, once Ted is mentioned, "Tell me about Ted." Only afterward, when several people have been discussed (so that there is no emphasis on Ted), should the interview step to questions about touching.

As a related point, proper interviewing requires that the adult not "inject" his or her own ideas into the conversation. In other words, it should (with rare exceptions) be the child, not the adult, who first mentions an action, a body part, or a person. The adult should certainly avoid introducing new ideas via yes/no questions, such as "Has anyone ever touched your private area?" If "private areas" have not been mentioned previously in the interview, then this question puts the idea into play in a fashion initiated by the adult, not the child. In addition, the yes/no format of this question makes it all too easy for the child to make a false statement with just a single syllable.

There is another concern about yes/no questions (and close-ended questions in general): Evidence suggests that children are capable of telling lies at a surprisingly young age, and evidence for deliberate deception has been collected even for children as young as three years (Vrij, 2002). However, the earliest lies tend to be brief (assertions contained in a single word); early lies also include the deliberate withholding of information. For these reasons, close-ended questions actually make it easier for a child to lie, if he or she wishes to. Open-ended questions require longer answers and so would demand more elaborate lies if the child is trying to be deceptive; this increases the burden on a child seeking to lie and thus increases the likelihood of lie detection. (For more on lies and lie detection, see Chapter 7.) Open-ended questions also elicit more information, and this point, too, increases the chance of detecting the child who is withholding information.

Additionally, interviewers should, of course, avoid vocabulary unfamiliar to the child. Indeed, good interviewers routinely take notes during an interview, but this is generally not for purposes of documentation. (The documentation is, in these cases, provided in a far-better form via a video recording of the interview.) What the notes do provide, however, is a "vocabulary list." Specifically, the notes provide the interviewer with a ready-at-hand listing of the terms the child has already used in the conversation and the labels the child has assigned to people, actions, or body parts. Interviewers can then use these words in their own utterances—echoing the child's own usage and therefore ensuring that they do not introduce new, unfamiliar, or unknown labels or vocabulary.

Delayed Disclosure, Repeated Interviews

In an ideal world, an investigation of child victimization might unfold this way: A child spontaneously comes forward and tells a trusted adult about the abuse. Perhaps there is no history of questioning the child about abuse or discussing abuse-related issues in the household. The parents hear just a brief report from the child about a recent episode (perhaps, "Grandpa Billy touched me last week") and immediately call the police. The police conduct a brief visit to the home, talking with the parents and minimally (or perhaps not at all) with the child; they urge the parents not to discuss the abuse further with the child, at least until a formal interview has been conducted. The police explain the importance of this admonition, so that the parents will understand—and so be more likely to comply with—this instruction. Police then schedule a formal forensic interview to take place within a day or two. The forensic interview is properly conducted and properly documented, and, in that interview, the child repeats the same accusation and is able to fill out the story with appropriate detail.

The sequence just described is one in which the authorities would (and should) give the child's report considerable weight. Needless to say, however, many cases depart from this idealized scenario in important ways—and one common departure involves the timing. Often, children who have been abused choose not to report the abuse for some time, and the reasons for this nondisclosure are straightforward: Many children are confused, embarrassed, or ashamed about the events. A child may also be frightened about the possible repercussions (for the child, the family, or the accused) of reporting the troubling events. And sometimes the child does not realize the concerning events are actually bad things that should be reported.

For similar reasons, sometimes adults suspect abuse but the child, when questioned, insists that nothing bad has happened. Or perhaps the child feels comfortable enough with a family member to report on the abuse but, when talking with some stranger (a police officer or forensic interviewer), now denies the abuse.

What should an interviewer do in any of these situations? Actually, there are several options. Some children are hesitant to talk about abuse but (if they are old enough) will write about the abuse or draw pictures depicting the abuse. In these cases, however, let's flag the need for caution in interpreting a child's nonverbal communications. Pictures and gestures are often ambiguous, and care is obviously needed when investigators seek to interpret reports that hinge on nonlinguistic signals. (I have certainly reviewed cases in which an interviewer assumed a sexual meaning for a gesture that may well have had no such meaning in the child's mind.)

Other children just need time, within an interview, to grow comfortable with the interviewer. Sometimes, the interviewer needs also to approach the concerning events from several different angles—asking first, perhaps, about different people in the child's life (including the suspected abuser), and then asking about different activities in the child's life (including the activity within which the abuse is suspected to have occurred), then asking about different places in the child's life (including the place at which the abuse is suspected to have occurred), and so on. These further inquiries are fine as long as they remain open-ended and not guiding.

In other cases, the interviewer has no choice but simply needs to end an interview with no disclosure from the child, despite other indications that there may in fact be something to disclose. In such cases, the interviewer may well try again with a subsequent interview at some later point. This repeated interviewing, however, carries certain risks: We have mentioned the dangers inherent in repeated questions, and the repeated interview also entails some passage of time between the early interview and the later one. This interval creates a risk of the child forgetting important elements of what occurred and also a risk of questions or discussion by family members that may compromise the child's memory. These risks must be taken seriously, but, nonetheless, repeated interviews are sometimes necessary and appropriate, and they can be valuable if conducted with appropriate care both during the interviews themselves and during the time period between interviews (see, for example, La Rooy, Katz, Malloy, & Lamb, 2010; Orbach, Lamb, La Rooy, & Pipe, 2012).

Props

In some investigations, interviewers supplement their conversation with a child with props of various sorts—including human body diagrams (often crude outline drawings showing a naked male or female) and anatomically correct dolls. In some interviews, these props are offered as a means of encouraging a noncommunicative child to open up. (Perhaps the child is embarrassed to say out loud what happened, but will point to the body diagram in response to questions.) In other interviews, the child's narrative is unclear, and the props are used to gain clarity. (For example, the child might be asked to position the dolls in a fashion that shows the interviewer how the child and the alleged abuser were positioned.)

Research, however, offers a mixed review of these various props. To be sure, the props usually do succeed in eliciting more information from the child. However, this gain comes at a nontrivial cost. For example, in several studies, props have increased both the number of accurate details recalled and also the number of inaccurate details reported (Lamb et al., 2008; Melnyk, Crossman, & Scullin, 2007; Pipe, Lamb, Orback, & Cedebork, 2007; Poole, Bruck, & Pipe, 2011). Likewise, when children are asked specifically about touches, human body diagrams lead to a large number of reports about touches that never happened at all; in one study, use of a human body diagram doubled the rate of some forms of inaccurate information (Brown, Pipe, Lewis, Lamb, & Orbach, 2012).

Likewise, consider the use of detailed, anatomically correct dolls (typically, dolls that have somewhat realistic genitals). Several studies suggest that these dolls can lead to false reports of genital touching—perhaps because the unfamiliar form of the dolls draws a child's attention to (and may invite touching of) this unexpected body part. In addition, some researchers have questioned whether young children understand the full pattern of correspondence between the doll's body parts and their own body parts. As a result, some investigators have urged that the dolls not be used with children under the age of five (Hungerford, 2005); some researchers have gone further and questioned the value of these dolls for children of any age (Dickinson, Poole, &

Bruck, 2005; Orbach, Shiloach, & Lamb, 2007; for a broad assessment of both the value and concerns, see Brown, 2011).

These cautions, originating in the research community, have been echoed by some professional interviewers. For example, the American Professional Society on the Abuse of Children notes that "interview 'props,' aids, and media tap less accurate recognition memory rather than recall, [and] should be used with caution. Therefore, interviewers should have less confidence in the information gathered using only media" (APSAC, 2012, p. 13). With this, this Society urges that anatomical dolls should be used "***only if needed*** to assist the child in communicating details of what happened" (APSAC, 2012, p. 23, emphasis—conveyed both by boldface and by underlining—in the original).

Therapeutic Interviews

In the last sections, we have been discussing various aspects of the forensic interview—steps that should happen in these interviews, and steps that should be avoided. We need to consider, though, two other settings in which children can sometimes offer reports of abuse—in a therapeutic setting and in a medical examination.

Children for whom abuse is suspected are often provided with some sort of counseling or therapy. Sometimes there are behavioral problems to be addressed (e.g., perhaps the child is acting in an oversexualized manner, and adults may suspect this is the result of being abused). Or perhaps the child is suffering from anxiety or depression (and, again, adults may suspect these problems are the consequences of abuse). Or perhaps adults are worried about a level of fear or shame that apparently is inhibiting the child from reporting the abuse, and the adults want to help the child work through these feelings. For these (and other) reasons, it is common for children to go through some form of counseling prior to any disclosures and only later to report the abuse. It is also common for children to make some disclosure of abuse, then enter counseling, and later offer further disclosures, describing other episodes or other actions. (For a broad discussion of these issues, see Kuehnle & Connell, 2011.)

How should we think about this sequence? Bear in mind that therapy comes in many forms, and so it is difficult to make claims that apply to therapy in general. Even so, there are many ways in which a forensic interview is different from most therapeutic interviews. For example, a forensic interview will typically begin with a reminder that only true things will be discussed; this sort of interview is not the place for fantasy. A therapist, on the other hand, may not offer this instruction, in part because the therapist wants to encourage communication as much as possible, and that will often mean placing no limits, no constraints, on the communication. A therapist may also be interested in fantasy (on the idea that fantasy will sometimes offer insights into themes the child will not discuss directly); on that basis, a therapist may encourage a discussion of fantasy (both waking fantasy and dreams)—a stance that is obviously the opposite of the one needed for a forensic interview.

Likewise, consider the atmosphere of a forensic interview. A forensic interviewer needs to be friendly and encouraging, but also objective. Thus, forensic interviewers are, for example, routinely cautioned not to offer expressions of comfort in response to a comment about abuse. (The concern, of course, is that these expressions might reward abuse disclosures and thus shape the flow of the conversation in ways that could distort the child's report.) A therapist, in contrast, will generally try to encourage trust and rapport and will often seek to establish an "alliance" with the child. Thus, a therapist may well offer statements of comfort and support to a child who has just made a painful disclosure and may say things like, "Yes, he was a bad man," or "We'll do all we can to make sure he doesn't hurt you again." These comments seem entirely appropriate—and may be necessary—in a therapeutic context, but risk contamination of the child's report.

Moreover, most interviewing guidelines suggest an avoidance where possible of repeated questions or repeated interviews; we have discussed the reasons for this point in other settings. Therapy, in contrast, can continue for many months, with weekly or even more frequent sessions throughout that period. Guidelines for forensic interviews also emphasize the importance of documentation (preferably through video recording), so that we know exactly what questions were asked and what the child's response was. The confidentiality of therapy settings, in contrast, precludes this type of documentation.

Some forms of therapy also involve so-called "memory work": techniques specifically designed to unearth otherwise hidden memories (e.g., Lindsay & Read, 1995). These techniques can yield accurate memories, but can also encourage false memories and so provide yet another regard in which the therapeutic context, although surely valuable for its own sake, may be inappropriate for any sort of forensic investigation.

We should also mention the differences in training between forensic interviewers and therapists. Forensic interviewing involves a distinct form of questioning, with its emphasis on invitational and open-ended questions and its avoidance of yes/no questions; forensic interviewing also involves a specialized tone (open and encouraging, but otherwise neutral). These points are emphasized again and again in the training of forensic interviewers, and ongoing supervision ensures that these points are taken seriously. Training for therapists, in contrast, will often emphasize none of these points. Instead, the training emphasizes the skills needed for clinical assessment and for that mode of therapy. With these contrasts in view, it cannot be surprising that forensic interviewers are generally ill-prepared to do therapy, and therapists are generally ill-prepared for forensic interviewing.

Finally, let's also be clear about the difference in goals between a forensic interview and a therapeutic one. The chief purpose of a forensic interview is to gather information. To be sure, the interviewer hopes that the child will exit the interview feeling better (and often a forensic interview includes closing steps aimed at this target), but the main purpose of the interview is to find out what did or did not happen to the child. The entire design of the interview is shaped by this overarching goal, and, as part of this design, a forensic interviewer needs to be alert to the fact that there may have been no abuse.

In contrast, the chief purpose of a therapeutic encounter is to help the child—perhaps help her to deal with strong emotions, or to avoid troublesome behaviors, or to relate more appropriately to others. The purpose of therapy, in other words, is not simply to gather information, but to work toward change in the child's beliefs, feelings, and behavior. The therapist is likely to encourage thoughts that are helpful for the child's well-being and discourage thoughts that are harmful. These points make it virtually inevitable that the therapeutic environment—although immensely valuable for its own purposes—is of poor quality as a source of forensic evidence.

Let's be clear that the point in all of this is not to question the value of therapy. Indeed, there is no debate over whether therapy is valuable for many children, including children who have been abused and also children who have suffered no abuse but who are now confused and embarrassed by the investigation (and family conflicts) triggered by abuse allegations. Therapy can also be valuable for children whose history contains no hint of abuse but who suffer from other problems. However, none of this changes the fact that therapeutic interviews are not designed for forensic investigation, and information gathered in a therapeutic interview may be of uncertain value for forensic purposes.

Medical Examination of the Child

Forensic interviews are often paired with another assessment conducted by a medical professional. This assessment allows law enforcement to check broadly on the child's health and medical well-being, but it can also be a source of crucial evidence about the abuse (if, for example, there are scars or bruises). But this assessment also allows another conversation with the child—between the child and a medical doctor or nurse.

In many jurisdictions, the medical assessment is done before the videotaped forensic interview, and this sequence is important—and troubling—for several reasons. Let's start with the fact that, for privacy reasons, the medical examination is often not recorded (with neither video nor audio documentation). Let's also note that the exam necessarily involves some conversation with the child about body parts or about bodily problems or discomfort the child might have experienced. The medical assessment in many jurisdictions also includes discussion of the incidents or concerns that triggered the assessment in the first place.

In the context of the present chapter, the concerns here should be obvious. The medical professional is sure to be well-trained in medical issues but may have little training as a forensic interviewer. There is generally no recording of the interview itself, and so we cannot be certain what questions were asked, how the questions were framed, or whether the questions were repeated. We cannot know for sure how the child answered. And, because this assessment often precedes the forensic interview, the conversation here can potentially offer suggestions or guidance to the child that can compromise the forensic interview.

One plausible improvement in this situation would be a reversal of the sequence. If the medical assessment followed the forensic interview, it could not possibly compromise the forensic interview. Then, with the primary evidence from the child coming from the forensic interview, we could worry less about exactly what words had been spoken in the subsequent medical conversation. Finally, with the medical exam after the forensic interview, the exam could sometimes clarify points that had arisen in the earlier step. Thus, if a child says she was touched, and the touching was "inside," this point could be pursued in the medical exam (e.g., by having the child touch, with a cotton swab, the spot where she had been touched during the alleged abuse).

Some jurisdictions do use this "medical exam second" sequence. Other jurisdictions would be well-advised to consider this procedure.

C. DISTINGUISHING TRUE REPORTS FROM FALSE REPORTS

Some accusations of abuse are unquestionably fully accurate and reveal repugnant acts that deserve prosecution and punishment. There can likewise be no question that protecting children must be a high priority for the justice system, for law enforcement, and, indeed, for any sane society. There can also be no question, sadly, that some of the allegations of abuse that come forward are groundless, making it an urgent matter that we seek means of telling which allegations are accurate and which are not. Points raised in this chapter and the previous one can help us in this effort, specifically by helping us ascertain the level of risk that a report might be false. But can we do better than this and assess the allegations by examining the child's report itself?

Certainty and Demeanor

Often, triers of fact assess a child's report by examining two aspects of the child's testimony: First, does the child seem certain about what happened, or is the child tentative and equivocal? Second, what is the child's demeanor while testifying? Does the child seem sincere and show appropriate emotion while describing the alleged events?

It turns out that neither certainty nor demeanor are reliable indicators of a report's veracity. In earlier chapters (e.g., Chapters 3 and 4), we discussed the problems associated with overt assessments of certainty (as, for example, when someone says, "I'm sure," or "I remember it perfectly," or the like) and likewise with indirect indications of certainty (as, for example, when someone conveys, in the fluency of their report, or their tone of voice, that they are confident in their recollection). To reiterate the main concerns here, there is a statistical linkage, in many circumstances, between how certain someone is (whether that person is an adult or a child) and the likelihood of his memory being correct. However, the linkage is weak—and so high-confidence recollection is often inaccurate, and low-confidence recall sometimes is correct. More troubling, the linkage between certainty and accuracy is quite fragile, and many factors can erode this linkage. We referred to this fragility in earlier chapters with the term "confidence malleability" and so, for example, feedback of various sorts can inflate someone's confidence in his recall, but with no effect on accuracy, thus driving a wedge between confidence and accuracy. Likewise, repeated reports of the same event can increase confidence with no benefit for accuracy, again undercutting the linkage between these two factors. As a result, investigators, advocates, judges, and jurors are probably overrelying on a child's degree of certainty and so may end up overbelieving children who express confidence in their reports and (just as bad) underbelieving children who are tentative in their reports.

The pattern of evidence is similar for demeanor. A child's demeanor in reporting on previous events is often indicative of sincerity. However, bear in mind that false reports from children will often be false memories, not lies, and false memories are sincere: By definition, a false memory is one that the child honestly and candidly believes to be correct, and so a child offering a false memory is not in any way being deceptive; instead, the child is simply confused. Thus, indications of sincerity are valueless as a means of detecting false memories.

Consistency

Another often-used criterion in assessing children's memories is the consistency of the memory. In many proceedings, I have heard investigators opine that children are generally not skilled in lying and therefore often have trouble maintaining their own stories. In other words, children will have a hard time remembering what they said when they last recited the lie and so may end up offering a different account on this recitation. On this basis, consistency in the report is an indication that the report is likely to be correct.

These assertions are plausible but unhelpful. Again, let's note that our concern is often that a child is offering a report based on a false memory, not a lie. (Indeed, even if the report came into being initially as a lie, it may have evolved into a false memory—see Chapter 10.) The traits of lies, therefore, are irrelevant here.

Moreover, let's bear in mind that false memories are, of course, *memories*, and so any report based on a false memory will depend on the same mechanisms and the same skills that the child uses for other memories. As a result, false memories will be neither more nor less consistent from one telling to the next than are accurate memories (cf. Ghetti, Goodman, Eisen, Qin, & Davis, 2002; Melnyk et al., 2007).

Indeed, for both true and false memories, children are often inconsistent in their reports. Perhaps they change their minds about what is interesting and worth reporting in the event. Or perhaps different aspects of the event come to mind when they try the second time to recall what happened. Whether for these or other reasons, though, children's reports on an event routinely do change. In one study, for example, children (aged three to five years) were asked on two separate occasions to recall a particular event (Fivush & Shukat, 1995); there was less than 10% overlap in the information provided by these two recall efforts. This shift in the children's report, however, was not indicative of falsehood; instead, the shift was merely a change in what the children happened to include the second time around.

Changes in a child's report seem especially likely in cases involving abuse allegations. One reason is that children reporting abuse will not know at the outset which aspects of the episode are of special interest to investigators. Later, cued by the investigators' questions, children may add information about those aspects to their report—not because their memory has changed, but because the child has a new understanding of what is worth including in the report (cf. La Rooy, Malloy, & Lamb, 2011). In addition, sometimes children may not appreciate the consequentiality of their own reports, and, once they perceive adults' responses to their allegations, they may become frightened and recant or perhaps alter their account in hopes of diminishing this response. Or, as yet another possibility, a child may find it aversive to talk about an abuse incident and, having once relayed the event, may now refuse to speak further of it. In all of these ways, it is plausible that a child's report of an actual incident of abuse may be quite inconsistent—sometimes adding information as time goes by, sometimes removing information, sometimes explicitly recanting on earlier statements.

Notice, in addition, that the considerations in the previous paragraph do not in any fashion depend on whether the child's report is correct or not. As a result, these various sources of inconsistency apply equally to true and false memories. This leads us once again to the idea that consistency will be of little value as a criterion for evaluating memories.

As yet a further concern, let's also bear in mind that, in some cases, children are called on to tell and retell what happened in an earlier event, and this process can be thought of as "practice" or "rehearsal." As one might expect, this rehearsal tends to "stabilize" a performance, and so, with more opportunities to relate a previous event, the child's report will likely settle into a consistent form (in overall content, in detail, in sequence). Hence, the multiple questions asked of a child during an investigation can sometimes create the very consistency that the justice system will later use as an indication of the report's veracity.

Putting all of these pieces together, then, consistency cannot be used as an indicator of veracity. False reports can be consistent, especially if the false report has been offered several times. And, for multiple reasons, accurate reports can be inconsistent. This pattern is the reality we are stuck with. We can document this pattern by observing children's memories and how these memories change from one telling to the next. We can also confirm this pattern by considering (as we have here) the various forces that can promote inconsistency in a child's report. And, finally, we can confirm this pattern by surveying professionals who work with children who have allegedly been abused. In one study, Berliner and Conte (1993) asked clinicians what signs they find especially helpful in deciding whether a child's allegations are accurate or not. A clear majority of the clinicians indicated that consistency in the child's report was a good indicator of veracity; indeed, this criterion was endorsed by 96% of the professionals surveyed. However, many of the same clinicians—60% of professionals in the survey—were ready to endorse the opposite view, noting that recantations (so that less information is included in later reports), gradual recall (so that more information is included in later reports), and conflicted reports (so that different information emerges in various reports) are all common in truthful descriptions of abuse. For these reasons, the professionals indicated, *inconsistency* is a hallmark of veracity. Thus, in short, the clinicians are telling us that true abuse allegations can sometimes be consistent and sometimes inconsistent—plainly underscoring the difficulties in relying on consistency when we evaluate a child's recall.

Level of Detail

As an alternative approach, some investigators rely on the level of detail as an indication of whether a child's account is true or not, based on the idea that true memories are likely to be more vivid, more detailed, than lies or false memories. This notion, however, is not well founded, and, in examining an individual memory, there is no level of detail that is reliably diagnostic of whether the memory is true or false.

Even so, forensic interviewers are well-advised to solicit as much detail from a child as possible, for several reasons. First, we mentioned earlier that false memories take time to grow and evolve. To see how this matters, imagine a case in which a child's report is quite detailed just a day or two after the concerning events are alleged to have taken place. In this setting, the claim of a false memory seems implausible because there has not been enough time for a false memory to have evolved into an elaborate form; this setting, therefore, would be one in which concerns about false memory are diminished.

A second point is related. Let's imagine that a 15-year-old is offering a detailed narrative describing abuse that took place a year earlier. In this setting, there has been enough time for a false memory to grow and evolve. Nonetheless, we'd still want to ask whether the likely influences on this child are proportional to the extensiveness of the memory. After all, we noted in Chapter 10 that larger memory errors, involving more complex events, are more difficult to produce than smaller memory errors. Therefore, a more elaborate memory (especially if the complaining witness is of a less-suggestible age) places a greater burden on anyone seeking to argue that the memory is false. A defender would, for example, have to argue that the child had been exposed to sufficient influence to create a memory at this level of detail.

Third, the details of a child's story can often provide a further check on the story, a point highlighted in the guidelines offered by the American Professional Society on the Abuse of Children Practice Guidelines: "Interviewers should always attempt to elicit information about specific facts that can be verified later—during a search of the scene as well as during interviews with other witnesses and the suspect" (APSAC, 2012, p. 4). To put this more broadly, we can often assess a child's story by asking: Do the details fit together, or do some of the details contradict others? (For example, the child might supply that the event took place during a snowy winter but that she went out afterward to ride her bicycle.) Likewise, do the details fit with other facts, external to the child's narrative? (The child might mention that her parents were away at the time of the alleged episode, when, in truth, we can confirm that they were not.)

We need to be careful on these points, however: In Chapter 10, we distinguished between memory for gist and memory for detail, and it is certainly possible for a child to be correct in recalling gist but be wrong in many details. Errors on the details, therefore, cannot be a sufficient basis for dismissing the child's overall report. Nonetheless, assessment of these points can provide at least some indication of the child's likely accuracy.

Privileged Knowledge

Detail from a child can also provide another assessment: Sometimes children include details in their narrative that invite us to ask: *How did the child find out about that?* Imagine, for example, that a child includes, in his narrative, knowledge about an adult's intimate anatomy or about sexual behaviors. In such cases, we need to ask whether the child might have acquired this knowledge from some source other than the alleged abuse itself. If not, then these points can be a powerful indication that the child's account is accurate.

Similarly, a child might know about a suspect's preferred style and color of underwear or the color of the suspect's bed sheets. Here, too, we need to ask: How did the child learn these things? To be sure, many children's narratives do not provide information that can be used in this fashion. And when a child's report does contain this information, there may be noncriminal reasons why the child knows these things. Even so, investigators and attorneys should be alert to these details because they can provide potent forms of evidence.

Symptom Evidence

Abuse of children is not just morally offensive; the abuse is also condemnable because of the harm it does to a child—both medically and psychologically. This harm adds to the tragedy of the abuse but can also be a source of evidence. Bruises and tears, for example, often provide evidence that directly indicates abuse.

But what about other types of harm to the child—psychological or behavioral problems that (we suspect) are related to the abuse? Can we use these problems as evidence that the abuse really did occur? The answer to these questions is generally "no." A number of studies have examined children for whom we have documentation of abuse, asking what problems the children suffer in the days (or years, or decades) following the abuse. For comparison, these studies have also examined children for whom we are reasonably sure there has been no abuse, asking what problems they suffer (e.g., see Kendall-Tackett, Williams, & Finkelhor, 1993, for a synthesis of 45 separate studies; see also Berliner & Conte, 1993; also Clancy, 2010). The data confirm that abuse does cause a variety of problems, both in the child's behavior (e.g., sexualized behavior) and in the child's emotions (including a type of post-traumatic stress disorder, although, on this issue, also see Clancy, 2010). But the data also remind us that children are resilient creatures, and many abuse victims (perhaps a third or more; see Kendall-Tackett et al., 1993) end up with none of these symptoms. Therefore, the absence of problems does not provide exoneration for a suspect.

Another result of these studies, however, is also important: The behavioral and psychological problems produced by abuse are often serious and long-lasting, but, crucially, the problems are "nonspecific." In other words, these problems are not in any way unique to abuse victims. Thus, children who have been abused often develop highly sexualized behavior, but children who have not been abused can also, through a variety of paths, develop sexualized behavior. Children who have been abused can become anxious and develop low self-esteem, but the same can be said for children who have not been abused; they, too, can develop these problems. In short, the presence of these various problems is not incriminating: Perhaps the problems were caused by abuse, but perhaps the problems have some other root.

This point is often misunderstood, and so an analogy may be helpful: The flu commonly leads to a fever. The flu is the cause, and the fever is the resulting symptom. However, this symptom is not, on its own, an indication that someone has the flu because there are myriad other medical problems that can also lead to a fever. Thus, the claim "If flu, then fever" is often correct, but the inverse, "If fever, then flu" is wrong. The point is the same for the various problems that can be caused by abuse. These problems are often tragic and are consistent with an allegation of abuse, but they are surely not diagnostic of abuse.

Cross-Examination

Where are we? Investigators and the justice system often rely on a child's confidence, demeanor, consistency, or level of detail in assessing the child's veracity, and, as we have discussed, none of these indices turns out to be reliable. Investigators sometimes rely on symptom evidence—oversexualized behavior or concerns about a depressed state—to corroborate allegations of abuse, but this strategy, too, is unwarranted.

In some cases, the content of a child's report allows the evaluation we need: If the report includes details that make no sense or do not fit with other facts, this can sometimes undermine a child's credibility. On the other side, if the report is elaborate, detailed, and reporting on recent events, the claim of a false memory seems implausible. And, of course, if the report contains privileged knowledge, knowledge we would not have expected the child to have, this point can powerfully bolster the child's credibility.

A different path focuses less on the report itself and more on the history and growth of the report: How did the report first arise? What influences or guides has the child been exposed to, perhaps influencing (or contaminating) the report? By assessing this history, we can often assess the risk of contamination and thus the risk of memory error.

There is, however, one last tool open to the justice system, and it is a tool commonly used for examining evidence. That tool, of course, is cross-examination. What happens when we cross-examine a child? Can this questioning put us in a better position to evaluate the child's testimony? Can cross-examination somehow improve a child's report, perhaps weeding out errors, or peeling back the effects of earlier influence?

A number of studies have pursued this issue (e.g., Zajac & Hayne, 2003; 2006; also see Krähenbühl, Blades, & Eiser, 2009). In one procedure, five- and six-year old children experienced a salient event—a visit to a police station in which (among other steps) they had their thumbprint recorded and they watched as a police officer turned the lights and siren on in one of the police cars. Afterward, some of the children were repeatedly given misinformation about the event, so that their recall would include a mix of accurate and inaccurate statements. Months later, these children were questioned, with the scripted questions containing a number of challenges similar to those used in cross-examination: The questioning challenged the child's certainty about some points (asking "Are you sure that . . .?") and expressed disbelief about other points ("I don't think that really happened. I think someone told you to say that"). The children were also given various reasons for the disbelief. In some cases, the disbelief was aimed at things the child had already said, with the goal of persuading the child to back away from testimony (e.g., "I think it happened to your friend and not you," or "But if your teacher said that didn't happen, she'd be right, wouldn't she?"). In other cases, the disbelief was aimed at things the child had not said, with the goal of gaining new admissions (e.g., "I think it did happen, but you just can't quite remember it," or "But if your teacher said that *did* happen, wouldn't she be right?").

These steps were impressively effective. In the study, 85% of the children changed at least one of their responses when challenged; 33% changed all of their original responses. The deep problem, though, is that these changes were independent of whether the child's initial answer had been accurate or not. In other words, when challenged in these ways, children were just as likely to abandon an initially correct answer as they were to abandon a mistaken answer.

In short, cross-examination can lead a child to change his or her story. And, in fact, this cannot be surprising, given our comments in the previous chapter about how suggestible children are and how easily bad questioning during an investigation can shape a child's report. The positive side of this, of course, is that cross-examination provides an effective means of getting a child to back off from a false report and to replace it with the truth. But, at the same time, cross-examination is just as likely to persuade a child to shift away from a true report and replace it with a false one. Thus, cross examination seems not to be a reliable means of moving children toward more accurate, more truthful testimony. (For more on cross-examination of children, see Henderson, 2002; Spencer, 2011.)

Investigating Children's Memory: Some Final Remarks

Before closing this chapter, we should reiterate one last point. In this chapter and in the previous one, we have not offered diagnostics or criteria that will tell us whether a specific child's allegations are mistaken. Indeed, throughout this book, we have not offered principles that will allow us to decide whether a particular identification is mistaken or whether a particular confession is false. What we have offered instead is information that can guide a "risk assessment." What is the risk that a particular identification is mistaken? How seriously should we entertain the possibility, for a particular confession, that the confession is false? Or, for the case before us in this chapter, how worried should we be that a particular child's allegations are mistaken, and, with this, how much weight should we give to the child's report?

We argued at the book's start that this information about risk can be used to guide investigative procedures: Once we know the factors that encourage error, we can avoid these factors and thus diminish the risk of error. But this information can also be valuable in the courtroom. Again, the available science will not allow a research-trained expert to offer "ultimate opinion" testimony about the veracity of this or that identification, this or that confession, this or that child. (And, indeed, in most courtrooms, a judge would forbid the expert from offering this sort of ultimate opinion testimony.) But the expert can provide information about the level of danger of falsity in each of these cases. Then it is up to the trier of fact to use this information, translating an estimate of "risk of error" into a decision, for that particular case, about whether an error had actually been made—in the identification, in the interrogation room, or in the child's report.

This translation is not a mechanical one. To put the issue metaphorically, not everyone who stands on thin ice (i.e., is at high risk) falls into the water below, and some people standing on seemingly thick ice (at low risk) fall through nonetheless. Even so, in choosing a place to stand, one surely wants to know how thick the ice is. In the same way, in choosing how much credence to give a memory-based report, it seems of obvious value to know the risk for a memory error. In this way, we hope, the science can allow the justice system to make sophisticated, well-informed, sensible judgments of these risks, so that all in the system can be intelligently guided as they assess the memory- and perception-based evidence that enters our legal system.

Epilog

A few years back, a friend confronted me with a challenge. Many jurors, he pointed out, are skeptical about scientific evidence, and why shouldn't they be? After all, the jurors have, in their day-to-day lives, likely seen example after example of arguments in which scientists contradict each other, and news report after news report in which this year's results reverse last year's. Thus, mammograms are recommended for younger women, and then they're not; salt in the diet is a health hazard, and then it isn't; playing Mozart for your newborn will improve the child's intelligence, and then it won't. Why, then, should jurors trust scientists—including scientists offering information about perception and memory? Why shouldn't they instead travel the obvious path and trust their own common sense assessment in evaluating witness evidence?

The jurors' skepticism is sensible but, for several reasons, not fair to the scientific enterprise overall. As one broad concern, we've discussed the scientific community's rigidly enforced mechanisms for quality control, but these mechanisms do little to shape the science that's most visible to the broad populace. Indeed, many of the studies showcased by journalists, bloggers, or radio hosts have not yet made it through the process of peer review and so have not yet been evaluated, much less endorsed, by other researchers. As a result, some of the studies reported to nonscientists are of high quality, but some are not—and the broader audience often has no means of separating the wheat from the chaff.

Another problem is one of *timing*. Science moves at a slow pace. The peer-review process itself can stretch out over many months. Then, once a finding is published, scientists may need a decade or more to corroborate the finding, or perhaps to challenge it or, quite commonly, to discover the "boundaries" on a result—that is, to define the circumstances in which the result emerges and the circumstances in which it does not. In sharp contrast, journalists and bloggers want to move forward quickly, reporting on studies that are novel in some interesting way and breaking new ground. Their work involves prompt reporting, even though that often means they are reporting results that have not yet been refined or fully tested in the ways that science demands.

In addition, what makes a study attractive to the broader public may be rather different from what makes a study valuable for the scientific community. To put the matter bluntly, studies are often showcased in the media or on the Internet because the studies are *cute*—relying on a miniaturized analog to the phenomenon we ultimately hope to understand. (Thus, a study might examine, say, consumer preferences for product logos flashed briefly on a computer screen, as an analog for consumers making choices in a supermarket aisle.) Often these analogs are valid and valuable, but sometimes they are misleading—but this is a point often neglected when a result is reported to a lay audience. Similarly, often experiments are conducted under tightly controlled circumstances, and, as we have discussed in earlier chapters, science gains powerful advantages from this control. Even so, these controlled studies sometimes provide a poor reflection of how events unfold in the more complicated "real world," and so extrapolation from these studies may be unwarranted.

For all of these reasons, skepticism about prominently reported scientific results is often justified, and it cannot be surprising that many people draw a broad lesson from this—and end up distrusting of scientists in general. This distrust is then amplified when, for example, scientific results bear on issues of public policy. (The policy debates concerning climate change provide a good illustration, with challenges to the climate science often fueled as much by ideology as by substantive concerns.) And, returning to more immediate issues, the reception for scientific data can be even chillier in the adversarial climate of the justice system, with scientific experts retained by one side vociferously challenged by attorneys for the other side.

All of this brings me back to my friend's concern—and it's a concern that we have to take seriously. How can we get jurors (and attorneys, and judges, and policy makers) to step away from their skepticism, especially since the skepticism may be justified in light of the perhaps lower quality "scientific studies" these individuals have encountered? How can we get these groups to respect the lessons drawn from careful, high-quality science? There is, I believe, a powerful answer to these questions, although it's not one that can be expressed in a fast sound bite. Instead, it's an answer rooted in points that I hope have been in view throughout this book. Specifically, psychology's contribution to the justice system is based on studies that have survived the scientific community's quality control—and that means the peer-review process, and then the test of time that has allowed other researchers, over a period of many years, to scrutinize a result and, if appropriate, challenge the result. Our research contribution relies on a wide fabric of studies—some focused directly on the issues under scrutiny, and some providing the broader scientific foundation for claims pertinent to the issues at hand. The summary of the data is not provided by some sort of qualitative cherry-picking but is instead the result of a thorough and objective process such as meta-analysis. When our studies involve analogs to real-world phenomena or are conducted in controlled settings, we provide the appropriate assurances that extrapolations from the results are indeed warranted. And, finally, when the data are not yet clear or the hypotheses not yet tested, we keep quiet and don't try to offer claims that are not yet justified. (As we noted in Chapter 1, scientists prefer to say nothing rather than to say something wrong.)

In short, the response to my friend's challenge is a recitation of methodological principles, and I'm convinced that the science in this book has met the burden established through those principles. Many trial judges have agreed and have allowed researchers to testify on these issues (in both *Frye* and *Daubert* jurisdictions). Many police departments have agreed and have adopted procedural steps recommended by the research community. And, on at least some topics, state Supreme Courts have carefully reviewed the scientific evidence and taken judicial notice of the relevant studies. New Jersey and Oregon have been the pioneers on this front (in their rulings in *State v. Henderson* and *State v. Lawson*, respectively); I expect other states to follow their lead.

Even so, we face an uphill climb in putting the science to full use. Cross-examination of scientific experts is often hostile. Sometimes the attacks are substantive. Sometimes the attacks are ad hominem. A larger obstacle, though, doesn't hinge on the contest between prosecution and defense. Instead, the obstacle grows out of the contest between the science and widely held "common-sense" beliefs: As already mentioned, common sense often leads people to distrust science. Common sense also encourages us to trust someone who expresses confidence in a memory, even though this trust is surely misplaced. Common sense tells us that sane, innocent people would not confess to actions they did not commit; the science says otherwise. Common sense indicates that a witness's demeanor is a decent basis for assessing that witness's veracity; the science challenges this idea. And so on.

How can we address these points? We should, of course, celebrate the (many) points for which common sense gets things right. But we also need to find a way to get beyond common sense for those cases for which common-sense views are unjustified, overstated, or just wrong. For this purpose, the key, in just one word, is education. The research community needs to "get the word out"—sometimes in testimony, but preferably in continuing-education sessions with attorneys and law enforcement and in books like this one. We can hope that this effort will put the scientific evidence into view and thus reassure all parties that the research is objective, persuasive, and genuinely helpful. The research can (and should) be presented in a context removed from the contentious setting of a particular litigation, so that all parties can evaluate the evidence in a fashion not guided by immediate self-interest. And, perhaps more importantly, we can hope that this effort will undercut the contest between science and common-sense beliefs, especially since (as we noted in Chapter 1) any "evaluation of lay knowledge has a limited shelf life" (Desmarais & Read, 2011, p. 208). The hope, in other words, is that putting the science into plain view will reshape "common sense" and bring widespread beliefs into better accord with the facts.

It may help to put all of this into a broader context: The problems at issue throughout this book—the potential concerns in witness (or victim) perception and memory—are obvious to all. Indeed, consider this excerpt from the Oregon Supreme Court's unanimous *Lawson* ruling, in 2012:

> Because of the alterations to memory that suggestiveness can cause, it is incumbent on courts and law enforcement personnel to treat eyewitness memory just as carefully as they would other forms of trace evidence, like DNA, bloodstains, or

fingerprints, the evidentiary value of which can be impaired or destroyed by contamination. Like those forms of evidence, once contaminated, a witness's original memory is very difficult to retrieve; it is, however, only the original memory that has any forensic or evidentiary value.

These sentences are remarkable in many regards, including how broadly framed they are. (Note that the sentences don't refer to adult memory or child memory, or to memory for voices or faces or events; instead, the sentences simply refer to *memory*—presumably, memory in all people and all circumstances.) The sentences also offer the strong (and I believe appropriate) assertion that memory is just another form of "trace evidence," and thus needs to be collected, preserved, and interpreted as carefully as any other bit of trace evidence. But, above all, note that these sentences are accompanied by no scholarly references; the Court apparently regarded these points as self-evident on their own.

In addition, let's bear in mind that the justice system will forever rely on witness evidence. We need this evidence to settle civil litigations, to prosecute criminals, and, in some cases, to exonerate those who have been wrongfully accused. And, in some regards, difficulties and ambiguities in this evidence are inevitable. Indeed, we argued in Chapters 2 and 3 that some of the seeming "flaws" in perception and memory are the byproducts of mechanisms that, in most settings, serve us very well; we therefore would not want to alter these mechanisms, even if the alterations might improve the cause of justice. But, even so, we can certainly take steps toward diminishing the problems that these "flaws" can create for the justice system. Those steps will require some education of judges, attorneys, policy makers, and ordinary citizens. (That's what my friend's challenge is ultimately all about.) But those steps can provide a huge pay off—in promoting justice and in promoting public safety. This book is my contribution to this broader effort.

REFERENCES

Abberton, E., & Fourcin, A. J. (1978). Intonation and speaker identification. *Language and Speech*, *21*, 305–318.

Ackil, J. K., & Zaragoza, M. S. (1998). Memorial consequences of forced confabulation: Age differences in susceptibility to falsememory. *Developmental Psychology, 34*, 1358–1372.

Ackil, J. K., & Zaragoza, M. S. (2011). Forced fabrication versus interviewer suggestions: Differences in false memory depend on how memory is assessed. *Applied Cognitive Psychology*, *25*, 933–942.

Akehurst, L., Bull, R., Vrij, A., & Köhnken, G. (2004). The effects of training professional groups and lay persons to use criteria-based content analysis to detect deception. *Applied Cognitive Psychology*, *18*, 877–891.

Akehurst, L., Manton, S., & Quandte, S. (2011). Careful calculation or a leap of faith? A field study of the translation of CBCA ratings to final credibility judgments. *Applied Cognitive Psychology*, *25*, 236–243.

Alexander, K. W., Quas, J. A., Goodman, G. S., Ghetti, S. G., Edelstein, R. S., Redlich, A. D., et al. (2005). Traumatic impact predicts long-term memory for documented child sexual abuse. *Psychological Science*, *16*, 33–40.

Alonzo, J. D., & Lane, S. M. (2009). Saying versus judging: Assessing knowledge of eyewitness memory. *Applied Cognitive Psychology*, *24*, 1245–1264.

American Bar Association. (2000). *Model rules of professional conduct*. Chicago: Author.

American Professional Society on the Abuse of Children. (2012). *Forensic interviewing in cases of suspected child abuse*. Elmhurst, IL: Author.

Amishav, R., & Kimchi, R. (2010). Perceptual integrality of componential and configural information in faces. *Psychonomic Bulletin & Review*, *17*, 743–748.

Anderson, J., Ellefson, J., Lashley, J., Miller, A. L., Olinger, S., Russell, A., Stauffer, J., & Weigman, J. (2010). The CornerHouse forensic interview protocol: RATAC. *Thomas M. Cooley Journal of Practical and Clinical Law*, *12*, 193–332.

Anzures, G., Quinn, P. C., Pascalis, O., Slader, A. M., Tanaka, J. W., & Lee, K. (2013). Developmental origins of the other-race effect. *Current Directions in Psychological Science*, *22*, 173–178.

Appleby, S., Hasel, L., & Kassin, S. M. (2013). Police-induced confessions: An empirical analysis of their content and impact. *Psychology, Crime and Law*, *19*, 111–128.

Arrigo, J. M., & Pezdek, K. (1997). Lessons from the study of psychogenic amnesia. *Current Directions in Psychological Science*, *6*, 148–152.

Asch, S. E. (1956). Studies of independence and conformity: A minority of one against a unanimous majority. *Psychological Monographs: General and Applied*, *70*, 1–70.

Attard, J., & Bindemann, M. (2014). Establishing the duration of crimes: An individual differences and eye-tracking investigation into time estimation. *Applied Cognitive Psychology*, *28*, 215–215.

Austin, J. L., Zimmerman, D. M., Rhead, L., & Kovera, M. B. (2013). Double-blind lineup administration: Effects of administrator knowledge on eyewitness decisions. In B. L. Cutler (Ed.), *Reform of eyewitness identification* (pp. 139–160). Washington, DC: American Psychological Association.

Badham, S. P., Wade, K. A., Watts, H. J. E., Woods, N. G., & Maylor, M. (2012). Replicating distinctive features in lineups: Identification performance in young versus older adults. *Psychonomics Bulletin & Review, 20,* 289–295.

Bahrick, H. P., Bahrick, P. O., & Wittlinger, R. P. (1975). Fifty years of memory for names and faces: A cross-sectional approach. *Journal of Experimental Psychology: General, 104,* 54–75.

Bahrick, L. E., Parker, J. F., Fivush, R., & Levitt, M. (1998). The effects of stress on young children's memory for a natural disaster. *Journal of Experimental Psychology: Applied, 4,* 308–331.

Bailey, P. J., & Mecklenburg, S. H. (2009). The prosecutor's perspective on eyewitness experts in the courtroom. In B. L. Cutler (Ed.), *Expert testimony on the psychology of eyewitness identification* (pp. 223–248). New York: Oxford University Press.

Baker, F., Johnson, M. W., & Bickel, W. K. (2003). Delay discounting differs between current and never-smokers across commodities, sign, and magnitudes. *Journal of Abnormal Psychology, 112,* 382–392.

Baker-Ward, L., & Ornstein, P. A. (2002). Cognitive underpinnings of children's testimony. In H. L. Westcott, G. M. Davies, & R. H. C. Bull (Eds.), *Children's testimony: A handbook of psychological research and forensic practice* (pp. 21–35). New York: Wiley.

Baker-Ward, L., Ornstein, P. A., & Starnes, L. P. (2009). Children's understanding and remembering of stressful experiences. In J. A. Quas, & R. Fivush (Eds.), *Emotion and memory in development: Biological, cognitive, and social considerations* (pp. 28–59). New York: Oxford University Press.

Bartlett, F. C. (1932). *Remembering: A study in experimental and social psychology.* Cambridge: Cambridge University Press.

Bartlett, J. C., & Memon, A. (2006). Eyewitness memory of young and older eyewitnesses. In R. C. L. Lindsay, D. F. Ross, J. D. Read, & M. P. Toglia (Eds.), *The handbook of eyewitness psychology: Volume 2. Memory for people* (pp. 309–338). Mahwah, NJ: Lawrence Erlbaum.

Behrman, B. W., & Davey, S. L. (2001). Eyewitness identification in actual criminal cases: An archival analysis. *Law and Human Behavior, 25,* 475–491.

Behrman, B. W., & Richards, R. E. (2005). Suspect/foil identification in actual crimes and in the laboratory: A reality monitoring analysis. *Law and Human Behavior, 29,* 279–301.

Behrmann, M., & Avidan, G. (2005). Congenital prosopagnosia: Face-blind from birth. *Trends in Cognitive Sciences, 9,* 180–187.

Bembibre, J., & Higueras, I. (2012). Comparative analysis of true and false statements with the source monitoring model and the cognitive interview: Special features of the false accusation of innocent people. *Psychology, Crime & Law, 18,* 913–928.

Ben-Shakhar, G., & Elaad, E. (2003). The validity of psychophysiological detection of information with the Guilty Knowledge Test: A meta-analytic review. *Journal of Applied Psychology, 88,* 131–151.

Benton, T. R., Ross, D. F., Bradshaw, E., Thomas, W. N., & Bradshaw, G. S. (2006). Eyewitness memory is still not common sense: Comparing jurors, judges, and law enforcement to eyewitness experts. *Applied Cognitive Psychology, 20,* 115–129.

Berliner, L., & Conte, J. (1993). Sexual abuse evaluations: Conceptual and empirical obstacles. *Child Abuse & Neglect, 17,* 111–125.

Berman, G. L., & Cutler, B. L. (1996). Effects of inconsistencies in eyewitness testimony on mock-juror decision making. *Journal of Applied Psychology, 81,* 170–177.

Berman, G. L., Narby, D. J., & Cutler, B. L. (1995). Effects of inconsistent statements on mock jurors' evaluations of the eyewitness, perceptions of defendant culpability and verdicts. *Law and Human Behavior, 19,* 79–88.

Berntsen, D. (2002). Tunnel memories for autobiographical events: Central details are remembered more frequently from shocking than from happy experiences. *Memory & Cognition, 30,* 1010–1020.

Bickel, W. K., & Marsch, L. A. (2001). Toward a behavioral economic understanding of drug dependence: Delay discounting processes. *Addiction, 96,* 73–86.

Bickel, W. K., Odum, A. L., & Madden, G. L. (1999). Impulsivity and cigarette smoking: Delay discounting in current, never, and ex smokers. *Psychopharmacology, 146,* 447–454.

Blagrove, M. (1996). Effects of length of sleep deprivation on interrogative suggestibility. *Journal of Experimental Psychology: Applied, 2,* 48–59.

Blair, I. V., Judd, C. M., Sadler, M. S., & Jenkins, C. (2002). The role of Afrocentric features in person perception: Judging by features and categories. *Journal of Personality and Social Psychology, 83,* 5–25.

Blandón-Gitlin, I., Sperry, K., & Leo, R. (2011). Jurors believe interrogation tactics are not likely to elicit false confessions. *Psychology, Crime and Law, 17,* 239–260.

Bond, C. F., & DePaulo, B. M. (2006). Accuracy of deception judgments. *Personality and Social Psychology Review, 10,* 214–234.

Bond, G. D. (2008). Deception detection expertise. *Law and Human Behavior, 32,* 339–351.

Bond, G. D. (2012). Focus on basic cognitive mechanisms and strategies in deception research (and remand custody of "wizards" to Harry Potter movies). *Journal of Applied Research in Memory and Cognition, 1,* 128–130.

Bornstein, B. (2006). Court review: Judges vs. juries. *Journal of the American Judges Association, 43,* 56–58

Bornstein, B. H., Deffenbacher, K. A., Penrod, S. D., & McGorty, E. K. (2012). Effects of exposure time and cognitive operations on facial identification accuracy. *Psychology, Crime and Law, 18,* 473–490.

Bourg, W., Broderick, R., Flagor, R., Kelly, D. M., Ervin, D. L., & Butler, J. (1999). *A child interviewer's guidebook.* Thousand Oaks, CA: Sage.

Boyce, M., Beaudry, J. L., & Lindsay, R. (2007). Belief of eyewitness identification evidence. In R. C. L. Lindsay, D. F. Ross, J. D. Read, & M. P. Toglia (Eds.), *The handbook of eyewitness psychology: Volume 2. Memory for people* (pp. 501–525). Mahwah, NJ: Lawrence Erlbaum.

Boydell, C. A., Barone, C. C., & Read, J. D. (2013). 'You caught 'em!' . . . or not? Feedback affects investigators recollections of speech cues thought to signal honesty and deception. *Legal and Criminological Psychology, 18,* 128–140.

Bradfield, A. L., & Wells, G. L. (2000). The perceived validity of eyewitness identification testimony: A test of the five *Biggers* criteria. *Law and Human Behavior, 24,* 581–594.

Bradfield Douglas, A., & Pavletic, A. (2012). Eyewitness confidence malleability. In B. L. Cutler (Ed.), *Conviction of the innocent: Lessons from psychological research* (pp. 149–165). Washington, DC: American Psychological Association.

Bradford, D., Goodman-Delahunty, J., & Brooks, K. R. (2013). The impact of presentation modality on perceptions of truthful and deceptive confessions. *Journal of Criminology, 2013,* 1–10.

Brainerd, C. J. (2013). Developmental reversals in false memory: A new look at the reliability of children's evidence. *Current Directions in Psychological Science, 22,* 335–341.

Brainerd, C. J., Reyna, V. F., & Zember, E. (2011). Theoretical and forensic implications of developmental studies of the DRM illusion. *Memory & Cognition, 39,* 365–380.

Bransford, J. D. (1979). *Human cognition: Learning, understanding and remembering.* Belmont, CA: Wadsworth.

Bransford, J. D., & Johnson, M. K. (1972). Contextual prerequisites for understanding: Some investigations of comprehension and recall. *Journal of verbal learning and verbal behavior, 11,* 717–726.

Brédart, S., & Barsics, C. (2012). Recalling semantic and episodic information from faces and voices. *Current Directions in Psychological Science, 21*, 378–381.

Brewer, N., Keast, A., & Rishword, A. (2002). The confidence-accuracy relationship in eyewitness identifications: The effects of reflection and disconfirmation on correlation and calibration. *Journal of Experimental Psychology: Applied, 8*, 44–56.

Brewer, N., & Wells, G. L. (2005). The confidence-accuracy relationship in eyewitness identification: Effects of lineup instructions, foil similarity, and target-absent base rates. *Journal of Experimental Psychology: Applied, 12*, 11–30.

Brewer, W. F., & Treyens, J. C. (1981). Role of schemata in memory for places. *Cognitive Psychology, 13*, 207–230.

Bricker, P. D., & Pruzansky, S. (1966). Effects of stimulus content and duration on talker identification. *Journal of the Acoustical Society of America, 40*, 1441–1449.

Brigham, J. C., & Bothwell, R. K. (1983). The ability of prospective jurors to estimate the accuracy of eyewitness identifications. *Law and Human Behavior, 1*, 19–30.

Brigham, J. C., Bennett, L. B., Meissner, C. A., & Mitchell, T. L. (2007). The influence of race on eyewitness memory. In R. C. L. Lindsay, D. F. Ross, J. D. Read & M. P. Toglia (Eds.), *The handbook of eyewitness psychology: Volume 2. Memory for people* (pp. 257–281). Mahwah, NJ: Erlbaum.

Brigham, J. C., Maass, A., Snyder, L. D., & Spaulding, K. (1982). Accuracy of eyewitness identification in a field setting. *Journal of Personality and Social Psychology, 42*, 673–681.

Brigham, J. C., & Wolfskeil, M. P. (1983). Opinions of attorneys and law enforcement personnel on the accuracy of eyewitness identifications. *Law and Human Behavior, 7*, 337–349.

Brown, A. S., & Murphy, D. R. (1989). Cryptomnesia: Delineating inadvertent plagiarism. *Journal of Experimental Psychology: Learning, Memory, and Cognition, 15*, 432–442.

Brown, D., Pipe, M. -E., Lewis, C., Lamb, M. E., & Orbach, Y. (2012). How do body diagrams affect the accuracy and consistency of children's reports of bodily touch across repeated interviews? *Applied Cognitive Psychology, 26*, 174–181.

Brown, D. A. (2011). The use of supplementary techniques in forensic interviews with children. In M. E. Lamb, D. J. La Rooy, L. C. Malloy, & C. Katz (Eds.), *Children's testimony: A handbook of psychological research and forensic practice* (2nd ed., pp. 217–249). New York: Wiley-Blackwell.

Brown, D. A., Lamb, M. E., Lewis, C., Pipe, M. -E., Orbach, Y., & Wolfman, M. (2013). The NICHD Investigative Interview protocol: An analogue study. *Journal of Experimental Psychology: Applied, 19*, 367–382.

Brown, E., Deffenbacher, K., & Sturgill, W. (1977). Memory for faces and the circumstances of encounter. *Journal of Applied Psychology, 62*, 311–318.

Brown, R., & Kulik, J. (1977). Flashbulb memories. *Cognition, 5*, 73–99.

Bruce, V., Burton, M., & Hancock, P. (2007). Remembering faces. In R. C. L. Lindsay, D. F. Ross, J. D. Read, & M. P. Toglia (Eds.), *The handbook of eyewitness psychology: Volume 2. Memory for people* (pp. 87–100). Mahwah, NJ: Erlbaum.

Bruck, M., Ceci, S. J., & Francoeur, E. (1999). The accuracy of mothers' conversations with their preschool children. *Journal of Experimental Psychology, 5*, 89–106.

Bruck, M., Ceci, S. J., Francoeur, E., & Barr, R. J. (1995). "I hardly cried when I got my shot!" Influencing children's reports about a visit to their pediatrician. *Child Development, 66*, 193–208.

Bruck, M., Ceci, S. J., & Hembrooke, H. (1998). Reliability and credibility of young children's reports: From research to policy and practice. *American Psychologist, 53*, 136–151.

Bruck, M., Hembrooke, H., & Ceci, S. J. (1997). Children's reports of pleasant and unpleasant events. In D. Read & S. Lindsay (Eds.), *Recollections of trauma: Scientific research and clinical practice* (pp. 199–219). New York: Plenum.

Bruck, M., & Melnyk, L. (2004). Individual differences in children's
   suggestibility: A review and synthesis. *Applied Cognitive Psychology, 18*, 947–996.
Bruton v. United States. 391 U.S. 123. (1968).
Buchanan, T. W., & Adolphs, R. (2004). The neuroanatomy of emotional memory in
   humans. In D. Reisberg & P. Hertel (Eds.), *Memory and emotion. series in affective
   science* (pp. 42–75). New York: Oxford University Press.
Buckley, J. P. (2006). The Reid technique of interviewing and interrogation. In T. Williamson
   (Ed.), *Investigative interviewing: Rights, research, regulation* (pp. 190–206). Devon,
   UK: Willan.
Buckley, J. P. (2012). Detection of deception researchers need to collaborate with
   experienced practitioners. *Journal of Applied Research in Memory and Cognition, 1*,
   126–127.
Bull, R. (2010). The investigative interviewing of children and other vulnerable
   witnesses: Psychological research and working/professional practice. *Legal and
   Criminological Psychology, 15*, 5–23.
Bull, R., & Clifford, B. R. (1984). Earwitness voice recognition accuracy. In G. L. Wells, &
   E. F. Loftus (Eds.), *Eyewitness Testimony: Psychological Perspectives* (pp. 92–123).
   New York: Cambridge University Press.
Burgwyn-Bailes, E., Baker-Ward, L., Gordon, B. N., & Ornstein, P. A. (2001). Children's
   memory for emergency medical treatment after one year: The impact of
   individual differences variables on recall and suggestibility. *Applied Cognitive
   Psychology, 15*, S25–S48.
Burke, A. S. (2010). Prosecutorial agnosticism. *Ohio State Journal of Criminal Law, 8*,
   79–100.
Burke, A. S., Heuer, F., & Reisberg, D. (1992). Remembering emotional events. *Memory
   & Cognition, 20*, 277–290.
Burton, A. M., Young, A. W., Bruce, V., Johnston, R. A., & Ellis, A. W. (1991).
   Understanding covert recognition. *Cognition, 39*, 129–166.
Busey, T. A., Tunnicliff, J., Loftus, G. R., & Loftus, E. F. (2000). Accounts of the
   confidence-accuracy relation in recognition memory. *Psychonomic Bulletin &
   Review, 7*, 26–48.
Butler, B. (2007). The role of death qualification in jurors' susceptibility to pretrial
   publicity. *Journal of Applied Social Psychology, 37*, 115–123.
Buzsáki, G. (1998). Memory consolidation during sleep: A neurophysiological
   perspective. *Journal of Sleep Research, 1*, 17–23.
Cahill, L., & McGaugh, J. L. (1995). A novel demonstration of enhanced memory
   associated with emotional arousal. *Consciousness and Cognition, 4*, 410–421.
California Commission on the Fair Administration of Justice. (2008). *Final report.*
   Retrieved from http://www.ccfaj.org/documents/CCFAJFinalReport.pdf
Carlson, C. A., Gronlund, S. D., Weatherford, D. R., & Carlson, M. A. (2012). Processing
   differences between feature-based facial composites and photos of real faces.
   Applied Cognitive Psychology, 26, 525–540.
Carpenter, S. K., Pashler, H., & Cepeda, N. J. (2009). Using tests to enhance 8th grade
   students' retention of U.S. history facts. *Applied Cognitive Psychology, 23*,
   760–771.
Carter, C. A., Bottoms, B. L., & Levine, M. (1996). Linguistic and socio-emotional
   influences on the accuracy of children's reports. *Law & Human Behavior, 20*,
   335–358.
Casey, B. J., Jones, R. M., & Hare, T. A. (2008). The adolescent brain. *Annals of the
   New York Academy of Sciences, 1124*, 111–126.
Ceci, S. J., Crossman, A. M., Scullin, M. H., Gilstrap, L., & Huffman, M. L. (2002).
   Children's suggestibility research: Implications for the courtroom and the
   forensic interview. In H. L. Westcott, G. M. Davies, & R. H. C. Bull (Eds.),
   Children's testimony: A handbook of psychological research and forensic practice
   (pp. 117–130). New York: Wiley.

Ceci, S. J., Crotteau-Huffman, M., Smith, E., & Loftus, E. W. (1994). Repeatedly thinking about non-events. *Consciousness & Cognition*, 3, 388–407.

Cerrato, L., Falcone, M., & Paoloni, A. (2000). Subjective age estimation of telephonic voices. *Speech Communication*, 31, 107–112.

Chabris, C., & Simons, D. J. (2010). *The invisible gorilla; How our intuitions deceive us.* New York: Crown Archetype.

Chae, Y., Ogle, C. M., & Goodman, G. S. (2009). Remembering negative childhood experiences: An attachment theory perspective. In J. A. Quas, & R. Fivush (Eds.), *Emotion and memory in development: Biological, cognitive, and social considerations* (pp. 3–27). New York: Oxford University Press.

Chan, J. C., Thomas, A. K., & Bulevich, J. B. (2009). Recalling a witnessed event increases eyewitness suggestibility: The reversed testing effect. *Psychological Science*, 20, 66–73.

Charman, S. D., & Wells, G. L. (2007). Eyewitness lineups: Is the appearance-changes instruction a good idea? *Law and Human Behavior*, 31, 3–22.

Charman, S. D., & Wells, G. L. (2012). The moderating effect of ecphoric experience on post-identification feedback: A critical test of the cues-based inference conceptualization. *Applied Cognitive Psychology*, 26, 243–250.

Charman, S. D., Wells, G. L., & Joy, S. W. (2011). The dud effect: Adding highly dissimilar fillers increases confidence in lineup identifications. *Law and Human Behavior*, 35, 479–500.

Charniak, E. (1972). Toward a model of children's story comprehension. Cambridge, MA: Artificial Intelligence Laboratory, M. I. T.

Chojnacki, D. E., Cicchini, M. D., & White, L. T. (2008). An empirical basis for the admission of expert testimony on false confessions. *Arizona State Law Journal*, 40, 1–45.

Christiaansen, R. E., Sweeney, J. D., & Ochalek, K. (1983). Influencing eyewitness descriptions. *Law and Human Behavior*, 7(1), 59–65.

Christianson, S. A., & Hübinette, B. (1993). Hands up! A study of witnesses' emotional reactions and memories associated with bank robberies. *Applied Cognitive Psychology*, 7, 365–379.

Chrobak, Q. M., & Zaragoza, M. S. (2008). Inventing stories: Forcing witnesses to fabricate entire fictitious events leads to freely reported false memories. *Psychonomic Bulletin & Review*, 15, 1190–1195.

Clancy, S. A. (2005). *Abducted: How people come to believe they were kidnapped by aliens.* Cambridge, MA: Harvard University Press.

Clancy, S. A. (2010). *The trauma myth: The truth about the sexual abuse of children—and its aftermath.* New York: Basic Books.

Clare, I. C., & Gudjonsson, G. H. (1995). The vulnerability of suspects with intellectual disabilities during police interviews: A review and experimental study of decision-making. *Mental Handicap Research*, 8, 110–128.

Clark, H. H. (1996). *Using language* (vol. 4). Cambridge, UK: Cambridge University Press.

Clark, S. E. (2005). A re-examination of the effects of biased lineup instructions in eyewitness identification. *Law and Human Behavior*, 29, 575–604.

Clark, S. E. (2012). Costs and benefits of eyewitness identification reform: Psychological science and public policy. *Perspectives on Psychological Science*, 7, 238–259.

Clark, S. E., Marshall, T. E., & Rosenthal, R. (2009). Lineup administrator influences on eyewitness identification decisions. *Journal of Experimental Psychology: Applied*, 15, 63–75.

Clark, S. E., Moreland, M. B., & Gronlund, S. D. (2014). Evolution of the empirical and theoretical foundations of eyewitness identification reform. *Psychonomic Bulletin & Review*, 21, 251–267.

Clark, S. E., Rush, R. A., & Moreland, M. B. (2013). In B. L. Cutler (Ed.), *Reform of eyewitness identification* (pp. 87–112). Washington, DC: American Psychological Association.

Clark, S. E., & Tunnicliff, J. L. (2001). Selecting lineup foils in eyewitness identification: Experimental control and real-world simulation. *Law and Human Behavior, 25*, 199–216.

Clifford, B. R., & Hollin, C. R. (1981). Effects of the type of incident and the number of perpetrators on eyewitness memory. *Journal of Applied Psychology, 66*, 238–259.

Colomb, C., Ginet, M., Wright, D., Demarchi, S., & Sadler, C. (2013). Back to the real: Efficacy and perception of a modified cognitive interview in the field. *Applied Cognitive Psychology, 27*, 574–583.

Colorado v. Connelly. 497 U.S. 107 S.Ct. 515. (1986).

Compo, N. S., Evans, J. R., Carol, R. N., Villalba, D., Ham, L. S., Garcia, T., & Rose, S. (2012). Intoxicated eyewitnesses: Better than their reputation? *Law and Human Behavior, 36*, 77–86.

Connelly, M. (2011). *The fifth witness.* New York: Little, Brown.

Connors, E., Lundregan, T., Miller, N., & McEwen, T. (1996). *Convicted by juries, exonerated by science: Case studies in the use of DNA evidence to establish innocence after trial.* Washington, DC: U.S. Department of Justice.

Conway, M. A., Cohen, G., & Stanhope, N. (1992). Very long-term memory for knowledge acquired at school and university. *Applied Cognitive Psychology, 6*, 467–482.

Cooper, B. S., Kennedy, M. A., Hervé, H. F., & Yuille, J. C. (2002). Weapon focus in sexual assault memories of prostitutes. *International journal of law and psychiatry, 25*, 181–191.

Cooper, L. A., & Shepard, R. N. (1973). The time required to prepare for a rotated stimulus. *Memory & Cognition, 1*, 246–250.

Correll, J., Park, B., Judd, C. M., & Wittenbrink, B. (2002). The police officer's dilemma: Using ethnicity to disambiguate potentially threatening individuals. *Journal of Personality and Social Psychology, 83*, 1314–1329.

Correll, J., Park, B., Judd, C. M., Wittenbrink, B., Sadler, M. S., & Keesee, T. (2007). Across the thin blue line: Police officers and racial bias in the decision to shoot. *Journal of Personality and Social Psychology, 92*, 1006–1023.

Corriveau, K. H., Kim, A. L., Schwalen, C. E., & Harris, P. L. (2009). Abraham Lincoln and Harry Potter: Children's differentiation between historical and fantasy characters. *Cognition, 113*, 213–225.

Corwin, D., & Olafson, E. (1997). Videotaped discovery of a reportedly unrecallable memory of child sexual abuse: Comparison with a childhood interview videotaped 11 years before. *Child Maltreatment, 2*, 91–112.

Costanzo, M., Shaked-Schroer, N., & Vinson, K. (2010). Juror beliefs about police interrogations, false confessions, and expert testimony. *Journal of Empirical Legal Studies, 7*, 231–247.

Crombag, H. F., Wagenaar, W. A., & Van Koppen, P. J. (1996). Crashing memories and the problem of "source monitoring." *Applied Cognitive Psychology, 10*, 95–104.

Crombie, D. (2011). *No mark upon her.* New York: Harper Collins.

Cruse, D., & Browne, B. A. (1986). Reasoning in a jury trial: The influence of instructions. *Journal of General Psychology, 114*, 129–133.

Cuc, A., Ozuru, Y., Manier, D., & Hirst, W. (2006). On the formation of collective memories: The role of a dominant narrator. *Memory & cognition, 34*, 752–762.

Cutler, B. L. (2006). A sample of witness, crime, and perpetrator characteristics affecting eyewitness identification accuracy. *Cardozo Public Law, Policy, and Ethics Journal, 4*, 327–340.

Cutler, B. L., & Penrod, S. D. (1988). Improving the reliability of eyewitness identification: Lineup construction and presentation, *Journal of Applied Psychology, 73*, 281–290.

Cutler, B. L., & Penrod, S. D. (1989). Forensically relevant moderators of the relation between eyewitness identification accuracy and confidence. *Journal of Applied Psychology, 74*, 650–652.

Cutler, B. L., & Penrod, S. D. (1995). *Mistaken identification: The eyewitness, psychology and the law*. New York: Cambridge University Press.

Cutler, B. L., Penrod, S. D., & Dexter, H. D. (1990). Juror sensitivity to eyewitness identification evidence. *Law and Human Behavior, 14*, 185–191.

Cutler, B. L., Penrod, S. D., & Dexter, H. R. (1989). The eyewitness, the expert psychologist, and the jury. *Law and Human Behavior, 13*, 311–332.

Cutler, B. L., Penrod, S. D., & Martens, T. K. (1987). Improving the reliability of eyewitness identification: Putting context into context. *Journal of Applied Psychology, 72*, 629–637.

Damasio, A. R., Tranel, D., & Damasio, H. (1990). Face agnosia and the neural substrates of memory. *Annual Review of Neuroscience, 13*, 89–109.

Darling, S., Valentine, T., & Memon, A. (2008). Selection of lineup foils in operational contexts. *Applied Cognitive Psychology, 22*, 159–169.

Daubert v. Merrell Dow Pharmaceuticals, Inc. (1993). 509 U.S. 579, 113 S. Ct. 2786, 125 L. Ed. 2d 469.

Davies, G. M., Shepherd, J. W., & Ellis, H. D. (1979). Similarity effects in face recognition. *American Journal of Psychology, 92*, 507–523.

Davies, G. M., & Valentine, T. (2007). Facial composites: Forensic utility and psychological research. In R. C. L. Lindsay, D. F. Ross, J. D. Read, & M. P. Toglia (Eds.), *The handbook of eyewitness psychology: Volume 2. Memory for people* (pp. 59–83). Mahwah, NJ: Erlbaum.

Davis, D., & Friedman, R. D. (2007). Memory for conversation: The orphan child of witness memory researchers. In M. P. Toglia, J. D. Read, D. F. Ross, & R. C. Lindsay (Eds.), *The handbook of eyewitness psychology: Volume 1. Memory for events* (pp. 3–52). Mahwah, NJ: Erlbaum.

Davis, D., & Loftus, E. F. (2007). Internal and external sources of misinformation in adult witness memory. In M. P. Toglia, J. D. Read, D. F. Ross, & R. C. Lindsay (Eds.), *The handbook of eyewitness psychology: Volume 1. Memory for events* (pp. 195–237). Mahwah, NJ: Erlbaum.

Davis, D., & Loftus, E. F. (2012). Inconsistencies between law and the limits of human cognition. In L. Nadel & W. P. Sinnott-Armstrong (Eds.), *Memory and law* (pp. 29–58). New York: Oxford University Press.

Davis, D., Loftus, E. F., Vanous, S., & Cucciare, M. (2008). "Unconscious transference" can be an instance of "change blindness." *Applied Cognitive Psychology, 22*, 605–623.

Davis, D., Lopez, P., Koyama, M., Knaack, D., Kusal, T., et al. (2005). *Memory for threats in conversation enhanced by later knowledge of violence between participants*. Presented at the American Psychological Society, Los Angeles, CA.

Davis, M., Markus, K. A., & Walters, S. B. (2006). Judging the credibility of criminal suspect statements: Does mode of presentation matter? *Journal of Nonverbal Behavior, 30*, 181–198.

De Jong, M., Wagenaar, W. A., Wolters, G., & Verstijnen, I. M. (2005). Familiar face recognition as a function of distance and illumination: A practical tool for use in the courtroom. *Psychology, Crime & Law, 11*, 87–97.

De Renzi, E., Faglioni, P., Grossi, D., & Nichelli, P. (1991). Apperceptive and associative forms of prosopagnosia. *Cortex, 27*, 213–221.

Defeldre, A. C. (2005). Inadvertent plagiarism in everyday life. *Applied Cognitive Psychology, 19*, 1033–1040.

Deffenbacher, K. A., Bornstein, B., & Penrod, S. (2006). Mugshot exposure effects: Retroactive interference, mugshot commitment, source confusion, and unconscious transference. *Law and Human Behavior, 30*, 287–307.

Deffenbacher, K. A., Bornstein, B. H., McGorty, E. K., & Penrod, S. D. (2008). Forgetting the once-seen face: Estimating the strength of an eyewitness's memory representation. *Journal of Experimental Psychology: Applied, 14*, 139–150.

Deffenbacher, K., Bornstein, B., Penrod, S., & McCorty, E. (2004). A meta-analytic review of the effects of high stress on eyewitness memory. *Law and Human Behavior, 28*, 687–706.

Deffenbacher, K. A., Cross, J. F., Handkins, R. E., Chance, J. E., Goldstein, A. G., Hammersley, R., & Read, J. D. (1989). Relevance of voice identification research to criteria for evaluating reliability of an identification. *Journal of Psychology: Interdisciplinary and Applied, 123*, 109–119.

Deffenbacher, K. A., & Loftus, E. F. (1982). Do jurors share a common understanding concerning eyewitness behavior? *Law and Human Behavior, 6*, 15–30.

DePaulo, B., Lindsay, J., Malone, B., Muhlenbruck, L., Charlton, K., & Cooper, H. (2003). Cues to deception. *Psychological Bulletin, 129*, 74–118.

DePaulo, B. M., Charlton, K., Cooper, H., Lindsay, J. J., & Muhlenbruck, L. (1997). The accuracy-confidence correlation in the detection of deception. *Personality and Social Psychology Review, 1*, 346–357.

DePaulo, B. M., Lanier, K., & Davis, T. (1983). Detecting the deceit of the motivated liar. *Journal of Personality and Social Psychology, 45*, 1096–1103.

Deslauriers-Varin, N., Lussier, P., & St-Yves, M. (2011). Confessing their crime: Factors influencing the offender's decision to confess to the police. *Justice Quarterly, 28*, 113–145.

Desmarais, S. L., & Read, J. D. (2011). After 30 years, what do we know about what jurors know? A meta-analytic review of lay knowledge regarding eyewitness factors. *Law and Human Behavior, 35*, 200–210.

Devenport, J. L., Kimbrough, C. D., & Cutler, B. L. (2009). Effectiveness of traditional safeguards against erroneous conviction arising from mistaken eyewitness identification. In B. L. Cutler (Ed.), *Expert testimony on the psychology of eyewitness identification* (pp. 51–68). New York: Oxford University Press.

Devine, D. (2012). *Jury decision making: The state of the science*. New York: New York University Press.

Devine, D. J., Buddenbaum, J., Houp, S., Studebaker, N., & Stolle, D. O. (2009). Strength of evidence, extraevidentiary influence and the liberation hypothesis: Data from the field. *Law and Human Behavior, 33*, 136–148.

Dexter, H. R., Cutler, B. L., & Moran, G. (1992). A test of voir dire as a remedy for the prejudicial effects of pretrial publicity. *Journal of Applied Social Psychology, 22*, 819–832.

Diamond, R., & Carey, S. (1986). Why faces are and are not special: An effect of expertise. *Journal of Experimental Psychology: General, 115*, 107–117.

Diamond, S. S., & Rose, M. R. (2005). Real juries. *Annual Review of Law and Social Science, 1*, 255–284.

Dickinson, J. J., Poole, D. A., & Bruck, M. (2005). Back to the future: A comment on the use of anatomical dolls in forensic interviews. *Journal of Forensic Psychology Practice, 5*, 63–74.

Dickinson, J. J., Poole, D. A., & Laimon, R. L. (2005). Children's recall and testimony. In N. Brewer & K. D. Wilson (Eds.), *Psychology and law: An empirical perspective* (pp. 151–176). New York: Guilford Press.

DiMatteo, M. R. (1985). Physician-patient communication: Promoting a positive health care setting. In J. C. Rosen & L. J. Solomon (Eds.), *Prevention in health psychology* (pp. 328–365). Hanover, NH: University Press of New England.

Dixon, T., & Linz, D. (2002). Television news, prejudicial pretrial publicity and the depiction of race. *Journal of Broadcasting and Electronic Media, 46*, 112–136.

Dobolyi, D. G., & Dodson, C. S. (2013). Eyewitness confidence in simultaneous and sequential lineups: A criterion shift account for sequential mistaken identification overconfidence. *Journal of Experimental Psychology, 19*, 345–357

Douglass, A., Neuschatz, J., Imrich, J., & Wilkinson, M. (2010). Does post identification feedback affect evaluations of eyewitness testimony and identification procedures? *Law and Human Behavior, 34*, 282–294.

Douglass, A. B., Brewer, N., & Semmler, C. (2010). Moderators of postidentification feedback effects on eyewitnesses' memory reports. *Legal and Criminological Psychology, 15*, 279–292.

Drews, F. A., Pasupathi, M., & Strayer, D. L. (2008). Passenger and cell phone conversations in simulated driving. *Journal of Experimental Psychology: Applied, 14*, 392–400.

Drizin, S. A., & Leo, R. A. (2004). The problem of false confessions in the post-DNA world. *North Carolina Law Review, 82*, 891–1004.

Dror, I. E., & Charlton, D. (2006). Why experts make errors. *Journal of Forensic Identification, 56*, 600–616.

Dudai, Y. (2004). The neurobiology of consolidations, or, how stable is the engram? *Annual Review of Psychology, 55*, 51–86.

Dunning, D., & Perretta, S. (2002). Automaticity and eyewitness accuracy: A 10- to 12-second rule for distinguishing accurate from inaccurate positive identifications. *Journal of Applied Psychology, 87*, 951–962.

Dysart, J., Lindsay, R., MacDonald, T., & Wicke, C. (2002). The intoxicated witness: Effects of alcohol on identification accuracy from showups. *Journal of Applied Psychology, 87*, 170–175.

Dysart, J. E., Lawson, V. Z., & Rainey, A. (2012). Blind administration as a prophylactic against the postidentification feedback effect. *Law and Human Behavior, 36*, 312–319.

Dysart, J. E., & Lindsay, R. C. L. (2007b). The effects of delay on eyewitness identification accuracy: Should we be concerned? In R. C. L. Lindsay, D. F. Ross, J. D. Read, & M. P. Toglia (Eds.), *The handbook of eyewitness psychology: Volume 2. Memory for people* (pp. 361–376). Mahwah, NJ: Erlbaum.

Dysart, J. E., & Lindsay, R. C. L. (2007a). Show-up identifications: Suggestive technique or reliable method? In R. C. L. Lindsay, D. F. Ross, J. D. Read & M. P. Toglia (Eds.), *The handbook of eyewitness psychology: Volume 2. Memory for people* (pp. 137–153). Mahwah, NJ: Erlbaum.

Dysart, J. E., Lindsay, R. C. L., & Dupuis, P. R. (2006). Show-ups: The critical issue of clothing bias. *Applied Cognitive Psychology, 20*, 1009–1023.

Ebbinghaus, H. (1885/1913). Memory. A contribution to experimental psychology. New York: Dover. (Original work published in 1885: Translated in 1913)

Eberhardt, J. L., Goff, P., Purdie, V. J., & Davies, P. G. (2004). Seeing Black: Race, crime, and visual processing. *Journal of Personality and Social Psychology, 87*, 876–893.

Edelson, M., Sharot, T., Dola, R. J., & Dudai, Y. (2011). Following the crowd: Brain substrates of long-term memory conformity. *Science, 333*, 108–111.

Edelstein, R. S., Alexander, K. W., Goodman, G. S., & Newton, J. W. (2004a). Emotion and eyewitness memory. In D. Reisberg & P. Hertel (Eds.), *Memory and emotion* (pp. 308–346). New York: Oxford University Press.

Edelstein, R. S., Alexander, K. W., Shaver, P. R., Schaaf, J., Quas, J. A., Lovas, G. S., & Goodman, G. S. (2004b). Adult attachment style and parental responsiveness during a stressful event. *Attachment and Human Development, 6*, 31–52.

Ekman, P. (2009). *Telling lies: Clues to deceit in the marketplace, politics, and marriage.* New York: W. W. Norton.

Ekman, P., & Friesen, W. V. (2003). *Unmasking the face.* Cambridge: Malor Books.

Ekman, P., & O'Sullivan, M. (1991). Who can catch a liar? *American Psychologist, 46*, 913–920.

Ekman, P., O'Sullivan, M., & Frank, M. G. (1999). A few can catch a liar. *Psychological Science, 10,* 263–266.

Erickson, W. B., Lampinen, J. M., & Leding, J. (2014). The weapon focus effect in target-present and target-absent line-ups: The roles of threat, novelty, and timing. *Applied Cognitive Psychology, 28,* 349–359.

Evans, J. R., Schreiber Compo, N., & Russano, M. B. (2009). Intoxicated witnesses and suspects: Procedures and prevalence according to law enforcement. *Psychology, Public Policy, and Law, 15,* 194–221.

Fahsing, I. A., Ask, K., & Granhag, P. A. (2004). The man behind the mask: Accuracy and predictors of eyewitness offender descriptions. *Journal of Applied Psychology, 89,* 722–729.

Fawcett, J. M., Russell, E. J., Peace, K. A., & Christie, J. (2013). Of guns and geese: A meta-analytic review of the "weapon focus" literature. *Psychology, Crime & Law, 19.*

Fiedler, K., Schmid, J., & Stahl, T. (2002). What is the current truth about polygraph lie detection? *Basic and Applied Social Psychology, 24,* 313–324.

Finger, K., & Pezdek, K. (1999). The effect of cognitive interview on face identification accuracy: Release from verbal overshadowing. *Journal of Applied Psychology, 84*(3), 340–348.

Finlay, W. M., & Lyons, E. (2002). Acquiescence in interviews with people who have mental retardation. *Mental Retardation, 40,* 14–29.

Fisher, J. (2008). *Forensics under fire: Are bad science and dueling experts corrupting criminal justice?* Newark, NJ: Rutgers University Press.

Fisher, R. P., & Schreiber, N. (2007). Interviewing protocols to improve eyewitness memory. In M. P. Toglia, J. D., Read, D. F. Ross, & R. C. L. Lindsay (Eds.), *The handbook of eyewitness psychology: Volume 1. Memory for events* (pp. 53–80). Mahwah, NJ: Erlbaum.

Fitzgerald, R. J., Price, H. L., Oriet, C., & Charman, S. D. (2013). The effect of suspect-filler similarity on eyewitness identification decisions: A meta-analysis. *Psychology, Public Policy, and Law, 19,* 151–164.

Fivush, R. (1998). The stories we tell: How language shapes autobiography. *Applied Cognitive Psychology, 12,* 483–487.

Fivush, R. (2002). The development of autobiographical memory. In H. L. Westcott, G. M. Davies, & R. H. C. Bull (Eds.), *Children's testimony: A handbook of psychological research and forensic practice* (pp. 55–68). New York: Wiley.

Fivush, R., Haden, C., & Reese, E. (2006). Elaborating on elaborations: Role of maternal reminiscing style in cognitive and socioemotional development. *Child Development, 77,* 1568–1588.

Fivush, R., Hazzard, A., McDermott Sales, J., Sarfati, D., & Brown, T. (2003). Creating coherence out of chaos? Children's narratives of emotionally positive and negative events. *Applied Cognitive Psychology, 17,* 1–19.

Fivush, R., Hudson, J., & Nelson, K. (1984). Children's long term memory for a novel event: An exploratory study. *Merrill Palmer Quarterly, 30*(3), 303–317.

Fivush, R., & Nelson, K. (2004). Culture and language in the emergence of autobiographical memory. *Psychological Science, 15,* 573–577.

Fivush, R., & Sales, J. M. (2004). Children's memories of emotional events. In D. Reisberg & P. Hertel (Eds.), *Memory and emotion* (pp. 242–271). New York: Oxford University Press.

Fivush, R., & Shukat, J. R. (1995). Content, consistency and coherence in early autobiographical recall. In M. S. Zaragoza, J. R. Graham, G. C. N. Hall, R. Hirschman, & Y. S. Ben-Porath (Eds.), *Memory and testimony in the child witness* (pp. 5–23). Thousand Oaks, CA: Sage.

Flowe, H., Finklea, K., & Ebbesen, E. (2009). Limitations of expert psychology testimony on eyewitness identification. In B. Cutler (Ed.), *Expert testimony on the psychology of eyewitness identification* (pp. 201–221). New York: Oxford University Press.

Flowe, H. D., & Humphries, J. E. (2011). An examination of criminal face bias in a random sample of police lineups. *Applied Cognitive Psychology, 25,* 265–273.

Flowe, H. D., Mehta, A., & Ebbesen, E. B. (2011). The role of eyewitness identification evidence in felony case dispositions. *Psychology, Public Policy, and Law, 17,* 140–159.

Formby, D. (1967). Maternal recognition of infant's cry. *Developmental medicine and child neurology, 9,* 293–298.

Frank, M. G., & Svetieva, E. (2012). Lies worth catching involve both emotion and cognition. *Journal of Applied Research in Memory and Cognition, 1,* 131–133.

Freitas-Magalhães, A. (2012). Microexpression and macroexpression. In V. S. Ramachandran (Ed.), *Encyclopedia of human behavior* (vol. 2, pp. 173–183). Oxford, UK: Elsevier/Academic Press.

Frenda, S. J., Nichols, R. M., & Loftus, E. F. (2011). Current issues and advances in misinformation research. *Current Directions in Psychological Science, 20,* 20–23.

Freyd, J. J. (1996). *Betrayal trauma: The logic of forgetting childhood abuse.* Cambridge, MA: Harvard University Press.

Freyd, J. J. (1998). Science in the memory debate. *Ethics & Behavior, 8,* 101–113.

Frowd, C. D., Bruce, V., Smith, A. J., & Hancock, P. J. (2008). Improving the quality of facial composites using a holistic cognitive interview. *Journal of Experimental Psychology: Applied, 14,* 276–287.

Frye v. United States, 293 F. 1013. (D.C. Cir. 1923).

Fulero, S. (2002). The past, present, and future of applied pretrial publicity research. *Law and Human Behavior, 26,* 127–133.

Fulero, S. M. (2009). System and estimator variables in eyewitness identification: A review. In D. A. Krauss & J. D. Lieberman (Eds.), *Psychological expertise in court* (pp. 57–78). Burlington, VT: Ashgate.

Fulero, S. M., & Everington, C. (1995). Assessing competency to waive Miranda rights in defendants with mental retardation. *Law and Human Behavior, 19,* 533–543.

Fulero, S. M., & Everington, C. (2004). Assessing the capacity of persons with mental retardation to waive Miranda rights: A jurisprudent therapy perspective. *Law & Psychology Review, 28,* 53–69.

Gallo, D. A., Roberts, M. J., & Seamon, J. G. (1997). Remembering words not presented in lists: Can we avoid creating false memories? *Psychonomic Bulletin & Review, 4,* 271–276.

Garrett, B. (2008). Judging innocence. *Columbia Law Review, 108,* 55–142.

Garrett, B. (2010). The substance of false confessions. *Stanford Law Review, 62,* 1051–1119.

Garrett, B. L. (2012). *Convicting the innocent: Where criminal prosecutions go wrong.* Cambridge, MA: Harvard University Press.

Garrioch, L., & Brimacombe, C. A. E. (2001). Lineup administrators' expectations: Their impact on eyewitness confidence. *Law and Human Behavior, 25,* 299–314.

Garry, M., Manning, C. G., Loftus, E. F., & Sherman, S. J. (1996). Imagination inflation: Imagining a childhood event inflates confidence that it occurred. *Psychonomic Bulletin & Review, 3,* 208–214.

Garry, M., & Wade, K. (2005). Actually, a picture is worth less than 45 words: Narratives produce more false memories than photographs do. *Psychonomic Bulletin & Review, 25,* 359–366.

Garven, S., Wood, J. M., Malpass, R. S., & Shaw, J. S. (1998). More than suggestion: The effect of interviewing techniques from the McMartin preschool case. *Journal of Applied Psychology, 83,* 347–359.

Gauthier, I. L., & Bukach, C. (2007). Should we reject the expertise hypothesis? *Cognition, 103,* 322–330.

Geis, G., & Loftus, E. F. (2009). *Taus v. Loftus*: Determining the legal ground rules for scholarly inquiry. *Journal of Forensic Psychology Practice, 9,* 147–162.

General Electric Company v. Joiner, 522 U.S. 136. (1997).

Geraerts, E., Lindsay, D. S., Merckelbach, H., Jelicic, M., Raymaekers, L., Arnold, M. M., & Schooler, J. W. (2009). Cognitive mechanisms underlying recovered-memory experiences of childhood sexual abuse. *Psychological Science, 20,* 92–98.

Geraerts, E., Schooler, J. W., Merckelbach, H., Jelicic, M., Hauer, B. J., & Ambadar, Z. (2007). The reality of recovered memories corroborating continuous and discontinuous memories of childhood sexual abuse. *Psychological Science, 18,* 564–568.

Ghetti, S., Edelstein, R. S., Goodman, G. S., Cordòn, I. M., Quas, J. A., Alexander, K. W., Redlich, A. D., & Jones, D. P. (2006). What can subjective forgetting tell us about memory for childhood trauma? *Memory & Cognition, 34,* 1011–1025.

Ghetti, S., Goodman, G. S., Eisen, M. L., Qin, J., & Davis, S. L. (2002). Consistency in children's reports of sexual and physical abuse. *Child Abuse & Neglect, 26,* 977–995.

Giesbrecht, T., Lynn, S. J., Lilienfeld, S. O., & Merckelbach, H. (2008). Cognitive processes in dissociation: An analysis of core theoretical assumptions. *Psychological Bulletin, 134,* 617–647.

Gilbert, J. A. E., & Fisher, R. P. (2006). The effects of varied retrieval cues on reminiscence in eyewitness memory. *Applied Cognitive Psychology, 20,* 723–739.

Godfrey, R. D., & Clark, S. E. (2010). Repeated eyewitness identification procedures: Memory, decision making, and probative value. *Law and Human Behavior, 34,* 241–258.

Gogtay, N., Nugent, T. F., Herman, D. H., Ordonez, A., Greenstein, D., Hayashi, K., Clasen, L., Toga, A., Gledd, J., Rapoport, J., & Thompson, P. M. (2006). Dynamic mapping of normal human hippocampal development. *Hippocampus, 16,* 664–672.

Goldstein, N. E. S., Condie, L. O., Kalbeitzer, R., Osman, D., & Geier, J. L. (2003). Juvenile offenders' Miranda rights comprehension and self-reported likelihood of offering false confessions. *Assessment, 10,* 359–369.

Goleman, D. (1996). *Vital lies, simple truths: The psychology of self-deception.* Simon and Schuster.

Gonzalez, R., Ellsworth, P. C., & Pembroke, M. (1993). Response biases in lineups and showups. *Journal of Personality and Social Psychology, 64,* 525–537.

Goodman, G. S., Ghetti, S., Quas, J. A., Edelstein, R. S., Alexander, K. W., Redlich, A. D., et al. (2003). A prospective study of memory for child sexual abuse: New findings relevant to the repressed-memory controversy. *Psychological Science, 14,* 113–118.

Goodman, G. S., Sharma, A., Thomas, S. F., & Considine, M. (1995). Mother knows best: Effects of relationship status and interviewer bias on children's memory. *Journal of Experimental Child Psychology, 60,* 195–228.

Goodsell, C. A., Wetmore, S. A., Neuschatz, J. S., & Gronlund, S. D. (2013). Showups. In B. L. Cutler (Ed.), *Reform of eyewitness identification* (pp. 45–63). Washington, DC: American Psychological Association.

Goodwin, D. W. (1995). Alcohol amnesia. *Addiction, 90,* 315–317.

Goodwin, D. W., Crane, J. B., & Guze, S. B. (1969). Alcoholic "blackouts." A review and clinical study of 100 alcoholics. *American Journal of Psychiatry, 126,* 191–198.

Goodwin, D. W., Cranke J. B., & Guze, S. B. (1969b). Phenomenlogical aspects of the alcoholic "blackout." *British Journal of Psychiatry, 115,* 1033–1038.

Goodwin, D. W., Othmer, E., & Halikas, J. A. (1970). Loss of short-term memory as a predictor of the alcoholic "black-out." *Nature, 227,* 201–202.

Goodwin, K. A., Kukucka, J. P., & Hawks, I. M. (2013). Co-witness confidence, conformity, and eyewitness memory: An examination of normative and informational social influences. *Applied Cognitive Psychology, 27,* 91–100.

Granhag, P. A., Strömwall, L. A., & Allwood, C. M. (2000). Effects of reiteration, hindsight bias, and memory on realism in eyewitness confidence. *Applied Cognitive Psychology, 14,* 397–420.

Greathouse, S., & Kovera, M. (2009). Instruction bias and lineup presentation moderate the effects of administrator knowledge on eyewitness identification. *Law and Human Behavior, 33*, 70–82.

Greene, E. L., & Wade, R. (1988). Of private talk and public print: General pretrial publicity and juror decision-making. *Applied Cognitive Psychology, 1*, 1–13.

Gregory, A. H., Schereiber,-Compo, N., Vertefeuille, L., & Zambrusky, G. (2011). A comparison of U.S. police interviewers' notes with their subsequent reports. *Journal of Investigative Psychology and Offender Profiling, 8*, 203–215.

Griesel, D., & Yuille, J. C. (2007). Credibility assessment in eyewitness memory. In M. P. Toglia, J. D. Read, D. F. Ross, & R. C. Lindsay (Eds.), *The handbook of eyewitness psychology: Volume 1. Memory for events* (pp. 339–370). Mahwah, NJ: Erlbaum.

Grisso, T. (1998). *Forensic evaluation of juveniles.* Sarasota, FL: Professional Resource Press.

Grisso, T., Steinberg, L., Woolard, J., Cauffman, E., Scott, E., Graham, S., Lexcen, F., Reppuci, N. D., & Schwartz, R. (2003). Juveniles' competence to stand trial: A comparison of adolescents' and adults' capacities as trial defendants. *Law and Human Behavior, 27*, 333–363.

Gronlund, S. C., Anderen, S. M., & Perry, C. (2013). Presentation methods. In B. L. Cutler (Ed.), *Reform of eyewitness identification* (pp. 113–138). Washington, DC: American Psychological Association.

Gronlund, S. D., Carlson, C. A., Dailey, S. B., & Goodsell, C. A. (2009). Robustness of the sequential lineup advantage. *Journal of Experimental Psychology: Applied, 15*, 140–152.

Gronlund, S. D., Goodsell, C. A., & Andersen, S. M. (2012). Lineup procedures in eyewitness identification. In L. Nadel & W. P. Sinnott-Armstrong (Eds.), *Memory and law* (pp. 59–83). New York: Oxford University Press.

Gronlund, S. D., Wixted, J. T., & Mickes, L. (2014). Evaluating eyewitness identification procedures using receiver operating characteristic analysis. *Current Directions in Psychological Science, 23*, 3–10.

Gross, S. R., Jacoby, K., Matheson, D. J., Montgomery, N., & Patil, S. (2005). Exonerations in the United States 1989 through 2003. *Journal of Criminal Law and Criminology, 95*, 523–560.

Grossman, D., & Siddle, B. K. (2004). Critical incident amnesia: The physiological basis and the implications of memory loss during extreme survival stress situations. *The Firearms Instructor: The Official Journal of the International Association of Law Enforcement Firearms Instructors, 31.*

Gudjonsson, G., Hannesdottir, K., Agustsson, T., Sigurdsson, J., Gudmundsdottir, A., Dordardottir, D., Tyrfingsson, D., & Petursson, H. (2004). The relationship of alcohol withdrawal symptoms to suggestibility and compliance. *Psychology, Crime & Law, 10*, 169–177.

Gudjonsson, G. H. (2003). *The psychology of interrogations and confessions: A handbook.* New York: Wiley.

Gudjonsson, G. H., Sigurdsson, J. F., & Sigfusdottir, I. D. (2009). Interrogation and false confession among adolescents in seven European countries: What background and psychological variables best discriminate between false confessors and non-false confessors? *Psychology, Crime, and Law, 15*, 711–728.

Haber, R. N., & Haber, L. (November, 2001). *A meta-analysis of research on eyewitness lineup identification accuracy.* Paper presented at the Annual Convention of the Psychonomics Society, Orlando, Florida.

Hafstad, G. S., Memon, A., & Logie, R. (2004). Post-identification feedback, confidence and recollections of witnessing conditions in child witnesses. *Applied Cognitive Psychology, 18*, 901–912.

Halamish, V., & Bjork, R. A. (2011). When does testing enhance retention? A distribution-based interpretation of retrieval as a memory modifier. *Journal of Experimental Psychology: Learning, Memory, and Cognition, 37*, 801.

Hamann, S. (2001). Cognitive and neural mechanisms of emotional memory. *Trends in Cognitive Sciences, 5,* 394–400.

Hammersley, R., & Read, J. D. (1985). The effect of participation in a conversation on recognition and identification of the speakers' voices. *Law and Human Behavior, 9,* 71.

Hammersley, R., & Read, J. D. (1996). Voice identification by humans and computers. In S. Ludwig, R. S. Malpass, G. Kowehnken (Eds.), *Psychological issues in eyewitness identification* (pp. 117–152). Hillsdale, NJ: Lawrence Erlbaum.

Harris, D. (2012). *Failed evidence: Why law enforcement resists science.* New York: New York University Press.

Harris, P. (2000). *The work of the imagination.* New York: Oxford University Press.

Harrison, Y., & Horne, J. A. (2000). The impact of sleep deprivation on decision making: A review. *Journal of Experimental Psychology: Applied, 6,* 236–249.

Hartshorne, H., & May, M. A. (1928). *Studies in the nature of character: I. Studies in deceit.* New York: Macmillan.

Hartwig, M., Granhag, P. A., Strömwall, L. A., & Andersson, L. O. (2004). Suspicious minds: Criminal's ability to detect deception. *Psychology, Crime and Law, 10,* 83–95.

Hartwig, M., Granhag, P. A., Strömwall, L. A., & Kronkvist, O. (2006). Strategic use of evidence during police interviews: When training to detect deception works. *Law and human behavior, 30,* 603–619.

Hartzler, B., & Fromme, K. (2003). Fragmentary blackouts: Their etiology and effect on alcohol expectancies. *Alcohol Clinical & Experimental Research, 27,* 628–637.

Harvey, A. J., Kneller, W., & Campbell, A. C. (2013). The elusive effects of alcohol intoxication on visual attention and eyewitness memory. *Applied Cognitive Psychology, 27,* 617–624.

Hasel, L. E. (2012). Evidentiary independence. In L. Nadel & W. P. Sinnott-Armstrong (Eds.), *Memory and law* (pp. 142–158). New York: Oxford University Press.

Hasel, L. E., & Kassin, S. M. (2009). On the presumption of evidentiary independence: Can confessions corrupt eyewitness identifications? *Psychological Science, 20,* 122–126.

Hasselmo, M. E. (1999). Neuromodulation: Acetylcholine and memory consolidation. *Trends in Cognitive Sciences, 3,* 351–359.

Hauch, V., Sporer, S., Michael, S. W., & Meissner, C. A. (2010, June). Does training improve detection of deception? A meta-analysis. Paper presented at the annual Conference of the European Association of Psychology and Law, Gothenburg, Sweden.

Havard, C., Memon, A., Clifford, B., & Gabbert, F. (2010). A comparison of video and static photo lineups with child and adolescent witnesses. *Applied Cognitive Psychology, 24,* 1209–1221.

Havard, C., Memon, A., Laybourn, P., & Cunningham, C. (2012). Own-age bias in video lineups: A comparison between children and adults. *Psychology, Crime & Law, 18,* 929–944.

Haw, R. M., & Fisher, R. P. (2004). Effects of administrator-witness contact on eyewitness identification accuracy. *Journal of Applied Psychology, 89,* 1106–1112.

Heathcote, A., Freeman, E., Etherington, J., Tonkin, J., & Bora, B. (2009). A dissociation between similarity effects in episodic face recognition. *Psychonomic Bulletin & Review, 16,* 824–831.

Hefferman, W. (2010). *The dead detective.* New York: Akashic Books.

Henderson, E. (2002). Persuading and controlling: The truth of cross-examination in relation to children. In H. L. Westcott, G. M. Davies, & R. H. C. Bull (Eds.), *Children's testimony: A handbook of psychological research and forensic practice* (pp. 279–293). New York: Wiley.

Henkel, L. A., Coffman, K. A. J., & Dailey, E. M. (2008). A survey of people's attitudes and beliefs about false confessions. *Behavioral Sciences and the Law, 26,* 555–584.

Heuer, L., & Penrod, S. (1994). Juror notetaking and question asking during trials. *Law and Human Behavior, 18*, 121–150.

Hilliar, K. F., Kemp, R. I., & Denson, T. F. (2010). Now *everyone* looks the same: Alcohol intoxication reduces the own-race bias in face recognition. *Law and Human Behavior, 34*, 367–378.

Hirst, W., Coman, A., & Stone, C. B. (2012). Memory and jury deliberation: The benefits and costs of collective remembering. In L. Nadel & W. P. Sinnott-Armstrong (Eds.), *Memory and law* (161–184). New York: Oxford University Press.

Hirst, W., Phelps, E. A., Buckner, R. L., Budson, A. E., Cuc, A., Gabrieli, J. D., et al. (2009). Long-term memory for the terrorist attack of September 11: Flashbulb memories, event memories, and the factors that influence their retention. *Journal of Experimental Psychology: General, 138*, 161–176.

Hockley, W. E., Hemsworth, D. H., & Consoli, A. (1999). Shades of the mirror effect: Recognition of faces with and without sunglasses. *Memory & Cognition, 27*, 128–138.

Hoiberg, B. C., & Stires, L. K. (1973). The effect of several types of pretrial publicity on the guilt attributions of simulated jurors. *Journal of Applied Social Psychology, 3*, 267–275.

Hollien, H. (1990). *The acoustics of crime: The new science of forensic phonetics.* New York: Plenum.

Hollien, H., Bennett, G., & Gelfer, M. P. (1983). Criminal identification comparison: Aural versus visual identifications resulting from a simulated crime. *Journal of Forensic Sciences, 28*, 208–221.

Hollien, H., Majewski, W., & Doherty, E. T. (1982). Perceptual identification of voices under normal, stress and disguise speaking conditions. *Journal of Phonetics, 10*, 129–148.

Hollien, H., & Martin, C. A. (1996). Conducting research on the effects of intoxication on speech. *Forensic Linguistics: The International Journal of Speech, Language and the Law, 3*, 107–127.

Hollien, H., & Schwartz, R. (2000). Aural-perceptual speaker identification: Problems with noncontemporary samples. *Journal of Forensic Linguistics, 7*, 199–211.

Holtgraves, T. M. (2002). *Language as social action: Social psychology and language use.* New York: Psychology Press.

Honts, C. R., & Kircher, J. C. (1994). Mental and physical countermeasures reduce the accuracy of polygraph tests. *Journal of Applied Psychology, 79*, 252–259.

Hope, L., Lewinski, H., Dixon, J., Blocksidge, D., & Gabbert, F. (2012). Witnesses in action: The effect of physical exertion on recall and recognition. *Psychological Science, 23*, 386–390.

Hope, L., Memon, A., & McGeorge, P. (2004). Understanding pretrial publicity: Predecisional distortion of evidence by mock jurors. *Journal of Experimental Psychology: Applied, 10*, 111–119.

Hope, L., Ost, J., Gabbert, F., Healey, S., & Lenton, E. (2008). "With a little help from my friends . . .": The role of co-witness relationship in susceptibility to misinformation. *Acta Psychologica, 127*, 476–484.

Horry, R., Halford, P., Brewer, N., Milne, R., & Bull, R. (2014). Archival analyses of eyewitness identification test outcomes: What can they tell us about eyewitness memory? *Law & Human Behavior, 38*, 94–108.

Horry, R., Memon, A., Wright, D. B., & Milne, R. (2012). Predictors of eyewitness identification decisions from video lineups in England: A field study. *Law and Human Behavior, 36*, 257–265.

Horry, R., Palmer, M., & Brewer, N. (2012). Backloading the sequential lineup prevents within-lineup criterion shifts that undermine identification performance. *Journal of Experimental Psychology: Applied, 18*, 346–360.

Hosch, H., Jolly, K., Schmersal, L., & Smith, B. (2009). Expert psychology testimony on eyewitness identification: Consensus among experts. In B. L. Cutler (Ed.),

Expert testimony on the psychology of eyewitness identification (pp. 143–168). New York: Oxford University Press.

Hosch, H. M., Beck, E. L., & McIntyre, P. (1980). Influence of expert testimony regarding eyewitness accuracy on jury decisions. *Law and Human Behavior, 4,* 287–296.

Hosch, H. M., & Cooper, D. S. (1982). Victimization as a determinant of eyewitness accuracy. *Journal of Applied Psychology, 67,* 649–652.

Hosch, H. M., Leippe, M. R., Marchioni, P. M., & Cooper, D. S. (1984). Victimization, self-monitoring, and eyewitness identification. *Journal of Applied Psychology, 69,* 280–288.

Huffman, M. L., Warren, A. R., & Larson, S. M. (1999). Discussing truth and lies in interviews with children: Whether, why, and how? *Applied Developmental Science, 3,* 6–15.

Hulse, L. M., & Memon, A. (2006). Fatal impact? The effects of emotional arousal and weapon presence on police officers' memories for a simulated crime. *Legal and Criminological Psychology, 11,* 313–325.

Hungerford, A. (2005). The use of anatomically detailed dolls in forensic investigations: Developmental considerations. *Journal of Forensic Psychology Practice, 5,* 75–87.

Huntley, J., & Costanzo, M. (2003). Sexual harassment stories: Testing a story-mediated model of juror decision-making in civil litigation. *Law and Human Behavior, 27,* 29–51.

Hvistendahl, J. K. (1979). The effect of placement of biasing information. *Journalism Quarterly, 56,* 863–865.

Hyman, I. E. (Ed.). (2000). The memory wars. In U. Neisser & I. Hyman (Eds.), *Memory observed: Remembering in natural contexts* (pp. 374–380). New York: Macmillan.

Hyman, I. E., Boss, S. M., Wise, B. M., McKenzie, K. E., & Caggiano, J. M. (2010). Did you see the unicycling clown? Inattentional blindness while walking and talking on a cell phone. *Applied Cognitive Psychology, 24,* 597–607.

Hyman, I. E., Husband, T. H., & Billings, F. J. (1995). False memories of childhood experiences. *Applied Cognitive Psychology, 9,* 181–197.

Iacono, W. G., & Lykken, D. T. (1997). The validity of the lie detector: Two surveys of scientific opinion. *Journal of Applied Psychology, 82,* 426–433.

Ihlebaek, C., Løve, T., Eilertsen, D. E., & Magnussen, S. (2003). Memory for a staged criminal event witnessed live and on video. *Memory, 11,* 319–327.

Imrich, D. J., Mullin, C., & Linz, D. (1995). Measuring the extent of pretrial publicity in major American newspapers: A content analysis. *Journal of Communication, 45,* 94–117.

Inbau, F. E., Reid, J. E., Buckley, J. P., & Jayne, B. C. (2011). *Criminal interrogation and confessions* (4th ed.). Gaithersburg, MD: Aspen.

James, W. (1890). *The principles of psychology,* vol. 1. New York: Dover.

Jelicic, M., Smeets, T., Peters, M. J., Candel, I., Horselenberg, R., & Merckelbach, H. (2006). Assassination of a controversial politician: Remembering details from another non-existent film. *Applied Cognitive Psychology, 20,* 591–596.

Jenkins, F., & Davies, G. (1985). Contamination of facial memory through exposure to misleading composite pictures. *Journal of Applied Psychology, 70,* 164–176.

Jenkins, R., White, D., Van Montfor, X. V., & Burton, A. M. (2011). Variability in photos of the same face. *Cognition, 121,* 313–323.

Jennison, K. M., & Johnson, K. A. (1994). Drinking-induced blackouts among young adults: Results from a national longitudinal study. *International Journal of Addictions, 29,* 23–51.

Jessen, M. (1997). Phonetic manifestations of cognitive and physical stress in trained and untrained police officers. *Forensic Linguistics, 4,* 125–147.

Joëls, M., Fernandez, G., & Roozendaal, B. (2011). Stress and emotional memory: A matter of timing. *Trends in cognitive sciences, 15,* 280–288.

Johnson, M. K., Kahan, T. L., & Raye, C. L. (1984). Dreams and reality monitoring. *Journal of Experimental Psychology: General, 113*, 329–344.

Johnson, M. K., & Raye, C. L. (1981). Reality monitoring. *Psychological Review, 88*, 67–85.

Julien, R. M., & DiCecco, K. (2010). To intend or not to intend: That is the question. *Journal of Legal Nurse Consulting, 21*, 10–14.

Karpicke, J. D. (2012). Retrieval-based learning: Active retrieval promotes meaningful learning. *Current Directions in Psychological Science, 21*, 157–163.

Karpicke, J. D., & Blunt, J. R. (2011). Retrieval practice produces more learning than elaborative studying with concept mapping. *Science, 331*, 772–775.

Karpicke, J. D., & Roediger, H. L. (2010). Is expanding retrieval a superior method for learning text materials? *Memory & cognition, 38*, 116–124.

Kassin, S. M. (2005). On the psychology of confessions: Does innocence put innocents at risk? *American Psychologist, 60*, 215–228.

Kassin, S. M. (2008). The psychology of confessions. *Annual Review of Law and Social Science, 4*, 193–217.

Kassin, S. M. (2012). Why confessions trump innocence. *American Psychologist, 67*, 431–445.

Kassin, S. M., Appleby, S. C., & Torkildson Perillo, J. (2010a). Interviewing suspects: Practice, science, and future directions. *Legal and Criminological Psychology, 15*, 39–55.

Kassin, S. M., & Barndollar, K. A. (1992). The psychology of eyewitness testimony: A comparison of experts and potential jurors. *Journal of Applied Social Psychology, 22*, 1241–1249.

Kassin, S. M., Bogart, D., & Kerner, J. (2012). Confessions that corrupt: Evidence from the DNA exoneration case files. *Psychological Science, 23*, 41–45.

Kassin, S. M., Drizin, S. A., Grisso, T., Gudjonsson, G. H., Leo, R. A., & Redlich, A. D. (2010b). Police-induced confessions, risk factors, and recommendations: Looking ahead. *Law and Human Behavior, 34*, 49–52.

Kassin, S. M., Dror, I. E., & Kukucka, J. (2013). The forensic confirmation bias: Problems, perspectives, and proposed solutions. *Journal of Applied Research in Memory and Cognition, 2*, 42–52.

Kassin, S. M., Ellsworth, P. C., & Smith, V. L. (1989). The "general acceptance" of psychological research on eyewitness testimony: A survey of the experts. *American Psychologist, 44*, 1089–1098.

Kassin, S. M., & Fong, C. T. (1999). "I'm innocent!": Effects of training on judgments of truth and deception in the interrogation room. *Law and Human Behavior, 23*, 499–516.

Kassin, S. M., Goldstein, C. J., & Savitsky, K. (2003). Behavioral confirmation in the interrogation room: On the dangers of presuming guilt. *Law and Human Behavior, 27*, 187–203.

Kassin, S. M., & Gudjonsson, G. H. (2004). The psychology of confessions: A review of the literature and issues. *Psychological Science in the Public Interest, 5*, 33–67.

Kassin, S. M., & Kiechel, K. L. (1996). The social psychology of false confessions: Compliance, internalization, and confabulation. *Psychological Science, 7*, 125–128.

Kassin, S. M., Leo, R. A., Meissner, C. A., Richman, K. D., Colwell, L. H., Leach, A. M., & La Fon, D. (2007). Police interviewing and interrogation: A self-report survey of police practices and beliefs. *Law and Human Behavior, 31*, 381–400.

Kassin, S. M., & McNall, K. (1991). Police interrogations and confessions. *Law and Human Behavior, 15*, 231–251.

Kassin, S. M., Meissner, C. A., & Norwick R. J. (2005). "I'd know a false confession if I saw one": A comparative study of college students and police investigations. *Law and Human Behavior, 29*, 211–227.

Kassin, S. M., & Neumann, K. (1997). On the power of confession evidence. *Law and Human Behavior, 21*, 469–484.

Kassin, S. M., & Sukel, H. (1997). Coerced confessions and the jury: An experimental test of the "harmless error" rule. *Law and Human Behavior, 21*, 27–46.

Kassin, S. M., Tubb, V. A., Hosch, H. M., & Memon, A. (2001). On the "general acceptance" of eyewitness testimony research: A new survey of the experts. *American Psychologist, 56*, 405–416.

Kassin, S. M., & Wrightsman, L. S. (1980). Prior confessions and mock juror verdicts. *Journal of Applied Social Psychology, 10*, 133–146.

Kassin, S. M., & Wrightsman, L. S. (1985). Confession evidence. In S. Kassin & L. Wrightsman (Eds.), *The psychology of evidence and trial procedure* (pp. 67–94). Beverly Hills, CA: Sage.

Keenan, J. M., MacWhinney, B., & Mayhew, D. (1977). Pragmatics in memory: A study of natural conversation. *Journal of verbal learning and verbal behavior, 16*, 549–560.

Kelley, D. M. (2005). Hypovolemic shock: An overview. *Critical Care Nursing Quarterly, 28*, 2–19.

Kemp, R., Towell, N., & Pike, G. (1997). When seeing should not be believing: Photographs, credit cards and fraud. *Applied Cognitive Psychology, 11*, 211–222.

Kemp, S., & Burt, C. D. B. (2006). Memories of uncertain origin: Dreamt or real? *Memory, 14*, 87–93.

Kemp, S., Burt, C. D. B., & Sheen, M. (2003). Remembering dreamt and actual experiences. *Applied Cognitive Psychology, 17*, 577–591.

Kendall-Tackett, K. A., Williams, L. M., & Finkelhor, D. (1993). Impact of sexual abuse on children: A review and synthesis of recent empirical studies. *Psychological Bulletin, 113*, 164–180.

Kerr, N. L., Kramer, G. P., Carroll, J. S., & Alfini, J. J. (1991). On the effectiveness of voir dire in criminal cases with prejudicial pretrial publicity: An empirical study. *American University Law Review, 40*, 665–693.

Kerstholt, J. H., & Jackson, J. L. (1998). Judicial decision making: Order of evidence presentation and availability of background information. *Applied Cognitive Psychology, 12*, 445–454.

Kerstholt, J. H., Jansen, N. J. M., Amelsvoorty, A. G., & Broeders, A. P. A. (2006). Earwitnesses: Effects of accent, retention and telephone. *Applied Cognitive Psychology, 20*, 187–197.

Kihlstrom, J. F., & Schacter, D. L. (2000). "Functional amnesia." In F. Boller & J. Grafman (Eds.), *The Handbook of neuropsychology* 2nd ed., vol. 2 (pp. 409–427). Amsterdam: Elsevier.

Kim, J. J., Song, E. Y., & Kosten, T. A. (2006). Stress effects in the hippocampus: Synaptic plasticity and memory. *International Journal on the Biology of Stress, 9*, 1–11.

Kintsch, W., & Bates, E. (1977). Recognition memory for statements from a classroom lecture. *Journal of Experimental Psychology: Human Learning and Memory, 3*, 150–159.

Kircher, J. C., Horowitz, S. W., & Raskin, D. C. (1988). Meta-analysis of mock crime studies of the control question polygraph technique. *Law and Human Behavior, 12*, 79–90.

Kleider, H. M., Cavrak, S. E., & Knuycky, L. R. (2012). Looking like a criminal: Stereotypical black facial features promote face source memory error. *Memory & Cognition, 40*, 1200–1213.

Knight, J. R., Palacios, J. N., & Shannon, M. (1999). Prevalence of alcohol problems among pediatric residents. *Archives of Pediatric and Adolescent Medicine, 153*, 1181–1183.

Koenig, M. A., & Sabbach, M. (2013). Selective social learning: New perspectives on learning from others. *Developmental Psychology, 49*, 399–403.

Köhnken, G., Milne, R., Memon, A., & Bull, R. (1999). The cognitive interview: A meta-analysis. *Psychology, Crime & Law, 5*, 3–27.

Kollins, S. H. (2003). Delay discounting is associated with substance use in college students. *Addictive Behaviors, 28*, 1167–1173.

Köster, O., & Schiller, N. O. (1997). Different influences of the native language of a listener on speaker recognition. *Forensic Linguistics, 4*, 18–28.

Köster, O., Hess, M. M., Schiller, N. O., & Künzel, H. J. (1998). The correlation between auditory speech sensitivity and speaker recognition ability. *Forensic Linguistics, 5*, 22–32.

Kovera, M. B., Penrod, S. D., Pappas, C., & Thill, D. L. (1997). Identification of computer-generated facial composites. *Journal of Applied Psychology, 82*, 235–246.

Krafka, C., & Penrod, S. (1985). Reinstatement of context in a field experiment on eyewitness identification. *Journal of Personality and Social Psychology, 49*, 58–69.

Krähenbühl, S., Blades, M., & Eiser, C. (2009). The effect of repeated questioning on children's accuracy and consistency in eyewitness testimony. *Legal and Criminological Psychology, 14*(2), 263–278.

Kramer, G. P., Kerr, N. L., & Carroll, J. S. (1990). Pretrial publicity, judicial remedies, and jury bias. *Law and Human Behavior, 14*, 409–438.

Krauss, R. M., Freyberg, R., & Morsella, E. (2002). Inferring speakers' physical attributes from their voices. *Journal of Experimental Social Psychology, 38*, 618–625.

Kuehnle, K., & Connell, M. (2011). Managing children's emotional and clinical needs. In M. E. Lamb, D. J. La Rooy, L. C. Malloy, & C. Katz (Eds.). (2011). *Children's testimony: A handbook of psychological research and forensic practice* (2nd ed., pp. 179–198). New York: Wiley-Blackwell.

Kumho Tire Company v. Carmichael. 119 S. Ct. 1167. (1999).

Künzel, H. J. (2000). Effects of voice disguise on speaking fundamental frequency. *International Journal of Forensic Linguistics, 7*, 149–179.

La Rooy, D., Katz, C., Malloy, L. C., & Lamb, M. E. (2010). Do we need to rethink guidance on repeated interviews? *Psychology, Public Policy & Law, 16*, 373–392.

La Rooy, Malloy, L. C., & Lamb, M. E. (2011). The development of memory in childhood. In M. E. Lamb, D. J. La Rooy, L. C. Malloy, & C. Katz (Eds.). *Children's testimony: A handbook of psychological research and forensic practice* (2nd ed., pp. 49–68). New York: Wiley-Blackwell.

Laible, D., & Panfile, T. (2009). Mother-child reminiscing in the context of secure attachment relationships. In J. A. Quas & R. Fivush (Eds.), *Emotion and memory in development: Biological, cognitive, and social considerations* (pp. 166–195). New York: Oxford University Press.

Lamb, M. E., Hershkowitz, I., Orbach, Y., & Esplin, P. W. (2008). *Tell me what happened: Structured investigative interviews of child victims and witnesses.* New York: Wiley.

Lamb, M. E., Malloy, L. C., & La Rooy, D. J.(2011a). Setting realistic expectations: Developmental characteristics, capacities and limitations. In M. E. Lamb, D. J. La Rooy, L. C. Malloy, & C. Katz (Eds.), *Children's testimony: A handbook of psychological research and forensic practice* (2nd ed., pp. 15–48). New York: Wiley-Blackwell.

Lamb, M. E., La Rooy, D. J., Malloy, L. C., & Katz, C. (Eds.). (2011b). *Children's testimony: A handbook of psychological research and forensic practice* (2nd ed.). New York: Wiley-Blackwell.

Lamb, M. E., Orbach, Y., Sternberg, K. J., Hershkowitz, I., & Horowitz, D. (2000). Accuracy of investigators' verbatim notes of their forensic interviews with alleged child abuse victims. *Law and Human Behavior, 24*, 699–708.

Lamb, M. E., Orbach, Y., Warren, A., Esplin, P., & Hershkowitz, I. (2007). Enhancing performance: Factors affecting the informativeness of young witnesses. In M. P. Toglia, J. D. Read, D. F. Ross, & R. C. Lindsay (Eds.), *The handbook of eyewitness psychology: Volume 1. Memory for events* (pp. 429–451). Mahwah, NJ: Erlbaum.

Lampinen, J. M., Meier, C. R., Arnal, J. D., & Leding, J. K. (2005). Compelling untruths: Content borrowing and vivid false memories. *Journal of Experimental Psychology: Learning, Memory, and Cognition, 31,* 954.

Lancaster, G. L. J., Vrij, A., Hope, L., & Waller, B. (2013). Sorting the liars from the truth tellers: The benefits of asking unanticipated questions on lie detection. *Applied Cognitive Psychology, 27,* 107–114.

Laney, C. (2013). The sources of memory errors. In D. Reisberg (Ed.), *The Oxford handbook of cognitive psychology* (pp. 232–242). New York: Oxford University Press.

Laney, C., Heuer, F., & Reisberg, D. (2003). Thematically-induced arousal in naturally-occurring emotional memories. *Applied Cognitive Psychology, 17,* 995–1004.

Laney, C., & Loftus, E. F. (2005). Traumatic memories are not necessarily accurate memories. *Canadian Journal of Psychiatry, 50,* 823–828.

Laney, C., Morris, E. K., Bernstein, D. M., Wakefield, B. M., & Loftus, E. F. (2008). Asparagus, a love story: Healthier eating could be just a false memory away. *Experimental Psychology, 55,* 291.

Langleben, D., & Campbell, J. C. (2013). Using brain imaging for lie detection: Where science, law, and policy collide. *Psychology, Public Policy, and Law, 19,* 222–234.

LaPaglia, J. A., & Chan, J. C. K. (2012). Retrieval does not always enhance suggestibility: Testing can improve witness identification performance. *Law and Human Behavior, 36,* 478–487.

Lassiter, G. D., & Geers, A. L. (2004). Bias and accuracy in the evaluation of confession evidence. In D. Lassiter (Ed.), *Interrogations, confessions, and entrapment* (pp. 197–214). New York: Kluwer Academic/Plenum.

Lassiter, G. D., Geers, A. L., Handley, I. M., Weiland, P. E., & Munhall, P. J. (2002). Videotaped interrogations and confessions: A simple change in camera perspective alters verdicts in simulated trials. *Journal of Applied Psychology, 87,* 867–874.

Leach, A. M., Lindsay, R. C. L., Koehler, R., Beaudry, J. L., Bala, N. C., Lee, K., & Talwar, V. (2009). The reliability of lie detection performance. *Law and Human Behavior, 33,* 96–109.

Leach, A. M., Talwar, V., Lee, K., Bala, N., & Lindsay, R. C. L. (2004). "Intuitive" lie detection of children's deception by law enforcement officials and university students. *Law and Human Behavior, 28,* 661–685.

Lee, H., Roh, S., & Kim, D. J. (2009). Alcohol-induced blackout. *International Journal of Environmental Research and Public Health, 6,* 2783–2792

Leichtman, M. D., & Ceci, S. J. (1995). The effects of stereotypes and suggestions on preschoolers' reports. *Developmental Psychology, 31,* 568–578.

Leins, D. A., Fisher, R. P., & Vrij, A. (2012). Drawing on liars' lack of cognitive flexibility: Detecting deception through varying report modes. *Applied Cognitive Psychology, 26,* 601–607.

Leippe, M., & Eisenstadt, D. (2007). Eyewitness confidence and the confidence-accuracy relationship in memory for people. In R. C. L. Lindsay, D. F. Ross, J. D. Read, & M. P. Toglia (Eds.), *The handbook of eyewitness psychology: Volume 2. Memory for people* (pp. 377–425). Mahwah, NJ: Erlbaum.

Leippe, M., & Eisenstadt, D. (2009). The influence of eyewitness expert testimony on jurors' beliefs and judgments. In B. L. Cutler (Ed.), *Expert testimony on the psychology of eyewitness identification* (pp. 169–199). New York: Oxford University Press.

Leo, R. A., & Liu, B. (2009). What do potential jurors know about police interrogation techniques and false confessions? *Behavioral Sciences and the Law, 27,* 381–399.

Leo, R. A., Neufeld, P. J., Drizin, S. A., & Taslitz, A. E. (2013). Promoting accuracy in the use of confession evidence: An argument for pre-trial reliability assessments to prevent wrongful convictions. *Temple Law Review, 85,* 759–802.

Lepore, S., & Sesco, B. (1994). Distorting children's reports and interpretations of events through suggestion. *Journal of Applied Psychology, 79,* 108–120.

Levett, L. M. (2013). Co-witness information influences whether a witness is likely to choose from a lineup. *Legal and Criminological Psychology, 18,* 168–180.

Levett, L. M., Danielsen, E. M., Kovera, M. B., & Cutler, B. L. (2005). The psychology of jury and juror decision making. In N. Brewer & K. D. Williams (Eds.), *Psychology and law: An empirical perspective* (pp. 365–406). New York: Guilford Press.

Levin, D., Momen, N., Drivdahl, S., & Simons, D. (2000). Change blindness: The metacognitive error of overestimating change-detection ability. *Visual Cognition, 7,* 397–412.

Levine, L. J., & Pizarro, D. A. (2004). Emotion and memory narrowing: A grumpy overview. *Social Cognition, 22,* 530–554.

Lieberman, J. (2009). The psychology of the jury instruction process. In J. Lieberman & D. Krauss (Eds.), *Jury psychology: Social aspects of trial processes* (pp. 129–156). Burlington, VT: Ashgate.

Lieberman, J., & Arndt, J. (2000). Understanding the limits of limiting instructions: Social psychological explanations for the failures of instructions to disregard pretrial publicity and other inadmissible evidence. *Psychology, Public Policy, and Law, 6,* 677–711.

Lindsay, D. S. (2002). Children's source monitoring. In H. L. Westcott, G. M. Davies, & R. H. C. Bull (Eds.), *Children's testimony: A handbook of psychological research and forensic practice* (pp. 83–98). New York: Wiley.

Lindsay, D. S., Hagen, L., Read, J. D., Wade, K. A., & Garry, M. (2004). True photographs and false memories. *Psychological Science, 15,* 149–154.

Lindsay, D. S., & Read, J. D. (1995). "Memory work" and recovered memories of childhood sexual abuse: Scientific evidence and public, professional, and personal issues. *Psychology, Public Policy, and Law, 1,* 846–908

Lindsay, R. C. L., & Wells, G. L. (1980). What price justice? Exploring the relationship between lineup fairness and identification accuracy. *Law and Human Behavior, 4,* 303–314.

Lindsay, R. C. L., Wells, G. L., & Rumpell, C. M. (1981). Can people detect eyewitness-identification accuracy within and across situations? *Journal of Applied Psychology, 66,* 79–89.

Lindsay, R. C. L., Semmler, C., Weber, N., Brewer, N., & Lindsay, M. R. (2008). How variations in distance affect eyewitness reports and identification accuracy. *Law and Human Behavior, 32,* 526–535.

Linton, M. (1975). Memory for real-world events. In D. H. Norman & D. E. Runelhart (Eds.), *Exploration in cognition* (pp. 376–404). San Francisco: Freeman.

Linton, M. (1978). Real world memory after six years: An in vivo study of very long term memory. In Gruneberg, M. M., Morris, P. E., & Sykes, R. N. (Eds.), *Practical aspects of memory* (pp. 69–76). New York: Academic Press.

Linton, M. (1982). Transformations of memory in everyday life. In U. Neisser (Ed.), *Memory observed: Remembering in natural contexts* (pp. 77–92). San Francisco: Freeman.

Linton, M. (1986). Ways of searching and the contents of memory. In D. C. Rubin (Ed.), *Autobiographical memory* (pp. 50–67). Cambridge, England: Cambridge University Press.

Liu, C. H., Chen, W., Han, H., & Shan, S. (2013). Effects of image preprocessing on face matching and recognition in human observers. *Applied Cognitive Psychology, 27,* 718–724.

Liu, D., Vanderbilt, K. E., & Heyman, G. D. (2013). Selective trust: Children's use of intention and outcome of past testimony. *Developmental Psychology, 49,* 439–445.

Loftus, E. F. (1979). Reactions to blatantly contradictory information. *Memory & Cognition, 7*(5), 368–374.

Loftus, E. F. (2003). Make-believe memories. *American Psychologist, 58*, 867–873.

Loftus, E. F. (2004). Memories of things unseen. *Current Directions in Psychological Science, 13*, 145–147.

Loftus, E. F., Garry, M., & Feldman, J. (1994). Forgetting sexual trauma: What does it mean when 38% forget? *Journal of Consulting and Clinical Psychology, 62*, 1177–1181.

Loftus, E. F., & Greene, E. (1980). Warning: Even memory for faces may be contagious. *Law and Human Behavior, 4*, 323–334.

Loftus, E. F., & Guyer, M. J. (2002a). Who abused Jane Doe?: The hazards of the single case study: Part I. *Skeptical Inquirer, 26*, 24–32.

Loftus, E. F., & Guyer, M. J. (2002b). Who abused Jane Doe?: Part 2. *Skeptical Inquirer, 26*, 37–40, 44.

Loftus, E. F., & Ketcham, K. (1996). *The myth of repressed memory: False memories and allegations of sexual abuse.* New York: St. Martin's Griffin.

Loftus, E. F., Loftus, G. R., & Messo, J. (1987). Some facts about "weapon focus." *Law and Human Behavior, 11*, 55–62.

Loftus, E. F., & Palmer, J. C. (1974). Reconstruction of automobile destruction: An example of the interaction between language and memory. *Journal of Verbal Learning and Verbal Behavior, 13*, 585–589.

Loftus, E. F., Schooler, J. W., Boone, S. M. N., & Kline, D. (1987). Time went by so slowly: Overestimation of event duration by males and females. *Applied Cognitive Psychology, 1*, 3–13.

Loftus, G. R. (1985). Picture perception: Effects of luminance on available information and information-extraction rate. *Journal of Experimental Psychology: General, 114*, 342–356.

Loftus, G. R., & Harley, E. M. (2005). Why is it easier to identify someone close than far away? *Psychonomic Bulletin and Review, 12*, 43–65.

Luus, C. A. E., & Wells, G. L. (1991). Eyewitness identification and the selection of distracters for lineups. *Law and Human Behavior, 15*, 43–57.

Luus, C. A. E., & Wells, G. L. (1994). The malleability of eyewitness confidence: Co-witness and perseverance effects. *Journal of Applied Psychology, 79*, 714–723.

Lynn, S. J., Neuschatz, J., Fite, R., & Rhue, J. R. (2001). *Hypnosis and memory: Implications for the courtroom and psychotherapy.* New York: Guilford Press.

Lyon, T. D. (2002). Child witnesses and the oath. In H. L. Westcott, G. M. Davies, & R. H. C. Bull (Eds.), *Children's testimony: A handbook of psychological research and forensic practice* (pp. 245–260). New York: Wiley.

Lyon, T. D. (2011). Assessing the competency of child witnesses: Best practice informed by psychology and law. In M. E. Lamb, D. J. La Rooy, L. C. Malloy, & C. Katz (Eds.), *Children's testimony: A handbook of psychological research and forensic practice* (2nd ed., pp. 69–86). New York: Wiley-Blackwell.

Lyon, T. D., Malloy, L. C., Quas, J. A., & Talwar, V. (2008). Coaching, truth induction, and young maltreated children's false allegations and false denials. *Child Development, 79*, 914–929.

Lyon, T. D., & Saywitz, K. J. (2000). *Qualifying children to take the oath: Materials for interviewing professionals.*

Maass, A., & Köhnken, G. (1989). Eyewitness identification: Simulating the "weapon effect." *Law and Human Behavior, 13*, 397–408.

Mack, A., & Rock, I. (1998). *Inattentional blindness.* Cambridge, MA: MIT Press.

Mack, J. E. (1994). *Abduction: Human encounters with aliens.* New York: Charles Scribner's Sons.

MacLin, O. H., & Malpass, R. S. (2003). The ambiguous-race face illusion. *Perception, 32*, 249–252.

Madon, S., Yang, Y., Smalarz, L., Guyll, M., & Scherr, K. (2013). How factors present during the immediate interrogation situation produce short-sighted confession decisions. *Law and Human Behavior*, *37*, 60–74.

Magnussen, S., & Melinder, A. (2012). What psychologists know and believe about memory: A survey of practitioners. *Applied Cognitive Psychology*, *26*, 54–60.

Malloy, L. C., Shulman, E. P., & Cauffman, E. (2014). Interrogations, confessions, and guilty pleas among serious adolescent offenders. *Law and Human Behavior*, *38*, 181 193.

Malpass, R., Ross, S., Meissner, C., & Marcon, J. (2009). The need for expert psychological testimony on eyewitness identification. In B. L. Cutler (Ed.), *Expert testimony on the psychology of eyewitness identification* (pp. 3–27). New York: Oxford University Press.

Malpass, R. S., Tredoux, C. G., & McQuiston-Surrett, D. (2007). Lineup construction and lineup fairness. In R. C. L. Lindsay, D. F. Ross, J. D. Read, & M. P. Toglia (Eds.), *The handbook of eyewitness psychology: Volume 2. Memory for people* (pp. 155–178). Mahwah, NJ: Erlbaum.

Malpass, R. S., Tredoux, C. G., & McQuiston-Surrett, D. (2009). Public policy and sequential lineups. *Legal and Criminological Psychology*, *14*, 1–12.

Mann, S., Vrij, A., & Bull, R. (2004). Detecting true lies: Police officers' ability to detect suspects' lies. *Journal of Applied Psychology*, *89*, 137–149.

Mann, S. A., Vrij, A., Fisher, R. P., & Robinson, M. (2008). See no lies, hear no lies: Differences in discrimination accuracy and response bias when watching or listening to police suspect interviews. *Applied Cognitive Psychology*, *22*, 1062–1071.

Manson v. Brathwaite. 432 U.S. 98, 97 S. Ct. 2243. (1977).

Mansour, J. K., Beaudry, J. L., Bertrand, M. I., Kalmet, N., Melsom, E. I., & Lindsay, R. C. L. (2012). Impact of disguise on identification decisions and confidence with simultaneous and sequential lineups. *Law and Human Behavior*, *36*, 513–526.

Marche, T. A., Brainerd, C. J., & Reyna, V. (2010). Distinguishing true from false memories in forensic contexts: Can phenomenology tell us what is real? *Applied Cognitive Psychology*, *24*, 1168–1182.

Masip, J., Herrero, C., Garrido, E., & Barba, A. (2011). Is the Behavior Analysis Interview just common sense? *Applied Cognitive Psychology*, *25*, 593–604.

Matsumoto, D., & Hwang, H. S. (2011a). Evidence for training the ability to read microexpressions of emotion. *Motivation and Emotion*, *35*(2), 181–191.

Matsumoto, D., & Hwang, H. S. (2011b). Judgments of facial expressions of emotion in profile. *Emotion*, *11*, 1223–1229.

Mauldin, M. A., & Laughery, K. (1981). Composite production effects on subsequent facial recognition. *Journal of Applied Psychology*, *66*, 351–357.

Mayall, B. (2008). Conversations with children. In P. Christensen & A. James (Eds.), *Research with children: Perspective and practices* (2nd ed., pp. 109–122). New York: Routledge.

Mazzoni, G., & Lynn, S. J. (2007). Using hypnosis in eyewitness memory: Past and current issues. In R. C. L. Lindsay, D. F. Ross, J. D. Read & M. P. Toglia (Eds.), *The handbook of eyewitness psychology: Volume 2. Memory for people* (pp. 3–34). Mahwah, NJ: Erlbaum.

Mazzoni, G., & Memon, A. (2003). Imagination can create false autobiographical memories. *Psychological Science*, *14*(2), 186–188.

Mazzoni, G. A., Loftus, E. F., & Kirsch, I. (2001). Changing beliefs about implausible autobiographical events: A little plausibility goes a long way. *Journal of Experimental Psychology Applied*, *7*, 51–59.

McAllister, H. A, Dale, R. H. I., Bregman, N. J., McCabe, A., & Cotton, C. R. (1993). When eyewitnesses are also earwitnesses: Effects on visual and voice identifications. *Basic and Applied Social Psychology*, *14*, 161–170.

McDaniel, M. A., Roediger, H. L., & McDermott, K. B. (2007). Generalizing test-enhanced learning from the laboratory to the classroom. *Psychonomic Bulletin & Review, 14*, 200–206.

McDermott, K. B., & Roediger III, H. L. (1998). Attempting to avoid illusory memories: Robust false recognition of associates persists under conditions of explicit warnings and immediate testing. *Journal of Memory and Language, 39*, 508–520.

McGaugh, J. L. (2000). Memory—a century of consolidation. *Science, 287*, 248–251.

McKone, E., & Robbins, R. (2007). The evidence rejects the expertise hypothesis: Reply to Gauthier & Bukach. *Cognition, 103*, 331–336.

McNally, R. J. (2003). *Remembering trauma*. Cambridge, MA: Belknap Press of Harvard University Press.

McNally, R. J., Lasko, N. B., Clancy, S. A., Macklin, M. L., Pitman, R. K., & Orr, S. P. (2004). Psychophysiological responding during script-driven imagery in people reporting abduction by space aliens. *Psychological Science, 15*, 493–497.

McQuiston, D. E., & Malpass, R. S. (2002). Validity of the mockwitness paradigm: Testing the assumptions. *Law and Human Behavior, 26*, 439–453.

McQuiston-Surrett, D. E., Malpass, R. S., & Tredoux, C. G. (2006). Sequential vs. simultaneous lineups: A review of methods, data, and theory. *Psychology, Public Policy and Law, 12*, 137–169.

Mecklenburg, S. H., Bailey, P. J., & Larson, M. R. (2008). The Illinois field study. *Law and Human Behavior, 32*, 22–27.

Megreya, A. M., Bindemann, M., Havard, C., & Burton, A. M. (2012). Identity-lineup location influences target selection: Evidence from eye movements. *Journal of Police and Criminal Psychology, 27*, 167–178.

Meijer, E., & Verschuere, B. (2010). The polygraph and the detection of deception. *Journal of Forensic Psychology Practice, 10*, 325–338.

Meissner, C. A., & Brigham, J. C. (2001). Thirty years of investigating the own-race bias in memory for faces: A meta-analytic review. *Psychology, Public Policy and Law, 7*, 3–35.

Meissner, C. A., & Kassin, S. M. (2002). "He's guilty!": Investigator bias in judgments of truth and deception. *Law and Human Behavior, 26*, 469–480.

Meissner, C. A., Redlich, A. D., Bhatt, S., & Brandon, S. (2012). Interview and interrogation methods and their effects on true and false confessions. Final report to the Campbell Collaboration. Available at www.campbellcollaboration. org.

Meissner, C. A., Sporer, S. L., & Schooler, J. W. (2007). Person descriptions as eyewitness evidence. In R. C. L. Lindsay, D. F. Ross, J. D. Read & M. P. Toglia (Eds.), *The handbook of eyewitness psychology: Volume 2. Memory for people* (pp. 3–34). Mahwah, NJ: Erlbaum.

Meissner, C. A., Sporer, S. L., & Susa, K. J. (2008). A theoretical and meta-analytic review of the relationship between verbal descriptions and identification accuracy in memory for faces. *European Journal of Cognitive Psychology, 20*, 414–455.

Melnyk, L., Crossman, A. M., & Scullin, M. H. (2007). The suggestibility of children's memory. In M. P. Toglia, J. D. Read, D. F. Ross, D. F., & R. C. L. Lindsay (Eds.), *The handbook of eyewitness psychology: Volume 1. Memory for events* (pp. 401–427). Mahwah, NJ: Erlbaum.

Memon, A., Fraser, J., Colwell, K. Odinot, G., & Mastroberadino, S. (2010). Distinguishing truthful from invented accounts using reality monitoring criteria, *Legal and Criminological Psychology, 15*, 177–194.

Memon, A., Havard, C., Clifford, B., Gabbert, F., & Watt, M. (2011). A field evaluation of the VIPER system: A new technique for eliciting eyewitness identification evidence. *Psychology, Crime and Law, 17*, 711–729.

Memon, A., & Higham, P. A. (1999). A review of the cognitive interview. *Psychology, Crime & Law, 5*, 177–196.

Memon, A., Hope, L., & Bull, R. (2003). Exposure duration: Effects on eyewitness accuracy and confidence. *British Journal of Psychology, 94*, 339–354.

Memon, A., Meissner, C. A., & Fraser, J. (2010). The cognitive interview: A meta-analytic review and study space analysis of the past 25 years. *Psychology, Public Policy and Law, 16*, 340–372.

Mickes, L., Flowe, H. A., & Wixted, J. T. (2012). Receiver operating characteristic analysis of eyewitness memory: Comparing the diagnostic accuracy of simultaneous versus sequential lineups. *Journal of Experimental Psychology: Applied, 18*, 361–376.

Mitchell, T., Haw, R., Pfeifer, J., & Meissner, C. (2005). Racial bias in mock juror-decision-making: A meta-analytic review of defendant treatment. *Law and Human Behavior, 29*, 621–637.

Molinaro, P. F., Arndorfer, A., & Charman, S. D. (2013). Appearance-change instruction effects on eyewitness identification accuracy are not moderated by amount of appearance change. *Law and Human Behavior, 37*, 432–440.

Moran, G., & Cutler, B. L. (1991). The prejudicial impact of pretrial publicity. *Journal of Applied Social Psychology, 21*, 345–367.

Morgan, C., Hazlett, G., Doran, A., Garrett, S., Hoyt, G., Thomas, P., Baronoski, M., & Southwick, S. (2004). Accuracy of eyewitness memory for persons encountered during exposure to highly intense stress. *International Journal of Law and Psychiatry, 27*, 264–279.

Morgan, C., Southwick, S., Steffian, G., Hazlett, G., & Loftus, E. F. (2013). Misinformation can influence memory for recently experienced, highly stressful events. *International Journal of Law and Psychiatry, 36*, 11–17.

Moriarty, J. C. (2008). Flickering admissibility: Neuroimaging evidence in the U.S. courts. *Behavioral Sciences & the Law, 26*, 29–49.

Mueller-Johnson, K., & Ceci, S. J. (2004). Memory and suggestibility in older adults: Live event participation and repeated interview. *Applied Cognitive Psychology, 79*, 918–930.

Mullennix, J. W., Ross, A., Smith, C., Kuykendall, K., Conard, J., & Barb, S. (2011). Typicality effects on memory for voice: Implications for earwitness testimony. *Applied Cognitive Psychology, 25*, 29–34.

Mullennix, J. W., Stern, S. E., Grounds, B., Kalas, R., Flaherty, M., Kowalok, S., May, E., & Tessmer, B. (2010). Earwitness memory: Distortions for voice pitch and speaking rate. *Applied Cognitive Psychology, 24*, 513–526.

Murphy, G. L., & Shapiro, A. M. (1994). Forgetting of verbatim information in discourse. *Memory & Cognition, 22*, 85–94.

National Children's Advocacy Center. (2012). *The National Children's Advocacy Center's Child Forensic Interview Structure*. Huntsville, AL: Author.

National Research Council, Committee on Evaluation of Sound Spectrograms. (1979). *Theory and practice of voice identification*. Washington, DC: National Academies Press.

National Research Council, Committee on Identifying the Needs of the Forensic Sciences Community. (2009). *Strengthening forensic science in the United States: A path forward*. Washington, DC: National Academies Press.

National Research Council, Committee to Review the Scientific Evidence on the Polygraph, Division of Behavioral and Social Sciences and Education. (2003). *The polygraph and lie detection*. Washington, DC: National Academies Press.

Neel, R., Becker, V., Neuberg, S., & Kenrick D. (2012). Who expressed what emotion? Men grab anger, women grab happiness. *Journal of Experimental Social Psychology, 48*, 583–586.

Neil v. Biggers, 409 U.S. 188 (1972).

Neisser, U. (1981). John Dean's memory: A case study. *Cognition, 9*, 1–22.

Neisser, U., & Becklen, R. (1975). Selective looking: Attending to visually specified events. *Cognitive Psychology, 7,* 480–494.

Neisser, U., & Harsch, N. (1992). Phantom flashbulbs: False recollections of hearing the news about Challenger. In E. Winograd & U. Neisser (Eds.), *Affect and accuracy in recall studies of "flashbulb" memories* (pp. 9–31). New York: Cambridge University Press.

Nelson, E. C., Heath, A. C., Bucholz, K. K., Madden, P. A., Fu, Q., Knopik, V., Lynskey, M. T., Whitfield, J. B., Statham, D. J., & Martin, N. G. (2004). Genetic epidemiology of alcohol-induced blackouts. *Archives of General psychiatry, 61,* 257–263.

Nelson, K., & Fivush, R. (2000). Socialization of memory. In E. Tulving & F. I. M. Craik (Eds.), *The Oxford handbook of memory* (pp. 283–295). New York: Oxford University Press.

Neuschatz, J. S., Lawson, D. S., Swanner, J. K., Meissner, C. A., & Neuschatz, J. S. (2008). The effects of accomplice witnesses and jailhouse informants on jury decisionmaking. *Law and Human Behavior, 32,* 137–149.

Neuschatz, J. S., Preston, E., Burkett, A., Toglia, M. P., Lampinen, J. M., Neuschatz, J. S., Fairless, A. H., Lawson, D. S., Powers, R. A., & Godsell, C. A. (2005). The effects of post-identification feedback and age on retrospective eyewitness memory. *Applied Cognitive Psychology, 19,* 435–453.

Newman, M. L., Pennebaker, J. W., Berry, D. S., & Richards, J. M. (2003). Lying words: Predicting deception from linguistic styles. *Personality and Social Psychology Bulletin, 29,* 665–675.

Nirider, L. H., Tepfer, J. A., & Drizin, S. A. (2012). Combating contamination in confession cases. *University of Chicago Law Review, 79,* 837–862.

Noon, E., & Hollin, C. R. (1987). Lay knowledge of eyewitness behavior: A British Survey. *Applied Cognitive Psychology, 1,* 143–153.

Norris, R. J., & Redlich, A. D. (2012). At-risk populations under investigation and at trial. In B. L. Cutler (Ed.), *Conviction of the innocent: Lessons from psychological research* (pp. 13–32). Washington, DC APA.

Nysse-Carris, K. L., Bottoms, B. L., & Salerno, J. M. (2011). Experts' and novices' abilities to detect children's high-stakes lies of omission. *Psychology, Public Policy and Law, 17,* 76–98.

Oberlander, L. B., & Goldstein, N. E. (2001). A review and update on the practice of evaluating Miranda comprehension. *Behavioral Sciences and the Law, 19,* 453–471.

O'Connell, M. J., Garmoe, W., & Goldstein, N. E. S. (2005). Miranda comprehension in adults with mental retardation and the effects of feedback style on suggestibility. *Law and Human Behavior, 29,* 359–369.

Odinot, G., Wolters, G., & Lavender, T. (2009). Repeated partial eyewitness questioning causes confidence inflation but not retrieval-induced forgetting. *Applied Cognitive Psychology, 23,* 90–97.

Oeberst, A. (2012). If anything else comes to mind . . . better keep it to yourself? Delayed recall is discrediting–unjustifiably. *Law and Human Behavior, 36,* 266–274.

Oeberst, A., & Blank, H. (2012). Undoing suggestive influence on memory: The reversibility of the eyewitness misinformation effect. *Cognition, 125,* 141–159.

Ogloff, J. R. P., & Vidmar, N. (1994). The impact of pretrial publicity on jurors: A study to compare the relative effects of television and print media in a child sex abuse case. *Law and Human Behavior, 5,* 507–525.

Ogloff, R. P., & Rose, G. (2005). The comprehension of judicial instructions. In N. Brewer & K. D. Wilson (Eds.), *Psychology and Law: An empirical perspective* (pp. 407–444). New York: Guilford Press.

Oorsouw, K., & Merckelbach, H. (2012). The effects of alcohol on crime-related memories: A field study. *Applied Cognitive Psychology, 26,* 82–90.

Oppenheim, D., & Koren-Karie, N. (2009). Mother-child emotion dialogues. In J. A. Quas & R. Fivush (Eds.), *Emotion and memory in development: Biological, cognitive, and social considerations* (142–165). New York: Oxford University Press.

Orbach, Y., Hershkowitz, I., Lamb, M. E., Sternberg, K. J., Esplin, P. W., & Horowitz, D. (2000). Assessing the value of scripted protocols for forensic interviews of alleged abuse victims. *Child Abuse and Neglect, 24,* 733–752.

Orbach, Y., Lamb, M. E., La Rooy, D., & Pipe, M. E. (2012). A case study of witness consistency and memory recovery across multiple investigative interviews. *Applied Cognitive Psychology, 26,* 118–129.

Orbach, Y., Shiloach, H., & Lamb, M. E. (2007). Reluctant disclosers of child sexual abuse. In M. E. Pipe, M. E. Lamb, Y. Orbach, & A. C. Cedeborg (Eds.), *Child sexual abuse: Disclosure, delay, and denial* (pp. 115–134). Mahwah, NJ: Lawrence Erlbaum.

Ost, J., Vrij, A., Costall, A., & Bull, R. (2002). Crashing memories and reality monitoring: Distinguishing between perceptions, imaginations and "false memories." *Applied Cognitive Psychology, 16,* 125–134.

O'Sullivan, M., & Ekman, P. (2004). The wizards of deception detection. In P. A. Granhag & L. A. Stromwall (Eds.), *Deception detection in forensic contexts* (pp. 269–286). Cambridge, UK: Cambridge University Press.

Otto, A. L., Penrod, S. D., & Dexter, H. R. (1994). The biasing impact of pretrial publicity on juror judgments. *Law and Human Behavior, 18,* 453–469.

Owen-Kostelnik, J., Repucci, N. D., & Meyer, J. R. (2006). Testimony and interrogation of minors. *American Psychologist, 61,* 286–304.

Owens, J., Bower, G. H., & Black, J. B. (1979). The "soap opera" effect in story recall. *Memory & Cognition, 7,* 185–191.

Padawer-Singer, A., Singer, A., & Singer, R. (1977). Legal and social-psychological research in the effects of pretrial publicity on juries, numerical makeup of juries, nonunanimous verdict requirements. *Law and Psychology Review, 3,* 71–79.

Pardo, M. S., & Patterson, D. (2013). *Minds, brains, and law: The conceptual foundations of law and neuroscience.* N.Y.: Oxford University Press.

Patihis, L., Ho, L. Y., Tingen, I. W., Lilienfeld, S. O., & Loftus, E. F. (2013). Are the "memory wars" over? A scientist-practitioner gap in beliefs about repressed memory. *Psychological Science, 25,* 519–530.

Palmer, M. A., Brewer, N. W., Weber, N., & Nagesh, A. (2013). The confidence-accuracy relationship for eyewitness identification decisions: Effects of exposure duration, retention interval, and divided attention. *Journal of Experimental Psychology: Applied, 19,* 55–71.

Pashler, H., Rohrer, D., Cepeda, N. J., & Carpenter, S. K. (2007). Enhancing learning and retarding forgetting: Choices and consequences. *Psychonomic Bulletin & Review, 14,* 187–193.

Paterson, H., & Kemp, R. I. (2006). Comparing methods of encountering post-event information: The power of co-witness suggestion. *Applied Cognitive Psychology, 20,* 1083–1099.

Patihis, L., Ho, L. Y., Tingen, I. W., Lilienfeld, S. O., & Loftus, E. F. (2014). Are the "memory wars" over? A scientist-practitioner gap in beliefs about repressed memory. *Psychological Science, 25,* 519–530.

Patterson, K. E., & Baddeley, A. D. (1977). When face recognition fails. *Journal of Experimental Psychology: Human Learning & Memory, 3,* 406–417.

Payne, J. D., Nadel, L., Britton, W. B., & Jacobs, W. J. (2004). The biopsychology of trauma and memory. In D. Reisberg & P. Hertel (Eds.), *Memory and emotion. Series in affective science.* New York: Oxford University Press.

Paz-Alonso, P. M., & Goodman, G. S. (2008). Trauma and memory: Effects of post-event misinformation, retrieval order, and retention interval. *Memory, 16,* 58–75.

Peace, K. A., & Porter, S. (2004). A longitudinal investigation of the reliability of memories for trauma and other emotional experiences. *Applied Cognitive Psychology, 18*, 1143–1159.

Peace, K. A., & Porter S. (2011). Remembrance of lies past: A comparison of the features and consistency of truthful and fabricated trauma narratives. *Applied Cognitive Psychology, 25*, 414–423.

Pennington, N., & Hastie, R. (1993). The story model for juror decision making. In R. Hastie (Ed.), *Inside the juror: The psychology of juror decision making* (pp. 192–221). New York: Cambridge University Press.

Penrod, S., & Cutler, B. (1995). Witness confidence and witness accuracy: Assessing their forensic relation. *Psychology, Public Policy and Law, 1*, 817–960.

Perillo J. T., & Kassin, S. M. (2011). Insider interrogation: The lie, the bluff, and false confession. *Law and Human Behavior, 35*, 327–337.

Perry v. New Hampshire, 132 S. Ct. 716. (2012).

Perry, P. J., Argo, T. R., Barnett, M. J., Liesveld, J. L., Liskow, B., Hewrnan, J. M., Trnka, M. G., & Brabson, M. A. (2006). The association of alcohol-induced blackouts and grayouts to blood alcohol concentrations. *Journal of Forensic Science, 51*, 896–899.

Peters, D. O. (1988). Eyewitness memory and arousal in a natural setting. In M. M. Gruneberg, P. E. Morris & R. N. Sykes (Eds.), *Practical aspects of memory: Current research and issues* (vol. 1, pp. 89–94). New York: John Wiley and Sons.

Peterson, A. C. I., & Wright, D. B. (2002). Do differences in event descriptions cause different duration estimates? *Applied Cognitive Psychology, 16*, 769–783.

Peterson, C. (2010). "And I was very very crying": Child self-descriptions of distress as predictors of recall. *Applied Cognitive Psychology, 24*, 909–924.

Peterson, C. (2012). Children's autobiographical memories across the years: Forensic implications of childhood amnesia and eyewitness memory for stressful events. *Developmental Review, 32*, 278–306.

Peterson, C., & McCabe, A. (1994). A social interactionist account of developing decontextualized narrative skill. *Developmental Psychology, 30*, 937–948.

Peterson, C., & Warren, K. L. (2009). Injuries, emergency rooms, and children's memory: Factors contributing to individual differences. In J. A. Quas & R. Fivush (Eds.), *Emotion and memory in development: Biological, cognitive, and social considerations* (pp. 60–85). New York: Oxford University Press.

Pezdek, K. (2009). Content, form, and ethical issues concerning expert psychological testimony on eyewitness identification. In B. L. Cutler (Ed.), *Expert testimony on the psychology of eyewitness identification* (pp. 29–50). New York: Oxford University Press.

Pezdek, K. (2012). Fallible eyewitness memory and identification. In B. L. Cutler (Ed.), *Conviction of the innocent: Lessons from psychological research* (pp. 105–124). Washington, DC: American Psychological Association.

Pezdek, K., & Blandón-Gitlin, I. (2011). Imagining implausible events does not lead to false autobiographical memories: Commentary on Sharman & Scoboria (2009). *Applied Cognitive Psychology, 25*, 341–343.

Pezdek, K., Blandon-Gitlin, I., & Gabbay, P. (2006). Imagination and memory: Does imagining implausible events lead to false autobiographical memories? *Psychonomic Bulletin & Review, 13*, 764–769.

Pezdek, K., Finger, K., & Hodge, D. (1997). Planting false childhood memories: The role of event plausibility. *Psychological Science, 8*, 437–441.

Pezdek, K., & Hinz, T. (2002). The construction of false events in memory. In H. L. Westcott, G. M. Davies, & R. H. C. Bull (Eds.), *Children's testimony: A handbook of psychological research and forensic practice* (pp. 99–116). New York: Wiley.

Pezdek, K., Morrow, A., Blandon-Gitlin, I., Goodman, G. S., Quas, J. A., Saywitz, K. J., et al. (2004). Detecting deception in children: Event familiarity affects

Criterion-Based Content Analysis ratings. *Journal of Applied Psychology, 89*, 119–126.

Pezdek, K., O'Brien, M., & Wasson, C. (2012). Cross-race (but not same-race) face identification is impaired by presenting faces in a group rather than individually. *Law and Human Behavior, 36*, 488–495.

Phelps, E. A. (2012). Emotion's impact on memory. In L. Nadel & W. P. Sinnott-Armstrong (Eds.), *Memory and law* (pp. 7–26). New York: Oxford University Press.

Philippon, A., Cherryman, J., Bull, R., & Vrij, A. (2007). Earwitness identification performance: The effect of language, target, deliberate strategies and indirect measures. *Applied Cognitive Psychology, 21*, 539–550.

Phillips, M. R., McAuliff, B. D., Kovera, M. B., & Cutler, B. L. (1999). Double-blind photoarray administration as a safeguard against investigator bias. *Journal of Applied Psychology, 84*, 940–951.

Pickel, K. L. (1998). Unusualness and threat as possible causes of "weapon focus." *Memory, 6*, 277–295.

Pickel, K. L. (2006). Remembering and identifying menacing perpetrators: Exposure to violence and the weapon focus effect. In R. C. L. Lindsay, D. F. Ross, J. D. Read & M. P. Toglia (Eds.), *The handbook of eyewitness psychology: Volume 2. Memory for people* (pp. 339–359). Mahwah, NJ: Lawrence Erlbaum.

Pickel, K. L., & Staller, J. B. (2012). A perpetrator's accent impairs witnesses' memory for physical appearance. *Law and Human Behavior, 36*, 140–150.

Pigott, M. A., & Brigham, J. C. (1985). Relationship between accuracy of prior description and facial recognition. *Journal of Applied Psychology, 70*, 547–555.

Pigott, M. A., Brigham, J. C., & Bothwell, R. K. (1990). A field study on the relationship between quality of eyewitnesses' descriptions and identification accuracy. *Journal of Police Science and Administration, 17*, 84–88.

Pinker, S. (1994). *The language instinct: How the mind creates language*. London: Viking.

Pipe, M. -E., Lamb, M. E., Orbach, Y., & Cederborg, A. -C. (2007a). *Child sexual abuse: Disclosure, delay, and denial*. Mahwah, NJ: Erlbaum.

Pipe, M. -E., Lamb, M. E., Orbach, Y., & Esplin, P. W. (2004). Recent research on children's testimony about experienced and witnessed events. *Developmental Review, 24*, 440–468.

Pipe, M. -E., Thierry, K. L., & Lamb, M. E. (2007b). The development of event memory: Implications for child witness testimony. In M. P. Toglia, J. D. Read, D. F. Ross & R. C. Lindsay (Eds.), *The handbook of eyewitness psychology: Volume 1. Memory for events* (pp. 453–478). Mahwah, NJ: Erlbaum.

Pipe, M. -E., & Wilson, J. C. (1994). Cues and secrets: Influences on children's event reports. *Developmental Psychology, 30*, 515–525.

Piper, A., Lellevik, L., & Krizer, R. (2008). What's wrong with believing in repression? A review for legal professionals. *Psychology, Public Policy and Law, 14*, 223–242.

Platz, S., & Hosch, H. (1988). Cross-racial/ethnic eyewitness identification: A field study, *Journal of Applied Social Psychology, 18*, 972–984.

Pollack, I., & Pickett, J. M. (1964). Intelligibility of excerpts from fluent speech: Auditory vs. structural context. *Journal of Verbal Learning and Verbal Behavior, 3*, 79–84.

Poole, D. A., Bruck, M., & Pipe, M. -E. (2011). Forensic interviewing aids: Do props help children answer questions about touching? *Current Directions in Psychological Science, 20*, 11–15.

Poole, D. A., & Lamb, M. E. (1998). *Investigative interviews of children: A guide for helping professionals*. Washington, DC: American Psychological Association.

Poole, D. A., & Lindsay, D. S. (1995). Interviewing preschoolers: Effects of nonsuggestive techniques, parental coaching, and leading questions on reports of nonexperienced events. *Journal of Experimental Child Psychology, 60*, 129–154.

Poole, D. A., & Lindsay, D. S. (2001). Children's eyewitness reports after exposure to misinformation from parents. *Journal of Experimental Psychology: Applied, 7*, 27–50.

Poole, D. A., & Lindsay, D. S. (2002). Reducing child witnesses' false reports of misinformation from parents. *Journal of Experimental Child Psychology, 81*, 117–140.

Poole, D. A., & White, L. (1991). Effects of question repetition on the eyewitness testimony of children and adults. *Developmental Psychology, 27*, 975–986.

Pope Jr., H. G., Gruber, A. J., Hudson, J. I., Huestis, M. A., & Yurgelun-Todd, D. (2001). Neuropsychological performance in long-term cannabis users. *Archives of General Psychiatry, 58*(10), 909–915.

Popper, K. R. (1963). *Conjectures and refutations: The growth of scientific knowledge.* London: Routledge.

Porter, D., Moss, A., & Reisberg, D. (2013). The appearance-change instruction does not improve line-up identification accuracy. *Applied Cognitive Psychology, 28*, 151–160.

Porter, S., & Peace, K. A. (2007). The scars of memory a prospective, longitudinal investigation of the consistency of traumatic and positive emotional memories in adulthood. *Psychological Science, 18*, 435–441.

Porter, S., & ten Brinke, L. (2008). Reading between the lies: Identifying concealed and falsified emotions in universal facial expressions. *Psychological Science, 19*, 508–514.

Posey, D., & Mozayani, A. (2007). The estimation of blood alcohol concentration. *Forensic Science, Medicine, and Pathology, 3*, 33–39.

Powell, M., & Thomson, D. (2002). Children's memories for repeated events. In H. L. Westcott, G. M. Davies, & R. H. C. Bull (Eds.), *Children's testimony: A handbook of psychological research and forensic practice* (pp. 69–82). New York: Wiley.

Pozzulo, J. (2006). Person description and identification by child eyewitnesses In R. C. L. Lindsay, D. F. Ross, J. D. Read, & M. P. Toglia (Eds.), *The handbook of eyewitness psychology: Volume 2. Memory for people* (pp. 283–308). Mahwah, NJ: Lawrence Erlbaum.

Principe, G., Kanaya, T., Ceci, S. J., & Singh, M. (2006). Believing is seeing: How rumors can engender false memories in preschoolers. *Psychological Science, 17*, 243–249.

Prinzmetal, W., Presti, D. E., & Posner, P. I. (1986). Does attention affect visual feature integration? *Journal of Experimental Psychology, 12*, 361–369.

Pritchard, M. E., & Keenan, J. M. (2002). Does jury deliberation really improve jurors' memories? *Applied Cognitive Psychology, 16*, 589–601.

Procter, E. E., & Yarmey, A. D. (2003). The effect of distributed learning on the identification of normal-tone and whispered voices. *Korean Journal of Thinking & Problem Solving, 13*, 17–29.

Purnell, T., Idsardi, W., & Baugh, J. (1999). Perceptual and phonetic experiments on American English dialect identification. *Journal of Language and Social Psychology, 18*, 10–30.

Quas, J. A., Goodman, G. S., Bidrose, S., Pipe, M. -E., Craw, S., & Ablin, D. S. (1999). Emotion and memory: Children's long-term remembering, forgetting, and suggestibility. *Journal of Experimental Child Psychology, 72*, 235–270.

Quas, J. A., Malloy, L. C., Melinder, A., Goodman, G. S., D'Mello, M., & Schaaf, J. (2007). Developmental differences in the effects of repeated interviews and interviewer bias on young children's event memory and false reports. *Developmental Psychology, 43*, 823–837.

Quinlivan, D. S., Neuschatz, J. S., Cutler, B. L., Wells, G. L., McClung, J., & Harker, D. L. (2012). Do pre-admonition suggestions moderate the effect of unbiased lineup instructions? *Legal and Criminological Psychology, 17*, 165–176.

R. v. J. (J. L.). [1999] 130 C.C.C. (3d) 541 (Que. C.A.).

R. v. Mohan. [1992] 2 S.C.R. 9.

Radelet, M. L., Bedau, H. A., & Putnam, C. E. (1992). *In spite of innocence: Erroneous convictions in capital cases.* Boston: Northeastern University Press.

Raichle, M. E. (2001). Cognitive neuroscience: Bold insights. *Nature, 412,* 128–130.

Rakover, S. (2013). Explaining the face-inversion effect: The face-scheme incompatibility (FSI) model. *Psychonomic Bulletin & Review, 20,* 665–692.

Raskin, D. C., & Esplin, P. W. (1991). Statement Validity Assessment: Interview procedures and content analysis of children's statements of sexual abuse. *Behavioral Assessment, 13,* 265–291.

Read, J. D. (1999). The recovered/false memory debate: Three steps forward, two steps back? *Expert Evidence, 7,* 1–24.

Read, J. D., & Connolly, D. A. (2007). The effects of delay on long-term memory for witnessed events. In M. P. Toglia, J. D. Read, D. F. Ross, & R. C. Lindsay. (Eds.), *The handbook of eyewitness psychology: Volume 1. Memory for events* (pp. 117–155). Mahwah, NJ: Erlbaum.

Read, J. D., & Desmarais, S. (2009). Expert psychology testimony on eyewitness identification: A matter of common sense? In B. L. Cutler (Ed.) *Expert testimony on the psychology of eyewitness identification* (pp. 115–141). Mahwah, NJ: Erlbaum.

Read, J. D., Tollestrup, P., Hammersley, R., McFadzen, F., & Christensen, A. (1990). The unconscious transference effect: Are innocent bystanders have misidentified? *Applied Cognitive Psychology, 4,* 3–31.

Read, J. D., Vokey, J. R., & Hammersley, R. (1990). Changing photos of faces: Effects of exposure duration and photo similarity on recognition and the accuracy-confidence relationship, *Journal of Experimental Psychology: Learning Memory & Cognition, 16,* 870–882.

Reder, L. M., Victoria, L. W., Manelis, A., Oates, J., Dutcher, J. M., Bates, J. T., Cook, S., Aizenstein, H. J., Quinlan, J., & Gyulai, F. (2013). Why it's easier to remember seeing a face we already know than one we don't: Preexisting memory representations facilitate memory formation. *Psychological Science, 24,* 363–372.

Redlich, A. D. (2007). Double jeopardy in the interrogation room for youths with mental illness. *American Psychologist, 62,* 609–611.

Redlich, A. D., Kulish, R., & Steadman, H. J. (2011). Comparing true and false confessions among persons with serious mental illness. *Psychology, Public Policy and Law, 17,* 394–418.

Reisberg, D. (2013a). *Cognition: Exploring the science of the mind* (5th ed.). New York: W. W. Norton.

Reisberg, D. (2013b). Visual imagery, spatial imagery. In D. Reisberg (Ed.), *The Oxford handbook of cognitive psychology.* New York: Oxford University Press.

Reisberg, D., & Hertel, P. (2004). *Memory and emotion.* New York: Oxford University Press.

Reisberg, D., & Heuer, F. (2004). Remembering emotional events. In D. Reisberg & P. Hertel (Eds.), *Memory and emotion* (pp. 3–41). New York: Oxford University Press.

Reisberg, D., McLean, J., & Goldfield, A. (1987). Easy to hear but hard to understand: A lip-reading advantage with intact auditory stimuli. In R. Campbell & B. Dodd (Eds.), *Hearing by eye: The psychology of lip-reading* (pp. 97–114). Hillsdale, NJ: Erlbaum.

Reyna V. F., & Farley, F. (2006). Risk and rationality in adolescent decision making. *Psychological Science in the Public Interest, 7,* 1–44.

Reyna, V. F., Mills, B., Estrada, S., & Brainerd, C. J. (2007). False memory in children: Data, theory, and legal implications. In M. P. Toglia, J. D. Read, D. F. Ross, & R. C. L. Lindsay (Eds.), *The handbook of eyewitness psychology: Volume 1. Memory for events* (pp. 479–507). Mahwah, NJ: Erlbaum.

Reynolds, B., Richards, J. B., Horn, K., & Karraker, K. (2004). Delay discounting and probability discounting as related to cigarette smoking status in adults. *Behavioral Processes, 65*, 35–42.

Rhodes, G. (2013). Face recognition. In D. Reisberg (Ed.), *The Oxford Handbook of Cognitive Psychology* (pp. 46–68). New York: Oxford University Press.

Rhodes, M. G., & Anastasi, J. S. (2012). The own-age bias in face recognition: A meta-analytic and theoretical review. *Psychological Bulletin, 138*, 147–174.

Rice, A., Phillips, P. J., Natu, V., An, X., & O'Toole, A. J. (2013). Unaware person recognition from the body when face identification fails. *Psychological Science*.

Rivard, J. M., Dietz, P., Martell, D., & Widawski, M. A. (2002). Acute dissociative responses in law enforcement officers involved in critical shooting incidents: The clinical and forensic implications. *Journal of Forensic Science, 47*, 1–8.

Robben, J. (2012). "I'll remember you—or someone I *think* was you": How memory affects our work as lawyers. *Oregon State Bar Bulletin*.

Roberts, K. P., & Lamb, M. E. (2010). Reality-monitoring characteristics in confirmed and doubtful allegations of child sexual abuse. *Applied Cognitive Psychology, 24*, 1049–1979.

Roediger, H. L., & McDermott, K. B. (1995). Creating false memories: Remembering words not presented in lists. *Journal of Experimental Psychology-learning memory and cognition, 21*, 803–814.

Roese, N. J., & Vohs, K. D. (2012). Hindsight bias. *Perspective on Psychological Science, 7*, 411–426.

Rollings, H. E., & Blascovich, J. (1977). The case of Patricia Hearst: Pretrial publicity and opinion. *Journal of Communication, 27*, 58–65.

Rose, M., & Diamond, S. (2008). Judging bias: Juror confidence and judicial rulings on challenges for cause. *Law and Society Review, 42*, 513–548.

Rosenfeld, J. P., Ben-Shakhar, G., & Ganis, G. (2012). Detection of concealed stored memories with psychophysiological and neuroimaging methods. In L. Nadel & W. P. Sinnott-Armstrong (Eds.), *Memory and law* (pp. 263–303). New York: Oxford University Press.

Rosnow, R. L., & Rosenthal, R. (2003). Effect sizes for experimenting psychologists. *Canadian Journal of Experimental Psychology, 57*, 231–237.

Ross, D. F., Benton, T. R., McDonnell, S., Metzger, R., & Silver, C. (2007). When accurate and inaccurate eyewitnesses look the same: A limitation of the "pop-out" effect and the 10- to 12-second rule. *Applied Cognitive Psychology, 21*, 677–690.

Ross, D. F., Ceci, S. J., Dunning, D., & Toglia, M. (1994). Unconscious transference and mistaken identity: When a witness misidentifies a familiar but innocent person. *Journal of Applied Psychology, 79*, 918–930.

Ross, L. (1977). The intuitive psychologist and his shortcomings: Distortions in the attribution process. *Advances in experimental social psychology, 10*, 173–220.

Rubin, D. C., & Berntsen, D. (2009). Most people who think that they are likely to enter psychotherapy also think it's possible that they could have forgotten their own memories of childhood sexual abuse. *Applied Cognitive Psychology, 23*, 170–173.

Ruby, C. L., & Brigham, J. C. (1997). The usefulness of the criteria-based content analysis technique in distinguishing between truthful and fabricated allegations: A critical review. *Psychology, Public Policy, and Law, 3*, 705–737.

Rush, E. B., Quas, J. A., & Yim, I. S. (2011). Memory narrowing in children and adults. *Applied Cognitive Psychology, 25*, 841–849.

Russano, M. B., Dickinson, J. J., Greathouse, S. M., & Kovera, M. B. (2006). "Why don't you take another look at number three?" Investigator knowledge and its effects on eyewitness confidence and identification decisions. *Cardozo Public Law, Policy, and Ethics Journal, 4*, 355–379.

Russano, M. B., Meissner, C. A., Narchet, F. M., & Kassin, S. M. (2005). Investigating true and false confessions within a novel experimental paradigm. *Psychological Science, 16*, 481–486.

Ruva, C. L., Guenther, C., & Yarbrough, A. (2011). Positive and negative pretrial publicity: The roles of impression formation, emotion, and predecisional distortion. *Criminal Justice and Behavior, 38*, 511–534.

Ruva, C. L., & LeVasseur, M. A. (2012). Behind closed doors: The effect of pretrial publicity on jury deliberations. *Psychology Crime & Law, 18*, 431–452.

Ruva, C. L., & McEvoy, C. (2008). Negative and positive pretrial publicity affect juror memory and decision making. *Journal of Experimental Psychology: Applied, 14*, 226–235.

Ruva, C. L., McEvoy, C., & Bryant, J. B. (2007). Effects of pre-trial publicity and jury deliberation on juror bias and source memory errors. *Applied Cognitive Psychology, 21*, 45–67.

Ryback, R. S. (1970). Alcohol amnesia: Observations in seven drinking inpatient alcoholics. *Quarterly Journal of Studies on Alcohol, 31*, 616–632.

Sachs, J. S. (1967). Recognition memory for syntactic and semantic aspects of connected discourse. *Perception & Psychophysics, 2*, 437–442.

Salmon, K., Price, M., & Pereira, J. K. (2002). Factors associated with young children's long-term recall of an invasive medical procedure: A preliminary investigation. *Developmental and Behavioral Pediatrics, 23*, 347–352.

Sampaio, C., & Brewer, W. F. (2009). The role of unconscious memory errors in judgments of confidence for sentence recognition. *Memory & Cognition, 37*, 158–163.

Sarason, I. G., & Stroops, R. (1978). Test anxiety and the passage of time. *Journal of Consulting and Clinical Psychology, 46*, 102–108.

Satel, S., & Lilienfeld, S. O. (2013). *Brainwashed: The seductive appeal of mindless neuroscience*. New York: Basic Books.

Saykaly, C., Talwar, V., Lindsay, R. C. L., Bala, N. C., & Lee, K. (2013). The influence of multiple interviews on the verbal markers of children's deception. *Law and Human Behavior, 37*, 187–196.

Saywitz, K. J. (2002). Developmental underpinnings of children's testimony. In H. L. Westcott, G. M. Davies, & R. H. C. Bull (Eds.), *Children's testimony: A handbook of psychological research and forensic practice* (pp. 3–19). New York: Wiley.

Saywitz, K. J., & Camparo, L. B. (2014). *Evidence-based child forensic interviewing: The developmental narrative elaboration interview*. New York: Oxford University Press.

Saywitz, K. J., Snyder, L., & Nathanson, R. (1999). Facilitating the communicative competence of child witness. *Applied Developmental Science, 3*, 58–68.

Saywitz, K. S. (1995). Improving children's testimony. The question, the answer, and the environment. In M. S. Zaragoza, J. R. Graham, G. C. N. Hall, R. Hirschman, & Y. S. Ben-Porath (Eds.), *Memory and testimony in the child witness* (pp. 113–140). Thousand Oaks, CA: Sage.

Schacter, D. L., Chamberlain, J., Gaesser, B., & Gerlach, K. D. (2012). Neuroimaging of true, false, and imaginary memories. In L. Nadel & W. P. Sinnott-Armstrong (Eds.), *Memory and law* (pp. 233–262). New York: Oxford University Press.

Schacter, D. L., Dawes, R., Jacoby, L. L., Kahneman, D., Lempert, R., Roediger, H. L., & Rosenthal, R. (2008). Policy forum: Studying eyewitness investigations in the field. *Law and Human Behavior, 32*, 3–5.

Schacter, D. L., & Loftus, E. F. (2013). Memory and law: What can cognitive neuroscience contribute? *Nature Neuroscience, 16*, 119–123.

Schmechel, R., O'Toole, T., Easternly, C., & Loftus, E. (2006). "Beyond the ken?" Testing jurors' understanding of eyewitness reliability evidence. *Jurimetrics, 46*, 177–214.

Schneider, C. E. (1998). *The practice of autonomy: Patients, doctors, and medical decisions*. New York: Oxford University Press.

Schooler, J. W. (1999). Discovered memories and the" delayed discovery doctrine": A cognitive case based analysis. In S. Taub (Ed.), *Recovered memories of child sexual abuse: Psychological, social, and legal perspectives on a contemporary mental health controversy* (pp. 121–141). Springfield: Charles C. Thomas.

Scoboria, A., Mazzoni, G., Kirsch, I., & Jimenez, S. (2006). The effects of prevalence and script information on plausibility, belief, and memory of autobiographical events. *Applied Cognitive Psychology, 20*, 1049–1064.

Seamon, J. G., Philbin, M. M., & Harrison, L. G. (2006). Do you remember proposing marriage to the Pepsi machine? False recollections from a campus walk. *Psychonomic Bulletin & Review, 13*, 752–756.

Seltzer, R., Venuti, M., & Lopes, G. M. (1990). Juror ability to recognize the limitations of eyewitness identifications, *Forensic Reports, 3*, 121–127.

Semmler, C., & Brewer, N. (2006). Postidentification feedback effects on face recognition confidence: Evidence for metacognitive influences. *Applied Cognitive Psychology, 20*, 895–916.

Semmler, C., Brewer, N., & Bradfield Douglass, A. (2012). Jurors believe eyewitnesses. In B. L. Cutler (Ed.), *Conviction of the innocent: Lessons from psychological research* (pp. 185–209). Washington, DC: American Psychological Association.

Senese, L. C. (2005). *Anatomy of interrogation themes: The Reid Technique of Interviewing and Interrogation*. Chicago: John E. Reid.

Shapiro, P., & Penrod, S. (1986). Meta-analysis of facial identification studies. *Psychological Bulletin, 100*, 139–156.

Sharman, S., & Scoboria, A. (2011). Event plausibility and imagination inflation: A reply to Pezdek and Blandon-Gitlin. *Applied Cognitive Psychology, 25*, 344–346.

Sharman, S. J., & Barnier, A. J. (2008). Imagining nice and nasty events in childhood or adulthood: Recent positive events show the most imagination inflation. *Acta Psychologica, 129*, 228–233.

Sharman, S. J., Manning, C. G., & Garry, M. (2005). Explain this: Explaining childhood events inflates confidence for those events. *Applied Cognitive Psychology, 19*, 67–74.

Sharman, S. J., & Powell, M. B. (2012). A comparison of adult witnesses' suggestibility across various types of leading questions. *Applied Cognitive Psychology, 26*, 48–53.

Shaw, D. J., Vrij, A., Leal, S., Mann, S., Hillman, J., Granhag, P. A., & Fisher, R. P. (2013). Expect the unexpected? Variations in question type elicit cues to deception in joint interviewer contexts. *Applied Cognitive Psychology, 27*, 336–343.

Shaw, J. A. (1996). Increases in eyewitness confidence resulting from postevent questioning. *Journal of Experimental Psychology: Applied, 2*, 126–146.

Shaw, J. A., & Budd, E. D. (1982). Determinants of acquiescence and nay saying of mentally retarded persons. *American Journal of Mental Deficiency, 87*, 108–110.

Shaw, J. S., McClure, K. A., & Dykstra, J. A. (2007). Eyewitness confidence from the witnessed event through trial. In M. P. Toglia, J. D. Read, D. F. Ross, & R. C. Lindsay (Eds.), *The handbook of eyewitness psychology: Volume 1. Memory for events* (pp. 371–397). Mahwah, NJ: Erlbaum.

Shiffman, H. R., & Bobko, D. J. (1975). Effects of stimulus complexity on the perception of brief temporal intervals. *Journal of Experimental Psychology, 103*, 156–159.

Sigler, J. N., & Couch, J. V. (2002). Eyewitness testimony and the jury verdict. *North American Journal of Psychology, 4*, 143–148.

Sigurdsson, J. F., & Gudjonsson, G. H. (1996). The psychological characteristics of "false confessors." A study among Icelandic prison inmates and juvenile offenders. *Personality and Individual Differences, 20*, 321–329.

Simmons v. United States. 390 U.S. 377. (1968).

Simon, D. (2012). *In doubt: The psychology of the criminal justice system*. Cambridge, MA: Harvard University Press.

Simon, R. J., & Eimermann, T. (1971). The jury finds not guilty: Another look at media influence on the jury. *Journalism Quarterly, 48*, 343–344.

Simons, D. J., & Ambinder, M. S. (2005). Change blindness: Theory and consequences. *Current Directions in Psychological Science, 14*, 44–48.

Simons, D. J., & Chabris, C. F. (1999). Gorillas in our midst: Sustained inattentional blindness for dynamic events. *Perception, 28*, 1059–1074.

Simons, D. J., & Chabris, C. F. (2011). What people believe about how memory works: A representative survey of the U.S. population. *PLos, 6*, 1–7.

Simons, D. J., & Rensink, R. A. (2005). Change blindness: Past, present, and future. *Trends in Cognitive Sciences, 9*, 16–20.

Sinha, P., & Poggio, T. (1996). I think I know that face. *Nature, 384*, 404.

Skagerberg, E. M. (2007). Co-witness feedback in line-ups. *Applied Cognitive Psychology, 21*, 489–497.

Slater, A. (1994). *Identification parades: A scientific evaluation*. London: Police Research Group, Home Office.

Smalarz, L., & Wells, G. L. (2013). Eyewitness certainty as a system variable. In B. L. Cutler (Ed.), *Reform of eyewitness identification procedures* (pp. 161–178). Washington, DC: American Psychological Association.

Smalarz, L., & Wells, G. L. (2014). Post-identification feedback to eyewitnesses impairs evaluators' abilities to discriminate between accurate and mistaken testimony. *Law and Human Behavior, 38*, 194–202.

Smeets, T., Telgen, S., Ost, J., Jelicic, M., & Merckelbach, H. (2009). What's behind crashing memories? Plausibility, belief and memory in reports of having seen non-existent images. *Applied Cognitive Psychology, 23*, 1333–1341.

Smith, A. M., & Cutler, B. L. (2013). Introduction: Identification procedures and conviction of the innocent. In B. L. Cutler (Ed.), *Reform of eyewitness identification* (pp. 3–21). Washington, DC: American Psychological Association.

Smith, S. M., & Gleaves, D. H. (2007). Recovered memories. In M. P. Toglia, J. D. Read, D. F. Ross, & R. C. Lindsay (Eds.), *The handbook of eyewitness psychology: Volume 1. Memory for events* (pp. 299–320). Mahwah, NJ: Erlbaum.

Smith, S. M., Lindsay, R. C., & Pryke, S. (2000). Postdictors of eyewitness errors: Can false identifications be diagnosed? *Journal of Applied Psychology, 85*, 542–550.

Snyder, M., & Swann, W. B. (1978). Hypothesis testing processes in social interaction. *Journal of Personality and Social Psychology, 36*, 1202–1212.

Snyder, M., Tanke, E. D., & Berscheid, E. (1977). Social perception and interpersonal behavior: On the self-fulfilling nature of social stereotypes. *Journal of Personality and Social Psychology, 35*, 656–666.

Solan, L. M., & Tiersma, P. M. (2003). Hearing voices: Speaker identification in court. *Hastings Law Journal, 54*, 373–390.

Soraci, S. A., Carlin, M. T., Read, J. D., Pogoda, T. K., Wakeford, Y., Cavanagh, S., & Shin, L. (2007). Psychological impairment, eyewitness testimony, and false memories: Individual differences. In M. P. Toglia, J. D. Read, D. F. Ross, & R. C. Lindsay (Eds.), *The handbook of eyewitness psychology: Volume 1. Memory for events* (pp. 261–297). Mahwah, NJ: Erlbaum.

Spanos, N. P., Burgess, C. A., Burgess, M. F., Samuels, C., & Blois, W. O. (1999). Creating false memories of infancy with hypnotic and non-hypnotic procedures. *Applied Cognitive Psychology, 13*, 201–218.

Spencer, J. R. (2011). Evidence and cross examination. In M. E. Lamb, D. J. La Rooy, L. C. Malloy, & C. Katz (Eds.), *Children's testimony: Handbook of psychological research and forensic practice* (2nd ed., pp. 285–307). Wiley.

Spiegel, D. (1995). Hypnosis and suggestion. In D. Schacter (Ed.), *Memory distortion: How minds, brains, and societies reconstructed the past* (pp. 121–142). Cambridge, MA: Harvard University Press.

Sporer, S. (2004). Reality monitoring and detection of deception. In Granhag, P. A. & Strömwall, L. A. (Eds.), *The detection of deception in forensic contexts* (pp. 64–96). New York: Cambridge University Press.

Sporer, S. (2014, March). Weighting guidelines for content cues to deception: Do they improve accuracy. Paper presented at the annual meeting of the American Psychology-Law Society, New Orleans, LA.

Sporer, S., Penrod, S., Read, D., & Cutler, B. L. (1995). Choosing, confidence, and accuracy: A meta-analysis of the confidence- accuracy relation in eyewitness identification studies. *Psychological Bulletin, 118,* 315–327.

Stanny, C. J., & Johnson, T. C. (2000). Effects of stress induced by a simulated shooting on recall by police and citizen witnesses. *American Journal of Psychology, 113,* 359–386.

Stark, L. J., & Perfect, T. J. (2006). Elaboration inflation: How your ideas become mine. *Applied Cognitive Psychology, 20,* 641–648.

Starr, D. (2013, December 9). The Interview. *New Yorker,* pp. 42–49.

State v. Lawson. 291 P.3d 673, 352. (Or. 2012).

Steblay, N. K. (1992). A meta-analytic review of the weapon focus effect. *Law and Human Behavior, 16,* 413–424.

Steblay, N. K. (2011). What we know now: The Evanston Illinois field lineups. *Law and Human Behavior, 35,* 1–12.

Steblay, N. K. (2013). Lineup instructions. In B. L. Cutler (Ed.), *Reform of eyewitness identification* (pp. 65–86). Washington, DC: American Psychological Association.

Steblay, N. K., Besirevic, J., Fulero, S. M., & Jiminez-Lorente, B. (1999). The effects of pretrial publicity on juror verdicts: A meta-analytic review. *Law and Human Behavior, 23,* 219– 235.

Steblay, N. K., Dietrich, H. L., Ryan, S. L., Racyzynski, J. L., & James, K. A. (2011). Sequential lineup laps and eyewitness accuracy. *Law and Human Behavior, 35,* 262–274.

Steblay, N. K., Dysart, J., Fulero, S., & Lindsay, R. C. L. (2003). Eyewitness accuracy rates in police showup and lineup presentations: A meta-analytic comparison. *Law and Human Behavior, 27,* 523–540.

Steblay, N. K., Dysart, J., Fulero, S., & Lindsay, R. C. L. (2001). Eyewitness accuracy rates in sequential and simultaneous lineup presentations: A meta-analytic comparison. *Law and Human Behavior, 25,* 459–473.

Steblay, N. K., Dysart, J. E., & Wells, G. L. (2011). Seventy-two tests of the sequential lineup superiority effect: A meta-analysis and policy discussion. *Psychology, Public Policy, and Law, 17,* 99–139.

Steblay, N. K., Hosch, H. M., Culhane, S. E., & McWethy, A. (2006). The impact on juror verdicts of judicial instruction to disregard inadmissible evidence: A meta-analysis. *Law and Human Behavior, 30,* 469–492.

Steblay, N. K., Wells, G. L., & Douglass, A. B. (2014). The eyewitness post identification feedback effect 15 years later: Theoretical and policy implications. *Psychology, Public Policy, and Law, 20,* 1–18.

Steblay, N. K., Tix, R. W., & Benson, S. L. (2013). Double exposure: The effects of repeated identification lineups on eyewitness accuracy. *Applied Cognitive Psychology, 27,* 644–654.

Steblay, N. M. (1997). Social influence in eyewitness recall: A meta-analytic review of lineup instruction effects. *Law and Human Behavior, 21,* 283–297.

Stevenage, S. V., Howland, A., & Tippelt, A. (2011). Interference in eyewitness and earwitness recognition. *Applied Cognitive Psychology, 25,* 112–118.

Storms, M. D. (1973). Videotape and the attribution process: Reversing actors' and observers' points of view. *Journal of personality and social psychology, 27,* 165–175.

Strayer, D. L., Drews, F. A., & Crouch, D. J. (2006). A comparison of the cell phone driver and the drunk driver. *Human Factors, 48,* 381–391.

Strayer, D. L., & Johnston, W. A. (2001). Driven to distraction: Dual-task studies of simulated driving and conversing on a cellular telephone. *Psychological Science, 12*, 462–466.

Studebaker, C. A., & Penrod, S. D. (1997). Pretrial publicity: The media, the law and common sense. *Psychology, Public Policy and Law, 3*, 428–460.

Studebaker, C. A., & Penrod, S. D. (2005). Pretrial publicity and its influence on juror decision making. In N. Brewer & K. D. Williams (Eds.), *Psychology and law: An empirical perspective* (pp. 254–275). New York: Guilford Press.

Studebaker, C., Robbennolt, J., Penrod, S., Pathak-Sharma, M., Groscup, J., & Devenport, J. (2002). Studying pretrial publicity effects: New methods for improving ecological validity and testing external validity. *Law and Human Behavior, 26*, 19–41.

Sue, S., Smith, R. E., & Gilbert, R. (1974). Biasing effects of pretrial publicity on judicial decisions. *Journal of Criminal Justice, 2*, 163–171

Sue, S., Smith, R. E., & Pedroza, G. (1975). Authoritarianism, pretrial publicity, and awareness of bias in simulated jurors. *Psychological Reports, 37*, 1299–1302.

Swanner, J. K., & Beike, D. R. (2010). Incentives increase the risk of false but not true secondary confessions from informants with an allegiance to a suspect. *Law and Human Behavior, 34*, 418–428.

Talarico, J. M., & Rubin, D. C. (2003). Confidence, not consistency, characterizes flashbulb memory. *Psychological Science, 14*, 455–461.

Talarico, J. M., & Rubin, D. C. (2007). Flashbulb memories are special after all: In phenomenology, not accuracy. *Applied Cognitive Psychology, 21*, 557–578.

Tanaka, J. W., & Farah, M. J. (1993). Parts and wholes in face recognition. *Quarterly Journal of Experimental Psychology, 46*, 225–245.

Tavris, C. (2008). Whatever happened to "Jane Doe"? *Skeptical Inquirer, 32*, 28–30.

ten Brinke, L., & Porter, S. (2012). Cry me a river: Identifying the behavioral consequences of extremely high-stakes interpersonal deception. *Law and Human Behavior, 36*, 469–477.

Tenney, E. R., MacCoun, R. J., Spellman, B. A., & Hastie, R. (2007). Calibration trumps confidence as a basis for witness credibility. *Psychological Science, 18*, 46–50.

Terr, L. (1991). Childhood trauma: An outline and overview. *American Journal of Psychiatry, 148*, 10–20.

Terr, L. (1994). *Unchained memories*. New York: Basic Books.

Terr, L. C. (1988). What happens to early memories of trauma? A study of twenty children under age five at the time of documented traumatic events. *Journal of the American Academy of Child and Adolescent Psychiatry, 27*, 96–104.

Thomas, A. K., & Loftus, E. F. (2002). Creating bizarre false memories through imagination. *Memory & Cognition, 30*, 423–431.

Thompson, C. P. (1987). A language effect in voice identification. *Applied Cognitive Psychology, 1*, 121–131.

Thompson, P. (1980). Margaret Thatcher: A new illusion. *Perception, 9*, 483–484.

Thompson-Cannino, J., Cotton, R., & Torneo, E. (2009). *Picking cotton: Our memoir of injustice and redemption*. New York: Macmillan.

Thomsen, D. K., & Berntsen, D. (2009). The long-term impact of emotionally stressful events on memory characteristics and life story. *Applied Cognitive Psychology, 23*, 579–598.

Tollestrup, P. A., Turtle, J. W., & Yuille, J. C. (1994). Actual victims and witnesses to robbery and fraud: An archival analysis. In D. F. Ross, J. D. Read, & M. P. Toglia (Eds.), *Adult eyewitness testimony: Current trends and developments.* (pp. 144–160). New York: Cambridge University Press.

Tredoux, C. G., Meissner, C. A., Malpass, R. S., & Zimmerman, L. A. (2004). Eyewitness identification. In C. Spielberger (Ed.), *Encyclopedia of applied psychology* (pp. 875–887). San Diego, CA: Academic Press.

Tunnicliff, J. L., & Clark, S. (2000). Foils for identification lineups: Matching suspects or descriptions. *Law and Human Behavior, 24,* 231–258.

Valentine, T., Davis, J. P., Memon, A., & Roberts, A. (2012). Live showups and their influence on a subsequent video line-up. *Applied Cognitive Psychology, 26,* 1–23.

Valentine, T., & Heaton, P. (1999). An evaluation of the fairness of police line-ups and video identifications. *Applied Cognitive Psychology, 13,* S59–S72.

Valentine, T., & Mesout, J. (2008). Eyewitness identification under stress in the London Dungeon. *Applied Cognitive Psychology, 23,* 151–161.

Valentine, T., Pickering, A., & Darling, S. (2003). Characteristics of eyewitness identification that predict the outcome of real lineups. *Applied Cognitive Psychology, 17,* 969–993.

Van Koppen, P. J., & Lochun, S. K. (1997). Portraying perpetrators: The validity of offender descriptions by witnesses. *Law and Human Behavior, 21,* 661–685.

Van Lancker, D., Cummings, J., Kreiman, J., & Dobkin, B. (1988). Phonagnosia: A dissociation between familiar and unfamiliar voices. *Cortex, 24,* 195–209.

Van Lancker, D., Kreiman, J., & Emmorey, K. (1985). Familiar voice recognition: Patterns and parameters. Part I. Recognition of backwards voices. *Journal of Phonetics, 13,* 19–38.

Van Lancker, D., Kreiman, J., & Wickens, T. (1985). Familiar voice recognition: Parameters and patterns. Part II: Recognition of rate-altered voices. *Journal of Phonetics, 13,* 39–52.

Van Oorsouw, K., & Merckelbach, H. (2012). The effects of alcohol on crime-related memories: A field study. *Applied Cognitive Psychology, 26,* 82–90.

Verkampt, F., & Ginet, M. (2010). Variations of the cognitive interview: Which one is the most effective in enhancing children's testimonies? *Applied Cognitive psychology, 24,* 1279–1296.

Vidmar, N. (2002). Case studies of pre- and midtrial prejudice in criminal and civil litigation. *Law and Human Behavior, 26,* 73–105.

Vidmar, N., & Judson, J. (1981). The use of social sciences in a change of venue application. *Canadian Bar Review, 59,* 76–102.

Vrij, A. (2002). Deception in children: A literature review and implications for children's testimony. In H. L. Westcott, G. M. Davies, & R. H. C. Bull (Eds.), *Children's testimony: A handbook of psychological research and forensic practice* (pp. 175–194). New York: Wiley.

Vrij, A. (2004). Why professionals fail to catch liars and how they can improve. *Legal and Criminological Psychology, 9,* 159–181.

Vrij, A. (2005). Criteria-based content analysis: A qualitative review of the first 37 studies. *Psychology, Public Policy, and Law, 11,* 3–41.

Vrij, A., Edward, K., & Bull, R. (2001). Police officers' ability to detect deceit: The benefit of indirect deception detection measures. *Legal and Criminological Psychology, 6,* 185–197.

Vrij, A., & Granhag, P. A. (2012). Eliciting cues to deception and truth: What matters are the questions asked. *Journal of Applied Research in Memory and Cognition, 1,* 110–117.

Vrij, A., Granhag, P. A., & Porter, S. (2010). Pitfalls and opportunities in nonverbal and verbal lie detection. *Psychological Science in the Public Interest, 11,* 89–121.

Vrij, A., & Mann, S. (2006). Criteria-based content analysis: An empirical test of its underlying processes. *Psychology Crime and Law, 12,* 337–349.

Vrij, A., Mann, S., & Fisher, R. P. (2006). Information-gathering vs accusatory interview style: Individual differences in respondents' experiences. *Personality and Individual Differences, 41,* 589–599.

Vrij, A., Mann, S. A., Fisher, R. P., Leal, S., Milne, R., & Bull, R. (2008). Increasing cognitive load to facilitate lie detection: The benefit of recalling an event in reverse order. *Law and Human Behavior, 32,* 253–265.

Wade, K. A., Garry, M., Read, J. D., & Lindsay, D. S. (2002). A picture is worth a thousand lies: Using false photographs to create false childhood memories. *Psychonomic Bulletin & Review*, *9*, 597–603.

Wagenaar, W. A., & Groeneweg, J. (1990). The memory of concentration camp survivors. *Applied Cognitive Psychology*, *4*, 77–87.

Wagenaar, W. A., & Van der Schrier, J. H. (1996). Face recognition as a function of distance and illumination: A practical tool for use in the courtroom. *Psychology, Crime & Law*, *2*, 321–332.

Wagner, A. D. (2010). Can neuroscience identify lies? In M. S. Gazzaniga & J. S. Rakoff (Eds.), *A judge's guide to neuroscience: A concise introduction* (pp. 13–25) Santa Barbara: University of California, Santa Barbara.

Wallace, D. B., & Kassin, S. M. (2012). Harmless error analysis: How do judges respond to confession errors? *Law and Human Behavior*, *36*, 151–157.

Warren, A. R., & Woodall, C. E. (1999). The reliability of hearsay testimony: How well do interviewers recall their interviews with children? *Psychology, Public Policy and Law*, *5*, 355–371.

Waterman, A., Blades, M., & Spencer, C. (2002). How and why do children respond to nonsensical questions? In H. L. Westcott, G. M. Davies, & R. H. C. Bull (Eds.), *Children's testimony: A handbook of psychological research and forensic practice* (pp. 147–159). New York: Wiley.

Waterman, A., Blades, M., & Spencer, C. (2004). Indicating when you do not know the answer: The effect of question format and interview knowledge on children's "don't know" responses. *British Journal of Developmental Psychology*, *22*, 335–348.

Weber, N., Brewer, N., Wells, G. L., Semmler, C., & Keast, A. (2004). Eyewitness identification accuracy and response latency: The unruly 10-12-second rule. *Journal of Experimental Psychology: Applied*, *10*, 139.

Weber, N., & Perfect, T. J. (2012). Improving eyewitness identification accuracy by screening out those who say they *don't know*. *Law and Human Behavior*, *36*, 28–36.

Weissenborn, R., & Duka, T. (2000). State-dependent effects of alcohol on explicit memory: The role of semantic associations. *Psychopharmacology*, *149*, 98–106.

Wells, G. L. (1978). Applied eyewitness-testimony research: System variables and estimator variables. *Journal of Personality and Social Psychology*, *36*, 1546–1557.

Wells, G. L. (1984a). How adequate is human intuition for judging eyewitness testimony. In G. L. Wells & E. L. Loftus (Eds.), *Eyewitness testimony: Psychological perspectives* (pp. 256–272). New York: Cambridge University Press.

Wells, G. L. (1984b). The psychology of lineup identifications. *Journal of Applied Social Psychology*, *14*, 89–103.

Wells, G. L. (1985). Verbal descriptions of faces from memory: Are they diagnostic of identification accuracy? *Journal of Applied Psychology*, *70*, 619–626.

Wells, G. L. (1993). What do we know about eyewitness identification? *American Psychologist*, *48*(5), 553–571.

Wells, G. L. (2014). Eyewitness identification: Probative value, criterion shifts, and policy regarding the sequential lineup. *Current Directions in Psychological Science*, *23*, 11–16.

Wells, G. L., & Bradfield, A. L. (1998). "Good, you identified the suspect": Feedback to eyewitnesses distorts their reports of the witnessing experience. *Journal of Applied Psychology*, *83*, 360–376.

Wells, G. L., & Bradfield, A. L. (1999). Measuring the goodness of lineups: Parameter estimation, question effects, and limits to the mock witness paradigm. *Applied Cognitive Psychology*, *13*, S27–S39.

Wells, G. L., Charman, S. D., & Olson, E. A. (2005). Building face composites can harm line-up identification performance. *Journal of Experimental Psychology: Applied*, *11*, 147–156.

Wells, G. L., Greathouse, S. M., & Smalarz, L. (2012). Why do motions to suppress suggestive eyewitness identifications fail? In B. L. Cutler (Ed.), *Conviction of the innocent: Lessons from psychological research* (pp. 167–184). Washington, DC: American Psychological Association.

Wells, G. L., & Hasel, L. E. (2007). Facial composite production by eyewitnesses. *Current Directions in Psychological Science, 16,* 6–10.

Wells, G. L., & Hryciw, B. (1984). Memory for faces: Encoding and retrieval operations. *Memory and Cognition, 12,* 338–344.

Wells, G. L., Lindsay, R. C. L., & Ferguson, T. J. (1979). Accuracy, confidence, and juror perceptions in eyewitness identification. *Journal of Applied Psychology, 64,* 440–448.

Wells, G. L., Memon, A., & Penrod, S. D. (2006). Eyewitness evidence: Improving its probative value, *Psychological Science in the Public Interest, 7,* 45–75.

Wells, G. L., Olson, E. A., & Charman, S. D. (2002). The confidence of eyewitnesses in their identifications from lineups. *Current Directions in Psychological Science, 11*(5), 151–154.

Wells, G. L., Olson, E. A., & Charman, S. D. (2003). Distorted retrospective eyewitness reports as functions of feedback and delay. *Journal of Experimental Psychology: Applied, 9,* 42–52.

Wells, G. L., & Quinlivan, D. S. (2009). Suggestive eyewitness identification procedures and the Supreme Court's reliability test in light of eyewitness science: 30 years later. *Law and Human Behavior, 33,* 1–24.

Wells, G. L., Rydell, S. M., & Seelau, E. P. (1993). The selection of distractors for eyewitness lineups. *Journal of Applied Psychology, 78,* 835–844.

Wells, G. L., Small, M., Penrod, S., Malpass, R. S., Fulero, S. M., & Brimacombe, C. E. (1998). Eyewitness identification procedures. *Law and Human Behavior, 22,* 603–647.

Wells, G. L., Steblay, N. K., & Dysart, J. E. (2012). Eyewitness identification reforms: Are suggestiveness-induced hits and guesses true hits? *Perspectives on Psychological Science, 7,* 264–271.

Wetherill, R. R., & Fromme, K. (2011). Acute alcohol effects on narrative recall and contextual memory: An examination of fragmentary blackouts. *Addictive Behaviors, 36,* 886–889.

White, A. M. (2003). What happened? Alcohol, memory blackouts, and the brain. *Alcohol Research and Health, 27,* 186–196.

White, A. M., Jamieson-Drake, D. W., & Swartzwelder, H. S. (2002). Prevalence and correlates of alcohol-induced blackouts among college students: Results of an e-mail survey. *Journal of American College Health, 51,* 117–119, 122–131.

White, A. M., Signer, M. L., Kraus, C. L., & Swartzweider, H. S. (2004). Experiential aspects of alcohol-induced blackouts among college students. *American Journal of Drug and Alcohol Abuse, 30,* 205–224.

White, D., Kemp, R. I., Jenkins, R., & Burton, A. M. (2014). Feedback training for facial image comparison. *Psychonomic Bulletin & Review, 21,* 100–106.

White, T. L., Leichtman, M. D., & Ceci, S. J. (1997). The good, the bad, and the ugly: Accuracy, inaccuracy and elaboration in preschoolers' reports about past events. *Applied Cognitive Psychology, 11,* S37–S54.

Wilford, M. M., & Wells, G. L. (2010). Does facial processing prioritize change detection? Change blindness illustrates costs and benefits of holistic processing. *Psychological Science, 21,* 1611–1615.

Wilford, M. W., & Wells, G. L. (2013). Eyewitness system variables. In B. L. Cutler (Ed.), *Reform of eyewitness identification* (pp. 23–43). Washington, DC: American Psychological Association.

Williams, L. M. (1994). Recall of childhood trauma: A prospective study of women's memories of child sexual abuse. *Journal of Consulting and Clinical Psychology, 62,* 1167–1176.

Williams, L. M. (1995). Recovered memories of abuse in women with documented child sexual victimization histories. *Journal of Traumatic Stress*, *8*, 649–673.

Wilson, T. D., & Brekke, N. (1994). Mental contamination and mental correction: Unwanted influences on judgments and evaluations. *Psychological Bulletin*, *115*, 117–142.

Wise, R. A., Safer, M. A., & Maro, C. M. (2011). What U.S. law enforcement officers know and believe about eyewitness factors, eyewitness interviews and identification procedures. *Applied Cognitive Psychology*, *25*, 488–500.

Wixted, J. T., Gronlund, S. D., & Mickes, L. (2014). Policy regarding the sequential lineup is not informed by probative value but is informed by receiver operating characteristic analysis. *Current Directions in Psychological Science*, *23*, 17–18.

Wogalter, M. S., Malpass, R. S., & McQuiston, D. E. (2004). A national survey of police on preparation and conduct of identification procedures. *Psychology Crime & Law*, *10*, 69–82.

Woolnough, P. S., & MacLeod, M. (2001). Watching the birdie watching you: Eyewitness memory for actions using CCTV records of actual crimes. *Applied Cognitive Psychology*, *15*, 395–411.

Wright, D. B., & Carlucci, M. E. (2011). The response order effect: People believe the first person who remembers an event. *Psychonomics Bulletin & Review*, *18*, 805–812.

Wright, D. B., & Loftus, E. F. (2008). Eyewitness memory. In Cohen, G., & Conway, M. A. (Eds.), *Memory in the real world* (3rd ed.) (pp. 91–106). New York, N.Y.: Psychology Press.

Wright, D. B., & McDaid, A. T. (1996). Comparing system and estimator variables using data from real line-ups. *Applied Cognitive Psychology*, *10*, 74–84.

Wright, D. B., & Skagerberg, E. M. (2007). Postidentification feedback affects real eyewitnesses. *Psychological Science*, *18*, 172–178.

Wright, D. B., & Stroud, J. N. (2002). Age differences in lineup identification accuracy: People are better with their own age. *Law and Human Behavior*, *26*, 641–654.

Yarbus A. L. (1967). *Eye movements and vision*. New York: Plenum Press.

Yarmey, A. D. (1986). Verbal, visual, and voice identification of a rape suspect under different levels of illumination. *Journal of Applied Psychology*, *71*, 363–370.

Yarmey, A. D. (1991). Voice identification over the telephone. *Journal of Applied Social Psychology*, *21*, 1868–1876.

Yarmey, A. D. (2000). Retrospective duration estimations for variant and invariant events in field situations. *Applied Cognitive Psychology*, *14*, 45–57.

Yarmey, A. D. (2001). Earwitness descriptions and speaker identifications. *Forensic Linguistics*, *8*, 113–122.

Yarmey, A. D. (2007). The psychology of speaker identification and earwitness memory In R. C. L. Lindsay, D. F. Ross, J. D. Read & M. P. Toglia (Eds.), *The handbook of eyewitness psychology: Volume 2. Memory for people* (pp. 101–136). Mahwah, NJ: Erlbaum.

Yarmey, A. D., & Yarmey, M. J. (1997). Eyewitness recall and duration estimates in field settings. *Journal of Applied Social Psychology*, *27*, 330–344.

Yarmey, A. D., Yarmey, M. J., & Yarmey, A. L. (1996). Accuracy of eyewitness identifications in showups and lineups. *Law and Human Behavior*, *20*, 459–477.

Yin, R. K. (1969). Looking at upside-down faces. *Journal of Experimental Psychology*, *81*, 141.

Young, A. W., Hellawell, D., & Hay, D. C. (1987). Configurational information in face perception. *Perception*, *16*, 747–759.

Yuille, J. C., & Cutshall, J. L. (1986). A case study of eyewitness memory of a crime. *Journal of Applied Psychology*, *71*, 291–301.

Yuille, J. C., Davies, G., Gibling, F., Marxsen, D., & Porter, S. (1994). Eyewitness memory of police trainees for realistic role plays. *Journal of Applied Psychology, 79*, 931–936.

Zajac, R., & Hayne, H. (2003). I don't think that's what really happened: The effect of cross-examination on the accuracy of children's reports. *Journal of Experimental Psychology: Applied, 9*, 187–195.

Zajac, R., & Hayne, H. (2006). The negative effect of cross-examination style questioning on children's accuracy: Older children are not immune. *Applied Cognitive Psychology, 20*, 3–16.

Zajac, R., & Henderson, N. (2009). Don't it make my brown eyes blue: Co-witness misinformation about a target's appearance can impair target-absent lineup performance. *Memory, 17*, 266–278.

Zaragoza, M. S., Payment, K. E., Ackil, J. K., Drivdahl, S. B., & Beck, M. (2001). Interviewing witnesses: Forced confabulation and confirmatory feedback increase false memories. *Psychological Science, 12*, 473–477.

Zhu, B., Chen, C., Loftus, E. F., Lin, C., & Dong, Q. (2010). Treat and trick: A new way to increase false memory. *Applied Cognitive Psychology, 24*, 1199–1208.

INDEX

Figures are indicated by an " *f*" after the page number.

Blair, I. V., 116
Blandón-Gitlin, I., 73, 74, 242
Blank, H., 69
Blascovich, J., 228
Blocksidge, D., 60
blogs, PTP on, 225
Blois, W. O., 73
blood alcohol levels, 57–58
blood-brain barrier, 54
blood pressure tests, 180
Blunt, J. R., 84
Bobko, D. J., 52
bodily touching, false memories of, 260, 269–270
Bogart, D., 219
Bond, C. F., 176, 183
Bond, G. D., 176, 177
Boone, S. M. N., 52
Bora, B., 79
Bornstein, B., 60, 113, 146, 244
Bornstein, B. H., 43, 83
Boss, S. M., 33
Bothwell, R. K., 21, 52, 104, 238
Bottoms, B. L., 178, 250
Bourg, W., 261, 277
Bower, G. H., 65
Boyce, M., 238
Boydell, C. A., 157
Bradfield, A. L., 50, 79, 131, 238
Bradfield Douglass, A., 142, 238
Bradford, D., 183
Bradshaw, E., 16, 92
Bradshaw, G. S., 16, 92
brain
    brain wave patterns, 188
    effects of emotions on, 89
    effects of injuries on, 54–55, 98–99
    facial recognition systems, 99–100
    familiarity vs. recollection systems, 143–144
    prefrontal cortex, 201
Brain Fingerprinting, 188
Brainerd, C. J., 81, 247, 250
Brandon, S., 217
Bransford, J. D., 164, 165
Brédart, S., 155
Bregman, N. J., 126, 156
Brekke, N., 19
Brewer, N. W., 41, 76, 77, 79, 105, 128, 143, 238
Brewer, W. F., 53, 79
Bricker, P. D., 158
Brigham, J. C., 21, 52, 75, 104, 115, 118, 186, 238
Brimacombe, C. A. E., 50, 138

Britain (United Kingdom)
    identification suites, use of, 124
    Police and Criminal Evidence Act, 216
Britton, W. B., 91
Broeders, A. P. A., 158
Brooks, K. R., 183
Brown, A. S., 170
Brown, D. A., 277, 283, 284
Brown, E., 146
Brown, R., 86
Brown, T., 274
Browne, B. A., 224
Bruce, V., 99, 101, 117
Bruck, M., 171, 251, 252, 262, 264, 270, 283–284
Bruton v. United States, 193
Bryant, J. B., 229, 230
Buchanan, T. W., 90
Buckley, J. P., 191, 199, 206, 218
Budd, E. D., 201
Buddenbaum, J., 227
Bukach, C., 100
Bulevich, J. B., 69
Bull, R., 43, 66, 97, 105, 110, 156, 158, 176, 179, 183, 191, 207, 261
bullying, by police, 197–198
Burgess, C. A., 73
Burgess, M. F., 73
Burgwyn-Bailes, E., 257
Burke, A. S., 89, 220
Burt, C. D. B., 70
Burton, A. M., 43, 99, 104
Burton, M., 101
Busey, T. A., 76
Butler, B., 234
Buzsáki, G., 54
bystanders vs. participants, as witnesses, 6–7

Caggiano, J. M., 33
Cahill, L., 59
calibration curve, for confidence, 77
California, *Frye* criteria, use of, 16
California Commission on the Fair Administration of Justice, 122, 136
camera angle, 243
cameras, light sensitivity, 109
Camparo, L. B., 277
Campbell, A. C., 56
Campbell, J. C., 188
Canada, admissibility of expert testimony in, 7
Carey, S., 99
Carlson, C. A., 119, 127
Carlson, M. A., 119

Carlucci, M. E., 237
Carpenter, S. K., 84
Carroll, J. S., 227
Carter, C. A., 250
case studies, of facial recognition,
103–104
Casey, B. J., 201
Cauffman, E., 194
Cavrak, S. E., 116
CBCA (Criteria-Based Content Analysis),
80, 185–186, 189
Ceci, S. J., 80, 144, 171, 261, 262, 264,
265, 269, 270
Cederborg, A.-C., 245, 283
cell phone conversations, distracting
power of, 33
Cepeda, N. J., 84
Cerrato, L., 157
certainty
vs. accuracy of memories, 75–80
confidence malleability and, 142, 288
as factor in determining truth of
children's reports, 287–288
of flashbulb memories, 86–87
of identification in lineups, 142
as indicator of witness reliability, 238
in lie detection, 177, 179, 183
in voice identifications, 159
Chabris, C. F., 20, 32, 33
Chae, Y., 252
Chamberlain, J., 188
Chan, J. C. K., 69, 119
Charlton, D., 219
Charlton, K., 177, 183
Charman, S. D., 76, 78, 79, 119, 130,
137
Charniak, E., 166
Chen, C., 72
Chen, W., 40, 104
Cherryman, J., 156
child abuse, 272–276, 282–283, 287–294
See also children, proper investigations
with
child-mother conversations, 171–172
children
CBCA scores in, 186
confessions offered by, 196
detecting lies of, 177–178
false confessions by, 194, 200–201
false memories in, 71–72
memory differences among, 251–253
school-aged, 177–178, 250–251
suggestive questioning of, 171–172
as witnesses, identification errors of,
125

See also adolescents; children's
memories
children, proper investigations with,
272–294
abuse, initial reports of, 272–276
delayed disclosure and repeated
interviews, 282–283
ground rules, 279 280
interviews, start of, 278–279
medical examinations, 286–287
overview, 276–277
proper questions, 280–281
props, use of, 283–284
report truth, certainty and demeanor
and, 287–288
report truth, consistency and, 288–290
report truth, cross-examination and,
292–293
report truth, level of detail, 290–291
report truth, privileged knowledge and,
291
report truth, symptom evidence and,
291–292
role of science in, 277–278
therapeutic interviews, 284–286
children's memories, 245–271
differences among children, 251–253
gist vs. source memory, 246–247
language acquisition and, 247–249
memory errors, 269–271
Mr. Science experiment, 259–260
overview, 245
paths toward suggestion, 268–269
in preschool-aged children, 249–250
in school-aged children, 250–251
significant events, remembering,
256–258
suggestibility, factors shaping, 260–268
trial competence and, 253–254
truth and lies, distinguishing, 254–256
Chinese (ancient), lie detection by, 180
choices, confessions as, 195–196
Chojnacki, D. E., 241
Christensen, A., 144
Christiaansen, R. E., 70
Christianson, S. A., 97
Christie, J., 48
Chrobak, Q. M., 69, 71, 74
Cicchini, M. D., 241
circularity, in Manson logic, 150–151
CIT (Concealed Information Test, Guilty
Knowledge Test), 187–189
Clancy, S. A., 73, 291
Clare, I. C., 201
Clark, H. H., 168

Clark, S. E., 118, 127, 130, 135, 138, 146
clean comparisons, 5
Clifford, B., 125
Clifford, B. R., 158
clinical psychologists, 1–2, 25
clinical psychology, 1–3
clinicians, on consistency of children's reports, 289
Clinton-Gore illusion, 113, 114
closed-ended vs. open-ended questions, 250, 260, 280
clothing bias, 124
coerced confessions, overbelief in, 241–242
Coffman, K. A. J., 241
cognition of jurors. *See* jurors' cognition
cognitive interviews, 85–86, 117
cognitive load, 190–192
cognitive psychologists, 3
cognitive science, 2–3
Cohen, G., 165
Cohen's *d* statistic, 23
coin tosses, null hypothesis and, 11–12
Colomb, C., 85–86
Colorado v. Connelly (1986), 193
Colwell, K., 187
Colwell, L. H., 194
Coman, A., 236
Committee on Scientific Approaches to Understanding and Maximizing the Validity and Reliability of Eyewitness Identification in Law Enforcement and the Courts (U.S. National Academy of Sciences), 147
common ground, in conversations, 163, 166, 168–169, 214
common sense, 17–22, 297
common-sense indicators of lies, 182–183, 191, 240
completeness, of emotional memories, 89
complexity, lie detection and, 191
compliance and suggestibility, false confessions and, 202–203
Compo, N. S., 56, 57
composite drawings, for facial recognition, 119–120
composite effect, 100
Concealed Information Test (CIT, Guilty Knowledge Test), 187–189
Condie, L. O., 201
cones (photoreceptors), 34, 38, 109
confessions, 193–223
    application of research to, 222–223
    coerced, overbelief in, 241–242
    contamination of, 218–219, 242

corroborations for, 217–220
duress and, 204–205
false, frequency of, 193–195
false, people at risk for, 200–204
interrogations, video records of, 220–222
PEACE model for interrogations and, 216–217, 222
reasons for, 195–200
Reid interrogations and, 205–216
confidence. *See* certainty
confidence malleability, 142, 288
confirmation bias, 208, 219–220, 231–232
conflicted reports, 289–290
confrontation, in Reid-related interrogations, 211–213
confusing questions, children's responses to, 249–250
conjunction error, 44
connections, in memory, 63–65
Connell, M., 284
Connelly, Michael, 179
Connolly, D. A., 83
Connors, E., 102
conscious inference, 144
Considine, M., 263
consistency, 26, 81, 238, 252–253, 288–290
Consoli, A., 113
constructiveness, 31, 36–37, 51
contact lenses, 41
contamination, of confessions, 218–219
Conte, J., 291, 298
context reinstatement effects, 57, 85
continuances, PTP and, 230, 232
continuous vs. discontinuous memories, 94–96
Control Question Test (CQT), 180, 181, 188
controlled settings, field settings vs., 5–7
conversations
    mother-child conversations, 171–172
    parent-child conversations, 273–274
    perceptual salience in, 221
conversations, memory for, 162–172
    common ground, importance of, 168–169
    filling-in and, 166–167
    initial observations on, 162–163
    interviews and interrogations, 170–172
    and knowledge, roles of, 169–170
    mishearing, risk of, 167–168
    overview, 162
    source confusion, 170, 218

empirical claims, 3, 16–17
en bloc blackouts, 58
Erickson, W. B., 48
error rates, 10–13, 122–124
  See also accuracy
error size, of false memories, 72
errors, risks vs., 26
  See also false memories; source confusion
Esplin, P. W., 186, 245, 258, 277, 278
estimator variables, 107–108
Estrada, S., 247
Etherington, J., 79
Evans, J. R., 57
event complexity, 44
event duration, 43, 52, 158
Everington, C., 201
evidence
  admissibility of, 180, 186, 213
  anecdotal, 22
  checking confessions against other, 219–220
  children's suggestibility and, 263
  fictitious, 211–213, 222, 263
  guidelines for collecting eyewitness, 128–129, 133
  hiding of, during interviews, 190
  improving quality of, 29
  jurors' memories for, 234–237
  polygraph evidence, 180
  promoting false memories, 71, 72
  See also eyewitness identification
exact words, memory for, 139, 158–159, 163–164, 165–166
examinations, memory retention and, 84
exoneration cases, 194
  See also DNA exonerations
expectations, effects on perceptions, 52–54
expert-level discrimination of individuals, 99
expert testimony, 21
  See also Daubert standard, admissibility of psychological science under; *Frye* standard
eye movements, 45, 46f, 48
eyeglasses, 41
eyes, 30–31, 34–35, 109
eyewitness identifications, 98–120
  faces, specialness of, 98–100
  facial recognition, accuracy of, 100–108
  facial recognition, factors affecting, 108–116
  facial recognition, post-crime factors affecting, 116–120
  See also mistaken identifications
eyewitnesses, lineup responses of, 139–143

face-voice interactions, 156
faces, specialness of, 98–100
Facial Action Coding System, 184
facial expressions, microexpressions, 184, 189
facial recognition, accuracy of, 100–108
  archival studies, evidence from, 105–106
  case studies, evidence from, 103–104
  composite drawings and, 119–120
  descriptions vs., 118
  DNA exonerations and, 102–103
  general impairment vs. suspect bias, 108
  limits to, 104–105
  recognition vs. identification, 101–102
  system and estimator variables, 107–108
  target-present vs. target-absent, 106–107
  verbal descriptions and, 118
facial recognition, factors affecting, 108–120
  alcohol, 112–113
  attention, 35, 110–111
  disguises, 113–115
  eyeglasses, 41
  instructions, 118–119
  interaction among, 149
  lighting, 37–39, 40, 109
  post-crime factors, 116–120
  race, 113–115
  time, passage of, 116, 149
  viewing distance, 41, 109, 149
  viewing duration, 43, 110
  viewing quality, 109
  weapon focus, 111–112
factual elements, of PTP, 225, 226, 232
factual innocence, 203–204
Faglioni, P., 99
Fahsing, I. A., 118
fail-safe numbers, 24–25, 228
Falcone, M., 157
false alarms (type 1 errors), 11–12
false confessions
  evidence confirming, 219–220
  false evidence and, 212–213
  frequency of, 193–195
  identifying risks for, 222–223
  interrogation duration and, 205
  isolation and, 211
  minimization technique and, 215
  PEACE interviews and, 217
  people at risk for, 200–204
  See also false memories; Reid interrogations

guilty knowledge, 187–189, 218, 242
Guilty Knowledge Test (Concealed
    Information Test, CIT), 187–189
Guyer, M. J., 93, 97
Guyll, M., 205
Guze, S. B., 58

Haber, L., 6
Haber, R. N., 6
Haden, C., 248
Hafstad, G. S., 79
Hagen, L., 71
Halamish, V., 84
Halford, P., 105
Hamann, S., 59, 90
Hammersley, R., 77, 144, 155, 159,
    165
Han, H., 40, 104
Hancock, P., 101, 117
Handley, I. M., 221
Hare, T. A., 201
Harley, E. M., 41, 42
Harris, D., 28
Harris, P. L., 255
Harrison, L. G., 69
Harrison, Y., 205
Harsch, N., 87
Hartshorne, H., 253
Hartwig, M., 190
Hartzler, B., 57, 58
Harvey, A. J., 56
Hasel, L. E., 119, 135, 193, 210, 213, 218,
    219
Hasselmo, M. E., 91
Hastie, R., 235, 238
hats, effects on facial recognition, 113,
    114
Hauch, V., 186
Hauer, B. J., 96
Havard, C., 115, 125
Haw, R., 224
Haw, R. M., 138
Hawks, I. M., 79
Hayne, H., 293
Hazzard, A., 274
Healey, S., 69
hearsay confessions, 162
Heathcote, A., 79
Heaton, P., 125
Heffernan, William, 179–180
Hembrooke, H., 264, 270
Hemsworth, D. H., 113
Henderson, E., 293
Henderson, N., 69
Henderson, State v. (2011), 103, 147

Henkel, L. A., 21, 241
Herrero, C., 21
Hershkowitz, I., 172, 245, 258, 277
Hervé, H. F., 48
Heuer, F., 48, 59, 88, 89
Heuer, L., 237
Heyman, G. D., 263
Higham, P. A., 86
Higueras, I., 85
Hilliar, K. F., 116
Hinz, T., 269
Hirst, W., 86, 236
Ho, L. Y., 92
Hockley, W. E., 113
Hoiberg, B. C., 227
holistic cognitive interviews, 117
holistic perception, 100, 110–111, 118
Hollien, H., 154, 156, 160
Hollin, C. R., 21
Holtgraves, T. M., 168
Honts, C. R., 182
Hope, L., 43, 60, 69, 110, 192, 231
Horn, K., 203
Horne, J. A., 205
Horowitz, D., 172
Horowitz, S. W., 181
Horry, R., 39, 41, 43, 105, 106, 128
Hosch, H. M., 6, 16, 21, 104
hospital visits, childrens' memories of,
    257
Houp, S., 227
Howland, A., 156
Hryciw, B., 118, 119
Hübinette, B., 97
Hudson, J., 256
Hudson, J. I., 56
Huestis, M. A., 56
Huffman, M. L., 255, 261
Hulse, L. M., 91
Humphries, J. E., 129
Hungerford, A., 283
Huntley, J., 235
Husband, T. H., 71
Hvistendahl, J. K., 227
Hwang, H. S., 184
hybrid studies, 6
Hyman, I. E., 33, 71, 74, 80
hypovolemic shock, 54–55

Iacono, W. G., 16, 181
IACP (International Association of Chiefs
    of Police), 122, 123, 147
identification procedures, 121–152
    admissibility, pretrial assessments of,
    147–151

Krähenbühl, S., 262, 293
Kramer, G. P., 227
Kraus, C. L., 57
Krauss, R. M., 157
Kreiman, J., 154, 155
Krizer, R., 92
Kronvist, O., 190
Kuehnle, K., 284
Kukucka, J. P., 28, 79, 208
Kulik, J., 86
Kulish, R., 202
Kumho Tire Co. v. Carmichael, 7
Künzel, H. J., 156

La Fon, D., 194
La Rooy, D. J., 251, 255, 277, 283, 289
Laible, D., 274
Laimon, R. L., 251, 280
Lamb, M. E., 172, 187, 245, 248, 249, 250, 251, 255, 258, 261, 270, 277, 278, 283, 284, 289
Lampinen, J. M., 48, 79
Lancaster, G. L. J., 192
Lane, S. M., 20
Laney, C., 48, 59, 69, 71, 94
Langleben, D., 188
language skills, of children, 247–249, 251–252, 254, 278–279
Lanier, K., 176
LaPaglia, J. A., 119
Larson, John August, 180
Larson, M. R., 106, 127
Larson, S. M., 255
Lassiter, G. D., 221, 243
Laughery, K., 119
Lavender, T., 78
Lawson, D. S., 162
Lawson, State v. (2012), 147, 148, 151, 297–298
Lawson, V. Z., 79
Laybourn, P., 115
Leach, A. M., 176, 177, 194
leading questions (directive questioning), 18–19, 67–68, 261, 273
Leding, J., 48, 79
Lee, H., 58
Lee, K., 177, 178
Leichtman, M. D., 264, 265
Leins, D. A., 191
Leippe, M. R., 6, 21, 142
Lellevik, L., 92
leniency, implied, in interrogations, 169, 196, 212–216, 241
Lenton, E., 69

Leo, R. A., 21, 194, 195, 201, 205, 219, 221, 242
Lepore, S., 262
LeVasseur, M. A., 232
level of detail. *See* detail, level of
leverage via others, in interrogations, 215
Levett, L. M., 135
Levin, D., 36
Levine, L. J., 59, 89
Levine, M., 250
Levitt, M., 256
Lewinski, H., 60
Lewis, C., 283
liars. *See* lies and liars
lie-detection wizards, 177, 184
Lieberman, J., 224, 233
lies and liars, 174–192
    children as liars, 252–253
    children's lies of omission, 178, 281
    detection of, via signs of emotion, 179–184
    improving detection of, 189–192
    jurors' detection of, 240–241
    knowing too much or too little, 185–189
    lies, accuracy of detection of, 174–179, 240
    lies, common-sense indicators of, 182–183, 191, 240
    lies and false memories, connection between, 267
    microexpressions and, 184
    motivations for, 74
lies and truth, children's distinguishing of, 254–256, 280
lighting, effects on facial recognition, 109
Lilienfeld, S. O., 92, 97, 188, 189
limits, of lie detection, 192
Lin, C., 72
Lindsay, D. S., 71, 246, 259, 260, 285
Lindsay, J. J., 177, 183
Lindsay, M. R., 41
Lindsay, R. C. L., 41, 52, 56, 71, 75, 107, 112, 116, 122, 124, 127, 141, 143, 177, 178, 238
line-length perception study, 197, 212
lineups
    fillers for, 78, 128–130
    instructions for, 134–137
    live, vs. photos, 124–126
    misidentifications in, 105–106
    mock-witness paradigm, 130–133
    nominal vs. functional size of, 129
    pictures, altering of, 133–134
    showups vs., 107, 121–123

Moreland, M. B., 127, 130
Morgan, C., 60, 86, 91, 112
Moriarty, J. C., 188
Morris, E. K., 71
Morsella, E., 157
Moss, A., 137
mother-child conversations, 171–172
motivation
    for lies, 175, 176, 186
    role of, in false memories, 74
Mozayani, A., 58
Mr. Science study, 259–260, 269, 273
Mueller-Johnson, K., 144
mug-shot bias, 146
Muhlenbruck, L., 177, 183
Mullennix, J. W., 156
Munhall, P. J., 221
Murphy, D. R., 170
Murphy, G. L., 165
musicians, voice recognition by, 160

Nadel, L., 91
Nagesh, A., 77
Narby, D. J., 238
Narchet, F. M., 215
Nathanson, R., 249
National Academy of Sciences, 2, 182
National Academy of Sciences, Committee
    on Scientific Approaches to
    Understanding and Maximizing the
    Validity and Reliability of Eyewitness
    Identification in Law Enforcement
    and the Courts, 147
The National Children's Advocacy Center,
    277
National Registry of Exonerations, 102
National Research Council, 28, 155, 212
Natu, V., 125
Neel, R., 44
negative feedback, 79
Neil v. Biggers (1972), 19, 50, 147
Neisser, U., 32, 87, 170
Nelson, E. C., 57
Nelson, K., 248, 256
nervous system, alcohol's effects on, 58
network, memory as, 63–67
Neuberg, S., 44
Neufeld, P. J., 219
neuroscience, 3
Neuschatz, J. S., 79, 85, 121, 162
neutral interviewing of children. See
    children, proper investigations with
New Jersey Supreme Court, 103, 147
New York, Frye criteria, use of, 16
Newman, M. L., 191

Nichelli, P., 99
Nichols, R. M., 69
Nirider, L. H., 219
Nixon, Richard, 170
No Lie MRI, 188
No Mark Upon Her (Crombie), 179
Nobel prizes, 2
nominal vs. functional size, of lineups, 129
Noon, E., 21
Norris, R. J., 201
Norwick, R. J., 242
note-taking, during trials, 237
novel science, admissibility of, 7
null hypothesis, 11
Nysse-Carris, K. L., 178

Oberlander, L. B., 201
O'Brien, M., 116
Ochalek, K., 70
O'Connell, M. J., 201
oddball bias, 129–130, 132, 161
oddball triggers, in brain wave patterns, 188
Odinot, G., 78, 187
Odum, A. L., 203
Oeberst, A., 69, 239
Ogle, C. M., 252
Ogloff, J. R. P., 228
Ogloff, R. P., 224, 235, 237
Olafson, E., 93
Olson, E. A., 76, 79, 119
Oorsouw, K., 56
open-ended vs. closed-ended questions,
    250, 260, 280
Oppenheim, D., 274
Orbach, Y., 172, 245, 258, 277, 278, 283,
    284
Oregon Supreme Court, 147, 148, 151,
    297–298
orienting response (OR), 187–188
Oriet, C., 130
Ornstein, P. A., 250, 257
Osman, D., 201
Ost, J., 66, 69
O'Sullivan, M., 176, 177, 179
other people, interrogation leverage via,
    215
O'Toole, A. J., 125
O'Toole, T., 20
Otto, A. L., 228
Owen-Kostelnik, J., 201
Owens, J., 65
Ozuru, Y., 236

p-values, 12–13
Padawer-Singer, A., 228

painful events, 260, 269
  See also traumatic events, memory of
Palacios, J. N., 58
Palmer, J. C., 67
Palmer, M. A., 77, 128
Panfile, T., 274
Paoloni, A., 157
Pappas, C., 119
Pardo, M. S., 188
parent-child conversations, 273–274
Park, B., 53
Parker, J. F., 256
participants, in lineups. *See* lineups
participants vs. bystanders, as witnesses,
  6–7
Pashler, H., 84
passing time. *See* time, passage of
Pasupathi, M., 33
Paterson, H., 69
Pathak-Sharma, M., 228
patient-doctor discussions, 168–169
Patihis, L., 92
Patil, S., 103, 194
patterns, consistency vs. universality of,
  26
Patterson, D., 188
Patterson, K. E., 113
Pavletic, A., 142
Payment, K. E., 69
Payne, J. D., 91
Paz-Alonso, P. M., 90
Peace, K. A., 48, 90
PEACE model for interviewing, 216–217,
  222
pedestrians, cell phones as distractions
  to, 33
Pedroza, G., 228
peer review and publication of scientific
  results, 9–10
peers, information from, children's
  suggestibility and, 263–264
Pembroke, M., 121
Pennebaker, J. W., 191
Pennington, N., 235
Penrod, S. D., 15, 17, 21, 43, 48, 60, 75,
  76, 77, 78, 83, 104, 110, 113, 119,
  125, 135, 141, 146, 149, 227, 228,
  233, 234, 237, 238
People v. Adrian P. Thomas (2014), 213
perception and memory
  children, investigations with, 272–294
  children's memories, 245–271
  confessions, 193–223
  foundational issues, 1–29
  identification procedures, 121–152

interplay of, 49
jurors' cognition, 224–244
lies, 174–192
memory, in general, 62–97
overview, 1–29
summary, 295–298
voices and conversations, memory for,
  153–173
witness evidence, 98–120
witnesses' perceptions, 30–61
perceptions (witnesses'), 30–61
  alcoholic blackouts and, 57–59
  angle of illumination and, 40
  attention and, 44–46
  constructiveness of, 36–37
  darkness and, 37–39
  distance and, 41–42, 149
  drugs and alcohol, effects of, 55–57
  emotional arousal and, 59–60
  event complexity and, 44
  event duration and, 43
  expectations, effects of, 52–54
  eyeglasses and, 41
  grand illusion of, 35–36
  injuries, effects of, 54–55
  memory of event duration and viewing
    distance and, 52
  memory of viewing opportunity and,
    49–51
  overview, 30–31
  perception and memory interplay and,
    49
  rule of 15 and, 39
  selectiveness of, 32–35
  special circumstances and, 37
  stress and, 60
  summary, 61
  traits of, 31–32
  viewing angle and, 42–43
  weapon focus and, 46–49
perceptions, of witnesses by jurors,
  237–243
perceptual salience, in conversations, 221
Pereira, J. K., 258
Peretta, S., 143
Perfect, T. J., 140, 170
Perillo, J. T., 212
Perry, C., 127
Perry, P. J., 57
Perry v. New Hampshire (2012), 147–148
Peters, D. O., 60
Peterson, A. C. I., 52
Peterson, C., 248, 250, 252, 257, 278
Pezdek, K., 73, 74, 90, 116, 117, 136, 149,
  186, 269

Pfeifer, J., 224
Phelps, E. A., 89
Philbin, M. M., 69
Philippon, A., 156
Phillips, M. R., 138
Phillips, P. J., 125
phoneticians, voice recognition by, 160
photo lineups (photospreads)
  altering photographs for, 133–134
  biased, 108
  choosing fillers for, 128–130
  live lineups vs., 124–126
  mock-witness paradigm for, 130–133
  sequential vs. simultaneous, 126–128
  viewing quality for, 109
photopic vision, 38
photoreceptors, 34, 38
Pickel, K. L., 48, 160
Pickering, A., 48, 105
Pickett, J. M., 166
pictures, 133–134, 282
Pigott, M. A., 52, 104, 116, 118
Pike, G., 104
Pinker, S., 166
Pipe, M.-E., 245, 248, 251, 252, 255, 258,
    278, 283
Piper, A., 92, 94
pitch changes, as vocal disguises, 160
Pizarro, D. A., 59, 89
Platz, S., 6, 104
plausibility, 73–74, 264–265
plausibility bias, 129, 130, 132, 161
Poggio, T., 113
Police and Criminal Evidence Act (1984),
    216
police officers, effects of stress on
    memories of, 60
Pollack, I., 166
polygraphs, 180–182, 188, 212
Poole, D. A., 251, 255, 259, 260, 262, 277,
    280, 283–284
Pope, H. G., Jr., 56
Porter, D., 137
Porter, S., 17, 90, 97, 176, 177, 184, 192,
    207
Posey, D., 58
Posner, P. I., 44
Powell, M., 258
Powell, M. B., 69
Pozzulo, J., 125, 245
practicing (report retelling), 289
prefrontal cortex, 201
preinstruction, research on benefits of, 235
preschool-aged children, memories of,
    249–250

Presti, D. E., 44
pretrial publicity (PTP), 225–234
  confirmation bias and, 231–232
  documentation of, 225–226
  effects of, 227–229
  remedies for, 230–234
  research methods for study of, 226–227
  source confusion and, 229–230
Price, H. L., 130
Price, M., 258
Principe, G., 264
Prinzmetal, W., 44
prior bad acts, 231
prior knowledge, source confusion and, 170
Pritchard, M. E., 230
privileged knowledge, 291
procedures, for identification. See
    identification procedures
Procter, E. E., 160
professional interviewers, 172
proper investigations with children. See
    children, proper investigations with
propositional content, of conversations,
    163
props, use in interviewing children,
    283–284
prosopagnosia, 99
Pruzansky, S., 158
Pryke, S., 143
psychological research, 1–7
Psychological Review (journal), 2
psychological science, admissibility of
  as beyond common sense, 17–22
  under Daubert standard, 7–16
  under Frye standard, 16–17
Psychological Science in the Public Interest
    (journal), 17
psychometric properties, 14
P300 brain wave pattern, 188
PTP. See pretrial publicity
puberty, effects on children's response to
    sexuality-linked questions, 251
publication and peer review of scientific
    results, 9–10
pullover caps, effects on facial recognition,
    113
Purdie, V. J., 116
Purnell, T., 157
Putnam, C. E., 105

Qin, J., 288
quality control, in science, 296
Quandte, S., 186
quantitative reviews (meta-analyses),
    22–25

Quas, J. A., 60, 255, 257, 264, 269
questions
  closed-ended vs. open-ended, 250, 260, 280
  confusing, children's responses to, 249–250
  control questions, 181
  leading (directive questioning), 18–19, 67–68, 261, 273
  proper, for interviewing children, 280–281
  repeated, 262–263, 274–275
  unexpected, 192
  yes/no questions, 281
Quinlivan, D. S., 135, 138, 141, 147, 149, 150

R. v. J. (J. L.), 7
R. v. Mohan, 7, 18
race
  effects on facial recognition, 6, 115–116
  effects on weapon perception, 53
Radelet, M. L., 105
Raichle, M. E., 54
Rainey, A., 79
Rakover, S., 99
Raskin, D. C., 181, 186
Raye, C. L., 70, 80, 187
Read, J. D., 20, 21, 71, 76, 77, 83, 97, 144, 155, 157, 159, 165, 285, 297
real-world cases, applicability of psychological research to, 4–7
reality and fantasy, children's distinguishing of, 178, 252, 253, 254–256
reality monitoring, 80, 81, 254
reality-monitoring (RM) approach to lie detection, 187, 189
recantations, 289–290
receptive vocabularies, 252
recognition memory, speed of, 142
recognition vs. identification, 101–102, 143, 154
recollection vs. familiarity, in identifications, 143–144
reconstructive memory, 51, 67, 91–92
recovered memories, 92–97
recreational drugs, 56
Reder, L. M., 101
Redlich, A. D., 201, 202, 217, 221, 242
Reese, E., 248
refusal of denials, 211
rehearsing (report retelling), 289
Reid, John E., 181, 206
Reid interrogations, 206–216

behavior analysis interviews, 206–207, 222
confrontation and refusal of denials, 211
confrontation via evidence, 211–213
effectiveness of, 215–216
guilt presumptive nature of, 207–209
isolation and, 210–211
leverage via others, 215
minimization in, 213–215
Reisberg, D., 33, 35, 43, 48, 59, 63, 89, 137, 164, 168, 208, 231, 236
rejection rates, for scientific papers, 8
relative-judgment strategy, for lineup identification, 126, 134, 139
relevant information, hiding of, during interviews, 190
relevant questions, 181
reliability, of measurement scales, 14
remembered vs. documented factors, 150
Rensink, R. A., 35
repeated events, children's remembering of, 258
repeated interviews, of children, 282–283
repeated questions, 262–263, 274–275
repeated testimony, 78
replication, importance of, 3–4
reports from children, truth and falsity of
  certainty and demeanor and, 287–288
  consistency and, 288–290
  cross-examination and, 292–293
  level of detail and, 290–291
  privileged knowledge and, 291
  symptom evidence and, 291–292
repression of memories, 92–94, 95–96
Repucci, N. D., 201
research
  confessions, application to, 222–223
  error rates for, 10–13
  on false confessions, paradigm for, 199
  on jury instructions, 224
  methods for PTP studies, 226–227
  on preinstruction, 235
  psychological, 1–7, 28–29
  scientific, general acceptance of, 15, 16–17
  standard research methods, 13
research literature, 9–10
research psychologists, 2, 25
research psychology, 1–3, 10, 27–28
resemblance, of individuals, 26
response criterion, 53
retention intervals, 83, 116, 158
retina, 34
retrieval failure, 83, 85, 95–96
retrieval paths (for memories), 63, 64, 66

retroactive fragmentary blackouts, 58
retrograde amnesia, 55
Reyna, V. F., 17, 81, 247, 250
Reynolds, B., 203
Rhead, L., 137
Rhodes, M. G., 115
Rhue, J. R., 85
Rice, A., 125, 140
Richards, J. B., 203
Richards, J. M., 191
Richards, R. E., 105
Richman, K. D., 194
Rishword, A., 76
risk assessments, 61
risks, 26, 75
risky predictions, 8
Rivard, J. M., 91
RM (reality-monitoring) approach to lie
     detection, 187, 189
Robbenolt, J., 228
Robbins, R., 100
Roberts, A., 123
Roberts, K. P., 187
Roberts, M. J., 65
Robinson, M., 183
Rock, I., 32, 35
rods (photoreceptors), 34, 38
Roediger, H. L., III, 65, 76, 84
Roese, N. J., 94
Roh, S., 58
Rohrer, D., 84
Rollings, H. E., 228
Roozendaal, B., 91
Rose, G., 224, 235, 237
Rose, M. R., 234, 244
Rosenfeld, J. P., 187, 188
Rosenthal, R., 138, 228
Rosnow, R. L., 228
Ross, D. F., 16, 92, 143, 144
Ross, L., 242
Ross, S., 3, 105, 149
Rubin, D. C., 73, 87
Ruby, C. L., 186
rule of 15 (for visual perception), 39, 41
Rumpell, C. M., 238
Rush, E. B., 60, 257
Rush, R. A., 130
Russano, M. B., 57, 138, 215
Russell, E. J., 48
Ruva, C. L., 226, 229, 230, 231, 232
Ryback, R. S., 57
Rydell, S. M., 119, 130

Sabbach, M., 263
Sadler, C., 85–86

Sadler, M. S., 116
Safer, M. A., 20
Salermo, J. M., 178
Salmon, K., 258
same-race identification, 6
Sampaio, C., 79
Samuels, C., 73
San Francisco Police Department, 109
sanctions, as standards enforcement,
     14–15
Sanford, A., 104
Sarason, I. G., 52
Sarfati, D., 274
Satel, S., 188, 189
Saver, P. R., 257
Savitsky, K., 209
Saykaly, C., 178
Saywitz, K. J., 249, 254, 262, 277, 280
scales of measurement, 14
Schaaf, J., 257
Schacter, D. L., 81, 97, 106, 127, 188
schema-based errors (in memories),
     66–67
     See also intrusion errors
schematic knowledge (schema effects), 62,
     64–65, 82, 235–236
Scherr, K., 205
Schiller, N. O., 160
Schmechel, R., 20, 21
Schmersal, L., 21
Schmid, J., 181
Schneider, C. E., 168
school-aged children, 177–178, 250–251
Schooler, J. W., 52, 94, 96, 118
Schreiber-Compo, N., 57, 172
Schwalen, C. E., 255
science
     common sense vs., 297
     definition of, 3
     juror's skepticism of, 295–296
     quality control in, 296
     replication in, 3–4
     role in setting interviewing procedures
        for children, 277–278
     scientific claims, falsifiability of, 8
scientific journals, 9–10
Scoboria, A., 74
scotopic vision, 38
scripts (in memory organization),
     235–236, 258
Scullin, M. H., 245, 261, 283
Seamon, J. G., 65, 69
secondary gains, from memories, 74
Seelau, E. P., 119, 130
selectiveness, of perceptions, 31, 32–35

statement-validity assessment, 185–186
states, using *Frye* criteria, 16
Steadman, H. J., 202
Steblay, N. K., 23, 24, 48, 79, 105, 106,
107, 122, 123, 127, 128, 135, 142,
146, 224, 233
stereotype induction, 265
Stern, S. E., 156
Sternberg, K. J., 172
Stevenage, S. V., 156
stimulus materials, for lie detection,
175–176
Stires, L. K., 227
Stolle, D. O., 227
Stone, C. B., 236
Storms, M. D., 221
story cues, for lies, 240
story model, for jury decision making,
235–236
strategic use of evidence, 190
Strayer, D. L., 33
stress
effects on facial recognition, 111–112
effects on memory of event duration,
52
effects on perceptions, 5, 60, 198
impact on childrens' memories,
256–257
traumatic memories and, 91, 93
Strömwall, L. A., 78, 190
Stroops, R., 52
Stroud, J. N., 115
Studebaker, C. A., 227, 228, 233, 234
Studebaker, N., 227
students, 84, 176
Sturgill, W., 146
substance use, 203
Sue, S., 228, 233
sufficient evidence of scientific research,
15–16
suggestibility
of adolescents and mentally impaired,
201
false confessions and, 198, 202–203
suggestibility, in children, 258–271
cross-examinations and, 292–293
factors affecting, 260–268
Mr. Science experiment, 259–260
overview, 258–259
paths toward suggestion, 268–269
possible memory errors, 269–271
suggestibility, in children, factors
affecting, 260–268
basis in truth, 265–266
delay, 266–267

directive questioning, 261
dreams and imagination, 267–268
feedback, 261–262
information from peers, 263–264
initial lies, 267
other evidence, 263
plausibility, 264–265
repeated questions, 262–263
stereotype induction, 265
trustworthy sources, 263
suggestive identifications, 147, 152
Sukel, H., 241
Supreme Court, U.S.
on admissibility of identifications, 141
on admissibility of polygraph evidence,
180
on confessions, 193
on level of certainty, 19
on scientific conclusions, 25
on suggestive identifications, 147–148
Supreme Judicial Court Study Group on
Eyewitness Evidence, 147
surveys
documenting common sense, 19–21
general acceptance surveys, 16–17
suspect bias vs. general impairment in
facial recognition, 108
suspect identification. *See* identification
procedures
Svetieva, E., 191
Swann, W. B., 208
Swanner, J. K., 162
Swartzwelder, H. S., 57, 58
Sweeney, J. D., 70
symptom evidence, as factor in truth of
children's reports, 291–292
system variables, 107–108, 121

Talarico, J. M., 87
Talwar, V., 177, 178, 255
Tanaka, J. W., 111
Tanke, E. D., 208
target-present (TP) vs. target-absent (TA)
procedures
cueing during, 138
for lineups, 106–107, 110, 126–127
MOMN instructions and, 135
for showups, 122–124
target-absent voice lineups, 155
Taslitz, A. E., 219
Tavris, C., 93
Telgen, S., 66
tells (cues), for lie detection, 177, 179–180,
182–184, 207
ten Brinke, L., 184, 192

Tenney, E. R., 238
Tepfer, J. A., 219
Terr, L. C., 92, 249
Tesmer, B., 156
testing, 4–5, 8
themes, for admission of crimes, 213
therapeutic interviews, 284–286
therapists, recovered memories and, 98
Thierry, K. L., 248
Thill, D. L., 119
Thomas, A. K., 69, 74
Thomas, S. F., 263
Thomas, W. N., 16, 92
Thompson, C. P., 160
Thompson, P., 99
Thompson-Cannino, Jennifer, 103
Thomsen, D. K., 90
Thomson, D., 258
Tiersma, P. M., 158, 172
time, passage of
    effects on children's suggestibility, 266
    effects on facial recognition, 116, 149
    effects on memory, 83, 95
    effects on voice memory, 158
    source confusion and, 230, 232
timing
    effects of, on memory of voices,
        157–158
    of science, 295
    See also duration
Tingen, I. W., 92
Tippelt, A., 156
Tix, R. W., 146
Toglia, M., 144
Tollestrup, P. A., 48, 144
Tonkin, J., 79
top-down processes, 53, 173
    See also filling-in
Torkildson Perillo, J., 217
Torneo, E., 103
Towell, N., 104
trace evidence, 297–298
trained investigators, memory for
    conversations, 172
training
    of forensic interviewers vs. of
        therapists, 285
    in how to remember, for children, 248
    in lie detection, 178–179
traits
    of memory, in general, 62–63
    of witnesses' perceptions, 31–32
Tranel, D., 99
traumatic events, memory of, 90–97
    in children, 258

continuous vs. discontinuous
    memories, 94–95
critical-incident amnesia, 91–92
recovered memories, evaluation of,
    96–97
remembering trauma, 90–91
repression, 92–94
retrieval failure vs. repression, 95–96
Tredoux, C. G., 43, 128, 133
Treyens, J. C., 53
trial competence of children, 253–254
trial evidence, jurors' memories for. See
    jurors' cognition
true and false reports from children,
    distinguishing. See reports from
    children, truth and falsity of
trustworthy sources, children's
    suggestibility and, 263
truth and lies, children's distinguishing of,
    254–256, 280
    See also reports from children, truth
    and falsity of
Tubb, V. A., 16
tunnel vision (memory narrowing), 47,
    56, 59, 88
Tunnicliff, J. L., 76, 118, 130
Turtle, J. W., 48
type 1 and type 2 errors, 11–12

ultimate opinion testimony, 294
unconscious plagiarism, 170
unconscious transference, 144
understood gist, memory for, 164–165,
    171
unexpected questions, 192
unfamiliar faces, 101–102, 104
United Kingdom. See Britain (United
    Kingdom)
United States, photo lineups, use of, 124
universality vs. consistency, of patterns,
    26

vague theories, 8
Valentine, T., 48, 60, 105, 116, 118, 119,
    123, 125, 130, 145
validity, of measurement scales, 14
Van der Schrier, J. H., 38, 39, 41
Van Koppen, P. J., 66, 118
Van Lancker, D., 154, 155
Vanderbilt, K. E., 263
Vanous, S., 144
variables, control of, 5
Venuti, M., 21
veracity of witnesses, psychological
    research and, 27

verbal descriptions of faces, problems of, 117–119
verbal material. *See* conversations, memory for
verbal maturity, of children, 247–248, 249, 251–252, 254, 278–279
verbal overshadowing, 118–119
verbatim wording, memory of, 139, 158–159, 163–164, 165–166
Verschuere, B., 180
Verstijnen, I. M., 39
Vertefuille, L., 172
Video Identification Parade Electronic Recording (VIPER) system, 124–125
video lineups, 124–125
video recorder view of memories, 20, 30–31, 81–82
video records, of interrogations, 220–222
video surveillance, viewing angle of, 43
Vidmar, N., 226, 228
views and viewing
    in facial recognition, 99, 109
    viewing angle, effects on perceptions, 42–43
    viewing distance, 52, 109, 149
    viewing duration, 110
    viewing opportunity, memory of, 49–51
Vinson, K., 241
VIPER (Video Identification Parade Electronic Recording) system, 124–125
visual acuity, 34
visual illusions, 36–37
vocabularies, of children, 252
Vohs, K. D., 94
voice-face interactions, 156
voice identification, 154–156, 159, 160–161
voice recognition, accuracy of, 125
voices, memory for, 150–162
    describing voices, 157
    exact words and, 158–159
    face-voice interactions, 156
    identifier's characteristics, 160
    overview, 153
    proper identification procedures, 161–162
    recognition vs. identification, 154
    summary, 172–173
    timing, effects of, 157–158
    voice changes, effects of, 160–161
    voice identifications, 154–156, 159
voiding cystourethrogram (VCUG) procedures, 257–258
voir dire, PTP and, 231, 232, 233–234

Vokey, J. R., 77
Von Montfor, X. V., 43, 104
Vrij, A., 17, 66, 80, 156, 176, 177, 178, 179, 183, 186, 190, 191, 192, 207, 281

Wade, K. A., 71, 134
Wade, R., 227
Wagenaar, W. A., 38, 39, 41, 66
Wagner, A. D., 189
Wakefield, B. M., 71
Wallace, D. B., 242
Waller, B., 192
Walters, S. B., 183
Warren, A. R., 172, 245, 255, 277
Warren, K. L., 250, 252, 257, 278
Washington, George, grandmothers' names, 80
Washington state, *Frye* criteria, use of, 16
Wasson, C., 116
Watergate Scandal, 170
Waterman, A., 250
Watts, H. J. E., 134
weapon focus, 35, 46–49, 111–112
Weatherford, D. R., 119
Weber, N., 41, 77, 140, 143
websites
    for American Judicature Society lineup study, 127
    National Registry of Exonerations, 102
    PTP on, 225
Wee Care Nursery School, 271
Weiland, P. E., 221
Weissenborn, R., 57
Wells, Gary L., 17, 48, 50, 75, 76, 77, 78, 79, 103, 105, 107, 108, 118, 119, 127, 128, 130, 131, 135, 137, 138, 141, 142, 143, 147, 149, 150, 238, 240
Wetherill, R. R., 57
Wetmore, S. A., 121
whispering, 156, 160
White, A. M., 56, 57, 58
White, D., 43, 104
White, L., 262
White, L. T., 241
White, T. L., 264
white noise, 167
white papers, 17
Wicke, C., 56, 112
Wickens, T., 155
Widawski, M. A., 91
Widmark calculations, 57–58
Wilford, M. M., 107, 108, 141
Wilkinson, M., 79
Williams, L. M., 93–94, 291

Wilson, J. C., 255
Wilson, T. D., 19
Wise, B. M., 33
Wise, R. A., 20
witness evidence. *See* eyewitness
    identification
witnesses
    confidence of identification in lineups,
        142
    influences on, 148
    participants vs. bystanders as, 6–7
    possible effects of stress on, 5
    speed of choice of identifications,
        142–143
    veracity of, psychological research and,
        27
    See also perceptions (witnesses')
witnesses, jurors' perceptions of, 237–243
    camera angle, importance of, 243
    coerced confessions, overbelief in,
        241–242
    confessions, assessment of, 241
    lies, detection of, 240–241
    witness's recall, persuasiveness of,
        238–240
Wittenbrink, B., 53
Wittlinger, R. P., 102
Wixted, J. T., 128
Wogalter, M. S., 124, 136
Wolfskiel, M. P., 75
Wolters, G., 39, 78
Wonder Woman, 180
Wood, J. M., 270

Woodall, C. E., 172
Woods, N. G., 134
Woolnough, P. S., 97
wording, of conversations, memory for,
    139, 158–159, 163–164, 165–166
Wright, D. B., 52, 68, 79, 85–86, 105, 115,
    237
Wrightsman, L. S., 241
writing, as children's abuse reporting, 282

Yang, Y., 205
Yarbrough, A., 226
Yarbus, A. L., 45
Yarmey, A. D., 38, 52, 124, 126, 154, 155,
    156, 157, 158, 159, 160, 161, 238
Yarmey, A. L., 124
Yarmey, M. J., 124
yelling, 160, 167
yes/no questions, 281
Yim, I. S., 60, 257
Yin, R. K., 99
Young, A. W., 99, 100
"Your mother told me…" statements, 263
Yuille, J. C., 5, 48, 97, 181, 186
Yurgelun-Todd, D., 56

Zajac, R., 69, 293
Zambrusky, G., 172
Zaragoza, M. S., 69, 71, 74, 267
Zember, E., 250
Zhu, B., 72
Zimmerman, D. M., 137
Zimmerman, L. A., 43